Contents

❖ PART 1 ❖

The Nature of Jesus' Family

← PART 2 →

THE NATURE OF THE JERUSALEM CHURCH

← PART 3 →

THE NATURE OF JEWISH CHRISTIANITY

THE
BROTHER
OF
JESUS
AND THE
LOST TEACHINGS
OF
CHRISTIANITY

JEFFREY J. BÜTZ

Inner Traditions
Rochester, Vermont

Inner Traditions
One Park Street
Rochester, Vermont 05767
www.InnerTraditions.com

Library of Congress Cataloging-in-Publication Data
Bütz, Jeffrey.
  The brother of Jesus and the lost teachings of Christianity / Jeffrey Bütz.
      p. cm.
  Includes bibliographical references and index.
  ISBN 1-59477-043-3
  1. James, Brother of the Lord, Saint. 2. Apocryphal books (New Testament)—
Criticism, interpretation, etc. I. Title.
  BS2454.J3B88 2005
  225.9'2—dc22
                                    2004021976

Printed and bound in the United States by Lake Book Manufacturing, Inc.

10 9 8 7 6 5 4 3 2

Text design and layout by Rachel Goldenberg
This book was typeset in Sabon with Charlemagne as the display typeface

✦ PART 4 ✦

THE NATURE OF ORTHODOXY

ACKNOWLEDGMENTS

I wish to thank all of my professors at Moravian Theological Seminary, where I earned my M.Div., for shaping my theology in an ecumenical fashion and rescuing me from fundamentalism. A special debt of gratitude to Dr. Glenn Asquith and the Rev. Otto Dreydoppel, Jr., for early encouragement of my writing. You were the first to make me realize I could write.

I also thank all of my professors at the Lutheran Theological Seminary at Philadelphia, where I earned my S.T.M., for refining my scholarship. I especially thank Dr. Erik Heen for initially sparking my interest in the historical Jesus (which led to my interest in James) and for all his patience and wise advice as my thesis advisor. I also thank my reader, Dr. John Reumann, for drilling into me the need for rigorous testing of evidence and caution in coming to conclusions when doing historical research. Thanks also to Dr. Walter Wagner of Moravian Theological Seminary and Dr. Peter Pettit, director of the Institute for Jewish Christian Understanding, for their generous gift of time and advice when the results of my research made me fear I was lapsing into heresy.

A special debt of gratitude to fellow Inner Traditions author Steve Sora for his generous advice and, especially, for encouraging my writing and enabling me to believe that I could turn my research into a popular book. Thanks also to the staff at Inner Traditions International for their hard work on my behalf, especially Jon Graham for his enthusiastic support from the beginning, to Jeanie Levitan and Vickie Trihy for their guidance of this project, and to my copy editor, who prefers to remain anonymous, for her astute analysis of my writing and meticulous attention to detail.

I also need to express my gratitude to those scholars and writers who have opened my eyes to astounding new vistas while bravely bucking the tides of scholarly consensus: Michael Baigent, Richard Leigh, and Henry Lincoln (whose work changed my life), Margaret Starbird, Robert Eisenman, Hyam Maccoby, Hugh Schonfield, John Painter, and Richard Bauckham. And to those whose writing and art molded me and inspired me from an early age: Arthur C. Clarke, Stanley Kubrick, Roger Barrett, David Gilmour, Nick Mason, Roger Waters, and Richard Wright.

Finally, a personal note of thanks to Rick Cardona, Dave Cardona, and Randy Overly whose friendship inspired me in ways they cannot imagine. To Deborah Buskirk for her unfailing interest in my work, engaging conversation, and gentle debate throughout our many theological changes over the years. To the Rev. Laura Klick for her personal and pastoral guidance. And, most especially, to my eternal soul mate— my wife, Katherine, and our truly wonderful children, Rachel and David, for their unfailing love and for doing without my time and attention (yet again!) while this book was being researched and written.

And, of course, thanksgiving *ad majorem Dei gloriam* to Messiah Jesus and his brother.

PREFACE

It is the glory of God to conceal a thing;
but the honor of kings is to search out a matter.

PROVERBS 25:2

I did not learn my theology all at once,
but have always had to dig deeper and deeper.

MARTIN LUTHER

After years of research, I have come to the conclusion that the role of James in the early church has been marginalized over the centuries—both consciously and unconsciously—and continues to be repressed today. The purpose of this book is to explain why this marginalization of James has occurred and to articulate the controversy that has surrounded the brother of Jesus for almost two millennia. It is my belief that understanding the role of James in the early church will make for no less than a revolution in our understanding of Jesus, the nature of the early church, and the relationship of Christianity to Judaism and Islam.

My fascination with James, the brother of Jesus, can be traced to a course I took in graduate school called the Quest for the Historical Jesus. This course led to my concentrating in the discipline of historical Jesus studies for a Master of Sacred Theology (S.T.M.) degree and eventually to my thesis topic: James.

In the course of my early research, I came across a volume of some thousand pages on the subject of the historical James entitled *James the Brother of Jesus* by Robert Eisenman, professor of Middle Eastern Religions at California State University. I opened to the introduction and read:

It is to the task of rescuing James, consigned either on purpose or through benign neglect to the scrapheap of history, that this book is dedicated . . .

Mentioned in various contexts in the New Testament, James the Just has been systematically downplayed, or written out of the tradition . . .

. . . but in the Jerusalem of his day in the 40s to 60s C.E., he was the most important and central figure of all—the "Bishop" or "Overseer" of the Jerusalem church.[1]

This certainly captured my attention. Eisenman's opening statements made it sound as though an outright conspiracy was afoot to erase James from history. I found the book riveting, but also quite at odds with the mainstream biblical scholarship taught in most seminaries. I soon discovered that while Eisenman has impeccable academic credentials, his theories are considered rather *outré* (to put it politely) by most scholars. Infamous in academic circles for waging a long campaign to prove that the sectarian writings of the Essene community (the community that collected the Dead Sea Scrolls) are in fact the writings of the early Christian movement, Eisenman argues that the Essenes *were* the early Christians. This has been a highly controversial and mostly rejected theory that has been proposed by various scholars ever since the discovery of the Dead Sea Scrolls. Even more controversially, Eisenman purports that the enigmatic leader of the Essene community, known only as the "Teacher of Righteousness" in the community's writings, is actually James; and his nemesis, who is called the "Spouter of Lies," is actually Paul, the apostle to the Gentiles. This is highly controversial stuff, indeed, and the advice given me was to cast a wary eye on Eisenman.

Nevertheless, Eisenman's book opened up a window on the importance of James in the early church about which I had been oblivious. The more I delved into James, the more I became increasingly fascinated by a figure who was obviously of major importance and influence in the early church, but whose role is indeed, as Eisenman claims, curiously muted in the New Testament and generally ignored in modern scholarship. Because of the few overt references to James in the New Testament, his great significance, which is plainly demonstrable, has gone largely unrecognized. Here was a mystery I could not resist, and I ended up focusing my research on James.[2] I had no inkling when I completed my thesis in the spring of 2002 that James would soon rise to international prominence.

That fall came the announcement of the discovery of an artifact claimed to be James's ossuary, or burial box, an archaeological windfall that created international headlines and quickly directed a long overdue spotlight on James.[3] Now, thanks to major articles in national news magazines and front page headlines in newspapers across the globe, it seems that everyone knows that Jesus had a brother. Yet, despite all this recent attention, there is a dearth of major studies on James. Aside from Eisenman, the only other comprehensive study is Australian scholar John Painter's 1997 book, *Just James: The Brother of Jesus in History and Tradition*. While *Just James* is the work of a more mainstream scholar, Painter's thesis echoes Eisenman:

> The study of James remains neglected. I hope that *Just James* will encourage a recovery of the recognition of how significant James was in the history of earliest Christianity and provide some explanation of how and why that significance has been obscured in most of the surviving traditions.[4]

Except for Eisenman and Painter, there were no other major studies of James published in English when I wrote my thesis. At the time, the only other scholar who had done significant work in the area of the historical James was British scholar Richard Bauckham, who had published one extended essay on James and the Jerusalem church and a book on the rest of Jesus' family, entitled *Jude and the Relatives of Jesus in the Early Church*.[5] All other information that existed had to be gleaned mainly from commentaries and papers on books in the New Testament, particularly those in which James plays a major role—the epistle of James, Acts (chapters 15 and 21), and Galatians (chapter 2).

But there are signs that scholars are beginning to pay attention. In response to Eisenman and Painter, several scholarly colloquies on James have convened, one result of which has been the publication of two volumes of research papers on James.[6] Interestingly, these scholars came to the same conclusion as Eisenman and Painter before them: "The lack of serious and sustained investigation of the historical figure of James 'the Just,' brother of Jesus, is one of the curious oversights in modern critical study of Christian origins."[7]

The book you are now reading is an attempt to correct this "curious oversight" and make the findings of an intriguing scholarly debate available to a wider audience. The work that has been done on James has been written by scholars for scholars, and the general public remains uninformed. The recently published popular work on the discovery of the James ossuary, *The Brother of Jesus,* by Hershel Shanks and Ben Witherington, is intended for a general audience, yet leaves much to be desired. The second part of the book, written by Witherington, a noted conservative historical Jesus scholar, gives a well-summarized overview of what we presently know about James, but does not touch upon much of the scholarly controversy surrounding James. Although a first-class scholar, Witherington adheres to the traditional representation of James and unveils little of the man who has been emerging in the research of the past century and a half. I propose to present here the far more controversial face of James. If many Christians are shocked to discover that Jesus had a brother, they will be even more shocked to discover what recent research into James is revealing about the nature of the early church and the beliefs and teachings of Jesus.

In the course of this book, we shall examine all of the primary historical sources on James and the major sources of secondary interpretation that have appeared since the rise of modern critical scholarship in the early 1800s. Having been personally influenced by the current renaissance in historical Jesus studies,* my overall methodology is primarily historical-critical.

Bruce Chilton, in his introduction to the recent compendium *James the Just and Christian Origins,* expresses disdain for recent efforts to recover the historical Jesus, an endeavor that he characterizes as hopeless and bankrupt.[8] I could not disagree more. I have come to believe that historical "questing" is of vital importance to Christian theology in today's postmodern world where many academics now consider the possibility of attaining any certain historical knowledge an impossibility, a trend in theology that began with Rudolph Bultmann.

In the early 1990s, the widely respected New Testament scholar James Dunn expressed strong support for historical methodologies at a

---

*The so-called new quest or third quest for the historical Jesus.

time when scholars were increasingly turning away from historical criticism to pursue the trendiest areas of literary research:

> [E]ndless fascination with Jesus and the beginnings of Christianity is well reflected in a seemingly non-stop flow of films, plays, musicals and documentaries on these themes. We have responsibility to ensure that such curiosity of the "person in the street" is met with well researched answers—otherwise it will be the imaginative storylines of the merely curious, or the tendentious portrayals of those with an axe to grind, or the fantasizing of the sensation-mongers which will set the images for a generation addicted to the television screen.
>
> It is hardly surprising that all these factors have given rise to what is often now referred to as "the third quest of the historical Jesus"— where it is *precisely the readiness to recognize and give weight to the Jewish context and character of Jesus* . . . which has provided the fresh stimulus and the new angle of entry into the Jesus-tradition.[9]

In light of the enormous popularity of Mel Gibson's *The Passion of the Christ* and Dan Brown's *The Da Vinci Code*, Dunn's rationale is even more cogent today. My personal predilection is for this type of "third quest" approach taken by scholars such as E. P. Sanders, Geza Vermes, and N. T. Wright, which takes seriously the thorough Jewishness of Jesus. It is, above all, the Jewishness of Jesus to which modern research into James points; and, as we shall see, it is the Jewishness of Jesus and James that was a major reason for James's leading role in the early church being suppressed; and it is still the reason why the findings of recent research into James continue to be resisted by most Christian scholars.

On a personal level, my research into James has proven to be an incredibly enriching and rewarding spiritual exercise, opening my eyes to whole new vistas on Jesus and the origins of the Christian church. The past years have also been a time of great spiritual wrestling for me, causing me to question and reexamine some of my most deeply held theological beliefs. Discovering what James believed about his older brother has forced me to significantly change my understandings of Jesus and the beginnings of Christianity. But my overriding goal all along has been a quest for truth—no matter where it may lie, and no matter what inherited dogmas may need to be abandoned in order to attain it.

It is my hope that the fruits of my struggles—contained in this book—can be a guide to future researchers and spiritual pilgrims in making their way through the dangerous minefield one encounters when trying to recover the historical James after nearly twenty centuries of neglect and abuse. And I have an even grander hope that the insights and understandings that James provides us on his brother Jesus might at long last bring healing to the festering wounds of the Western world caused by the misunderstanding, hatred, and warfare among the three great Western religions and their political heirs.

→←

Unless otherwise indicated, all scripture quotations are from the New Revised Standard Version (NRSV) of the Bible. A list of abbreviated source titles can be found in the back of the book.

CHRONOLOGY

6–4 B.C.E.	The birth of Jesus
27–29 C.E.	The ministry of John the Baptist
30–33*	The ministry of Jesus
30–33	The crucifixion and resurrection of Jesus
32–35	The conversion of the apostle Paul
34–38	Paul's first visit to Jerusalem (James already an acknowledged leader of the Jerusalem church)
41–44	The imprisonment of Peter (traditional date that James succeeds Peter as head of the Jerusalem church)
44	James, son of Zebedee, becomes first martyred apostle
47–56	Paul conducts missionary tours among the Gentiles
48–49	Paul's second visit to Jerusalem
49	Jerusalem Conference held (First Apostolic Council), Apostolic Decree issued
50	Paul writes earliest letters (1 and 2 Thessalonians)
55	Galatians composed
56	Paul's final visit to Jerusalem
62	James's death; Jesus' cousin Symeon succeeds James as head of Jerusalem church
66–73	Jewish revolt against Rome; Jewish Christians flee to Pella
70	Destruction of Jerusalem and the Temple

---

*Some authorities postulate 27–30 as the period of Jesus' ministry.

66–70	The gospel of Mark composed
80–85	The gospel of Matthew composed
85–90	The gospel of Luke and Acts composed
81–96	Domitian searches for Davidic pretenders and interrogates the grandsons of Jude
90–95	The gospel of John composed
100–110	Justus succeeds Symeon as head of the Jerusalem church
132–35	Second Jewish Revolt, Hadrian expels Jews from Jerusalem
150–80	Hegesippus composes *Memoranda*
300–324	Eusebius composes *Ecclesiastical History*
325	Council of Nicaea
610	Muhammad receives first revelation

INTRODUCTION:
OF REVOLUTIONS
AND PARADIGM SHIFTS

As we enter the third millennium, our human community is rent by war, increasing distrust, and the loss of a sense of our common nature and past. We seem to be more tempted than ever to define ourselves in opposition to the Other and more threatened than ever by a paradigm, or worldview, that separates rather than unites us. Yet things are not as they seem, and James, the brother of Jesus, is the key to understanding ourselves differently.

This book is an examination of an emerging paradigm shift in the field of New Testament studies, specifically in our understanding of Christian origins and the nature of the early church. Within these pages we shall uncover the beginnings of a revolution that has the potential to change our understanding of Western religion forever. This emerging paradigm shift has yet to be recognized by the majority of biblical scholars and theologians, even though the evidence has been plainly staring us in the face from the pages of the Bible for two millennia. The obvious is not always so easy to see.

Three philosophical revolutions in human understanding have taken place since the rise of modern science. The philosopher of science Thomas Kuhn coined the term "paradigm shift" to describe the sweeping changes in worldview that accompany such revolutions. The first of these paradigm shifts was caused by the implications of the mathematical calculations of the astronomer Nicholas Copernicus (subsequently confirmed by the telescopic observations of Galileo) that we live in a heliocentric (sun-centered), not a geocentric (earth-centered) solar system. Such was the enormity of the change in worldview caused by this discovery that it has rightly come to be called the Copernican Revolution. As with most scientific revolutions, the Copernican Revolution was vehemently opposed by the Christian church.

The second such revolution was the more recent Darwinian Revolution. If the paradigm shift that accompanied the Copernican Revolution displaced humanity from the center of the universe, the Darwinian Revolution and its accompanying paradigm shift humbled us even further, demoting humans from their status as the "crown" of God's relatively recent supernatural creation to a modest rank as a by-product of natural evolution. The third revolution began in the 1920s, and the full impact of its accompanying paradigm shift has yet to be fully felt. While not a commonly accepted term, I would dub it the Hubble Revolution, after the American astronomer Edwin Hubble, who first came to the conclusion that our Milky Way galaxy—thought at the time to comprise the entire universe—was merely one single "island universe" in a seemingly infinite sea of hundreds of billions of other galaxies. The paradigm shift necessitated by the Hubble revolution makes the downsizing of humanity's significance that followed the Copernican and Darwinian revolutions pale in comparison.

Amid all of the religious and societal upheaval engendered by these three major paradigm shifts in human awareness, smaller and lesser known paradigm shifts have more quietly occurred in many fields of human endeavor. A prime example is the grudging acceptance of the theory of continental drift by geologists in the 1960s. Since the discovery of the Americas, many had taken notice of the curious fact that the shorelines of the eastern coasts of North and South America, and the western coasts of Europe and Africa seemed to match up like perfectly fitting jigsaw-puzzle pieces. The vast majority of scientists shrugged this off as nothing more than an interesting coincidence. Still, a few people harbored a suspicion that the almost perfect match of the continental shorelines was more than coincidence. In 1911, the geologist Alfred Wegener was the first to seriously propose that the Americas and Europe and Africa really *were* once connected. Wegener and the few who agreed with him were widely ridiculed. Wegener's problem was that he could not provide an explanation of *how* continents could drift, but despite the censure of his peers, Wegener, like Galileo before him, bravely stood by the commonsensical conviction of what his eyes showed him.

It was not until the 1950s that oceanographers mapping the Atlantic Ocean floor made the startling discovery of the Mid-Atlantic Ridge, the biggest mountain chain on earth (located in the middle of the Atlantic Ocean). All along this mountain chain, lava is continuously spewing up from the earth's mantle, literally pushing the ocean floor apart and slowly but inexorably pushing the Americas and Europe and Africa away from each other. Sea-floor spreading, as this process came to be called, was the needed explanation for how continents could move. Almost overnight the theory of continental drift went from the category of quack theory to proven fact, and it was quickly christened with the more academically respectable name of "plate tectonics." It is enlightening to note that as late as 1960 geologists or oceanographers who dared to say they believed in continental drift would pretty much ruin their academic careers. Less than ten years later, any scientist who *denied* the new scientific dogma of plate tectonics had become the pariah.

History has proven, through many such examples, that the human mind is inherently conservative. The obvious is not always easily seen, and the truth is often firmly resisted in order to hold onto the "assured results" of authoritative scholarship. It is not, of course, news that humans have an innate tendency toward conservatism that impels us to quash contrary opinions, no matter how self-evident. The great Galileo was placed under house arrest by the church for going public with the evidence his eyes showed him. But it is not only scientists who have been forced to pay high prices for redefining the way we understand our world. Such injustices happen in all fields of research, perhaps none more so than the field of theology. Theologians who dare to challenge theological dogma are as ostracized by their peers as scientists who challenge scientific dogma. Just one of many recent examples is the shameful treatment of the Dead Sea Scrolls scholar Robert Eisenman, whose peers in an effort to discredit his theories on James and Christian origins went so far as to publicly accuse him of plagiarism (unjustly, as it turned out).[1] Paradigm challenges are never suffered lightly by the orthodox establishment in any field.

In some ways, challenging paradigms is harder today than it ever has been because the modern academic world is a world of minute specialization. As a result, today's scientists, philosophers, and theologians often suffer from severe myopia, their noses so buried in the details of their particular fields of research that the forest is often missed for the trees. The days of the classic philosopher, whose job it once was to fit the pieces of research from various fields together into larger theoretical pictures, is gone. The branch of philosophy known as metaphysics, whose task it originally was to systematically organize all knowledge into overarching paradigms, is frowned upon today. Postmodern thinking has declared such efforts bankrupt. This book, however, dares to synthesize all the evidence we have about James and the early church, and the result is a view of the man and the church that is radically at odds with accepted wisdom and scholarship. The theories I present in this book are not new. They have all been proposed before, but have either been sheepishly ignored or unfairly discredited. To rectify matters, we will here survey all the extant evidence that exists on James, along with running commentary by scholars that shows how this material has been interpreted. You will find that I have let the scholars speak largely for themselves, and I have worked hard to let all of the voices—both liberal and conservative—be heard.

In part 1 we will examine the nature of Jesus' family. After an overview of the evidence for James's relationship to Jesus and James's role in the early Christian community in chapter 1, in chapter 2 we undertake a detailed examination of the nature of Jesus' family as seen in the four gospels, which will lay a firm foundation for all that follows. The exact familial relationship of Jesus to his brothers and sisters has been a matter of controversy between Roman Catholic, Eastern Orthodox, and Protestant Christians, and Jesus' relationship to his family during his ministry has largely been misinterpreted by almost all Christian scholars, with tangible consequences in the history of Christianity.

In part 2 we investigate the nature of the earliest Christian community—generally referred to as the Jerusalem church—of which James was the leader. In chapter 3 we examine the evidence from the New Testament about this community, particularly the testimony of the early church history written by Luke (the book of Acts) and the invaluable firsthand testimony of Paul, particularly his letter to the Galatians. In chapter 4 we undertake an analysis of two watershed events in the history of earliest Christianity: the Apostolic Council held in Jerusalem (described in Acts 15), and the incident at Antioch where Peter and Paul come to loggerheads over the issue of table fellowship between Jews and Gentiles. Both these events provide us with significant amounts of information about James's leadership role in the Jerusalem church. In chapter 5 we will discuss the dynamics and friction between Paul and the Jerusalem Christians that finally sparked when Paul made his final visit to Jerusalem and which led to his arrest and imprisonment in Rome. We will also take at look at the fascinating account of James's martyrdom from the respected Jewish historian Josephus.

Part 3 examines the nature of a fascinating phenomenon in early Christianity that scholars generally refer to as Jewish Christianity, a widespread community that retained its Jewish roots, beliefs, and practices while adhering to Jesus as the Messiah of Israel and revering the memory of James. Chapter 6 surveys the literature on James and Jewish Christianity that exists in the writings of early church historians and the church fathers, while chapter 7 surveys the writings on James that come from later Jewish Christian and Gnostic communities whose beliefs caused them to be branded as heretics by the Catholic Church.

In light of the first three parts, part 4 examines the nature of orthodoxy and heresy. Here we shall be led to some startling conclusions about who were the orthodox and who were the heretics in early Christianity. We shall see why Christianity inevitably parted ways with parent Judaism, and why there continues to be an impassible divide between Christians, Jews, and Muslims—one that has led to the precarious state of political affairs in the Western world today and even to which the blame for such tragic events as 9/11 can be attributed. Finally, in part 5 we shall endeavor to synthesize all of our information into a new paradigm that can perhaps repair the tragic breach between the children of Abraham.

If I have made any original contribution to the debate about James, it is simply in performing the philosophical task of bringing others' findings together to allow a bigger picture to emerge. Many theologians would prefer for this emerging picture not to be put on public display, for its implications will have major repercussions not only on the average Christian, but on Jews and Muslims as well. If and when it is ever fully realized, the emerging paradigm shift presented here could forever change how the three great Western religions—the "people of the Book," as the Qur'an calls the descendants of Abraham—understand their holy scriptures and their relationship to each other. This paradigm shift could even help to usher in—at long last—peace in the Middle East.

The story of this nascent revolution begins at the epicenter of Western religion: the city of Jerusalem, where Jews and Christians first parted ways almost two millennia ago. Our story begins with two first-century Jewish brothers named Jesus and James.

1

THE NATURE OF JESUS' FAMILY

1

PERSONA NON GRATA:
JAMES THE BROTHER OF JESUS

*Jesus . . . came to his hometown . . . On the Sabbath he
began to teach in the synagogue, and many who heard
him were astounded. They said, "Where did this man
get all this? What is this wisdom that has been given to
him? What deeds of power are being done by his hands!
Is not this the carpenter, the son of Mary and the
brother of James and Joses and Judas and Simon, and
are not his sisters here with us?"*

THE GOSPEL ACCORDING TO MARK 6:1–3

Jesus had siblings. This simple, seemingly innocuous statement actually
raises a host of profound questions, the answers to which have startling
implications. Perhaps it is because these questions are so sensitive to some
Christians—indeed, divisive—that the subject of Jesus' brothers and sisters has largely been ignored both by biblical scholars and by the
Christian church. Yet the evidence of Jesus' siblings is so widespread that
there can be no doubt of their existence. The amount of information that
exists on Jesus' brothers, particularly James, is quite surprising. As we see
above, Mark even provides the names of Jesus' four brothers; nonetheless,
in my experience both as a pastor of a Lutheran church and an instructor
of world religions in a public university, people are almost always incred-
ulous when told that Jesus had brothers and sisters. This is not something
they have usually been taught in church or Sunday School.

The recent discovery, in 2002, of an ancient Middle Eastern ossuary (a burial box) made international headlines because of the startling inscription on the box, which identified this particular ossuary as once containing the bones of "James, son of Joseph, brother of Jesus." This find was shocking both to the academic community and the general public for two reasons. First, if genuine (and this is still a hotly debated question), the artifact would be the first archaeological evidence—literally written in stone—of the existence of Jesus, but even more intriguing to the public was the fact that this burial box was purported to be that of *James*, whom the New Testament refers to in several places as the "brother" of Jesus. The many newspaper and magazine articles that appeared after the announcement of this discovery all gave short shrift to the ossuary itself and devoted the majority of space to the controversy over whether Jesus could have had a brother. That is what most fascinated the public.

FROM JACOB TO JAMES

We shall not go here into the particulars of the discovery and testing of the ossuary, which has been amply documented elsewhere;[1] instead, our focus will be on the person whose bones are claimed to have once been entombed in that box: the brother of Jesus, most commonly known in church tradition as "James the Just" (because of his exceeding righteousness) or "James of Jerusalem" (his base of operations) or, much more rarely, "James the Brother of Jesus."

James's name is derived from one of the great patriarchs of Jewish history—Jacob. "James" is the English translation of the Greek *Iakob*, which is itself a translation of the Hebrew *Ya'akov*. In the English translation of the Greek New Testament, *Iakob* is always translated as "Jacob" when referring to Old Testament figures, and as "James" when referring to Christian figures. This is interesting because, as we shall see, James represents a bridge between Judaism and Christianity. The Greek "Jacob" became the English "James" by way of Latin, in which *Jacobus* and *Jacomus* are variations of the same name. The Latin also explains why in European history the dynasty of King James is referred to as "Jacobite" or "Jacobean."

Iakob was an exceedingly common name in first-century Israel, as evidenced by the fact that eight different people in the New Testament bear the name. The scholarly consensus is that half of the occurrences of the name in the New Testament refer to James the son of Zebedee (the brother of John, also referred to as James the Elder), one of two apostles who bear the name. A third of the occurrences of the name refer to Jesus' brother, who is, unfortunately, often confused with the James known as James the Less, but James the Less is correctly James the son of Alphaeus, the second of the two apostles who bear the name. That the brother of Jesus has sometimes been called James "the Less" is just one example of the many slights and indignations he has been forced to bear.

It is surprising that such widespread ignorance of Jesus' siblings exists, for, besides the New Testament itself, there exist quite a number of non-canonical writings from the earliest days of the church that provide absolutely reliable evidence that Jesus not only had siblings, but that some (if not all) of his brothers played significant roles in the leadership of the early church. In fact, James was considered by many early Christians to be the first "bishop" of the church, the successor to Jesus following the crucifixion, making James in essence the first "pope," not Peter as Catholic tradition has maintained. The church father Clement of Alexandria in his work *Hypostases* (Outlines), written at the beginning of the third century, makes the following rather startling statement: "After the ascension of the savior, Peter, James [the Son of Zebedee], and John did not claim pre-eminence because the savior had specifically honored them, but chose James the Just as Bishop of Jerusalem."[2] While Clement's use of the title "bishop" is certainly an anachronism, it is a term that, as we shall see, does accord well with James's role in the church as it is described in both the book of Acts, Luke's history of the early church from the ascension of Jesus to Paul's imprisonment in Rome, and in Paul's letter to the Galatians, where Paul describes two meetings he had with James and the other apostles in Jerusalem.

James the Just, as Clement calls him, is the appellation by which Jesus' brother has most commonly been known in the church's writings. It is a title originally bestowed upon James by early Jewish-Christian groups such as the Nazoreans, the Ebionites, and the Elkesaites, who revered James for his outstanding righteousness under the Law and considered him to be the leader of the apostles after the death of Jesus. These Jewish-Christian sects claimed to be the remnants of the original Jerusalem church which had been scattered and dispersed after the siege of Jerusalem by the Romans in 70 C.E., a claim that, if true, would make them direct successors to the apostles. These groups and their startling claims will be discussed in part 4.

In light of the widespread esteem for James in many quarters of the early church, we are compelled to ask why it is that he is almost completely unknown among modern-day Christians. It can justifiably be said that of all the figures in the New Testament, he is the most mysterious. If one reads through the New Testament from the beginning, the first major reference to James comes at Acts 12:17, where Peter goes to the house of Mary, the mother of Mark, after miraculously escaping from prison, and urges her to "Tell this to James and the brethren." What is curious here is that the reader is given no explanation of who James is, an omission that is especially striking because he has not been mentioned before in Acts. The only logical conclusion one can come to is that James was of such stature in the early Christian community that Luke (the author of Acts) simply assumed his readers were well aware of who James was. He was obviously important enough that Peter wanted the news of his escape from prison to reach James first. It would also seem from Peter's statement that James was the leader of "the brethren," since he is singled out by name. Note well that this would mean James was the leader of the Jerusalem church by at least the early 40's C.E., when this incident most likely occurred (Jesus' crucifixion is generally dated between 30 and 33).

Just as puzzling as this reference in Acts is Paul's mention of James in his first letter to the Christian community in Corinth—his famous list of those to whom Jesus appeared after his resurrection:

> [H]e appeared to Cephas [Peter], then to the twelve. Then he appeared to more than five hundred brothers and sisters at one time, most of whom are still alive, though some have died. Then he appeared to James, then to all the apostles. (1 Cor. 15:5–7)

Here, as in Acts, Paul apparently assumes his audience is well acquainted with James, for again no identification is given. It is significant that of all of those to whom Jesus appeared only Cephas (Cephas is Aramaic for Peter) and James are important enough to be singled out by name. So while James is almost completely unknown to modern readers, it would seem that the early readers of the New Testament writings were well acquainted with him and that in the earliest days of Christianity he was a major figure, equal in stature to Peter, well known to the earliest Christians, and not easily confused with any other James (of whom there were many).

BISHOP OF THE CHURCH

As one reads further in Acts, the significance of James's role in the affairs of the earliest Christian community in Jerusalem—commonly referred to as the "Jerusalem church"—becomes clear. At some point early on, James becomes the head of the Jerusalem church (if he hadn't always been so, a question we shall examine shortly), apparently having authority even over Peter, who has traditionally been considered the leader of the disciples following Jesus' death. In Acts 15, James is clearly the central figure in the great debate about how Jewish law applied to Gentile converts and is even portrayed as the final arbiter at the so-called Jerusalem Conference, convened to decide this question, and as the author of the "Apostolic Decree" that was issued there.

James's leadership of the Jerusalem church is surprising for a number of reasons. First, the impression one gets from the gospels is that Jesus' brothers did not believe in him and were opposed to his mission. For example, the gospel of John shows Jesus' brothers apparently challenging him:

> Now the Jewish festival of booths was near. So his brothers said to him, "Leave here and go to Judea so that your disciples also may see the works you are doing; for no one who wants to be widely known acts in secret. If you do these things show yourself to the world." (For not even his brothers believed in him.) (John 7:2–5)

John's parenthetical comment makes clear why *he* believed Jesus' brothers challenged him.

A second reason that the evidence for James's leadership of the Jerusalem church comes as such a surprise is that Peter is traditionally thought of as the leader of the apostles, the "rock" on which Jesus built his church, in Roman Catholic tradition the first pope, or spiritual leader. It is therefore astounding to discover such clear evidence in the New Testament, as well as in later history and tradition, that James was actually the leader of the Jerusalem church. As we shall see, even Peter bows to his authority.

A number of scholars have pointed out that if anyone deserves the title of first pope, by virtue of being the first leader of the Christian church, it is James, not Peter. So how do we account for James's rapid rise to such prominence (especially if James had been a nonbeliever, as is traditionally assumed), and why has James's prominent role become so obscured? As we investigate these questions, we shall see that a real revolution is under way in our understanding of the history and development of the early church. James turns out to be the key that unlocks a dusty old vault containing a treasure trove of information that the ecclesiastical powers-that-be have attempted to conceal for close to two millennia.

BROTHER OF JESUS

Connected to these questions about James's role in the church is the more imposing question of his relationship with his brother Jesus, as well as the question of Jesus' relationship to the rest of his family. As we have already seen, certain statements in the gospels seem to imply that the members of Jesus' family did not believe in Jesus' work and ministry during his lifetime. Traditionally, both scholars and clergy have considered Jesus' family highly skeptical of—and even opposed to—Jesus' mission, a conclusion based mainly on the following passage from the gospel of Mark:

> Jesus went back home, and once again such a large crowd gathered that there was no chance even to eat. When Jesus' family heard what he was doing, they thought he was crazy and went to get him under control. (Mark 3:20–21, CEV)

Given that portrayal of the family, it is puzzling to note how quickly they must have converted from nonbelievers to believers after the crucifixion; for opposed to the picture that Mark paints, the first chapter of Acts clearly demonstrates a close bond between Jesus' family and the disciples not long after the crucifixion:

> Then they returned to Jerusalem from the mount called Olivet . . . When they had entered the city, they went to the room upstairs where they were staying, Peter, and John, and James, and Andrew, Philip and Thomas, Bartholomew and Matthew, James son of Alphaeus, and

Simon the Zealot, and Judas son of James. All these were constantly devoting themselves to prayer, together with certain women, *including Mary the mother of Jesus, as well as his brothers.* (Acts 1:12–14; italics mine)

Here we have evidence that Jesus' mother and brothers were not only all present in Jerusalem within weeks of the crucifixion, but that they also spent intimate time in prayer with Jesus' disciples, which is unlikely if they had been opposed to Jesus and the apostles' mission. We also have evidence here that Jesus' brothers are *not* to be identified with the apostles, refuting the commonly heard argument from some quarters that references to Jesus' brothers in the Bible are to be understood as meaning his "spiritual" brothers, that is, his disciples.

While biblical evidence states clearly that Jesus had brothers, the exact relationship of Jesus to those whom the New Testament calls his "brothers and sisters" has been hotly debated by scholars and theologians, many contending that these are not actually *blood* brothers and sisters. By the end of the fourth century, three positions on this question had been established. According to the so-called Epiphanian view, named after its main proponent, the fourth-century bishop Epiphanius, and championed by the third-century theologian Origen and fourth-century bishop Eusebius, the "brothers" and "sisters" mentioned in the New Testament are all older than Jesus—sons of Joseph from a previous marriage, and hence only stepbrothers of Jesus. This view is still the official position of the Eastern Orthodox churches. Another viewpoint, the Hieronymian theory, was first proposed by the church father Jerome and argues that those whom the New Testament calls brothers and sisters were actually Jesus' *cousins*—children of Mary's sister. This remains the official Roman Catholic position. How these ideas arose will be examined later, but for now, it is sufficient to point out that these positions were developed early on to uphold the emerging dogma of the perpetual virginity of Mary. An ever-virgin Mary obviously could not have had children other than Jesus unless they had also been miraculously conceived.

The stance taken in this book is the position traditionally known as the Helvidian view, after the Roman theologian Helvidius, which understands the brothers and sisters of Jesus cited in the New Testament to be full siblings of Jesus, born to Mary and Joseph after the firstborn Jesus. This understanding is able to retain the doctrine of the virgin birth, but does not claim an ever-virgin Mary. This has been the traditional Protestant position. It is the most natural reading of all the New Testament citations that we shall examine, and requires no bending or stretching of the plain reading of the original Greek text. Also in support of this view we have Luke's famous words in the Nativity story: "And she gave birth to her *first-born* son and wrapped him in bands of cloth, and laid him in a manger, because there was no place for them in the inn" (Luke 2:7). If Jesus was an only child, why would Luke use the term "first-born"? Another piece of evidence for Mary and Joseph having normal conjugal relations after the birth of Jesus, comes from the gospel according to Matthew: "This is how the birth of Jesus Christ came about: His mother Mary was pledged to be married to Joseph, but *before they came together*, she was found to be with child through the Holy Spirit" (Matt. 1:18, NIV). "Before they came together" is a classic biblical euphemism along the lines of "Adam knew Eve."

The number of references in the New Testament to Jesus having natural siblings is not insignificant. Mention is made of Jesus' brothers in all four gospels. There are seven references altogether: Mark 3:31–35 and 6:3; Matthew 12:46–50 and 13:55–56; Luke 8:19–21; and John 2:12 and 7:3–5. James is cited several times in the book of Acts, where he plays a huge role in the leadership of the disciples in the decades following Jesus' crucifixion (Acts 12:17; 15:13–21; 21:17–26). Paul speaks of meeting with James in his letter to the Galatians (1:19 and 2:1–12), giving us the most solid and undisputed evidence we have that James was a prominent leader of the Jerusalem church. In all these instances, James clearly seems to be understood as the natural brother of Jesus. Further evidence for the role of Jesus' brothers is found in 1 Corinthians, where we learn not only that James was a witness to the Resurrection, but also that Jesus' other brothers were traveling evangelists. Paul states in passing:

> This is my defense to those who would examine me. Do we not have the right to our food and drink? Do we not have the right to be accompanied by a believing wife, as do the other apostles and the brothers of the Lord and Cephas? (1 Cor. 9:5)

Paul's words are startling. Not only does this passage provide further evidence that Jesus' brothers are not to be identified with the apostles, but it also claims that Jesus' brothers and the apostles (including

Peter) were *married*; a two-fold strike against the traditional Catholic teaching that bases the requirement of priestly celibacy on the understanding that Jesus and his apostles were not married.* In fact, according to Mark's gospel, one of Jesus' first miracles is curing Peter's mother-in-law of a fever.†

Finally, in addition to all of the other evidence to be found in the New Testament, there are two letters attributed to brothers of Jesus— the letters of James and Jude—although their actual authorship is a much debated question.

EARLY HERO

References to James also abound outside of the Bible. First and foremost, independent attestation to the remarkable role James played in apostolic times is found in the writings of the revered Jewish historian Josephus, whose works *The Wars of the Jews* and *The Antiquities of the Jews* are contemporaneous with the New Testament. In these highly regarded histories, Josephus actually discusses James at greater length than Jesus.

Many early church Fathers also discuss James, including Clement, Eusebius, Hegesippus, Jerome, and Origen. James is also highly regarded—indeed, revered—in many of the apocryphal books that were excluded from the New Testament, such as the *Gospel of the Hebrews* and the *Protevangelium of James*—a book wholly about James. The famous cache of Gnostic writings discovered at Nag Hammadi in 1945 includes several works that bear James's name in their titles, such as the *Apocryphon of James*, the *First Apocalypse of James,* and the *Second Apocalypse of James*. There are also references to James in the now highly regarded *Gospel of Thomas,* championed by many scholars as a legitimate "fifth gospel." These writings all bear witness to the high esteem in which James was held among early Christians.

James is looked to as the apostle *par excellence* by early Jewish-Christian sects such as the Ebionites and Elkesaites, who revered James

---

*As we shall see in chapter 9, the tradition of priestly celibacy in the Catholic church goes back primarily to Jerome and the emergence of the doctrine of the perpetual virginity of Mary.

†See Mark 1:30–31; see also Mathew 8:14–15 and Luke 4:38–39.

while disdaining Paul and his desire to jettison the requirement that Gentile converts adhere to Jewish law. As we shall see, James is at the storm-center of the early debate over how the Jewish law applied to Gentile converts to Christianity. It was James's exceeding righteousness under the Law that led to these Jewish-Christian groups giving him the epithet "the Just." It was their desire to adhere to James's upholding of faith *and* works (see James 1:17) rather than Paul's teaching of faith in Christ as a replacement for the Law, that caused these early Jewish-Christian sects to be labeled as heretics by the emerging Catholic orthodoxy. Many scholars today are beginning to recognize that an understanding of the phenomenon generally referred to as "Jewish Christianity" is vital to our understanding of how and why Christianity parted ways with Judaism to become a distinct religion.

The importance of Jewish Christianity for an understanding of the early church was first recognized by the notorious liberal German scholar Ferdinand Christian Baur of Tübingen University, who in the early 1800s proposed that the accepted idea of unity and harmonious cooperation among the earliest Christians was a fiction. Baur and his followers (the so-called Tübingen school) posited a sharp division, even an outright battle, between Paul and Jesus' apostles over the issue of Jewish law. While conservative scholars forcefully opposed Baur's theories and his ideas fell out of favor by the early 1900s, a number of major scholars today are beginning to reevaluate Baur in light of the most recent understandings of the thorough Jewishness of Jesus exemplified in the writings of such respected scholars as E. P. Sanders, Geza Vermes, and James Dunn.

The rediscovery of the Jewishness of Jesus is causing a renaissance of sorts in the study of the historical Jesus, a subject that is as fraught with lack of consensus in its current manifestation as it was back in the days of Albert Schweitzer and his groundbreaking work *The Quest of the Historical Jesus*. James actually provides one of the most solid pieces of evidence we have in the often illusory quest for the historical Jesus. Indeed, James is a vital key to an understanding of the beliefs and teachings of Jesus. As maverick scholar Robert Eisenman starkly puts it: "Once James has been rescued from the oblivion into which he was cast . . . [it] will no longer be possible to avoid . . . the obvious solution to the problem of the Historical Jesus . . . the answer to which is simple. Who and whatever James was, so was Jesus."[3]

FORGOTTEN HERO

Regrettably, the memory of James, his relationship to his brother Jesus, and his significant contributions to the early church became lost in the official history and teaching of Christianity for reasons both benign and malignant. James's story is thus a tragic one. Because the knowledge we have of Jesus' siblings is threatening to those with vested theological or ecclesiastical interests, James was forgotten, downplayed, and even intentionally suppressed. In the Roman Catholic and Eastern Orthodox traditions, adherence to the doctrine of the perpetual virginity of Mary makes the notion of Jesus having natural siblings scandalous. In the Protestant tradition, James's seeming support for "works righteousness," especially as it was understood from the New Testament letter of James ("Faith without works is dead," James says in chapter 1), was viewed as antithetical to the all-important Protestant doctrine of *sola fide* (faith alone). It was for this reason that Martin Luther referred to the epistle of James as an "epistle of straw," and would have much preferred its removal from the New Testament. From about the fourth century, disdain for James and his teachings—and even for acknowledging his existence—spread wide. As a result, his vital contributions to the early church were lost. Nonetheless, when the role of James is recovered and objectively assessed, it can justifiably be said that James is the great "lost hero" of Christianity.

My research into James's understanding of the Jewish law has impelled me, as a Lutheran pastor, to come to grips with the question of where Jesus would have stood in the debate over the Law in the early church. Frankly, I have been swayed by the evidence to believe that Jesus was much more Law-oriented than most Protestants (and Lutherans especially) have ever realized. I have come to harbor a strong suspicion that Protestantism may have carried the doctrine of *sola fide* to an extreme that Jesus himself would not have advocated.

The so-called new perspective on Paul and Second Temple Judaism that has been burgeoning in recent decades has attempted to correct this Protestant misunderstanding by demonstrating that the Law-oriented Judaism of Jesus' day valued salvation by grace much more than Christians have ever realized. While it may come as quite a surprise to most Protestant Christians, the widely respected New Testament scholar James Dunn has shown that the Father of the Reformation,

Martin Luther, who based his insights on "salvation by grace through faith" in Paul's writings, largely misunderstood Paul's theology:

> Luther read his own experience back into Paul. He assumed that Paul too must have been confronted by a dominant tradition which taught justification by works . . . that the Judaism of Paul's day must have taught the equivalent of the Catholicism of Luther's day . . . Unfortunately the grid remained firmly in place for Protestant scholarship thereafter.[4]

The conservative Protestant scholar, Richard Bauckham, has also recognized this:

> [A] theological tradition which originated with Martin Luther subordinates [the epistle of] James to Paul . . . Luther famously deplored James's contradiction of the Pauline . . . doctrine of justification by faith alone . . . and relegated James to a virtually apocryphal status on the margin of the canon.[5]

Undoubtedly, this is the major reason for the marginalization of James in the Protestant tradition.

Current research into Paul is making it quite obvious that the early Protestant reformers, due to the pressing issues of the Reformation, grossly misunderstood the Judaism of Jesus' day, the Judaism to which both Jesus and James adhered. A recovery of James's understanding of the Law can provide a much-needed correction to this misunderstanding, just one more example of why recovering James is so important to Christianity today. Recovering James and his teaching is not only an important step toward resolving the centuries-old Catholic-Protestant debate over the relative merits of works and faith, but it is also vital to expanding the interfaith dialogue between Christians, Jews, and Muslims. James may well be the missing link that can bring peace and reconciliation to "the people of the Book."

As should be obvious by now, salvaging James from the distortion, misrepresentation, abuse, and neglect to which he has been subjected will necessitate exploring many different avenues of research. So let us turn now to an investigation of how James and Jesus' other siblings are portrayed in the only biographies we have of Jesus—the four gospels. Many more surprises await us.

2

A FAMILY DIVIDED: JESUS' FAMILY IN THE GOSPELS

> *Then Jesus entered a house, and again a crowd gathered,*
> *so that he and his disciples were not even able*
> *to eat. When his family heard about this, they went to*
> *take charge of him, for they said, "He is out of his mind."*
> THE GOSPEL ACCORDING TO MARK 3:20–21 (NIV)

> *For not even his brothers believed in him.*
> THE GOSPEL ACCORDING TO JOHN 7:5 (NRSV)

Because of statements in the gospels such as those above, the vast majority of scholars and theologians have understood Jesus' family to be opposed to (or at least highly skeptical of) Jesus' ministry and mission during his lifetime. A standard reference work found on the bookshelves of almost all clergy, *The Interpreter's Dictionary of the Bible*, unequivocally states that Jesus' brothers:

> did not approve of Jesus' ministry. This is clear in the . . . gospels. Jesus himself . . . said that a prophet is without honor "in his own house" (Matt. 13:57; Mark 6:4). This clearly implies opposition within his own family.[1]

Many standard preaching commentaries of a prior generation share this assessment. For example, Barclay's *Daily Study Bible* in its commentary

20

on Mark 3:20–21 says: "Jesus' own family had come to the conclusion that He had taken leave of his senses."[2] The *Cambridge Bible Commentary* concurs: "Jesus' own relations think he must be mad: instead of following his father's trade and settling down to an ordinary life, he is mixed up . . . so they try to rescue him."[3]

Uncritical acceptance of such commentary has left the impression in many people's minds that Jesus' rejection by his family is historical fact. Some recent scholarship, however, presents a more nuanced view, suggesting that passages such as Mark 3:20–21 are open to divergent interpretations and may even turn the traditional interpretation on its head. If one accepts the standard line that Jesus' family was opposed to his mission, some interesting questions are raised when one moves from the gospels to the book of Acts and the letters of Paul. As mentioned in the previous chapter, the speed with which Jesus' mother and brothers shifted from being nonbelievers to believers after the crucifixion is perplexing in light of what the gospels say about them. As the *Interpreter's Dictionary of the Bible* summarizes the situation: "The [New Testament] . . . regards the brothers of the Lord as . . . unresponsive to his preaching during his earthly ministry, but active and leading members of the church from the beginning of the apostolic age."[4]

The widely respected evangelical scholar, F. F. Bruce, succinctly puts the question this way: "How . . . did it come about that [Jesus'] relatives, who did not figure at all among his followers before his death, should so soon afterwards be found taking a leading place among them?"[5] This question has usually been answered, as Bruce does, by citing the resurrection appearance to James, which, it is believed, resulted in a sudden, dramatic conversion experience similar to the one that changed Paul from a persecutor of Christianity into its most ardent spokesman when Christ appeared to him. This solution reasonably claims that the empty tomb and the subsequent resurrection appearances had the same galvanizing effect on James and Jesus' family that it did on the apostles, but it raises other questions: Since we are told by Paul that Jesus' other brothers became Christian evangelists, are we to suppose that they *all* received resurrection appearances? Or was the rest of the family converted by the witness of James? Or is there, perhaps, another answer?

The two primary scholars who have done in-depth research into Jesus' family, John Painter and Richard Bauckham, have put forth another answer that is as surprising as it is sensible: Perhaps Jesus' family was never opposed to his ministry in the first place. There is ample evidence that Jesus' family were not, in fact, unbelievers. Painter and Bauckham propose that the gospel passages that have traditionally been understood as showing Jesus' family in opposition to his mission (including the seemingly damning Mark 3:21 and John 7:5) have been misunderstood and need not be read in a negative light. Painter in particular believes that Jesus' family was *never* opposed to his mission, that they were actually supporters of his ministry from its inception.

In point of fact, the *only* two passages in either the New Testament or any other early Christian literature that seem to show Jesus' family opposing his mission are the aforementioned Mark 3:21 and John 7:5. But Mark 3:21 in particular is quite convoluted in the original Greek and has engendered a number of quite varied translations. And John 7:2–5, except for the author's parenthetical comment, can also be interpreted in other ways. Yet these two brief passages have influenced our understanding of Jesus' relationship to his family far beyond their merit.

In the rest of this chapter, we will focus primarily on an investigation of Mark 3:20–21 and its parallels in the other synoptic gospels, Matthew and Luke.* We will be going into some depth here, but the detail is vital for laying a firm foundation for the arguments that follow. Until we can get past Mark 3:21, we cannot begin to reimagine the character and role of James and the nature of early Christianity.

We will also examine the handful of other passages in the gospels that make mention of Jesus' family for the light they can shed on the historical traditions that might lie behind Mark 3:20–21. Our goal will be to work our way back through what scholars refer to as the three stages of gospel formation: from *stage three* (the stories as we have them written in the pages of the gospels) back to *stage two* (the oral traditions that were in circulation before the gospels were written down, and which served as the basis for the written gospels) to *stage one*—the elusive holy grail of historical Jesus studies: the actual historical events that gave rise to both the oral tradition and the later written accounts.

---

*The term "synoptic" comes from the Greek, meaning to "see together" and refers to the fact that Matthew, Mark, and Luke essentially tell the same story. John's gospel is quite different in style and content from the three synoptic gospels.

Such work requires a thorough investigation; we will need to rigorously process a mass of evidence with the eye of a forensic scientist searching for clues at the scene of a crime.

THE FAMILY ACCORDING TO MARK

Almost all scholars today agree that Mark is the earliest gospel, composed about 70 C.E., and that the authors of Matthew and Luke used it as a blueprint in composing their own gospels. To begin our investigation, let us take a look at Mark 3:20–21 in its immediate context. As any beginning Bible student is taught, it can be dangerous to pull individual Bible verses out of their context in support of an argument. Mark 3:20–21 is a classic example. Let us first examine the entire *pericope** of Mark 3:20–35 as translated in the popular Revised Standard Version (second edition):

> Then he [Jesus] went home; 20 and the crowd came together again, so that they could not even eat. 21 And when his family heard it, they went out to seize him, for people were saying, "He is beside himself." 22 And the scribes who came down from Jerusalem said, "He is possessed by Beelzebul, and by the prince of demons he casts out the demons." 23 And he called them to him, and said to them in parables, "How can Satan cast out Satan? 24 If a kingdom is divided against itself, that kingdom cannot stand. 25 And if a house is divided against itself, that house will not be able to stand. 26 And if Satan has risen up against himself and is divided, he cannot stand, but is coming to an end. 27 But no one can enter a strong man's house and plunder his goods, unless he first binds the strong man; then indeed he may plunder his house.
>
> 28 "Truly, I say to you, all sins will be forgiven the sons of men, and whatever blasphemies they utter; 29 but whoever blasphemes against the Holy Spirit never has forgiveness, but is guilty of an eternal sin"—30 for they had said, "He has an unclean spirit."
>
> 31 And his mother and his brothers came; and standing outside they sent to him and called him. 32 And a crowd was sitting about him; and they said to him, "Your mother and your brothers are outside, asking for

---

Pericope is a term scholars use to refer to a complete literary unit in the Bible.

you." 33 And he replied, "Who are my mother and my brothers?" 34 And looking around on those who sat about him, he said, "Here are my mother and my brothers! 35 Whoever does the will of God is my brother, and sister, and mother."

First, it is interesting that there is an ancient variation of this passage, known as the "Western text" by scholars, which makes a subtle but striking change to verse 21. Instead of reading "when his family heard it," the Western text reads, "When *the scribes and the others* heard about him." It would seem obvious here that someone intentionally "monkeyed" with this text.* The prime suspect would be a devout ancient copyist who meant no harm, but substituted the words "the scribes and others" for "his family" in an attempt to cope with the embarrassment of Jesus' own family taking action against him because they think he's insane.

The variation found in the Western text is not the only attempt that has been made to relieve the discomfort that this passage causes. With the voluminous number of Bible translations produced in the past few decades, Mark 3:20–21 has seen some other significant variations in its translation. Even the Revised Standard Version, the favorite of Protestants for over a hundred years, significantly altered its translation of verse 21 between editions, greatly impacting the interpretation of this passage. The second edition is quoted above. The first reads (italics mine):

> And when *his friends* heard it, they went out to seize him, for *they* said, "He is beside himself."

The earlier RSV translation followed the lead of the King James Version, which translates verse 21 thus:

> And when his friends heard of it, they went out to lay hold on him: for they said, He is beside himself.

---

*"Monkeying with a text" is a phrase I have borrowed from a beloved professor from my seminary days, Dr. Arthur Freeman, bishop in the Moravian Church, who believes there are more than a few passages in the New Testament that were "monkeyed with" by scribes and copyists.

Obviously, these translations do not shed any negative light on Jesus' family. Rather, the opposition comes from "his friends" (whoever they might be; obviously, they could include Jesus' family, but this would be stretching the interpretation), and it is these friends who say Jesus is "beside himself," which is a bit more polite than saying Jesus was "out of his mind."

Before examining the reasons for these significant changes in translation, let us look at how some other important translations have handled this delicate passage (italics again mine):

New Revised Standard Version (a mainline* ecumenical translation):

> When *his family* heard it, they went out to restrain him, for *people* were saying, "He has gone out of his mind."

New International Version (an evangelical Protestant translation):

> When *his family* heard about this, they went to take charge of him, for *they* said, "He is out of his mind."

The Anchor Bible (a mainline ecumenical commentary):

> On hearing of this, *his family* set out to take charge of him, for *people* were saying that he was out of his mind.

Word Biblical Commentary (an evangelical Protestant commentary):

> When *his people* heard, they set out to take him into their custody. For *they* said, "He was out of his mind."

The New American Bible (a Roman Catholic translation):

> When *his relatives* heard of this they set out to seize him, for *they* said, "He is out of his mind."

---

*In biblical studies, the term *mainline* refers to those churches directly descended from the Catholic Church.

The Scholar's Version (a liberal secular translation):

> When *his relatives* heard about it, they came to get him. (You see, *they* thought he was out of his mind).

Obviously, these variations in translation allow for significantly different interpretations of this critical passage. Whether it is Jesus' family or the crowd or "people" who are saying he is "beside himself" or "out of his mind" or "crazy," and whether it was his family or his friends or his "people" who came to "seize him" or "restrain him" or "get him under control"—these details significantly affect our understanding of this passage.

To fully understand how these variations are possible, it is necessary to engage in the somewhat unpleasant task of dissecting the original Greek in which this passage was written. Here is how the all-important verse 21 looks in the original Greek:

> καὶ ἀκούσαντες οἱ παρ' αὐτοῦ ἐξῆλθον κρατῆσαι αὐτόν· ἔλεγον γὰρ ὅτι ἐξέστη.

If this is "all Greek to you," here is a transliteration from Greek characters into English characters:

> *Kai akousantes hoi par autou exelthon kratesai auton; elegon gar hoti exeste.*

A literal, word-for-word translation is:

Kai akousantes	*hoi par autou*	*exelthon*	*kratesai auton;*
And hearing [it],	the ones with him	went forth	to seize him;
elegon gar	*hoti exeste.*		
for they said	that he is beside himself.		

There are essentially two main issues of translation here that bear significantly on the interpretation of this passage and that have shown up in variant ways in English:

1. Is *hoi par autou* (the ones with him) best translated as "his family," or "his friends," or "his people"?

2. Who is the "they" who say that he is "beside himself"? Is it people in general, or was it his family or his friends?

How these translation decisions are made ultimately depends on a given passage's context, as I will explain in a moment. Thus, translations of this critical verse are more exactly *interpretations* based on the verse's surrounding text rather than exact word-for-word translations. But before moving on to investigate the surrounding context of this verse, let us first place under the microscope the extremely critical translation of *hoi par autou*, literally, "the [ones] with him," or "the [ones] from him." The mother of all Greek reference books, Walter Bauer's *Greek-English Lexicon of the New Testament and Other Early Christian Literature*, tells us that this phrase, "nearly always . . . denotes a person, and indicates that something proceeds from this person . . . *from (the side of)*."[6] Specifically referring to its use in Mark 3:21, the lexicon states that, "The [Greek] also uses this expression to denote others who are intimately connected with someone, e.g. *family, relatives*."[7] About this matter, the *Anchor Bible* commentary states:

> The Greek phrase covers all manner of meanings, from "envoys" and "adherents" to "neighbors and family." The sense is correctly conveyed by the Vulgate [the Latin translation] *sui* (his own). The reference is to immediate family, and not to disciples, still less to critics.[8]

But how does one make the jump from a phrase that at face value literally means "the ones with him" to "his own," implying "immediate family," as the Anchor Bible insists? And not only the Anchor Bible. "His family" has become so accepted that only older translations such as the King James and the first edition of the Revised Standard Version say "his friends." One modern translation, the *Word Biblical Commentary*, does vary, translating *hoi par autou* as "his people." But even this translator, Robert Guelich, accepts that "family" is implied. In his commentary, Guelich states:

> "His people" renders an ambiguous Greek construction . . . which generally means "envoys" or "adherents" but *on occasion* can mean "relatives". . . . *Mark 3:31 makes clear that Jesus' "family" is meant.*[9] (italics mine)

Here Guelich reveals that the reason most translators favor rendering *hoi par autou* in verse 21 as "his family," even though it is a less common usage, is *the passage's relationship to* Mark 3:31—"And his mother and his brothers came; and standing outside they sent to him and called him." But quite a jump is being made here. Note well that the translation of the phrase in verse 21 is being decided based on another statement that comes *ten verses later*. In the *New International Commentary*, William L. Lane elaborates on this link:

> Because the expression is clearly colloquial it is difficult to be certain of its exact nuance. The translation "his friends" or "associates" is adopted by the AV [Authorized Version, better known as the King James] . . . and is supported by C. F. D. Moule, *An Idiom Book of New Testament Greek* . . . Papyri support for the rendering "friends," "neighbors," "associates" is not lacking . . . *[T]he context would seem to demand that the family of Jesus is in view*. . . . It is natural . . . to find *in Ch. 3:31–35* the proper sequel to Ch. 3:20 . . . [T]he group of people described colloquially in verse 21 *is further defined by verse 31* as including Jesus' mother and his brothers.[10] (italics mine)

Lane's comments clarify that the critical decision to translate *hoi par autou* as "his family" is driven by the context provided by verse 31: "And his mother and his brothers came . . ." But if Jesus' mother and brothers only arrive on the scene in verse 31, where is the justification in translating verse 21 as "his family"? The older English translations such as the King James and the RSV did not, although it could be argued that the translators of the King James were perhaps hesitant to cast the family in a bad light (as we saw with the ancient Western text) and the RSV simply followed suit.

There is, however, another way of looking at this passage that does not negatively reflect on the family. In his 1972 article (bearing the wonderfully right-to-the-point title "Mark 3:21—Was Jesus Out of His Mind?") in the prestigious journal *New Testament Studies*, Henry Wansbrough offered the following alternative:

> The Jerusalem Bible translates Mark iii.21 "When his relatives heard of this, they set out to take charge of him, convinced he was out of his mind." This way of construing the verse goes back at least as far as the Vulgate . . . and in its general lines seems to be accepted without ques-

tion by all modern commentators. Nevertheless, it appears to me to be at least disputable and probably wrong. The understood subject of *exeste* [out of his mind or crazy] is not Jesus but *ho ochlos* [the crowd].[11]

Making this switch, Wansbrough renders the translation thus: "When they heard it [the crowd], his followers went to calm it down, for they said it was out of control with enthusiasm."[12]

Wansbrough's proposal led to a lively debate in the pages of *New Testament Studies* in the early 1970s. In a follow-up article, Ernest Best pointed out that Wansbrough's understanding was not new, but went back to a view that was

> originally advanced by G. Hartmann in 1913 which dissociates [verses 20–21] from vv. 31–35. They argue that: (a) vv. 31–35 do not take up the theme of v. 21, for the family of Jesus in vv. 31–35 is not actively hostile to him in v. 21; (b) [*exeste*] does not normally refer to madness and in Mark always carries the connotation "wonder, amazement"; (c) [*hoi par autou*] has usually a wider meaning than "family, kinsmen" . . . They therefore take [*hoi par autou*] to refer to the disciples who are with Jesus in the house and who go out [*exelthon*] to the crowd [*auton*] to curb its enthusiasm for they (the disciples) were saying that the crowd was amazed.[13]

As Best notes, Wansbrough and others are only able to hold that *hoi par autou* does *not* refer to family by dissociating verses 20–21 from verses 31–35. Again we see that it is the context of verses 31–35 that forces the decision of how to translate *hoi par autou*.

Around the time of this debate, an ecumenical task force composed of Protestant and Roman Catholic scholars produced the landmark work in Protestant-Catholic understanding, *Mary in the New Testament*. In considering the implications for Jesus' mother in Mark 3:20–21, they concluded that while the majority of scholars are probably correct in translating *hoi par autou* as "his family," what we are reading in this passage only represents, ". . . Mark's *own interpretation* of the attitude of Jesus toward his physical family"[14] (italics mine).

In point of fact, Mark may have had a motive for intentionally casting Jesus' family in a bad light, an issue we will discuss in the next section, but even if this is the case, the gospel is still no closer to historical fact than stage three—Mark's interpretation of events. The deeper question we want to address in our investigation is whether any animosity between Jesus and his family existed in the second-stage traditions that lie behind Mark's written account. To answer this question, we now examine the context of the disputed passage.

ANALYZING THE SYNOPTIC ACCOUNTS

The pericope found in Mark 3:20–35 is a classic example of what scholars call Mark's "sandwich technique," where, quite often in his gospel, Mark places filler material in between two associated episodes in order to connect them. The following outline of Mark 3:20–35 illustrates how Mark has done this:

Introduction: A crowd assembles at the house—Jesus can't eat (verse 20)

(A)   Jesus' "own" set out to seize him (verse 21)
    21a: "His own" hear of his activity and set out to seize him
    21b: Their reason: "He is beside himself"

(B)   The dialogue between Jesus and the Jerusalem scribes (verses 22–30)
    22a: The first charge of the scribes: "He is possessed by Beelzebul."
    22b: The second charge: "By the prince of demons he casts out demons."
    23–27: Jesus replies to the second charge
    28–30: Jesus replies to the first charge

(A')   Jesus' mother and brothers arrive and ask for him, resulting in Jesus' pronouncement of who his "real" family is (verses 31–35)

Here we can graphically see the three basic units that make up Mark's "sandwich." Many scholars believe that this passage is a combination of earlier traditional stories that were in circulation. Robert Guelich notes:

> 3:20–35 consists of a collection of originally discrete traditions. That leaves us with the questions about when these traditions were combined and what role, if any, did the evangelist [Mark] have in bringing together and modifying the material.[15]

Guelich concludes that the story of Jesus' family (3:20–21 and 31–35) was originally a single unit into which the controversy with the scribes was interjected by Mark.[16] Why would Mark do this? Many scholars believe it was expressly for the purpose of subtly casting a shadow upon the family. Interposing the scribes' accusation that Jesus was in league with Satan between the two references to his family could be Mark's subtle way of making the point that Jesus' family was no better than the scribes in their opposition to Jesus.

Before investigating Mark's possible motives for such a startling act of misrepresentation, let me first demonstrate that there is other evidence of Mark intentionally arranging his narrative for the purpose of denigrating Jesus' family. To do so, we must step back and look at the big picture—the larger context into which Mark has placed 3:20–35. Verses 20–35 follow immediately upon the famous story of Jesus choosing the twelve apostles (3:13–19), a passage that is the first part of an even bigger "sandwich" (which scholars call an *inclusio)* that is completed with the sending forth of the apostles in 6:7–13. Looked at from this distance, the sequence of narrated events reveals a pattern that provides a clue to Mark's motive. Mark places an incident involving Jesus' family just prior to the sending of the Twelve: the rejection of Jesus by the people of his hometown (6:1–6). Here is the larger pattern:

(A)   Choosing of the Twelve (3:13–19)

(B)   Family controversy (3:20–35, discussed above)

(C)   Chapters 4 and 5—The Parable of the Seeds and Healing Stories (the "filler")

(B')   Family controversy (6:1–6, the people of Nazareth reject Jesus)

(A')   Sending of the Twelve (6:6–13)

This larger pattern reinforces the smaller one we saw in 3:20–35. John Painter feels that the crucial verses, 3:20–21, are a "bridging summary" into the next pericope,[17] and the fact that verses 20–21 follow immediately upon the choosing of the Twelve means that *hoi par autou* refers to the *apostles,* and not Jesus' family. This seems quite logical. While most commentators look ahead to verses 31–35 for the clue to how to interpret *hoi par autou,* it makes far more sense to look at the immediately preceding verses for the context rather than looking ahead ten verses. Painter does not believe that verses 20–21 are in any way linked to 31–35:

It is asking too much of the reader to recognize the vague expression
in 3:21 as a reference to the family members who are not specifically
mentioned until 3:31. If the *disciples* are in view in 3:20–21, the narrative continues their presence with Jesus from 3:13–19. This reading
seems more obvious.[18] (italics mine)

In Painter's interpretation, it is the *disciples* who question Jesus' sanity,
not his family. This makes significantly more sense. But, as we saw with
the obviously matching continental shorelines that so many were able
to ignore, the obvious is not always easily recognized.

Further support for Painter's theory is found in the well-known fact
that Mark consistently portrays the apostles as quite human and quite
fallible—at times dense and uncomprehending, at times cowardly, at
times egotistical. Many scholars conclude that Mark had negative feelings toward the Twelve, as we will discuss shortly. So it is indeed quite
probable, as Painter proposes, that it is the *apostles* whom Mark
intended to be understood by *hoi par autou; they* are the ones who, as
so often in Mark, misunderstand and question Jesus. Painter thinks that
there are in fact *four* different groups that fall under Mark's stinging
critique in verses 20–35: first the disciples, then the crowd, then the
scribes, and finally Jesus' family (but in verses 31–35, *not* in 20–21). *All*
misunderstand Jesus.

However we interpret *hoi par autou* in verse 20 (as family, friends,
or disciples), Jesus *does* contrast his family with the disciples in Mark
3:31–35. But if we could imagine reading verses 31–35 without having
any prior knowledge of verses 20–21, there is really nothing deroga-
tory in Jesus' words. Jesus simply says that those who listen to him are
his brothers and sisters, just as much as his real brothers and sisters.
This is apparently the way that both Matthew and Luke interpreted
this passage when they adapted it for use in their own gospels.
Comparing the pertinent passages in Mark to parallel passages in
Matthew and Luke uncovers telling differences.* The most obvious
difference between the three synoptics is that Matthew and Luke have

---

*While Matthew and Luke used Mark as the basis for their gospels (scholars call this
the theory of Markan priority), they also added their own unique oral traditions (which
scholars call the special M and L sources). Comparing the three synoptics provides some
evidence of what those unique traditions were.

no parallels to verses 20–21—they are unique to Mark! There are parallels to the Beelzebul controversy with the scribes, but they are removed from the context in which they are found in Mark and placed elsewhere (see Matthew 12:35–37 and Luke 11:17–23). So our main clues in Matthew and Luke are found in the parallels to verses 31–35 in Mark:

Matthew 12:46–50

> 46 While he was still speaking to the people, behold, his mother and his brothers stood outside, asking to speak to him. 47 Someone told him, "Your mother and your brothers are standing outside, asking to speak to you." 48 But he replied to the man who told him, "Who is my mother, and who are my brothers?" 49 And stretching out his hand toward his disciples, he said, "Here are my mother and brothers! 50 For whoever does the will of my Father in heaven is my brother, and sister, and mother."

Luke 8:19–21

> 19 Then his mother and his brothers came to him, but they could not reach him for the crowd. 20 And he was told, "Your mother and your brothers are standing outside, desiring to see you." 21 But he said to them, "My mother and my brothers are those who hear the word of God and do it."

It is immediately obvious that the absence of Mark's verses 20–21 removes any negative motive for Jesus' family seeking him. It is possible that Matthew and Luke deleted these verses because the potential implications made them nervous (as we saw it did the scribe who produced the Western Text). Neither Matthew nor Luke, however, shows any animosity between Jesus and his family. In their versions, his family is simply seeking to see him. In fact, some scholars see a positive evaluation of Jesus' family in Luke because Jesus' statement, "my mother and my brothers are those who hear the word of God and do it" could well include both Jesus' natural family and his disciples. Evangelical Christian scholar Ralph P. Martin, who wrote the commentary on the epistle of James for the Word Biblical Commentary, believes that Luke "openly associates the family of Jesus with potential discipleship. . . The inference is that Jesus' family—both spiritual and natural—are in Luke's sights here."[19] The widely respected Catholic New Testament scholar Joseph A. Fitzmyer, who wrote the commentary on Luke for the eminent *Anchor Bible* series, goes further. Fitzmyer believes that Luke "presents Jesus' mother and his brothers . . . as *model disciples*. They are the prime examples of those who listen to the word of God 'with a noble and generous mind' (8:15)"[20] (italics mine). Fitzmyer appeals to a literal translation of the Greek for support: "The phrase is actually . . . '(as for) my mother and brothers, *they* are the ones who listen.' So runs the literal translation of Luke's Greek, other attempts to interpret these words not withstanding." So not only do Matthew and Luke soften Mark's hostile stance toward Jesus' family, but Luke even portrays them positively.

This reappraisal by Matthew and Luke of Mark's seemingly negative understanding of Jesus' family is also in evidence in one other passage involving Jesus' family—the famous story of Jesus' first return to his hometown after becoming a celebrated figure throughout Galilee. The following are the parallel accounts of the reaction of Jesus' former neighbors when he returns home for the first time:

Mark 6:1–4

> He left that place and came to his hometown, and his disciples followed him. 2 On the Sabbath he began to teach in the synagogue, and many who heard him were astounded. They said, "Where did this man get all this? What is this wisdom that has been given to him? What deeds of power are being done by his hands! 3 Is not this the carpenter, the son of Mary and the brother of James and Joses and Judas and Simon, and are not his sisters here with us?" And they took offense at him. 4 Then Jesus said to them, "Prophets are not without honor, except in their hometown, and among their own kin, and in their own house."

Matthew 13:54–58

> 54 He came to his hometown and began to teach the people in their synagogue, so that they were astounded and said, "Where did this man get this wisdom and these deeds of power? 55 Is not this the carpenter's son? Is not his mother called Mary? And are not his brothers James and Joseph and Simon and Judas?

56 And are not all his sisters with us? Where did this man get all this?" 57 And they took offense at him. But Jesus said to them, "Prophets are not without honor except in their own country and in their own house."

Luke 4:22–24

22 All spoke well of him and were amazed at the gracious words that came from his mouth. They said, "Is not this Joseph's son?" 23 He said to them, "Doubtless you will tell me this proverb, 'Doctor, cure yourself!' And you will say, 'Do here in your hometown the things that we have heard you did in Capernaum.'" 24 And he said, "Truly I tell you, no prophet is accepted in the prophet's hometown."

These accounts are fascinating, for they report the purported words of those people who knew Jesus and his family ever since Jesus was a child. These are also the only accounts in the gospels where Jesus' brothers are named.* It is said that familiarity breeds contempt, which was apparently the case here, for this is where Jesus utters his famous saying, "Prophets are not without honor except in their own . . ." Exactly where and among whom a prophet is without honor depends on whether we read Mark, Matthew, or Luke's version. Mark says: ". . . in their hometown, and among their own kin, and in their own house." Tellingly, Matthew drops "hometown" and "kin" and says: ". . . in their own country and in their own house." Luke simply says: ". . . in the prophet's hometown."

The wording of Luke's account is so different from Mark's and Matthew's that some scholars think Luke is not relying on Mark for this information, but on a separate tradition he had at his disposal, which scholars call the special "L source." Once again, as we move from Mark to Mathew to Luke, a progressive softening of Mark's antifamily stance is plainly seen. And in *none* of the three gospels is Jesus' family identified outright as taking offense at him—it is only the townspeople who do so.

---

*The brothers are most likely listed in order of age (the convention followed by writers of ancient literature), and it is on the basis of James's name coming first in the list that he has been universally accepted as the oldest of the four.

Once again, the most negative representation of the family is in Mark, where Jesus specifically says prophets are without honor "among their own kin, and in their own house." While the widely accepted theory of Markan priority sees Matthew and Luke as making alterations to Mark, it also needs to be kept in mind that Mark made alterations to the traditional material on which he based his gospel. So it is also possible that Matthew and Luke did *not* delete Mark's reference to kin, but that Mark *added* it to the tradition for the intentional purpose of showing that Jesus' family, like the apostles and everyone else in his gospel, misunderstood Jesus. In the next verses (5–6), Mark immediately adds: "And he could do no deeds of power there . . . And he was amazed at their unbelief." The point is clear: those who knew Jesus best—the people of his hometown, his friends and neighbors, and even his family—did not believe in him.

Now is a good time for a recap of where our investigation has thus far led us. To sum up our findings to this point, we have before us three possibilities:

1. Jesus' family really was in opposition to him.
2. Jesus' family was not in opposition to him—the main source for concluding an antagonistic relationship, Mark 3:20–21, has been misinterpreted.
3. Jesus' family was not in opposition to him, but Mark deliberately painted them in this light for reasons yet to be uncovered.

Thus far, we have seen a lot of evidence favoring the latter two possibilities, each of which challenges received wisdom in both academia and the church. Yet as compelling as the evidence may be, it does not by itself actually overturn the traditional paradigm. To do that, more supporting evidence will be needed. Further evidence can be found in the fourth gospel—the Gospel According to John. While John does not report any parallel to the story of Jesus' family that we have been examining, the gospel does present a unique and fascinating encounter between Jesus and his brothers following the story of the wedding banquet at Cana, to which we now turn.

THE FAMILY ACCORDING TO JOHN

In John we find the only evidence anywhere in the gospels that Jesus' family may have been a part of his following *during his ministry*. The first reference to Jesus' family in John is in the famous story of the wedding banquet at Cana (John 2:1–12), where Jesus, at his mother's urging, performs his first miracle by turning the water in six vast stone water jars (John tells us each contained twenty to thirty gallons) into wine, thus saving a lavish wedding banquet from ruin. Not only is Mary the protagonist in this story, but she could be said to inaugurate Jesus' ministry by impelling him to perform his first miracle. What is most significant for our purposes is that Mary does not seem at all skeptical of Jesus here.

The seemingly innocuous transition statement that follows upon the banquet scene has even more interesting implications: "After this he went down to Capernaum with his mother, his brothers, and his disciples; and they remained there a few days" (2:12). This is the first mention of Jesus' brothers in John, yet they are introduced in a remarkably nonchalant way, reminiscent of James's introduction in Acts and Galatians. When one stops to think about it, John's seemingly offhand transition actually speaks volumes about Jesus' brothers. John Painter, in his major study *Just James*, perceptively articulates the significance of this deceptively simple verse:

> The mention of the brothers in 2:12 is completely gratuitous. They are mentioned at neither the Cana wedding nor the subsequent events in the Temple. Had the evangelist freely composed 2:12, those mentioned in the linking verse might be expected to be present in the preceding and succeeding incidents. What 2:12 does is to create the impression that *the brothers were an essential part of the following of Jesus.*[21] (italics mine)

Painter would likely be more hesitant to come to such a startling conclusion if 2:12 were the only such evidence that Jesus' family was part of his ministry, but it is not. If Painter's surmise is correct, we may now be starting to hit some historical bedrock—the elusive first-stage history that is the ultimate goal of historical Jesus scholarship.

Another piece of evidence pointing in this direction is, surprisingly, the seemingly damning account of Jesus' brothers in John 7:1–5:

> After this Jesus went about in Galilee. He did not want to go about in
> Judea because the Jews were looking for an opportunity to kill him.
> 2 Now the Jewish festival of booths was near. 3 So his brothers said to
> him, "Leave here and go to Judea so that your disciples also may see
> the works you are doing; 4 for no one who wants to be widely
> known acts in secret. If you do these things, show yourself to the
> world." 5 (For not even his brothers believed in him.)

If we read between the lines here, we are once again left with the
impression (despite both the brothers' seemingly sarcastic challenge to
Jesus and John's comment on the brothers' unbelief) that Jesus' brothers were regularly in his company, and certainly not estranged from
him. To resolve the seeming contradiction between the subtext (that the
brothers were commonly with Jesus) and the overt message (that they
did not believe in him) of verse 5, we can turn to John Painter:

> [H]ow are we to take the statement that "his brothers did not believe
> in him?" From [John's] perspective, belief prior to the resurrection/
> glorification of Jesus is thought to be suspect, so that right at the end of
> his farewell discourses Jesus challenges the affirmation of belief by the
> disciples, "Do you now believe?" (16:31) . . . If Jesus puts the belief of
> the disciples in question at this point, we should hesitate before con-
> cluding that the narrator's comment in 7:5 indicates that the brothers
> were total unbelievers.[22]

Painter is here pointing to a well-known theme in John's gospel:
Everyone, including the apostles (and particularly Peter), misunder-
stands Jesus and the nature of his messianic mission. In John's gospel,
no one truly believes in Jesus until after the resurrection when all is
made clear. Therefore, it may be less accurate to say that John singles
Jesus' brothers out when he accuses them of unbelief than to say that
he comments on them to make the point that *even* Jesus' brothers—
along with everyone else—did not have true belief. John's comment
may not at all imply that Jesus' brothers were opposed to his ministry,
and it does not at all rule out the possibility that, as Painter puts it, "the
brothers were an essential part of the following of Jesus."

At first glance, one might get the impression from John 7:3–4 that
Jesus' brothers are being sarcastic or are perhaps taunting Jesus, but
that idea is also garnered from John's parenthetical comment in verse 5

(and perhaps also from a subliminal carryover of the traditional under-standing of Mark 3:21). If we can try to erase John 7:5 and Mark 3:21 from our memory, there really is nothing at all sinister or even sarcas-tic in the brothers' statements in verses 3 and 4. In fact, it could be argued that they are actually supporting Jesus and urging him on to more fully reveal himself to his disciples in Judea.

These possibilities become even more plausible when we consider that except for the single aside in 7:5 (which, moreover, could be a later editor's addition to the original text), John's gospel is more pro-family than the three synoptic gospels. In addition to the key role that Jesus' mother plays in inaugurating his ministry, Mary is also present at the cross (with at least one other female relative—Mary of Clopas, Jesus' aunt), and one of Jesus' last acts is to entrust her care to the "Beloved Disciple." John Painter concludes of the evidence in John:

> Had the presence of the brothers with Jesus during his ministry not been traditional, they would have played no part in the gospel narrative. Even in the evangelist's interpretation of their role, they are portrayed as "fal-lible followers" rather than as outright unbelievers. In this their por-trayal does not differ greatly from that of the disciples . . .
>
> The overall effect . . . is to lead the reader to the conclusion that the mother and brothers of Jesus were among his intimate supporters.[23]

By now the reader should begin to see a clear pattern emerging. When one assesses *all* of the evidence in the gospels, on balance *there is more evidence to support a positive role for Jesus' family in his ministry than a negative one.* This is one of the first firm conclusions to which the evidence all points. We can now discard the notion that Jesus' fam-ily really was in opposition to him. Based solely on the evidence we have thus far, we can conclude that Jesus' family were not opponents, but followers of his ministry.

As for Mark 3:21, we are now left to decide between the other two possibilities: either 3:21 does *not* refer to Jesus' family or it does, and Mark intentionally composed the verse to cast the family in a bad light. If the latter, we may reasonably ask why Mark would pursue such a goal. We turn now to some contemporary scholarly theories that attempt to account for Mark's motives.

ANALYZING MARK'S AGENDA

A growing trend among scholars (that has practically reached a consensus) understands Mark as a gospel with a hidden agenda. Two of today's leading historical Jesus scholars, John Dominic Crossan and Burton Mack, see Mark as writing polemically against the leadership of the mother church in Jerusalem, specifically, the role played in the Jerusalem church by Jesus' apostles and his family.[24] This rather startling idea goes back to a theory first promulgated in the early 1970s by Theodore Weeden in his book *Mark—Traditions in Conflict* (based on his doctoral dissertation, "The Heresy That Necessitated Mark's Gospel"). Weeden was one of the first to notice a pattern in Mark which scholars up to that point had failed to see—that Mark portrays the disciples, without exception, negatively:

> What . . . scholars have refused to consider is the possibility that
> these Markan episodes in which the disciples are placed in such an
> unfavorable light may be more than just the result of the passing on
> of tradition or the consequence of the development of a theological
> motif . . . They have failed to consider seriously the possibility that
> the evangelist might be attacking the disciples intentionally, for
> whatever reason.[25]

Weeden noted that the groundwork for this revolutionary theory was laid in the early 1960s by two scholars named Johannes Schreiber and Joseph Tyson, both of whom argued that:

> Mark's portrayal of the disciples must be seen as a literary device in
> the service of a polemic against a conservative Jewish Christian group
> in Palestine which placed no positive meaning in Jesus' death, held to
> the long-established Jewish practices, and rejected the necessity of the
> gentile mission.[26]

The "conservative Jewish Christian group" that Weeden refers to as being the object of Mark's polemic is the same group that Paul rails against in many of his letters. Christian scholars have traditionally used the rather anti-Semitic term "Judaizers" to describe this group—followers of Jesus who wanted to maintain their Judaism by continuing to adhere to the Torah, and who were in opposition to Paul's mission to the Gentiles (at least in the way in which Paul wanted to carry it out). In later chapters we shall examine rather astounding evidence that this Jewish Christian group against whom Mark was contending (in the late 60s C.E.) was actually the second generation leadership of the Jerusalem church, and claimed the support of James and the apostles for their teachings and practices.

Scholars today realize that early Christianity was by no means homogeneous; there were many competing factions within the early church, each holding different interpretations of Jesus. Tensions and disagreements, especially over the nature of Jesus (i.e., whether he was human or divine) built up over the years and were eventually resolved (certainly not to everyone's satisfaction) at the Council of Nicaea in 325 C.E. Those who disagreed with the majority vote at Nicaea were forever afterward declared to be heretics.

These disagreements between the various Christian communities in the fourth century had their roots already among the earliest Christian communities of the first century, especially in the rival interpretations of Jesus held by the earliest Jewish Christian and Gentile Christian communities. As noted earlier, the German scholar F. C. Baur was the first to recognize that all was not peaceful between Paul and the Jerusalem church. After Baur, many scholars began to reread the New Testament in the light of this friction, and after falling out of favor for more than a century, there is a strong resurgence of Baur's ideas today. British scholar Micheal Goulder, for example, in his recent book *St. Paul versus St. Peter: A Tale of Two Missions*, examines the tendencies of the gospel writers in light of the friction between the Jewish Christian community centered in Jerusalem and the Gentile Christian communities centered on Paul's teachings. Goulder summarizes:

> Mark looks like a Pauline, hostile toward Jesus' family who ran the Jerusalem mission in his time, ambivalent about [the disciples], but down on their followers if they started talking about authority. Matthew steadily exonerates both groups, and seems if anything sympathetic to the Jerusalem leadership. Luke is an irenic character, friendly to both sides. As for John, he is an ultra-Pauline. . . . He tells us that Jesus' brothers did not believe in him (the fundamental sin in the Fourth Gospel); they tried to hustle Jesus to go to Jerusalem before his time . . .[27]

Goulder notes that Matthew and Luke remove the animosity toward the family that is present in Mark's gospel, and offers the following reason why:

> Matthew and Luke seem to have a tendency to exonerate Jesus' family; and we could explain this by the view that they were much more sympathetic to the Jerusalem church than Mark was. In the case of Luke, we really know this was so, because we have a second book Luke wrote, the Acts of the Apostles . . . Peter (and the other eleven) are the heroes in chs 1–12, and Paul is the hero in chs 13–28; and in ch 15, when the issue of Gentiles keeping the Law is discussed, everyone agrees with Paul, and the Gentiles are not made to observe it. So we know that Luke is a liberal Pauline . . . but he wants the church united and the two missions reconciled, and he will not tell stories in which Jesus' family come out badly.[28]

The possibility of animosity and rivalry among the early Christians can come as a shock to average Christians today, most of whom imagine a congenial picture of the early church, with Jesus' disciples living harmoniously in Christian love. In reality, it was simply not so, and we shall begin to see the actual history of muckraking, mudslinging, and backstabbing in the next chapter.

In fairness, it should be pointed out that some scholars caution against making so much of the gospel writers' polemical agendas that we fail to consider other reasons for the attitudes that emerge in their writing. Ernest Best, for example, has stated that "it seems that too much [New Testament] scholarship today begins with the question, 'Against whom is this written?'" Best thinks that Mark may have drawn a picture of the hostility of Jesus' family not for the purpose of polemicizing against them, but for the purpose of encouraging Christians who were experiencing opposition from their own families because of becoming Christians:

> Jesus is depicted as alienated from his family . . . Such an alienation from family must have been the experience of many of Mark's community . . . their families will have thought them out of their minds for becoming Christians. The family of Jesus is thus used homiletically [for teaching purposes]. Historically such opposition may have been their attitude—at any rate Mark has tradition to this effect—but he is

not interested . . . in how it could be used to tarnish a James-party, but instead in how his readers can be encouraged.[29]

As far as there being any actual animosity between Jesus and his family, note well that Best will only go so far as to say that Mark "has tradition to this effect." As we have emphasized, what was in the oral, or second-stage, tradition was not necessarily in the actual first-stage history. John Dominic Crossan believes that while tension between Jesus and his family may have been in the tradition that came down to Mark, Mark intensifies that animosity for polemical purposes:

> Even if there was some pre-Markan evidence of tension between Jesus and his relatives in the tradition . . . it is Mark himself who: (i) equated their attempt to restrain Jesus as one insane with the accusation of the Jerusalem scribes that he was possessed . . . and (ii) mentioned the relatives by name and then added that these also did not honor him [6:1–6].[30]

Crossan believes that Mark took this bold step because he was fighting on a "double front," both against Judaizing "heretics" within the Markan community who claimed the support of Jesus' family for their views (Weeden's theory), and also "in whole or in part, against the jurisdictional and doctrinal hegemony of the Jerusalem church," which, as we shall in the next chapter, was led by James. Crossan presents the following evidence:

> [T]he villains of Markan theology are not just the disciples in general but the inner three, Peter, James [Jesus' brother], and John in particular . . . To focus the failure of the disciples in general on the three in particular and most especially on Peter can hardly be derived merely from a desire to personify the heretics within the Markan community. It seems rather to point towards the Jerusalem mother-church where the importance of Peter, on the one hand, and of an inner three, on the other, is witnessed to by a text such as Gal. ii 7–10 . . .
>
> Secondly, the animosity of Mark to the relatives of Jesus points likewise against the Jerusalem church because it is there that James, the brother of the Lord, becomes important . . . The polemic against the disciples and the polemic against the relatives intersect as a polemic against the jurisdictional hegemony of the Jerusalem mother-church.

In other words, by the time Mark was writing in the late 60s, the Gentile churches outside of Israel were beginning to resent the authority wielded by Jerusalem (where James and the apostles were leaders), thus providing the motive for Mark's antifamily stance and his polemics against the apostles.

So we now have a motive that could account for Mark's unfavorable portrayal of Jesus' family in 3:21. Of course, that motive—no matter how clearly expressed elsewhere—may not apply to the critical understanding of 3:21 if *hoi par autou* was not intended by Mark to refer to Jesus' family. On this matter, then, we are still faced with making a decision between the two alternative possibilities enumerated earlier: either Mark has intentionally taken a swipe at Jesus' family in 3:21 or Mark never meant to imply Jesus' family with his use of the phrase *hoi par autou*. Although the evidence we saw strongly favors the latter theory, a definitive determination remains elusive. Fortunately for our concerns, either theory is acceptable because neither one is any longer an obstacle to our first major claim, that Jesus' family were followers of his ministry prior to the resurrection.

No matter what Mark's intention was in 3:21, it is highly unlikely that Jesus' family thought he was out of his mind and opposed his mission. The bottom line is that the well-attested evidence that Jesus' family were followers so soon after the crucifixion is hard to account for only by the attestation of a resurrection appearance to James which resulted in a sudden about-face. As one of the pioneer historical Jesus scholars, Johannes Weiss, observed a century ago, "there must accordingly have taken place a change in the attitude on the part of the brothers, sometime *before the appearance to James*"[31] (italics mine). Richard Bauckham, who has done as much research into Jesus' family as anyone, agrees:

> If James were in no sense a follower of Jesus until he met the risen
> Christ, this resurrection appearance would be comparable only to the
> appearance to Paul. It is more likely to imply that *James already
> belonged to the circle of the disciples of Jesus.*[32] (italics mine)

In other words, Jesus appeared to James after his resurrection not because James did *not* believe, but precisely because he *did*. Both Weiss and Bauckham, however, still work under the assumption of the old paradigm that Jesus' family was initially opposed to his mission, but at some point changed their minds and became supporters.

Our work in this chapter isn't paradigm-shattering in itself, yet by reevaluating the relationship between Jesus and his family as it is portrayed in the New Testament, we have changed a small part of the picture that most biblical scholars of the past two millennia have taken for truth and prepared the way for a more extensive revision of how we understand one of the central characters in the New Testament and the nature of early Christianity itself. As persuasive as the textual evidence presented in this chapter has been, these are not conclusions to be taken on textual evidence alone. Therefore, we shall now seek to uncover more supporting evidence from a historical analysis of the early Christian church. But before moving ahead in our investigation, let us pause to take stock of where the evidence has led us thus far.

THE FAITH OF THE FAMILY

To conclude this initial stage of our investigation into how James and the family of Jesus are portrayed in the gospels, let us summarize our findings to this point:

1. Despite a lack of certainty about Mark's intent in the use of the term *hoi par autou* in 3:21, there is *nothing* in the gospels that *incontrovertibly* shows opposition to Jesus by his family during his ministry.
2. The two leading scholars who have done the most in-depth investigation on these matters—Painter and Bauckham—have arrived at essentially the same conclusion: that Jesus' mother and brothers were followers of his ministry some time *prior to the crucifixion*. Their matching conclusions are all the more significant because Painter and Bauckham are not theologically in the same camp. John Painter is a liberal, a disciple of Rudolph Bultmann, while Richard Bauckham is a more conservative Christian scholar.

As the more cautious of the the two, Bauckham is hesitant to say that the members of Jesus' family were disciples from the outset of his ministry, or even an "essential part" of his following, as Painter does. Let us hear the final piece of testimony on Jesus' family from Bauckham:

From . . . the Gospels we may draw the following conclusions:

(1) During his ministry Jesus' relationship with his family was not
     entirely smooth . . . At least for part of his ministry they were not
     among his followers.

(2) According to . . . the Markan . . . traditions Jesus expected renuncia-
     tion of family relationships as part of the cost of discipleship . . . and
     it is not unreasonable to suppose that this was also the cost to him-
     self of his own mission.

(3) At least by the time of his last visit to Jerusalem, Jesus' relatives—
     his mother, brothers, his uncle Clopas and his wife, and probably
     another aunt—had joined his followers.[33]

Personally, I think Bauckham's conservatism causes him to be a bit
too circumspect here. He agrees with Painter that Jesus' family were followers before the crucifixion, and that the traditional account of James
becoming a believer only after a resurrection appearance does not
account for the data. Why, then, does Bauckham feel that they were not
always part of Jesus' ministry? He believes that they became followers
sometime *during* Jesus' ministry (which was at most one to three years).
If Jesus' family had been skeptical of his mission early on, as Bauckham
claims, we are still faced with question of what made them change their
minds. Certainly not the resurrection, since it had not yet happened.

Such lingering questions make me agree with Painter. It is far more
likely that Jesus' family had *always* been an "essential part" of his following. This conclusion makes the most sense out of all the evidence
without leaving any lingering questions or loose ends. Such a conclusion would *not*, however, mean that Jesus' family were always in total
agreement with him, even if, and perhaps especially if, they believed
him to be the Messiah. If indeed Jesus' family were part of his ministry
because they believed him to be the Messiah (a notion we shall address
later), there would almost certainly have been areas of heated debate
and disagreement, and perhaps it is this part of the historical tradition
that Mark acquired. Disagreements between Jesus and his family would
likely have arisen over some of the very same issues that aroused opposition from Jesus' detractors: Jesus' perceived flaunting of aspects of the
Law, his associating with "sinners," and the very nature of messiahship
itself and what that entailed (especially if, as many third-quest historical Jesus scholars now believe, Jesus understood his mission to be that

of a *suffering* Messiah, and not the traditional conquering Messiah of Jewish expectation).

This line of reasoning accounts for *all* of the data at our disposal. It not only explains the seemingly sudden post-crucifixion discipleship of the family (it *wasn't* sudden), but it also accounts for the presence in the tradition of some opposition between Jesus and his family without relying on theories of polemics (although polemics were also certainly involved to some extent). And if Mark and John *were* writing polemically, our theory is enhanced all the more.

To find further support for the new paradigm we are beginning to construct, let us now begin phase two of our investigation by focusing in on the Jerusalem church, starting with an examination of how James is portrayed in the book of Acts and in the letters of Paul.

2

THE NATURE OF
THE JERUSALEM CHURCH

3

JAMES OF JERUSALEM: THE
WITNESS OF LUKE AND PAUL

*Then after three years I went up to Jerusalem to visit
Peter, and remained with him fifteen days. But I saw
none of the other apostles except James the Lord's
brother.*

ST. PAUL, GALATIANS 1:18–19 (RSV)

In this chapter we shall open a file on James's activity in Jerusalem as
witnessed to by Luke in the book of Acts and by Paul in his letter to the
Galatians. Because the historicity of the accounts in the book of Acts has
been so contentious in modern scholarship, we shall rely on Galatians as
our primary witness, with Acts used as ancillary testimony. This will
place us on firmer historical ground: after all, Paul *was there*, his is an
eyewitness account, whereas Acts is a later historian's attempt to piece
together those same events. Nonetheless, so much historical information
can be gleaned from Acts that we will treat it at great length.

Most scholars today believe that Galatians was written around the
year 55 and Acts quite a bit later, somewhere between 85 and 90. This
is not to say that Paul's account is always more accurate. Paul had his
personal biases which may have both subtly and not-so-subtly influenced his account, perhaps especially in his heated arguments in
Galatians. In this epistle, Paul is arguing against the teaching of some
influential Jewish Christian leaders who have tried to convince the
Gentile Christians in Galatia that they needed to be circumcised and

obey the Law of Moses in order to attain salvation. Paul's argument is heated, and his personal agenda will, of course, have to be taken into consideration when analyzing his text for its historical accuracy.

As is well known, however, Luke had his own agenda, which affected his portrayal of the development of the early church. Noted Roman Catholic historical Jesus scholar John Meier has nicely summed up the scholarly debate concerning the historicity of Luke's representation of the early church in Acts:

> The author of Acts . . . has a noted tendency to smooth over fierce battles in the early church. To what extent his peaceful vision molded his narrative and, indeed, to what extent he enjoyed reliable sources for early Christianity, is still disputed among Lukan scholars . . . [I]t can be said with a certain amount of truth that the majority of Germans . . . have proven more reserved towards the historical reliability of Acts than the British and Americans . . . Faced with this disagreement . . . we would do well to pursue a middle course in which Acts is neither dismissed lightly as pure theologizing nor accepted naively as pure history. Each text must be judged on its own merits and on available information from other sources.[1]

This is wise advice from a wise scholar, and Meier's balanced approach is the one that will be taken here.

Luke himself makes it clear in the opening of his gospel that he did not personally know Jesus and therefore relied on earlier written sources, which in turn were dependent on even earlier oral tradition. At the outset of his gospel, he states:

> Many writers have undertaken to draw up an account of the events that have happened . . . following the *traditions handed down to us by the original eyewitnesses* . . . And so I in my turn . . . as one who has gone over the whole course of these events in detail, have decided to write a connected narrative (Luke 1:1–3, NEB).

This is certainly how all of the gospels were written, and we need to remember that the earliest gospel, Mark, which was one of Luke's sources, was itself composed some thirty-five to forty years after Jesus' death, while Luke's gospel and Acts were written over fifty years after the crucifixion. The reason for the delay is that the early Christian community saw no need to commit its history to writing—Jesus was expected to return at any time. It was only after decades had elapsed and it became obvious that Jesus' return (referred to by scholars with the Greek term *Parousia*) would not happen as soon as expected, that the need to commit things to writing became necessary. In light of the long interval between the events themselves and Luke's writing (c. 85–90), it is fortunate that we have Paul's firsthand account (in Galatians 2) of one of the key sections in Acts that concerns James— the all-important Jerusalem Conference in Acts 15. (We should note, however, that whether these two passages refer to the same event is one of the most debated questions in New Testament studies.) The other key passage in Acts that involves James is the account of Paul's final visit to Jerusalem, which we cannot, unfortunately, weigh against a parallel account from Paul. Happily, this is one of the "we sections" of Acts—passages that were written in the first person and purport to be eyewitness reports.

Due to such complicating factors, sorting through the accounts of Luke and Paul in an attempt to uncover reliable historical evidence on James requires some careful analysis. So, with the foregoing caveats in mind, let us turn our keen attention to James's earliest days in Jerusalem.

JAMES IN JERUSALEM

As we have already seen, in the very first chapter of Acts we are told that immediately after Jesus' ascension the apostles remained together in Jerusalem, "constantly devoting themselves to prayer, together with certain women, including Mary the mother of Jesus, as well as his brothers" (1:14). While he is not here mentioned by name, we can only assume that James, as the eldest brother of Jesus, would have been with them. Paul can at least attest that James was present at the time of his first visit to Jerusalem (Galatians 1:19, quoted at the beginning of the chapter), an initial consultation with Peter and James that is generally dated anywhere from 34 to 38, within just a few years of the crucifixion, which is universally accepted as occurring sometime between 30 and 33. Obviously, though, Paul's meeting with James cannot corroborate that James was present in Jerusalem within weeks of the crucifixion. Passages from the gospels however, do imply the presence of Jesus' family. John 19:25 tells of the presence of Jesus' mother at the crucifixion, and while Luke does not explicitly place Mary at the crucifixion in his own gospel, he does leave room for her presence when he writes, "the women who had followed [Jesus] from Galilee, stood at a distance, watching these things" (23:49).

So while Luke's gospel says nothing about Jesus' family being in his company during his ministry, in Luke's sequel—the book of Acts—they are suddenly, and without explanation, in the company of the apostles immediately after the crucifixion. It could be conjectured that they came along with Jesus and the apostles to celebrate Passover in Jerusalem, for Luke attests that "every year [Jesus'] parents went to Jerusalem for the festival of the Passover" (2:41). Thus, there was a solid precedent for Jesus' family being in Jerusalem at the time of his crucifixion (which happened at Passover). They were obviously a devout Jewish family with the financial means to make the annual pilgrimage to Jerusalem, something few were able to afford. And even if the family *had* been back in Galilee, news of Jesus' crucifixion would certainly have brought them hurriedly to Jerusalem. But all of this is speculation. It is much more plausible that the family was already there in Jerusalem with Jesus at the time of his arrest.

It is worth mentioning at this point that the historical Jesus scholar John Dominic Crossan has entertained some intriguing thoughts about the possibility of James having been in Jerusalem even *prior* to Jesus coming there in the final week of his life. In *Jesus: A Revolutionary Biography,* Crossan engages in a fascinating speculation:

> [H]ow long had [James] been in Jerusalem? We know for sure . . . that he was there by about 38 C.E., when Paul first met him. Did he come there only after the execution of Jesus, or *had he been there long before it?* I realize how tentative . . . this is, but much more explanation for James's presence and standing in Jerusalem needs to be given than is usually offered.[2]

Crossan admits that his suggestion is "terribly hypothetical," but bases his speculation on the high standing that James achieved in Jerusalem in a remarkably short period of time. From a logical standpoint, it is hard to believe that Jesus' apostles, who had been with him from the beginning, would have so quickly turned the reins of leadership over to James (his relationship to Jesus notwithstanding) if James had been at odds with Jesus and opposed to his mission. Crossan also bases his conjecture on the tumultuous reaction to the illegal execution of James, which, according to Josephus, aroused the ire of the leading Pharisees in Jerusalem.* It is difficult to believe that James would have been accorded such respect by leading Pharisees if he had not been entrenched for quite some time in a prominent position in Jerusalem.

Before we get too far ahead of ourselves, however, let us return to the beginning of Acts. Here we need to keep in mind, as already mentioned, the possibility of Luke's own ideology coloring his narrative. This is summed up nicely in an article in the invaluable reference guide the *Dictionary of Paul and His Letters:*

> Luke . . . had an apologetic purpose in mind in his presentation . . . [H]e sought to demonstrate . . . that Jerusalem had a central place in the divine plan. He begins his gospel in Jerusalem (Lk 1:5–23) and concludes at the same place (Lk 24:33–53). He begins Acts in Jerusalem as well (Acts 1:3–8) and patterns the spread of the gospel along the lines of the paradigm Jerusalem-Judea-Samaria-ends of the earth (Acts 1:8). The centrality of Jerusalem for Luke is also seen in its being the place of the church's origin (Lk 24; Acts 1) . . . It is the place where key theological debates are settled (Acts 15) and from where decrees are promulgated (Acts 15:19–35). Yet all this is certainly not . . . a purely literary fiction but based on reality. From the available evidence, the fact is that Jerusalem was indeed the center and the mother church of the Christian movement.[3]

As this commentary makes clear, Luke's concern with Jerusalem is wont to override his concern for historical accuracy. It is telling that Luke is the only gospel that places Jesus' resurrection appearances in *Jerusalem* rather than Galilee! The rather notorious German liberal theologian, Gerd Lüdemann, who is as careful a historicist as any New Testament scholar, gives a sober and well-reasoned summary of Jerusalem's actual historical significance:

> Although the Acts account of the earliest beginnings of Christianity in Jerusalem is certainly incorrect, there can be no doubt that not long

---

*As one of the major Jewish religious parties in New Testament times, the Pharisees were known for their strict adherence to the Law of Moses and were critical of the party of the Sadducees, who were the wealthy ruling elite in charge of the Jerusalem Temple. Christians today know the Pharisees mainly because the New Testament presents them as Jesus' opponents.

after the crucifixion of Jesus a considerable number of his followers, after having left the capital temporarily, established a church in Jerusalem which was of decisive importance for Christianity in and outside of Palestine up to the time of the Jewish War . . .

The first resurrection appearances occurred *in Galilee* (Mark 16:7; Matt. 28:16ff.; John 21), where Jesus' disciples had returned—or rather, fled . . .

Regarded historically . . . Peter reorganized the circle of the Twelve in Galilee and with them returned to Jerusalem. Thus with Peter as the leader the Twelve . . . assumed a position of leadership in the Jerusalem church.[4] (italics mine)

Lüdemann's conjecture that the apostles fled back to Galilee certainly makes sense in that, after the crucifixion, the disciples would have feared for their own lives and wanted to return to familiar territory as quickly as possible. Their equally hasty return to Jerusalem also makes sense when one considers the galvanizing effect that the empty tomb and the resurrection appearances would have had on the disciples. Their belief in Jesus' imminent Parousia would have impelled them to return to Jerusalem, for that is where, according to Old Testament prophetic tradition, the Messiah would appear and the apocalyptic "Day of the Lord" would commence.[5]

Whether the itinerary of James was the same as that of the apostles is an open question at this point. As fearful as the disciples were for their own lives following Jesus' crucifixion, James, as the next of kin, would have had even more to fear. If Jesus was, as the gospels attest and as most historical Jesus scholars agree, crucified for the crime of treason against the Roman Empire (as Pilate's placard on the cross, reading "the King of the Jews," plainly declared), the Romans would indeed have cast a wary eye on James, whom, as Jesus' eldest brother, they would have expected to be next in line to succeed him. The Romans kept close vigilance on anyone who might be a potential threat to the peace of Rome—the sacred *Pax Romana*.

JAMES AS APOSTLE

As to the whereabouts of James, in addition to the collected records of Luke, we also have the invaluable eyewitness testimony of Paul. In fact, our earliest written evidence about James's presence in Jerusalem comes from Paul's letter to the Galatians, written about thirty years after the crucifixion. In the first chapter of that letter, Paul gives a brief, but invaluable, autobiographical summary of his activity subsequent to his conversion experience on the Damascus Road (generally dated 32–35). Here, Paul reflects on his first visit to Jerusalem, dating it three years after his conversion from persecutor of Christians to apostle to the Gentiles: "Then after three years I went up to Jerusalem to visit Cephas [Peter], and remained with him fifteen days. But I saw none of the other apostles except James the Lord's brother" (Gal. 1:18–19, RSV). Here we have firm evidence that James was resident in Jerusalem by at least the mid-30s. Paul's statement also reveals that, *at least* by this time, James was a major figure in Jerusalem. F. F. Bruce has commented on the import of Paul's account of seeing James: "This may point to James as the second most important man in the church; at any rate, he was some-one whom it was important for Paul to see."[6] Or, as Oscar Cullmann succinctly puts it: "it was already impossible for a Christian believer to make a stay in Jerusalem without coming into contact with James."[7]

A crucial piece of evidence for James's standing is also to be found in Paul's turn of phrase in his seemingly off-the-cuff statement, "But I saw none of the other apostles except James the Lord's brother." Note well that Paul bestows upon James the title *apostle*. Naturally, there are other ways to interpret this verse, such as the translation found in the New International Version: "I saw none of the other apostles—only James, the Lord's brother." This could be taken to mean that James was *not* an apostle, but the vast majority of scholars take Paul's statement at face value to mean that Paul considered James to be an apostle of the same merit as the Twelve. F. F. Bruce sums up the argument:

> Paul certainly indicates that he regarded James as an apostle. If we were compelled to understand his words otherwise, they could be con-strued differently—as though he meant, "I saw none of the other apos-tles, but I did see James the Lord's brother"—but this is a less natural construction . . . unlike Luke, Paul does not confine the designation "apostles" to the twelve.[8]

It is well known that Paul uses the term *apostle* for any eyewitness to the resurrected Christ, which is the basis of his defense to his critics for being able to apply the title to himself. In 1 Corinthians, Paul asks: "Am I not an apostle? Have I not seen Jesus our Lord?" (9:1) That Paul would consider James an apostle in this sense (apart from the question of whether James was a follower prior to the resurrection) is attested to by Paul's listing of James as a witness to the resurrected Christ later in this same letter (1 Cor. 15:7).

A dissenting voice on this issue is that of conservative scholar Ralph P. Martin, who, in his commentary on the epistle of James, has this to say about how Paul viewed James:

> [Paul] recognized James as a leader who was prominent in the mother church. He appealed to James's authority as a witness of the resurrection, and claimed himself to be a member of that company. [But he] was reluctant to state plainly that James was, in Paul's own estimation, an apostle—according to what is perhaps the best conclusion we can reach on the ambiguous wording of 1 Cor 15:7.[9]

In support of his claim, Martin cites what he calls the "considered judgment" of New Testament scholar Walter Schmithals, whom he quotes:

> We can only conclude that [the] lack of clarity was intentional with Paul . . . Paul limits the assertion that he has seen no apostles besides Peter by leaving room for the possibility that one could, if need be, count James among the apostles—something he was not himself accustomed to doing.[10]

John Painter, however, strongly rebuts the interpretation of Martin and Schmithals, stating that theirs

> is an extraordinary reading of Gal 1:19. One reason for this seems to be the assumption that the status of true apostleship was limited to the twelve. Was Paul's claim to apostleship a claim to be one of the twelve? That is most unlikely. Rather Paul claimed apostleship of equal status with the twelve. The evidence of 1 Cor 15:7 implies that he recognized that James shared the status of "all the apostles." Thus the apostolic band included Peter and the twelve, James and all the apostles, and last of all Paul himself (15:5–8).[11]

Painter's last statement is undoubtedly the most accurate description of historical fact. There was an "apostolic band" that included, but was not limited to, the Twelve. The apostolic band would comprise all who had seen the risen Christ (Paul's criterion to be an apostle), which, according to 1 Corinthians, was a group of more than five hundred:

> [H]e appeared to Cephas [Peter], then to the twelve. Then he appeared to more than five hundred brothers and sisters at one time, most of whom are still alive, though some have died. Then he appeared to James, then to all the apostles. (1 Cor. 15:5–7)

To recap our findings to this point, in addition to Paul's testimony that James was a leading apostle in Jerusalem in the earliest days of the Christian movement, we have Luke's corroborating testimony that Peter wanted the news of his escape from prison to reach "James and the brethren" as soon as possible (Acts 12:17). It is likely that Luke's use of the term "brethren" here refers to the general community of believers, rather than Jesus' brothers, as it does also in Acts 1:15: "In those days Peter stood up among the brethren (the company of persons was in all about a hundred and twenty), and said, 'Brethren, the Scripture had to be fulfilled'" (RSV). Here we see that the "brethren" of the earliest Christian community were a group of slightly over a hundred people *in Jerusalem* (surely a realistic and not exaggerated figure), and surely there were more in Galilee.

JAMES AND PETER

F. F. Bruce points out a significant implication in Peter's words, "Tell this to James and the brethren":

> This implies that James and the brethren associated with him met in a different place from Peter's company—that they belonged, to use Pauline language, to a different house-church. . . . it may be inferred that even at this early date James was the leader of one group in the Jerusalem church and Peter was the leader of another.[12]

Bruce's hypothesis is contrary to the traditional understanding that Peter was the sole head of the early church. The vast majority of scholars have held that James succeeded Peter as head of the Jerusalem church only after Peter's escape from prison (generally dated 41–44), since Peter would then have been a fugitive and forced to flee Jerusalem. Acts 12:17 has often been understood as marking the "passing of the baton" from Peter to James, after which Peter became a traveling missionary to the Jews living in the Diaspora (i.e., outside of Palestine). Current scholars who support this view include the conservatives Richard Bauckham, Ralph P. Martin, and Luke Timothy Johnson—and also, interestingly, the extremely liberal Gerd Lüdemann. A maverick voice arguing for a different interpretation is, again, John Painter. Because Painter bucks the consensus, and because his explanation is extremely significant, it is worth quoting his rationale at length:

> It has been suggested that the narrative of Acts portrays the leadership of the Jerusalem church at first by the apostles, headed by Peter . . . Acts 12:1–24 can be read as a kind of flashback to explain how James came to leadership, Herod Agrippa had James the brother of John executed and Peter was thrown into prison.
>
> The transition of authority from Peter to James is often taken to be implied by Acts 12:17. [But if] James *were already the leader,* nothing would be more natural than for Peter to report back to him. This reading is at least as plausible as the one that takes Peter's message to be a passing on of the authority of leadership. If this is what Luke meant to convey, why does Peter not resume leadership on his return to Jerusalem? In Acts 15 James is portrayed as the leader of the Jerusalem church even though Peter was then present again. It seems that the prominence of Peter in Acts has been interpreted in terms of his leadership. But that prominence is described more in terms of his activity in relation to those outside the believing community than in terms of leadership of the community. Peter, like Paul, is portrayed as a "missionary" rather than as the leader of a settled community.
>
> Acts explicitly names no single leader of the Jerusalem church. The conclusion that Peter was the leader at first is the consequence of the influence of [a Catholic] interpretive tradition that has no support in relation to Jerusalem. Nothing in Acts supports this view. Indeed, the tradition that Peter was the leader runs contrary to tradition that concerns the Jerusalem church. [This] tradition names James as the first leader ("bishop"). The nomenclature is anachronistic, but the leadership of James is supported by the way in which James is cited in both Acts 15 and 21 as well as in Paul's letter to the Galatians.[13] (italics mine)

We will be examining the James tradition to which Painter refers in a later chapter. For now, note well that Painter is cautious to say that his interpretation of James's leadership from the beginning is only "at least as plausible" as the prevailing interpretation that James succeeded Peter. Painter cautiously adds:

> [I]n Acts and Galatians the sole leadership of James is not explicit. More than likely James was one of a group of leaders among whom he stood out, from the beginning, as the leading figure and dominant influence. Upon this basis the tradition of James as the first bishop of Jerusalem was developed.

Another factor that needs to be considered in assessing the case for James's early leadership of the Jerusalem church is that Peter may have always been a *traveling* evangelist, while James is always portrayed as rooted in Jerusalem. Support for this is found in 1 Corinthians, where Paul rousingly defends his claim to the entitlements of apostleship against his critics who deny he is an apostle:

> Do we [Paul and Barnabas] not have the right to our food and drink? Do we not have the right to be accompanied by a believing wife, as the other apostles *and the brothers of the Lord and Cephas?* Or is it only Barnabas and I who have no right to refrain from working for a living? (1 Cor. 9:4–6)

Some have said that here Paul is drawing a contrast between Jesus' brothers and the apostles, and therefore, Jesus' brothers were not apostles, but that interpretation leads necessarily to the conclusion that *Peter* was not an apostle because he is also mentioned separately from the apostles. So it is clearly not Paul's intent to imply that Jesus' brothers were not apostles. But we do have here firm support that Peter and Jesus' brothers were traveling evangelists. Whether James was also a traveling evangelist, or was permanently based in Jerusalem, is another question. Ralph Martin argues for traveling: "At 1 Cor 9:5 there is a[n] . . . allusion to 'the Lord's brothers,' among whom James is certainly to be numbered . . . Here . . . there is evidence that James was known . . . at Corinth to have sponsored missionary activity."[14] Of course, there is a big difference between *sponsoring* missionary activity and taking part in that activity oneself. In fact, Martin's suggestion that James sponsored missionary activity fits perfectly with the general picture of James we are beginning to see—that he was the settled overseer of the Jerusalem church, one who would indeed sponsor *all* missionary activity. It is hard to believe that James could have carried out the administrative role of leading the Jerusalem church while actively engaging in far-flung missionary activity.

This brings us to the next firm conclusion of our investigation: *At least by the time that Peter became a traveling missionary, if not earlier, James held the reins of leadership of the entire early Christian community both in Jerusalem and beyond.*

It can also be argued that the leadership of James is not explicit in either Acts or Galatians simply because *it was common knowledge.* Luke and Paul only tacitly imply James's leadership role for the same reason that they give him no introduction the first time he is mentioned: they would have been stating the obvious for readers familiar with James's person and position. While Painter's theory that James was *always* the leader of the Jerusalem church has not yet persuaded the majority of scholars, it makes the best sense out of the biblical evidence and ties together many loose ends. Logically, nothing would be more natural, especially in Jewish society, than for the reins of leadership to be handed after Jesus' death to his eldest brother, especially if Jesus' role as Messiah was tied directly to his descent from King David. German theologian Ethelbert Stauffer was the first to champion the idea of Jesus' brothers and family forming a Christian "caliphate" after his death, a proposal for which there is reliable evidence in the later history and tradition of the Jerusalem church.

Galatians 1:19 might, however, seem to unseat any theory of James gripping the reins of leadership from the beginning. Paul asserts plainly that he "went up to Jerusalem to visit Cephas." If James were the acknowledged leader, why would Paul have gone to Jerusalem with the express purpose of seeing *Peter*? Painter again provides a plausible answer: "Paul might have chosen to see Peter because Peter was perceived to be more sympathetic to Paul's cause. James, as the leader, was too important to be missed, and Peter may have effected an introduction for Paul."[15] This is, of course, speculation on Painter's part, but at the least, his argument adds to the probability of James having been the leader from the beginning and reminds us again how difficult it is to achieve absolute historical certainty.

JAMES AND THE RESURRECTION

For another piece of evidence in favor of James's early standing, let us look again at Paul's intriguing list of resurrection appearances in 1 Corinthians 15:3–7:

> 3 For I handed on to you as of first importance what I in turn had received: that Christ died for our sins in accordance with the scriptures, 4 and that he was buried, and that he was raised on the third day in accordance with the scriptures, 5 and that he appeared to Cephas, then to the twelve. 6 Then he appeared to more than five hundred brothers and sisters at one time, most of whom are still alive, though some have died. 7 Then he appeared to James, then to all the apostles. 8 Last of all, as to one untimely born, he appeared also to me.

The vast majority of scholars are agreed that here Paul has preserved a traditional list that had been handed down to him, as Paul himself states in verse 3: "For I handed on to you as of first importance *what I in turn had received.*" This is a very early list, and it provides essential evidence that very early on—*perhaps even already at the time of Jesus' death*—James was considered an apostle. F. F. Bruce argues in favor of this:

> "[A]ll the apostles" should certainly be interpreted as a wider body than "the twelve" and equally certainly James is to be regarded as one of those "apostles" as Peter is one of "the twelve." The appearance of the risen Lord to James was no doubt something of which Paul heard from James himself during his first post-conversion visit to Jerusalem just as he would have heard of the appearance to Peter from Peter himself.[16]

While there is scholarly unanimity about the authenticity of Paul's list, there is much debate over the order in which the appearances took place (a very heated debate in the early church too). The scholarly debate today concerns whether Paul meant for his list to be understood in a temporal sequence (an In Order of Appearance listing, so to speak), or whether Paul did not intend such, but rather combined two lists that represented rival traditions in which one early Christian community claimed that the first appearance was to Peter, and another community claimed that James was the first to see the resurrected Christ. The idea of rival traditions (called *Rivalitätsformel* by the German liberal theologians who first proposed the idea) has a long history in scholarship. Today, Gerd Lüdemann upholds the classic German understanding, which goes back to the legendary Adolf von Harnack:

> The formula in 1 Cor 15:7 grew out of the fact that disciples of James claimed for their leader the primacy that Peter enjoyed by virtue of having received the initial resurrection appearance. To support this claim they constructed the formula of 15:7, patterned after that of 15:5. Although Paul . . . is reporting in chronological order, it is still questionable whether this development had occurred prior to Paul's first visit to Jerusalem. In any case, at that time James already had a group of disciples in Jerusalem, although Cephas was still the leading figure. Still, the process of a gradual shifting of authority from Peter to James can be traced in the life of the Jerusalem church.[17]

The pro-James community to which Lüdemann refers probably supported their claim with an apocryphal work, *The Gospel of the Hebrews*, that makes the astounding claim that the first resurrection appearance was to James: "And when the Lord had given the linen cloth [his burial shroud] to the servant of the priest, he went to James and appeared to him."[18]

John Painter proposes a surprising twist to the accepted German idea of rival formulas, which upholds the possibility that the first resurrection appearance really *was* to James, despite Paul's sequence, thus making James the leader of the Jerusalem church from its inception:

> According to Adolf von Harnack, the tradition assumes that Jesus first appeared to Peter in Galilee . . . and that the appearance to James was subsequent to the appearance to the five hundred brethren at Pentecost. Harnack argues that 15:5 and 15:7 reflect a shift from the leadership of Peter . . . to . . . James. [Wilhelm] Pratcher, building on the work of von Harnack, argues that 15:7 is based on 15:5 . . . reflecting the rivalry between the followers of James and the followers of Peter. Lüdemann develops a similar position . . . If the original leadership of Peter is accepted the *Rivalitätsformel* reflects a change of leadership in the Jerusalem church. Alternatively, we have argued that there was continuing tension between James and Peter (Galatians

2:11–14). . . . . *it is possible to see the imposition of Petrine leadership as the later move.*[19] (italics mine)

In other words, Painter is positing that James had *always* been the leader of the Jerusalem church because Jesus appeared to him first. Later, a community loyal to Peter created a rival tradition, claiming that Peter had been the first recipient of a resurrection appearance. Painter essentially turns the traditional understanding on its head, and again shows us the slippery slope that threatens the quest for historical certainty.

To explore the farthest reaches of historical *un*certainty, let us now turn to an examination of the event known as the Jerusalem Conference (the very first "apostolic council" of the church) and the so-called Apostolic Decree that was promulgated there. While even more scholarly debate surrounds this episode (it is, in fact, another of the much-debated issues in New Testament studies), here the leadership of James is clearly undeniable, as is Peter's deference to him.

4

POPE JAMES: THE FIRST APOSTOLIC COUNCIL AND THE INCIDENT AT ANTIOCH

After the ascension of the savior, Peter, James, and John did not claim pre-eminence . . . but chose James the Just as Bishop of Jerusalem.

CLEMENT OF ALEXANDRIA, *HYPOSTASES*

Clement of Alexandria wrote sometime early in the third century, and thus might not at first seem to merit the claim of historical reliability. His use of the term *bishop* to describe James is certainly an anachronism. In his own time, James would have been called an overseer (*episkopos* in Greek), which is the word translated as "bishop" in the New Testament. But while the term *bishop* is not applied to James in the New Testament, as we shall see in this chapter it is absolutely an accurate description of the role that James played in the Jerusalem church.

As mentioned previously, in the beginning of his letter to the Galatians Paul provides a brief biographical summary of the first few years after his conversion experience. This account provides scholars with invaluable information for dating key events in the life of the early church, as well as providing us with important information regarding James's leadership role. The first two chapters of the letter to the Galatians are priceless; without them, our knowledge of early

Christianity would be gravely impoverished. Here is a condensation of the material crucial to our concerns, taken from Galatians 1 and 2:

> 13 You have heard, no doubt, of my earlier life in Judaism. I was violently persecuting the church of God and was trying to destroy it . . .
> 15 But when God, who had set me apart before I was born and called me through his grace, was pleased 16 to reveal his Son to me, so that I might proclaim him among the Gentiles, I did not confer with any human being, 17 nor did I go up to Jerusalem to those who were already apostles before me, but I went away at once into Arabia, and afterward I returned to Damascus.
>
> 18 Then after three years I did go up to Jerusalem to visit Cephas and stayed with him fifteen days; but I did not see any other apostle except James the Lord's brother . . .
>
> 1 Then after fourteen years I went up again to Jerusalem with Barnabas, taking Titus along with me. 2 I went up in response to a revelation. Then I laid before them (though only in a private meeting with the acknowledged leaders) the gospel that I proclaim among the Gentiles, in order to make sure that I was not running, or had not run, in vain.

Whether Paul counts his "fourteen years" in 2:1 from the time of his conversion or from the time of his first visit to Jerusalem (three years after his conversion) is a matter of some debate, though most scholars favor the former interpretation. In any case, Paul's second visit to Jerusalem to meet with the apostles is generally dated around 48–49. While there is great uncertainty among scholars about when James came to be head of the Jerusalem church, there is *no* debate that by the time of Paul's second visit James held the reins of leadership.

It is fascinating (and surprising, if one is familiar with Paul) that in 2:2 Paul seems to submit his work among the Gentiles to the leaders of the church for their approval. Logically, such a move makes sense for a new missionary like Paul, especially in light of his former life as a persecutor of the church. Still, Paul's seeming submission to the Jerusalem leaders is curious in light of the lengths to which he goes elsewhere in his letters to assert the complete independence of his mission from that of the other apostles. Noted early twentieth-century scholar A. S. Peake provides this sound rationale for Paul's unusual humility:

> The impulse for the journey . . . was to secure both his previous and his future mission from the risk of failure. By this he does not mean that he had any misgivings as to the truth of his gospel or thought that his seniors could correct any mistaken view which he might hold . . . But he was well aware how disastrous might be the consequences for his mission if a different form of the Gospel should be preached in the Gentile world with the prestige of the original apostles attaching to it . . . [H]e realized how much he would be hampered if the leaders of the Church at Jerusalem, the apostles who beyond all others might be expected to know the mind of their Master, had thrown the weight of their influence against his presentation of Christianity.[1]

As Peake points out, it would have been widely assumed that the original apostles knew Jesus' teachings better than anyone. In Jesus' absence, *they* were the authorities, and even as independent and authoritative a figure as Paul needed to evaluate his mission in light of their judgment of its conformity to Jesus' teaching. This has important ramifications for our understanding of James's role. It is quite likely that much of the prestige that James enjoyed, and a major reason for his rapid rise to leadership, was the perception that, as Jesus' eldest brother, he knew the "mind of the Master" better than anyone. And if indeed he did, Christians today are going to have to reevaluate some of their most deeply held assumptions and beliefs about Jesus and his teaching.

THE CIRCUMCISION QUESTION

Succeeding verses of Galatians 2 explain that there was more to Paul's visit than simply seeking approval for his mission to the Gentiles—namely, addressing the crucial question of whether his Gentile converts needed to be circumcised in order to become Christians. That Paul needed to confer with the leadership in Jerusalem over this question speaks volumes. It shows that Paul was questioning a widely held assumption that Gentile converts *were* in fact required to undergo circumcision—in essence, to become a Jew—in order to follow Christ.

This requirement makes sense when we remind ourselves that at this point Christianity was a *Jewish* phenomenon. It was not yet a separate and distinct religion, but rather a sect of Judaism. At this early time, the *only* thing that distinguished Jesus' followers from any other Jews was their belief that, in Jesus, the long-awaited Messiah of Israel had arrived. Originally, they were not even called Christians, but "Nazarenes" (see Acts 24:5), the implications of which we shall discuss later. Acts attests clearly to their continued regular attendance at the services of the Temple and the goodwill they had from their fellow Jews, demonstrating that the disciples' faith and practice remained thoroughly Jewish:

> All who believed were together and had all things in common; they would sell their possessions and goods and distribute the proceeds to all, as any had need. Day by day, as they spent much time together in the temple, they broke bread at home and ate their food with glad and generous hearts, praising God and having the goodwill of all the people. (Acts 2:44–47)

The Jewish scholar, Hyam Maccoby, has pointed out some fascinating implications of the fact that the disciples continued to worship in the Temple in Jerusalem after Jesus' death and resurrection, the Temple that had been the central focus of Jewish religious life since the days of King Solomon:

> The book of Acts does not disguise the fact that the Nazarenes of Jerusalem, in the days immediately following the death of Jesus, consisted of observant Jews, for whom the Torah was still in force. For example, we are told that 'they kept up their daily attendance at the Temple' (Acts 2:46). Evidently, then, Jesus' followers regarded the services of the Temple as still valid, with its meat and vegetable offerings, its Holy of Holies, its golden table for the showbread, and its *menorah* or candelabra with its seven branches symbolizing the seven planets. All these were venerated by the followers of Jesus, who made no effort to set up a central place of worship of their own . . . Also, their acceptance of Temple worship implied an acceptance of the Aaronic priesthood who administered the Temple. Though Jesus' movement had a system of leadership of its own, this was not a rival priesthood.[2]

Maccoby's stark conclusion is not often considered by Christian scholars for obvious reasons. Until only very recently, Christian scholarship has instead viewed Christianity as representing a complete and total break with Judaism from the time of Jesus' death;* whereas, in fact, Christianity became distinct from Judaism through a slow and gradual process, a process that has been accurately described by James Dunn in his enlightening volume, *The Partings of the Ways.*

In the eyes of Jesus' original Jewish followers, any Gentile who wanted to become a follower of Jesus was, in fact, becoming a follower of Judaism. But as Paul's evangelism brought in ever-larger numbers of Gentile converts, the issue of just how far these converts had to go in order to become followers became very difficult. New Gentile believers who were male would, quite understandably, want to put off circumcision if at all possible. Jewish believers, on the other hand, fretted that relaxing the circumcision requirement could potentially threaten all the requirements of the Torah. As Paul's ministry grew, the issue became increasingly urgent. Was any relaxing of the Law of Moses possible in these new circumstances? These are the questions that the Jerusalem Conference was called to decide.

THE JERUSALEM CONFERENCE

The Jerusalem Conference, described in Acts 15 as a meeting of all the key leaders of the primitive church, can legitimately be called the church's first apostolic council. There has been an enormous amount of debate over whether the meeting with the apostles that Paul discusses in Galatians is in fact the Jerusalem Conference, or perhaps a different meeting, a debate we shall examine momentarily. In any case, as we read Paul's description of his meeting with the apostles in Galatians 2, we come to a startling realization. It is quite obvious that Paul harbors some resentment toward the apostles in Jerusalem, for his tone is nothing short of sarcastic:

> And from those who were supposed to be acknowledged leaders (what they actually were makes no difference to me; God shows no partiality)—those leaders contributed nothing to me. On the contrary, when

---

*This precept has been supported by statements in the gospels such as Matthew 27:50–51: "Then Jesus cried again with a loud voice and breathed his last. *At that moment* the curtain of the Temple was torn in two, from top to bottom."

they saw that I had been entrusted with the gospel for the uncircumcised, just as Peter had been entrusted with the gospel for the circumcised (for he who worked through Peter making him an apostle to the circumcised also worked through me in sending me to the Gentiles), and when James and Cephas and John, who were acknowledged pillars, recognized the grace that had been given to me, they gave to Barnabas and me the right hand of fellowship, agreeing that we should go to the Gentiles and they to the circumcised. They asked only one thing, that we remember the poor, which was actually what I was eager to do. (Gal. 2:6–10)

First, note Paul's listing of the leaders: "James and Cephas and John, who were acknowledged pillars." Most scholars believe that James's position in the list clearly implies that he was the most important of the three. As F. F. Bruce comments, "Next time Paul visited Jerusalem, James's leading role had been established . . . the order in which [the] names are given tells its own story, which is confirmed by the general impression made by all the relevant evidence."[3]

Second, Paul's use of the term "acknowledged pillars" to describe James, Peter, and John is significant. The generally accepted meaning behind Paul's usage of the term *pillars* is given in an article on James in the standard reference *The Anchor Bible Dictionary*:

> The metaphor could be an eschatological one which originated not with Paul but with the Jerusalem Christians. Paul was apparently aware that they spoke of their leading apostles as "pillars" because of the positions of importance they believed [they] would occupy in the eschatological temple in the age to come.[4]

The term *eschatological* refers to beliefs concerning the "end times" or the "last things," what the Jews of Jesus' time called the Day of the Lord, which had been foretold by prophets. Following Jesus' resurrection from the dead, his followers believed that the Day of the Lord and the final judgment was imminent. The popular historical Jesus scholar N. T. Wright has taken up the idea championed by the legendary Albert Schweitzer a century ago, that Jesus fully believed his messianic mission would usher in the Day of the Lord and the final judgment. Wright has proposed that Jesus viewed his ministry as the establishing of a new messianic community that would be a replacement for the Temple, which he had predicted would soon be destroyed, marking the end of the age (see Mark 13). James, Peter, and John were thus looked upon after Jesus' death and resurrection as the "pillars" of the new eschatological "Temple" of the New Jerusalem in the soon-to-be-realized Kingdom of God.

While Paul acknowledges their role as pillars, and seems to defer to their leadership by asking their approval for his mission to the Gentiles, he betrays a definite note of condescension when he refers to them as, "those who were *supposed* to be acknowledged leaders (what they actually were makes no difference to me; God shows no partiality)—those leaders contributed nothing to me." Scholars agree that here Paul is trying to impress upon the Galatians the independence of his mission from the Jerusalem leadership by implying that his mission does not require the blessing of James, Peter, and John to be valid; for, as Paul argues elsewhere, his mission was received as a direct commission from the risen Christ himself. Paul therefore believed he had full independent authority and need not submit to anyone, including the pillar apostles. Paul's very first words in Galatians emphasize this: "Paul an apostle—sent neither by human commission nor from human authorities, but through Jesus Christ and God the Father."

Some scholars have seen Paul's tone in Galatians 2 as evidence of a much deeper rift between Paul and the pillar apostles than Paul was at liberty to divulge in a publicly circulated epistle. F. C. Baur was the first to propose, in the 1800s, that there was outright animosity between Paul and the pillar apostles. Baur, affectionately referred to as the Old Master of Tübingen by his students, was one of the founders of the so-called Tübingen school which arose at Tübingen University, and which influenced continental European Protestant theology for almost a century. Baur's theory of outright opposition between Paul and the pillar apostles generally fell out of favor after World War I, especially in light of the burgeoning influence of Rudolph Bultmann's antihistorical methodology.* But Baur's ideas

---

*Bultmann proposed that we could know next to nothing about the historical Jesus, that the *kerygma* (proclamation) of his message was all that mattered. This idea held sway among liberal scholars until the 1950s when some of Bultmann's own pupils initiated the so-called new quest for the historical Jesus.

never completely died, and they have been revived in modern times by liberal scholars such as Gerd Lüdemann and Michael Goulder, and by Jewish scholars such as Hyam Maccoby and Hugh Schonfield. While such theories are generally belittled by conservative Christian and most mainstream scholars, the widely respected mainstream scholar James Dunn has called for a reappraisal and reappropriation of Baur's theories.[5] Even the popular evangelical scholar Luke Timothy Johnson, who is quite hesitant to ascribe any animosity between Paul and the Jerusalem leadership, still acknowledges that Paul's tone toward the pillar apostles

> indicates some reservation by Paul concerning their reputation . . .
> But although his tone is cool, Paul does not question the authority
> of the three leaders. Indeed he comes prepared to submit . . . for their
> consideration the gospel he preaches among the Gentiles, and specif-
> ically states his willingness to defer to their judgment, "lest I am run-
> ning or have run in vain" (2:2). His claim that they imposed no
> further obligation on him (2:6) . . . and that they recognized the
> legitimacy of the gift God had given him for his mission to the
> Gentiles (2:9) is implicit acknowledgment of their authority to dis-
> cern and judge.[6]

Whatever the actual state of affairs was between Paul and Jerusalem, the bottom line would seem to be given in Galatians 2:9: "[W]hen James and Cephas and John . . . recognized the grace that had been given to me, they gave to Barnabas and me the right hand of fellowship, agreeing that we should go to the Gentiles and they to the circumcised." According to Paul, a demarcation of mission territories had been amicably agreed to.

It is this official agreement that seems to be the basis of the trouble that necessitated Paul's rather angry letter to the Galatians. Apparently, influential people from Jerusalem had journeyed to the Galatians to inform them that they needed to be circumcised in order to be saved. Their influence was such that the Galatian Christians had begun to practice circumcision. Thus it is that at the beginning of his letter to the Galatians, Paul says:

> I am astonished that you are so quickly deserting the one who called
> you in the Grace of Christ and are turning to a different gospel . . .

> [T]here are some who are confusing you and want to pervert the gospel . . . But even if we or an angel from heaven should proclaim to you a gospel contrary to what we proclaimed to you, let that one be accursed! (Gal. 1:6–8)

That those who are proclaiming the "contrary gospel" are respected, leading figures necessitates Paul's assertion that it doesn't matter whether an *angel* proclaimed it—it would still be in error. There are some scholars who believe this is an indirect reference to the pillar apostles themselves.

We may at this point ask: What exactly is the contrary gospel that so upset Paul? The answer is to be found in Acts 15, where Luke describes the turmoil that had erupted in the Gentile church in Antioch, which precipitated the need for the Jerusalem Conference:

> Then certain individuals came down from Judea and were teaching the brothers, "Unless you are circumcised according to the custom of Moses, you cannot be saved." And after Paul and Barnabas had no small dissension and debate with them, Paul and Barnabas and some of the others were appointed to go up to Jerusalem to discuss the question with the apostles and the elders. (Acts 15:1–2)

Although Acts is describing a situation in Antioch, the problem was the same in Galatia. In fact, the same perpetrators ("certain individuals . . . from Judea") seem to have been at work in both places, teaching that the circumcision of Gentile converts was a necessity for salvation, not faith in Christ alone as Paul taught. That is, the passage in Acts seems to explain the purpose of Paul's second visit to Jerusalem which he describes in Galatians, and the reason for the meeting and the cast of characters seem to be the same in both accounts.

Scholars, however, have long noticed discrepancies between Acts 15 and Galatians 2 that call into question whether Luke and Paul are in fact describing the same meeting. Seemingly irreconcilable differences in the two accounts have led many scholars to conclude that the Jerusalem Conference described in Acts 15 actually happened *after* Paul wrote his letter to the Galatians, and that the meeting Paul discusses in the letter was an earlier, less official assembly. Whatever the case, here is the account of the Jerusalem Conference as described by Luke in Acts 15:

4 When they [Paul and the delegation from Antioch] came to Jerusalem, they were welcomed by the church and the apostles and the elders, and they reported all that God had done with them. 5 But some believers who belonged to the sect of the Pharisees stood up and said, "It is necessary for them [the Gentiles] to be circumcised and ordered to keep the law of Moses."

6 The apostles and the elders met together to consider this matter. 7 After there had been much debate, Peter stood up and said to them, "My brothers, you know that in the early days God made a choice among you, that I should be the one through whom the Gentiles would hear the message of the good news and become believers. 8 And God, who knows the human heart, testified to them by giving them the Holy Spirit, just as he did to us; 9 and in cleansing their hearts by faith he has made no distinction between them and us. 10 Now therefore why are you putting God to the test by placing on the neck of the disciples a yoke that neither our ancestors nor we have been able to bear? 11 On the contrary, we believe that we will be saved through the grace of the Lord Jesus, just as they will."

12 The whole assembly kept silence, and listened to Barnabas and Paul as they told all the signs and wonders that God had worked through them among the Gentiles.

Here we see that certain believers in Jerusalem, who were members of the Pharisaic (conservative) party, believed strongly that circumcision and adherence to the Law was a strict requirement for Gentile converts. And the question obviously had not yet been decided. It cannot be stressed enough, that *Jesus and his earliest followers were thoroughly Jewish in their beliefs and practices.* What later became the distinct religion of Christianity began as a messianic movement within Judaism, and the *only* thing that distinguished the members of the Jerusalem church from their fellow Jews was their firm belief that Jesus was the Messiah of Israel. Therefore, it was only natural for those first believers in Jesus to expect that anyone wishing to follow Jesus would become a Jew. They were in fact becoming part of the Israel of which Jesus was the Messiah.

At the opening of this crucial meeting between the delegates from Antioch and the leaders of the Jerusalem church, Peter, Paul, and Barnabas (Paul's missionary companion) give testimony to how God has been at work though the Holy Spirit among the Gentiles. The conversion of so many Gentile believers was seen by many (Paul most of all) as a fulfilling of the biblical prophecies that at the end of the age the nations would come streaming into Jerusalem acknowledging the God of Abraham, Isaac, and Jacob as the God of all the world, culminating in the establishment of the Kingdom of God on earth with Jesus as the eternal Davidic king.

Paul pushed the question that was most painfully at the forefront of the Gentile mind: Was circumcision really a necessary requirement for Gentiles to become part of Jesus' new kingdom? And here we come to a vital bit of information. According to the account in Acts, it is not Peter, but *James* who makes the final call on this crucial issue, which speaks volumes about James's sole leadership role in the Jerusalem church:

> 13 After they [Paul and Barnabas] finished speaking, James replied, "My brothers listen to me. 14 Simeon has related how God first looked favorably on the Gentiles, to take from among them a people for his name. 15 This agrees with the words of the prophets, as it is written,
>
> 16 'After this I will return,
> And I will rebuild the dwelling of David,
> which has fallen;
> from its ruins I will rebuild it,
> and I will set it up,
> 17 so that all other peoples may seek the Lord—
> even all the Gentiles over whom my name has been called.
> Thus says the Lord, who has been making these things
> 18 known from long ago.'
>
> 19 Therefore I have reached the decision that we should not trouble those Gentiles who are turning to God, 20 but we should write to them to abstain only from things polluted by idols and from fornication and from whatever has been strangled and from blood. 21 For in every city, for generations past, Moses has had those who proclaim him, for he has been read aloud every Sabbath in the synagogues."

Thus ends the speech of James, which, except for the epistle of James, are the only words in the New Testament attributed directly to him. Whether they are the actual words of James is, of course, impossible to prove. But while many scholars have doubted the historicity of this account in Acts, there are solid reasons to trust it. First and foremost, James's leadership is plainly demonstrated, which ironically suggests that it is more trustworthy than less. Luke is widely accepted as an advocate of Pauline doctrine, meaning that he had no reason to invent a situation where James had the final say and where his arguments carried the day. And James does indeed issue the final word on the matter in the so-called Apostolic Decree.

THE APOSTOLIC DECREE

Immediately following James's speech in Acts 15, we are told that an official letter regarding the matter was composed and sent back with Paul and Barnabas:

> 22 Then the apostles and the elders, with the consent of the whole church, decided to choose men from among their members and to send them to Antioch with Paul and Barnabas. They sent Judas, called Barsabbas, and Silas, leaders among the brothers, 23 with the following letter: "The brothers, both the apostles and the elders, to the believers of Gentile origin in Antioch and Syria and Cilicia, greetings. 24 Since we have heard that certain persons who have gone out from us, though with no instructions from us, have said things to disturb you and have unsettled your minds, 25 we have decided unanimously to choose representatives and send them to you, along with our beloved Barnabas and Paul, 26 who have risked their lives for the sake of our Lord Jesus Christ. 27 We have therefore sent Judas and Silas who will themselves tell you the same things by word of mouth. 28 For it has seemed good to the Holy Spirit and to us to impose on you no further burden than these essentials: 29 that you abstain from what has been sacrificed to idols and from blood and from what is strangled and from fornication. If you keep yourselves from these, you will do well. Farewell."

The four requirements of this Apostolic Decree—abstaining from food offered to idols, from fornication, from eating animals that have been strangled, and from eating rare meat ("from blood")—are ancient regulations found in the Law of Moses. In the section of the Law given in Leviticus 17, known as the Holiness Code, these same requirements are listed in the same order. These were known as the Noahide Laws (named after Noah) and were the minimum requirements for observance of the Law imposed upon Gentiles who wished to follow Judaism without taking the step of being circumcised and becoming full Jews. Such partial converts were known as "God-fearers." That these requirements are correctly listed in the Apostolic Decree certainly lends it authenticity, belying the notion that Luke, himself a Gentile, freely composed this section. Logically, it would only be natural for James and the Torah-observant apostles and elders to look to the Torah for guidance on the question of requirements for Gentile converts. Adding support to this line of reasoning is the fact that James quotes the Hebrew prophet Amos in support of his argument (compare Acts 15:16–18 with Amos 9:11–12). Here we have a poetic rendering of the concept, also expressed by Isaiah, that on the eschatological Day of the Lord, the Gentiles will come streaming into the Temple in Jerusalem proclaiming Yahweh as the God of all the earth.

The main proponent of James's speech being authentic is Richard Bauckham, who examines it in great detail in his groundbreaking essay "James and the Jerusalem Church." Bauckham sees James's use of Amos 9:11–12 as a vital piece of evidence in favor of the speech's authenticity:

> Many other prophecies portrayed the Temple of the messianic age as a place where the Gentiles would come into God's presence . . . There were also prophecies predicting that the Gentile nations would become, like Israel, God's own people . . . But in most cases such texts *could* be taken to mean that these Gentiles would be proselytes, undergoing circumcision as the corollary of their conversion . . . These texts could not decisively settle the issue. But Amos 9:11–12 could, for it states that the nations [as] Gentile nations belong to [Yahweh]. Precisely as "all the nations" they are included in the covenant relationship . . . Probably no other scriptural text could have been used to make this point so clearly.[7]

As to the overall authenticity of James's speech, Bauckham concludes:

> The argument which James's speech represents . . . is exactly the kind of argument about the relation of Gentile Christians to the Law of

Moses which we should expect from the Jerusalem church leaders. It
. . . skillfully deploys the exegetical methods of contemporary Jewish
exegesis. It employs the notion of the Christian community as the messianic Temple, which we know to have been important to the
Jerusalem church under James's leadership. It deals with the question
of Gentile Christians in a way which by no means sets aside the
authority of the Law of Moses but fully upholds it . . .

These considerations make the Jerusalem church leadership, with
James at its head, very plausibly the source of the apostolic decree
. . . It is almost universally agreed, for good reasons, that the decree
itself is not a Lukan invention . . . though many scholars doubt that
Luke can have correctly described the circumstance of its formulation.[8]

By the "circumstance of its formulation," Bauckham is referring to
the notorious difficulty scholars face in trying to reconcile the way the
Apostolic Decree is described in Acts with Paul's understanding of the
result of the meeting he had with the apostles as described in Galatians
2:10. The Apostolic Decree places four binding stipulations upon
Gentile converts, but in Galatians 2:10, Paul says, "They asked *only
one thing,* that we remember the poor," referring to the collection for
the poor in Jerusalem, which he enthusiastically supported throughout
his mission. If there were any other requirements, Paul does not mention them. But an even more problematic issue is this: If there had
indeed been an official Apostolic Decree issued that stated that circumcision was not necessary for Gentiles, *why doesn't Paul cite the
decree in his argument with the Galatians?* This, more than anything
else, has led the majority of scholars to believe that the account of the
Jerusalem Conference in Acts 15 occurred *after* Paul wrote his letter to
the Galatians.

RECONCILING ACCOUNTS

The problem of reconciling Acts 15 with Galatians 2 has long been one
of the thorniest issues in the history of New Testament scholarship. The
Dictionary of Paul and His Letters summarizes the many and various
ways that scholars have tried to reconcile the two accounts, some quite
ingenious. According to the *Dictionary,* at least eight different propos-
als have been advanced (my own annotations are in brackets):[9]

1. Galatians 2 = Acts 15.
2. Galatians 2 = Acts 11 [Paul's famine-relief visit].
3. Galatians 2 = Acts 11 = Acts 15 (Luke, or his traditions, has mis-interpreted what happened in the visit of Galatians 2 and erro-neously reported it twice).
4. Galatians 2 = Acts 18 [Paul's brief visit to Jerusalem after his sec-ond missionary journey].
5. Galatians 2 = Acts 15:1–4 [only].
6. Galatians 2 = Acts 11 + Acts 15 (Luke, or his traditions, has mis-interpreted what happened in the visit of Galatians 2 and erro-neously reported what happened on this occasion as occurring at two separate times).
7. Galatians 2 is not reported in Acts.
8. Galatians 2 = Acts 9 [Paul's first post-conversion visit to Jerusalem].

The *Dictionary* identifies solutions 1, 2, and 6 as the most proba-ble and widely accepted. Perhaps the most even-handed assessment of the situation comes, once again, from the venerable A. S. Peake, whose 1929 analysis of the matter is well worth quoting at length:

[T]he identification of the visit in Gal. ii. 1–10 with that in Acts xv. is favoured . . . if we remember that Paul is writing with the inside knowledge of one who had been a party to the discussion and who was stating his own position as he saw it, while Luke describes the events as they appeared to the community in general. Paul is not con-cerned with the general assembly of the Church, though his language seems to imply that the larger body met; much more important to him is the private conference at which the leaders of the mother Church recognized the vocation of himself and Barnabas and delimited their spheres of work . . . It must be conceded that Paul, in perfect good faith, is telling the story from his own point of view, and that if we had the account of Peter or James the impression of the incidents and the discussion might be modified. But be that as it may, it would be per-ilous to use the narrative in the Acts to discredit, or even to modify the account given by Paul. Luke had no first-hand knowledge of the facts but was dependent on what information he could collect when in Palestine; and as a Gentile he was less qualified to grasp the full sig-nificance of the events than a Jew would have been.[10]

Among contemporary scholars, the more conservative scholars generally believe that Acts 15 and Galatians 2 are describing the same event, while more liberal scholars think that Luke has freely composed Acts 15 to sum up his interpretation of events. But, again, there are exceptions. Gerd Lüdemann, who resides near the radical left end of the theological spectrum, believes that Acts 15 is basically historical as it stands. The Roman Catholic historical Jesus scholar John P. Meier believes that Acts 15 and Galatians 2 essentially describe the same event, with the caveat that the Apostolic Decree was a later addition by Luke. Among conservatives, F. F. Bruce believes that the Jerusalem Conference described in Acts 15, while historical, was a later meeting held sometime after an earlier, private meeting with the pillar apostles that Paul describes in Galatians. Lending weight to this idea is Paul's description of the meeting in 2:2 as "only . . . a private meeting with the acknowledged leaders." Finally, Richard Bauckham, along with most conservatives, believes the two accounts can be completely reconciled.[11]

Indeed, the accounts *can* easily be reconciled, and without a lot of mental gymnastics, if one simply makes the assumption that Paul wrote Galatians *before* the Jerusalem Conference and the issuance of the Apostolic Decree, and this position has therefore become the most widely held. It is the only solution that answers the simple question: Why didn't Paul cite the decree? Walter Schmithals summed up scholarship on this issue midcentury, and his assessment remains true today: "Most commentators today assume that [the Apostolic Decree] originated in the period *after* the [Antioch incident] and was recommended by the Jewish Christians to the Gentile Christians in order to make table-fellowship possible between them."[12] The evidence for this is to be found in the event that Paul describes next in Galatians 2, a major crisis that is curiously not mentioned in Acts, where Peter and Paul nearly come to blows.

THE INCIDENT AT ANTIOCH

We know of the incident at Antioch solely from Paul. Luke may not have wished to include this account in his history of the church because serious conflict between church leaders disrupted his intent to portray a harmonious community. Paul's brutally honest account in Galatians 2, therefore, belies Luke's idealized picture all the more. Note well the implications of Paul's reference to James:

> 11 But when Cephas came to Antioch, I opposed him to his face, because he stood self-condemned; 12 for *until certain people came from James*, he used to eat with the Gentiles. But after they came, he drew back *for fear of the circumcision faction*. 13 And the other Jews joined him in the hypocrisy, so that even Barnabas was led astray by their hypocrisy. 14 But when I saw that they were not acting consistently with the truth of the gospel, I said to Cephas before them all, "If you, though a Jew, live like a Gentile and not like a Jew, how can you compel the Gentiles to live like Jews?"

This is one of the more revealing passages in the New Testament for what it tells us about the composition and beliefs of what we call the early "church." It becomes more and more obvious that the first followers of Jesus thought of themselves as nothing other than Jews. What Paul says of Peter in verse 14 speaks volumes: "If you though a *Jew* . . ." And notice how Paul refers to the other believers in verse 13: "And the other *Jews* joined him . . ." Plainly, they, and Peter, still think of themselves as Jews. Indeed, Acts itself says that Jesus' followers were not called "Christians" for many years after Jesus' death: "and it was in Antioch that the disciples were first called 'Christians'" (Acts 11:26). Before this they were sometimes called "Nazarenes," a designation with important ramifications which we shall examine later. Their being called Nazarene (in Greek *Nazorean*) may well imply their thorough *Jewishness,* for as we shall see in the next chapter, Nazarene may be a term associating them with the strict ascetic Jewish group known as the Nazirites.

The second startling point about the account of the Antioch incident is the plain fact that Paul and Peter are at cross-purposes, and the reason for their coming to loggerheads is *James.* Paul, the newcomer, the former persecutor of Christians, who we know aided and abetted in the stoning of Stephen,* dares to take Peter to task. The issue? A delicate one to be sure: Jews sharing meals with Gentiles. It is one thing to say that Gentiles may become part of the Christian

---

*See Acts 7:58: "Then they dragged him [Stephen] out of the city, and began to stone him; and the witnesses laid their coats at the feet of a young man named Saul." See also Acts 8:1: "And Saul approved of their killing him." Saul was Paul's Jewish name prior to his conversion.

community without being circumcised and may observe only a very limited part of the Law; it is another to figure out how Jews and Gentiles could share table-fellowship. Resolving this issue wasn't just a matter of Gentiles agreeing to "eat kosher" when with Jews. As we know from the trouble Jesus often got himself into, Jews were not allowed to share meals with Gentiles *under any circumstances.* Gentiles were "unclean" according to the Law of Moses. Peter, however, apparently in line with the practice of Jesus, had no problem sitting down and breaking bread with non-Jewish converts. Key to our purposes is James's role in the matter. Taking Paul's words at face value, a delegation sent by James from Jerusalem caused not only Peter, but Paul's close companion Barnabas to stop sharing meals with the Gentiles—and Paul reacts vigorously.

James obviously wielded quite a bit of power. Even this point, however, is not undisputed. Once again, more conservative scholars, hesitant to see any serious differences between Paul and James, have proposed that the "certain people . . . from James" did *not* come with any official backing from James, but were stricter Law-observant "Judaizers" who wished to turn back the clock on open relations with the Gentiles, and who only used James's name and claimed his support. Advocates of this position point to James's speech at the Jerusalem Conference to show that he, in line with Jesus' teaching, took a liberal position on how the Law applied to Gentiles and would not have forbidden Peter from table-fellowship with them. The credibility of this view, of course, depends on whether one purpose of the Apostolic Decree was to enable table-fellowship between Jews and Gentiles. Alternatively, the decree could simply address the minimum dietary laws Gentiles were required to follow, without setting any precedent on the subject of breaking bread with Jews. Conservative scholars also point to Paul's statement that Peter and Barnabas withdrew from table-fellowship "for fear of the circumcision faction," a faction scholars argue was an ultra-conservative "Judaizing" group at odds with James, who had heard their demands about circumcision at the Jerusalem Conference and disagreed (at least according to Luke).

But if the men from Jerusalem were not sent by James, why in the world would both Peter and Barnabas yield to their demands? It would seem that the *only* person powerful enough to have influenced Peter and Barnabas in this way would be Jesus' brother. The only logical conclusion would then seem to be that these men were indeed sent by

James to check up on the rumors of laxity regarding the observance of the Law by Jewish Christians at Antioch.

There are other possibilities to consider, however—first, that the decree may not yet have been issued at the time of the Antioch incident. The very existence of the circumcision faction points to this, for it is unlikely that such a faction would exist if the Apostolic Decree was in force. Of course, a conservative faction opposed to the decree could have survived after the Jerusalem Council, but would Peter and Barnabas have bowed to them when the decree had been issued by apostolic fiat? The only other possibility, already alluded to, is that the Apostolic Decree did not really enable table-fellowship, but rather spoke only to Gentile requirements without loosening any requirements for Jewish Christians. A. S. Peake supports this solution:

> It is important to realize that the question at issue [at Antioch] was not that which had been decided at the Council at Jerusalem. At this the Gentiles . . . had been exempted from circumcision and obedience to the Law. But nothing had been said as to the relationship in which the Jewish Christians stood to the Law. In a purely Jewish church the members would go on keeping it. . . . the question had not been considered what course should be followed in a church with both Jews and Gentiles in its membership.[13]

Richard Bauckham also follows this line of reasoning: "the enabling of table fellowship [is not the Decree's] primary purpose. Galatians 2:11–14 may describe . . . the situation that required a decision by the Jerusalem leaders."[14]

A more controversial line of thought is pursued by John Painter, who, along with F. C. Baur and the nineteenth-century Tübingen school, does not think that James was as liberal on these issues as most scholars suppose. Painter says bluntly: "The circumcision party *is to be identified with James* and those who had come representing him to Antioch"[15] (italics mine). Painter sees no need to place the Antioch incident prior to the formulation of the Apostolic Decree; rather,

> [t]he situation in Antioch provided the first test of the accord . . . and it was James who gave the definitive Jerusalem position, and Peter bowed to his leadership . . . Given the status and standing of Peter,

some great authority must have been behind the circumcision party and been the source of his fear. This can only be James.

Painter's latter statement is difficult to argue with, given Peter's undisputed prominence in the church's hierarchy. If this interpretation is correct (and it is the *only* interpretation that takes Paul's words at face value), then Galatians 2:11–14 gives us firm evidence that James was a conservative when it came to the Law, at least insofar as the Law applied to Jewish Christians. That James threw his support behind Paul's mission at the Jerusalem Conference by requiring only minimal observance of the Law from *Gentile* Christians does not mean that James believed that the Law was any less fully in effect for *Jewish* Christians. To wit, New Testament scholar David Catchpole made a rather daring proposal in the 1970s that makes eminent sense of the situation:

> So precise and so exact is the correspondence between the demands involved in the Gal. ii 11–14 situation and the demands expressed in the Decree that we are, I believe, driven to one and only one conclusion: the demands laid down in Antioch are none other than the demands of the Decree. That is, the emissaries who came from James to Antioch brought the Decree.[16]

If the Apostolic Decree is indeed historical, and if it was already in effect at the time of the Antioch incident, then the differing stances of Peter, Paul, and James would seem to show that the decree was open to interpretation regarding mixed table fellowship—James taking a conservative stance, Paul a liberal one, and Peter, as usual, waffling. Under pressure, Peter and Barnabas both agreed with the view of James, which has significant implications for our understanding of the historical Jesus, as we shall soon see.

Before we turn from the Antioch incident, there is one more piece of evidence regarding James's power and influence that must not escape our notice: Not only did Peter withdraw from table-fellowship with the Gentiles, but so did Paul's fellow missionary Barnabas. In fact, it was immediately after this conflict that Paul and Barnabas, after many missionary journeys together, went their separate ways. Let us hear a concluding word about the ramifications of all of this from the evenhanded James Dunn, who explains that the trail of evidence has led us far from the traditional Christian understanding that at Antioch Paul was in the right and Peter stood corrected:

> We naturally tend to assume that Paul made his point and won the day—Peter admitting his mistake, and the previous practice being resumed. But Paul does not actually say so . . . if Paul had won, and if Peter had acknowledged the force of his argument, Paul would surely have noted this, just as he strengthened his earlier position by noting the approval of the "pillar apostles" in 2.7–10. In the circumstances then, *it is quite likely that Paul was defeated at Antioch* . . .
>
> Whatever the precise facts of the matter then it is evident that *there was a much deeper divide between Paul and the Jewish Christianity emanating from Jerusalem than at first appears* . . . [T]he fierceness of his response to Peter at Antioch . . . may well have been a contributing factor of some significance in fuelling that antagonism of Jewish Christianity towards Paul.[17]

The growing animosity between Paul and the Jewish Christians comes even more sharply into focus in the account of Paul's final journey to Jerusalem, where his very presence in the Temple sparks rioting in the streets by the Jerusalem Christians, and Paul has to be taken into protective custody by a Roman tribune. On the very steps of the Temple, the growing animosity between Paul and Jerusalem comes to a shocking head.

5

APOSTOLIC INTRIGUE: PAUL'S FINAL VISIT TO JERUSALEM AND THE DEATH OF JAMES

The judges of the Sanhedrin . . . brought before them a man named James, the brother of Jesus, who was called the Christ . . .

JOSEPHUS, *ANTIQUITIES OF THE JEWS*

The final piece of evidence regarding James to be found in the New Testament is the dramatic account in Acts 21 of Paul's last visit to Jerusalem, generally dated around the year 56. This is one of the "we sections" of Acts—apparently a firsthand account, often thought to be written by Luke himself, and generally considered historically accurate by almost all scholars. The section relevant to James begins:

17 When we arrived in Jerusalem, the brothers welcomed us warmly.
18 The next day Paul went with us to visit James; and all the elders were present. 19 After greeting them, he related one by one the things that God had done among the Gentiles through his ministry.

Of note here is the fact that James is singled out as being the leader of the elders, the main person Paul is there to see. What the elders relate to Paul, after hearing of his successful ministry among the Gentiles, is filled with intrigue:

20 When they heard it, they praised God. Then they said to him, "You see, brother, how many thousands of believers there are among the Jews, and they are all zealous for the law. 21 They have been told about you that you teach all the Jews living among the Gentiles to forsake Moses, and that you tell them not to circumcise their children or observe the customs. 22 What then is to be done? They will certainly hear that you have come."

Extremely interesting developments! It is plain that James and the elders are quite proud of the zeal for the Law that the Jewish believers possess. It is almost as if the elders of the Jewish Christians are trying to top Paul's achievement after he relates his great success among the Gentiles. One can almost hear their subtext: "Oh, yes? Well, wait till you hear how many thousands of *Jews* we've converted! And *they* obey the *Law!*"

Naturally, the elders exhibit quite a bit of concern about the reputation that Paul is garnering among the Jewish believers in Jerusalem, a reputation based on stories circulating that Paul is turning Jews living outside of Palestine away from the Law. And they seem to show concern not only for Paul's reputation, but also for his safety: "What then is to be done?" they ask. "They will certainly hear that you have come."

It is interesting that earlier, in Acts 21:11, a prophet name Agabus had warned that Paul would be in danger from "the Jews in Jerusalem," and Paul's companions strongly urged him not to go there. Their misgivings would, unfortunately, soon be borne out. Fearing for his safety, the elders prescribe a course of action for Paul that will publicly demonstrate to all that he is in fact loyal to the Law of Moses:

23 "So do what we tell you. We have four men who are under a vow. 24 Join these men, go through the rite of purification with them, and pay for the shaving of their heads. Thus all will know that there is nothing in what they have been told about you, but that you yourself observe and guard the law. 25 But as for the Gentiles who have become believers, we have sent a letter with our judgment that they should abstain from what has been sacrificed to idols and from blood and from what is strangled and from fornication."

More interesting developments. As a public demonstration of his orthodoxy, Paul is advised to financially sponsor some men who are apparently taking what was known as a Nazirite vow. The Nazirites were a strict Jewish religious order that observed ascetic practices such as abstaining from alcohol, fasting, refraining from cutting their hair, and rigorously upholding the Law. The great biblical hero and Israelite judge, Samson, despite his well-known lust for women, was a Nazirite. In urging Paul to make a public demonstration of his loyalty by publicly sponsoring these Nazirite novices, James and the elders appear to be supporting Paul, and they seem to realize that the charges against him are untrue. Indeed, while Paul fought for a minimum adherence to the Law for Gentiles, it is quite unlikely that he would have taught Jews to abandon the Law. But, rightly or wrongly, the majority of Jewish Christians in Jerusalem were not at all supportive of Paul, to put it mildly.

Perhaps the most interesting thing in this section is that, quite oddly, the elders inform Paul about the terms of the Apostolic Decree as if Paul had never heard of it before. It could, therefore, be speculated that Paul is silent about the decree in his letter to the Galatians because he has not heard of it before. As we saw in the last chapter, however, all the pertinent evidence leads to the conclusion that the decree was in place already at the time of the Antioch incident, and it is hard to believe that Luke, who has described the Jerusalem Conference and the issuance of the Apostolic Decree only six chapters earlier, would let such an editorial blunder slip through. The more likely explanation for the inclusion of verse 25 is that it is instead an editorial insertion for the benefit of the *readers,* in order to jog our memories on the terms of the decree.

In any event, Paul does as the elders urge him, sponsors the men, and goes into the Temple with them to undergo the rite of purification. Toward the end of this seven-day-long ritual, however, the fears of all are realized when some "Jews from Asia" (i.e., Asia Minor, modern-day Turkey) see Paul in the Temple and a riot ensues:

> 27 When the seven days were almost completed, the Jews from Asia, who had seen him in the temple, stirred up the whole crowd. They seized him, 28 shouting, "Fellow Israelites, help! This is the man who is teaching everyone everywhere against our people, against our law, and this place . . ." 30 Then all the city was aroused, and the people rushed together. They seized Paul and dragged him out of the temple, and immediately the doors were shut. 31 While they were trying to kill him, word came to the tribune of the cohort that all Jerusalem was in

> an uproar. 32 Immediately he took soldiers and centurions and ran down to them. When they saw the tribune and the soldiers, they stopped beating Paul. 33 Then the tribune came, arrested him and ordered him to be bound.

Paul, likely owing his life to the quick intervention of the Roman tribune and his cohort, is taken into protective custody and a series of trials ensues in the Roman courts. Because Paul is a Roman citizen, he manages to have his case taken all the way to the imperial court of the Roman governor, Festus, as Acts goes on to relate.

In all of this, Luke seems to be quite candid in his depiction of the very real friction between Paul and the Jewish Christians, but, then, this passage *is* an eyewitness account written in the first person, so candor here is not so surprising. Still, we have to wonder how much is left unsaid because of Luke's well-known tendency to whitewash antagonisms within the church. The way Luke depicts the event, James and the elders showed genuine support for Paul, and the trouble that erupted was due to a simple misunderstanding among those "zealous for the law." One has to wonder, though, whether James and the elders couldn't have simply explained the truth about Paul to their more conservative brethren in the Jerusalem church. Would they not have listened?

Some intriguing questions have been raised around these issues by James Dunn, who also indicates the importance of what Luke does *not* say in Acts:

> when Paul was arrested and put on trial we hear nothing of any Jewish Christians standing by him, speaking in his defence—and this despite James's apparent high standing among orthodox Jews . . . Where were the Jerusalem Christians? It looks very much as though they had washed their hands of Paul, left him to stew in his own juice. If so it implies *a fundamental antipathy on the part of the Jewish Christians to Paul himself and what he stood for.*[1]

Some scholars go even further than Dunn, claiming that James and the elders purposely lured Paul into a trap.[2] If such an idea appears totally unfounded, note the end of verse 30: "They seized Paul and dragged him out of the temple, *and immediately the doors were shut.*" Such speculations are little more than conjecture, yet Dunn's assertion—

while a sour note in the harmonious song the church has sung about itself throughout the centuries—is congruous with all the other evidence we have examined to this point. It should be quite obvious by now that Paul was despised by the Jewish Christians.

THE COLLECTION FOR THE POOR

It is also curious in Acts 21 that Luke makes no mention of Paul's reason for visiting Jerusalem—to deliver the collection that he had gone to such great lengths throughout his journeys to take up on behalf of "the poor" in Jerusalem. This is a highly unusual omission of what would certainly have been a momentous event in the history of the church, and Acts' silence about the delivery of the collection has caused more than a few scholars to conclude that the collection was actually rejected by the elders. That would have been a bitter pill for Paul to swallow, and if indeed the collection was rejected, it is reasonable to suppose that Luke—always at pains to portray the church harmoniously—would have covered up incontrovertible evidence of a rift between Paul and Jerusalem. Luke's silence on the collection speaks loudly.

If it is true that the collection was rejected, then relations between Paul and Jerusalem had indeed reached the breaking point. Even conservative Ralph P. Martin admits that, by the time of Paul's final visit to Jerusalem, his "ministry was decisively rejected by James and the Jerusalem leadership."[3] The official acceptance of a collection gathered from Paul's Gentile congregations would have been seen as tacit approval of Paul's teachings. But this line of reasoning would not seem to be supported by Paul's statement in Galatians 2:10: "*They asked only one thing, that we remember the poor, which was actually what I was quite eager to do.*" Why, if the collection was at the request of James, Peter and John, and was so desperately needed, would the collection have been rejected when it was at hand?

The answer may be that the collection meant different things to Paul and the Jerusalem leadership, and Paul's acceptance of the commission from the elders does not necessarily mean they were in accord. German scholar, Dieter Georgi, has thoroughly researched this issue in *Remembering the Poor: The History of Paul's Collection for Jerusalem.* Georgi begins by noting that Paul's willingness to agree to the collection was seen as being the fatal flaw in F. C. Baur's theory of a fundamental antipathy between Paul and the Jerusalem "pillars." If Paul and Peter and James were at such bitter odds, why would Paul have put such effort into carrying out their wishes? Georgi notes that Baur and the Tübingen theologians solved this seeming discrepancy, "by ascribing the initiating and the carrying out of the collection to Paul personally."[4] Georgi notes that the German theologian Karl Holl solved this problem in another way by positing that the collection "was a tax demanded by the leaders of the Jerusalem church corresponding to the traditional Jewish temple tax. Paul, on the other hand, tried to instill an entirely different meaning for the collection."

While the idea of the collection being a kind of Temple tax has not withstood the test of time, Georgi has run with the idea that Paul imbued the collection with a deeper theological meaning, that the collection was of great theological importance to Paul for reasons that go beyond helping the needy in Jerusalem. Georgi points out that Holl, "was the first to realize that it had been the *eschatological expectation* that prompted the Jewish believers in Jerusalem to participate actively in promoting the plan" (italics mine). This idea has gained a lot of ground among scholars. As we noted earlier, part of the preeminence that the Jerusalem church enjoyed was due to its being at "ground zero"—the site of the expected Parousia of Jesus. It was here that the new eschatological Temple would be built over the ruins of the old Temple, which Jesus had predicted would be destroyed (see Mark 13). Thus it was that James, Peter, and John were considered the "pillars" of that coming eschatological Temple. In light of all this eschatological expectation, Jerusalem had deep theological significance for the early Christian community throughout the Mediterranean basin. Jerusalem was the Mother Church, and it is not at all hard to see why even the Gentile churches founded by Paul would pay heed to representatives from Jerusalem—which is, of course, what happened at Antioch and Galatia that so aggravated Paul.

There is also evidence that the believers in Jerusalem were called "the poor" not so much because of their economic status (which may well have been quite poor), but because of their eschatological status. "The poor" was actually a title of honor and respect, as Georgi explains:

Being "the poor" appears to be the essential dignity held by the congregation in Jerusalem, to be granted and respected by all other Jesus congregations. The absolute use of this appellation in Galatians 2:10

and the fact that it does not need any explanation show that it must have been a title commonly bestowed upon that congregation . . .

This titulary usage was modeled after other, previously existing . . . examples in the Jewish Bible. . . . the name "the poor" . . . is used synonymously with such designations as "pious" and "just" [think James]. Since the Maccabean wars [second century B.C.E.] . . . "the poor" had been used as a self-designation by a variety of Jewish groups, all of whom meant to express that they alone were the true devotees, the true Israel, the "Holy Remnant."[5]

Despite the religious prestige that the Jerusalem Christians enjoyed, they may also have been economically poor as well. We know that, in an interesting social experiment akin to modern socialism, the Jerusalem Christians gave all their possessions to the church and shared all things in common (see Acts 2:44–45). The Jerusalem missionaries did not hold jobs, but lived off charity, following the example of Jesus (see Mark 6:8–10). Therefore, the collection may well have been important for economic survival, but it was even more important theologically. The offerings of the Gentiles were no doubt seen by all as a sign that the eschatological Day of the Lord was at hand. As Georgi explains:

Mount Zion and God's city were considered the goal of the forthcoming eschatological pilgrimage not only of the Jews but also of the nations of the world. The heathen peoples would come there and bring all the riches of the Earth to Jerusalem to pay homage to Yahweh and his people, and serve them.

Such an eschatological pilgrimage had been envisioned by prophets such as Isaiah and Micah, and is also reflected in the theology of the book of Revelation. Most pertinent is Isaiah's prophecy:

Nations shall come to your light,
And kings to the brightness of your dawn.
Lift up your eyes and look around;
They all gather together. They come to you . . .

Then you shall see and be radiant;
your hearts shall thrill and rejoice,

Because the abundance of the sea
Shall be brought to you,
The wealth of nations shall come to you. (Isa. 60:3–5)

Certainly Paul thought of his mission to the Gentiles in such terms. His mission was the fulfilling of the ancient prophecies. It was with such weighty theological expectations that Paul looked upon the collection, and this was the source of his zeal for completing the collection and handing it to the Jerusalem leaders in person, with what he surely anticipated would be great fanfare and acclaim. Paul likely hoped that the delivering of the collection would heal all wounds and unite the Jewish and Gentile wings of the church, perhaps even usher in the return of Jesus. This is surely why he forged ahead to Jerusalem despite the warnings and misgivings of his companions.

Georgi also goes on to show that the use of the term "remembering" in association with "the poor" meant more than a monetary remembering. "Remembering the poor,"

stipulated that the Gentile Jesus believers were to give recognition to the exemplary [ethical] performance on the part of their fellow believers in Jerusalem. In other words, the agreement was about the recognition of the Jerusalem congregation's ongoing and self-forgetful eschatological effort.[6]

Like their kindred community, the Essenes of Qumran, the Jerusalem Christians believed they could help to usher in the Day of the Lord by rigorously adhering to the Law, fulfilling for the entire Jewish community the righteousness that the majority of the people were not able to attain to. This understanding is seen in James's title, "the Just." In the next chapter we shall examine the evidence for the rigorous and ascetic lifestyle that James led.

No matter how one explains Luke's silence on the matter of Paul's delivery of the collection, or what significance it held for Paul or James, examining the topic forces us to confront the evidence that two Christian missions existed in the early church, and that the one with the greater prestige was the one led by James and the Jerusalem Christians. This understanding begs us to ask larger, more provocative questions. As Professor Erik Heen of the Lutheran Theological Seminary at Philadelphia has asked:

> Did this exceptional eschatological status (based on a very particular role) demand a particularly "rigorous" orientation to the Law that was not a demand of Jewish Christian communities outside Jerusalem? Were the purity requirements different given this understanding of the *particular* eschatological significance of Jerusalem? (How else do you move from Jesus' rather "liberal" attitude towards the law . . . [to] the seemingly rigorist attitude of the Jerusalem "messianic" community?)[7]

In short, Heen cuts to the heart of our concerns in reevaluating James. How *does* one reconcile Jesus' seemingly free-spirited attitude toward the Law in the gospels with the seemingly rigorous, Pharisaic approach of James and the Jerusalem church? Following Georgi, Heen suggests that James and the Jerusalem community took a particularly rigorous approach to following the Law in light of their being the vanguard of the new eschatological community that God was establishing. It is for this same reason that the Essenes retreated to the desert commune at Qumran and practiced such strict asceticism and adherence to the Torah—to help usher in the Day of the Lord. As Heen suggests, this eschatological orientation of the Jerusalem church also provides an alternative way of understanding the purity requirements of the Apostolic Decree.

There are only two other possibilities. The first has been the church's traditional answer to the conundrum we are facing: James, the apostles, and the rest of the Jewish Christians began slowly but inexorably to fall back (or "backslide" as evangelical Christians like to put it) into their old strict observance of the Law because Jesus was no longer present to remind them that they need only believe in him to be saved. In this view, it is the "enlightened" Paul who takes up the new gospel of freedom from the Law that Jesus had directly entrusted to him and proclaims the "true gospel." It is based on this traditional Christian understanding that Paul's letter to the Galatians has sometimes been referred to as the "Magna Carta" of Christian liberty.

The only other possibility is that Jesus may have been much more Law conformant than the Pauline tradition has led most Christians (and Protestants especially) to believe. This conclusion would, obviously, have revolutionary implications for the church's traditional understanding of Jesus, but it is also where the evidence is inexorably leading us, and it is where we shall concentrate our efforts in the rest of this investigation. Further evidence for this working theory is to be found in the invaluable accounts of the famed Jewish historian Josephus.

THE DEATH OF A CHRISTIAN PHARISEE

Before bringing our account of James's presence and activities in Jerusalem to a close, we must step outside of the New Testament for the first time and look at Josephus' report of how James met his demise in Jerusalem. Apparently, James never lived anywhere else subsequent to Jesus' death. Therefore, for at least thirty-two years— from the time of Jesus' death until his own death, which can reliably be dated in 62, James was a permanent resident of Jerusalem.

Here is the tale of how James met his martyrdom as told by Josephus in his acclaimed history, the *Antiquities of the Jews*:

> Upon learning of the death of Festus [the Roman governor of Judea], Caesar sent Albinus to Judea as procurator. The king removed Joseph from the high priesthood, and bestowed the succession to this office upon the son of Ananus, who was likewise called Ananus . . . The younger Ananus . . . was rash in his temper and unusually daring. He followed the school of the Sadducees . . . Ananus thought that he had a favorable opportunity because Festus was dead and Albinus was still on the way. And so he convened the judges of the Sanhedrin and brought before them a man named James, the brother of Jesus who was called the Christ, and certain others. He accused them of having transgressed the law and delivered them up to be stoned. Those of the inhabitants of the city who were considered the most fair-minded and who were in strict observance of the law were offended at this. They therefore secretly sent to King Agrippa urging him . . . to order [Ananus] to desist from any further such actions . . . King Agrippa . . . deposed him from the high priesthood which he had held for three months and replaced him.[8]

In chapter 3, we considered John Dominic Crossan's hypothesis that James might have been a resident of Jerusalem even prior to Jesus' crucifixion. It is, in fact, Josephus' account of James's death that spurred Crossan to speculate along these lines. Why? Let us hear Crossan's fascinating commentary on this passage:

Josephus tells us that Ananus was a Sadducee, but he was much more than that. His father, Ananus the Elder, was high priest from 6 to 15 C.E., and is known to us from the gospels as Annas. The elder Ananus was father-in-law of Joseph Caiaphas, High Priest from 18 to 36 C.E., a figure also known to us from the gospels [the priest who tried Jesus]. He was furthermore the father of five other High Priests . . . The immediate family of Ananus the Elder had dominated the high priesthood for most of the preceding decades, with eight high priests in sixty years, *yet the execution of James resulted in the deposition of Ananus the Younger after only three months in office.* An abstract illegality could hardly have obtained such a reaction, so *James must have had powerful, important, and even politically organized friends in Jerusalem.* Who were they? Josephus' phrase "inhabitants . . . who were in strict observance of the law" probably means Pharisees. *Was James a Pharisee?* . . . we need to think much more about James and how he reached such status among Jewish circles that, on the one hand, he had to be executed by a Sadducee and that, on the other, his death could cause a High Priest to be deposed after only three months in office.[9] (italics mine)

Now we are in a much better position to understand Crossan's conjecture. The events surrounding his death point to James having been an influential figure in Jerusalem even before Jesus began his ministry. Crossan goes on to ask:

Did [James] leave Nazareth long before [Jesus' crucifixion] and become . . . involved within scribal circles in Jerusalem? Could his earlier presence there and Jesus' (single?) visit to Jerusalem be somehow connected . . . Above all, was he in Jerusalem long before Jesus' death, and did his presence there invite, provoke, challenge Jesus' only journey to Jerusalem?

While Crossan's speculations are indeed just that—speculations—it would be foolish not to at least keep these possibilities open. The hypothesis that James was a respected Pharisaic leader in Jerusalem even before Jesus' crucifixion goes a long way toward explaining many of the enigmas about James's presence and standing in Jerusalem that we have encountered.

In truth, it should not really surprise us that James could have been a prominent Pharisee. One of the few reliable outcomes of current historical Jesus scholarship has been the increased awareness that Jesus and the Pharisees were not the stalwart enemies that tradition has pictured them as being (as is exemplified in the work of E. P. Sanders and Geza Vermes). Rather, Jesus and the Pharisees were like-minded rabbis arguing fine points of legal interpretation. And let us not forget that Jesus was indeed a rabbi. The most common title by which he is addressed in the gospels is "teacher," which is a direct translation of the Aramaic word *Rabbouni* (Rabbi) in the Greek New Testament.

Already in the 1960s, an early James investigator by the name of Kenneth Carroll anticipated this growing trend in modern scholarship and saw its implications for James. Writing in 1961, Carroll's words could just as easily have been written last year:

> One of the great achievements of modern scholarship has been the establishment of the Pharisees as a group worthy of respect. Jesus was much closer to the Pharisees than to any other group in Jewish religious life. They represented the best in Judaism. Yet, at certain points, the Gospels show Jesus criticizing the Pharisees. Only in one or two instances does Jesus clearly criticize the Pharisaic interpretation of Scripture. In other cases he simply goes farther in the extension of privilege. Most of the Christian scholars who have worked on this problem . . . have suggested that Jesus was not attacking the Pharisees as a whole (since his own ethical and religious beliefs were almost wholly in agreement with theirs), but that he was attacking those Pharisees who took advantage of their position of authority to exploit or suppress the Jewish masses. . . .
>
> Some of the scholars . . . have suggested that the authors of the Gospels were more hostile to the Pharisees than Jesus himself was—so that our canonical Gospels possess a bias against this religious group.[10]

Of James's relation to the Pharisees, Carroll starkly concludes: "James . . . was a Christian Pharisee."

In fact, we would do well to consider whether both Jesus and James were Pharisees. Pharisaism is certainly the Jewish school of thought that lies closest to the teaching of Jesus, and it is important to keep in mind that the Pharisees were not a monolithic party. There were both liberal Pharisees (as exemplified by the school of Rabbi Hillel) and conservative

Pharisees (exemplified by the school of Rabbi Shammai). Rabbis Hillel and Shammai both lived into the early decades of the first century, so it is quite possible that Jesus could have come under the influence of Hillel, and James could have fallen in with Shammai.

The difference between the two schools has been summarized in a classic rabbinical anecdote. The story goes that a Gentile asked the temperamental and strict Shammai to sum up the Torah "while standing on one foot":

> Appalled that anyone could be simple enough to imagine that the profundities of the Mosaic revelation could be articulated in a single phrase, Shammai sent the Gentile packing. Undaunted, the Gentile then went to Hillel with the same question. Taking the man's inquiry as sincere, Hillel is said to have replied: "Do not do to your neighbor what is hateful to yourself. That is the entire Torah. All the rest is commentary."[11]

It is interesting that, in the gospel of Matthew, Jesus is also challenged to sum up the Law by a group of Pharisees (Matt. 22:34–40) and responds with a very similar answer: "You shall love you neighbor as yourself."

We should remember, too, that despite his well-known disagreements with the Pharisees, Jesus was friendly with many. It was while dining in the home of a Pharisee that a woman famously anoints Jesus' feet (Luke 7:36–49). Luke also records that it was a group of Pharisees who saved Jesus' life by tipping him off that Herod was seeking to kill him (13:31). On all major matters, Jesus and the Pharisees were in agreement. Unlike the Sadducees, Jesus and the Pharisees believed in the imminent eschaton (the end of the present age) and a final judgment; they believed in the resurrection of the dead and in the existence of angels and demons—all of which the Sadducees denied. Let us also not forget that *Paul* had been a Pharisee and had studied under the famous Pharisaic teacher, Gamaliel. It is intriguing that Acts records how Gamaliel defended and protected the early Jesus movement in Jerusalem (see Acts 5:33–39).

Finally, let us not forget that Matthew's gospel paints Jesus as virtually a spokesman for Pharisaism. Listen to Jesus' words in the Sermon on the Mount:

Do not think that I have come to abolish the law or the prophets; I have come not to abolish but to fulfill. For truly I tell you, until heaven and earth pass away, not one letter, not one stroke of a letter, will pass from the law until all is accomplished. Therefore, whoever breaks one of the least of these commandments, and teaches others to do the same, will be called least in the kingdom of heaven; but whoever does them and teaches them will be called great in the kingdom of heaven. For I tell you, unless your righteousness exceeds that of the scribes and Pharisees, you will never enter the kingdom of heaven. (Matt. 5:17–20)

A more stirring defense of the Pharisees would be hard to find! Clearly, if one can remove the blinders of twenty centuries of Pauline influence, and some five centuries of Lutheran influence, the differences between Jesus and the Pharisees are few.

THE RISE OF PAULINE CHRISTIANITY

In our summary of part 1, we reached two conclusions:

1. There is nothing in the gospels that incontrovertibly shows opposition to Jesus by his family during his ministry.
2. Jesus' mother and brothers were followers of his ministry prior to the crucifixion.

In our investigation of James's role in the Jerusalem church in the last three chapters, we have seen nothing that would cause us to question these conclusions, and much, in fact, that further supports them. Therefore, onto the two initial conclusions, we can now add the following:

3. James was the leader of the Jerusalem church from its inception following Jesus' death and resurrection.
4. James's theological stance was that of Pharisaism. By implication, and as is attested by independent evidence, it is likely that Pharisaism was also the theology of Jesus.

Like Alfred Wegener's matching continental shorelines that were ignored for centuries, the evidence for these four propositions has been staring out at us from the pages of the New Testament for almost two millennia. Quite simply put, James could not have become a believer *post*-resurrection: He would never have gained authority over Peter and the other apostles so quickly, especially if he had been a nonbeliever while Jesus was alive. Moreover, the fact that Peter and the other apostles did hand the reins of leadership to James after Jesus' death strongly suggests that James's teachings and sympathies were in line with Jesus' own.

Given this understanding, we must now ask how James's leadership role became so obscured that it was virtually unrecognizable until only recently. On this question, let us hear a word from John Painter that will set the tone for the third and final phase of our investigation:

> [I]t is clear that James was the leading figure in the Jerusalem church. In spite of this fact, Luke mentions him on only three occasions (Acts 12:17; 15:13; 21:18). This is puzzling. [German scholar] Martin Hengel has described the presentation of James in the New Testament as one-sided and tendentious. Luke may have known of the martyrdom of James in the year 62 C.E. but chose not to mention the event because of the prestige attached to James as a martyr . . . [I]t is as if Luke has pushed James into the background, but, because of his prominence, has been unable to obscure totally his leading role. He sought to minimize the role of James because he was aware that James represented a hard-line position on the place of circumcision and the keeping of the law, a position that Luke himself did not wish to maintain.[12]

By the time that Luke wrote his two-part history of the church near the end of the first century, the church had largely been transformed from a Jewish phenomenon into a Gentile phenomenon. Therefore, the beliefs and teachings of James slowly were subsumed under the beliefs and teachings of Paul. This also led to a not-so-subtle prejudice against the thoroughly Jewish form of Christianity that the Jerusalem church and its leaders represented, which ultimately led to the elision of James and the ostracizing of the Pharisees in the New Testament.

While James had unflagging zeal for the Law, it was Paul's relentless zeal for the mission to the Gentiles that won the day. Due almost single-handedly to Paul's ceaseless efforts, Christianity increasingly became a Gentile movement, and the importance of Jewish law naturally waned. There were also factors beyond either James's or Paul's control—namely, the Jewish revolt against Rome in the year 66 and the resultant sack of Jerusalem in 70, resulting in the second diaspora of the Jewish people. After 70, the Jewish form of Christianity that James had represented, and that was so thoroughly rooted in Jerusalem, found it difficult to survive in the Gentile world, while Paul's Gentile form of Christianity flourished and soon evolved into Christianity as we know it today.

The emerging Catholic Church quickly abandoned the dogmas associated with adherence to the Law, but it soon developed dogmas of its own to replace them, one of which was the doctrine of the virgin birth. With the rise of this doctrine, and especially with the growth of the belief in the *perpetual* virginity of Mary, James and the rest of Jesus' siblings became an embarrassment that needed to be hidden in the closet. Soon the memory of their importance, and even of their existence, was tragically lost.

But not lost by all. There were those who tended the memory of James and upheld his theology and teachings. It is to their tragic story that we now turn.

3

THE NATURE OF
JEWISH CHRISTIANITY

6

KEEPING THE CANDLE BURNING: JAMES IN HISTORY AND TRADITION

James, whom the people of old called the Just because of his outstanding virtue, was the first, as the records tell us, to be elected to the Episcopal throne of the Jerusalem church.

EUSEBIUS, *ECCLESIASTICAL HISTORY*

When one moves beyond the New Testament, literature about James becomes both surprisingly plentiful and surprisingly reverential. There are at least thirteen extra-biblical sources that treat of him. We have already examined the report of James's death from Josephus, almost unanimously considered historically trustworthy. While the other sources generally possess less historical reliability, at the very least they contain valuable information that shows how later generations of Jewish Christians, Gnostic Christians, Coptic Christians, and others managed, under some extremely difficult conditions, to keep the memory of James alive. Because all of these later reports about James are relatively brief, it is possible to offer the reader a comprehensive survey, which we shall now undertake as the last phase of our investigation.

Scholarly opinion about the historical reliability of the sources we will be examining falls all over the spectrum. So, unlike the prior phases of our investigation, here we shall for the most part lay aside the scholarly debate on the material. Instead, we shall simply let the accounts speak for themselves and see what historical nuggets we can mine from this material based on the insights gleaned in parts 1 and 2. We turn first to our most plenteous source of information on James outside of the New Testament—the church father and historian Eusebius.

EUSEBIUS' *HISTORY OF THE CHURCH*

Eusebius was Bishop of Caesarea from 313–339. A careful historian, his *Ecclesiastical History* (a.k.a. *History of the Church* and hereafter abbreviated by the standard Latin abbreviation *HE*) was written between 300 and 324 and is one of the very first historical works to contain citations of sources. Eusebius relies heavily on the earlier work of Clement of Alexandria (c. 150–215, a later Clement than Clement of Rome), Hippolytus (c. 170–236, the most important third-century theologian of the Roman church), and Hegesippus (a second-century church historian who was a converted Jew). In Eusebius, as in almost all of the non-canonical literature, we find exalted terminology used in reference to James. As we have already seen, it is in this text that James is often referred to as the "Bishop of the Church," and is even called the "Brother of God" (Greek *adelphotheos*), perhaps a not-unexpected usage in light of Mary being called the "Mother of God" by this time. In English translations, the near-divinity implied in the epithet "the Brother of God" is, not surprisingly, toned down as "the brother of *the Lord*."

It is Eusebius' belief, based on his sources, that the twelve apostles elected James as the first bishop of the church after Christ's ascension to heaven. John Painter notes that, "Eusebius provides no evidence of any implied early leadership of Peter . . . Eusebius asserts the leadership of James more or less from the beginning."[1] To wit, in the second chapter of the *Ecclesiastical History,* Eusebius tells us:

> Then there was James, who was called the Lord's brother; for he too was named Joseph's son . . . This James, whom the people of old called the Just because of his outstanding virtue, was the first, as the records tell us, to be elected to the Episcopal throne of the Jerusalem church. Clement, in *Outlines*, book six, puts it thus:

> > "After the ascension of the savior, Peter, James, and John [the brothers James and John, sons of Zebedee] did not claim

pre-eminence because the savior had specifically honored them, but chose James the Just as Bishop of Jerusalem."

In book seven of the same work the writer makes this further statement:

"James the Just, John, and Peter were entrusted by the Lord after his resurrection with the higher knowledge. They imparted it to the other apostles, and the other apostles to the Seventy, one of whom was Barnabas. There were two Jameses, one the Just, who was thrown down from the parapet and beaten to death with a fuller's club, the other the James who was beheaded."

James the Just is also mentioned by Paul when he writes, "Of the other apostles I saw no one except James the brother of the Lord." (*HE* 2.1.2–5; Williamson translation)

The first item of note here is Eusebius' statement that "the people of old" called James "the Just because of his outstanding virtue." How far back the use of "the Just" as an appellation for James goes is difficult to say. While it does not appear in the New Testament, it was obviously already traditional at the time Eusebius wrote. We shall encounter it many more times in our survey. "James the Just" has in fact survived down to our own times as the most common appellation for James.

CLEMENT'S *OUTLINES*

While Clement's *Outlines* (*Hypostases* in Greek), which Eusebius used as a source, has sadly not survived, there is no reason not to trust Eusebius' citation of it. The real question here is the reliability of Clement. Clement's writings are from the early third century, and scholarly opinion on their historical reliability is divided.

There are three items in the citations from Clement that are debatable. First, while the use of the term *bishop* is almost certainly a retrojection of a term in use in Eusebius' day, there is, as we have seen, no reason to dismiss the very real possibility that James was indeed chosen to lead the community of believers after Jesus' ascension. John Painter's well-considered arguments impel us, at the very least, to not rule out the possibility.

The second item that raises an eyebrow is Clement's claim of "higher knowledge" being imparted to the three pillar apostles, a claim that sounds remarkably Gnostic in flavor. The Gnostics were an early Christian sect that taught that salvation was attained through the acquiring of secret knowledge (*gnosis* in the Greek) that Jesus had entrusted to only a few. For obvious reasons, Gnosticism became one of the first heresies that the emerging Catholic Church battled against. Yet despite his talk about "higher knowledge," Clement himself was actually a staunch defender of emerging Catholic orthodoxy against the growing tide of Gnosticism. Here we actually see Clement using a defensive approach that his student Origen would later use to great effect—taking over Gnostic language and terminology in order to use it against the claims of the Gnostics.

Another common feature of Gnostic literature is the elevation of James over Peter and Paul, which is also a common feature of the Jewish Christian writings we will be examining shortly. Clement, therefore, was apparently careful to assert that James's leadership was the result of the apostles giving authority to James. In other words, James's leadership was not a matter of dynastic succession, nor was it a case of Jesus himself handing the reins of leadership to his brother, both of which were common claims of the Gnostic and Jewish Christian groups Clement opposed. That Clement's agenda was taken up by Eusebius becomes apparent in two further remarks that Eusebius makes:

> [The Jews] turned against James, the brother of the Lord, to whom the throne of the bishopric in Jerusalem had been allotted *by the apostles*. (*HE* 2.23.1; italics mine)

> James . . . was the first to receive *from the savior and the apostles* the episcopate of the church at Jerusalem. (*HE* 7.19.1)

In the latter item, Eusebius asserts that the "episcopate" was given to James by Jesus *and* the apostles. Here Eusebius may be drawing from a different, unnamed source, or more likely, he had no need to carefully omit Jesus from the event because the struggle against Gnostic and Jewish Christian heresy was no longer a burning issue when he wrote. Or perhaps Eusebius' attention simply lapsed for a moment.

At any rate, what is most striking here is that Eusebius does not dispute the priority of James—it was obviously accepted as fact in the early 300s. If this is the case—and all the evidence we have seen supports it—then the knowledge of James's leadership role was either distorted or suppressed sometime later on. Indeed, the obfuscation of James's role was the result of the later church's efforts (beginning with the Council of Nicaea in 325) to officially establish what was orthodoxy and what was heresy, one major factor of which was the status of Jesus' brothers and sisters vis-à-vis the emerging dogma of the perpetual virginity of Mary.

The third item of note in the citations from Clement is the claim that James was martyred by being "thrown down from the parapet [of the Temple] and beaten to death with a fuller's [laundryman's] club." This is a bit different from Josephus' account which says that James was stoned to death. It is possible that Clement was drawing on an alternate tradition that was independent of Josephus. If Clement was aware of Josephus' account, he either deemed this alternate account more reliable or had a particular (perhaps polemical) reason for using it. John Painter theorizes:

> Perhaps stoning implied a more lawful execution than Clement wished to portray . . . Even so, the use of the club is somewhat puzzling. Given that there is a tendency [in Eusebius] to portray James as a priest or even a high priest (see *HE* 2.23.6), it is possible that the punishment was specifically related to some supposed priestly offense. According to [Jewish law], a priest performing Temple service while unclean was to be taken out of the Temple court by the young priests and his skull was to be split with clubs.[2]

The notion that James was a Temple priest is another one of those startling things that jumps out from the noncanonical literature and grabs you. While the idea may at first seem patently absurd, Eusebius actually goes on to report it in detail. But first, Eusebius provides some other surprising details concerning the death of James.

EUSEBIUS AND THE DEATH OF JAMES

Referring to the failed attempt on Paul's life in Acts 21, Eusebius makes the claim that "the Jews" next plotted the death of James:

> When Paul appealed to Caesar and was sent to Rome by Festus the Jews were disappointed of the hope in which they had laid their plot against him and turned against James the brother of the Lord, who

had been elected to the Episcopal throne of Jerusalem by the apostles. This is the crime that they committed against him. They brought him into their midst and in the presence of all the people demanded a denial of his belief in Christ. But when, contrary to all expectation, he spoke as he liked and showed undreamt of fearlessness in the face of the enormous throng, declaring that our savior and Lord Jesus was the son of God, they could not endure his testimony any longer, since he was universally regarded as the most righteous of men because of the heights of philosophy and religion which he had scaled in his life. So they killed him, using anarchy as an opportunity for power since at that moment Festus had died in Judaea, leaving the province without governor or procurator. How James died has already been shown by the words of Clement already quoted, narrating that he was thrown down from the parapet and clubbed to death. (*HE* 2.23.1–3)

Eusebius was apparently either familiar with Josephus' account (note his reference to James's death occurring in the period between governors) or drew on an independent source. If he knew Josephus' account, he apparently preferred Clement's version of James's execution either because he believed it more reliable or because he found it more theologically agreeable.

Another item of note here is Eusebius' claim that James was "universally regarded as the most righteous of men because of the heights of philosophy and religion which he had scaled in his life." This is an unexpected claim in light of the traditional understanding of Jesus and his family as relatively uneducated. That James and Jesus could have been highly educated is certainly not implausible, but it is also possible that Eusebius is merely trying to make James appealing to his Greco-Roman readers.*

---

*There is, however, a fascinating account in *HE* 1.13.1–22 that shows that Eusebius believed Jesus could read and write. Eusebius claims to have found two letters written in Syriac (a dialect of Aramaic, the language Jesus spoke) in archives located in Edessa (today known as Urfa, in eastern Turkey). In the first letter, King Abgar V of Edessa is writing to Jesus from his deathbed, asking that Jesus might cure him. The second letter is claimed to be Jesus' response, in which Jesus promises to send one of his disciples to cure him. Eusebius goes on to say that, after Jesus' ascension, Thomas sent the apostle Addai (Syriac for Thaddeus) to Edessa to effect a cure for Abgar that resulted in the entire population of Edessa converting to Christianity (*HE* 2.2.2–5).

Eusebius notes that of all his sources, "the most detailed account of [James] is given by Hegesippus," and indeed we gain some remarkable information from Eusebius' extracts:

Control of the church passed together with the apostles, to the brother of the Lord James, whom every one from the Lord's time till our own has named the Just, for there were many Jameses, but this one was holy from his birth; he drank no wine or intoxicating liquor and ate no animal food; no razor came near his head; he did not smear himself with oil, and he took no baths. He alone was permitted to enter the Holy Place [the Holy of Holies in the Temple], for his garments were not of wool but of linen. He used to enter the Sanctuary alone, and was often found on his knees beseeching forgiveness for the people. Because of his unsurpassable righteousness he was called the Just and *Oblias*—in Greek "Bulwark of the people and Righteousness"— fulfilling the declarations of the prophets regarding him.

Representatives of the seven [Jewish] sects already described by me asked him what was meant by "the door of Jesus," and he replied that Jesus was the Savior. Some of them came to believe that Jesus was the Christ: the sects mentioned above did not believe either in a resurrection or in one who is coming to give every man what his deeds deserve, but those who did come to believe did so because of James. Since therefore many even of the ruling class believed, there was an uproar among the Jews and scribes and Pharisees, who said there was a danger that the entire people would expect Jesus as the Christ. So they collected and said to James: "Be good enough to restrain the people, for they have gone astray after Jesus in the belief that he is the Christ. Be good enough to make the facts about Jesus clear to all who come for the Passover Day . . . So make it clear to the crowd that they must not go astray as regards Jesus: the whole people and all of us accept what you say. So take your stand on the Temple parapet, so that from that height you may easily be seen, and your words audible to the whole people. For because of the Passover all the tribes have come together, and the Gentiles too."

So the scribes and Pharisees made James stand on the Sanctuary parapet and shouted to him: "Just one, whose word we are all obliged to accept, the people are all going astray after Jesus who was crucified; so tell us what is meant by 'the door of Jesus.'" He replied as loudly as he could: "Why do you question me about the Son of Man? I tell you, he is sitting in heaven at the right hand of the great power, and he will come on the clouds of heaven." Many were convinced and gloried in James's testimony, crying: "Hosanna to the Son of David!" Then again the scribes and Pharisees said to each other: "We made a bad mistake in affording such testimony to Jesus. We had better go up and throw him down, so that they will be frightened and not believe him." "Ho, ho!" they called out, "even the Just one has gone astray!"—fulfilling the prophecy of Isaiah: "'Let us remove the Just one, for he is unprofitable to us.' Therefore they shall eat the fruit of their works."

So they went up and threw down the Just one. Then they said to each other, "Let us stone James the Just," and began to stone him, as in spite of his fall he was still alive. But he turned and knelt, uttering the words: "I beseech thee, Lord God and Father, forgive them; they do not know what they are doing." While they pelted him with stones, one of the descendants of Rechab the son of Rechabim—the priestly family to which Jeremiah the prophet bore witness, called out, "Stop! What are you doing? The Just one is praying for you." Then one of them, a fuller, took the club which he used to beat clothes, and brought it down on the head of the Just one. Such was his martyrdom. He was buried on the spot, by the Sanctuary, and his headstone is still there by the Sanctuary. He has proved a true witness to Jews and Gentiles alike that Jesus is the Christ.

Immediately after this Vespasian began to besiege them. (*HE* 2.23.3–18)

Eusebius is quoting here from the *Memoranda* (*Hypomneumata* in Greek) of Hegesippus, and we can plainly see his reliance on his source. However, while the *Memoranda* is generally dated 150–180 (bringing us much closer to apostolic times than Eusebius' own work), it is obvious that some of Hegesippus' account is largely legendary. Ultimately, what is claimed here about James depends on the reliability of Hegesippus.

Hegesippus' reporting is so detailed that initially one is inclined to consider it factual, especially as much of what Hegesippus describes fits what we have already learned about James. There are, however, several problematic items, such as James praying for forgiveness for his persecutors in the exact words of Jesus: "Father, forgive them; they do not know what they are doing." While this anecdote is likely legendary, it is at least possible that James might have chosen to die repeating the famous prayer that his brother prayed for his accusers at his death. Unlike Eusebius, Hegesippus did not cite his sources. It is possible he drew on Josephus for the details of James being stoned, but he apparently combined Josephus with a tradition, which Clement also knew, of James being thrown down from the parapet and beaten with a fuller's club.

The overall tone of Hegesippus is clearly Jewish Christian. He describes James in terms that make him appear to be a Nazirite, claiming that James "was holy from his birth; he drank no wine or intoxicating liquor and ate no animal food; no razor came near his head." These are the promises of the Nazirite vow (see Numbers 6), and Nazirites were sometimes dedicated at birth by their parents, such as was the case with the Israelite Judge Samson of "Samson and Delilah" fame (see Judges 13). The overall description of James's ascetic behavior betrays the Jewish Christian origins of this passage. Nevertheless, none of what Hegesippus says is actually unacceptable. In fact, it all accords well with Luke's depiction, in Acts 21, of James as someone with close Nazirite affinities.

What is most surprising (and dubious) in Hegesippus is his claim that James was a high priest, able to enter the Holy of Holies on the Day of Atonement. While this may seem patently absurd, it is not impossible. We saw James's close ties to the Temple in Acts, and we know from Josephus of the sympathy that leading Jews in Jerusalem had for James. There is also a genuine element of veracity in Hegesippus' assertion that James was buried "by the Sanctuary, and his headstone is still there by the Sanctuary," which would be something verifiable by Hegesippus' readers, leading one to conclude that James was in fact buried there.* And surely not just anyone would be buried near the Temple—certainly not someone who was considered a heretic by his fellow Jews. The only conclusion would seem to be that James was considered orthodox by the Temple priests and was a respected Jewish leader as well. A priest? Not at all implausible. A high priest? Quite unlikely, but not completely outside the realm of possibility. That

---

*It is interesting that the James ossuary is purported to have come from an area near the Temple. See Shanks and Witherington, *The Brother of Jesus,* for details.

James was a priest assigned to the Temple would account for his being the only key apostle never to conduct missionary journeys. In fact, in all the accounts we have of James, he is *always* in Jerusalem.

Eusebius himself did not doubt Hegesippus' reliability, asserting that he was in fact a Jewish Christian who used the *Gospel of the Hebrews* (an apocryphal Jewish Christian gospel we shall examine later) as a source and calling his account of the martyrdom of James the "most accurate" and "most careful" (2.23.3), more accurate even than Josephus'. The majority of modern scholars, however, consider Hegesippus' account to be largely legendary. As we have seen, Josephus associates James with the Pharisees (as do several modern scholars) which would make a priestly James unlikely, since it was the Sadducees who oversaw the Temple and the priests. The Pharisees were in strong opposition to the Sadducean leaders, perceiving them as being in league with Rome.

Another discrepancy that brings Hegesippus into question is that he concludes that it was immediately after James's death that the Roman siege of Jerusalem under Vespasian began; however, we have the rather firm evidence from Josephus that James died in 62, and the siege of Jerusalem did not begin until 67. What we likely see here in this anachronism is a common feature of the Jewish Christian writings—to make the death of James the cause of the destruction of Jerusalem. In fact, Hegesippus' use of the term *Oblias* (bulwark) may hint at the Jewish Christian belief that the Roman attack had been divinely forestalled until after James's death. Eusebius provides a concluding summary to the Hegesippus account, which states this explicitly:

> This account is given at length by Hegesippus, but in agreement with Clement. Thus it seems that James was indeed a remarkable man and famous among all for righteousness, so that the wise even of the Jews thought that this was the cause of the siege of Jerusalem immediately after his martyrdom, and that it happened for no other reason than the crime they had committed against him. (*HE* 2.23.19)

Of course, "immediately" can be a relative term, especially when one is writing decades (Hegesippus) or centuries (Eusebius) later; but Eusebius goes on to claim that Josephus (who was *not* writing a long time after) also believed that the siege of Jerusalem was caused by the death of James:

And indeed Josephus did not hesitate to write this down in so many words: "These things happened to the Jews to avenge James the Just, who was a brother of Jesus who is called Christ, for the Jews put him to death in spite of his great righteousness." (*HE* 2.23.20)

Unfortunately, this quote is not extant in the existing manuscripts of Josephus. This might seem to throw Eusebius' own reliability into question, especially as the purported words of Josephus echo the Jewish-Christian line. However, Eusebius immediately regains his credibility by quoting in full and without any deviation Josephus' account of James's martyrdom as it appears in the *Antiquities of the Jews* (2.23.21–24). Eusebius then concludes his discussion:

Such is the story of James, to whom is attributed the first of the "general" epistles. Admittedly, its authenticity is doubted, since few early writers refer to it, any more than to "Jude's," which is also one of the seven called general. But the fact remains that these two, like the others, have been regularly used in very many churches. (*HE* 2.23.24–25)

Here Eusebius shows that in his day the authenticity of the two letters attributed to brothers of Jesus was in doubt.* After the reference to Jude, Eusebius considers the rest of Jesus' brothers and their descendants, simply fascinating material that we shall examine in a moment. But, first, there are a few odds and ends to note.

After this detailed look at James, there are only a few scattered references to him in the rest of the *Ecclesiastical History*. One is a summary of the early Christian martyrdoms:

After the ascension of our savior, the Jews had followed up their crime against him by devising plot after plot against his apostles. First they stoned Stephen to death; then James the son of Zebedee and brother

---

*The authenticity of the letters of James and Jude is still doubted by the majority of scholars, most believing that these are pseudepigraphal—written in the names of James and Jude by later disciples. Both are clearly Jewish Christian in character. Unfortunately, a fair examination of the letter of James is beyond the scope of this present book, although we shall say something of its main arguments later.

of John was beheaded; and finally James, the first after our savior's ascension to be appointed to the bishop's throne there, lost his life in the way described, while the remaining apostles, in constant danger from murderous plots, were driven out of Judaea. (*HE* 3.5.2–3)

Here again Eusebius asserts that James held the first bishop's "throne" in Jerusalem.

Later, Eusebius states unequivocally that it was James's presence that held off the Roman siege, but links the siege to Jesus' death rather than to James's:

After the savior's passion . . . disaster befell the entire nation . . . But . . . certain facts bring home the beneficence of all gracious providence, which for forty years after the crime against Christ delayed their destruction. All that time most of the apostles and disciples, including James himself, the first bishop of Jerusalem, known as the Lord's brother, were still alive, and by remaining in the city furnished the place with an impregnable bulwark. (*HE* 3.7.7–9)

Despite Eusebius' earlier citation of Josephus, which laid the blame for the siege on the death of James, here he asserts that it was due to Jesus' death. It seems as though Eusebius wants to make the crucifixion the actual cause of the destruction of Jerusalem and the Temple, but has a hard time doing so because of the large interval of time (about forty years) between the two events. Therefore, he upholds the idea that it was the presence of James and the apostles that was responsible for a four-decade delay in what would otherwise have been the immediate destruction of Jerusalem as divine retribution for the crucifixion of Jesus.

DYNASTIC SUCCESSION

Eusebius' account of the early martyrs also presents intriguing evidence that the leadership of the Jerusalem church may have been a matter of dynastic succession:

After the martyrdom of James and the capture of Jerusalem which instantly followed, there is a firm tradition that those of the apostles and disciples of the Lord who were still alive assembled from all parts together with those who, humanly speaking, were kinsmen of the Lord—for most of them were still living and they all took counsel together concerning whom they should judge worthy to succeed James and to the unanimous tested approval it was decided that Symeon, son of the Clopas, mentioned in the gospel narrative, was worthy to occupy the throne of the Jerusalem see. He was, so it is said, a cousin of the savior, for Hegesippus relates that Clopas was the brother of Joseph. (*HE* 3.11.1)

It is interesting that Eusebius upholds this account as "a firm tradition," rather admitting that there were other traditions that were not as reliable. This, however, was firm: that Jesus' family and disciples held an assembly following the siege to choose a successor to James. That they chose Symeon the son of Clopas, who was a cousin to Jesus, has caused some scholars to see a dynastic succession at work here.

Eusebius then relates stories about the descendants of Jesus' family. Most notably, he states that Hegesippus recorded how, after the siege of Jerusalem, the Roman emperor Vespasian inflicted great persecution on many Jews in the course of a search he conducted to find those who were of the house of David. When referring to the relatives of Jesus, Eusebius uses the term *desposynoi* (those who belong to the Master), a word he took over from the early historian Julius Africanus and that has remained standard scholarly jargon for Jesus' family to this day. Later, Eusebius records another such search for *desposynoi* by the emperor Domitian, who reigned from 81 to 96:

Domitian ordered the execution of all who were of the family of David, and there is an old and firm tradition that a group of heretics accused the descendants of Jude—the brother, according to the flesh, of the savior—alleging that they were of the family of David and related to Christ himself. Hegesippus relates this as follows:

Now there still survived of the family of the Lord the grandsons of Jude—who was said to be his brother according to the flesh—and they were informed against as being of the family of David. These the *evocatus* [official] brought before Domitian Caesar. For he was afraid of the coming of Christ as Herod also. He asked them if they were descended from David and they admitted it. Then he asked them how much property they owned or how much money they controlled. They replied that they possessed only nine thousand *denarii* between them, half belonging to each, and this, they said, was not available in cash but was the estimated value of only thirty nine *plethora* [about a half acre] of land on which they paid their taxes and lived on by their work.

They showed him their hands, putting forward as proof of their toil the hardness of their bodies. . . .

On hearing this Domitian did not condemn them but despised them as simple folk, released them, and decreed an end to the persecution against the church. When they were released they were the leaders of the churches, both because of their testimony and because they were of the family of the Lord and remained alive in peace which lasted until Trajan. This we learn from Hegesippus. (*HE* 3.19.1–3.20.7)

Eusebius later relates another story about the grandsons of Jude in the time of the emperor Trajan (98–117), and tells of the martyrdom of Symeon, the successor to James:

[O]ther descendants of one of the so-called brothers of the savior named Jude lived on into the same reign [of Trajan] after they had given, in the time of Domitian, the testimony in behalf of the faith of Christ already recorded of them. [Hegesippus] writes thus:

Consequently they came and presided over every church, as witnesses and members of the family of the Lord, and since profound peace came to every church they survived until the time of Trajan Caesar, until the time of the son of the Lord's uncle, the aforesaid Simon the son of Clopas, was similarly accused by the sects on the same charge before Atticus the consular. He was tortured for many days and gave his witness so that all, even the consular, were astounded that at the age of one hundred and twenty he could endure it, and he was ordered to be crucified. (*HE* 3.32.1–6)

Obviously, there are legendary elements here, such as the claim that Symeon lived to be 120 years old,* but both John Painter and Richard Bauckham consider the accounts of Jesus' family found in Eusebius to be essentially reliable.[3] Painter highlights the importance of this material for our understanding of James:

> The continuing importance of the family of Jesus in the Jerusalem church and indeed in the churches at large . . . depended on the recognition of members of the human family of Jesus. Reservations about leaders being part of the family belong more to the time of Eusebius, and qualification [e.g., "so-called"] is normally present in those passages composed by him, even when he is summarizing sources from which it is absent. The qualification is generally absent from quotations from Hegesippus . . . For the early church, two centuries before Eusebius, the important issue for leadership was membership in the family of Jesus, a position that would be destroyed by the denial of the reality of that relationship.[4]

What Painter emphasizes here is that the dynastic succession claimed by Hegesippus and Eusebius is indeed historical, and that this dynastic succession was being downplayed and suppressed by the Catholic Church of Eusebius' day. Painter concludes:

> This view is consistent with our reading of the New Testament evidence. The link with the family of Jesus runs against the theological tendencies affirming his unique significance. The emerging orthodoxy of the early church tended to isolate Jesus from all but Mary, his virgin mother.[5]

In other words, the fact that the stories of Jesus' brothers and their descendants relayed by Hegesippus and Eusebius are in conflict with the emerging belief in the perpetual virginity of Mary validates their authenticity.

Gerd Lüdemann, along with a majority of scholars, is skeptical of such claims. Lüdemann does not think that there was any actual Davidic descent in the family of Jesus:

---

*It is worth noting that the book of Genesis says that 120 is the age to which God allowed people to live just prior to the flood (see Gen. 6:3).

> In my opinion, the claim to Davidic descent for the grandsons of Jude
> can only be considered to be redactional [the creation of Hegesippus
> or Eusebius]. At the time the story was composed (the beginning of the
> second century), Davidic sonship was already an element of christo-
> logical doctrine . . .[6]

In other words, any claim that Jesus or his family were *actually* of
Davidic descent is fictional. Lüdemann holds that all such references in
the New Testament, or any other early Christian literature, are the creation of the early church. Painter, however, specifically rebuts
Lüdemann:

> It is sometimes claimed that the Davidic messianic motif fits the agenda
> of the early church and probably does not belong to the early tradition.
> But there is independent evidence of messianic activity among the Jews,
> and, at least in the second of the two [Jewish] wars, Symeon bar
> Kochba was perceived by both sides to be a messianic leader.[7]

Painter is here referring to the second revolt of the Jews against
Rome, the so-called bar Kochba revolt (132–135 C.E.). Bar Kochba
and many other messianic pretenders claimed Davidic descent in order
to bolster their claims, and what Painter is pointing out is that Davidic
descent was a prerequisite for anyone claiming to be the Messiah.
Being of the line of David was a universal Jewish expectation based on
the everlasting covenant that God made with David—that a Davidic
descendant would reign as Messiah forever. It is therefore difficult to
agree with Lüdemann and so many others who claim that the Davidic
descent of Jesus is purely a creation of the early church. One of the few
solid conclusions of current historical Jesus research is the increasing
recognition that Jesus was indeed crucified by the Romans for sedition
and treason—for claiming to be "the King of the Jews," as the official
charge against Jesus read on the placard that Pilate ordered attached
to his cross. This is the source of the ancient Christian symbol INRI,
the Latin abbreviation for *Iesus Nazarenus Rex Iudaeorum*—Jesus of
Nazareth, King of the Jews. If this biblical account is historical, that
placard speaks volumes about the true identity of Jesus.

The person who has done the most in-depth research into the
matter of the *desposynoi* is conservative scholar Richard Bauckham.
He takes the middle ground and summarizes the debate thus:

The observation that not only James, but also other members of the family of Jesus were prominent in the leadership of the churches of Palestine down to at least the early second century prompted a series of scholars from Harnack to Schoeps to speak of a Christian "caliphate" or of a dynastic form of Christianity . . . This thesis of a dynastic succession in Palestinian Jewish Christianity was strongly attacked by von Campenhausen, whose article provoked an equally strong defence and reaffirmation of the thesis by Stauffer.

Our investigation . . . allows us to acknowledge some truth in the arguments of both von Campenhausen and Stauffer. The thesis of a strictly dynastic succession cannot be maintained, but it has to be admitted that the family relationship to Jesus played some part in the prominence of the *desposynoi* in the leadership of the Palestinian churches.[8]

While acknowledging where the evidence is pointing, Bauckham is more hesitant to accept the conclusion to which that evidence points than is the more liberal Painter. Here again we see the "matching coastline" factor at work. All the evidence points to the importance of Jesus' family both during his ministry and after his death, but scholars, like scientists, are in general inherently resistant to accepting new paradigms.

Eusebius actually supplies a complete list of the bishops of the Jerusalem church and attests to the thoroughgoing Jewishness of their leadership, a bit of candor quite remarkable for the (anti-Semitic) time in which Eusebius wrote:

All are said to be Hebrews in origin . . . at that time their whole church consisted of Hebrew believers who had continued from apostolic times down to the later siege in which the Jews . . . were overwhelmed in a full-scale war.

As this meant an end to the bishops of the circumcision, it is now necessary to give their names from the first. The *first* then was James who was called the Lord's brother; after whom Symeon was *second;* Justus third; Zacchaeus fourth; fifth Tobias; sixth Benjamin; John seventh; eighth Matthias; ninth Philip; tenth Seneca; eleventh Justus; Levi twelfth; Ephres thirteenth; fourteenth Joseph; and last, fifteenth Judas. Such were the bishops in the city of Jerusalem from the apostles down to the time mentioned; they were all of the circumcision. (*HE* 4.5.1–4)

The length of Eusebius' list of bishops causes most scholars to doubt the list's veracity because the Jerusalem church as such likely came to an end after the second Jewish revolt (132–135), which resulted in the banning of Jews from Jerusalem. Some scholars speculate that the list might actually be a sequential catalog of those who replaced the original twelve apostles as they were successively martyred, but it is likely that the "Jerusalem" church continued in Pella or elsewhere and that Eusebius lists the leaders there.

Unfortunately, in a bitter irony, the very thing that tied the Jerusalem church to Jesus' family—"they were all of the circumcision"—proved to be its undoing, as we shall see. The most significant factor was the loss of Jerusalem itself. Eusebius goes on to say that after the final Roman siege in the time of the emperor Hadrian, Jerusalem became a Gentile city (*HE* 4.6.4).

Later, Eusebius makes one final mention of James:

> Now the throne of James, who was the first to receive from the savior and the apostles the episcopate of the Jerusalem church and who was called a brother of Christ, as the divine books show, has been preserved to this day; and by the honor that the brethren in succession pay there to it, they show clearly to all the reverence in which the holy men were and still are held by the men of old time and those in our day, because of the love shown them by God. (*HE* 7.19.1)

Eusebius is apparently referring to an actual physical throne that was believed to have belonged to James. While the authenticity of such a holy relic seems unlikely, that such an object was believed in Eusebius' day to have belonged to James, and was venerated as such, is not at all unlikely. In fact, this throne is claimed to be the one that is preserved in the Armenian cathedral of St. James in Jerusalem to this day.

Another item of note here is the reverence that was paid to James even in the time of Eusebius, when the church had long been a Gentile form of Christianity. As mentioned earlier, James's suppression clearly came at a later time.* We noted earlier that Eusebius states that the

---

*The *Ecclesiastical History* was completed by 324. The Council of Nicaea was held in 325 and marks the beginning of James's erasure from orthodoxy; Eusebius, being the Bishop of Caesarea, was a delegate to the council.

"episcopate" was given to James by both Jesus *and* the apostles. Again, this emphasis was likely put forth to counter the claim in both Gnostic Christian and Jewish Christian circles that the risen Lord appeared first to James, not Peter. John Painter notes that

> Eusebius, like Clement, was conscious of a tradition that elevated James the Just in order to subvert apostolic succession. That alternative tradition is found in the Nag Hammadi documents that honor James . . . as well as in the [Jewish Christian] works . . . Clement and Eusebius were unwilling to give James up and attempted to reclaim him by placing him under the umbrella of apostolic authority.[9]

Here we see that there were those (mainly Gnostic and Jewish Christians) who early on were opposed to the idea of apostolic succession. In their eyes, succession to the leadership of the church was based on family ties—on dynastic, not apostolic, succession. It is to these pesky Gnostic and Jewish Christians that we turn next in our investigation.

7

THE BROTHER OF GOD: JAMES, GNOSTICISM, AND JEWISH CHRISTIANITY

The disciples said to Jesus, "We know that you are going to leave us. Who will be our leader?" Jesus said to them, "No matter where you are, you are to go to James the Just, for whose sake heaven and earth came into being."
THE GOSPEL OF THOMAS, LOGION 12 (SV)

By chance, in the year 1945, an Egyptian farmer unearthed what is perhaps the most important biblical archaeological discovery of modern times. While digging for natural fertilizer in the town of Nag Hammadi, Mohammad Ali and his brother discovered an ancient pottery jar that contained within it thirteen leather-bound books made of papyrus (called *codices* by scholars). The Nag Hammadi library, as these books have come to be called, contains more than fifty individual works, mainly alternative Christian gospels and other writings that were not included in the final canon of the New Testament. The Nag Hammadi codices are almost all written in the Coptic language and are translations from original Greek documents. They include titles such as the *Gospel of Truth*, the *Gospel of the Egyptians*, the *Acts of Peter and the Twelve Apostles*, and the *Apocalypse of Peter*. Most pertinent to our concerns are the *Apocryphon of James (AJ)*, the *First Apocalypse of James (FAJ)*, the *Second Apocalypse of James (SAJ)*, and the now famous *Gospel of*

123

Thomas (GT). All of these writings exhibit the theological beliefs of the early Christian sect known as the Gnostics, who, as we saw earlier, believed that Jesus transmitted secret teaching to certain apostles.

THE *GOSPEL OF THOMAS*

The most well-known of the Nag Hammadi texts is the *Gospel of Thomas*, which an increasing number of scholars believe may be as old as the canonical gospels. Some scholars see Thomas as a legitimate "fifth gospel," although it is quite different in nature from the four canonical gospels. Thomas is made up entirely of individual sayings of Jesus with no connecting narrative. The hypothetical document called "Q" (from the German *quelle*—"source"), which almost all scholars have long held to be one of the sources used by Matthew and Luke as the basis for their gospels, is, interestingly, also believed to have been entirely a collection of Jesus' sayings. A few scholars are wondering if the *Gospel of Thomas* might in fact *be* the missing Q document. Whatever the case may be, what has attracted the public's attention is that many of the sayings in Thomas are not found in the canonical gospels. Could they really be authentic lost sayings of Jesus? An increasing number of scholars think that at least some of them are.

Pertinent to our concerns is a single reference to James in the *Gospel of Thomas:* logion, or saying, 12, quoted above. Here we clearly have a rival tradition to that found in the canonical gospels, a tradition that portrays James as the leader of the apostles rather than Peter. What is especially significant is that the *Gospel of Thomas* is not a Jewish Christian writing, but a Gnostic one. So we know that two traditions outside the mainstream claimed priority for James. Is it possible that the canonical gospels have it wrong?

The *Gospel of Thomas* not only elevates James over Peter, but also elevates Thomas, for whom the gospel is named. In logion 13 (immediately following the James logion) there is an astounding parallel to the famous canonical story at Caesarea Philippi where Jesus questions the disciples as to who people believe he is. In the synoptic gospels, Peter gives his famous response, "You are the Messiah!" (Mark 8:27–30; Luke 9:18–21; Matthew 16:13–20). In Matthew, Jesus then designates Peter as the "rock" on which he will build his church, and this single statement has been the underlying source for the Roman Catholic Church's claim to apostolic authority to this day.

Strikingly, in logion 13 of the *Gospel of Thomas*, it is *Thomas* who gives the correct response, while Peter incorrectly identifies Jesus as an angel! Jesus then takes Thomas aside and reveals three secret teachings to him alone. This is the basis for the claim made in the opening of the *Gospel of Thomas*: "These are the secret sayings that the living Jesus spoke and Judas Thomas the Twin recorded."[1] The Gnostic Christians believed that Thomas the Twin (as he is called in the canonical gospels) was actually the twin brother of Jesus. While this sounds outlandish to modern ears, it was a common belief of a significant number of early Christians, derived from two facts: Thomas was known to be a twin, and his first name was Judas. According to the *Gospel of Thomas*, some early Christians identified this Judas with Jesus' brother Judas (also known as Jude). While their understandings may have been mistaken, the Gnostic writings clearly demonstrate that more than one early Christian community gave priority to the brothers of Jesus.

The handing on of the reins of leadership to James in logion 12 bears one significant difference from Clement's depiction of it in the account preserved in Eusebius' *Ecclesiastical History*. There, as we saw, both Jesus *and* the apostles hand the reins to James. In Thomas, it is Jesus alone who directs the apostles to James as their leader. Most striking is the exalted language used of James: "for whose sake heaven and earth came into being." John Painter notes that such language should not necessarily be all that surprising, for this is actually, "an expression which is comparable to other sayings concerning 'the righteous,' including Abraham and the patriarchs generally, Moses, David, and the Messiah, as well as Israel as a whole."[2] Painter refers to examples such as 2 Baruch 14:19—"the world was created for the righteous" (the words "righteous" and "just" are interchangeable).

Painter concludes of the evidence in Thomas: "The recognition of the leadership of James and the veneration of the family of Jesus signal that this tradition originated in a form of Jewish Christianity with a continuing memory of the role of Jesus and his family."[3] This trend in Jewish Christianity is everywhere evident in the Gnostic literature.

THE *APOCRYPHON OF JAMES*

The *Apocryphon* (Secret Book) *of James* was actually known before its discovery at Nag Hammadi. This lost work was first brought to light by the great psychologist Carl Jung, who had a deep interest in Gnosticism and who arranged for a copy found in a Coptic monastery to be smuggled out of Egypt. While this manuscript has become known as the *Apocryphon of James,* the work actually bears no title, but it does claim to have been written by James. In the opening lines, the author identifies himself simply as "James" without any further elaboration (as is done also in the canonical epistle of James), perpetuating the trend that is characteristic of other scriptural writings such as Acts and Galatians, where James is introduced without any background or explanation. Over and over again, we are left with the impression that James was so well known that he simply needed no introduction.

The *Apocryphon* is composed in the form of a letter addressed to a single individual whose name is no longer identifiable in the damaged manuscript. It opens with the author explaining his purpose using typical Gnostic terminology:[4]

> James, writing to . . . Peace be with you from Peace! Love from Love! Grace from Grace! Faith from Faith! Life from holy Life!
>
> Since you asked me to send you a secret book revealed to me and Peter by the Lord, I could not turn you down or refuse you. So I have written it in Hebrew, and sent it to you, and only you. But, considering that you are a minister for the salvation of the saints, try to be careful not to communicate this book to many people, for the Savior did not even want to communicate it to all of us, his twelve disciples. (*AJ* 1:1–3)

Though the author's opening words say the book was revealed to both James and Peter, this does not place them on equal footing. As in all of the Gnostic literature, James is clearly the leader of the apostles and the guardian of his brother's secret teachings. What is most remarkable here is James's claim to be one of the Twelve, an assertion that has caused some scholars to theorize that the James of this work is the apostle James, the son of Zebedee. The vast majority of scholars, however, hold that this is indeed James the brother of Jesus. Is it possible that Jesus' brother was one of the Twelve? Since there are two other apostles named James, it is indeed possible that one of them was either mistakenly or intentionally substituted for Jesus' brother in the gospels to cover up the fact that James was one of the Twelve (as Robert Eisenman claims).

As in the *Gospel of Thomas*, the *Apocryphon* replaces Peter with James in stories that have parallels in the canonical gospels. For example, in Matthew 16:22 Peter rebukes Jesus for speaking of his impending suffering and death, but in the *Apocryphon* it is James who says, "Lord, do not speak of your cross and death to us, for they are far from you" (*AJ* 3:12). In Mark 10:28, Peter attests on behalf of all the apostles that they have left everything behind to follow Jesus. In the *Apocryphon*, it is James who says, "[W]e have left our fathers, our mothers, and our towns, and have followed you" (*AJ* 3:1). The leadership role of James is also in evidence at the end of the *Apocryphon*, where James assigns the disciples to different mission territories and he himself goes to Jerusalem (*AJ* 10:10). As we have seen, this is likely the actual history, thus lending credibility to the *Apocryphon*.

THE *FIRST APOCALYPSE OF JAMES*

The tendencies seen in the *Gospel of Thomas* and the *Apocryphon* continue in two other works found at Nag Hammadi, the *First Apocalypse of James* and the *Second Apocalypse of James*. Both of these manuscripts actually bear the same name, *The Apocalypse of James*, but they have been distinguished by scholars by the addition of "First" and "Second." They are again Coptic translations from the Greek and are generally dated early third century. Most scholars think that both works are based on earlier Jewish Christian writings emanating from a Jewish Christian community that survived in Syria. One piece of evidence for this is that the codices contain a series of post-resurrection dialogues between James and Jesus on the Syrian Mount Gaugela. The Jewish Christian nature of these writings is further evidenced by the fact that James repeatedly refers to his brother as "Rabbi."

The *First Apocalypse* can be broken down into three sections: (1) a dialogue between James and Jesus prior to the crucifixion; (2) a post-resurrection dialogue; (3) the foretelling of James's death by Jesus. Of significance in the first part is the close involvement between James and Jesus prior to the crucifixion, an intimacy that we also saw in the *Apocryphon* and that we will also see in another Jewish Christian work, the *Gospel of the Hebrews*. What is most telling here is that these works show James as a disciple of Jesus prior to the crucifixion *without placing any stress on it*. That James was a disciple prior to the crucifixion is simply unremarkable in this literature—as unremarkable as the introduction of James in Acts and Galatians.

While most of what James says in the *First Apocalypse* is related in the third person, the work opens with James speaking in the first person: "It is the Lord who spoke with me: 'See now the completion of my redemption. I have given you a sign of these things, James, my brother. For not without reason have I called you my brother, although you are not my brother materially'" (*FAJ* 24.14–15).[5] At first glance, it may seem that Jesus is denying a blood relationship to James ("you are not my brother materially"), but this is not the case. These words actually express one of the core beliefs of the Gnostics—that the transcendent Christ did not have a material body, but only appeared to be in human form (an early heresy known as docetism). This belief comes out clearly in a post-resurrection dialogue where Jesus says, "James, do not be concerned for me . . . I am he who was within me. Never have I suffered in any way, nor have I been distressed. And this people has done me no harm" (*FAJ* 31:15–24). The Gnostics did not believe that Christ could suffer. Only the human form of Jesus suffered, not the transcendent Christ, who only "possessed" the body of Jesus ("I am he who was within me").

Gnostic theology is also in evidence in a passage where Jesus tells James that he will be casting off the bonds of the flesh and returning to the place from whence he came, to again be part of the "One Who Is" (*FAJ* 24:19–24).

A tendency to highly elevate James, almost to the status of Jesus himself, appears in a passage where James's death is likened to Jesus' death in destroying the powers of darkness (*FAJ* 25:15–19). In this section, James is also warned to flee Jerusalem before its destruction, which may be the basis for an influential legend of the flight of the Jerusalem Christians to the city of Pella prior to the Roman invasion. In later centuries, Jewish Christian sects such as the Ebionites used the story of the flight to Pella as the basis for their claim of direct descent from the Jerusalem church. The historicity of this legend is one of the most debated issues in the study of early Jewish Christianity.

Another significant incident related in the *First Apocalypse* is an account of James rebuking the disciples, clearly demonstrating his authority over them (*FAJ* 42:20–24). James's priority also shows itself in the passage where Jesus appears to his brother after the resurrection while James is alone in prayer on the aforementioned Mount Gaugela. James embraces and kisses Jesus and, as in other Gnostic works, receives a secret revelation (*apokalypsis* in Greek) from Jesus. James is instructed to pass this revelation on to the disciple named Addai (Syriac for Thaddeus), the Thaddeus who purportedly took a letter of Jesus to King Abgar of Edessa, which is known to have been another center of Jewish Christianity (see chapter 6). Significantly, there is no discussion of Jesus assigning any final mission to the Twelve as he does at the conclusion of Matthew and Luke. In the *First Apocalypse,* that task is carried out by James.

THE *SECOND APOCALYPSE OF JAMES*

What we see in the *First Apocalypse* is the Gnostic and Jewish Christian belief that the mission of Jesus was handed on directly to James by Jesus. This understanding also underlies the *Second Apocalypse of James,* but in a slightly different form. Here, James divulges the secret revelation he has been given by Jesus to a Jewish Christian priest named Mareim, who commits it to writing. The church father Hippolytus apparently knew this story, for in his well-known antiheretical work *Refutation of All Heresies* (5:2) he notes that a Jewish Christian sect he calls the "Naassenes" venerated James as the one who transmitted the secret teachings of Jesus through "Mariamne." The Naasenes are almost certainly the same group we know as the Nazarenes or Nazoreans (i.e., the Jerusalem church or their descendants). In the *Second Apocalypse,* Mareim also serves as a juror at James's trial.

Whereas the *First Apocalypse* elevates James's status, the most notable feature of the *Second Apocalypse* is that James is exalted to a level far beyond that found in any other Gnostic or Jewish Christian writing. As in Hegesippus' *Memoirs* (which is likely the basis for the *Second Apocalypse*), James explains that the "door of Jesus" means the door to eternal life, or the door to heaven. In the Gnostic-flavored Gospel of John, Jesus speaks of himself as the "door" (see John 10:9). In the *Second Apocalypse,* James is portrayed as the keeper at the door to heaven, somewhat akin to the traditional role of St. Peter at the pearly gates. The *Second Apocalypse* even says that those who pass through the door to heaven belong to both Jesus and James! In one passage, James is referred to as the "illuminator and redeemer" (*SAJ* 55.17–18). In another, James is "he whom the heavens bless" (*SAJ* 55.24–25).

The *Second Apocalypse* also contains some fascinating statements about James's familial relationship to Jesus. At one point, James quotes his mother, Mary:

> [M]y mother said to me, "Do not be frightened, my son, because he
> [Jesus] said 'My brother' to you. For you were nourished with this
> same milk. Because of this he calls me 'My Mother.'" (*SAJ* 50:15–22)

There could certainly be no more "natural" way of attesting that James
and Jesus were natural brothers than to say they suckled at the same
breast. The statement, "Because of this he *calls* me 'My Mother,'" also
has Gnostic implications, suggesting the docetic belief that Jesus only
appeared human, and actually had no earthly mother.

The *Second Apocalypse* also trumps the *First Apocalypse* in the
scene where the risen Christ appears to James. Rather than James
embracing and kissing Jesus as in the *First Apocalypse,* here Jesus
takes the initiative. This intimate scene is described by James in the
first person:

> And he kissed my mouth. He took hold of me saying, "My beloved!
> Behold, I shall reveal to you those (things) that (neither) [the] heavens
> nor their archons have known . . . Behold I shall reveal to you every-
> thing, my beloved. (*SAJ* 50.15–22)

Jesus does indeed reveal everything to James. Even the prediction of the
destruction of the Temple, which is made by Jesus in the gospels, is here
predicted by James (*SAJ* 60.12–23). James even cites his impending
martyrdom as the reason for the Temple's doom. The assigning of the
blame for the siege of Jerusalem to James's death, which we also saw in
Clement and Hegesippus, is here put into James's own mouth. It is
telling that the *Second Apocalypse* agrees with Josephus (over against
the later Hegesippus) in laying the blame for James's unjust execution
at the feet of the Sadducees and priests, rather than the Pharisees and
scribes. As we have seen, it is far more likely that James was a Pharisee
than a Sadducee. The *Second Apocalypse* actually elaborates on the
legal details of the trial, details that give the account a ring of authenticity (or at the very least show that the author had a sound knowledge
of Jewish and Roman courtroom procedure).

John Painter believes that what we have in the *First* and *Second
Apocalypse of James* is evidence of a Gnostic Jewish Christian tradition
completely independent of Josephus, Hegesippus, or Clement.[6] We will
now turn an eye to this alternative Jewish Christian tradition to close
out our survey of the extra-biblical literature on James.

THE JEWISH CHRISTIAN COMMUNITIES

The phenomenon generally referred to as "Jewish Christianity" was not a monolithic entity (in this it is like all other Christian and Jewish sects). The groundbreaking work on the nature of Jewish Christianity, *Patristic Evidence for Jewish Christian Sects* by A. F. J. Klijn and G. J. Reinink, identifies five distinct Jewish Christian communities that existed in apostolic times: the Ebionites, the Elkesaites, the Nazoreans, the Cerinthians, and the Symmachians.[7] Though there is some diversity in the beliefs of these groups, James Dunn has identified three common characteristics that warrant placing each community under the umbrella label of "Jewish Christian":[8]

1. Faithful adherence to the Law of Moses.
2. The exaltation of James and the denigration of Paul.
3. A christology* of "adoptionism"—they all believed that Jesus was the natural born son of Joseph and Mary and was "adopted" by God as his Son upon his baptism by John.

We shall encounter all of these traits in the documents we examine next. In addition to these three criteria, there is also a growing consensus among scholars that most of these Jewish Christian groups were influenced to a greater or lesser extent by Gnosticism, which was well established throughout the Roman Empire by the end of the first century.

Despite the major commonalities between these groups, however, they may have been more diverse than has traditionally been supposed. One of the main criticisms that is leveled against F. C. Baur's theory of a polar opposition between a Petrine (Jewish) Christianity and a Pauline (Gentile) Christianity, is that Baur saw Jewish and Gentile Christianity too simplistically. Baur thought there was a single body of Jewish Christians led by Peter,† and a single body of Gentile Christians led by Paul. In actuality, these two bodies had developed early on into a variety of subgroups.

---

*The term *christology* refers to official doctrine or beliefs about the nature of Jesus.
†Baur did not realize the full significance of James and operated under the traditional understanding that Peter was the leader of the apostles.

The revered Roman Catholic scholar Raymond Brown first delineated the varieties of Jewish Christianity in his seminal article, "Not Jewish Christianity and Gentile Christianity, but Types of Jewish/Gentile Christianity."[9] Brown posits four distinguishable Jewish Christian groups. Type one is "Jewish Christians and their Gentile converts who practiced full observance of the Mosaic Law, including circumcision, as necessary for . . . salvation." Type two is like type one, but its members, "did not insist on circumcision as salvific for Gentile Christians but did require them to keep some purity laws." Brown believes that both James and Peter belong in this group (recall the terms of the Apostolic Decree). Type three Jewish Christians "did not insist on circumcision as salvific for Gentile Christians and did not require their observing Jewish purity laws." Type three Jewish Christianity "did not entail a break with the cultic practices of Judaism (feasts, Temple) nor did it impel *Jewish* Christians to abandon circumcision and the Law." Brown places Paul in this group. Finally, type four can hardly retain the title *Jewish* Christian for they "saw no abiding significance in the cult of the Jerusalem Temple." This type is thus almost completely Gentile in orientation, having lost all lingering connections to parent Judaism. It is important to note that among all of the earliest Jesus communities, this is the first group that can truly be called "Christian" in the modern sense.

James Dunn, in *The Partings of the Ways*, proposes a system similar to Brown's, but breaks down early Christianity even further—into six types, again ranging from conservative Jewish believers on one end to pure Gentiles on the other. As Dunn notes of both his work and Brown's, "The value of all this has been to bring home . . . the *diversity* of first-century Christianity." But Dunn also warns against maintaining such a typology too rigidly: "A closer approximation to first-century reality is to see it as a more or less unbroken spectrum across a wide front from conservative Judaizers at one end to radical Gentiles at the other."[10]

THE *GOSPEL OF THE HEBREWS*

The most important scripture for the more staunchly *Jewish* Christian communities was the aptly name *Gospel of the Hebrews*. Unfortunately, no copies of this gospel are extant today. Rather, we know of it only from extracts in other writings, and confusion about it abounds because it seems to have gone by several different names. The church fathers reference writings known as the *Gospel of the Nazareans* and the *Gospel of the Ebionites*. These may all have been one and the same gospel, though the majority of scholars believe the *Gospel of the Hebrews* to be a distinct work, certainly dating no later than the first half of the second century, and perhaps even earlier (in other words, not much later than the gospels of Luke and John).

Serendipitously, one of the few quotations that exists from the *Gospel of the Hebrews* concerns James (there were likely many more). The passage comes down to us in Jerome's *Lives of Illustrious Men,* where Jerome (translator of the first Latin Bible) informs us that he himself translated the *Gospel of the Hebrews* from the original Hebrew. That the *Gospel of the Hebrews* was originally written in Hebrew is certainly significant, as all four of the canonical gospels were written in Greek, perhaps indicating that the *Gospel of the Hebrews* could be *earlier* than the canonical gospels. In any event, here is the passage in question:

> The Gospel called according to the Hebrews which was recently translated by me into Greek and Latin, which Origen frequently uses, records after the resurrection of the Savior:

> And when the Lord had given the linen cloth [his burial cloth] to the servant of the priest, he went to James and appeared to him. For James had sworn that he would not eat bread from the hour in which he had drunk the cup of the Lord until he should see him risen from among them that sleep. And shortly thereafter the Lord said: Bring a table and bread! And immediately it is added: He took the bread, blessed it and brake it and gave it to James the Just and said to him: My brother, eat thy bread, for the Son of Man is risen from among them that sleep.[11]

Once again, the tendency to exalt James in Jewish Christianity is clearly in evidence, though it must be emphasized at this point that it is quite likely that James is not in fact being elevated over Peter as a rhetorical move on the author's part, but rather that the primacy of James is historical. Here James is the *first* recipient of a resurrection appearance. The *Gospel of the Hebrews* may in fact be the source of the rival James tradition that Paul makes use of when listing the resurrection appearances in 1 Corinthians 15.

Also of great significance is the tacit implication that James partook in the Last Supper: "he would not eat bread from the hour in which *he had drunk the cup of the Lord*." Again, the *tacit* assumption that James was present at the last supper, without any emphasis on the matter (a matter that to us today is highly remarkable) speaks volumes for the historical authenticity of this tradition. John Painter believes the *Gospel of the Hebrews* to be important evidence for James being a disciple prior to the crucifixion:

> This fragment is important . . . because it portrays James as belonging to the circle of disciples of Jesus during his ministry and those present at the last supper. It puts in question the notion that James joined the believing community only after . . . the appearance of Jesus to him. Recognition of the ideological stance adopted by the canonical Gospels puts in question the reading that concludes that the brothers of Jesus did not, during his ministry, believe in him.[12]

Of course, much of the real significance depends on the dating of the *Gospel of the Hebrews*. Gerd Lüdemann points out that for F. C. Baur and the Tübingen School, the *Gospel of the Hebrews* "was supposed to be the oldest gospel and the midpoint of the Jewish-Christian gospel literature, which was precipitated out into the canonical gospels."[13] Painter is a bit more cautious than Baur; he feels that while 1 Corinthians 15 presents clear evidence of a rivalry between the supporters of James and the supporters of Peter, ". . . it is unclear where the *Gospel of the Hebrews* fits into this history."[14]

Another set of writings that F. C. Baur considered to be very early and reliable, and that he made much use of in support of his theory of a Petrine/Pauline rivalry (as does Robert Eisenman today), is a collection known as the *Pseudo-Clementines*.

THE *PSEUDO-CLEMENTINES*

The term *pseudo* was applied to this collection of writings because of its original (now disputed) attribution to the church father Clement—not to be confused with author of the *Outlines,* Clement of Alexandria. This Clement was the Bishop of Rome at the end of the first century and the *Pseudo-Clementines* purport to tell his story. The vast majority of scholars today consider the *Pseudo-Clementines* to be no earlier than the fourth century, at least in its final form, but a few—such as Robert Eisenman—believe that the underlying traditions contained within it are much older. This is supported by the fact that that the *Pseudo-Clementines* is an anthology of smaller works. There are two main parts: the "Homilies" and the "Recognitions." These are both made up of yet smaller works: the *Ascents of James,* the *Epistula Petri,* and the *Kerygmata Petrou.*

The *Ascents of James,* which is part of the *Recognitions,* takes its name from an incident where James ascends the steps of the Temple to engage in a public debate over Jesus being the Messiah. It is a fitting title for today—since James is indeed "ascending" from the hidden depths in which he has been too long buried. The debate into which James enters is a dispute that had been started by Peter and Clement with Jewish opponents outside the Temple. James is on the verge of persuading the crowd of Jews to be baptized, when someone mysteriously referred to only as "the enemy" enters the Temple, creates an uproar, physically accosts James, and throws him down from the top of the steps. It soon becomes quite obvious that this unnamed "enemy" is none other than Saul (Paul prior to his conversion), engaging in one of his well-known acts of violent persecution against those who proclaimed Jesus to be the Messiah. Following this attack on the Temple steps, James sends Peter to spy on Saul and send back regular reports on his activities. Saul then attempts to arrest Peter, pursuing him as far as Damascus. Those scholars who believe the *Ascents* to be a late writing see this passage as a later reflection of the accounts of Paul's violent persecutions in Acts (see 8:3, and especially 9:1–2, where Paul goes to Damascus to seek out those who belong to "the Way"). It is certainly not impossible, however, that the *Ascents* records actual history. It is intriguing to speculate that it could have been while Paul was in pursuit of Peter on the road to Damascus that he had his dramatic encounter with the risen Christ, resulting in his conversion.

This intriguing story is but one of many examples of a virulent anti-Paulinism that pervades the *Pseudo-Clementines.* In light of Paul's track record, such an attitude on the part of the Jewish Christian community is certainly understandable. We know from Paul's own letters that he had indeed been a violent persecutor of the Christian community prior to his conversion. Acts tells of Saul aiding and abetting at the stoning of Stephen, even holding the cloaks of those who took part in the stoning. In light of Luke's well-known tendency in Acts to whitewash unseemly matters, and in light of Paul's well-known temper and preconversion hatred for followers of Jesus, it is certainly not improbable that Paul did more than just hold the cloaks of the perpetrators. Acts goes on to say: "And Saul approved of their killing him. That day a severe persecution began against the church in Jerusalem, and all except the apostles were scattered . . . Saul was ravaging the church by entering house after house; dragging off both men and women, he committed them to prison" (Acts 8:1–3).

In view of Paul's portrayal in Acts, it is not at all unlikely that the violent attack by Paul on James in the *Ascents of James* is factual. If the account is *not* historical, we must ask why the early Jewish Christians would invent such a story. Why would they need to, given that there were so many other well-known stories of Paul's violence against Christians? And if Paul did indeed attack James, then it is no wonder that James and Peter were as wary of Paul as they decidedly were. Paul's talk in Galatians of having cordial meetings with Peter and James in Jerusalem may simply have been rhetorical strategy, for Paul would certainly have had reason to downplay the fact that James and Peter were far less than receptive to his visits.

The part of the *Pseudo-Clementines* known as the *Epistula Petri* (the Epistle of Peter, sometimes called the Epistle of Peter to James) serves as an introduction to the *Kerygmata Petrou* (the Proclamation of Peter). In the epistle, Paul is again referred to obliquely, here as the "hostile man" who "teaches lawless doctrine." It is quite obvious to all scholars that the role played in this writing by a character called Simon Magus is a veiled allusion to Paul (Simon Magus appears in Acts 8:9–24 as a sorcerer who tries to buy the power of the Holy Spirit from Peter and John). Also striking in the *Epistula Petri* is that Peter addresses this letter to "James, the lord and bishop of the holy Church" (1.1) and expresses his concern to James that, "some from among the Gentiles have rejected my lawful preaching, attaching themselves to certain lawless and trifling preaching of the man who is my enemy" (2.3).[15] In light of all the other evidence we have uncovered, this letter could indeed be historical. There is certainly nothing implausible here.

Recognitions makes the interesting argument that Paul could not have received a revelation from Jesus because his teaching does not agree with that of James and Peter, and it is further argued that Paul cannot be considered an apostle because he is not one of the Twelve (4.35). Peter is upheld as the *true* apostle to the Gentiles, who gives them the genuine (Law-based) gospel. Books 4–6 of *Recognitions* tell of a missionary journey to Tripolis undertaken by Peter, who warns his audience there to beware of false apostles (Paul?) who might come after him: "[B]elieve no teacher, unless he brings from Jerusalem the testimonial of James the Lord's brother" (4.35). Peter refers to James as "our James" and "James the bishop" (1.66). He is also called the "chief of the bishops" and "archbishop" (1.68). Clement even addresses James as "my Lord James" (3.74). Many more such references from the *Pseudo-Clementines* could be presented, but the gist is that the anthology takes the themes of Jewish Christianity that we have encountered in our survey to the extreme. The community that produced them obviously fits Raymond Brown's description of a "type one" community.

The assumption of the basic authenticity of the *Pseudo-Clementines* underlay F. C. Baur's theories, and the *Pseudo-Clementines* is still key to the theories of today's scholars such as Robert Eisenman, Hyam Maccoby, and the late Hugh Schonfield. It is certainly significant that while Jewish scholars have little problem with the reliability of the *Pseudo-Clementines*, Christian scholars generally disparage it because of its denigration of Paul and upholding of Jewish Christian theology. Much more scholarly investigation of this anthology urgently needs to be undertaken. Even though the provenance and reliability of these controversial pieces presently remains in dispute, at the very least they reveal the heart of the concerns of later Jewish Christianity and reveal something of the theological battles that Jewish Christians waged against what they considered to be apostasy and heresy (but which we today call Christianity).

JEWISH CHRISTIAN ORTHODOXY

At the end of part 1, we had reached two conclusions:

1. There is nothing in the gospels that incontrovertibly shows opposition to Jesus by his family during his ministry.
2. Jesus' mother and brothers were followers of his ministry prior to the crucifixion.

By the end of part 2, we had added two more conclusions:

3. James was the leader of the Jerusalem church from its inception following Jesus' death and resurrection.
4. James's theological stance was that of Pharisaism. By implication, and as attested by independent evidence, it is likely that Pharisaism was also the theology of Jesus.

In our investigation of later history and tradition in the last two chapters, we have seen nothing that would cause us to question these conclusions, and much that further supports them. Onto these conclusions we can now add the following:

5. While the historicity of the Jewish Christian literature remains in dispute, these writings provide firm evidence that the early Jewish Christian community was firmly opposed to Paul and his theology.
6. All of the earliest followers of Jesus, up to the commencement of Paul's mission, thought of themselves as nothing other than loyal Jews.

Ultimately, all of these conclusions point to an unsettling prospect for many modern Christians. Bruce Chilton has asked a haunting question in his introduction to the compendium of research papers produced by the international Consultation on James, *James the Just and Christian Origins*. Chilton boils all of the evidence concerning James down to

a single, systemic concern: in its generative moment, was Christianity in fact, *as well as in its self-awareness,* a species of Judaism? That is why the relation between James and Jesus . . . is so important. If James self-consciously remained faithful to a received definition of Israel (as Paul did not), and if Jesus and James were indeed brothers of the flesh and in their affections, then the grounding conception of Christianity as a separate religion from Judaism, or even as offering a distinct revelation, is seriously compromised.[16]

In other words, if the first followers of Jesus—including the apostles and Jesus' own family—were thoroughly Jewish in their belief and practice and opposed to Paul's interpretation of the gospel, then just what is "orthodoxy" and what is "heresy"? Is Christianity, as it has come to be practiced for close to two millennia, in fact based on a heresy? And is the "heresy" of Jewish Christianity in fact the original orthodoxy?

These are disturbing questions indeed. To even consider them is heresy in the minds of many Christians today. But these questions are being addressed more and more by scholars, and if we want to learn the truth about James and Jesus, we must address them too.

4

THE NATURE OF ORTHODOXY

8

ORTHODOXY AND HERESY: JAMES AND THE QUEST FOR THE HISTORICAL JESUS

". . . believe no teacher, unless he brings from Jerusalem the testimonial of James the Lord's brother . . ."

ST. PETER PREACHING AT TRIPOLIS, *PSEUDO-CLEMENTINE RECOGNITIONS*

The historical and apocryphal works we examined in part 3 present us with two possibilities:

1. The Jewish Christian writings accurately portray Jesus' earliest followers as thoroughly Jewish in their beliefs and opposed to Paul's interpretation of Jesus' teachings.

or

2. The Jewish Christian writings are merely the attempt of a later generation of Jewish Christians to portray the apostles in a Jewish light in order to support their own Jewish understanding of Jesus.

The latter interpretation has, for obvious reasons, been the belief of the vast majority of Christian scholars. The mainstream Christian view is that the Jewish Christians painted their hero James as superior to Peter and pictured the apostles as strictly Law-observant and opposed to Paul because they had an axe to grind with him. In actuality, the mainstream theory goes, James and the apostles agreed with Paul about abandoning the Law for the Gospel of Jesus Christ. In support of this traditional understanding, we do know that a similar development occurred in the Johannine Christian community, which produced the gospel and epistles of John, a development that it would be enlightening to survey before we attempt to draw any final conclusions in our investigation.

A PARALLEL FROM JOHN

It is well known that the Gospel According to John portrays Peter negatively in relation to the anonymous "Beloved Disciple" who is portrayed as Jesus' "favorite"—the disciple who rests his head on Jesus' bosom at the Last Supper. This disciple is obviously the hero-founder of the Johannine community, for he appears only in John's gospel. Most significantly, in John it is the Beloved Disciple who is the first to believe that Jesus has risen from the dead (John 20:8). Yet, the Beloved Disciple is curiously absent in the synoptic gospels, although there have been many theories as to the Beloved Disciple being John the Son of Zebedee or another of the apostles.

John's gospel clearly demonstrates that there is a precedent for the sort of later reinterpretation of tradition (specifically in regard to the elevation of a particular apostle) that most scholars believe is at work with the elevation of James in the Jewish Christian literature. John Painter explains the correlation:

> We are reminded of the subservient role played by Peter in relation to the Beloved Disciple in the Fourth Gospel. Many scholars see in that account a struggle between the Johannine community . . . and emerging "Catholic" Christianity . . . the Beloved Disciple is also portrayed as the repository of secret tradition . . .The Johannine tradition was harnessed by the Great Church through the reconciliation of the role of Peter and the Beloved Disciple in the epilogue to the Gospel and through the acceptance of John as one of the four canonical gospels.[1]

As Painter points out, the gospel and epistles of John reveal the struggles of one particular Christian community whose beliefs and practices were in tension with other early Christian communities. Raymond

Brown has written the most enlightening account of this in his magnificent work, *The Community of the Beloved Disciple.*

It is also well known that the distinctly Gnostic flavor of John's gospel caused it to be scrutinized for its orthodoxy before it was allowed to join the synoptic gospels in the final canon of the New Testament. It was only in the late third and fourth century, when Christianity grew to the point where it became the official religion of the Roman Empire, that what was once a smattering of separate churches with differing, and oftentimes competing theologies and christologies, began to be pressured by political circumstances to circle around a common creed. Thus arose the impetus for the convening of the first church councils, such as Nicaea (325) and Chalcedon (451), where Western bishops and Eastern patriarchs, and their delegates from major cities around the Empire, hammered out which beliefs about Jesus were "orthodox," and which were to be forever after condemned as "heresy."

Long before these official councils, the theology expressed in the gospel of John had been unofficially declared orthodox by a majority of Christians simply by its popularity and increasing usage, and by the mid-second century it was accepted alongside the gospels of Matthew, Mark, and Luke as canonical. Like John, the synoptic gospels were also written by and for particular Christian communities. Of the four, Matthew's community was the most Jewish in nature. Only Matthew records these words of Jesus, which we looked at previously when we noted the Pharisaic character of Jesus' teaching:

> Do not think that I have come to abolish the law . . . I have come not to abolish but to fulfill. For truly I tell you, until heaven and earth pass away, not one letter, not one stroke of a letter, will pass from the law . . . Therefore, whoever breaks one of the least of these commandments, and teaches others to do the same, will be called least in the kingdom of heaven . . . For I tell you, unless your righteousness exceeds that of the scribes and Pharisees, you will never enter the kingdom of heaven. (Matt. 5:17–20)

These are some of the most debated words of Jesus in the New Testament. Both conservative and liberal scholars have tried hard to avoid their implications—liberal scholars declaring that these words were put into Jesus' mouth by the Jewish Christian Matthean community, and conservative scholars interpreting the passage as Jesus "preparing the way" for the Gospel by showing the impossibility of upholding the Law perfectly. In other words, Jesus didn't really *mean* what he said about the Law—he was simply using hyperbole to make the opposite point. These are attempts, by both liberals and conservatives, to avoid taking the implications of these words at face value— Jesus was more thoroughly Jewish than Christians throughout history have believed. If, in fact, we attribute these words to Jesus, and take them at face value, they are surely evidence of Jesus' alignment with the Pharisaic party, as a growing number of contemporary scholars are now beginning to accept.

Even more than John's gospel, the epistle of James was debated and its orthodoxy thoroughly analyzed. Well into the fourth century, James remained one of the most disputed of the popular Christian writings because of its obvious Jewish Christian theology and its apparent opposition to Paul's teaching of salvation by faith alone. This opposition doesn't get any more plain than James 2:14: "What good is it, my brothers and sisters, if you say you have faith but do not have works? *Can faith save you?*" This passage gets my vote as the most explained-away verse in the New Testament. Once again, theologians of every stripe have devised clever exegetical and hermeneutical tricks* to avoid taking this passage at anything but face value. But Martin Luther wasn't fooled. Luther knew *exactly* what James was saying. Given his preference, Luther would have excised the book of James from the Bible forever, along with Hebrews, Jude, and Revelation (the other thoroughly Jewish Christian books in the New Testament) and gladly tossed them all "into the Elbe River." In fact, when Luther translated the Bible into German, he relegated these four books to a separate section at the end of the Bible, not considering them of equal worth with the rest of the New Testament writings.

But the emerging Catholic Church had declared early on that the gospel of John was orthodox and had accepted it into the canon. So, too, the church finally accepted the epistle of James. John Painter explains that just as the emerging church needed to incorporate the

---

*Exegetical (from the Greek *exegesis,* literally "to draw out") and hermeneutical (from the Greek *hermēneutikos,* "to interpret") refer to methods of interpreting the meaning of scripture. Hermeneutical refers more specifically to interpreting a passage for preaching.

views of the Johannine community for the sake of political unity, it also needed to co-opt the views of the communities centered on James—but James's leadership role needed to be suppressed:

> There is evidence, in the tradition from Clement transmitted by Eusebius, of an attempt to harness the authority of James to the benefit of the emerging Catholic Church by rooting his authority in that of the apostles and by making him a co-recipient of the revelation with Peter and John. . . .
>
> Pauline opposition to the authority of James, the disappearance of the Jerusalem church [after the Roman invasion in 70], and the emergence of Peter as a more ecumenical transformation of the James tradition seems to have led to the suppression of James in the emerging catholic tradition. This was made easier by Luke's attempt to obscure the conflicts within the early church in his account in Acts. His harmonization obscured the leadership of James by assimilating the roles of Peter and James, but the cracks in this treatment appear when his account is read in the light of the letters of Paul.[2]

To be fair in weighing the evidence before us, because of the example of the Beloved Disciple in the gospel of John, we see that it is not unlikely that the Jewish Christian communities, in their struggles to retain their beliefs in response to the increasing dominance of Pauline Christianity, would have exaggerated the role of James and the importance of the Law in their writings. And while there is clearly a tendency in the later Jewish Christian literature to exalt James that sometimes borders on the unbelievable (and that might seem to dim the credibility of these writings), we must not forget that it is not only in the Jewish Christian literature that we see James elevated over Peter. *We also see this in Acts and in Galatians.* And it is also in Acts and Galatians that we see so much of the evidence for the thoroughgoing Jewishness of James and the apostles. So the leadership of James, and the strict Jewishness of the apostles, are clearly not total fabrications by the later Jewish Christian community. They may indeed be somewhat exaggerated, but they surely have a solid basis in fact.

When synthesized, the witness of the Jewish Christian literature and the evidence of the New Testament itself powerfully impel us to abandon the traditional understanding of the "heretical" nature of the Jewish Christian literature in favor of the first of the two possibilities enumerated at the beginning of this chapter: The Jewish Christian writings are indeed basically accurate in their portrayal of James's apostolic leadership and in their portrayal of James and the apostles as thoroughly Jewish in their beliefs and opposed to Paul's interpretation of Jesus' teachings.

Obviously, this is a revolutionary theory on the origins of Christianity, yet once one accepts this understanding as the inevitable outcome of an unbiased reevaluation of the evidence, the seemingly mismatched puzzle pieces in the New Testament suddenly fall into place and a bigger picture comes clearly into focus. The picture which emerges may shock many traditional Christians; for many it will be absolutely blasphemous. It is, moreover, a picture that has the potential to tear apart many cherished "truths" and to shatter a paradigm that has been in place for almost two millennia, but in its place, it is possible to see a truer and nobler picture emerging.

JESUS AND JUDAISM

The controversial (at least to Christians) Jewish scholars Hyam Maccoby, Hugh Schonfield, and Geza Vermes have seen all of this as clearly as anyone. Schonfield in particular has long anticipated this new paradigm.[3] Maccoby demonstrates how those who hold to the traditional Christian interpretation (that Paul and the apostles were in agreement in abandoning the Law) explain away the Law-observance of the Jewish Christians by representing it as "re-Judaization," nothing more than a case of backsliding into former beliefs and practices—beliefs and practices, moreover, that Jesus had come to do away with. As Maccoby sums up the traditional understanding,

> [l]ater movements in Christanity, such as the Ebionites, are regarded
> as re-Judaizing sects, which lapsed back into Judaism, unable to bear
> the newness of Christianity. Re-judaizing tendencies are . . .
> [believed to exist] in certain passages in the Gospels, especially that
> of Matthew, where Jesus is portrayed as a Jewish rabbi: this, the
> argument goes, is not because he was one, but because the author of
> the Gospel or the section of the church to which he belonged was
> affected by a re-Judaizing tendency, and therefore rabbinized Jesus
> and tempered the extent of his rebellion against Judaism. All the evi-
> dence of the Jewishness of Jesus in the Gospels, on this view, is due

to late tampering with the text, which originally portrayed Jesus as rejecting Judaism.

This is a line that was fashionable at one time and is still to be found in many textbooks. Its implausibility, however, has become increasingly apparent.[4]

The anti-Semitic undertones of the mainstream Christian view have also become increasingly apparent. It is a view that has led to some of the greatest atrocities that human has inflicted upon human. It is no exaggeration to state quite bluntly that the ultimate blame for the Crusades, the Inquisition, and the Holocaust can be squarely laid at the feet of this traditional understanding of Jesus and the early church.

But there is a new paradigm emerging today, one that is increasingly revealing the implausibility of the inherited paradigm. It is seen most clearly in the so-called third quest for the historical Jesus, an approach that understands Jesus as being thoroughly Jewish with no designs on starting a new religion. As was the case with Martin Luther vis-à-vis Catholicism, Jesus simply wanted to reform Judaism from within. The last thing Luther wanted to do was start a new church; the last thing Jesus wanted to do was start a new religion.

The third-quest approach to the historical Jesus is well summed up by one of the school's leading lights, the highly regarded E. P. Sanders (who sounds eerily similar to Maccoby here):

We have again and again returned to the fact that nothing which Jesus said or did which bore on the law led his disciples after his death to disregard it. This great fact, which overrides all others, sets a definite limit to what can be said about Jesus and the law.[5]

Indeed, this is the "great fact" that we have "again and again" run up against in our investigation into James. All of the evidence we have uncovered attests to the fact that James and the apostles retained their Jewish practice and belief, while adding to it their unique belief that Jesus was the promised Messiah of Israel. It can be claimed, as many have, that the apostles quickly "backslid" into Judaism after the death of Jesus, but Hyam Maccoby clearly shows that what we know of the earliest apostolic community disproves this claim:

The implausibility of the "re-Judaization" approach cannot be better illustrated than when it is applied to the Jerusalem movement led by James and the Apostles. This would mean that Jesus' new insights had been lost so quickly that his closest associates acted as if they had never been. Of course, it may be said that Jesus' closest associates never did understand him and, in support of this, various passages in the Gospels may be adduced; e.g., Peter's altercation with Jesus, upbraiding him for announcing the necessity of his sacrificial death . . . But here the following question is appropriate: which is more likely, that Jesus' closest disciples failed to understand his most important message, or that Pauline Christians, writing gospels about fifty years after Jesus' death, and faced with the unpalatable fact that the "Jerusalem Church" was unaware of Pauline doctrines, had to insert into their Gospels denigratory material about the Apostles in order to counteract the influence of the "Jerusalem Church"? Mark's story about Peter, so far from proving that Peter misunderstood Jesus, is evidence of the dilemma of Pauline Christianity, which was putting forward a view of Jesus that was denied by the most authoritative people of all, the leaders of the Jerusalem movement, the companions of Jesus.[6]

A difficult question that Maccoby raises here is whether the gospel writers were as guilty of putting a Pauline spin on things as the Jewish Christian writers were of putting a "Jamesian" spin on things. As Maccoby points out, the Pauline communities faced quite a dilemma in the fact that James and Peter—who any objective observer would agree knew the teachings of Jesus better than Paul (who did not know the historical Jesus at all)—disagreed with Paul's understanding of Jesus' teachings regarding the Law. Consequently, we see Paul constantly trying to prove that his teachings are valid, especially in his arguments in Galatians, but in most of his other letters as well. In fact, it could be said that the purpose of almost all of Paul's letters was to counteract the authority, beliefs, and practices of James and the Jerusalem church. We saw how Paul lost this battle at Antioch, when Peter and Barnabas, at the urging of James, parted ways with Paul over the issue of eating with Gentiles. On this issue, the book of Acts tries hard to "Paulinize" Peter by omitting the salient fact of Peter's break with Paul at Antioch.

That Acts does attempt to put a Pauline face on Peter is best illustrated in the famous scene where Peter receives a vision that teaches him that he should abandon Jewish dietary laws:

About noon the next day, as they were on their journey and approaching the city, Peter went up on the roof to pray. He became hungry and wanted something to eat; and while it was being prepared, he fell into a trance. He saw the heavens opened and something like a large sheet coming down, being lowered to the ground by its four corners. In it were all kinds of four-footed creatures and reptiles and birds of the air. Then he heard a voice saying, "Get up, Peter; kill and eat." But Peter said, "By no means, Lord; for I have never eaten anything that is profane or unclean." The voice said to him again, a second time, "What God has made clean, you must not call profane." (Acts 10:9–15)

This famous passage has traditionally been understood to mark the point where the cobwebs are swept from the brain of the dim-witted Peter, who is ever-so-slow to understand that Jesus had come to sweep away the Law. As Maccoby again astutely asks:

[W]hy was it necessary for Peter to have a special vision to tell him something that, according to the Gospels, he had already been taught by Jesus? Why does Peter say with such unthinking conviction that he even contradicts a voice from God in saying it, "No Lord, no: I have never eaten anything profane and unclean," *thus proclaiming his adherence to the Torah?* Peter, apparently, *has never heard of the abrogation of the Torah,* so that now, several years after the death of Jesus, he has to be slowly and painfully educated into abandoning his unquestioning loyalty to it. The answer given in the Gospels is that Peter and the other Apostles were thick-witted . . . To be quite so thick-witted, however, is incredible; and the solution, on the level of history, rather than pro-Pauline propaganda, is that *Jesus never did abrogate the Torah.* The adherence of the leaders of the so-called "Jerusalem Church" to Judaism proves that *Jesus was never a rebel against Judaism.* The Pauline Church, however, was not content to base its rejection of the Torah on Paul alone, for this would have meant the abandonment of the authority associated with the prestigious "Jerusalem Church," and would have left a suspicious gap between Jesus and Paul. . . . A gradual process of enlightenment is therefore ascribed to the leaders of the "Jerusalem Church," James and Peter, by which their obtuseness is slowly dispelled, and they reach at last the realization that Jesus, during his lifetime, was telling them something that they quite failed to comprehend at the time.[7] (italics mine)

As Maccoby points out, Pauline Christianity could not relinquish the prestigious mother church in Jerusalem. All of the evidence we have uncovered in our investigation into James has brought us smack up against the "wall" of the Jerusalem church, which increasingly stood as a dividing line between Jewish and Gentile Christianity. Maccoby nicely sums up the situation that confronts us at this point:

> [E]verything points to the conclusion that the leaders and members of the so-called "Jerusalem Church" were not Christians in any sense that would be intelligible to Christians of a later date. They were Jews, who subscribed to every item of the Jewish faith. For example, so far from regarding baptism as ousting the Jewish rite of circumcision as an entry requirement into the religious communion, they continued to circumcise their male children, thus inducting them into the Jewish covenant. The first ten "bishops" of the "Jerusalem Church" . . . were all circumcised Jews. They kept the Jewish dietary laws, the Jewish Sabbaths and festivals, including the Day of Atonement (thus showing that they did not regard the death of Jesus as atoning for their sins), the Jewish purity laws (when they had to enter the Temple, which they did frequently), and they used the Jewish liturgy for their daily prayers . . .
>   . . . the first follower of Jesus with whom Paul had friendly contact, Ananias of Damascus, is described as a "devout observer of the Law and well spoken of by all the Jews of that place." (Acts 22:12)

We have seen the evidence in Acts that the early Christian community was not only thoroughly Jewish, but on good terms with their fellow Jews and distinguished only by their belief that Jesus was the Messiah of Israel. And this was not at all unusual or heretical in the eyes of their fellow Jews. Many Jews around the time of Jesus believed that in other figures the Messiah had arrived. Many of the followers of John the Baptist believed that *he* was the Messiah. That Jesus' disciples claimed him to be the Messiah would not necessarily be seen as heretical, or even outlandish, by their fellow Jews, especially if Jesus and his family were of Davidic descent.

In fact, what is becoming increasingly accepted in historical Jesus studies, especially in the third-quest approach exemplified especially in the work of N. T. Wright, is that Jesus did indeed claim Davidic messiahship for himself.* Many beyond the circle of his immediate disciples also accepted that claim. Thus, it is becoming increasingly clear that the traditional understanding, portrayed in the gospels, of large numbers of Jews turning against Jesus as a false messianic claimant, and in fact calling for his death, is a ruinous anti-Semitism that appeared only decades after Jesus' death as the Pauline/Gentile form of Christianity grew and gained power. This development is seen especially in John, the latest of the four gospels.

Maccoby also points out some fascinating things about the way Jesus is portrayed in the book of Acts that most Christians miss, probably because Maccoby is reading the Christian literature through Jewish eyes. Intriguingly enough, he claims the accounts in Acts are "evidently based on early records of the Jerusalem Nazarenes":

> [N]othing is said here about the founding of a new religion. The doctrines characteristic of Christianity as it later developed under the influence of Paul are not present. Thus Jesus is not described as a divine figure, but as "a man singled out by God" [see Acts 2:22]. His resurrection is described as a miracle from God [see Acts 2:23], not as evidence of Jesus' own divinity; and Jesus is not even described as the son of God. Everything said, in fact, is consistent with the attitudes of a Jewish Messianic movement, basing itself entirely on the fulfillment of the Jewish scriptures, and claiming no abrogation or alteration of the Torah.
>
> The belief that Jesus had been resurrected was . . . the mark of the movement after Jesus' death. Without this belief, the movement would simply have ceased to exist, like other Messianic movements. But this belief did not imply any abandonment of Judaism, as long as it did not involve a deification of Jesus or the abrogation of the Torah as the means of salvation.

The belief in Jesus' resurrection was indeed the hallmark innovation (as Maccoby makes painfully clear, the *only* innovation) that the followers of Jesus brought into Judaism. Maccoby then goes on to conclude:

---

*Ever since Bultmann, belief in the literal Davidic descent of Jesus has been suspect in liberal Christian scholarship where the Davidic sonship of Jesus has been generally understood as metaphorical. Even the idea that Jesus claimed messiahship for himself has been suspect.

> It is abundantly clear . . . that James and his followers in the Jerusalem movement saw no contradiction between being a member of their movement and being a fully observant Jew; on the contrary, they expected their members to be especially observant and to set an example in this respect.

Since Hyam Maccoby is a Jew, many Christians will claim his view is biased, that he fails to understand the Gospel of Jesus Christ. But it is interesting that the conclusions of many contemporary Christian historical Jesus scholars, especially of the third-quest school, largely agree with Maccoby. Furthermore, the conclusions of the widely respected mainstream Christian scholar James Dunn sound remarkably like Maccoby:

> [I]t is evident that *the earliest* [Christian] *community in no sense felt themselves to be a new religion, distinct from Judaism* . . . [T]hey saw themselves simply as fulfilled Judaism, the beginning of eschatological Israel . . . Indeed we may put the point more strongly: . . . the earliest Christians were not simply Jews, but in fact continued to be quite orthodox Jews.
>   . . . [T]his is the group with whom Christianity proper all began. Only their belief in Jesus as Messiah and risen . . . mark them out as different from the majority of their fellow Jews. None of the other great Christian distinctives that come to expression in and through Paul are present . . .
>   If we now shift our glance from the beginning of Christianity forward 150 years or so into the second century and beyond, it at once becomes evident that the situation has significantly altered: Jewish Christianity, far from being the only form of Christianity, is now beginning to be classified as unorthodox and heretical.[8]

Dunn's analysis was in fact already recognized and accepted by liberal Christian scholars in Germany in the 1800s, most notably F. C. Baur. As Maccoby notes, "Nineteenth-century New Testament scholarship, on the whole, recognized these facts and gave them due weight. It has been left to twentieth-century scholarship, concerned for the devastating effect of this recognition on conventional Christian belief, to obfuscate the matter."[9]

THE LEGACY OF F. C. BAUR

It was in 1831 that F. C. Baur put forth the revolutionary hypothesis we have already examined that the supposedly united early Christian community was actually more like two clashing political parties, and that the two patron saints of the Christian church—Peter and Paul— were more akin to feuding cousins than brothers in the faith.

Baur was a remarkable man in many ways. A world-class scholar of undisputed integrity, and adept in many fields, he was legendary for his workaholism. In his office every morning by 4 A.M., by the end of his life, Baur had an average literary output equivalent to a five-hun- dred-page book every year for forty years!

What Baur shall be most remembered for, despite some glaring flaws in his work, is that he was the first New Testament scholar to recognize "the forest for the trees"—the first to see the larger picture of the first- century historical reality of Christian origins. Baur's proposal—first for- mally put forward in the article "The Christ Party in the Corinthian Church"—was the opening volley of a revolution in our understandings of Christian origins. But we can recognize today that Baur's theories, while basically accurate, were also biased to a large extent by a deep- rooted anti-Semitism that pervades his thought. Though Baur recognized the thoroughgoing Jewishness of James and the apostles, he, too, believed it to be a consequence of "re-Judaization." Though conserva- tive Christian scholars roundly attacked him for his "liberal" views, in hindsight Baur was still a traditional Pauline Christian who believed that Jesus came to found a new religion superior to Judaism.

One of Baur's most vocal critics in recent times was the esteemed New Testament scholar Johannes Munck. In his acclaimed work, *Paul and the Salvation of Mankind*, Munck succinctly summarizes Baur's theory and points out the inherent weakness in it:

> Baur's view of the development of early Christianity stresses the party contrast between the primitive Church and Paul. He makes the apostles and the whole Church stand on Jewish ground throughout, apart from their belief in the crucified Jesus as the coming Messiah. Everything about Jesus that was the expression of a new religion was either forgotten or completely disregarded in the apostles' memory. When Paul rediscovers the universalism and freedom that Jesus represented, it puts him out of line with the primitive Church, which refuses to approve his message.[10]

Munck then states what he believes to be the basic problem inherent in Baur's theory:

> [I]t is quite incredible that Jesus' disciples, who were those nearest to him during the whole of his ministry, learnt and retained nothing of his life and teaching, but continued to have a Jewish point of view—apart, of course, from their belief that the crucified Jesus was identical with the coming Messiah.

This quote could just as well have come from Maccoby's own hand. When bedfellows as odd as Munck and Maccoby agree on a point as salient as this one, we know we're on to something. Munck simply could not bring himself to believe that the disciples would have retained their traditional Jewish beliefs after being "enlightened" by Jesus, and this is why he rejected Baur's thesis. For his part, Baur was ahead of his time in insisting on the Jewishness of the Jerusalem church and the disharmony of the early church as a whole. What sets him apart from most of today's third-quest scholars is that he assigned the disciples' adherence to the Law to backsliding. But this is where Baur made his only real mistake. As all the evidence we have examined has shown us, the apostles' ongoing adherence to Jewish faith and practice was most emphatically *not* a case of "re-Judaization." As Maccoby starkly makes clear, the disciples had simply *never abandoned* their Jewish beliefs and practices. And the reason—a reason that slaps us modern-day Christians right across the face—is that *Jesus* had not abandoned those beliefs and practices.

Another component of Baur's theory that has remained influential is the idea that it was in the give-and-take (what scholars technically call "dialectic," following the philosopher G. W. F. Hegel) of the friction and struggles between the Jewish Christian and Gentile Christian churches that a new religion—Christianity as we know it today—emerged. Evangelical commentator Timothy George provides one of the best summaries I have come across of Baur's thinking on the dialectical origins of Christianity:

> Baur proposed that the history of early Christianity could be read in terms of the polar opposition between two rival factions. One, led by Paul and Apollos, emphasized the Christian mission to the Gentiles; the other, gathered around Peter and James, stressed the priority of the

Jerusalem church and the continuing validity of the Jewish law for Christian believers . . . According to this view, the Pauline party continued to become more and more radical in its break with Judaism until it was ultimately absorbed into Gnosticism. The Petrine party, on the other hand, became more and more narrow, gradually evolving into such Jewish-Christian sectarian groups as the Ebionites. Eventually a synthesis between the Pauline and Petrine extremes was achieved in the emergence of "early Catholicism."[11]

Hegel's influence on Baur is obvious. Hegel understood all of history to proceed "dialectically": in the struggle between a "thesis" and an "antithesis," a new "synthesis" occurred. In the case of the early church, it was in the struggle between Jerusalem-based Jewish Christianity and Pauline-based Gentile Christianity that the synthesis of Catholic Christianity emerged. It is possible to see this theory played out in the pages of the New Testament. The Jewish Christian "thesis" is represented in the books of Hebrews, James, Jude, and Revelation; the Pauline corpus represents the "antithesis"; and the conciliatory Acts represents the earliest synthesis of the two poles.

Baur used as primary evidence of this struggle the arguments Paul makes against his opponents in Galatians, 1 and 2 Corinthians, and Philippians—opponents who would clearly seem to be strict Jewish Christians who want to "Judaize" Paul's Gentile converts. In Philippians, Paul writes bitterly of them: "Beware of the dogs, beware of the evil workers, beware of those who mutilate the flesh! For it is we who are the circumcision, who worship in the Spirit of God and boast in Jesus Christ and have no confidence in the flesh" (3:1–2). This is one of Paul's classic pieces of vitriol against those who claim that circumcision is necessary for salvation. In Galatians, Paul is furious with the believers in Galatia for being deceived by these "Judaizers": "You foolish Galatians! Who has bewitched you? . . . Did you receive the Spirit by doing the works of the law or by believing what you heard? Are you so foolish? Having started with the Spirit, are you now ending with the flesh?" (3:1–3). In 2 Corinthians, Paul similarly rails against the Corinthian Christians for their gullibility:

I am afraid that as the serpent deceived Eve by its cunning, your thoughts will be led astray . . . For if someone comes and proclaims another Jesus than the one we proclaimed . . . or a different gospel from the one you accepted, you submit to it readily enough. I think that I am not in the least inferior to these super-apostles. (11:3–5)

Just who these "super apostles" are who have been "deceiving" the believers in Corinth is another of the greatly debated questions in New Testament scholarship. Paul goes on to mysteriously describe them as "false apostles, deceitful workers, disguising themselves as apostles of Christ. And no wonder! Even Satan disguises himself as an angel of light. So it is not strange if his ministers also disguise themselves as ministers of righteousness" (1 Cor. 11:13–15). It is these words that caused Baur to come to the conclusion that these "super apostles" were none other than the original apostles. One can see why Baur would think so. Ever since Baur first put forth his disturbing theory, all kinds of exegetical and hermeneutical gymnastics have been performed to conclude otherwise, but Baur's main thesis remains sound.

In the 1800s, Baur's theories were vociferously attacked as heresy. It is no exaggeration to say that he was one of the first victims of the modern academic inquisition. The two leading disciples of the "old master of Tübingen," Eduard Zeller and Albert Schwegler (both brilliant scholars in their own right), were driven out of teaching because of their views. Unfortunately, truth often comes at a perilous price. As Jesus taught, prophets are without honor in their own time.

Baur can also be justifiably criticized for portraying too simplistically a bipolar rivalry between Jewish and Gentile Christianity, an issue that scholars today realize was much more complex than a simple two-party battle. As we have seen, there were many competing factions within the early church, falling along a continuum from conservative "Judaizers" to liberal Hellenistic Christians. James Dunn has summarized how some early attempts were made in the late nineteenth century to amend Baur's theory:

Early on [Baur's theory] was qualified by the recognition that his portrayal of early Christianity in terms of a confrontation between two monolithic blocks was too much of an oversimplification. The Jewish Christians could not be lumped together as a single group opposed to Paul. "Strict or extreme Judaizers" were to be distinguished from "moderate Jewish Christians," and while the former could be linked to Jerusalem, Peter was to be distinguished from

them, with the question whether James should be reckoned a
Judaizer a subject for some debate.[12]

This, then, became a generally accepted alternative to Baur's theory.
Dunn goes on to explain that over a century later scholars were still
attempting to avoid the implications of the original Tübingen theory by
positing other possibilities for the identity of Paul's opponents:

> Baur's basic claim, that the opposition to Paul during his mission
> should be designated as "Judaizers," Jewish Christians who insisted
> that Paul's Gentile converts must be circumcised and become Jews,
> was widely accepted, and indeed became axiomatic in most of the dis-
> cussions of the next hundred years . . .
>
> This broad consensus has received two major challenges in the
> twentieth century . . . W. Lütgert saw Paul's chief opponents at
> Corinth as spiritual enthusiasts, an early type of gnostic libertines . . .
> and saw them also alongside the [Judaizers] as a second front in
> Galatians. And W. Schmithals pushed the case further by arguing that
> in Galatians there are no judaizers in view at all, only Jewish Gnostic
> Christians, with similar claims for Corinthians and Philippians . . .
>
> J. Munck developed the reaction against Baur and the Tübingen
> school on another front by arguing that there was no judaizing party in
> Jerusalem and by rejecting the "pan-Judaizer" hypothesis . . . Paul's let-
> ters were addressed to different situations with different opponents. . . .
> The judaizing opponents in Galatians are *Gentile* Christians keen to
> adopt the practices of the Law . . . the compulsion to "Judaize" did not
> come from Jewish Christianity, which was concerned only for its mis-
> sion within Israel, but was a *Gentile* Christian "heresy." (italics mine)

Gentile Christians *keen* to adopt the practices of the Law? Gentile *men*
keen to be circumcised? The illogic of all this is rather obvious. While
one could assert that the fervor with which many people even today
embrace the religions they convert to could show that Gentiles might
have been willing and even eager to fulfill all the requirements of the
Law, including circumcision, there is evidence to reject this hypothesis.
As we have noted, there were many "God-fearers," Gentiles who
adopted the Jewish faith, but they were only expected to adhere to the
minimal Noahide laws (the regulations stipulated in the Apostolic
Decree). In fact, it was the unworkability of requiring adherence to the

Law for Gentiles that fueled Paul's mission. Although Munck's theories gained much attention from scholars eager to dismiss the Tübingen theory, in hindsight it is quite obvious that Munck's is a last-gasp effort to avoid the increasingly obvious—but for many, unpalatable—facts that Baur first saw almost two centuries ago.

Many others have attempted in the past 175 years to offer viable alternatives to Baur's description of an early church fraught with discord, but the alternatives all falter on the balance beam of common sense. Simply put, we know that Paul faced opposition. That opposition was, in fact, the impetus for the writing of almost all of his letters. Now, if we look at the situation objectively—just based on a commonsense approach to these basic facts—who else could these opponents possibly have been other than *Jewish* Christians, and not just any Jewish Christians, but the apostolic leadership itself? At the time that Paul wrote, *less than twenty years* after the crucifixion, there simply would not have been enough time for "heresies," such as the Gnosticism that Munck and others proposed, to have permeated the widespread Christian communities. Munck's hypothesis, that Paul's opponents were *Gentile* Christians who were enthusiastic for the Law, strains credibility.

Even if, for arguments's sake, there *were* such a thing as Gnostic or Gentile "Judaizers" early on, such novel groups would certainly not have been able to exert any great influence on the communities established by Paul and his missionary companions. And certainly such fledgling heretical groups would not yet have the logistical capability or the necessary authority (which can only come with time or with one's close relationship to the founders) to be sending missionaries to far-flung parts of the empire to convert established Gentile churches to Jewish practice (especially if, as the theory goes, they themselves were not Jewish). And, last but certainly not least, Paul would surely not refer to them as *apostles*, as he does in 2 Corinthians.

Simply put, Who else but the apostles themselves would have had the motive, the ability, and, most importantly, the *authority* (already in the years circa 45–50) to send emissaries to so many far-flung Gentile communities—including Antioch, Corinth, Philippi, and Galatia—to preach adherence to the Law? That it could have been anyone other than the apostles defies all logic. No one other than Jesus' own apostles would posses the authority to influence these new Christians on such an important matter, especially when it was a matter in such serious disagreement with the highest authority in the Gentile churches—Paul himself. No one other than the apostles would dare to take on Paul. And not only challenge Paul, but win!

F. C. Baur was indeed on the right track. He saw the "matching shorelines," but couldn't quite make all the pieces fit since he lacked the proper supporting mechanism, just as Alfred Wegener in his theory of continental drift lacked the supporting evidence of seafloor spreading, which wasn't discovered until later. The most damaging criticism of Baur, in fact, is not that he oversimplified the division in the early church or that he erroneously believed that the Jewish Christians were "backsliders," but rather that his theory as a whole is anti-Semitic insofar as it understands Christianity to be the superior replacement for an inferior Judaism. What has often been little understood is the extent to which he perpetuated an ancient tradition of Christian supersessionism (i.e., that Christianity supersedes Judaism). How this latent anti-Semitism detracts from Baur's theory is revealed quite well in an article in the *Dictionary of Paul and His Letters,* which highlights the all-too-common belief (perpetuated by Baur) that Christianity is a universal religion that God intended to be a superior replacement for the outmoded particularistic religion of Judaism:

> Paul is seen too much as an isolated apostle who alone truly understands the universalism and freedom that Jesus represented. Apparently in the memory of the other leading apostles this has either been forgotten, misunderstood or compromised. A misleading contrast informed Baur's and many of his followers' theology—they posited an absolute opposition between particularism [Judaism] and universalism [Christianity]; . . . from this perspective Paul was seen as a lone contender for the universalism of the gospel in contrast to the primitive church, whose leaders were in varying degrees tribalistic or particularistic in their ongoing commitment to Judaism.[13]

Both in spite of and because of this serious shortcoming of the Tübingen theory, a revival of Baur's theories is occurring under the influence of the third-quest school of thought, especially in the writings of extremely liberal Christian scholars, such as Micheal Goulder and Gerd Lüdemann, and controversial Jewish scholars, such as Robert Eisenman and Hyam Maccoby. Even mainstream Christian scholars, such as James Dunn and Bruce Chilton, and conservative scholars, such as Craig A. Evans, are opening the door to a new acceptance of Baur's theories, but in a revised form that more accurately reflects the complexity and diversity of early Christianity. Dunn, however, warns against falling into the trap that caught Baur: There was no polar opposition between two monolithic camps. In line with his emphasis on the wide but continuous spectrum of belief in the early church, Dunn says, "I go along with the older F. C. Baur thesis at least to the extent that emerging catholicism was a catholic synthesis of several strands and tendencies (and factions) within earliest Christianity."[14]

This leaves us still facing the vital question, Amid all of the variety of early Christian belief, what was the original "orthodoxy"? What was the nature of the originating source from which all of these "strands and tendencies" first divided, and then late re-coalesced to produce a "catholic synthesis"?

THE FIRST ORTHODOXY

James Dunn, like Maccoby, believes that when one tries to get to the root of the earliest, most primitive strand of belief from which the diversity of early Christianity sprang, one is led right back to Jewish Christianity. This might seem rather obvious since Jesus, his family, and his apostles were all Jews. But while this is usually obvious to someone coming at it from outside the Christian tradition, for those inside the Christian tradition the obvious has not always been easy to recognize. In this case, the overgrown and tangled branches of accumulated Christian tradition obscure the forest. Just as often, traditional Christian scholars have harbored a subconscious desire not to *want* to know the truth, which, of course, makes it all the more difficult to see the real picture.

James Dunn is one leading scholar who has made the effort to rise above the treeline. In his examination of the three distinguishing features of later Jewish Christian communities such as the Ebionites (faithful adherence to the Law of Moses, reverence for James, and an adoptionist christology), Dunn sees something the majority of Christian scholars would prefer to ignore:

> If these are indeed the three principal features of heretical Jewish Christianity, then a striking point immediately emerges: *heretical*

Jewish Christianity would appear to be not so very different from the faith of the first Jewish believers.[15]

The three main tenets of Jewish Christian belief and practice that Dunn enumerates are what led to the Jewish Christians being labeled as heretics by the emerging Catholic Church. The Jewish Christians, on the other hand, thoroughly rooted in the teachings of James and the apostles, thought of the Pauline churches as the heretics. And this brings us to the trickiest question in the study of Christian origins: What is orthodoxy, and what is heresy? Dunn notes that by the second century

> there was no uniform concept of orthodoxy at all—only different forms of Christianity competing for the loyalty of believers. In many places, particularly Egypt and eastern Syria [centers of Jewish Christianity], it is . . . likely that what later churchmen called [Jewish] Christianity was the initial form of Christianity . . . The concept of orthodoxy only began to emerge in the struggle between different viewpoints—the party that won claimed the title "orthodox" for itself![16]

Or, to put it in other words, orthodoxy is merely the most successful heresy.

These observations on the nature of orthodoxy and heresy become clearer when one understands that the word "heresy" comes from the Greek *haeresis,* which carries the root meaning of an "opinion" or a "party line." Therefore, in the strict sense of the word, all of the early Christian communities had their own heresy—their own opinion about who Jesus was. It was only many years later—at the Council of Nicaea in 325—that by majority vote it was permanently decided what would forever be the acceptable heresy, which then, by definition, became orthodoxy. Walter Bauer (no relation to F. C. Baur), most well known today for his monumental Greek-English Lexicon, wrote the seminal volume on this idea, *Orthodoxy and Heresy in Earliest Christianity,* in 1934, a groundbreaking work that has had an ever-increasing influence on New Testament scholarship. Bauer powerfully demonstrated that it is difficult to maintain that there ever was any pristine unified doctrine in the early church, only many competing heresies. British scholar, Michael Goulder, who is one of today's strongest supporters of the Tübingen theory, provides a succinct analysis of the situation revealed to us in the light of the ideas of Baur and Bauer:

> When in church life there is an irreconcilable difference over important doctrine, there are winners and losers. The winning party becomes the church, and its opinion is orthodoxy . . . the losing party is driven out of the church and becomes a sect . . . or heresy . . . In the early Christian church the Petrines won at Antioch (Gal. 2.11–14); but Paul played his cards carefully, and did not split away. In the second century the Paulines won and the Aramaic [Jewish Christian] churches split away . . . and became heretical sects called the Ebionites and the Nazarenes.[17]

As we have noted before, the Ebionites claimed that they were in fact the direct descendants of the Jerusalem church. Wishing to keep its blinders on, most Christian scholarship has dismissed this claim, but there is the fascinating legend recorded in Eusebius and Epiphanius of the escape of the Jerusalem Christians prior to the Roman invasion thanks to the warning of a prophecy, whence they fled to Pella in Transjordan. If this legend has any basis in fact (and most legends have at least some basis in fact), it would be from Pella that the later Jewish Christian communities such as the Nazoreans, the Ebionites, and the Elkesaites developed. The flight to Pella could explain how the Jewish Christian "heresy" spread beyond Palestine.

One of the first heresy hunters of the emerging Catholic Church was the church father Irenaeus, who wrote the mammoth five-volume *Against Heresies*. Irenaeus sums up the distinctive beliefs and practices of the heretical Ebionites thus:

> They use the gospel according to Matthew only, and repudiate the apostle Paul, maintaining that he was an apostate from the Law . . . [T]hey practice circumcision, persevere in those customs which are enjoined by the Law, and are so Judaic in their style of life that they even adore Jerusalem as if it were the house of God. (*AH* 1.26.2)

We can see from Irenaeus's description that the Ebionites plainly fit the criteria of "Jewish Christian." It is quite likely that all of the later Jewish Christian groups ultimately derived from a Nazirite movement in Jerusalem in which, as we saw in Acts 21, James was closely involved.

Mainstream Anglican scholar Bruce Chilton, one of the organizers of the international Consultation on James, has come to the conclusions that James was indeed a Nazirite, that he most likely had at least some connection with this strict sect, and that this is the most likely reason that Jesus was called Jesus "of Nazareth":

> [M]y suggestion that James was a Nazirite, and saw his brother's movement as focused on producing more Nazirites, enables us to address an old and as yet unresolved problem of research. Jesus, bearing a common name, is sometimes referred to as "of Nazareth" in the Gospels . . . There is no doubt but that a geographical reference is involved (see John 1:45–46). But more is going on here. Jesus is rarely called "of Nazareth" or "from Nazareth" . . . He is usually called "Nazoraean" or "Nazarene." Why the adjective, and why the uncertainty in spelling? The Septuagint [the Greek translation of the Hebrew Bible] shows us that there were many different transliterations of "Nazirite": that reflects uncertainty as to how to convey the term in Greek . . . Some of the variants are in fact very close to what we find used to describe Jesus in the Gospels. . . .
>
> For James and those who were associated with him, Jesus' true identity was his status as a Nazirite.[18]

Conservative scholar, Craig Evans, coeditor with Chilton of the compendium of research papers *James the Just and Christian Origins*, follows the trail of evidence to another startling conclusion. He notes some astonishing commonalities between James and Jesus regarding the reason for their deaths:

> According to the four New Testament Gospels, Jesus engaged in controversy with the ruling priests, a controversy which included a demonstration in the Temple precincts, and was subsequently handed over to the Roman governor, who executed him as the "king of the Jews.". . .
>
> Although different at points, the fate that overtook James, the brother of Jesus, is similar . . .
>
> Jesus had been accused of blasphemy, while James later was accused of being a lawbreaker. Both were condemned by High Priests—High Priests who were related by marriage. Jesus was handed

over to the Roman governor, who complied with the wishes of the ruling priests, while James was executed without the approval of Roman
authority . . . In the case of Jesus, Pilate saw warrant in execution, for
a serious political charge could be made (i.e., "king of the Jews"). In
the case of James, however, evidently no such compelling case could
be made.[19]

Of this interesting set of parallels, Evans reaches a conclusion quite
similar to that of John Dominic Crossan:

> That both brothers, Jesus and James, should be done away by
> Caiaphas and his brother-in-law Ananus is surely more than mere
> coincidence. A Davidic element . . . complete with devotion to the
> Temple . . . and probable criticism of Temple polity . . . seems to be
> the thread that runs throughout.
>
> The line of continuity between Jesus and brother James, the leader
> of the Jerusalem church, supports the contention that Jesus and James
> may very well have advanced the same agenda over against the Temple
> establishment, and both suffered the same fate at the hands of essen-
> tially the same people . . . The subsequent, partially parallel career of
> James moves us to view the activities of his brother Jesus in terms of
> the Jewish Temple and teachings that his contemporaries understood
> as holding serious implications for this sacred institution. For this rea-
> son we must eschew recent faddish scholarship that minimizes the role
> of the Temple in the life and ministry of Jesus.

In the scholarship of Evans and Crossan, we find another instance
of scholars from the conservative and liberal camps reaching the same
conclusion on the thorough Jewishness of James and Jesus. One of the
very few common conclusions reached by the many scholars engaged in
the current quest for the historical Jesus is that Jesus' arrest and crucifixion were a direct result of his terroristic protest in the Temple, which
is, significantly, one of the few stories relayed in all four Gospels (Matt.
21:12–17; Mark 11:15–18; Luke 19:45–48; John 2:13–22).

According to the synoptic gospels, Jesus was arrested not long after
his attempt to cleanse the Temple. And if Jesus was indeed of the line of
David, this attempt to purify the Temple would have been his royal pre-
rogative. This was the temple envisioned by David and built by his son,
Solomon. And the Temple was the house of God (in Jesus' words, "my

Father's house," as stated in Luke 2:49 and John 2:16). Jesus and James apparently shared the same agenda of reforming (or perhaps even doing away with) the corrupt leadership of the aristocratic ruling Sadducees.

And let us not forget that Jesus was executed on the Roman charge of treason—for claiming to be the "king of the Jews." While most modern scholars have eschewed the idea that Jesus was actually of Davidic descent (the generally accepted idea being that this was a later claim of the early church), the Davidic ancestry of Jesus is one of the core claims of the New Testament. It is rather ironic that Jewish scholars have taken the Davidic claim more seriously than Christian scholars. Again, Hyam Maccoby notes what many Christian scholars have failed to see:

> [T]he Gospels say quite distinctly that Jesus founded a Church. Why, then, did the Apostles of Jerusalem act as if no Church had been founded, and they were still members of the Jewish religious community? This leads to the further puzzling question: if Jesus, as the Gospels say, chose Peter as the leader of the Church, why were the Nazarenes, after Jesus' death, led not by Peter, but by James . . . a person who is not even mentioned in the Gospels as a follower of Jesus in his lifetime? This is the kind of contradiction that, if logically, considered, can lead us to the true picture of the history of Jesus' movement in Jerusalem, as opposed to the picture which the later Church wished to propagate.[20]

The two questions that Maccoby puts forth are the main questions we have had to face in our investigation into the mystery of James. The answers are obvious when we fully understand the reasons for which Jesus and James were put to death. Maccoby's explanation is well worth quoting at length as a summary of where we have arrived in our own investigation:

> To understand . . . we must remind ourselves of what Jesus really was. He was not the founder of a Church, but a claimant to a throne. When Peter . . . hailed Jesus as "Messiah," he was using the word in its Jewish sense, not in the sense it acquired in the later Christian church. In other words, Peter was hailing Jesus as King of Israel. Jesus' response was to give Peter his title of "Rock" and to tell him that he would have "the keys of the kingdom of Heaven." The meaning of this phrase, in its Jewish context, is quite different from what later

Christian mythology made of it, when it pictured Saint Peter standing at the gates of Heaven, holding the keys, and deciding which souls might enter . . . the reference is not to some paradise in the great beyond, but to the Messianic kingdom on Earth, of which Jesus had just allowed himself to be proclaimed King—i.e., the Jewish kingdom, of which the Davidic monarch was constitutional ruler, while God was the only real King.

By giving Peter the "keys of the kingdom," Jesus was appointing him to be his chief minister . . .

. . . This explains fully the relationship between Peter and James . . . in the movement, and why James suddenly rises to prominence at this point. When Jesus became King, his family became the royal family, at least for those who believed in Jesus' claim to the Messiahship. Thus, after his death, his brother James, as his nearest relative, became his successor; not in the sense that he became King James, for Jesus was believed to be alive, having been resurrected by a miracle of God, and to be waiting in the wings for the correct moment to return to the stage as the Messianic King. James was thus a Prince Regent, occupying the throne temporarily in the absence of Jesus.

Further proof that this was the situation can be derived from what is known about other members of Jesus' family. After James . . . was executed . . . he was succeeded by another member of Jesus' family, Simeon, son of Cleophas, who was Jesus' cousin. This again shows that the structure of the "Jerusalem Church" was monarchical, rather than ecclesiastical. Moreover, there is evidence that the Romans saw the matter in this light, for they issued decrees against all the descendants of the house of David, ordering them to be arrested; and Simeon . . . was eventually executed by the Romans as a pretender to the throne of David.

Maccoby's assessment neatly ties together all of the evidence we have evaluated in our investigation of James. Another controversial Jewish scholar, Robert Eisenman, summarizes the conclusion our investigation has brought us to quite succinctly: "Once James has been rescued from the oblivion into which he has been cast . . . [it] will . . . no longer be possible to avoid, through endless scholarly debate and other evasion syndromes, the obvious solution to the problem of the Historical Jesus . . . the answer to which is simple. Who and whatever James was, so was Jesus."[21]

The answer is indeed quite obvious, once one sees the larger picture that comes into view when all of the puzzle pieces are put together. But the emergent picture is not easy for many Christians to take in all at once. Now that we have completed the puzzle, we find ourselves facing a revolutionary (not to say heretical) paradigm—that not only were James and the apostles thoroughly Jewish in their beliefs and practice, but so was Jesus: the original orthodoxy was in fact a strict form of messianic Judaism. And we have been led to this conclusion, inexorably and step by step, by none other than the brother of the Messiah himself, James the Just—the unsung hero of Christianity.

9

THE FORGOTTEN HERO: JAMES AND THE ORIGINS OF CHRISTIANITY

*"Do not think that I have come to abolish the law . . .
I have come not to abolish but to fulfill."*

JESUS, MATTHEW 5:17

In light of the previous chapters, it should be quite clear why James lies at the storm-center in the struggles of the early church to decide what was orthodoxy and what was heresy. It is certainly no coincidence that he is connected with so many defining events in the development of the early church, both within his lifetime and for centuries afterward. James's undisputed leadership of the Jerusalem church for thirty years after Jesus' death, his unquestioned wisdom and vision at the Jerusalem Council, and his exalted status in the memory of the later Jewish Christian communities, all attest to the paramount role that James played in the struggles of the early church to define its theology vis-à-vis parent Judaism.

SPLITTING UP THE FAMILY

Two of the most important Christian articles of faith that developed in conjunction with the emergence of the embryonic Catholic Church were the doctrine of the virgin birth and its codicil, the doctrine of the perpetual virginity of Mary. As these Marian beliefs became ever more central to Christian theology, early church Fathers such as Origen, Epiphanius, Eusebius, and Jerome began to seek alternative explanations for the relationship of Jesus to those whom the early Christian writings call his "brothers" and "sisters." This brings us to a fascinating apocryphal writing, generally dated early third century, known as the *Protevangelium of James* which I have intentionally reserved for now. Although quite popular in its time, the *Protevangelium* (Proto-gospel) was rejected by Jerome as heresy, and its use in the Western (but not the Eastern) Churches of the Roman Empire soon died out. The *Protevangelium* is a nativity story akin to the nativity stories in Matthew and Luke, but with some surprising differences. In the *Protevangelium*, the birth of Jesus takes a backseat to the details of Mary's virginity. Here, a midwife who aids in Jesus' delivery discovers upon inspection that Mary's virginity is miraculously intact after the delivery of Jesus. We can starkly see the earliest traces of a belief in the perpetual virginity of the Mother of Jesus.

The *Protevangelium* also portrays Joseph as a widower with children from a previous marriage, thus explaining away Jesus' siblings. In a rather sublime passage in the *Protevangelium*, a youthful James leads the ass on which the pregnant Mary rides as the family makes their way to Bethlehem (17.2). This became a beloved story in the Eastern Orthodox Church, where the theme worked its way into art. A famous fourteenth-century painting by Giotto, the *Flight into Egypt*, depicts a variation of the story, with James leading the ass on which Mary is tenderly carrying the infant Jesus as the family flees King Herod's massacre of the infants. A more poignant statement of the essence of the Epiphanian theory—that Jesus' siblings were actually step-siblings—would be hard to find.

Jerome, however, rejected the *Protevangelium* because it did not go far enough in dissociating Joseph's children from Jesus. Jerome, who was the person mainly responsible for priestly celibacy in the Catholic Church, also advocated virginity for Joseph. Jerome proposed that the "brothers" and "sisters" mentioned in the New Testament were actually Jesus' *cousins*, based on an eisegesis ("reading into" a passage, essentially a wishful interpretation) of two statements in Mark and John. In John, one of the women standing alongside Jesus' mother at the cross is her sister, who seems, curiously, to also be named Mary: "Meanwhile, standing near the cross of Jesus were his mother, and his mother's sister, Mary the wife of Clopas, and Mary Magdalene" (19:25). Depending on how one interprets the syntax of this sentence, there could be three or four women here.

"Mary the wife of Clopas" could refer back to "his mother's sister," making it a total of three women; or Mary's sister could be unnamed, making it four women at the cross. Jerome concludes that Mary the wife of Clopas is "his mother's sister," thus making her Jesus' aunt. Jerome further concludes that this is the same Mary mentioned in Mark: "There were also women looking on from a distance; among them were Mary Magdalene, and Mary the mother of James the younger and Joses, and Salome" (15:40). Proceeding under two unfounded assumptions (that "Mary the mother of James the younger and Joses" is the same Mary mentioned in John and that she is Jesus' aunt), Jerome then makes the further jump that "James the younger and Joses" must be the same James and Joses named in Matthew 6:3 as being two of Jesus' "brothers," thus actually making them Jesus' *cousins!* By this exegetical sleight of hand, Jerome rescues both Mary *and* Joseph from the stain of sexual intercourse.

Due to Jerome's powerful influence, this understanding came to be Roman Catholic dogma. Since James was now no longer the brother of Jesus, any lingering interest in the erstwhile bishop of the church quickly waned. Thus it was that James the Just, the eldest brother of Jesus, and *the* leading figure in earliest Christianity, became a forgotten man.

THE FALLOUT OF WAR

One other significant event conspired to sweep James into the dustbins of history. The siege of Jerusalem by the Romans in 70 C.E. resulted in the dissolution of the Jerusalem church and the scattering of those who upheld Jewish Christian beliefs into the Diaspora. Living in the Gentile world, where their position was far less influential, any esteem that the Jewish Christians had enjoyed quickly diminished, especially as the Gentile churches flourished (with Paul's letters forming the basis for their theology). The final nail in the coffin for Jewish Christianity came when the Jewish Christian views about Jesus began to be declared officially heretical by the growing power of the dominant church in Rome.

With the loss of the Temple and the central authority of Jerusalem, infant Christianity was soon weaned of its Jewish sustenance and nurtured almost exclusively on Pauline teachings and Gentile understandings. Then, in its later adolescence, Gentile Catholic Christianity severed any lingering ties with mother Judaism and based its theology completely on Paul's teaching of faith in Christ as the replacement for the Law. At the same time, Jesus' crucifixion came to be interpreted as the atoning sacrifice by which God's new covenant with humanity was consummated and sealed with blood. Bereft of its Jewish roots, the church came to understand the new covenant through Jesus as a complete replacement for the "old" covenant that God had made with the Jews. And once the child rebelled against the parent to the extent that it declared the old covenant no longer effectual even for Jews, the ugly roots of anti-Semitism began to take hold.

This brings us now to the bottom-line question: What would Jesus have thought of the development of the early church? Would Jesus have agreed with how Paul interpreted his ministry and his message? In short, is the Christian church that emerged as the official religion of the Roman Empire what Jesus would have wanted? Paul's teachings are being seen by a rapidly growing number of modern scholars and writers as a distortion of what Jesus taught, and the development of the Christian church as a travesty of the original Jewish beliefs and teachings of Jesus. Yet, in the end, the Christian Church that developed was actually the salvation of Jesus' teaching, for without the rise to power of the Church of Rome, the Christian movement would surely have died out, and Jesus' message would have faded into obscurity. Though many contemporary scholars have claimed (with some justification) that Paul essentially "invented" Christianity, without the theological innovations that Paul brought into it, the Jesus movement would surely have died. While the Christian church that emerged indeed has many flaws, and has committed many grievous sins, it has managed (to some extent despite itself) to preserve the essential story and teaching of Jesus for the ages.

PARTICULARISM AND UNIVERSALISM

Pauline Christianity survived because it was the most successful of all the early heresies (or parties) of the Christian movement. And it was the most successful heresy for a simple and quite legitimate reason—it had the most universal appeal. James and the Jewish Christians saw their mission as being almost exclusively to the *Jews*. And it must be emphasized yet again that James's mission was the continuation of Jesus' mission. John Painter comments:

> The evidence of the Gospels suggests that James, in limiting his active
> role in mission to the Jews, was consistent with the practice of Jesus for
> whom, according to the Gospels (which reflect the reality of the mission
> to the nations), mission beyond the people of Israel was exceptional.

James, centered in Jerusalem with a focus on the mission to the Jews, had every right to think that his approach to mission was true to the mission of Jesus and that the mission of Paul was without adequate precedent in the practice of Jesus . . . Nevertheless . . . evidence suggests that Jesus was not strictly observant of Jewish purity laws, and it can be argued that the Law-free mission to the nations is an extension of the logic arising from the exceptional practice of Jesus.[1]

With only a very few exceptions (at least as far as we know from the gospels), Jesus' mission was aimed exclusively at the people of Israel and James's mission clearly reflects this, but as Painter notes, Paul's Gentile mission had its roots in the practice of Jesus as well: "The Pauline position was an extension of the exceptional practice of Jesus, which did not wait until Israel first enjoyed the blessings and was satisfied before extending the blessing to the nations."

The prime example of Jesus' "exceptional practice" is the well-known story of the Gentile woman who begs Jesus to heal her demon-possessed daughter (Matthew 15:21–28; Mark 7:24–30). Here is Matthew's version:

> Jesus left that place and went away to the district of Tyre and Sidon. Just then a Canaanite woman from that region came out and started shouting, "Have mercy on me, Lord, Son of David; my daughter is tormented by a demon." But he did not answer her at all. And his disciples came and urged him, saying, "Send her away, for she keeps shouting after us." He answered, "I was sent only to the lost sheep of the house of Israel." But she came and knelt before him, saying, "Lord, help me." He answered, "It is not fair to take the children's food and throw it to the dogs." She said, "Yes, Lord, yet even the dogs eat the crumbs that fall from their master's table." Then Jesus answered her, "Woman, great is your faith! Let it be done for you as you wish." And her daughter was healed instantly.

Quite surprisingly, Jesus is hesitant to help this needy woman, even likening her to a dog (a Jewish term of derision for Gentiles) begging for scraps at the table prepared for God's children, the Jews. Many defensive explanations have been offered for Jesus' most un-Jesus-like behavior here (I must confess to having used these myself in sermons to try to "explain away" the import of this passage), but Jesus' hesitancy to reach beyond Israel is quite clear from his blunt response to the woman: "I was sent only to the lost sheep of Israel." Of course, he does in fact end up helping her, after she dares to rebut him.

The traditional Christian explanation for Jesus' behavior in this passage is that Jesus' mission *during his lifetime* could only be focused on the Jews, but later, through his post-resurrection commissioning of Paul as the Apostle to the Gentiles, Jesus also brought the Gospel to the nations. As we have seen, traditional Jewish belief was that the salvation of the Gentiles would come *through Israel,* an idea rooted in scriptures such as Isaiah's prophecy of the Gentile nations carrying their treasures into the Temple in Jerusalem on the Day of the Lord. The prophets likened the Temple on Mt. Zion to a beacon on a hill, bringing light and salvation to all nations.

In light of this image of the beacon, it is fascinating to look again at James's adjudication of the Jerusalem Council, called to decide the question of the salvation of the Gentiles (most emphatically, those in attendance, including Paul, were not concerned about the salvation of the Jews). In his concluding remarks at the Council, James quoted the prophet Amos:

> *After this I will return,*
> *And I will rebuild the dwelling of David,*
> *which has fallen;*
> *from its ruins I will rebuild it,*
> *and I will set it up,*
> *so that all other peoples may seek the Lord—*
> *even all the Gentiles over whom my name has been called.*

For as much distance as is often put between James and Paul, James did support Paul's mission to the Gentiles; and, conversely, Paul continued to uphold the centrality of the Jerusalem church. Paul believed that through his mission, and especially through his collection for the Jerusalem church, he was fulfilling the prophecies of the streaming of the Gentiles into Jerusalem, thus ushering in the Day of the Lord. In the end, James's concerns and Paul's concerns were the same: to bring God's salvation to all people through Messiah Jesus.

One of the main purposes of the Jerusalem Council was to delineate the parameters for the twin missions to the Jews and Gentiles. While the goal was the same—to proclaim the Good News of Christ's resurrection

IN BED that night, Jacques pulled the blankets up round his shoulders. There was no fat on his body, where the first muscles of manhood were packed firm and taken carelessly for granted. As he lay, he knew what Olivier meant by the feeling that came into the body at this age, the sensation of permanent excitement, as though he was continually crouched at the starting line, waiting for a race to begin. He gripped the blanket in both hands and vowed never to give in to compromise and fatigue. However rocky the path, he would not look down at his feet and allow his life to contract within that view: he would keep his gaze fixed on the widest horizon. The words of the psalm they had sung in church came back to him: "I will lift up mine eyes unto the hills . . ." That line would be his reminder, his coat of arms.

He relaxed his grip on the blanket and allowed himself a silent smile. He was a practical youth who made tables and had taught himself to dissect rats; as such, he knew that there was a much more immediate problem to be solved: he must find a way to study and a means of support.

His smile broadened in the darkness. I am too young, he thought. I am, perhaps, absurd. Now I shall sleep, and think about the fence, the roof, my mother and the chance of goose rillettes from the market.

But then he thought again. Dear God, make me great. Make me good. Amen.

THE FOLLOWING evening, when Jacques returned from the woods, he heard the unusual sound of voices coming from his father's house. They reached him as he opened the gate into the orchard and there was something in them that made him hurry. He ran round to the front of the house and let himself into the parlor.

Grand-mère stood with her back to the scullery door, rigid, with her arms at her sides; Tante Mathilde was screaming, red-faced and tearful in the middle of the room, and at the foot of the stairs was the encrusted, tangled figure of Olivier. He held in his right hand one of the saw blades from Jacques's table, with which he appeared to have gouged a hole in his left forearm. Blood ran in narrow streams down over his open palm and onto the floor.

Tante Mathilde screamed incoherent abuse. "You madman. You wretched lunatic! What have you done to your father's house? Kill yourself for all I care. Go on. Take the blade and cut your throat. Why don't you? You wicked, wicked man!"

Olivier took two paces toward her, still sawing at his arm.

"Don't bring that thing near me! Did you see that, Grand-mère? He's trying to attack me. He wants to kill me! Jacques, do something. Get the blade off him."

"It's all right," said Jacques. "He doesn't want to hurt anyone, do you, Olivier?" He did not want to touch his brother, but tried to catch his eye. Olivier's gaze was turned wholly inward; Jacques had never seen him so far away.

"What happened?" said Jacques.

Grand-mère at last gave voice. It was thin, but firm, with a strong local accent. "I heard a noise from my room. Upstairs. I went to look and found . . ." She seemed to struggle for a name, ". . . him . . . Olivier. He was in your room. He'd smashed everything. All the jars and everything. He'd written words on the walls. It was a mess. I told him to go back to his stable. Then he came down here and started shouting at Mathilde."

"That's right," said Mathilde. "He wants to kill me, I know it. He's always hated me. We should send him away somewhere. Get rid of him. But your father's too kindhearted."

Jacques cautiously put his hand on Olivier's arm. "What is it, Olivier? What's the matter? You can tell me. No one's going to hurt you. Tell me. Like old times. Like the old days when we used to talk."

Olivier turned to face Jacques. His tongue emerged from the hair that covered his mouth; it moved along a line where the lips must be. He swallowed and said, "I had to kill the spiders that were in me. They were laying eggs in my arm, under the skin. I was told to kill them."

"Where are they now, Olivier?"

"I killed them, I killed them."

"I'm going to get the gendarme," said Tante Mathilde.

"No," said Jacques. "There is no gendarme in Saint Agnès. Anyway, Olivier is all right. You'll be all right, won't you, Olivier? Shall we go to the stable? And I'll bring you something to eat. Would you like a glass of water?"

"Put him in with the pig," said Tante Mathilde. "Until your father gets home. Look at him. He doesn't know his own name."

"Olivier?" said Jacques.

"You see. He didn't answer. And who's this?" She poked Jacques in the ribs. "Go on. Tell me. Who's this? See! He doesn't know his own brother."

"Leave him alone," said Jacques. "I can manage him." He took a pace toward Olivier, who thrust the blade out toward Jacques's chest.

"These are my instructions," Olivier said.

Grand-mère edged back toward the scullery, then turned and scuttled out. They heard the door of her room slam shut and a bolt being drawn.

"I'm going to get help," said Tante Mathilde. "I'm going to get him taken away from here. I'm going—"

"I have an idea," said Jacques. "Why don't we go and get the Curé? He'll know what to do. He's a man of God and he was a doctor before that. He knows what—"

"Doctor! He doesn't need a doctor, he needs to be in prison. As for saying his prayers, it's a bit late for that, isn't it?"

Jacques looked at his stepmother. For the first time in his life, he had the intoxicating certainty that he knew more than a superior.

"Tante Mathilde, if I stay with Olivier, I can make sure he does no more damage. And if you go to the Curé, you'll be safe. He'll know what to do. He knows people, the kind of people we don't. And my father would be pleased, would he not, that you had turned to the right person for help?"

Grumbling, Tante Mathilde went to fetch her bonnet and coat.

"Please tell him it's urgent. Say I asked him to come as quickly as possible."

When Tante Mathilde had gone, Jacques took Olivier to the scullery, took the blade from him, pumped some water into a bucket and washed his arm over the stone sink. In the drawer of an old dresser, Jacques found a white cloth which he tore into pieces; he packed the wound with them and tied one strip tightly round the forearm. While he had him there, he took the opportunity to wash his brother's filth-encrusted hands in the bucket.

"Do you want to come up to your room? Would you like to sit on your old bed?" It occurred to him that, until help came, his brother had a short spell of freedom that he might enjoy.

Olivier made no reply; he had started the head-rolling with which Jacques had become anxiously familiar. Jacques led the way upstairs and Olivier, after hesitating for a moment, followed him along the landing.

Jacques turned in horror to Olivier when he saw the inside of his room. The jars along the windowsill had been smashed on the floor, leaving their contents where the vinegar ate into the bare wood of the boards. His collection of moths and butterflies had been ripped from their mounts; his notes and exercise books were torn up or disfigured by Olivier's scrawl, hastily done with the pen Jacques had left on the table. The pieces of machinery were scattered on the floor, while on the wall Olivier had written with his finger in black ink. The words were unfamiliar to Jacques, though the drag of flesh through ink on the white plaster gave them a fearful look, like the words at Belshazzar's feast.

"Come," said Jacques. He took Olivier's arm awkwardly, a young man with no experience of tenderness toward another. "Come and sit here. Why don't you lie down and rest if you'd like to? It's your old bed." He swept some moth wings from the cover.

Olivier perched on the edge of the mattress, rocked his head back and forth and scraped at the hair on his cheek.

It was the first time Jacques had seen his face in full daylight for a year, and he was surprised by how much of the boy he remembered was still visible behind the matted beard. The blue eyes with their hazel flecks, the soft, unmarked skin beneath the eyes, with a handful of childish freckles. Was it possible that his invisible mouth was twitching into its old half-smile? What was missing, he thought, was Olivier. Some invader had taken control of his body and had assumed his voice; it was not an impersonation, it was an inhabitation. He was possessed. How fragile had he been, how slight his own character that it had been so utterly displaced?

Jacques sat down next to Olivier and took his washed hands between his own. The surge of adult confidence he had felt with Tante Mathilde had now deserted him; he was like a child again.

"I don't mind about the room. I can do the drawings again."

Olivier began to moan and move his head up and down; his eyes moved rapidly from side to side.

Jacques held his brother's hands tight between his own. "Olivier, I will do everything I can for you. I will try to make you well. I swear to you."

"I forbid you," said Olivier.

"I'll ask the Curé if he knows where—"

"The Curé does what I tell him."

Olivier stood up and pulled his hands away. He stood among the debris of his brother's endeavors, bits of animal and glass about his feet.

Jacques said, "If I can just get away from here, Olivier . . . Someone will help me. Perhaps the Curé. I will come for you. I will return."

He made his way across to Olivier and held out his hand. "I will make it the mission of my life," he said.

He offered his hand again, palm up, to his brother. Very slowly, Olivier moved toward him, half a step at a time. When they were almost touching, Olivier looked straight past him and laughed.

From downstairs, they heard voices.

Old Rebière had returned from work to find the new Curé in his parlor and his wife in tears.

"He tried to kill me!" said Tante Mathilde. "He was waving his knife at me."

"What's he doing here?" Rebière gestured toward Abbé Henri.

"Oh," said Tante Mathilde, "Jacques said I should go and get help. I don't know why. I was just glad to be out of harm's way."

"I am a friend of your son's," said Abbé Henri. "It is natural that he should turn to me at a difficult moment."

"Yes, Father," said Rebière, as though remembering himself. "Where is the boy?"

"Upstairs," said Jacques from the doorway. "He's all right. He is quite calm."

Rebière went and stood with his back to the stone chimneypiece while the others waited for him to speak.

"We shall have to get rid of him. There are places where they can be locked up. I know. He has been in one before."

"They are not the kind of thing you would want for your son," said Abbé Henri. "In the countryside we have always looked after our own. It is God's way."

"And is it God's choice that he should be a lunatic?"

"All such afflictions are part of the divine plan. God in the end is merciful."

"And is it God's way that he should live with the horse?"

"No, Monsieur. I understand that was your decision."

Rebière snorted. "I shall see what I can arrange when I next go to Vannes. He can't stay here anymore."

Jacques said, "Father, couldn't Olivier come and sleep in my room? Perhaps he would feel safer if he was back in the house."

Rebière shook his head. "He had his chance. You can all go about your business now. Leave this to me."

Olivier had silently descended the stairs and was now standing in the doorway next to Jacques.

Abbé Henri took a step forward into the smoky gloom of old Rebière's parlor. His hair, prematurely gray and worn long at the back, covered the square white collar and touched the shoulders of the soutane; his unbearded face appeared anxious in the candlelight.

"Here is your son, Monsieur, a fine-looking young man who needs only a bath and visit to the barber. You cannot wish for him to live among the lunatics at the mad-hospital. I have visited such places and I would not send my dog there to die, Monsieur. I beg you to find some accommodation for the boy at home. One day such poor unfortunates will be cured, as modern medicine has cured so many illnesses that baffled our ancestors. It is Olivier's misfortune to have been born too soon for our medical knowledge. Have pity on him, Monsieur. I beg you."

"Chains," said Rebière. "I suppose that might be an answer. If we kept him chained he couldn't run out and attack my wife."

Everyone looked at Olivier, who was now still, almost serene, like a John the Baptist whose message had been delivered, waiting for another voice to call him in the wilderness.

"Father," said Rebière, "you may go. Jacques, take Olivier to the stable and make sure the door is bolted. Mathilde, tell Grand-mère to put dinner on the table. Good night, Father. This way, please."

Rebière held the door open for the priest, who, with a glance back to Jacques and Olivier, stepped out reluctantly into the night.

THE BLACKSMITH lived at the bottom of the main street in Saint Agnès; the open top half of his door revealed a scruffy parlor through which his wife led Jacques out into a yard, on the other side of which was the forge.

The blacksmith was working a horseshoe on the anvil when Jacques, against his will, went and stood opposite him. When he had finished hammering the metal into shape, he tossed it casually into a stone water trough where it hissed for a moment, then was still. Only then did he look up to Jacques.

"What do you want?"

"Some chains, a ring that can be fixed and two . . . circular pieces that can be closed."

"Manacles?" The blacksmith, a slight man with a grayish face, was known as someone who spoke little.

"Well," said Jacques. "Like manacles, I suppose. That shape."

"What's it for?"

"I don't know. My father . . . Something for his employer. A tenant wanted them."

"How big?"

"About . . . I suppose . . ." Jacques made a circle with his hands, roughly wrist-sized.

"How much chain?"

Jacques spread both his arms out wide. "About twice that much."

"You can come tomorrow evening, at the same time."

Two days later Jacques was excused work by his father and sent to the stable. First, he took out the mare and tethered her outside; then he shoveled up the old straw and excrement and dumped them in the midden on the far side of the yard. Under Olivier's uninterested gaze, he swept the stone floor with water, then took the hefty ring he had collected from the blacksmith and hammered it by its attached point through the back wall of the stable. The point had screw threads that went through a horizontal plate, so that when the nut was tightened, it was braced against the outside wall. Inside, Jacques ran the chain through the loop and attached it at each end, as instructed, to the manacles.

He filled the stable with fresh straw and led the horse back into her stall. He looked at Olivier. Thus far, he had managed without difficulty: something about the large hammer, the weight and swing of it in his hand, the wood on the soft skin of his palm, was reassuringly mundane. It was like putting up a fence.

When it came to asking Olivier to go back inside, however, he began to falter. His brother was so docile. In the morning, he had helped Olivier to wash beneath the pump and change his clothes; now when he put his arm round him, he felt his soft hair and it reminded him of when they had been children and had wrestled together on the floor: a memory from before he was even fully conscious, of a blessed time. Olivier sat on the fresh straw and allowed Jacques to close the manacles round his wrists and to lock them as the blacksmith had showed him.

Olivier said nothing until it was done, then he looked up at Jacques with his eyes full of bewilderment, and Jacques knelt down beside him, sobbing, smelling Olivier's special sweet smell, feeling his brother's heart against his ribs.

II

IN ENGLAND, THE WEEK BEFORE CHRISTMAS 1876 WAS COLD, NO-
where more so than in the wind-troubled flatlands whose coast lies
between the Wash and the Humber estuary. In Torrington, a village
twelve miles as the angels flew from the cathedral spire of Lincoln, the
boys ran down to the frozen duck pond on the green. Those without
skates slid back and forth in their boots, gathered snow from the light fall
at the edge of the water and hurled it at one another. From her bedroom
window in Torrington House, Sonia Midwinter watched enviously,
wishing that the dignity of her eighteen years had not disqualified her
from joining in. A low but unclouded sun struck crystals from the frozen
water, from the white-dusted reeds at its edge and from the icy twigs on
the boughs of oak that overhung the pond. Sonia shivered behind the
leaded lights of her window; she was wearing only her underclothes,
while on the bed behind her lay stockings, bodices and skirts from her
still-unfinished dressing.

She put a log on the small fire and wrapped a gown round her shoulders. She glanced out of the window. It was nearly noon, and already the
sun seemed to be failing in its ascent of the sky, flattening into a tired
ellipse that would see it subside before the day had really started. Sonia
could make out her younger brother, Thomas, on the pond, a strong,
mysterious boy who teased her more than his two years' juniority
should have allowed. She licked her lips and swallowed. In an hour or
so she would be meeting Mr. Prendergast and his family—honorable

Nottingham people, her father had informed her, manufacturers of fine lace. Mr. Richard Prendergast, their elder son, had been introduced to Sonia at her aunt's house the previous Christmas; she had had at the time no idea that it was anything other than a chance meeting, though was later aware of murmured discussions in the drawing room of Torrington House from which she made out the words "wait a year," and saw her father emerge with the look of purse-lipped satisfaction that she recognized as his "business done" face.

She sighed and picked up a plum-colored silk dress with a tight bodice and a full skirt that gave glimpses of her slender feet, which, her mother assured her, were her best feature. How plain must I be, thought Sonia at her dressing table, that my feet are prettier than my face? She rubbed a hint of red coloring into her lips and tied her hair back with a black ribbon. Her eyes were dark and rapid, her skin was pale and prone to flushing; at the top of her cheeks minute capillaries were visible where the translucent covering of babyhood had never fully thickened into adult skin. She powdered over them and smiled at herself in the glass. Her elder brother, Edgar, once told her, "You're a pretty girl, Sonia," though he had, sadly, never repeated the compliment; Thomas occasionally called her the Queen of Sheba, spoiling the exotic comparison with some qualification about "the half was not told unto me." Her father appeared uneasy about Sonia's presence in the house, embarrassed by her woman's bust and dresses and ball invitations. Mrs. Midwinter spoke to her with the firm encouragement she showed to Amelia, the more backward of her Dalmatian bitches.

Sonia went along the landing to her mother's bedroom on the south side of the house, pausing on the polished boards to knock. Mrs. Midwinter was also at her toilet, seated on an upholstered stool that her flesh overflowed in downward-pouring, silk-covered waves.

"What have you got on your lips?"

"Just the smallest touch of—"

"Take it off, for heaven's sake. What would Mr. Prendergast think?"

"What are you going to wear, Mama?"

"I shall wear my black dress with the white lace at the cuff. You should go and see how Miss Brigstocke's getting along in the kitchen."

Sonia grimaced. "What is she preparing?"

"Sole, if the fishmonger remembered to get any. Then some con-sommé. I asked her for a saddle of mutton, but you know what she's like. Some fowl to follow, I think. Your father will have found her something in the game larder, if Amelia hasn't had it."

"I hope the Prendergasts are good eaters," said Sonia.

"They will need something after that long journey." Mrs. Midwinter rose from her stool and moved slowly over to the oak wardrobe, taking a sugar-dusted bonbon from a saucer on the way. "Don't forget what a favor they are doing us."

"I shan't forget, Mama."

Sonia ran along the cold landing to her room, reluctantly removed the color from her lips, and went down the narrow back staircase, with its powerful hundred-year-old scent of lime wood, into the servants' hall. She hurried over the patterned tiles, past the butler's pantry (they had not had a butler for years) and into the cavelike kitchen, where Miss Brigstocke, angular and flushed, was leaning over a two-gallon boiling pot, prodding the contents with a long-handled spoon.

"Hello, May," Sonia said to the kitchen maid, who looked up from her potato peeling and smiled apprehensively. "What's in your cauldron, Miss Brigstocke? What does it look like?"

"It looks like what it ought to look like," said Miss Brigstocke, neither smiling nor apprehensive. "If you don't mind me saying so."

Like Mr. Midwinter, she had difficulty in adjusting to Sonia's almost-adulthood; after ten years of shooing her and spanking her and telling her to mind her p's and q's, she had not found an idiom in which to defer to the young mistress.

"Is there anything I can—"

"We're doing very well, thank you, Miss. Aren't we, May? It would be different if we was at Torrington Manor, I dare say, Miss, where, as you know—"

"Indeed, I do, Miss Brigstocke. Where you worked as a scullery maid for ten years and then for five as—"

"Be that as it may, Miss—"

"Before you took the position in our poor house without so much as an underfootman to—"

"Be that as it may, Miss," said Miss Brigstocke a little more firmly. "I shouldn't have to pluck and clean the birds myself as well as light the range if I was at the Manor, should I? Do you imagine Mrs. Turney ever dirtied her hands with making a sheep's pluck or a proper pig's fry, with all liver, lights and chitterlings like what I have to when Mrs. Midwinter's having one of her—what do you call 'em?"

"Thrift weeks?" said Sonia.

"Offal weeks, I call 'em. I'm up to my elbows in the cavity of the pig, even if Jenkins has made the cut. Well, you don't have to do that sort of thing at the Manor. They get all their pies and that sent from Lincoln, from Trubshawe's, ready made."

"Ah, the Manor, the Manor," laughed Sonia. "Wouldn't it be splendid if we lived at the Manor instead of the Laceys! Papa would be the Member of Parliament and Mama would be a shadow of herself and wear those pastel satins that are all the fashion in London. And I should be Miss Jane. And Edgar would inherit the village. Wouldn't we all be happy? And you, Miss Brigstocke, should have all the help you wanted. Instead of which we're stuck in the rotten old House!"

"And what about Master Thomas? What would he be at the Manor?" said May.

"Oh dear," said Sonia. "I'd forgotten Master Thomas. There's no equivalent of him, is there? Why do you ask, May?"

May looked back quickly to her potatoes.

"Sometimes I wonder," said Sonia, standing on tiptoe and leaning over Miss Brigstocke's shoulder to look into the pot, "what world Thomas does belong to."

May laughed, but stopped when Miss Brigstocke caught her eye.

Sonia turned back into the room, wanting to say something, but managing to control herself. "It's very gloomy in here, isn't it?" she said.

"These dark days," said Miss Brigstocke. "All the light's gone off by noon. And I did ask for more lamps. We shall have to wash the plates by candlelight."

So much of the room was dark, besides the blackened range; the framed silhouettes on the wall, to either side of it, were black, as were the pots and pans on the open shelf of the dresser; the ceiling was stained by years of dark fumes; but it was not a cheerless room. Sonia had spent many afternoons of childhood sitting at the big deal table, drawing, talking to bad-tempered Mrs. Travers, Miss Brigstocke's predecessor, or Elmley, the last butler, and inhaling the aromas of the range, all of which were exotic to her young senses, whether onions frying, cooked apples, melted cheese or the powerful scent of roasting meat that would come with a roar and hiss when Mrs. Travers opened the oven door, and stood up scarlet-faced, flapping her white cloth.

"I must leave you to it, I'm afraid," said Sonia. "That man's coming from the village to help. You know. Mr. Fisher, the one who came when Papa had to give that dinner."

"Lord help us," said Miss Brigstocke.

"I think we're supposed to pretend he's the butler," said Sonia, "as though he works here all the time."

"Well, he'll have to do a better job of knowing where things is kept. And not spill the wine this time."

"That's your responsibility, Miss Brigstocke. Don't let him anywhere near that bottle of Madeira."

May giggled as Sonia went out through the far door, down a dim, paneled passage and out into the bright side of the house.

Though well lit by the tall windows that overlooked the drive, the main hall was cold, and Sonia put some logs onto the mean flame that flickered in the fireplace. A circular table in the middle of the space held a vase of winter blooms in icy water, which she rearranged to look more welcoming.

What now? She wiped her hands down the front of her dress and looked into the dining room to make sure the places were properly set. May was only fifteen years old and was learning the job as she went along, from what gruff hints she could squeeze from Miss Brigstocke. Sonia straightened a setting on the table. For years she had considered Miss Brigstocke only as she presented herself—a bossy, disappointed servant of the kind you might find in any cold house in Lincolnshire; then one day Sonia had discovered a lascivious and private part of her life, far from regular, involving the lampman, Jenkins, and, she suspected, other men as well.

As Sonia went back into the hall, the double front doors opened noisily and her father appeared, banging the snow from his hat, then using it to drive a dancing Dalmatian away from him.

"Where is your mother, Sonia? They'll be here at any minute. Is that what you're wearing? Never mind. Is Fisher here yet? Get off, Dido!"

Mr. Midwinter went up the front stairs, calling to his wife. A carriage arrived, bringing Edgar and his pale young wife, Lucy. Fisher, the occasional butler, walked up the frosty path through the kitchen garden and let himself in at a back door. May came scurrying through from the kitchen with a message from Miss Brigstocke asking how long she was supposed to wait before sending the lunch through.

"OH, YES please," said Mr. Richard Prendergast. "A man can't have too much caper sauce, that's what I always say. And what's sauce for the goose . . ." He looked at Mrs. Midwinter, then at Sonia, and winked, as he helped himself from the silver jug that Fisher held at his shoulder.

"Nice bit of mutton, Midwinter," said Mr. Prendergast the elder, wiping his mouth on a white napkin and settling back in his chair with a glass of claret. "Keep your own sheep, do you?"

"There's a small farm, a house, a few cottages. I let the tenants do what they please. I have too much to do in town to give it much attention."

Mrs. Prendergast, a tall woman with a high color who had spoken very little, said, "I suppose you have ever such a large staff here."

"Yes," said Mr. and Mrs. Midwinter together. She retreated. "Of course," he went on, "it's not as easy to get the servants you want these days, but we have to look after the place. It's ours in trust, that's how I see it, to hand on to the next generation. And we have to make sure our daughter's well cared for, don't we?"

"Yes, Papa." Sonia wondered whether he was implying that she had a maid of her own.

"And has the house been in the family for long?" said Mrs. Prendergast.

"It's only a hundred years old," said Mr. Midwinter. "Completed in the year of American Independence. There's a date carved above the door. I'll show you afterward, if you like."

"And do you live in Nottingham itself?" said Mrs. Midwinter, helping herself to sauce. Sonia noticed the way she had saved her husband from having to make any more ancestral claims.

Mrs. Prendergast stretched her long back a little further up in her seat. "We have two houses, as a matter of fact."

"Oh." Mrs. Midwinter deflated visibly, but only for a moment. "And are they both in the town?"

"No fear!" said Richard Prendergast. "Pater's a great one for the fresh air. Riding to hounds, all that sort of thing. Pass me a bit more of the wine, will you, Fisher, there's a good chap."

Fisher stiffened, but managed to extend a yellowish, choreatic hand to the decanter on the sideboard and pour another glassful for the guest.

Richard Prendergast had fair curly hair, some of which he was losing at the temples and from the crown, giving him a half-plucked appearance. He had a small mouth set in red cheeks and blue eyes which moved rapidly from face to face without seeming to take much in.

"Good man, Fisher!" he said, drinking deep of the claret that Fisher had extracted from the cellar's furthest bin.

". . . quite a responsibility," Mrs. Prendergast was saying, "living in the manor house. Do you ask all the villagers in at Christmas?"

"Not all of them," said Mrs. Midwinter vaguely. "So much to do, now Edgar and Lucy are married. And there's a baby due in the New Year, isn't there, Lucy?"

Sonia covered her mouth with her napkin. "Manor House!" she imagined Miss Brigstocke spluttering, "I'll show them the Manor House . . ."

Edgar Midwinter, a solemn young man of twenty-four, cleared his throat and addressed himself to Richard Prendergast. "And are you following your father's line of business, sir?"

"Me? Good heavens, no! There are enough lace cuffs in the world, don't you think? No. No, I'm starting a venture with some chums in London. You just can't go wrong at the moment. Of course, you have to know the right people, that's what I always say."

"What sort of business?" said Mr. Midwinter keenly.

"Sugar."

"And will you just import or—"

"We expect to act as brokers," said Richard.

"I see. And do you have your residence in London?"

"Not yet. I'm still lodged with the long-suffering parents. But I intend to move. I have my eye on a place in Mayfair. Just as soon as I can . . ." He

coughed and held his hand in front of his mouth. "Make my arrangements."

Sonia found Lucy looking at her across the table, her eyes wide with
theatrical excitement.

"Mama," she said into a silence that had swiftly and uncomfortably
fallen on the room, "shall I ask May to clear the plates?"

"Thank you," said Mrs. Midwinter. "Fisher, tell Miss Brigstocke she
may send in the dessert."

Sonia left the dining room discreetly, squeezing the oak door closed,
then ran down the passage to the kitchen.

"Miss Brigstocke!" she said irrupting into the smoky cavern.

"What's the matter, Miss Sonia?"

Sonia sat at the table and put her hand to her head. "Nothing." She
laughed and sat up. "Nothing's the matter. It's just rather . . . I wanted to
escape. I keep wanting to giggle. I feel someone's going to make a fool of
themselves, and it might be me."

"What's he like then?" said Miss Brigstocke.

"Who?"

May giggled.

"The young man."

"I don't know what you mean, Miss Brigstocke. I've come to tell you
that you may send through the dessert."

"Very well, Miss."

"He's very . . ." Sonia put her hand to her mouth. "Curly."

May snorted.

"And he's going to move to London, and live in Mayfair."

"London," said Miss Brigstocke sepulchrally, as though it were
Gomorrah. "Well, well, well. Now then, May, get those jellies from the
larder and put the cloth on the tray. Go on."

Sonia stood up. "I suppose I'd better go back. They liked the mutton,
Miss Brigstocke."

"Good. And the fish? Did Mrs. Midwinter like the fish?"

Sonia stopped in the doorway and looked back, grave in her plum-
colored dress. "I was not going to mention the fish, Miss Brigstocke."

The flow of conversation at the dining table had divided. Sonia
resumed her seat and tried to decide whether she should join her father

and Mrs. Prendergast, who were talking about the breeding of horses, or save Lucy from Mr. Prendergast's inquiries about her pregnancy.

The door of the room rattled loudly and swung open to reveal Thomas Midwinter, covered in mud and snow, clutching his left arm in his right, pale, with gray lips and a thin line of blood running down his cheek. He had been in a fight with some boys from the village and lost track of time; he thought he might have broken his arm.

"For heaven's sake go and get washed," said Mrs. Midwinter. "You can come and join us when you've changed. Fisher, see if Miss Brigstocke can keep something hot for him."

"I'm sorry about that," said Mr. Midwinter as the door closed. "My younger son. He lives in a world of his own, I'm afraid." He spoke without enthusiasm.

There was a murmur of sympathy.

"But never mind about him. Where were we?"

It was quite dark by the time Thomas came downstairs and joined the rest of the party in the dining room, where the light from the small fire had been augmented by that of two pewter candelabra that Fisher had set uncertainly on the table. Thomas had dressed himself properly, in a jacket, white necktie and waistcoat, but he looked pale, Sonia noticed, and he used only one hand to eat the plate of mutton that was brought to him.

Thomas had untidy chestnut hair, and eyes that were the opposite of Richard Prendergast's: brown, steady and liable to remain fixed for a long time on a single person as though he was making an examination, dispassionate and not necessarily kind. Suddenly, his body might be galvanized by a thought, a spasm of laughter or by the physical turbulence of being sixteen years old, and he would speak fast, fluently, in his recently acquired baritone voice. Then his eyes flashed, no longer still, but often filled with affection, a little for his parents and elder brother, but mostly toward Sonia, to whom his gaze seemed often to return.

When the meal was finally done, Mrs. Midwinter took the women upstairs to her bedroom, while her husband circulated some port among the men.

"In due course," said Mr. Midwinter, "Edgar will take over my business, just as he will inherit the house. After he completed his studies, I

sent him away to Canada to learn about grain. He's going to start working for me next year."

Mr. Midwinter was the third generation to manage the company of
Chas. Midwinter & Sons, grain merchants, but he felt sure that the previous two had never had to work so hard. Harvest, yields, transport,
markets . . . Nothing was predictable except the fierceness of the competition and the narrowness of his own margins of profit.

"I see," said Mr. Prendergast. "And what about you, young man?" He
turned to Thomas. "I suppose it's the church or the army for you, is it?"
He laughed richly.

"As a matter of fact, he's very keen on the Bible, aren't you?"

"I like the stories, Father," said Thomas. "I like the tales of people lost
in the wilderness. But I don't think that makes me a likely priest."

"But it's still the Bible, isn't it? You spend hours with your nose in it."

"They are stories, like Homer. I love Homer, too. Or Shakespeare's
plays."

"Oh, dear. Don't start on the theater," said Mr. Midwinter. "Our
guests don't want to hear about all that. Hamlet's ghost and three
witches and heaven knows what."

"It's Hamlet's father's ghost, in fact, who—"

"He pesters me all the time to let him go to London, to Drury Lane or
some such place."

Richard Prendergast laughed. "I suppose the young fellow wants to
meet all the pretty actresses."

"It's really only Shakespeare I like," said Thomas. "He tells you
things that he's discovered, like a great inventor."

"And there were we," said Richard, "thinking the play was an
evening's entertainment!"

Thomas's eyes grew narrow, but he said nothing.

"I suppose we shall have to send him to the university," said Mr. Midwinter, "like his brother."

"Oh yes?" Mr. Prendergast seemed taken aback.

"Yes, indeed," repeated Mr. Midwinter, as though worried that his
guest had not quite understood. "The University at Cambridge is the
Midwinter tradition now."

Prendergast rallied politely. "I see. So you will be joining the scholars in their caps and gowns, will you? And what will be your subject?"

"Well, sir," said Thomas. "I suppose it depends on whether my father will pay for me to go there."

"True enough," said Mr. Midwinter. "Fiendish expensive it is."

Thomas pushed his plate away, still nursing his left arm. He looked through the French doors over the darkened terrace at the side of the house. Beyond it, at the end of the crazy paving, above the stone gateposts, he could see a handful of low stars.

"If I could choose anything at all to study," he said, still looking into the clear winter sky, "I suppose it would be Shakespeare and some of the other English poets."

The others laughed again. "You are a buffoon, Thomas," said Edgar. "As though the fellows of the College would get together and teach you how to watch a play!"

Mr. Prendergast was purple with mirth. "Or read poetry to you!"

Mr. Midwinter was also smiling, though with plain embarrassment. "He's just pulling our leg, aren't you, Thomas? It's always been his way."

"Really," said Thomas. "They teach us grammar at school, how to read and write. Then they teach us to translate Homer and Euripides. Why should they not teach the depths of literature?"

"For heaven's sake," said Edgar, "you can't become a Bachelor of Arts in reading novels!"

"I meant poetry. Shakespeare drew a new map of the human mind as clearly as Newton mapped the heavens. Why is one considered science and the other fit only to be mocked with jokes about pretty girls and Drury Lane?"

"That's enough," said Mr. Midwinter, rising from the table. "Edgar, go and join the ladies in the morning room. Thomas, you go and make yourself useful. Prendergast, you come with me if you please, sir, and smoke a pipe in my study."

There, the two men stood on either side of the fireplace, approximately equal in height, dressed in similar clothes of good but not ostentatious quality, each wary, full of family pride, but willing, all other things being equal, to proceed.

"I like your house, Midwinter. And your family. Mrs. Midwinter, a very gracious lady if I may say so."

"Thank you." Mr. Midwinter inclined his head. "Mrs. Prendergast likewise. Do you have other children?"

"Another boy at home. But no girls. No dowries to find."

"Indeed . . . Indeed not."

There was an awkwardness. "And your young Thomas. He's a character, isn't he?"

"Oh, him?" Mr. Midwinter waved a hand. "He'll settle down. He'll study law like his elder brother in the end, I expect. He shall have to find a profession because I expect to have only one heir to my business and my house."

"He looks a decent lad, your Edgar."

"Yes. I couldn't ask for better." Mr. Midwinter took a half step forward, as though he had recovered from the thought of dowries and was now prepared to move cautiously on to the offensive.

"This sugar business," he said. "Is that likely to flourish?"

"Oh yes." Mr. Prendergast stuck his pipe into his mouth and pulled at his waistcoat with both hands. "I'll make sure the boy's well set up there. I know a few people in Cheapside who—"

"What? Usurers?"

"No, no, no," laughed Prendergast. "Useful folk for the boy to know. People who can put business his way."

"Will he have to travel? He can't rely on people in coffeehouses to do his work for him. And then he'd be away from . . . from home."

"We'll not let him come to any harm."

"Why does he not follow you into the family business? Would that not be more secure for him and his wife?"

Prendergast set down his pipe on the mantelpiece. "Let us talk about this straight," he said. "I have had a good look at your girl and I like what I have seen."

"She is an accomplished child. She—"

"I am not saying my Richard could not do better. But I am saying he could do worse."

Mr. Midwinter made as if to speak, then held back. It was a more delicate business than he had expected because he had no certain idea of how attractive Sonia might appear to a young man. Her figure was slender and womanly, he supposed; her manner was considerate yet lively: but was she beautiful? Did a young stranger see something to enchant him, or merely, as he himself did, the ghosts of the various stages of childhood and adolescence layered up one upon another, almost visible beneath her excitable skin?

He did not enjoy hearing his daughter discussed by this man as he presumably talked about a bolt of cloth to some Lancashire supplier, but he was obliged to listen; if Prendergast let slip that he or his son considered her attractive, then he might be able to offer a smaller dowry.

THOMAS MIDWINTER went up to his bedroom and took up the book he was reading, *Quentin Durward* by Sir Walter Scott. He had chosen it from the library because of a single line of Scott's poetry: "O, young Lochinvar is come out of the west." The last word suggested mists and freshness and romance—odd, he thought, when really the west was where the sun went down and the day ended. The word "young" made Lochinvar easy for Thomas to identify with (he felt sorry for old people) yet also worryingly vulnerable; and some terrible, precarious hope was in that sighing "O." What Thomas loved most about the line, however, was the word "is." In his grammar class the master had explained that this was an archaism, yet the two common letters sent shivers of delight through him.

Quentin Durward, on the other hand, was drudgery. At that moment, Louis XI was being reconciled, slowly, with Charles the Bold at Péronne, while Quentin's affairs had been left to drift. Thomas settled on the bed and pulled the candle closer to him. He was fairly certain that he had broken his left arm, but did not wish to intrude on the business of the day.

After a while he closed his eyes, folded the book on his chest and gave in to the ache of his limbs. Often at such moments he heard his voice. It was that of a narcoleptic man who had spoken to him regularly since childhood. It was not like hearing his own thoughts, which invariably came in fully formed sentences as though uttered by himself, silently, into his mind's ear (the sound of thoughts was similar to the sound of reading, when, however rapidly his eye skimmed the lines, the words did form and resonate, albeit inaudibly). His voice, by contrast, could be heard, like Edgar's voice or Sonia's; it was outside him, not produced by the workings of his own brain but by some other being.

Generally, it soothed him. It offered comments of an indifferent, sometimes inconsequential nature on what he was doing or thinking or proposing. It did not try to interfere with his life and he was not frightened of it. The voice was always slow and dream-weighted, as though its owner had drained off a bottle of laudanum before speaking. He heard it less and less often these days, but it had been for so long such an intimate part of his experience of living that he had never thought to question it; nor had he ever mentioned it to anyone.

There was no voice in the dark December afternoon, no sound at all in Thomas's bedroom or from outside, where the garden and the village lay beneath the muffling weight of snow. It was dark, dead winter, Saint Lucy's day, and the sequence of Thomas's thought broke up into single images, in whose hypnotic light he faded into sleep.

There was a knocking at the door. It rose through his dream, where it was briefly incorporated as a hammer on an anvil, then awoke him. He stood up and crossed the floor.

"Wake Duncan with thy knocking," he thought, "I would thou couldst . . . Sonia!"

"Can I come in?"

"Yes. What's going on?"

"They have been in the study for almost two hours."

"And still no puff of smoke?"

"Oh there's plenty of smoke. It is like a London fog."

"You know what I mean. Come and sit on the bed."

"I had to show Mrs. Prendergast round the house and then take her outside to look at the grounds. I saw that awful man Fisher swigging from a bottle in the kitchen garden. Luckily it was almost dark by then so I don't think she saw. Are you all right, Thomas? You look pale."

"It's my arm. I think it's broken."

"Then we must take you to a doctor at once. Or I'll send . . . I'll send . . ."

"Well, whom will you send? There's no one to send anymore, is there? Jenkins, I suppose. But listen, Sonia, it's all right. I'll get Edgar to take me when they've gone. I don't want to distract them from their business."

Thomas put his good hand in his sister's lap, where her own fingers were clasped together. "So," he said. "What do you think of him?"

"I do not love him."

"Really, Sonia. No one could expect that, not after two hours. Do you think you could marry him?"

Sonia looked toward the door. "I think you should marry someone you love."

"That is a very modern idea, I think. A very English idea. No one on the Continent of Europe would consider marrying for anything but social position."

"I know," said Sonia. "But I am an English girl, Thomas, and I don't live on the Continent of Europe."

Thomas was silent for a moment. Then he said, "His hair is very—"

"I know! But he's losing it at quite a rate. Soon there won't be any left."

"Yes. The silver lining. I like your dress, by the way. You look beautiful."

Sonia raised her eyes to her brother's face doubtfully. "The Queen of Sheba?" she said.

"More lovely, much more."

She pulled some thread from the cover on the bed. "It's easy for you," she said, "because you can have any profession you like. You can live where you want, you can marry the girl of your choice."

"Good Lord! If she'd have me. Anyway, I don't know what profession I should follow. They all laugh when I say I'm interested in literature. And where would that take me? I suppose I could become a schoolmaster, teaching grammar in Lincoln, but . . . Oh dear."

"Why don't you join the army? The Dragoons or the Hussars. You'd look handsome in that uniform."

"Yes, even I—"

"Even you, Thomas."

"Stop it, Queenie, or I shall go downstairs and tell young Mr. Prendergast that you still sleep with a doll and that I saw you kiss—"

"Thomas!"

"All right. But you are blushing."

"I know. But shall I marry Mr. Prendergast? That's what I want you to tell me."

"I am sixteen years old, Sonia."

"You have always been grown up for your age. Alas."

"Ow! My arm, my arm. You sat on my broken arm."

"Let us have a look at this arm, shall we? Hold it out for me. Now where is it supposed to be broken?"

"Here. Just above the wrist."

"Can you move it like this?"

"Ow!"

"And like this? Dearest, if it was broken, you could not move it at all. Do you know nothing about anatomy?"

"Not really."

"You are a hypochondriac, Thomas. And do you know why? Because you have never had a day of illness in your life. Not one."

"I had chicken pox."

"A handful of spots for half a day. And that is all, isn't it? That is why you always fancy you are ill, because you don't really know what being ill feels like!"

Sonia leaned forward on the bed and gently set Thomas's unbroken arm back by his side. "You are fascinated by illness. You love those long medical words even if you don't know what they mean. I heard you talking to Miss Brigstocke the other day about her scapula. She must have thought it was a kind of spoon for stirring soup."

"Like a spatula."

"But don't you see, Thomas?" Sonia stood up and walked over to the window; Thomas's room was on the second floor and the lights of the window were half obscured by the stone parapet outside. "I am excited by this."

"By what?"

"Thomas, don't be silly. This is what you should do. You should study to become a doctor. You could go to the university. Father would be happy and you could do all your play-reading and suchlike in the evenings after you had done your medical classes. It is perfect for you. Then you could become a doctor or a surgeon anywhere you liked. In London, in Edinburgh, Paris—or on board a ship."

"I am not going to be a barber surgeon cutting off the midshipman's leg. I want to—"

"But I am right, aren't I, Thomas? It is the perfect profession for you."

"And my qualification for it is that I am a hypochondriac."

"I think it is the ideal qualification. You have excellent health, which you will need, and at the same time a fascination with the morbid. What more could you ask?"

Thomas smiled at her but said nothing.

"Well?" said Sonia.

"I have heard you say more foolish things."

Sonia folded her hands. "And now that I have decided your life's course for you, it is your turn to help me with mine."

"Mr. Prendergast?"

Thomas sucked in his breath. He did not want Sonia to leave Torrington House because he would miss her; in the brief time he had known Richard Prendergast he had developed misgivings about him. He did not trust himself to advise his sister, however, because he knew little about such things; it all seemed so unpredictable to him, so lacking in pattern. All he could do was help her to elucidate her own thoughts.

"You think a girl should marry only for love?" he said.

"Not for love alone, but I think love must be there."

"And you do not love Mr. Prendergast?"

"Of course not. As you said, I barely know him. But Mother says that love will come."

"Love will come?"

"Yes. She said it came to her after she was married to Father."

"I see. And did it stay?"

"I did not ask."

Thomas could think of nothing more to say on the subject of love.

"Would you like to live in London?" he asked.

"I . . . I think so. It might be noisy and dirty but we could always come back here when we were tired of it."

"Or to Nottingham. Should you not go and see his family's house?"

"I imagine Father will go and see it. Anyway, as long as there is still this house, I should not have to go there if I didn't want to."

"I would miss you, Sonia."

"But you would come and stay in Mayfair. And from there you could walk to the theater every night of the week."

Thomas smiled. "Yes. I suppose I could. But I think . . ."

He was interrupted by the sound of his mother's voice calling up the stairs.

He raised his eyebrows. "Smoke?" he said.

Sonia licked her lips nervously. "Yes, perhaps smoke," she said.

"Sonia, you do not have to make a decision straight away. Be gentle. Be calm."

He felt her fingers lightly drum his sleeve. "I know, Thomas, I know."

AT MIDNIGHT, long after the last carriage had left, when the supper things were washed and tidied back into their cupboards by the sleepy May, when Dido and Amelia had been brought in from their kennel on account of the cold and given an old blanket in front of the range, there were still three people awake in Torrington House.

Sonia lay beneath her eiderdown, staring at the invisible ceiling. Her grandmother had told her when she was a child that it was the duty of a girl to do the bidding of her father. A woman's life, she said, was full of rewards so long as she knew how to please her husband; and as to who that man should be, Sonia must rely on the wisdom and experience of her parents. What she should avoid at all costs was becoming unattached; she must not allow her selfishness—and she did have a little willfulness, did she not—to remove her beyond the pale. If she was prepared to do as she was asked, then her life might be agreeable.

She did not like Richard Prendergast; she did not dislike him: what she wanted was for her life to begin. She was bored at Torrington House with only domestic duties to attend to, helping out here and there. She wanted to bring pleasure to her parents, to act out wholeheartedly the part they chose for her and to collect her reward in the approval of their eyes. She was fairly certain she would grow to love Richard, because he was blessed, raised in her view merely by being the choice of her family. And even if there was no flame, no anguish, no joy when he came home at night, still she could relish the business of being a wife, buoyed by the knowledge that she brought comfort to him, and pride to her father.

She turned onto her side. How, really, could she know? With what other man could a girl of eighteen compare Mr. Richard Prendergast? If she were allowed a rehearsal, an experiment, then she might make a graver, more informed decision. Life, however, never felt like that to her; it felt like something that she improvised from day to day. Having the idea of duty deep inside her head, and having—by some chance of birth—a hopeful temperament, she was always, she admitted, more likely to say yes than no.

MR. MIDWINTER stood in front of the fire in his study, his feet planted on the thin rug that covered the flags.

Occasionally, he had such moments alone, when he could step aside from the demands of his family and his clients. They were not glorious or exciting, these minutes of solitude, but they enabled him to correct the weight of anxiety and disappointment that were the burden of his days. His wife irritated him and his children were not what he had hoped; they would make no fortunes or conquests, would not become the cynosure of the county or the land. On the other hand, they were alive; the firm of Chas. Midwinter labored on beneath his direction; the house stood, his stomach was full and the dogs slept.

In the corner of the room were packages he had wrapped for Christmas, another duty discharged. He shifted, and felt the floor again through the leather soles of his boots.

This Richard Prendergast was not the kind of man he liked, and the parents were somehow a disappointment; he had felt no elation when he stood opposite the father after lunch: it had been a little like looking at himself in a dim glass. He told Prendergast the sum that he had put aside to settle on Sonia when she married, an amount his business manager told him he could not, under any circumstances, exceed. After half an hour of bargaining, he had agreed to raise it ten percent and they shook hands, each with satisfaction—Prendergast in the knowledge that he had secured a reluctant increase, Midwinter relieved that the sum was still lower than the figure he had actually resigned himself to losing.

THOMAS LAY nursing his arm, cold and unhappy beneath his blankets. He had one year left of Sonia's company before she would be removed to London by young Mr. Prendergast after their wedding. Much of that year would in any event be spent by Thomas at his boarding school and he felt that the best part of his childhood had been brought to a sudden close by an opportunist family raid. It was not fair on him; nor could it really be fair on poor Sonia, he thought, to ask her to venture into a fragile future with this Prendergast, with her hopeful disposition their only real asset. Thomas knew little of the economics of marriage, but he could not help feeling that his sister had been sold too cheap.

For himself, it was time to escape. Torrington without Sonia was unthinkable; he would stay there not a moment longer than was necessary to complete his education; and then . . . He would shock his parents with the brilliance of his plans; he would dazzle them and make them ponder, sadly, at what they themselves had overlooked. He would, like King Lear, do such things—what they were yet he knew not—but they should be the terrors of the earth.

He clenched his good fist beneath the bedclothes. If they would not let him become a doctor of literature, then perhaps he should accept Sonia's parting present—the bride's gift to her bachelor—and become a doctor of medicine. Why not bring the laborer, science, to do the mule's work in his greater project? Keats, after all, had been apprenticed to an apothecary and qualified as a surgeon.

Thomas's fretful ambitions, once they had blown and raged enough to keep him from sleeping, elicited from him a reluctant smile. Who would listen to an English boy, of no obvious abilities, invisible in the cold and silent countryside? How would they even know that he existed?

III

IN THE FOURTH YEAR OF HER MARRIAGE, SONIA ACCOMPANIED HER husband to the recently built French resort of Deauville. Richard Prendergast told her it would be good for his business to be seen mingling with fashionable Parisians, strolling along the seafront and sitting down at the gaming tables of the Trouville casino at night. He assured Sonia that he would gamble only small sums and that when it came to card games he had the luck of the devil. "Anyway," he said, taking her arm, "a change of air might help your . . ." He gestured toward the area of her abdomen, then overcame his diffidence as a thought apparently came to him. "Fresh air," he said, "for a fresh heir."

They took rooms in a boardinghouse some way back from the front, therefore less expensive than the principal hotels. Sonia had disliked the seaside since being immersed as a child in the freezing waves of Yarmouth and felt her spirits subside as the summer months approached. How was she to make conversation with the spinster ladies and retired Parisian stockbrokers who would constitute the clientele of the establishment? One day in April, as she was returning to her small house behind Curzon Street, she had an idea; she ran upstairs to the sitting room and pulled out a piece of paper.

Dear Thomas,

Thank you for your last letter. I am sorry you have been in trouble with the university authorities again. For heaven's sake,

do be careful or you will be sent down and then where will all
your plans be?

Now that is why I am writing to you, young man, as your
chaperone and Guiding Light. You shall have your bachelorhood
of science, your MB or whatever you may call it—provided you
can keep away from the low company you have described at
Emmanuel College and the taverns of Newmarket—but then
what? Are you to practice in Lincoln like poor old Dr. Meadowes
with his pony and trap and his gouty foot? Or is it to be the
fashionable women of Mayfair with their imaginary maladies?

Think hard, Thomas. You must be able to go where new
discoveries are being made, where the great men of science are
gathered together. You must learn to speak their language. I
know you were taught German at school, but you need to speak
French. You must be able to discourse as easily in Paris as in
Vienna. You must never—certainly not at this tender age—
allow your horizon to be limited.

To this effect, my dear brother, I have engaged a room for you
in a lodging house in the French resort of Deauville this summer.
There you will undergo an intensive course in the French
language, of which I know you already have the rudiments.
By the time you return to your Fenland rooms, you shall be
trilingual!

Father can be persuaded to pay, I suppose, in the name of
Education; if not . . . Well, I am not the kind of wife to play the
coquette, and anyway I do not think it would be profitable. But
you must come. It is a fine town, I am told, and a very fit place for
a young man to pass his twenty-first summer.

Respond at once, saying yes, to your ever-loving and -guiding

Sonia.

P.S. Please do say yes.

The atmosphere in the dining room in the Pension des Dunes was even
stuffier than Sonia had feared, since most of the residents appeared to

dread fresh air, frowning and clacking if the waiters left a sliver of door open. There were about forty guests in all, a few families whose small children were made to sit up straight with their hands visible on the table, but mostly gray-haired couples of long familiarity, who faced one another in committed silence.

Richard Prendergast ran his finger round the inside of his collar. "I wish they would open a window."

"We can have coffee outside," said Sonia. "There's a charming little garden. Did you see it?"

"Yes," said Thomas. "With lanterns and red creeper on the walls."

The waiter placed a tureen of soup on the table and invited them to serve themselves. Sonia lifted the lid and a smell of cress and summer savory floated upward.

"I see you have grown a beard, Thomas," said Richard. "Do all your fellow-students have beards beneath their scholar's caps?"

"Almost all. Do you like it?"

"It makes you look older," said Sonia.

"It's a bother keeping it trim."

"You should visit my barber in Leadenhall Street," said Richard. "Now let's hear some French from you, young man."

"After two days? You are a hard master. But I can speak to the waiter if you like. Shall I ask him for some wine?"

As Thomas looked about the room, he saw an unusual couple seated at a table by an enviably open window. One was a Curé, sweating a little beneath his soutane, the other a young man of about Thomas's age with black brows, a mustache and staring brown eyes. Something about his expression made Thomas want to smile.

"I wonder what brings them together," he said quietly to Sonia, gesturing with his head.

"I suppose the young man is being prepared for the priesthood."

"In Deauville?" said Thomas. "More likely to be prepared for the Turf here, isn't he? And somehow he doesn't have a devout look about him. He reminds me of a fellow I know in Trinity."

Their waiter was a tall, mournful man with a bald head and a thick mustache that gave him a look of the late Prince Albert. His manner was also regal, as he endowed the table with the burgundy; to each diner he offered a half glass of wine, then bowed slightly, and moved off on flat feet.

He returned a few minutes later with some plates of sole in a cream sauce and a china dish of *petits pois*.

"Nothing wrong in drinking red wine with fish," said Richard, looking round for the bottle which Prince Albert had secreted. "Drink what you dash well like, that's what I always say."

"The sole is good, isn't it?" said Sonia.

"Yes," said Thomas. "Has my sister proved a satisfactory housekeeper, Richard?"

"Adequate, thank you. We had to let the cook go at Christmas. Domestic economies, you see."

"I enjoy it," said Sonia. "It's a pleasure for me to make a dinner for Richard's friends, then to manage the budget with some modest suppers." She did not look up from her plate as she spoke.

In the garden after dinner, they found themselves seated at the table next to the Curé and his charge.

"Here's a chance," said Richard. "Ask the young fellow what he's doing. Let's see what your French is made of."

"Not much," said Thomas. "That's why I have come. Let me have a cognac, I need some courage. Sonia speaks better than I do. Papa once sent her for a summer to a family—in Brittany, I believe."

"That's enough excuses. Go on with you."

Thomas shifted his chair against the paved courtyard and cleared his throat as he leaned across the neighboring table. In an accent in which he himself could almost hear the roar of the Wash, he said, "Good evening. My sister and her husband and I, we were asking ourselves what was bringing you to Deauville this summer and if the boardinghouse pleases you."

"Good evening, Monsieur," said the Curé. "My friend and I have come for a week's holiday. I promised him that if he was successful in his examina-tions I should reward him with a week at the seaside. Although his family lives near the sea, he has never had a holiday in all his twenty years. As to the boardinghouse—"

"Me also," said Thomas, "I mean, I, too, have—am twenty years old. My name is Thomas Midwinter. I have come from England."

"I thought perhaps you did. We are from Brittany. May I introduce my friend Jacques Rebière, a great doctor of the future."

Jacques held out his hand to Thomas. "What did he say, Father?"

"He is the same age as you and he comes from England."

Thomas introduced Richard and Sonia.

"Do you speak English?" Thomas asked Jacques.

Jacques shook his head, looking startled.

"Jacques's education was late in starting," Abbé Henri said, "but every week he is making up the ground that he lost. And you yourself, sir, I presume you are studying at one of those fine old English universities."

"Yes. It is very ancient and very fine. My sister thinks I do not work enough, but this is not true. Each morning I must do a lecture and a practical demonstration of the anatomy."

"You speak very good French."

"No, this too is not true. This is why I am come here in France. When I speak then about lecture and anatomy it is easy because the words are the same thing in English. Like this I have the air of a good French. But it is not true."

Thomas noticed Jacques's tense expression resolve at last into a brief grin; it was an extraordinary expression, like a piece of fruit gashed by a cutlass. His mouth had a hundred shining teeth; then it was closed, the mustache realigned itself and the brows re-knitted in perplexity. Thomas felt his own lips twitch in amusement.

It transpired that Abbé Henri spoke some English and was able to make himself pleasant to Richard, who looked displeased at having been excluded from the conversation. One of Sonia's accomplishments, one of the makeweights in her father's downward adjustment of her dowry, was a fluent if idiosyncratic French; her accent was free of any Gallic influence, but she was able to understand almost everything and to reply at speed. At the end of the evening, they parted company in the hotel vestibule, but Thomas did not feel ready for bed.

He turned to Jacques. "Would you want to walk for a few minutes?"

Jacques shrugged one shoulder. "Yes."

"To the beach?"

"Yes."

"Good night, Sonia. Good luck at the tables, Richard."

It was a warm evening as they went down the streets toward the front, between the quiet villas and their tree-shaded gardens. Each took off his jacket and carried it over his shoulder. Thomas smiled encouragingly at Jacques in the darkness but could see no response.

When they arrived at the front, Jacques said something that Thomas did not understand. After some repetitions, it was agreed that they should walk on the sand, and they made their way past a series of small wooden changing huts and some bathing machines that had been pulled back from the tide.

Thomas took his shoes off and tied them round his neck, then put his socks in his pocket so he could feel the cold sand under his feet.

"It is good," he said, but Jacques merely shrugged and walked on. Thomas wondered what he would have to do to elicit another of those smiles.

"What do you study?" said Thomas.

"I am studying medicine in Paris."

"Does your family inhabit Paris?"

"My family is from a small village near the coast. Saint Agnès. No one has ever heard of it. It is very bare and bleak. Monsieur the Curé says even the rocks of the seashore cry out for God's mercy."

Jacques spoke rapidly, with no concession to his English listener; Thomas, struggling to follow, was not sure whether to be irritated or flattered. Perhaps Jacques was inhibited in some way by his presence, but there seemed little he could do about it, now that they were committed, close to the dark water's edge with no one else in sight.

They stared toward the sea in uncompanionable silence. It was a clear night, and beyond the bay of Trouville to their right Thomas could make out the distant lights of Le Havre; above them, the sky was smeared with stars.

Thomas pointed. "How do you call this star?"

"The polar star."

"We call it the North Star. Do you think there is an . . . intelligence there?"

"In the sky?"

"In the universe."

Jacques said nothing and Thomas wondered if he had insulted him. He knew that, although France was proud of the fact that it was a lay republic, most French people were still fierce in their Catholic beliefs; he feared that he had offended Jacques by questioning the existence of his god, though in fact he had meant to suggest something vaguer.

"I ask pardon if I . . ." He could not find the words.

"No, no." Jacques cut him off.

Thomas sat down on the sand. He would not give up yet, he thought; he would simply continue to talk without asking questions, and see if that way he could tempt Jacques to respond.

Laboriously, he set off. "My sister inhabits London. I like the theater. I go often to the theater. Do you like . . . I like Shakespeare. He is an English writer. Perhaps you do not know him at France. I am a student of medicine. I have one brother also, he is older and will take the work of my father and his house. I find interest in philosophy—same word in English—and the way in which functions the mind of the human."

"Stop! Stop! Wait there. I will be ten minutes. Don't move from there!" Jacques ran off, stumbling, back over the shallow waves of sand, then gained his footing more surely as he neared the road where, as Thomas watched in astonishment, he leapt the small brick wall beneath the streetlamp and ran back into the town.

Thomas lay flat on the sand and shook with laughter.

Ten minutes later, Jacques, panting, knelt down beside him. He carried a wicker basket, from which he took a bottle of wine, two glasses, a half-empty bottle of cognac, a Camembert, a loaf of bread and a box of violet-scented chocolates. He drew the cork and poured some wine into a glass which he handed to Thomas. His white teeth flashed in the darkness.

"Thank you," said Thomas. "Where have you found these things?"

"In the boardinghouse. I know where they are kept. Do you want some cheese?"

"Not now. And what—"

"Wait." Jacques put his hand on Thomas's arm. "I am always hungry, even after dinner. And the food at the pension, it's—"

"It's marvelous."

"Yes, it is. But wait. I want to talk to you, but it's difficult for me. My mother died when I was a baby and my elder brother is not well. I left school when I was young so I could go and work for my father, and Abbé Henri is the only real friend I have had. So when you began to talk—"

"Excuse me," said Thomas. "May you talk more slowly, please. Thank you."

"Ah, it's difficult." Jacques stood up. "I have so much to say and I sense that for the first time in my life I have found someone who can understand it. I only met you this evening, of course, but I know it . . . Here." He banged his sternum so hard with his closed fist that Thomas thought he must have hurt himself.

"Slowly," said Thomas. "Slowly. At least you may help teach me French."

"I will. At once. The best way to learn is to listen."

"Is that true?"

"Yes. Alas." They laughed at the same time.

Jacques began to describe his studies in physiology and anatomy, the lectures, the classes, the unforgiving timetable. "I sleep on the floor of another student. He is often out at night, so sometimes I climb into his bed. Abbé Henri has paid for my courses and I can't ask him for more money, so sometimes I have to work in the laundry or at a bar. I don't mind. My mind is so much on fire for what I'm learning, but I am frustrated because I want to move beyond the movement of the bowel or the function of the liver and—"

"Gently."

"Forgive me. When you spoke just now—what were the words you used? About the mind. It doesn't matter. I can come back to that. You see, I have this idea that we must somehow try to understand the meeting point between thought and flesh. That is what the next great aim and discovery of medical science will be. Are you with me?"

"I think so. I—"

"We have alienists in the asylums. We call them asylums but they are prisons, really. We have neurologists, great neurologists in this country, and in Germany, and of course we have physicians. Even in your country—forgive me—"

"It's all right, I—"

"Physicians by the score! But a medicine that would understand and cure those whose sickness is in the mind and which could determine its causes . . . That is something I dream about."

Thomas looked over his wineglass as Jacques's torrent slowed for a moment. He had understood most of it, he thought.

"I think the proposition," Thomas said, "is this. Forgive my French. To understand . . . to accomplish what you describe is a thing not only of medicine. I need, you need, also to see at what point the human being rests on his journey of evolution. You know the book of Mr. Darwin which comes out twenty years past?"

"In the year of my birth?"

"Exactly. Our birth, in effect. And for me there is also a question of psychology, such as the great writers speak of, which is important here also. I mean to say, it is more than a question of dissection of dead people to see the cause of a malady. And at last . . ."

Thomas found himself struggling, but thought it was important to continue, because this aspect of what he had to say was to him the most important. "There is at last the question of what we might call . . . how does one say . . . the sensation of being alive and of thinking . . ."

"Awareness?" said Jacques.

"Yes. To know if that is a faculty which also evolves. For some scientists, this power of—what are we calling it—awareness is that which separates humans from animals. It was God who provided it. But if this is a faculty of the mind which evolves as the human reason has evolved, or our ability to make things, then we are only animals after all. Forgive me. I explain myself badly. Or perhaps awareness is a thing which is there but which we do not yet completely see or use, as for many millions of years human beings did not have fire, or electricity. Then, once it is discovered, everyone has it."

Jacques grabbed his arm. "Exactly. Exactly. These are the questions I have been asking myself for a long time. I feel that there is an answer, perhaps a single answer, which may help us. But it is the project of a lifetime."

"I have a lifetime," said Thomas.

"And you have a project."

As Jacques began to talk again, Thomas began to see how aspects of his own interests and ambitions—things he had previously thought to be irreconcilable—might be brought together. Perhaps he and this extraordinary young man might really one day work together. And then, what might they not achieve? The discovery of new diseases that could be named after them—Midwinter's Disease, Rebière Syndrome; a great teaching hospital that would carry on their methods after their death; but, more than such conventional stuff: a map of the mind and its million pathways . . . As Jacques's ideas raged on in front of the gently breaking Channel waves, almost anything seemed possible. Thomas was thrilled not just by the exuberance of Jacques's talk, but by the certainty of the references. Although the Curé had said something about his education starting late, he clearly had a scientist's turn of mind; though there was also, in his gesticulating hands, a suggestion of the crusader.

If Jacques had begun with chemistry and moved through the elements of medicine to an interest in neurology and behavior, it might be, Thomas felt, almost a mirror of his own journey, which had begun in the abstract land of words and verses, taking half a handhold in psychology before he had acquainted himself with the rudiments of anatomy. If there was a common ground where they now met, it was unlikely that they would cross and diverge—that Jacques would ever end up reading Shakespeare or that he himself would master the details of chemical change. To this extent, their interests, while similar, also seemed to complement one another.

It was beginning to grow light, the color of darkness slowly receding from the sky over Le Havre, leaving the pallid gray of cliffs and clouds to reemerge from the mist. They still had a little cognac left, the last of which Thomas poured into the two glasses. They had been talking for more than six hours, yet he felt he had only begun to explore what needed to be said; he could not catch the next thought fast enough for his determination to do justice to the previous one.

As the night began to fade, Jacques drained his glass. "Shall I tell you something peculiar that has happened in the course of this conversation?" he said.

"What?"

"You have become fluent in French."

"Have I?"

"Yes. At the start you had all the words in the wrong order and you spoke slowly. Now you talk like a native. A native of Brittany, I am afraid, like me, with a Vannes accent, but at least you sound like a Frenchman."

Thomas felt gratified. "Now I shall have to teach you English."

"Dear God. Let us do the simple things first."

"Establish a new clinical method."

"Yes. And a map of the mind."

"Then English."

Thomas bent down and put on his socks and shoes. "We can continue our conversation," he said, "over breakfast. One of the cafés on the front should be open by now."

"Not the front. Let's find a back street. And before we go," said Jacques, "we should drink a toast to our future work."

Thomas lifted his glass. "All right," he said. "I propose we drink to that phrase of yours, if I remember it right. 'The meeting point of thought and flesh.'"

They drank solemnly. "Don't finish," said Jacques. "I have another. It was something you said, in your ancient French—your former language. It was a fine phrase and I think we should drink to that as well. It was the words that made me know you would be my friend, which is why I ran back to the pension to get food and drink. I propose a toast to: 'The way in which functions the mind of the human.'"

They drained their glasses. "If," said Thomas, "I am to be your friend and we are to speak in French, we will need to find some better words for 'mind.'"

"Very well. You can be the master of words."

"I may force some Anglo-Saxon distinctions on you, or we may improvise with German."

"Good. But now . . . To breakfast."

They labored back over the cold sand and walked into the town, heads down, glancing up only to see if they could find a café that was open.

THAT AFTERNOON, when Prince Albert had slowly cleared the plates of langoustine shells, the Muscadet bottle, peaches and grapes, Richard said he needed to go up to the room for a rest. He had returned at two in the morning from the gambling room of the Trouville casino and was enigmatic about how the night had gone for him. Sonia set off with Thomas to hire a boat.

"Do you know how to sail?" she asked, as they walked along the front.

"Yes. I learned that summer at Mablethorpe. But I imagine we would take a man with us."

It was a hot afternoon, and most of the holidaymakers stayed indoors behind the shutters of the new Norman villas. Sonia wore a wide-brimmed straw hat held in place and fastened beneath the chin by a pink scarf; even so, she felt uncomfortably warm in her long skirt and high-necked blouse.

"Do you like Deauville?" she said.

"It needs to be used a little more, doesn't it? I don't like the way that all the streets are at right angles to one another. I think I like the look of Trouville better. It has more character."

"That's where the boatman is."

"Perhaps we should stay and have dinner in a dirty old café after our sailing."

"I would love to. But . . . well, we can't, can we?"

"No."

There was a pause, then Sonia brightened. "And in any case the food at the pension—"

"I know. Those langoustines. And the little cheese things afterward. I could grow very fat in that dining room."

They came to the boatman's house down a small path on the hillside above the bay; it seemed to belong to an earlier century than the houses of the resort and there was a long silence after they had knocked at the splintery front door. They could hear an old man's voice calling out from inside, then the sound of boots crossing a flagged floor. The door scraped back and they found themselves looking into the startled face of a tousle-haired young man, whose eyes moved up and down Sonia's figure, from the bonnet to the boots, finally coming to rest on Thomas, somewhere in the region of his chest.

"Yes, yes, come in," he said, when Thomas explained why they were there. "Come and sit down for a moment." He pulled back two chairs from the table in the cool parlor and disappeared.

Sonia and Thomas looked round the room, where lobster pots and fishing tackle were piled up between the chairs. He raised one eyebrow.

"Can you swim, Queenie?"

"Stop it. You know I can."

The young man returned. "This is my grandfather. It is his boat."

Thomas held out his hand to be shaken by the owner and found it grasped with painful firmness.

"Guillaume," said the powerful old man. "You can call me that. My grandson is also Guillaume. Little Guillaume."

"And your son?" said Thomas. "Is he—"

"I have no son. The boy's mother is my daughter. I always wished for sons, but alas . . . So the lad and I run the business together. Staying in Deauville, are you? I remember when it was just a swamp. Even young Guillaume remembers, don't you? Where are you from?"

"From England," said Sonia.

The old man looked surprised. He rubbed his hand through the white bristles of his cheek. "We've never met a . . . Anyway, I will send the boy with you. Guillaume, don't forget to look at the pots on the way up this evening. Mind your step on the way down to the boat."

Young Guillaume beamed with impatience. "Shall we go?"

He went ahead and held out his hand for Sonia as she descended, lifting her skirts to avoid the sharpest of the small rocks. He took them to a jetty and helped them into a wooden skiff, which he then rowed out to an anchored sailing boat. When they were safely embarked, he took off his shirt and shoes and flung them down on the deck; then he rowed the skiff back and attached it to a wooden buoy closer to the shore; to Thomas and Sonia's surprise, he then dived over the side and swam back to them, hauling himself up into the sailing boat, disdaining Thomas's offer of help, and slithering aboard like a familiar dolphin, shaking off the drops of seawater as he set about rigging the sails. Sonia sat on a bench, her lips pressed together, trying not to catch Thomas's eye.

Guillaume soon had the boat heading out into the bay, picking up what small breeze fluttered in the torpid afternoon. He had replaced his shirt, with mumbled apologies, but his rolled cotton trousers still dripped onto the deck. As he whisked the tiller from side to side, shouting instructions when the boom swung across, he kept his gaze fixed on

Sonia, as though not quite able to believe that a woman as elegant as this was in his grandfather's battered craft. Thomas asked a few polite questions about the resort and the weather, which Guillaume answered without taking his eyes from Sonia.

Eventually, after a sudden change of tack, he found himself opposite Thomas. "And you, Monsieur, you are also from England?"

"No," said Thomas, "I am from Vannes. In Brittany. Do you know it?"

"No, no, we have not traveled far in my family."

"Really, Thomas," said Sonia in English, "you are a child sometimes."

"I know. But not for much longer. I shall soon be twenty-one and then I shall find the cares of the world pressing in on me. There's not much time left to be a child in."

"No. Not for either of us, I suppose." Sonia looked over the sea for a moment. "But he seemed to believe you, didn't he? I must say your French is extraordinary. What happened?"

"I did a rapid course last night. It lasted twelve hours, from when we said good night in the hall, to about ten this morning. I spent the whole time with Jacques, the young man from the boardinghouse. I have never met anyone like him. He is wonderful. He is just like me—"

"Is that why he is wonderful?"

"Let me finish! He is just like me, but completely different at the same time. He has had all the same thoughts yet they have come from a different life, a different world. It's like two men bumping into each other in the jungle when one started in Iceland and one in China—and finding they are reading the same book. He has a marvelous mind, he's so lucid, yet at the same time he makes me laugh. I want to laugh all the time when I'm with him, though I think he is a sad man, really. I have never had a friend like this, ever. The boys in the village, I mean, I liked fighting them and the boys at school, or at Cambridge there were one or two, of course, but that was like befriending the man in the next cell. But Jacques—Jacques, I feel as though I've been waiting all my life to meet him."

Sonia laughed. "My dear Thomas, you sound as if you are in love."

The boat tracked back and forth, heading west into the Deauville bay and then beyond.

"Stay out as long as possible," Sonia told Guillaume, who nodded vigorously. She rearranged her hat, to shade herself from the sun, and settled back against the side of the boat.

"And you?" said Thomas, looking up from where his fingers split the white water by the hull.

"Me what?"

"Are you in love?"

"Oh, Thomas, you cannot ask that question of a married woman." Sonia looked away.

Thomas knew the answer, but thought Sonia might like to tell. "Did love come?" he said. "As mother said it would?"

"It's not right to ask me such questions."

"Did it?"

"Yes," said Sonia. "Yes, if you really insist on knowing. I have great affection and respect for Richard. He has many fine qualities and I like trying to manage his house."

"It sounds as though you like the job of being a wife more than—"

"I do enjoy it. I like cooking, as you know. I try out some of the old receipts I learned from Mrs. Travers."

"Sheep's head broth?"

"Do you remember that?"

"I used to dread Tuesday suppers. Every day from the previous Wednesday."

Sonia laughed. "Kidney pudding he likes. And I got away with giblet pie."

"Why is money so short?"

"I think the sugar business has not proved as easy as we thought. There have been sugar brokers in London for a long time, and some of them are very large and powerful companies. And the partners in the business have been reckless. There's one called Jackman who has been especially ill-advised, I am told."

"Is it a problem with buyers or suppliers?"

"It's no use asking me. I don't understand how the business works and I have been told very little about it. My husband says it's not something for me to know about."

"And do you mind that?"

"Of course not. He does his work and I do mine. Though I wish sometimes he would not be quite so strict. My dress allowance has been cut to almost nothing. I made the curtains for the bedrooms myself. It's not that I mind or that I think it is beneath me, but he ordered four new coats for himself. He says he must have them to impress his clients. And I am hardly allowed out at all."

"Poor girl. No parties."

"I am not able to go to parties because he has sent the little coach away and I am forbidden to take a cab."

"Poor Queenie. I am sorry."

"It doesn't really matter. As long as I please him."

"And when will you start a family?"

Sonia stared at her hands, clasped in her lap. "I have been to see a doctor about it. He says he can see nothing wrong with me, but I fear there may be. Sir James Bannerman was his name. He has a brass plaque in Wimpole Street. I asked Mama if she would pay his account because I didn't want my husband to know."

"Did he have no solution at all?"

"He recommended patience."

"Might it not be worth Richard going to see a doctor?"

"No, no! I did mention it to him but he told me he was perfectly healthy. No, Thomas, I think the problem lies with me."

They were far from land and could make out no more than the smudges and outlines of the town.

"Sonia, would you mind if I went for a swim?"

"But you have no bathing costume."

"I know. But I love the feel of the water on my skin. It's one of the greatest feelings in the world, to swim in a deep sea."

"How will you dry yourself?"

"The sun will dry me quickly. I'll explain to Guillaume. You look the other way while I undress and dive in."

Guillaume grinned incredulously when the plan was explained; he slackened off the sail and a few moments later Thomas dived into the cold green water. He surfaced, spluttering and exclaiming.

"It's wonderful! I feel like a primitive animal in his element at last. Sonia, you must come in."

Sonia laughed. "You silly boy."

"I mean it!" Thomas disappeared under the water and reemerged on the other side of the boat. He gripped onto the side, gasping and laughing.

"It's so wonderful. You feel it wash you clean. It's like being an animal, a porpoise. I'm sure we must once have lived in the sea."

"Is it cold?"

"Not at all. Do come in, Sonia. I'll make Guillaume look the other way, then I'll hold up my shirt for you when you want to come back."

"Thomas, don't be ridiculous. I am a respectable married lady with—"

"No, you're not! You're little Sonia from Torrington. The little girl from the big house. Or the not so big house in fact, but don't tell your husband."

"I'm not telling him anything of this nonsense."

"Will you please do what I say, Sonia. Get in at once."

"You are a bully, Thomas."

"I am a strong character, Sonia. There is a difference."

In Sonia's green eyes he saw the look he had most loved in any human being in his short life, the look of modesty at war with daring. He admired both qualities in his sister, the fact that they could exist together and the way that daring always won.

He explained to Guillaume that he must fix his gaze on the land behind Trouville until such time as he was told otherwise.

"Sonia, tell me when you're about to be indecent and I shall dive under the waves. Then jump in."

He could see Sonia's skirt and stockings being laid on the bench on the other side of the sail; they were followed by some undergarments, and when she was dressed in only a shift she called out, "I'm coming!"

Thomas sank beneath the waves and held his nose for as long as he could. When he came up, it was to hear Sonia screaming from the other side of the boat. "It's freezing!"

He swam round to her, laughing so hard that he could barely breathe.

"Isn't it marvelous?"

"It's freezing! You horrible man, why didn't you tell me?"

"Swim up and down, you'll soon get warm."

Sonia did as she was told, her head above the gentle waves, its hair still neatly parted in the center as she cautiously breaststroked to and fro.

"You liar, you horrid liar," she spluttered through her chattering teeth.

"But you did it, you did it!"

"I know. And now I want to get out."

"All right. Look the other way while I clamber in. Then I'll hold up my shirt for you."

Thomas heaved himself up over the stern and pulled on his cotton drawers. "Trouville!" he shouted to Guillaume. "See if you can make out your grandfather's cottage. Tell me what he's cooking for your dinner. Come on, Sonia. Lift yourself up while I look toward England. I am holding up my shirt for you. Dear old England! If she only knew . . ."

Sonia managed to pull herself, shivering, back into the boat and put on Thomas's shirt. She went back to her place, shaking and laughing.

"You'll soon warm up," said Thomas. "Do you want my jacket?" He draped it round her shoulders and hugged her as he did so. "You are a sport, Sonia. Dear God, let no one in the world ever deny that." He kissed the salt water on her cheek.

"All right, Guillaume," he said, "you can look now, so—"

"No, he can't. My legs! Tell him to wait."

When Sonia was dry enough to dress again, Thomas went to sit with Guillaume in the bow until such time as Sonia said they could turn round.

Thomas pulled on his trousers and resumed his seat, allowing the early evening sun to dry his bare chest.

"All right, Guillaume, once round the bay, then home for dinner."

"Very well, Monsieur."

Sonia was still shivering slightly, but apart from that, and her damp hair, had so resumed her former bearing that no one could have told that she was not the most conventional young wife in Deauville.

THAT NIGHT Jacques packed his small suitcase to return home: a white shirt that was a patchwork of Tante Mathilde's repeated needlework, a dissecting knife, a pair of hairbrushes given to him by Abbé Henri. He stowed them neatly against the check lining of the cheap case, but as he did so, he felt sick. The months ahead were like a tundra, a gray plain through which he would have to drive himself until he could arrange to see Thomas again.

He sat down on a cane-seated chair in the window, where he parted the shutters and looked down onto the garden. Prince Albert was delivering what looked like a jug of *citron pressé* to Sonia and her husband at the table beneath the magnolia. Jacques felt his heart give another lurch. Sonia looked flushed beneath her hat and a little uneasy; there seemed an awkwardness between her and the English husband. Yet in her open face, her pale pink dress with its white sash and the gentle movements of her hands as she stirred her drink, Jacques saw all the qualities that had been absent from his life. Perhaps his anguish was more complicated than he had thought.

When they said goodbye on the beach the next morning, Jacques wanted Thomas to swear an oath in blood, a promise that they would always be friends, but feared that Thomas might think it puerile.

"But you will write a letter from England, won't you?"

"Yes, I will. There is not much to do on those cold evenings in East Anglia. And you will reply?"

"Of course," said Jacques.

They faced the sea for the last time. "One day, Thomas, we will work together. We will do great things to alleviate the suffering of human beings."

"I hope so, Jacques, if we are not—"

"No, we will do it. There are no ifs. It will happen."

"I was going to say, if we are not deflected by the petty demands of life, the need to make money, families, idleness . . ."

"My family does not really exist. As for money, we will make enough together. We will both be doctors of one kind or another and there is always a need for medicine."

"Will you come to England one day?"

"One day, Thomas. When I have some money. Tell me what your plans are now."

"I shall finish my degree. I will train further. I will travel. I don't know exactly." Thomas felt Jacques squeezing his arm ferociously. He laughed. "I am too young to be certain."

"But you will write. You will not lose touch."

"I promise. Anyway, what about you? What will you do next?" said Thomas.

"If I am to understand and cure the afflictions of the mind, I need to study them first. To try to understand. I am going to study further in Paris."

"All right," said Thomas. "For my part, I promise this. When I am ready, I will come to you. I will take no other work until we have tried together. Until we have tried to climb our mountain."

"Do you swear?"

"I swear." Thomas held out his hand and Jacques took it, then gathered Thomas in his arms. They embraced tightly.

No need for blood, thought Jacques.

The wind was beginning to moan softly and waves were starting to swell; there was the first rumble and spray of the coming autumn.

"I love you," said Jacques.

"What?" said Thomas, over the noise of the sea.

WHEN SONIA asked if he would like to go sailing again, Thomas told her that he needed to study that afternoon; she tried to persuade her husband to come instead, but he was having lunch with a man he had met the night before in Trouville, someone who, he told Sonia, might be the very person he had been looking for.

"He knows everyone in Paris, stockbrokers, people in the government," said Richard, flushed with excitement. "He is a marvelous fellow as well. I just know he is the man to turn our little craft about and head her into the wind. I shall telegraph to Jackman. Meanwhile I am taking him to the best lunch in town. You have to spend money to make money, that's what I always say."

So Sonia went alone to the next bay, feeling a little furtive, but not knowing why. When she knocked at the door of the fisherman's cottage there was no answer, and she went to sit in the garden until someone should return.

"Ah . . . Madame. Excuse me, I did not see you there." It was Guillaume. "Have you been waiting long?"

"No. I am sorry. I had no way of telling you I would be coming."

"I am afraid I cannot take you out this afternoon because my grand-father has the boat. He won't be back before nightfall."

"In that case," said Sonia, "I had better return to the hotel. Perhaps we could make an arrangement for tomorrow."

"Would you like a drink before you go back, Madame? It's hot, isn't it?" He gave an awkward laugh.

"Perhaps a glass of water."

In the cool of the parlor, Guillaume seated himself opposite her, with a jug of water and two glasses. He grinned repeatedly and, Sonia thought, if he had had a tail, it would have been thumping the wooden bench he sat on. This made her think of Dido, and Amelia, the force of whose wagging tail had once freed a frozen tap in the backyard, and she felt wistful for her old home.

Guillaume showed her some fishing hooks and floats he had made, but it soon became clear that what he wanted to talk about was her. Sonia could not think what made her life seem intriguing to him; she presumed it must be the fact that she was foreign, and Guillaume had never before spoken to a person from another country.

"What was your home like?" he said. "Not like this." He glanced round the jumble of nets, pots and clothes left to dry over the furniture.

"It was a happy home. We never had very much money, but that did not matter to Thomas and me. When he was young, he used to sleep in my room. I had always wanted to be a big sister because I have an elder brother and I grew tired of being the little one all the time. Thomas was a naughty boy. He made us all laugh. I used to read him stories before he could read for himself. He was always very violent in his feelings. Occa-sionally he seemed to see things I had not seen, so that I began to look forward to what he would say. Then when we were older I was sent away to learn to speak French and to practice the piano and all these things that make you a more valuable wife while Thomas stayed at school and learned many more things than I ever knew. And then there was a time when I felt he might leave me behind because he was impatient. But something seemed to stop him. Although he argued with my parents, he stopped short with me. It was as though he remembered the old days when we slept in the same room and fell asleep together each night by the light of the candle. And if it was cold, he would climb into bed with me. These are the things you remember about your home, I suppose. The pattern of the candle shadows on the wall, the fiery little boy who needs your arm round him to make him sleep. Nothing happens to make you happy. There are no prizes or thunderbolts or adventures. Just the shadow of the candle on the wall."

"I see," said Guillaume.

Sonia coughed. "Then one day, when you are grown up, you suddenly become aware that something has gone. In any event," she said, making an effort to recollect herself, "my husband and I live a very satisfactory life. In London. A very big city."

"I imagine."

Sonia smiled. "No one has ever asked me these questions. I am not sure that even I know the answers."

"Excuse me, Madame, I—"

"No, no. It's all right. In fact, I like it. It's . . . reassuring."

"You like to be reassured?"

"Yes."

"But why, Madame? You are—forgive me, beautiful, and wealthy and—"

"Not really. Neither."

"But look . . ." Guillaume gestured with outstretched hand to the messy parlor.

Sonia blushed. "Yes . . . but we are not rich, I promise you. And I am certainly not beautiful."

"But—"

"Ssh. Please. I know. My mother used to tell me my best feature was my feet." Sonia laughed. "Can you imagine?"

Guillaume also laughed. "Perhaps she did not mean that. Perhaps—"

"Now we will talk about something else."

"But, Madame, tell me one thing. Why is it that you need to be reassured? If I was like you I would wake up every day and thank God for everything he has given me. I would not need to be told every day how fortunate I was. I would still remember from the day before!"

Sonia began to laugh. "You are right, Guillaume. It is a mystery, an utter mystery. All I can say is that a plant needs water not once in its life but every evening, sometimes more often."

"Yes, Madame, but a plant—"

"I know. It was not a precise comparison."

Sonia took up her hat and prepared to leave. Richard would be waking from a sleep made heavy by the wine he would have taken with his new business friend; it was a slow and fractious time of the afternoon, before the cool of evening brought a change of clothes and a quickening of pace. She pictured him stirring, licking his dry lips and splashing water from the washstand into his face.

There was a loud knocking on the parlor door, which Guillaume went to open. Sonia, with her back to the door, recognized the English voice.

"I'm looking for my wife—ah, there she is. What on earth are you doing here?"

Sonia rose to greet her husband. To her annoyance, she found that her face was hot with shame. "Hello, Richard. This is where we come sailing. I—"

"I know it is. They told me at the hotel. Why aren't you sailing?"

"Guillaume's grandfather has the boat. I don't think he will be coming back until evening, so Guillaume kindly offered me a glass of water before I set off."

"Sonia, what on earth do you think you are doing?"

"I told you, Richard. How was your luncheon?"

Richard snorted. "The bounder didn't come. Wretched man. Made an ass of me, sitting there on my own at the best table with the confounded waiter hovering over me."

"I am sorry. What a disappointment. I imagine—"

"I think you imagine far too much. It is not your place to imagine, it is your place to be with your husband. Go back to the hotel at once. I will deal with this young man."

Richard's voice was shaking. Sonia had not seen him angry in this way before, yet she sensed that the rage had somehow accumulated in him and felt uneasy that she had been responsible for making it overflow.

"Guillaume has behaved with perfect propriety, so please . . ." Her voice faltered then died, as Richard came toward her.

"Get out of here! Go home."

She turned and hurried through the door, without glancing back.

IV

THE BUILDING BLOCKED THE DOWNLAND VIEW IN BOTH DIREC-
tions: low, brick upon brick, some livid, some ocher, stretching from one
horizon to the other. In the center of the monstrous construction was an
oddity: a bell tower like that of the cathedral in Siena; and such Italianate
fancy was not what Thomas had expected of the county lunatic asylum.

He entered by the guarded double iron gates where the coach had set
him down and walked slowly up the avenue in a mild September afternoon. It was Sunday, and he had been told to report at three o'clock
before the arrival of new patients at teatime. He clasped a leather bag
with his spare clothes in one hand and, in the other, the book he had
been reading on the coach, *A Manual of Psychological Medicine* by Bucknill and Tuke. Around him on the lawns, contained within the high
enclosing walls, were specimen trees, some with benches placed beneath
them; beyond a pale willow was an icehouse, and beyond that further
brick outbuildings, workshops, laundries and what looked to Thomas
like the back of pigsties. He walked confidently to the main door of the
building and pulled the bell. A spy hole swiveled, and he saw a single eye
inspect him before, with a grinding of numerous locks, half the door
was opened. In the entrance hall was a wooden booth with a glass front,
in which the porter who let him in had been reading a newspaper by
gaslight. Thomas's nostrils twitched at some unfamiliar smell.

"Dr. Midwinter. I am the new assistant medical officer. I believe Dr.
Faverill is expecting me."

"The superintendent's office is down the far end. The name's above the door." The porter spoke with a skeptical edge to his voice, as though not sure if Thomas was who he said he was. Thomas wondered if the man was a former patient.

"Shall I?" Thomas gestured toward the corridor on his left.

The porter looked at him, then said, "Walk outside the building. You don't have no keys yet. Take the green door at the end."

It was, although Thomas could not have said why, a relief to be in the open air again. He walked along the flank of the asylum, on a graveled path; at his feet were half-windows from the basement, barred, their lower lights underground. Occasionally he would go past a ground-floor window with the same arched top as the others, but bricked in. He was reluctant to turn his head to look, and kept his gaze ahead of him until he had reached the end of the wing, where he found the green door at the foot of one of the smaller bell towers.

Inside, he knocked on a door beside which was Dr. William Faverill's name, painted white on a black background, as his own had been at the foot of his staircase at Cambridge. He remembered the time he had climbed his college wall in the small hours after a visit to Newmarket to find that some vandal had painted out the letters "winter" from his name and substituted "night." He knocked. Faverill's office was full of smoke from a pile of coal in a small grate, beside which sat a woman in a shawl, rocking back and forth in her chair.

"Midwinter. Yes, of course." Faverill waved his arm toward a vacant seat. He was a gaunt, tallish man, with fair hair parted in the middle and swept into two curling wings above the ear; his beard was sparse on the upper cheeks, but dense and gray beneath the jaw. He looked at Thomas over the top of his spectacles, then through them, then peeled them off his face altogether as he sat down. "You are very welcome, sir. Matilda, this is Dr. Midwinter, who has come to assist us in our mission. Dr. Midwinter, this is Matilda, who helps me with all manner of details, domestic and medical. Forgive the smoke. It is our first fire of the year and I fear the chimney needs sweeping. Let me see." He picked up a piece of paper from the desk. "Cambridge. Edinburgh. Then St. Bartholomew's? Is that right? Is that where you completed your studies?"

"Yes."

"Very good. Commendable. You will enjoy meeting my colleague, the deputy superintendent, Mr. McLeish. A Scot. From which town is he, Matilda? A Fifer, I think. Not a real Highlander, though I have never been certain of Scotch tribal terms. An inspired people, though, and with a medical tradition second to none. McLeish is the lungs and liver of the asylum."

Thomas wondered who the heart was, but found it difficult to concentrate on what Faverill was saying because he was too interested in the rocking figure by the fire. If the porter was not a former lunatic, then this woman certainly exhibited florid symptoms of insanity, muttering to herself and grinding the fingers of one hand into the palm of the other.

The office was lined with bookshelves, and Thomas narrowed his eyes in an effort to read their titles through the smoke. Apart from some standard texts on anatomy and two editions of Bucknill and Tuke, there seemed to be little of any medical, let alone psychological nature; most of the space was taken up with books on botany, geography and philosophy. There was even, Thomas noticed, a shelf of novels by Sir Walter Scott. Well, he thought, psychiatry is a young discipline; that is part of its excitement.

"Now we shall have some tea," said Faverill. "I find it beneficial to have a refreshing cup before the arrival of our new patients. After the reception process is complete I sometimes take something a little stronger. Perhaps you would care to join me then. No, I have another idea. As your introduction to the asylum I shall allow you to write up the new arrivals. McLeish shall do the men and you may do the women."

Faverill busied himself with a kettle and teapot. "Numbers," he said, "that is the difficulty that is facing us, Midwinter. In a word. Numbers." Thomas was surprised that it was Faverill, not Matilda, who made the tea, but she seemed to expect nothing less, and took her steaming cup from him, as her due, when it was ready. Faverill sat in the rather beautiful wooden chair behind the desk, its walnut curve accommodating his frock-coated back, as he stretched out and placed his buttoned boots on the blotter. "Doubtless you are aware, Midwinter, that families once looked after their lunatics at home, but the great men of our calling—I hesitate to call it a profession until it is recognized as such by our equals—have demonstrated beyond contradiction that a well-run asylum can offer restorative benefits unavailable even to the most well-meaning family. Our fellow-countryman Samuel Tuke, among others, has shown that with kindness, a firm hand and tasks to occupy the mind most people can be helped in their affliction. The word 'asylum,' let us never forget, denotes safety." He sipped his tea.

"Oh yes," said Thomas, pleased to have a chance to show his enthusiasm. "I visited the York Retreat and was most impressed by what Mr. Tuke had established there. It was almost a model society, though of course its citizens were . . . eccentric." He did not look toward the fireside. "But the so-called moral treatment is certainly the best palliative that exists—until such time as we can establish the etiology of the different diseases."

He felt pleased with the rigorous way he had expressed himself; his superior would surely see in him an assistant of entirely scientific mind, not someone whose first interest had been in playgoing.

"Er . . . Yes," said Faverill. "Very possibly. But numbers, you see, Midwinter. That's the thing. We are nigh on two thousand. Your appointment here as additional medical officer has been authorized by the county council, but it was granted only after considerable pleading—yes, I think pleading is not too strong a word—on my part."

"Do you mean—"

"I mean that sometimes I find myself the captain of a stricken vessel. I have the stars by which to navigate; I try never to take my eyes from the heavens, because I know the constellations. I know the direction of our landfall. But on bad days I feel that we are holed below the waterline. Do you understand me?"

"I think so," said Thomas. A clearing in the smoke had just revealed the poetry of Tennyson and Wordsworth on a shelf behind the desk.

"Your task—one of your many tasks, I may say, but perhaps the most important single one—is to help me never to take my eyes from the stars in the sky."

Faverill stood up and walked round the desk. He smiled at Thomas. "Let us go then, you and I, Dr. Midwinter. We shall walk the length of the building, at the other end of which I shall introduce you to Mr. McLeish. Matilda, the keys, if you please."

Faverill put his arm round Thomas's shoulder and ushered him toward the door, clasping in his other hand a large iron ring that Matilda had passed him, from which hung a dozen keys.

From the inner vestibule, Faverill unlocked a double, iron-barred door which gave into a low-roofed corridor, whose walls and ceiling were tiled in white and whose floor was made of some kind of asphalt—spongy, uneven and disintegrating. There were dim gaslights at intervals of fifty feet or so, though not all were working; a sort of low mist seemed to have gathered from the damp floor, obscuring the way ahead, so that, as far as Thomas could see, the passageway was never-ending.

"This side is the ladies' wing," said Faverill, unlocking a smaller door to his left. He gestured Thomas into a large, twilit room with white-washed, unplastered walls, a brick floor and a fireplace, inactive, with a padlocked wire guard. Thomas estimated that there were about sixty patients.

Half a dozen women sat at a plain deal table in the center of the room, some dressed in black overalls and hobnailed boots, some in bombazine dresses and woolen shawls, a few in clothes they appeared to have stitched for themselves. An elderly, white-haired patient was banging her enameled tin bowl with a wooden spoon and screeching. Her nearest neighbor was a blank-faced young woman, clearly an idiot, Thomas thought, perhaps also deaf. On a bed behind them lay a woman who panted and moaned and mopped at her face, which even in the gloom Thomas could see was flushed; she appeared to have soiled the bed, though had not noticed in her delirium. Typhoid fever, he thought, with the reflex speed of diagnosis he had been taught in the acute wards; little could be done for her, and it would remit in time.

If there had been a meal, most of the women seemed to have finished and returned to their beds or to corners of the room. Some sat with their arms wrapped round their knees, hunched, waiting, rocking; many chattered, though without care for a listener, like rooks calling to an open sky.

A small woman with large eyes and ingratiating smile made her way across the room to them.

"Hello, Ruth," said Faverill. "This is Dr. Midwinter, my new assistant."

Thomas noticed that the woman wore a dress of toughened sailcloth with stitching that might have withstood a force-ten gale; the sleeves were sewn into the side of the dress so that her hands were allowed little movement. She was able, nonetheless, to stroke Faverill's sleeve as she spoke to him.

"Do me right now, sir," she said, and her voice had an undulating Welsh accent. "A little bit of what's good goes a long way, as the plowboy said to his master. When I was a girl, you know, they used to come from all parts just to look at me. Some of them wanted to touch me, but I said, 'No!' I was never like that. I was a proper girl from a good family. Twelve of us there were and went to chapel every day and twice on Sunday. So don't think that of me. Don't tell me you think I'm like that, now, please. When my father comes to collect me, now, he'll put you right. Have you heard from him yet? Did he write to you like he promised?"

She gripped Faverill's arm with her separated hands.

"Don't believe what they say about me, will you? I'm not that sort of lady, you should know that by now."

"It's all right, Ruth," said Faverill, freeing himself and moving away. "As you know very well, I have the highest regard for you."

"And you!" she said, turning toward Thomas. "Wouldn't you like to now? I can see from your eyes that you would. You filthy vermin!"

Thomas felt Faverill's hand on his elbow, moving him down the ward.

"The ways of gentleness," said Faverill vaguely.

"What?"

"It was a phrase used by Pinel. It describes the path we try to follow."

On either side of their slow progress were beds on which lay women with conditions that made them twitch or shake; some cried out as they trembled; one appeared to be at the start of an epileptic fit. Next to her sat a fat girl, no more than fifteen, with mongoloid features and filth-matted hair.

"Ruth," said Faverill, "is a good woman, I believe. She is educated, and she worked quite happily as a clerk in a tobacco company for some years."

"What brought her to you?"

"Mania."

"Do you have no more detail of her illness?"

"My dear Midwinter, we have more detail than we can record. The woman is a fountain of detail. For the purposes of the asylum and what we can do for her, however, she falls clearly into the category of mania. You are of course familiar with the categories?"

"Yes, sir," said Thomas. "Melancholia—"

"She is seldom melancholic. She has none of the chronic symptoms, no more than you or I."

"Idiocy."

"Quite the opposite, I should say."

"What do we know of her heredity?"

"Enough to say that there is no degenerative trend. Which leaves dementia. I have occasionally thought, Midwinter, that her mania has had elements of dementia in it. But it is sufficiently concentrated on one thing, what one might call the amorous—"

"Erotomania?"

Faverill sucked air over his teeth. "I recoil from diagnosing any lady so simply, but there is a certain consistency to her mental process." He picked his way with skilled elegance down the narrow space between the beds. "I shall show you the rooms we are proudest not to use. Come."

A back door from the main ward opened into a bathing area, stone floored, with three doorless cubicles. An attendant sat on a rush-seated chair by the entrance and Thomas wondered why she was sitting when there seemed so much to be done among the sixty or seventy beds that had been packed into the main part of the ward.

From the bathroom, Faverill pushed open another door into a small cell with ironwork over its window; the walls and floor were padded with canvas from which horsehair was spilling. "I am pleased to say that we have not had recourse to this room since I have been here. We leave the door unlocked. I made it my mission when I arrived never to resort to mechanical restraint. I was much influenced as a young man by a book written by a Mr. Conolly, an English alienist, on this very matter. Perhaps you have heard his name?"

"I have read his book, sir. It is inspiring."

"Indeed so," said Faverill. "It is one of the stars by which I navigate."

As they closed the door on the padded room, they were timidly approached by a young woman of about twenty years old, neater in her dress than most, but with troubled brown eyes.

"Sirs," she said, "if I could ask you . . . I am going crazy for want of something to do. I am locked in here for so many hours each day and I had the misfortune not to be taught to read when I was young. Not that there's books anyway."

"You have the airing court for exercise?" said Faverill.

"Yes, sir, I do and right glad we are of it." She had the accent of the county, Thomas noticed, but not the upward lilt of the voice it normally engendered; her tone was melancholic, and she appeared terrified that she had exceeded her rights and might at any moment, at the wave of a doctor's hand, be confined more strictly.

"I shall speak to the attendant," said Faverill, "and see if she cannot find you some work, on the farm or in the laundry. Should you like that?"

"Oh yes, sir. Yes, please, sir." The girl's eyes filled with tears, but she was not smiling. "You will not forget me, will you, sirs? My name is Daisy."

"I shall not forget," said Faverill.

Thomas smiled at the young woman as they left, reminding himself to remember her.

"What is her diagnosis?" he asked.

"I am not familiar with the young lady," said Faverill. "As I told you, we are close on two thousand now, and more than half are on the female side. You can find her name in the register with her admission notes. McLeish will show you. I suggest you look up her Christian name first because she may not have a surname."

"No surname?"

"Some have no names at all."

Faverill locked the door of the ward behind them, and they were once more in the infinite corridor. Faverill noticed Thomas's stretched, inquiring look as they set off. He smiled.

"It is built on an impressive scale, our asylum, is it not?"

"Indeed, sir," said Thomas.

The gas lamps grew less frequent as they walked on over the asphalt floor. Mingled with the damp that rose beneath their feet was an odor of missed excrement and saturated brick, a redolence of despair. This, with the failing light and the narrowing perspective, combined to give Thomas the impression that he was walking slightly downhill.

"Can you imagine," said Faverill, "the total length of passageway in this building?"

"I could not easily put a figure to it, sir."

"Including the first floor, where one's passage is through the wards themselves, we have six miles of corridors."

Thomas could think of nothing to say.

"Remarkable," said Faverill, "is it not? What a feat of engineering. It contains more than ten million bricks and was built in less than two years. And what generous intentions it bespeaks toward the unfortunate!"

Thomas could still not find anything to say; in any case, his mouth was dry, his throat was closed.

"In the circumstances," Faverill continued, "you will understand if I do not take you into every ward. We should need several days. This corridor alone is more than one-third of a mile long."

"One-third . . ." Thomas managed words at last.

"Indeed," said Faverill. "We believe it to be the longest corridor in Europe."

After fifteen minutes' walking, broken only by Faverill's occasional unlocking of a door, they reached the center of the building. Through an internal window they could see the hall with the wooden booth where Thomas had first entered. The porter smirked from behind the glass partition.

"Good afternoon, Grogan," called Faverill, moving smartly onward to a set of double iron-barred doors. "Now for the men," he said to Thomas, with a faint but noticeable dulling to the brightness of his manner. The doors swung to behind them.

"Grogan enjoys Sundays," said Faverill as they plunged down into the gloom again. "He is allowed to take supper with McLeish. When we have admissions, he takes pleasure in seeing the unfortunates as they arrive, knowing they will always outnumber those we release. It reassures him in his sense of singularity. He came here fourteen years ago, raving and incontinent. He spent six weeks naked in the safe room, covered in his own filth."

"And how was he cured?"

"My predecessor gave him henbane, camphor, morphine, I believe. I stopped that. I set him to work in the gardens and the farm. He revealed an extraordinary brain. He can calculate and keep records better than I can."

"Should he not have returned to his family?"

"We did ask." Faverill coughed. "I am sorry to say that they declined. He prefers living in the asylum in any case. If he goes outside the walls he hears voices. I use a number of the saner patients in positions of responsibility. The attendant you saw in the women's ward, for instance. She came to us three years ago with acute melancholia. She is paid a little now to help the other attendants. She is not a very active person, I'm afraid, but she is intelligent in her way and they tell me they can rely on her. She is very strong. You would not think it from so small a woman, but she can carry the dining table on her back."

Faverill pulled a watch from his waistcoat pocket, but it was too dark to see it until they reached the next gas lamp. "I have time to show you one men's ward," said Faverill. "McLeish shall have to show you the rest tomorrow. Where are we? Let me see. Number Twelve." He glanced at Thomas's young face in the half-light. "No. Perhaps not. Number Fourteen, I think. Yes, I think that might be better."

He fumbled at the ring of keys and opened a door on their left. The room was similar in shape and design to the women's ward they had visited, but with an asphalt floor and high, unopenable windows. A few men were playing whist, surrounded by half a dozen onlookers; many were walking up and down, talking to themselves or to the reeking air. It was striking how properly dressed most of them were, in frock coats, suits, white neckerchiefs, pinned stocks, white shirts with collars; so at first only the untrimmed beards and the laceless boots marred the impression of normality. As Thomas moved gingerly into the dense atmosphere, his senses took in other strangenesses. A gentleman with neatly parted gray hair and gold tie pin was masturbating at the dining table; opposite him, oblivious to his behavior, sat a clerkly looking man, bespectacled, with eyebrows thick as mustaches, who moved his head slowly up and down in time to an incantation he endlessly repeated, which, to Thomas's ears, sounded like, "Di-ater. Di-ater."

Round them in the teatime air rotated bootmakers and porters, domestic servants, glaziers and painters, drapers, fishmongers, chimneysweeps, watchmakers and nurserymen; adrift from their former selves, they argued, jabbered or stood motionless, listening to absent voices. Their experience of living, their awareness of the moment, was so individual, it seemed to Thomas, that it could find no true expression, let alone response or comprehension; it was so individual, in fact, that it could only be seen as part of a mass—a "mass of lunatics," he reflected, the most heterogeneous entity you could imagine, a perfect oxymoron.

Most men seemed too lost in their thoughts to register the doctors' presence in the room, though one man with a beard down to his chest wrapped his arms over his head and retreated to a corner, whimpering, crouched, looking back occasionally through his hands at the intruders. Faverill gestured to an attendant to come over.

"Tyson," he said, "this is Dr. Midwinter, our new assistant medical officer."

Tyson held out his hand, and Thomas noticed the bottom of a tattoo at his wrist as the sleeve rode up; he was a swarthy, muscular man with an unsmiling face.

Faverill gestured to the dining table. "Can you stop that man doing that? His organ appears to have become blistered."

"It bleeds," said Tyson. "He won't leave it alone."

"Have you given him potassium bromide?"

"Yes. And they put some ointment on the organ too."

"Liquor of Epispasticus," said Faverill to Thomas. "No wonder it is blistered. Have you tried sewing up the front of his trousers?"

"Yes," said Tyson. "He just takes them down."

"Does he ever find . . . relief?"

"No. We could use the straitwaistcoat. Nothing else can stop him."

"Then you had better leave him. Does it distress the others?"

Tyson pursed his lips and shook his head. "Not here, sir. They have other things on—"

"Yes. Quite. There is the most terrible stench in here, Tyson."

"It's this floor, isn't it? It absorbs it. Them that shits themselves."

Faverill began to edge away. "Do something. Find a mop."

As Tyson went reluctantly to the bathroom, Faverill said, "He used to be a merchant seaman. He has no training, but he has his uses. Good afternoon."

He spoke to a neatly dressed man, gray-haired, with a polite manner.

"Doctor Faverill, is it not? Might I beg a moment of your time among these poor lunatics? My brother has written to me, do you see, a long letter from the War Office where he works. As you know, I am a man of considerable means though through no fault of my own I am unable to pay my debts at the moment. Mr. Gladstone, who is a close friend of my wife's family, has graciously invited me to submit my patent for a new kind of warship, which was to have been commissioned next year. The editor of the *Pall Mall Gazette* has commissioned a lengthy article from me. I should very much like you to cast an eye over it."

Thomas felt Faverill's hand on his elbow again. They had to cross the room to reach the door back into the corridor, and Thomas sensed as they made their way through the press that something had changed in the atmosphere. They walked through the moaning and the shouting, with hands reaching out to them. Thomas bit his lip and remembered holding Jacques in his arms on the Deauville shore. From the corner of his eye, he saw Tyson wrestle someone down onto a bed; he felt his sleeve being pulled back roughly, wrenched himself free, and they were outside again, in the endless corridor.

As he inhaled deeply, Thomas realized he had tried not to breathe during his time in the ward.

Faverill consulted his watch. "Very well, Dr. Midwinter. It is now time for us to see Mr. McLeish. I know he will be looking forward to meeting you. We have ten minutes to get to the other end of the men's wing from here, so no dawdling, please."

As they tunneled onward, past the moans and cries that reached them from behind locked doors, Thomas felt afraid. Suppose I become separated from myself, he thought: the warship designer was once as steady and sane as I am. He brought to mind more homely images as he walked on: of Sonia sitting on his bed that cold Christmas at Torrington, inventing a profession for him; he pictured Jacques, his black eyebrows driven to an apex as he puzzled over some point of physiology before the light of victory came into his eyes. It felt important to keep these pictures near the front of his mind.

McLeish's office was, in design, the mirror image of Faverill's, but it had no printed books, Thomas noticed. Instead, there were several ledgers on a shelf by the window and two new ones, leather-bound, open on the desk. McLeish was bald, short and meticulously dressed; the shine on his toe caps was like a reflection of his polished head.

After a few pleasantries, McLeish said to Thomas, "The new patients will be arriving in ten minutes' time. The superintendent tells me that you are to book in the women."

"Yes, if you will show me what to do."

Although McLeish's Scots accent was mild, he pronounced the word "women" as "woman," as though there were one in particular that Thomas was to see. As he stood and gathered up the two open ledgers, a white bull terrier, hitherto concealed, heaved itself out from behind the desk. McLeish fastened a chain to its collar and went toward the door.

The three men walked back along the outside of the building to the entrance hall beneath the main tower, where Faverill left them and hurried back toward his own wing and toward whatever "something stronger" was awaiting him.

"Did you meet Grogan yet?" said McLeish as they went up to the main door.

"The porter? Yes."

McLeish unlocked the door. "We tried to discharge the little bastard last year but his family refused to take him back. In you go."

Grogan had set up two long trestle tables in the hall, behind each of which sat two attendants with papers and ink. "That chair's for you," said McLeish. "You take their papers, you classify, and the attendant will give them a ward number. Don't be long about it."

Thomas said, "I am going to wait outside for a moment."

The September dusk was falling swiftly on the parkland as he looked up the avenue toward the guarded gates where he had himself come in. A fine rain was beginning to drift across the lawns on the first winds of autumn.

It was all unreal. What fate, what loops of time or circumstance, he thought, decree that I stand here? It might as well be me descending now from the carriage that has brought these people from the railway station. In another life that I have lived but cannot recall, cannot quite touch with my mind, perhaps it was me; and in another time, it could be me again. As our real world runs parallel to that of these poor lunatics, to be seen but not inhabited, so other times and lives are separated from ours only by the dimmest veil, through which an awareness more developed, more evolved than mine could reach out.

The lunatics began to walk down the avenue, their heads low, some supported or cajoled by family, some resolutely alone. Many were in the clothes of the workhouse, some brightened with colorful additions, gifts or remembrances of home. For most of them, the journey was almost over: another hundred yards of park and drizzle, then the doors would swing shut behind them. In the terraces or slums, the farm cottages, shops or houses that had once been home, this evening would begin with candles, lamps or gaslight; there might be Bible reading and sewing; there might be strong drink and violence; but from all this and much more that passed for normal they were now removed. In a place of safety, in the name of comfort, they were hereafter free to relinquish their struggles with the life outside and battle only with their several realities.

Attendants brought the women one by one to Thomas when he took his seat behind the trestle. He was handed two doctors' reports for each patient. Some were cautious and detailed: "Patient imagines herself to have been hypnotized. She declares she hears voices, and instances one as saying that her brother has been shot. They order her to carry out various acts. She declares there is electricity in the air that acts in her. Her appetite is poor and she has become anemic." He looked up and saw a woman in a black dress, half bald, with strong features, and hands like a man's.

"Do you know where you are?" he asked. "What is your name?"

She had been transferred from a private asylum where she lay with sheets over her head, talking to voices in a state of agitated depression.

"How do you feel? We are going to make you better."

"Classification," muttered the female attendant on his right.

Thomas sighed. "Dementia."

"Refractory?"

"I cannot say after one minute with the patient."

"Looks like it. Look at the hair. Put her in Twelve B."

"B?"

"Basement. Refractories. If it turns out she's not, so much the better. They need some quiet ones even if it's just to help muck out the room."

"All right. What is your name?"

"Miss Whitman. Senior attendant, ladies." She spoke with a genteel, enunciated precision.

"Dr. Midwinter."

"I know. You have another customer."

"When can I see the first lady again?"

"Whenever you want, young man. There's no appointments books here!" Miss Whitman let out a deep laugh. "Come along now."

Some doctors' reports were more outspoken: "Acute maniacal excitement. Says she is pursued by animals and passes her nights in what she calls 'a sweat of death.' Uses foul language and displays her private parts. Clothes disheveled. Appearance that of a lunatic."

"How old are you?" said Thomas. "Do you have children?"

"They murdered my baby in the hospital. Stuck a needle through his throat till he choked on blood."

"Have you been in a hospital before?"

"Of course! That's what done for me."

Thomas was aware of McLeish barking out a single word every thirty seconds to his left as the queue of men diminished in front of his table: "Melancholia. Ward Fifteen. Epilepsy. Nine." His dog was snoring loudly.

Thomas turned to his attendant. "Do we have a ward for puerperal mania?"

"We don't say 'mania' in front of them, it gives them ideas," said Miss Whitman. "Just a number. Put her in Five."

"Not Basement?"

"Wait and see."

"Before you go." He looked down at the papers and saw her name. "Mildred. Do you have a husband, Mildred? A family? When you feel better you can go and see them. Did you know that?"

The woman laughed as she was led away into the corridor. Thomas watched her recede, slowly, into the narrowing, darkening distance.

Another patient was waiting. Thomas found that each time he

looked up from the doctors' reports to the woman herself, he hoped to meet the eye of understanding, to look into the face of someone whose awareness of the gloomy hall in which she stood was something like his own. Each time he was disappointed, and the notes he read, while full of individual incident, delusion of almost comic peculiarity, began to take on a strangely familiar air. "Convinced that a murderer is after her . . . incoherence of manner . . . thinks she is pregnant (which she is not) . . . careless and filthy about her person . . . injured herself with a breadknife . . . profound melancholia . . . believes God is coming for her . . . crimes she has not committed."

"Classification!"

"Ward Eight," said Thomas quietly. ". . . Unless we have a ward number for Unknown."

Alerted by some peculiarity, he stood up to examine the next patient, a girl of about twenty with a red bow in her hair, clear skin, full skirt and beige bodice, sweat-stained beneath the armpits.

"Where are the notes for this patient?"

"There are no notes. She's workhouse. No family."

Thomas laid his hand on the young woman's arm. "What is your name?"

She pulled her arm back, but did not speak.

"How old are you? May I touch your face? I promise I won't hurt. There. I didn't hurt you, did I?"

She shook her head.

"We must give you a name," said Thomas, "otherwise you will have no record and I fear you will disappear forever down that corridor. What name would you like?"

The woman said nothing, and Thomas peered closely into her fixed eyes. "Shall I choose a name for you? Will you be called . . . Mary?"

He touched her sleeve again to show her whom he was addressing; and very slightly, she inclined her head.

"Idiocy. Five," he heard from McLeish's table. "Aha. My final customer. This is a record time. It is not yet eight o'clock."

Thomas looked over Mary's shoulder where his line of waiting women stretched out into the night.

"Classification," said Miss Whitman sharply.

"Mary," said Thomas. "Tell me how many fingers I am holding before your face."

Mary lowered her head and mumbled some inaudible word. Thomas saw that the top of her scalp was raw where she had scratched it.

"Dr. Midwinter! Will you please tell me what to write down for this woman!"

"This woman," said Thomas, taking her hand as he spoke, "is blind."

IT WAS half past one when he finally finished writing up his new admissions. The patients themselves had been classified by ten, but he wanted, beneath the pasted-in notes of the examining doctors, to note down his own impressions in the ledger, while they were still clear in his mind. One of the problems was the simple question of identity. The majority of the women he admitted would not be released and most of them would receive no medical consultation while they were in the asylum. In addition to Faverill and himself, there was one other doctor, also with the rank of assistant medical officer. His name was Stimpson, and Thomas was due to meet him in the morning.

McLeish, it had transpired over a rushed supper in the kitchen, was not a doctor. After a spell in the county regiment, he had been the warehouse manager at a porcelain factory in Stoke-on-Trent, where he had shown unusual ability as an administrator. He had been hired by Faverill's predecessor on the recommendation of the governing body, who were reluctant to pay for medical expertise. One doctor to six hundred patients was a not abnormal ratio in the English county asylums, they concluded, and while Faverill's predecessor had the help of Stimpson, it was thought that a proven warehouseman would be more helpful than a third alienist.

Even with the most rigorous schedule and the briefest of consultations, it was clear to Thomas that he would not be able to follow the course of six hundred illnesses, let alone devote to them the long-term observation they required. From what McLeish told him, it did not appear in any case that patients were assigned to any medical officer in particular.

"Here, Captain." McLeish threw a piece of fat to his dog, who sat beneath the table, while he, Grogan and Thomas were completing their supper.

"Am I at least free to visit whichever patient I wish?" said Thomas.

McLeish laughed. "They don't expect to be visited. They are not here to tell you the story of their lives, young man. In fact, it is because they cannot tell you the story of their lives that they have been sent to us!"

"But I should like to find out more."

"You will find your time is full enough without trying to interfere with individual cases. There are six miles of madmen to be looked after. I think you will find that work enough."

Grogan held out his glass to be refilled from the jug of beer.

"Are you prescribing hyoscine?" said Thomas. "I believe it has had some good results."

"What is it?"

"It is a form of henbane, mightily toxic, but carefully administered it can bring relief in mania, I believe. Or paraldehyde? It is a sleeping medicine."

"I don't know," said McLeish. "Ask Stimpson. Is paraldehyde the one that makes them smell? We don't go in for treatments a great deal, that much I can tell you. From the last papers I had from the apothecary, I recall that the number of male patients taking physic was sixty-five out of nine-hundred-odd, and among the ladies it was seventy-nine out of almost eleven hundred."

"So that's about . . ."

"It is seven percent."

"And for the others? What treatment are they receiving?"

"They are receiving the treatment of the asylum," said McLeish. "They are given a safe home, free food and lodging; they are given tasks to perform in the grounds, the farm and the workshops. They are given exercise in the airing courts if they are not fit to work. They are given entertainments and distractions. Next Saturday evening they will have a visit from the Temperance Hand Bell Ringers."

Thomas did not wish to provoke McLeish, but he found his pride as a doctor a little scuffed by McLeish's warehouse manner. "Do you not think we might do more from a medical point of view?" he said.

"'We are an asylum, not a hospital,'" said McLeish. "'We are a hospital only in occasional instances, but we are an asylum always.'"

"Is that your belief?"

"Yes," said McLeish. "And not only mine. I was quoting from the report of the chairman of the Committee of Visitors. You would do well not to forget what the word 'asylum' means. From the Latin: *a*—without, *sylum*—cure. Get down, Captain."

Thomas suppressed the pedantic correction that occurred to him. "I accept what you say, Mr. McLeish. I respect your experience here. But I shall follow my own hopes in this establishment."

"You can follow what you like, young doctor. We have our successes, our cures, do we not, Billy?" Grogan nodded over his beer. "Some people do leave the asylum and return to their families. However, the weight of experience is the other way. More than ten years ago a state hospital in New York made it a point of policy that no patient should be discharged. They gave them-selves the honorable task of acting as custodians. Most of the hospitals in the United States have begun to follow that example, and I think you will find that our American cousins have the habit of always being a wee bit in advance of us."

Thomas left them to it and returned to his room to complete his notes on the admissions. He had been given a cubicle between wards Seven and Six on the female side; the attendant who normally occupied it had been discharged when she became pregnant and was yet to be replaced. Faverill promised Thomas a better room in one of the towers, above the babel, when one became available.

In addition to the narrow iron bed, there was a chest, a shelf and a writing table, on which Thomas had completed his notes by the light of an oil lamp. He put down his pen, rubbed his eyes and sat down on the edge of the bed. The question of identity. He could make small pencil sketches of each patient in the ledger, but it was hardly scientific. Who looked at the books, anyway? McLeish, probably. The Committee of Visitors. The Commissioners in Lunacy. They would not want to see Thomas's ungifted draftsmanship. He would have to write down brief, coded mnemonics to himself: red face, tremor, stench, scar; he could perhaps do it in Latin, in which language he would certainly escape detection by McLeish.

Or photographs. Would Faverill permit photography? He had heard
of an alienist in London who took pictures of the patients in his asylum
because he was an amateur of physiognomy, who wished to demonstrate the importance of race, interbreeding and cranial phenomena in
the process of morbid degeneration. He himself might use photographs
to a simpler end, he thought.

He took a wash bag from his case and went quietly out, across Ward
Seven to the bathroom, where he scrubbed his face and teeth. Back in
his cubicle, he undressed, put on a night shirt and pulled up the blanket
over him.

To his ears, from the wards on either side, came the moans and jab-
berings of shipwreck.

Oh Sonia, my sister, he thought. Oh Jacques, my dear friend. He tried
to sleep, but his head was filled with the faces of lunatics, their palsied
hands, their shattered eyes.

THERE WAS a meeting after breakfast in Faverill's office, and here
Thomas met the third alienist, Stimpson, a black-jawed man of forty or
so who smoked cigars and was interested in experimenting with different sedatives. He proposed that by default each patient should be dosed
daily, unless obviously in the category of idiot or epileptic, when such
medicine would be either useless or harmful. Support was lukewarm—
from McLeish in that he regarded his own methods of management as
sufficient, and from Faverill in that the proposal lacked any diagnostic
element. At the end of the meeting, also attended by Matilda, rocking by
the fire, Miss Whitman, the senior ladies' attendant, and by Tyson from
the men's side, the staff went their different ways.

"Come with me, Midwinter," Faverill said, and showed him to the
back of the building, where three high walls, together with the rear of
the asylum, made a square that had been laid to grass.

"Have you ever visited France?" said Faverill.

"Yes. I went with my sister to Deauville and I have a friend who is
studying medicine in Paris. I have been to visit him."

"There is a pleasant hillside, a sort of barrow, I suppose, that over-
looks the River Aisne. It is called the Chemin des Dames because it is

where the ladies of the court of Louis XIV used to take their exercise. I sometimes think of it when I come into this airing court. Alas, the view to the river here is blocked by the wall, but I feel it is important for the women to have something charming to look at."

In the center of the square was a decorative iron arch, up which wisteria was being encouraged; around it was a marquetry of graveled paths and triangular beds with ankle-high box at the edge. A simple lawn enclosed this cultivated centerpiece, stretching to a path that went round the perimeter of the square; the lawn was spotted with dandelions and grew ragged at the edges where it ran into the brick.

"One or two of them have cultivated flowers in the beds," said Faverill. "We cannot give them sharp implements, so it is a little haphazard. But I think it pleases them."

"It is admirable," said Thomas. "Very pleasant. And do the men have something similar?"

"Yes, a similar space, but they grow vegetables. We wanted to install a greenhouse for them, but alas . . . the glass, you see."

There was the sound of locks being turned in a battered, green-painted door and twenty or so "ladies" were ushered out into the airing court. An old white-haired woman, of the kind Thomas had seen a thousand times behind the counter of a confectioner's shop or pulling a grandchild along the street, walked to a decided spot on the grass, squatted down and defecated. None of the women spoke to one another; most seemed to have locomotive routines that involved pacing round the perimeter at speed, with stretched, unnatural stride or else making intricate but repeated patterns of steps: two to the left, one back, one to the right; and repeat. Two kept up shrill unending narratives; one stretched her neck and screamed. There was no horticulture that Thomas could see.

The men's airing court, to which Faverill next led him, was similar in the extent to which each man stood apart from the others. None attempted to communicate, and Thomas wondered if they noticed one another. One sat on the grass and rocked himself, with his temples between his hands, to an angle of about forty-five degrees each way; there were bald patches on the sides of his head where the insides of his wrists had rubbed away the hair. There was a rumbling of menace that had not been present on the female side, and when a stout, bearded man grabbed a vacant-looking youth by the throat and began to beat his head against the wall, a wail of fear ran through the court. The rocking man rocked harder and moaned under his breath; the striders at the edge strode faster, looking more fixedly ahead, and those measuring out their patterned steps did so with a whimpering precision that suggested that their safety depended on it. A scholarly looking man of sixty or so put his hand down his trousers, pulled out the feces that he found there and anxiously began to stuff them into his mouth, glancing guiltily this way and that as he did so. Two attendants took away the miscreant, and one of them gave the half-throttled youth a stick of licorice.

Faverill, who had a report to write, told Thomas to explore the grounds and the farm at his leisure and to take note of what he saw. "Come and report to me at five o'clock in my office when Matilda shall make us a cup of tea. A charming creature, is she not?"

"Yes, sir," said Thomas.

In Ward Four on the ladies' side he found Daisy, the young woman who had accosted him and Faverill the day before. His eyes met her impatient gaze as soon as he unlocked the door: she was sitting at the table in the middle of the room and sprang up when he entered.

Thomas smiled. "Steady! I had not forgotten. First I need to tell someone that I am taking you." He signed a daybook at the request of an attendant, then told Daisy to come with him, which she did, following so close to his heels that she tripped herself and stumbled as they left.

When they found themselves in the open air, Daisy gave a jump of elation, and held on hard to Thomas's arm, as though she feared someone might separate them and shove her back into the reeking atmosphere of the ward.

"How long have you been in the asylum?" he asked.

"I don't exactly know. I lost count of time. I've seen two Christmases here. We do it up nice at Christmas, all the wards. Nothing you can do with that corridor, though."

They were walking through the grounds, up toward the workshops. "And where were you before that?"

"I was in service, but they didn't need me so I was chucked out. I went to work in a pub, which is what I done when I was a little girl. My ma used to take me round and I did tricks for the customers, turn cartwheels, sing songs and suchlike. Then they'd give us a few pennies at closing time. This time I was seventeen and I was arrested for . . . for something I didn't understand what he was on about. Moral something. I got a fine from the magistrate but I didn't have no money. And my ma was dead so I was in the workhouse then, and it sort of drives you mad, that place." Daisy's contralto was more animated than on the previous day; there was something in her voice and manner that Thomas found charming.

"I see, "he said. "Have you been to the farm here? Or the laundry?"

"No. Never been out of Ward Four, except the airing court. They wouldn't let me go because they said I was . . . I don't know."

"I have not been able to find your notes," said Thomas. "I expect it is in there. Do you have a surname?"

"My ma never told me because she wasn't married, so I don't know. Her name was Wilkins. But no one ever called me that, just Daisy."

The redbrick outbuildings of the asylum were at the top of the gentle slope, most of them ranged about a rectangular yard; the layout reminded Thomas a little of the boarding school he had attended in Yorkshire.

"All right, Daisy. We shall find out together what lies behind these walls. You can tell me more about yourself while we look round. You decide which place you might like to work and I shall see if I can arrange it."

The metal and carpentry workshops were staffed entirely by men, who looked bewildered to be interrupted at their work by a doctor and a girl. The tailoring, upholstering and shoemaking were also done by men; so, of the buildings on the hillside, only the laundry was left. The atmosphere inside was shrill and tense. A few weeks earlier, a patient had drowned herself in the cold rinsing tank, and the number of attendants was higher here than in the other workrooms—large, muscular women in uniform black who kept watch over the steaming vats and the red-faced lunatics who struggled back and forth with tubs of washing balanced on their heads. Thomas felt Daisy's fingers grip his arm; she let out a small whinny of fear. Attached to the washing, drying and ironing rooms was a needlework studio, which, despite its vast size and the number of women employed in it, had a calmer atmosphere. The farm and the brewery were also reserved to male patients, so Daisy's choice, Thomas explained when they had finished their tour, was needlework, kitchens or helping on the ward.

"I must get out of that place," she said. "Anyway, that Miss Whitman, she don't like me, she wouldn't let me help. Can I work for you, doctor, like what that girl does for Dr. Faverill?"

"I could do with a secretary, or a clerk, someone to help me with the books."

"I can't read, can I? What's the bloody use? You must have known, you . . ."

"It's all right, Daisy. Be calm. Perhaps someone can teach you to read and write. Calm yourself. Don't cry."

The storm of anger passed quickly through Daisy's face, which then resumed its natural look of bovine hopefulness. "Will you teach me?"

"No," said Thomas. "I do not have time. My hours must be passed in medical research—in doing something to understand the people here. But I shall find someone who will."

They were walking down the slope, back toward the great building. "We shall make a deal, Daisy. I shall find you a teacher. You learn to read and write well, then you can come and help me with my books. Until then, it is kitchens or needlework."

Thomas knew there was no chance that Daisy would ever be skilled enough to work for him, but the deal still offered her a better life. He turned with some trepidation to see how she would respond. To his surprise, he saw her smile.

"Yes, doctor. Here's a bargain too. Take me out of here one evening. I know all the pubs. I would, wouldn't I? Take me out of this place one night, just for an evening out, and I'll tell you what you need to know for your . . . whatever you call them, medical researches."

Thomas laughed. "My dear Daisy, that would defeat my purpose. I should be dismissed and very likely prosecuted under some bylaw and you would be sent into a refractory ward."

"Me and you, we could do it clever, though, so we didn't get found out."

"Put the idea out of your mind and just tell me one thing. Sewing or kitchen?"

"Sewing. It gets me out of this building."

"I shall instruct the attendants that you start tomorrow. Good luck, Daisy. I shall come and see how you are getting on."

It was one o'clock in the morning before Thomas finally sat down at
the table in his cubicle. He pulled the writing paper toward him with the
intention of telling Jacques of his experiences, but he felt somehow not
ready yet; he needed to be less tired, perhaps, or to have formed a clearer
picture of his work. Instead, he wrote:

Dear Sonia,

How I miss you. How welcome you would be in this
extraordinary place. Across the downs you see this building, like
an Italian palace, the site of some Great Exhibition, but what it
exhibits is chaos and pity. Grand without; but inside, no thought
or money has been spent. A group of patients has painted the
ceiling in one of the men's wards, sky blue, and even that is some
relief to their eyes. Some of the women have pinned up small
pictures brought to them by visitors, sentimental scenes of
cottages or posies of flowers; it is most affecting to see them look
at these or at pictures of children, thinking of what was theirs.

How all this would benefit from a Sonia's eye or touch, when
instead they are tended by lumpish women (on the ladies' side;
men on the men's), some patients themselves, some former
patients, none qualified or with an interest in the mentally
unwell, many of the type washerwoman, fishwife or what Mama
would call "sulky shopgirl." The ordinary attendants are paid
£22 a year, so even with board, lodging and washing it is not
hard to see why such a poor class of person is all that can be
employed.

My colleagues here are good men, I think. Dr. Faverill, the
superintendent, is a man of science and learning, rather
grandiloquent, filled with the optimism of our time. He is a
believer in our ability to cure, to enlighten, to discover how the
mind works.

But, goodness, there is a great deal for me to do. This
morning I supervised the bathing treatment of some male
melancholics. This consisted of their being kept in a bath at a
temperature between 92 and 96 degrees while cold water was

intermittently poured upon their heads from a watering-can. Some great French alienists recommend cold shower baths of three minutes or more, but a man in a London asylum recently died from the weight of icy water pouring down on him. We have a Turkish bath here also, though it appears to be out of order.

I am writing to you from the cubicle in which I am temporarily lodged until the rooms, to which by virtue of my great rank here I am entitled, are redecorated or prepared (Dr. Faverill is unclear on this point) or perhaps just rid of their present occupant. It is past one in the morning and there is utter darkness all round. The governing body has only lately granted the expense of gaslight, and that only partially; so that the corridors (oh, the corridors . . .) are thus intermittently lit, and some of the wards, but not all; so here, for instance, the attendants are obliged to carry lamps with which to investigate the most outlandish of the nighttime noises (the merely bestial are ignored), while elsewhere many with suicidal thoughts or epileptic convulsion are not watched by light at all. I wonder what this enormous building must look like from the outside, as I write; often passersby do stop on the top road and peer down between the railings, though those going by now must be night-workers, or revelers. They could just make out this vast folly, if you will forgive the word, the million delusions of its inhabitants contained in utter darkness.

I am not allowed a holiday until the summer, when I shall return to Torrington. Perhaps you can manage to be there as well. Shall I send you my dates? In the meantime I am allowed one day of rest a week, which is hardly time enough to make the journey.

I am anxious to know how things are with you in your fashionable London house and whether you have managed to get to the theater at all. I send my regards to Richard and my love always to you, dear Sonia; forgive me if I write no more now, I am tired as a dog.

From yr affectionate brother, Thomas

Sonia read the letter as she walked upstairs to the drawing room of her house. She had not been to the theater for a year; she had not been out in the evening for almost three months, since the economy measures imposed by her husband now forbade all such frivolities. Richard Prendergast did himself venture out at night sometimes, but, as he explained to Sonia, his time was spent in cultivating his business acquaintance, so that even the occasional game of baccarat at a Pall Mall club might pay dividends. Sonia had the impression that victory at such games was, in fact, almost their last hope.

Five years had passed since her visit to Sir James Bannerman, the expensive gynecologist, and still there was no sign of an heir. In Richard's mind this was proof that Sonia had failed him; in Sonia's there lingered a doubt, because the act by which children were conceived had become so infrequent. Very occasionally, Richard returned late, flushed and breathing heavily, and made his way into her bedroom. Sonia did not mind these rare and abrupt intrusions; it was part of her duty, seriously undertaken and fully understood at the time (she had not been a particularly naïve girl, after all). Men needed certain things and were entitled to them; that was the arrangement; and even to be held roughly, for a short time, and then, when her function was performed, left to sleep alone, sometimes seemed better than not being held at all.

Thomas's letter amused but also worried her a little, which, she thought, was typical of her perpetually mingled feeling toward him. Her anxiety was over whether he had the strength for what sounded like life-sapping work; she felt certain that in addition to long hours, the circumstances in which he worked would tax his resilience. It was not necessary for him to describe the plight of the insane or the conditions in which they were kept: as a member of the local Dorcas Society, she had once visited Bethlem hospital to take flowers and fruits to the most mildly afflicted of the patients (and only those with a hope of cure were admitted to Bethlem, it had been explained), and even that solitary hour had marked her soul, she felt, with a profound unease about God's love and purpose.

Sonia's other anxiety for Thomas was less severe, and was to some extent contradictory. Suppose he was not worn down or exhausted by the work, but, on the contrary, overtaken by impatience, by that reckless side of him. Was he sufficiently serious for labor that showed no dividend? Was he by temperament really a scientist?

She had followed his life since the summer in Deauville with deep amusement and vicarious pleasure, but also with a thudding heart. After a short rustication from his college and two more contretemps with the university proctors, he had succeeded in obtaining his medical degrees; but before completing his qualification as a physician in London, he insisted on the need to improve his German because it was, according to him, "the language of the new psychological sciences." The self-tuition had taken him to the obvious centers of Munich and Vienna, but also to Heidelberg, where he had fallen in love with a nurse at the hospital.

He explained in a letter to Sonia that it was necessary for him to travel further to put this young woman out of his mind, and to that end he went on to Italy, guiding himself on a miniature grand tour, which he subsidized by teaching English, French and—his latest acquisition—German to the children of wealthy families he met at the Italian seaside. He assured Sonia that he read painstakingly in German at night and by the time he returned to England he could even manage to make his way in Italian. Still, Sonia thought, for all this admirable self-improvement, there was something unpredictable about him; something in the way those dark brown eyes lingered on your face that made you forever unsure which way he was going to leap.

That evening, after dinner, Richard Prendergast summoned Sonia to his study.

"There is something important I want to ask you," he said, packing the meerschaum pipe Thomas had brought him as a present from Vienna.

"Yes, of course." Sonia sat with her hands in her lap, pleased to be consulted.

"When we were married," said Richard, "your father passed over to me a sum of money by way of a gift or settlement."

"So I understand."

"There were some conditions attached to this sum of money." Richard looked down to the rug on the floorboards and Sonia noticed how there was no hair on the crown of his head; the curls that were left made an approximate half-circle from one ear to the other, giving him the look of a bald angel.

"If you say so," said Sonia, who knew nothing of conditions.

"I was not to invest the money in any business venture of my own, but to keep it in some sound scheme that would provide for you and our children."

Richard's manner was showing the defensive edge that always made Sonia uneasy. "I suppose he saw it as a family gift rather than an investment in your company," she said.

"Indeed. However, since the condition of the gift did not apply, I saw no reason to adhere to the detail of the understanding."

"I do not quite follow."

Richard coughed. "I mean that since you were barren, there was no need for me to put the money aside for the well-being or education of our children. I have therefore drawn substantially on the sum."

"How substantially?"

"To the extent that I need to seek further finance."

"From whom?"

"From your father."

"But surely, the bank—"

"The bank has disappointed me. Their outlook is shortsighted and they are unwilling to continue. Indeed, they are pressing me with quite unreasonable demands for interest on loans already made."

"There must be other sources of money, Richard. Your father, for instance."

"I have investigated every possibility, believe me. What do you imagine I do when I leave here at seven each morning? I have worked myself into the ground. And as for my father, he has not put a penny in the way of my business. From the day of our marriage he has dealt with me as though I were a burden of which he is pleased to be free."

"What will happen to the house?"

"I shall relinquish it at the end of the next quarter. There are rooms."

"Rooms?"

"Jackman has found me rooms somewhere in Clerkenwell."

"And me?"

"What?"

"You said, 'Jackman has found me rooms,' as though it was lodging for just one person."

"Well, of course you can come if you like."

Sonia said nothing. She wanted to be quite certain that she had heard correctly. Richard pushed at a loose thread on the rug with the toe of his shoe, and, in the silence, she could hear the ticking of the carriage clock on the mantelpiece. She did not wish to catch his eye; she wanted him to have time to consider.

She breathed in, but still did not speak. What Richard had indicated to her was that she was no longer essential to him, no longer required, except as a short-term financial intermediary between him and her father. Sonia knew that if her father could be persuaded to lend or give Richard more money it would be on this one occasion only; so that by the end of—what, tomorrow, next week?—her usefulness even in this limited role would have expired.

Eventually, she did meet her husband's gaze: he thrust his chin out for a moment, then looked sheepishly away, but his face made it clear that he did not retreat from the implications of what he had said. Sonia was grateful for the clarification; it seemed to her, in fact, that Richard had not only made his position clear but had done so in terms as delicate as could really be managed.

Why, then, did she feel this childish rage and indignation? Why was she convinced that she was entitled to better treatment; that she had, as it were, a right to love and respect? What "right" was this, and by whom granted? She had bound herself to this man for life, and what sort of person reneged on such a vow? Richard's wife was who she was, who she had freely chosen to be—and that partly, she admitted, from an unruly impatience for her own life to begin.

The choice was simple. There was her petulance and her desire for self-fulfillment on the one hand; and on the other, her honor, fidelity and devotion to a common venture on which she had entered gaily, of her own volition. The choice between the two imperatives was an easy one; the decisions that you made between such conflicting claims was the measure of your human worth.

She needed only to assure herself that her motives were pure. She said, "I suppose you have done well to last this long when the business has always struggled."

"We had our good times."

"Yes, but as long ago as Deauville, you were—"

"Yes. I know."

His crestfallen tone allayed her small doubt, and her eyes filled with compassion for him. She stood up and wrapped her arms round him, her heart burning with a sense of their shared failure.

"It's all right, dear Richard," she said, stroking his back. "We have lived too closely, been through too much. I will not leave you. I cannot, anymore than I can leave myself. Being your wife is what I am. We will manage together."

She drew determination from her own words and squeezed Richard more tightly, as though the resolve might flow from her fingers, through the thick cloth of his jacket and into his spine.

V

THE CORPSES WERE DELIVERED AT NOON TO THE ECOLE PRATIQUE d'anatomie and then distributed to the various dissecting rooms; by two o'clock, Jacques found himself up to his elbows in the abdominal cavity of an old woman whose blue eyes seemed to look down approvingly at his rapid scalpel work.

Behind him, a skeleton was suspended from a hook attached by a chain to the ceiling; an hour earlier it had been a fleshy young woman who had died in childbirth. Her uterus was on the cast-iron table next to Jacques, where two other students were bent over it.

Jacques had a splashed textbook of anatomy propped open next to his old lady; he wore a skullcap of the kind favored by Professor Charcot of the Salpêtrière hospital and paper sleeves over his shirt. He smoked powerful cheap cigars whose ash occasionally tumbled into the cavity. He thought this disrespectful, but had discovered, like other students, that it was the only way to tolerate the stench. The dozen bodies in the room were of different vintages, some having been retained by the supplying hospital for two or three days. Behind him, two cadavers had been prepared to show the workings of the nervous system, so that they looked, if he allowed himself to think so, like flayed martyrs.

He worked patiently but fast, because speed helped him to view the flesh as scientific material, not as a person who, a few hours earlier, had had thoughts and a name. The professor of anatomy, a tall, enthusiastic man with a glittering eye, strode among the carcases and organs like a sculptor in a studio of his apprentices, nodding his approval over Jacques's bench, pointing him to a previously prepared cadaver for purposes of comparison.

An impatient mop was shoved up against Jacques's feet by Bernard, the porter, who swabbed the worst of the blood from the floor and collected the offcuts into a galvanized bucket. In the courtyard were stray dogs, rounded up and tied at the ankle in readiness for their own dissection; into their latticed cages, Bernard poked the contents of his bucket. The dogs snarled at him as they grabbed the human pieces.

Every medical man has been through this, thought Jacques, lighting another cigar: therefore I must not complain. Thomas cut up corpses in a filthy shed in Cambridge and I cannot allow him to outstrip me in our partnership; I must have done as much as he has when we come to share our knowledge.

So he cut on dextrously, with the fixed concentration he had first cultivated in the bedroom at Saint Agnès. He could bear this bloody work. What he hated was when at last it was over and he staggered out into the Paris street, reeking, scalpel in one hand, textbook in the other; and, in the early darkness of the winter afternoon, he could just make out the look of distaste on the ladies he brushed past. Assaulted by the smell of his drenched clothes, they shrank back from what they took to be an ostler or a butcher's boy.

THOMAS, MEANWHILE, was told by Faverill that a room had been prepared for him on the second floor, and he went up the stone steps of the western tower two at a time. His new lodging had a window overlooking the downs to the south, a gas-lamp bracket and a washstand with an enamel basin; there was also a bookcase where he could at last set out not only the registers and records on which he was working, but the medical texts he had had sent on from Torrington. If only the room had been a little warmer, he might have felt almost at home, but the system of iron pipes that carried steam through the lower floors had not been extended to the upstairs parts of the asylum, and he was dependent on one bucket of coal a day, delivered after breakfast by a melancholic called Stevens.

That evening, Thomas took a taper from the mantelpiece and lit the splintered kindling in the grate; he knelt down and blew gently until he inhaled the sweetly acrid smell of the coals first catching. He stood and rubbed his hands, then moved over to the tea chest and started to unpack. He was proud of the number and variety of the volumes he had acquired; they were in French, German and Italian as well as in English, and he had paid for them by working at often uncongenial tasks. The books he piled onto the threadbare rug represented, he believed, everything that was known about madness.

The history of the subject was shameful and brief. There had been the dark ages, when wandering idiots were mocked or pilloried; there had been the superstitious centuries when people spoke of "possession" and other devilish nonsense; then there had been the era of cruelty, of imprisonment and taunting, when the idle sane paid to make faces at the lunatics. This had turned into the era of "restraint," earlier in the century, when the gathering of many mentally afflicted people in one place for the first time had necessitated the use of manacles, irons and straitwaistcoats. Even before such practices had become widespread, however, they were starting also to become obsolete under the influence of enlightened thinkers, some medical men and some, like the famous Mr. Tuke of the York Retreat, laymen of humane and philanthropic vision. This was, in Thomas's view, the true beginning of his medical discipline.

It was curious, he had to admit, that the first medicine was not a herbal preparation or a surgical procedure, but simple kindness; odd, because the struggle of the pioneering mad-doctors had always been to establish that illness of the mind was organic, a physical malfunction, to be treated in the same way as an illness of the liver or the foot, the brain being just such an organ, entirely comparable to the others—if more complicated. Yet one did not treat cirrhosis or a broken metatarsal with kindness, so here was a paradox. It was one that Thomas could explain to himself, however. Morally, it was right to grant gentle care to the sick; practically, if a cure worked (and private asylums of France and England had had some successes) then a doctor was obliged to use it. And medically, the use of sympathy and concern was not the primary but only the auxiliary treatment specific to this illness. To the patient with the broken tibia you gave a pair of crutches; to the one with the abscess, you gave a bandage, but surgery came before the crutch or dressing. Kindness to the lunatic was like the support or bandage; the odd thing about psychiatry, he had once explained to Sonia, was that its cart had come before its horse: its task was now to discover its primary treatments, the cures of surgeon or apothecary.

The bookcase had two long shelves, and on the top one Thomas placed, in approximate chronological order, the works of his century that he believed could be taken together to show a consensus of quickening advance. *On Insanity*, by a Florentine called Vincenzio Chiarugi, was strictly of the previous century, but Chiarugi's argument, that an asylum might in itself be therapeutic, seemed in spirit to belong to the modern era. Thomas, in any case, was fond of the three-volume edition he had bought from a barrow in Rome, because it was the only Italian book he had ever managed to read to the end.

Next to Chiarugi, he placed a copy of Johann Reil's *Rhapsodies of the Psychological Method of Cure in Mental Alienation*, the first book, as far as he knew, to have stated that madness was not a supernatural visitation, but an affliction of the tissues of the brain, in a way that pneumonia is an ailment of the lung, no less physical for being invisible. Next to that he placed *Traité médico-philosophique sur l'aliénation mentale* by the Frenchman Philippe Pinel, who was known even to the dreamy undergraduates in Thomas's lectures as the man who "struck the chains from the lunatics" at the Bicêtre hospital and the Salpêtrière in Paris. Thomas's professor had pointed out that Pinel had in fact replaced the chains with straitjackets and that his real contribution was to have believed that lunatics with periods of lucidity were curable.

In any event, there was something else Pinel had written that was of particular interest to Thomas because it seemed to have a bearing on the plight of Jacques's brother, Olivier. Pinel had noticed a particular group of symptoms that first afflicted young people, between puberty and adulthood; he seemed to have sensed, without stating it clearly, that this might be a distinct disease entity, and Thomas was convinced by what he had seen in the asylum that a large number of patients, particularly those demented and hearing voices, were suffering from what—for lack of any other term—he and Jacques had come to call "Olivier's disease."

On this point, Thomas was also excited by the writing of an English alienist, John Haslam, a medical officer at Bethlem. In *Observations on Insanity*, Haslam reported how he carried out postmortem inspections of twenty-nine Bethlem inmates and found that the lateral ventricles of the brain were noticeably larger than normal; he filled them with measured spoonfuls of water to prove it. If such physical phenomena could be shown by a teaspoon and a naked eye, Thomas thought, what might more advanced techniques not show? What, indeed, did Olivier's brain look like?

Had Sonia been able to see the care and respect with which Thomas shelved his small library, her anxieties for him might have been allayed. His own mind had been so inflamed by enthusiasm that he was almost immune to weariness; he felt the pity of what he saw about him in the asylum, but it did not touch him with despair; it inspired him: the slavering, the shouting and the shipwreck drove him on. Next to Haslam, he placed the three volumes of *Des maladies mentales*, published by Pinel's pupil, Jean-Etienne Esquirol, in 1838. Esquirol had become master of the asylum at Charenton, a place of cultivated gardens, billiards, dancing parties, tender nursing and something approaching *douceur de vivre*, from which patients had been sent home cured. Here, just outside Paris, the rising arc of enlightenment had seemed most exuberant.

Next to Esquirol, in the middle of the shelf, in a place of honor, Thomas placed *Die Pathologie und Therapie der psychischen Krankheiten*, the book most admired by the other alienists he had met. Its author, Wilhelm Griesinger, was a physician who insisted that, since lunatics suffered from a disease of the body in nerve and brain, psychiatry must become part of medicine as a whole. The training he devised bore out his belief: one of his student psychiatrists was instructed, in mid-tuition, to intervene in a complicated labor causing concern in the obstetric ward next to the lecture hall. Thomas had read Griesinger in Heidelberg; even with dictionaries to hand, he found the prose extremely difficult to understand, but all the students he had met in Germany knew by heart Griesinger's battle cry that psychiatry must emerge from its hermetic life as a kind of guild and become an integral part of medicine. Thomas was considerably irritated to discover, on his return home, that the book had been translated into English more than a decade earlier.

These were his heroes, respectfully shelved; but now psychiatry was in need of a new one. While he sincerely believed that there was a rapid increase of knowledge and a growing consensus of the wise, it had to be admitted that there was an insidious and growing countermovement. The setting up of public asylums in France and Britain had brought welcome seclusion to many and had ended the use of chains and irons; but before long the huge buildings had come to falter under the mounting weight of numbers—from the jabbering multitude forever at the gates. The trouble was that although the pioneering writers had humanely and beautifully described the problem, they had not found any cures. While Griesinger and the scholars scratched their heads, while they pored over corpses on the slabs, observed their patients and puzzled at the wondrous meeting of thought with cell, there came into being an alternative philosophy whose main tenet was simple: in the absence of cures, there can only be management. Such a brutal belief naturally did not need volumes to articulate itself, Thomas thought, because it found its purest expression in McLeish's bookless shelves.

The last volume he put away epitomized the urgent need for rapid advance. *The Physiology and Pathology of Mind* by Henry Maudsley argued that lunacy was passed on from generation to generation; that characteristics not only inborn but acquired by a parent could be transmitted to a child and that the mentally ill were therefore part of a process called "degeneration." As such, they were to be viewed as a waste product of healthy evolution and were fit only for excretion. Maudsley doubted whether asylums helped to cure patients and pointed out that many became better only when they were released; he thought sedation by narcotics not much better than imprisonment by ball and chain, and concluded that psychiatrists were well advised merely to watch and learn until such time as they were in possession of more information about their subject.

Maudsley was right about the need for further observation, Thomas thought, the need to study the whole length of a disease from childhood to postmortem; but such work needed time, and time was what a medical officer in a giant asylum never had. On the contrary, he had to rush and grasp at any evidence he could find in the rooms that opened off the reeking corridor. What laboratory conditions, Thomas thought. What carnival of delusion and inconsequence. What temptation to despair. A symptom that occurred in two people might be the central diagnostic point of the illness in one, and incidental in the other. Without time, though, how would he ever tell?

He relied on certain facts and insights provided by the authorities whose books he treasured and, to support them, he depended, to an extent he admitted was undesirable, on instinct. In the confusion and the headache, there were patterns, he was sure, and he could occasionally see them. There was, for a start, such a thing as Olivier's disease. He could predict how those afflicted by it would behave and report their symptoms; there were common, recurring factors that gave it a profound identity. A young German called Kahlbaum had also noticed the group of symptoms and called it "hebephrenia," or young madness. How it was to be cured, though, he could not say.

Then, thought Thomas, there was the case of the warship inventor, whose wife was such a friend of Gladstone and who daily expected a letter from the Queen. These symptoms were also predictable, consistent and apparently separable from other kinds of madness; they formed a stage in the general paralysis of the insane, which had been noted by Haslam and Esquirol many years before; some thought the source of the illness appeared to lie in youthful debauchery and use of prostitutes, and that it might be related to physical symptoms of syphilis earlier in life; but how it entered the mind was impossible to describe.

Thomas stood up and stretched. When he had committed himself to this life, he had been thrilled by the possibilities it offered: the chance to solve intractable problems, to bring relief to those afflicted and enlightenment to all mankind. The zeal remained—it had increased—but to it had been added, by his fuller understanding of where the science stood, a sense of urgency. If he and Jacques, and others like them, did not find solutions quickly, there was a chance that their work would be overwhelmed not only by the number of incurable patients but by the growing doctrines of despair within their own world.

SONIA'S FATHER arrived early, grumbling about the fare of the hansom cab he had taken from St. Pancras. Sonia kissed him warmly and took his travel-battered bag upstairs to the spare bedroom. In her absence, he looked about the scruffy hall, where a huge cobweb had been spun from the fanlight to the chandelier.

"What happened to the maid?" he said.

"Abigail? We had to let her go. Come up to the drawing room and have some tea. I've got in some of that fruitcake you said you liked from the baker in Mount Street."

In the absence of Richard, who was at his office, they were able to talk freely of the Midwinter family and its fortunes. Sonia's mother was suffering from rheumatism and had had to give up hunting; Edgar was proving bullish and astute in the family business, to his father's evident delight.

"Yes," he said, "and little Lucy, what a treasure she is. Such a pretty little thing. And three grandchildren already."

"Yes," said Sonia, looking down.

"I'm sorry, my dear, I didn't mean to—"

"No, no of course. Little Henry must be nine now, I suppose. How is he?"

"Quite off his head," laughed Mr. Midwinter. "And the twins. A merry little pair."

"Yes, I heard from Lucy that they are flourishing. She wrote me a letter a few weeks ago. And Thomas, do you hear from him?"

"Hmm," said Mr. Midwinter. "Occasionally we have a rushed line or two from that confounded asylum. What about you?"

"Yes, I have had two or three letters. He works such terrible long hours, from six in the morning until midnight some days, I believe. He seems happy in a Thomas-like way."

"I don't know what possessed him to be a mad-doctor. Your mother and I dined at the Manor the other day and I was sitting next to a very distinguished lady. She asked me about my children and I told her what you all did. She gave me a very clear impression that she did not consider medicine to be on the same level as the church, or even the law. She said that the surgeon who had operated on her husband had been not quite a gentleman."

Sonia laughed. "Nonsense, Papa. Thomas will make a great success of his life. You will see."

"Why is it that so many young medical men have to take unpaid work at the hospitals, then? What respectability is there in that?"

"I think it is just while they make a name for themselves. I believe it is difficult to make a start in private practice without being known and without having some experience."

"And is that what he intends to do? Private practice?"

"I believe so," said Sonia. She made no mention of Thomas's intention of setting up with a penniless Frenchman in a foreign country.

"But mad-doctors," said Mr. Midwinter. "Everyone knows they are the hopeless ones. I read an article in the paper the other day by one of the most famous mad-doctors, I forget his name, and he said that a fully qualified young man who chose to work as an alienist must be either desperate for cash or so wealthy that he doesn't mind the awful pay. He more or less admitted that it was not a proper branch of medicine."

"Well," said Sonia, "I think it is a fine and humane thing that he is doing. Now, let me take your teacup."

"Thank you, my dear. In the mean time, tell me about Mr. Prendergast."

"Oh," said Sonia airily, setting down the china cup with a rattle. "He is very well, thank you. As always, he is looking for new investors. And knowing your generosity, he—"

"Tell me, what staff do you have here?"

"Staff? A woman comes to clean the house. Sometimes."

"You have no carriage? What about a dress allowance?"

"I make do. Since I seldom go out, I have no need for new clothes."

Mr. Midwinter looked at his daughter. He had always been a little uneasy with her, unsure what girls or women wanted, but she had been a dependable source of order and good humor at Torrington. There had been awkward moments, it was true, but Sonia had provided something in the house that no one else could muster: a kind of poise. When he looked in her eyes now, she could not meet his gaze, but smiled and looked down at her lap; he saw with a pang of sadness that some light had been extinguished in her. He thought how much he missed having her in his house.

"Richard will be back presently," said Sonia. "I thought perhaps you should go to his office, but he said he preferred to meet here. I think I shall go out and leave you to discuss the business. I have some small matters of my own to see to."

The interview with Richard Prendergast did not go at all as Mr. Midwinter had foreseen.

"Take a glass of sherry wine, will you?" said Richard in a way that sounded more like an order than an offer. "We shall have some claret with dinner."

They were in the small morning room off the main hall on the ground floor. Richard had his foot on the low fender and an elbow on the mantelpiece; Mr. Midwinter stood opposite, watching him.

"I expect Sonia has told you where we stand," said Richard.

"No. She expects the men to do the business. She merely passed on your request to see me."

"Yes, but not just business. Rather . . . the whole picture."

"I don't know what you mean."

"Well, let's . . . let's do business. Business before . . . business first, that's what I always say."

"Very well. How much money do you want?"

Richard outlined at length the difficulties he was facing, and ended by naming a sum that was almost twice what Mr. Midwinter had allowed.

"What guarantees would I have of seeing this money again?"

"Guarantees?"

"I believe it is normal to secure a guarantee before making a loan."

"Alas, there is little . . . material that I can offer. The house, as you know, is not mine. I have a handful of securities in a safe box at the bank but they are pledged already. I can certainly ask Jackman whether he would consider granting you some share in our company at a future date."

"The guarantee cannot be attached to the speculation," said Mr. Midwinter. "That would defeat the purpose."

"Indeed. I suppose I had rather hoped that you would take a more, how shall I put it, familial attitude to the matter. It is money after all that could go to securing the future of your daughter."

They discussed the prospects of the business for a further twenty minutes. Mr. Midwinter had no doubt that from a commercial point of view it was a waste of money; he might as well have written out a check and thrown it on the meager fire between them. He was disinclined to continue with this young man in any event; there was something self-important yet pathetic in his manner; he was, in a phrase popular in the Midwinter warehouse, full of chaff. He had seemed a reasonable match for his daughter at the time, but the fortunes of Chas. Midwinter & Sons had since improved, and these days Sonia could have hoped for something better. There were the girl's own feelings to consider, however, and although he found it impossible to think that she might feel affection for this man, she did exhibit loyalty when she spoke about him.

He sighed, and named a sum that was half of what Richard had asked for. "And in order to be what you call 'familial,'" he said, "I should allow the loan to run over a period of five years with no interest payable. At the end of that time you would repay it in full and it would be understood that you would make no further calls on me."

Mr. Midwinter had expected his son-in-law to negotiate upward or—knowing him—to take the matter personally and make a stand on his affronted dignity. To his surprise, Richard did neither, but stroked his chin and looked into the fire.

"I wonder," he said at last, "if we are seeing this problem in the correct light. I appreciate your offer. It is not unreasonable in the circumstances. The provision for interest, or lack of it, is decidedly generous. I am concerned, however, by what you may gain from the arrangement."

"You are worried about my profit?" Mr. Midwinter was baffled.

"Not merely," said Richard, "in a strictly financial sense. I rather wondered whether in return for investing a larger sum you might not ask for more from me."

Mr. Midwinter opened his mouth to speak, then stopped. Surely Prendergast could not be suggesting . . . He thought again; this was a moment for extreme caution.

"You mean . . ." He opened his hands with an invitation to Richard to proceed.

Richard coughed and drained his glass of Marsala, then paused, as though waiting for the wine to lend him eloquence. He licked his lips. "We always try in our business to look ahead, to think in periods of five years. Then where shall we be?"

The debtors' prison in your case, thought Mr. Midwinter, but said nothing.

"The circumstances in which I married your daughter have changed. As you know, she is infertile and in that respect has failed me as a wife. She is no longer young and—"

"Sonia is not yet thirty years of age! She barely looks twenty. She has her life ahead of her."

"Exactly," said Richard. "She may indeed have a life ahead of her. A different life from this one. Or she may not. I suppose that, embarrassing though it is, onerous though the choice may be, it rather depends on me."

Mr. Midwinter looked at his son-in-law closely. "Are you suggesting—"

"I am not suggesting anything. Nor am I trying to raise the figure I originally mentioned. Supposing, however, we were to view that sum as a loan more or less without strings."

"A gift, you mean. Or to be precise, a payment."

"It is probably not necessary to be precise about the term we use. In return, you would have your daughter back. As you say, she is still a young woman, and she has admirers."

"What would Sonia think of such an arrangement?"

Richard sucked in the air over his lower teeth. "I think she might resist at first. But I imagine that she would find it difficult ultimately to prevail against the will of her father."

"And of her husband?"

"Indeed."

"I should require written assurances that you would never—"

"I took the liberty of having my lawyer draw up some heads of agreement, which I think you will find answer all your anxieties. I have a copy of it in my pocket. Perhaps you would care to peruse it in your room and let me know your decision after dinner." Richard handed over the paper and took out a watch from his waistcoat. "We dine in half an hour."

As Richard left the room, Mr. Midwinter found his mouth opening and closing. He had never felt so thoroughly outwitted in a business conversation; yet the resentment he felt was more than equaled by his pleasure at what seemed to him the advantageous terms of the deal that had been offered. As he took a cigar from the box on the table and walked over to look out of the window onto the traffic going down to Grosvenor Square, he wondered why, with skills like these, Richard Prendergast had not made more of his business.

THREE WEEKS later, at nine o'clock on a dry, cold evening, Thomas went quietly down the uncovered stone staircase and into Faverill's vestibule at the foot of the West Tower. He was certain that this was the time that McLeish took supper in the kitchen, usually with Tyson and Miss Whitman, so the wards would be watched only by junior attendants, slumbering in their cubicles or staring ahead into the turbulent darkness.

With the largest key on the ring, he unlocked the main doors into the corridor, then closed them gently behind him. He carried a candle, whose flame he protected with his hand against the fetid drafts. It took him ten minutes of slow tunneling, locking and unlocking, until eventually he arrived at the door of Daisy's ward. He swallowed and licked his lips. This was an act of madness, and he hoped that Jacques would never discover it; suppose he were struck off the medical register as a result? I don't care, he thought: I will practice in Bohemia with fake papers; I will continue my researches somehow; and what is the sane, the healthy life that we are trying to restore to the afflicted if it has no room for laughter and beer? He turned the key gently in the lock.

Daisy was waiting in the shadows near the door, as they had agreed, while Thomas went to find Maud Illsley, the attendant, and distract her attention.

She was sitting at the dining table, doing some needlework by candle-light; Thomas knew her to be timid, kind and unimaginative. She had worked in service until a year ago and saw her new duties as little more than tidying up and counting heads. She seemed surprised to see Thomas.

"Just making sure everything is all right," he said.

"Yes, thank you, Doctor."

"Good, I like to look in occasionally. I pick a ward at random, just to have a sense of how the patients are resting. They seem very quiet tonight. Well done, Maud. I shall lock the door as I go."

Outside, Daisy was leaning into the darkness of the low corridor; she grabbed at Thomas's arm as he emerged and he noticed that she was trembling.

"Are you all right?"

She put her arms round him and squeezed. He saw then that she was not trembling, but laughing.

"Come on. Follow close behind me. If anyone comes, though, remember what we said."

"We're not together."

"Yes, but I'll find an excuse for your being out." That was the plan, though he had in fact not yet been able to think of any reason for a patient to be out of the locked ward at night.

When they reached the end of the corridor, Thomas went ahead into the lit hallway and looked about before gesturing to Daisy to emerge. She ran out past him into the night while he locked the door back into the corridor.

She took his arm again as they walked up through the grounds toward the laundry and the farm.

"Are you good at climbing, Daisy? Are you acrobatic?"

"I should say so. That's how I used to make my living, remember? Doing cartwheels and that."

"Good. Because we're going out over the brewery gate. I can't use the main gate because Patterson's on duty and he might recognize you. I thought of passing you off as my sister but I haven't had a visitor signed in, so I can't."

Thomas had reconnoitered the means of escape and had concluded that the high walls were impassable except at this spot. Although the asylum was almost self-sufficient, there were sometimes heavy goods from outside, such as bricks or sacks full of hops, that were delivered through a pair of bolted wooden doors let into the perimeter wall next to the brewery. There was an iron manger for the dray horse attached to the brickwork, which Thomas believed would give him a foothold from which he could step onto the nub of the thick upper bolt and thence lever himself onto the top of the gate.

"I'll go first, Daisy. You watch what I do and follow me. When you get to the top you must swing over and hang down off your hands because it's too high to jump down."

Daisy put her hand over her mouth to stifle a giggle. They walked across the cobbled courtyard, trying to make no noise, though the hobnails of Daisy's boots clicked on the stones. The laundry cast a giant shadow in which the other brick workshops seemed shrunk, and deprived of their institutional grandeur—just buildings, idle and alone at night, thought Thomas, not mills where lives were ground out.

After four years of scaling walls and gates in Cambridge at odd hours of the night, he did not find the brewery gates a difficult proposition. He squatted on top for a moment to whisper encouragement to Daisy, then dropped down onto the path outside. A minute later, she was with him. They walked for a mile, away from the town, until they came to a village in which, Daisy said, there was a friendly inn where she had once performed as a child. They picked out the lights, some way back from the main road, and went down the path to a side entrance. Thomas looked through the window in the glow of lamps on the tables and the fluttering firelight.

"Try and keep your boots out of sight. Pull your skirt down over them when we sit at the table," he said, even though most of the men looked too inebriated to notice two strangers. They made their way over the stone flags to a corner, where Thomas sat Daisy down and brought some beer over from the bar. The landlord's eyes took in Thomas's frock coat and white tie with more curiosity than Daisy's shabby black dress.

At the table, Thomas raised his glass and clinked it against Daisy's. He noticed the reek of the ward on her clothes as she leaned in, but when he sat back against the wooden settle he saw that there were tears of exhilaration in her eyes.

"Good health, Daisy. May we never be found out, and may your life take a turn for the better."

"Already has, Doctor."

"Good. Drink up, then. You're almost as slow at drinking as my real sister. She takes an age to drink a glass of wine."

"What's her name?"

"Sonia."

"Is she married?"

"Yes."

"Tell me about her then. Talk to me, Doctor. You've no idea what it's like in there, how much I've wanted someone just to talk to."

Thomas told her about Sonia and a little about Richard Prendergast. At her prompting, he described Torrington House and what they had done as children.

"Sounds ever so grand. Sounds like where I used to be in service."

"Not really. It's a lovely house, but it's not grand. And they only have a cook and a maid to help. Though things have looked up, I believe, so maybe they have another pair of hands now."

He bought more beer and carried it back through the press. It was a Friday evening, and many of the customers had clearly just received their wages. They were in high spirits, which pleased Thomas because it meant they were not likely to pay much attention to him. One of them took out a fiddle and began to play, singing on his own at first, then with half a dozen others who gradually joined in.

Daisy leaned back and closed her eyes. Thomas noticed that she had combed her hair and put a ribbon in it; but her skin was mealy, blotched with sores around the lips; her red-rimmed eyes were circled with black arcs of weariness and there were streaks of grime appearing over the high-buttoned collar of her dress. He looked at the skin stretched over her temples and followed it with his eye to the hairline; as he did so, he could not help but envisage the frontal bone beneath the dermis, the rippling of sulcus and gyrus over the folded cortex inside.

Daisy, a little drunk from the beer, began to smile ecstatically, still with her eyes closed.

SONIA WAS sitting on the edge of her bed, staring straight ahead. Her father and her husband had colluded to decide the future of her life, and it seemed that there was nothing she could do to stop them. After dinner, she had been called back to the dining room and told to sit down. Her father took the lead in explaining the agreement, though Richard made it clear that he concurred by nodding his head at intervals.

"So," Mr. Midwinter concluded. "I think it is a solution that suits everyone. Mr. Prendergast shall have his investment and a chance to start a family, perhaps, with another wife. You can be free to do the things you enjoy, without the restrictions of economy and, who knows, you too may find another suitor, perhaps an older man, a widower with children of his own. Your mother and I can have our dear daughter back at the house, where there will always be plenty to occupy you."

"But I don't want to," said Sonia. "This is my home, here. I have put so much work into it, the curtains, the decoration, silly things, I know, but . . . And Richard is my husband. I married him for better or worse and though it has been in some ways worse than I foresaw, I am not in a position to abandon it. I cannot stop being who I am."

"Come, my dear," said Richard, "you cannot pretend that ours has been a marriage of romantic love or passion."

"I learned to become fond of you," said Sonia tightly. "Truly fond of you. I worked for you and with you. I took real pleasure in your occasional successes. And when you failed, I wept real tears for you."

The men eyed each other across the dining table, over the curling orange peel and the split walnut shells. Neither had suspected what they might unleash. Mr. Midwinter thought she was being perverse in clinging to a man she clearly did not love, yet as he moved to sweep aside her objections, he was caught by a sudden memory of her as a child, a naked three-year-old, dancing alone to imaginary music in the kitchen one summer day, and felt with a panicking lurch, that he had failed her.

"My dear . . ." Richard began.

"Don't call me that! How can I be dear to you if you can sell me off like this?"

"I thought," said Richard gently, "that it would please you. I know that I have disappointed you as a husband, in more ways than perhaps your father suspects. I honestly and truly thought that you would welcome your liberation from . . . from me."

There was something becoming in the way he spoke which made Sonia for a moment blink and look down to her lap. "I do not know how I am supposed to proceed," she said. "It is as though you were taking my name from me and telling me that from now on I am to be called something else. It is not that I love you so dearly, Richard, I suppose. It is that loving you as much as I have been able to manage has defined the person that I am. That is who I have become."

Neither man was able to answer. Sonia looked from one to the other, and eventually spoke herself.

"I suppose you will prevail. If a husband no longer wants to keep his wife, then that is the end of the matter. But I ask you both to reconsider this demeaning arrangement. I am happy to pretend that this conversation never took place. Discuss it between yourselves and tell me what you decide. If you want to agree that it never happened, I promise never to mention it or think of it again. If you still want to proceed, I will do as you wish. Meanwhile, I am going to visit my brother, who, I now see, is the only person I can trust, the only one who truly loved me."

She stood up, holding her hand across her trembling lip, and left the room with a rustle of silk. Her father and her husband grimaced at one another and at the closed door.

THEIR EXCURSION over, Thomas was cupping his hands to make a foothold for Daisy, so that she could pull herself up onto the top of the brewery gate. Twice she lost her balance and fell off, giggling; at the third attempt, she secured a handhold and hauled herself up, scrabbling at the wooden doors with her boots. Thomas himself was able to reach the top without help.

"I'll see you by the icehouse," he whispered to Daisy. "Are you all right?" he called after she had dropped down inside the walls.

"Yes."

He walked up to the main gate and hammered at the window of the small lodge. "Don't say anything about this, Patterson," he said, "and I won't report you for being asleep."

Patterson blinked several times, manifestly wondering how Thomas could be coming back when he had not gone out. Thomas ran down to the icehouse, where Daisy was waiting.

"The doors are barred inside at ten," he said, "so we shall have to climb the drainpipe at the back. I wedged the casement open on the first-floor landing, so we can get in there."

Daisy gripped his arm. "Listen," she said, "I must be the first lunatic to break into an asylum."

IT WAS decided by Dr. Faverill that in December the patients should have a ball. At the morning meeting in his office, he set out his plan to the staff.

"It is my intention that we should invite observers from outside, representatives of the Committee of Visitors, county councillors, the gentlemen of the press. They must be allowed to see how well our little society functions. I appreciate that all this will entail considerable preparation and, on the night itself, some vigilance."

Faverill looked round the faces in the room: McLeish skeptical but silent; Tyson and Miss Whitman exchanging worried glances; Matilda, rocking; Stimpson, puzzled, smelling of the pharmacy; and Thomas, tired but eager. It was not a difficult choice.

"Dr. Midwinter, I should like you to take charge of the preparations. I can make a small sum of money available to you, though most of the decorations, the refreshment and so forth will be homemade."

"I understand, sir," said Thomas.

"As for music," said Faverill, "Mr. McLeish, I believe that the asylum band is ultimately under your control. Please ensure that the conductor has a suitable program and that they are well rehearsed."

"Yes, sir. Tell me, where exactly do you envisage the revels taking place?"

"The central hall. What used to be the dining room."

"It's not been used these ten years, since we started to feed them in the wards."

"Well, ask Grogan to set to work. Detail some men from the farm to help. Clear it up and paint it. They should enjoy doing that."

"I see," said McLeish. "And what sort of numbers had you envisaged? And what manner and degree of affliction would you consider appropriate amongst the revelers?"

"I suppose we could manage two hundred patients. As to which ones, I imagine there will have to be a degree of selection."

"Aye."

"But I should not like to think it was merely the most presentable who are invited. You should also have in mind those who would most benefit from it. A dancing party can be therapeutic."

Thomas left the meeting with a youthful excitement at the prospect of a celebration, even a lunatics' ball, and found he was able to put to one side his misgivings about how much time the preparations might take from his already attenuated day: he would simply have to go to bed later, he thought. First, he needed to form a small committee.

Daisy would be a good lieutenant. He had, since their nighttime excursion, found her admission notes. "Overexcited and rambling in her discourse. Says she is afraid to sleep at night," the first doctor had recorded. The medical officer at the workhouse complained that "She keeps others awake at night by walking round. Has been seen engaging in self-abuse. Loud of voice, confused." She had been diagnosed, by McLeish, as suffering from mania. The only subsequent entry reported that her behavior was improved, but that she was moody and unpredictable. After reading the notes and talking to Daisy, Thomas could see no sure evidence of organic illness because there was little in her record that could not be explained as a reaction to the conditions in which she had found herself. Although he was wary of her, he did not see why she could not be trusted to help; the more he was able to remove her from the locked ward, the more lucid she appeared.

Thomas thought it would also be wise to have one of the potentially more recalcitrant staff on his side, so approached the muscular Tyson and flattered him with assurances that the success of Faverill's scheme depended on Tyson's ability to deliver the appropriate male patients, clean and compliant. Since Thomas had been given the task of admitting the women on his first day, he had become—by practice if not by any design—associated with the female side, so Tyson's help with the men was vital. There would need to be planning meetings, he added: in the evening, with beer.

The committee of three met in the kitchen at nine o'clock, over cheese, bread and half a gallon of the asylum's best bitter.

"We can disqualify all men with infectious diseases and all the chronic bedridden," said Tyson. "That gets rid of half."

"Daisy," said Thomas, "I would like you to ask round on the female side. I will tell the attendants that you have leave to wander. I should like you to ask the blind girl, Mary. It would be particularly good for her, I think. And any other odd cases like that."

"Yes, Doctor," said Daisy. She looked distrustfully over her beer at Tyson. "What about Ward Fifty-two? You going to invite anyone up from there?"

"What is Ward Fifty-two? I have never heard of it," said Thomas.

"There's no need," said Tyson. "It's a back ward."

"I am the senior assistant medical officer of this asylum. I think—"

"We can see about that later. Let's write down some names." Tyson pushed a pad of paper over the table to Thomas, who hesitated, then began to write.

McLeish, meanwhile, told the conductor of the asylum band, a former professional violinist called Brissenden, to report to Dr. Midwinter; and with that McLeish concluded his personal involvement in the festivities. Brissenden worked in the carpentry shop, and Thomas extracted him one morning to discuss the program. He was a tall, nervous man with woolly gray hair, and long fingers that he pulled till the joints cracked; he had an educated, high-pitched voice.

"Yes, indeed, Doctor. We could manage a waltz or two, a polka I have no doubt. Would you like a quadrille? No. Too tricky, I suppose. I wonder if in addition to the dances you would like a recital or some songs? A full dance program might overexcite some of the weaker brethren."

Thomas thought. "That might be a good idea. Perhaps we could have an interval in the dancing during which we could have these other—"

"Indeed, and perhaps some recitation," said Brissenden. "I believe Dr. Faverill could give us 'John Gilpin's Ride.'"

"You must come to the next meeting of our committee," said Thomas. "I shall speak to the attendant on duty in your ward. Then we can put together some sort of program that I can show to Dr. Faverill. Do you like beer?"

"Beer? Oh, dear me no." Brissenden's knuckles went off like a drumroll. "Alcohol was part of my undoing. I was principal violin with a distinguished orchestra in Portsmouth when—"

"Never mind, you can just have some chocolate. Where does the band normally rehearse? Do we have any good musicians?"

"Ah, rehearsal. Yes, a routine more honored in the breach than the observance. Still, I am certain the prospect of a ball will ensure a better turnout. It is a mixture of staff and lunatics. We have some fair woodwinds and a couple of good string players, rather too many percussionists. At the last count, we had only one horn player, very unreliable, and I fear he has been removed to a basement ward in any event. Do you play an instrument, Doctor?"

"I can play the piano, but not at all well."

"We have a most excellent pianist. A Miss Mary Ann Parker. A little inclined to rush ahead, but a most pleasing touch. We rehearse in the old dining hall, though of course the piano desperately needs tuning."

"Consider it done," said Thomas. "We shall meet on Friday evening at nine in the kitchen. I need to come and fetch you. Which ward are you in?"

"Number Eleven," said Brissenden. "The attendants call it CD, chronic demented. I call it Beethoven's Ninth. Confounded choirs. Never a moment's peace."

Over the days that followed, Thomas found time to submit a program for Faverill's approval and to send out invitations to the external visitors. The piano was tuned by a wary-looking man from the town and Tyson in due course delivered a list of men.

"Some of these will need to be dosed first," he said. "I'll speak to Dr. Stimpson. Half of them shouldn't have beer. The rest should be all right. I shall be on the lookout."

Thomas went to the old dining hall to hear the band rehearse. Among the patients were three attendants who helped Brissenden to produce a ragged but more or less recognizable series of tunes. The sound was quite well served by the high-ceilinged, empty space, which, Thomas noticed, like the dining hall of his college in Cambridge, had a gallery at the back. If they could find enough staff to supervise the movement of numbers, it seemed to him that many of those not invited to the dance itself might at least be taken by turns into the gallery to watch.

———

ON THE night of the ball, Thomas walked up to the main gates to welcome the visitors; a light fall of snow had frozen on the path and cracked
beneath his feet as he made his way up to where he could see the yellow
lamp outside Patterson's lodge. He rubbed his hands together in the
frosty darkness and paused for a moment to think how strange his life
had become. The asylum, for once, was lit from end to end, and from
Thomas's raised position at the gates, looked like an elongated vessel, its
bell towers funnels, built to the specifications of a crazed warlord determined to fill onlookers with despair and awe at the number of these
twinkling casements, each beaming its untrustworthy light into the surrounding sea.

When the dozen or so visitors were assembled, Patterson led the way
down through the grounds, holding a flaming torch above his head, so
that the distinguished visitors, reporters and representatives of the
townswomen's guild should not lose their footing before they reached
the revels. A number of chains and bolts had to be freed on the front
doors, by Grogan, at his least hurried, before they were finally admitted
to the place of entertainment. Access to the dining hall could not be
gained from the central tower, so Thomas had to unlock the doors into
the main corridor and gesture his guests to follow. He was aware of conversation dwindling, of anxious glances being exchanged, as they made
their apparent descent into the narrowing passageway, through more
chains, through air that began to carry feral odors and odd, disconnected cries.

At the foot of a ventilation tower, they finally left the corridor by a
small side door and emerged into a brighter area, a hallway lit by numerous candles. A banner had been strung from the banisters, over the
doorway and across to the opposite wall; its message was picked out in
winter flowers, white and pink, under Daisy's supervision: "WELLCOME,"
it said; and Thomas had not had the heart to demur.

Dr. Faverill showed the guests into the ballroom, where the selected
patients awaited them, lined up along the walls beneath streamers and
floral decorations. At one end of the room, the band was seated on a
raised platform, and at the other, the gallery was filled with faces, some
blank, some preoccupied, some craning to see the spectacle below.
Thomas had a moment of despair, as he always had when seeing

madness en masse, a sense of trying to empty the sea with a bucket. Then, as he made out people he knew, it began to pass and he remembered his own duties for the evening.

"Do we mix with the lunatics?" a female visitor asked him.

"I doubt whether any of them will ask you to dance. If they do, you are quite at liberty to decline the invitation—or to accept it. Entirely as you wish, Madam."

Brissenden tapped his music stand with the drumstick he used in place of a baton, and the band struck up a waltz. The attendants, as instructed, approached a patient each and led them onto the polished floorboards. The less demented of the male patients approached female partners and steered them round in approximate time to the music. Faverill watched anxiously from the doorway, running his hand back through his hair from time to time, stroking the beard beneath his jaw and rubbing it between thumb and forefinger into small gray twists.

There was the dogged scrape of the string section, a reedy whistle from the woodwinds and the occasional, plangent punctuation of the trumpet, like a foghorn or a battle cry to some engagement all its own; but apart from that, there was no sound in the hall, so that in the moments when Mary Ann Parker's piano had to pause to allow the others to catch up, Thomas could hear the slide of shoe leather on wood.

The dancers did not speak. They held each other at arm's length and watched the patterns of their feet in silence; it was as though the concentration required to make contact and move in time with another being left them no resource for speech. Thomas did not know all their names, but he recognized most of their faces and their ailments. The young man, about Olivier's age, whose thought was controlled by French spies stationed in the park, had so broken free of their influence as to be able to escort Miss Whitman repeatedly from one side to the other. He pushed her carefully, like a gardener with a wheelbarrow full of fragile pots. The old woman in Daisy's ward who wept when anybody spoke to her allowed herself to be rocked back and forth, gravely, on the spot, by the inventor of warships. The woman who had defecated on the grass of the airing court had devised a dance of her own: she made a trancelike pattern with both arms held out in front of her, as though perhaps rocking a large child in her arms, while her face, in which the mouth was puckered inward over blackened gums, was stretched by an expression of concentrated wonder.

Thomas moved down the line of female patients until he came to Mary, the blind girl he had admitted on his first day. He laid his hand gently on her arm, told her who he was, and asked if she would like to dance. She shook her head, but only slightly, more of a tremor than a denial, and it occurred to Thomas that she might not really know what dancing was.

"Will you trust me?"

She nodded, and he placed his arm round her waist, took her right hand in his left and guided her with all the delicacy he could manage onto the floor. He had never been much of a dancer—Sonia had laughed at him during the lessons they had had one Christmas—but he felt it necessary not to tread on Mary's foot or frighten her.

"What you do, Mary, is you allow yourself to move in time with the music. Do you see what I mean? You go with the tune, like this, and like this. The whole floor is full of people dancing, it is not just you and I. You have to hold on like this so we don't bump into someone. You're doing very well. Have you ever danced before?"

Mary's feet moved only a few inches on the wooden floor. She shuffled one boot forward, brought the other alongside, then slid the first one back. Through the waistband of her dress, however, Thomas could feel the faintest stir of rhythm in her spine. Her glaucous eyes were touched at the corner by what might have been the twitch of shyness, or of mirth, he could not say. The violins swept upward, urged on by the conductor, and Thomas felt Mary's diffident grasp tighten in his hand as her fingers squeezed down onto his shoulder. He saw the inflamed skin of her scalp as she laid her head against the bosom of his shirt, where it hung heavy, like ripe fruit. It was possible, he thought, that she had never before in her life been held in someone's arms. The music ended, and he led her back to her place by the wall.

He hesitated before leaving her. He should say something; he could not just cast her off, throw her back into the abyss of time. He moved away a step, then stopped. He wished that he had never patronized her with his kindness, because now he was obliged to her. But he had duties,

he had work to do with other patients, a difficult evening to negotiate—
and in truth he could not bear to look back at her face. He could not bear
it because, God forgive him, he was too young to take on the implications
of what he knew he would see.

He walked away. The mock-Ionic pillars of the dining hall were
wreathed with garlands of paper flowers and trails of ivy. On the
re-whitewashed walls were festive greetings painted onto boards, each
decorated with a sprig of holly. Beneath the central "Merry Christmas to
You All" were spread four long trestles, with beer, lemonade, hot chocolate, meat pies and pieces of cake for the dancers; attendants, three of
each sex, stood behind to make sure no patient took more than one
glass.

During supper, programs were circulated giving details of the entertainment that was to follow. "Reading: 'The Arab's Farewell to His
Steed': Dr. Faverill; Song: 'Trifles Light as Air': Miss Illsley; Recital: 'Mis-
adventures at Margate': Dr. Stimpson."

Thomas drank some asylum bitter and watched as Stimpson made
his way efficiently to the end of his piece. Few of the patients showed
much interest when Stimpson took to the stage, or when he came down
from it, though there was some shouting from the gallery and some off-
key laughter that was followed by the sounds of a scuffle and a slam-
ming door.

"I say," said the female visitor next to Thomas, "that gentleman in
the corner."

"Which one?"

She pointed toward a small bespectacled man who sat hunched on
the floor, moving his head convulsively from side to side and pulling at
an invisible thread on his trousers. "Is that Mr. Hayward?"

"I do not know his name, Madam."

"I am quite sure it is. He worked at Evans the draper's. For years and
years. My husband bought shirts from him when we were first married.
He was the outfitter for my children's school. What is the matter with
him?"

"He is afflicted with melancholy."

The lady visitor seemed a little affronted. "It seems hardly right. All
those years. And then to end up . . . like that . . . in here."

Thomas filled her glass with lemonade and looked down at his program: "Recital. 'Precepts of Politeness': Mr. Grogan." There was a listlessness among the patients when Grogan climbed onto the platform; they seemed anxious to return to the dancing, Thomas thought, and their mood was not helped by Grogan, whose attempt to introduce humor came over as a kind of leering. The climax of the interval entertainment was a duet: "'Grieve No More': Mr. Tyson, Daisy Wilkins, with Mary Ann Parker, pianoforte."

Tyson had a surprisingly pleasant tenor, and Daisy sang with conviction, a semitone sharp, occasionally missing a line to catch up with Mary Ann's restless fingers. Neither singer looked at the other; the trio performed as individuals, each apparently bent on completing an unpleasant duty as fast as possible, though in Thomas's mind there was never any doubt about the likely winner. Tyson shuffled his feet and swallowed his last, unsung half-line as the asylum band resumed their places on the platform behind him.

The couples once more took to the floor and resumed their silent marking out of space. Not even Brissenden's liveliest polka, the Louisa, could prompt them into speech, though Thomas noticed a disheveled old woman occasionally burst into harsh, irrelevant laughter. She tossed back her cropped white hair and showed her edentulous jaw, causing the man who held her at arm's length to pull back further. He was a former watchmaker, well known to the attendants for his conviction that only if he could compete in a walking race to Blackpool would his lost soul be returned to him by the group of Plymouth Brethren who had stolen it.

At a quarter to ten, Dr. Faverill took to the platform to declare the evening's festivities over. The double doors at once opened from the vestibule, and a dozen attendants came into the room, taking their appointed places by the wall and marking their patients out with warning eyes. Any escape from the asy-lum was deemed to be the relevant attendant's fault and the expense of recapture was deducted from wages.

". . . wonderful evening," Faverill was saying, "and I would like to thank our most distinguished visitors for taking the time to come and share in our seasonal celebrations. I feel sure that they will take away with them the most favorable impression of our asylum. It is an unusual household, we are the first to admit. We have our share of black sheep, of wicked uncles and long-lost cousins. But we have as well the comfort of a Christian faith, which teaches us that God loves each of us as His own. There is no man or woman here tonight whose life is not dear in the eyes of Our Lord. First, I would like to present a small bouquet to Mr. Brissenden, our most excellent bandmaster. There you are. Thank you, sir. And now I should like to ask Miss Whitman if she would be so kind as to present this bouquet to Mrs. Cunningham, wife of the chairman of the Committee of Visitors. Thank you, Miss Whitman.

"Before we all go off to our beds, I would like to conclude by thanking all of you, the patients, for coming tonight and making the evening so pleasant for us all. I have occasionally, I believe, compared myself to the captain of a ship—a somewhat vainglorious comparison, it now occurs to me. But on a night such as this, I feel proud to think that this vessel sails onward. The weather threatens, sometimes we may steer blind, but, if I may quote the Bard, "Though the seas threaten, they are merciful"; and we must not curse them without cause. The ways of the Almighty are mysterious to men. I cannot presume to unriddle to you the details of his intricate plan. I cannot begin to explain to you my own sense of the strangeness of our human lives and my conviction that it might so easily, with the merest tilt of the world on its axis, be so entirely different. One thing I can say with certainty is this. Tonight my heart is filled with love and pride in you, my dear friends, and I wish you with all the fervor I can command a safe and peaceful harbor at the end of the voyage the Almighty has set out before you. Ladies and gentlemen, good night."

The attendants moved into the room, gathering their charges. "Come on Alice, move along, girl. Don't do that, you filthy man. Come here, Jack. Put that down. Bedtime now, come along, come along."

Thomas stood in the vestibule as they marshaled their patients through the door and into the long corridor. In the ballroom, the instruments were already packed up and Tyson was turning off the gas lamps; Brissenden was the last to leave, walking silently across the floor with his gathered sheet music furling beneath his arm. He was humming to himself as he walked past and did not hear when Thomas wished him good night.

Dr. Faverill had already left the building to escort the visitors to their waiting carriages. Maud Illsley and Miss Whitman had put up stepladders to blow out the candles in the hall and take down Daisy's banner. Thomas stood for a moment, looking, hearing the rattle of keys and the clank of locks being turned, as through the length of the building the lamps were turned out. He took a candle to light his way through the resumed darkness.

VI

AS SONIA HAD FORESEEN, THERE WAS NOTHING SHE COULD DO TO affect the course her husband and father had chosen, and the practical details of a divorce were surprisingly easy to arrange; what was more complicated was the disarray in which she was left by her conflicting emotions. She sighed from the depths of her heart as she packed her trunks and locked up the rooms of the London house. She knew that it was perverse, almost comic, for her to be the last to abandon the marriage when she was the wronged party within it; yet the more her efforts to be a good wife were mocked, the more anxious she became to make them work. Of course, she had been too young to marry; but she was quite grown-up for her age, and she had deceived no one about the nature of her feelings. She had followed the good advice of those who knew better and was content to believe that love would come; or that in its absence, the pleasure she brought to her parents and husband would be reward enough. A sort of love had come—an absolute identification of her interests with Richard's and an anguished desire for him to prosper, which was tested but not shaken when she saw that as well as being socially inept, her husband was a bully. Any resentment she might have felt at this discovery was stifled by her guilt at being unable to conceive: Richard was entitled to be brusque when he had been disappointed in a man's simplest expectation.

In the months after their separation, when she had returned to live with her parents, Sonia endlessly reviewed the course of her marriage. She should perhaps have resisted acting as financial go-between; but there was a sense of unease in her that she had been influenced to marry in the first place by a degree of impatience. Maybe she ought to have left when he casually told her, of the rooms that had been found for him: "Of course you can come if you like." At the time she put her staying down to a sense of duty, a conviction that someone at least must behave with dignity; but had she really clung on from fear of the unknown?

It seemed to her, as she resumed her old duties at Torrington, that she had undoubtedly missed a chance, somewhere; she had been made a fool of, sold and rebought. Such was the effect on her self-respect, however, that she could feel little relief at being rid of a man she did not love, and one who had behaved unkindly toward her. So unsure was she now of what value to place on herself that she could not even feel affection for her father: he seemed to think that he had ransomed and redeemed her and to expect her gratitude in return, but she felt that he had merely dealt with her at Richard Prendergast's level.

For some months, Sonia wept at night from a sense of injustice. She even missed the rough embrace of her husband, alone as she was, and cast back into her child's bedroom. Then, very slowly, a little relief did find her; she became able to smile a little at the memory of some of Richard's absurdities, and her own. By the time the spring came, her grief had turned through tears into a kind of mute acceptance. She was in all probability unable to conceive, though this had not, in her view, been proved beyond doubt. Assuming the worst, however, her prospects as a wife were limited; but this was something she could adapt to, and need not circumscribe her life too narrowly. One thing in all the uncertainties did become clear to her: that she would never, in any circumstances, allow herself to be so used again. She held this determination tight in her heart, as some of the old lightness, her humor and her influence about the house began to return.

ONE MORNING in early summer Jacques received a package from England. Madame Maurel, his landlady, handed it over in person, curious that one of her tenants should have an overseas correspondent, but Jacques did not respond to her imploring glance as he walked out into the morning. As he tore open the envelope on his way to the hospital, two pieces of paper fell out: one was a folded English banknote, and the other . was a ticket, issued by Thomas Cook and Son, for the Channel steamer. There was also a brief accompanying letter in English from Thomas.

My dear Jacques,

I cannot bear your procrastination any longer. I am certain that your studies in neurology are most engrossing, but time is short and my asylum overlords allow me scant leave. Go to Calais. Take this ticket to the harbor and walk onto the vessel. You may study all you wish on the waves; no need even to raise your eyes from the book to view the white cliffs as they approach. The money will buy you a train ticket to London, a cab from Victoria to St. Pancras and a ticket to Lincoln. I shall be waiting for you at the station. What could be simpler?

At Torrington will be assembled: the undersigned; his sister Sonia (*sans* Prendergast, who has departed our lives); his aged parents; his brother Edgar, his wife Lucy and assorted children; Miss Brigstocke, a cook, and her maid, May; new girl, name as yet unknown; sundry Dalmatian dogs; pages, hautboys, drums &c. The action takes place in the space of a summer week. You need to bring one decent suit for dinner, otherwise clothes suitable for outdoor activity, fishing, riding and so forth. Your linen will be cared for by the maid, who, though nameless, is reported by my sister to be fair of face and "obliging in all things." What can she mean?

Please do not disquiet yourself about the money. My masters pay me a salary of £190 per year; my board, lodging, laundry and coals are understood in this sum. In the eight months I have been at the asylum I have contrived to spend no more than 24 guineas (beer, books, photographic equipment; it is hard to find anything at all—even my shoes are mended by the lunatics). So this is my first investment in our joint venture—which we will

discuss at length beneath the cedars of Torrington. You can
repay me out of your first check when we set up our clinic.

Do not reply; only come. We await you with impatience.

Sincerely
Thomas Midwinter

P.S. Have you heard of lawn-tennis? It is a game patented by
a British army officer a few years ago, an adaptation of the
original game to the exigencies of an ordinary lawn. It is
apparently popular in Lincolnshire. You are warned.

Jacques smiled as he tucked the letter away in his pocket. Presumably
Thomas had hoped to pique his interest by his mention of the new maid,
but it was not the presence of an anonymous girl that interested him.

HE SAT by the window on the hard bench of the Channel packet.
Although the function of the boat was to carry the mails, there were
about three dozen passengers, tradesmen he supposed, reading newspapers or books. Many had brought food and wine, which they spread
out beside them. A woman at the end of his bench produced a half
Camembert and a slab of terrine the size of a small headstone; she sliced
a loaf neatly, smeared it with butter from a paper packet and began to
pile up each oval plank with food. As she ate, she pulled the paper stop-
per from a bottle of red wine, which she upended against her pursed lips,
so thin red dribbles mingled with the excess of terrine on her dimpled
chin. The smell of pork and garlic caused Jacques's belly to make such
desperate noises that he had to move to a different seat.

The time had come, he thought, when he and Thomas would have to
start behaving like serious men. In the language of the student, which
had till then been their rhetoric, there was always comedy and exaggeration; there was the self-consciousness that sprang from the difference
between their private estimation of their worth and their knowledge of
the public fact that others, more eminent, had preceded them. There was
the self-mockery that was their preemptive defense against their elders,

and against the unyielding nature of the obstacles ahead. So many sentences in the conversations of students began with the words, "Apparently, they . . ." "They" were the masters, those who had gone before and probably sought, for no clear reason, to obstruct the young; and "apparently" showed how little students knew at first hand, how much of what they dealt in was hearsay.

Jacques felt it was time to take possession of the facts, to confront the "they" and to cease to hide behind self-mockery: to stare the world, unsmiling, in the face. At the same time, he was reluctant to lose the humor of his dialogue with Thomas. Three times since their meeting at Deauville, Thomas had visited him in Paris, where Jacques had been not only exhilarated to see him, but impressed by his determination. He had not retreated one pace, one half-pace, from the ambition of their shared objective and he had showed himself resolute in the surroundings of his English asylum. Having visited Olivier, Jacques knew what such places were like.

For almost ten years, Olivier had been in the public asylum. Jacques went to see him when he could, though the distance to be traveled and the hours of his work, first as a student, then as an intern, made it difficult. Olivier had intervals of lucidity, occasions when he seemed to know who Jacques was and to be able to communicate almost normally, but such times seemed to give him no insight into his condition. When he was better, he could not understand or picture himself when he was possessed; and when he was worse, he could not draw on any deposit of reason or comfort from his better periods, because he could not remember them.

Jacques had at first persuaded Abbé Henri to accompany him, but the Curé found the experience so harrowing that he had reduced his visits to one a year. He told Jacques that after each occasion it required several weeks of prayer and meditation to restore his faith: the sights he saw, the sounds, the parodies of human grace, made it hard for him to discern God's purpose. Jacques did not sympathize, but his debt to Abbé Henri was such that he could not express his misgivings.

At least the Curé did visit; old Rebière had not been once to see his son. Jacques could forgive Tante Mathilde, who was not related to Olivier, for not visiting, and Grand-mère, who was too frail to manage a journey by coach, but not his father, whose attitude to Olivier was that of a farmer rejecting ill-bred livestock at market: take it away, he seemed to say, it is of no value to me. Yet Olivier was his son, his firstborn, and in his blood and brain ran particles of Rebière's own transmitted self. As a consequence, Jacques had ceased to write to him and no longer visited Saint Agnès. Often in his narrow attic room at Madame Maurel's he dreamed of the fields and paths where he had grown up; he walked again along the shingled beach or emerged from the wood at dusk and saw the thin drift of smoke coming from the chimney of his father's house below: this was the country of his heart, and no human changes could supplant it.

His plan was to remove Olivier from the asylum as soon as he had a place for him to live and the money to support him. He did not share Thomas's view that living in an asylum could in itself be of benefit. Although Esquirol had had success with patients in his private hospital at Charenton, Jacques doubted the severity of their illness. Olivier's health had certainly not improved by his being incarcerated with other lunatics; and although he generally evinced little awareness of his sur-roundings, Jacques felt that in his periods of relative calm it could not be helpful to Olivier to see himself surrounded by others suffering, in squalor, the torments from which he had a brief remission. The only worthwhile thing that Olivier did in the asylum was to make drawings in his neat, clerk's hand; he had studied some architectural books and, in his saner interludes, drew up intricate plans for improved accommodation.

Jacques ordered some lamb cutlets and beer at a chop house in Dover and ate them wolfishly with some sort of suet pudding, unknown to him, in a dark savory broth. He seemed to have plenty of money left over when he took the train to London and watched the hopfields of Kent gliding past the window. This was England . . . pale, flat, lacking the grandeur and variety of Brittany, but pleasant in its own way. It was the first foreign country he had seen. Until he had met Thomas, he had given little thought to the island across the water; he knew that its people were warlike and practical, but they had, so far as he had been taught, contributed nothing original to civilization—some agricultural tools, a play or two, perhaps; but otherwise his own country had remained a self-sufficient universe, which had discovered or invented all it needed to make it, and keep it, preeminent. Yet Thomas had a sort of confidence, Jacques noticed, that was not a personal trait but seemed to spring from the power of a tradition, as though he were able to draw at will on some sort of inheritance; so as the train neared London, he decided he had better be watchful in what he assumed about this new country. He did not want to betray the fact that besides Olivier, whom he had lost, and Thomas, he had seen no need for friends and so had never dined in company or attended social events.

Thomas was waiting for him at the station with Jenkins the coachman. He squeezed Jacques so hard in his arms that Jacques began to cough and had to push him away.

"Tussis nervosa," said Thomas. "Jump in the coach. Quick. We can still be in time for dinner. I presume you are hungry?"

"Always."

"Drive like hell, Jenkins. We've killed the fatted calf. The fatted sow at any rate. What do you think of my country?"

"I love it," said Jacques. "I feel I am Englishman already."

"Good. Then you will want to ride with us tomorrow."

"Of course I will."

"I suppose that is another of your talents."

"We had a violent mare at home. If you could ride her, my father used to say, you could ride any horse in France."

Thomas laughed. "You wait till you try Achilles. Do you have a clean shirt and all that nonsense for dinner? Tell me about your journey. And what is happening in the world of the nervous system? Tell me everything."

"First, you tell me what I need to know for tonight. Who else will be there? What special customs do you have?" said Jacques, trying to sound facetious, not just worried. "What English rituals are there?"

"Early June," said Thomas. "The sacrifice of the virgins. You have missed the Maypole dancing, but it is the season for the burning of the Roman Catholics. I have told my father you would be happy to oblige."

"Delighted, of course. Provided that I am allowed to witness the sacrifice of the virgins."

"But of course. Noblesse oblige. And you pass the port to your left. Or is it your right? I can never remember. Do not kiss anyone. Do not shake hands. That is considered vulgar and foreign."

"And foreign things are bad?"

"Invariably. Is that not your experience?"

"It was until a few moments ago. Now I see possibilities. There is a part of me that feels almost English."

"Make sure it is a thinking part. We are entering the village of Torrington. They may never have seen a Frenchman before. I wish you good luck. After dinner we shall meet again."

The new maid, who turned out to be called Violet, showed Jacques to his bedroom and told him to be downstairs in ten minutes. Jacques had time to take out his best suit and shirt for dinner, to wash his face and hands and to check his appearance in the mirror on the dressing table. There was something about the room that pleased him—the planed and polished floorboards, the jar of fresh wildflowers, the selection of books on a side table: Atkinson's *Flora of Lincolnshire*, a translation of *Eugénie Grandet* and an old copy of *The Lancet*. Someone had been thoughtful on his behalf—that was what it was, more than the details of the room itself—and he was touched by it. He peered at his face one more time in the glass. Although he had slept only a few hours the night before in a Holborn inn, his brown eyes were bright, and the skin below was clear; he was excited for no reason he could tell, merely that he was young, there was an evening ahead, friendship, wine and much to say.

Thomas's family was in the library, to which the waiting Violet escorted him. "This way, sir." Jacques felt fraudulent, being called "sir" by a servant in a big house in a foreign country; he felt the gloom of his humble home envelop him like a flag that said "impostor." Thomas sprang from the sofa where he had been lounging and put his arm round Jacques's shoulders as he introduced him. Jacques's eyes took in people—English people, lumpish, powdery, stiff. He held out his hand, then, remembering, rapidly thrust it back behind him. On his shoulder was Thomas's arm—"My mother . . . father . . . Mrs. Meadowes . . ."—and round his knees were what appeared to be a pack of Dalmatian dogs, snuffling and grinning, thrashing his thighs with their tails. ". . . Dr. Meadowes . . . Stop it, Dido, get down. . . . Gordon, sit down. . . . And my sister, Sonia Prendergast, whom you will remember from Deauville."

Jacques found himself bowing, and as his eyes went down to the carpet saw a proffered pale hand briefly appear then vanish.

"I remember very well," he managed to say, looking up again into Sonia's slightly amused eyes, dark and rapid, exactly as he did indeed recall from the walled garden of the Pension des Dunes: that look—sardonic, but modest. She wore a dress of burgundy silk with a row of pearls; the skin of her throat and upper chest, Jacques noticed, was still that of a girl.

"Welcome to Torrington, Mr. Rebière," said Mrs. Midwinter. She stressed it on the first syllable, as though it were "Rebbier."

"A glass of Marsala, perhaps," said Mr. Midwinter. "Don't let the dogs do that or you'll have white hairs all over your trousers."

"Not black hairs," said Jacques, "from the spots? That would be preferable."

"No," said Mrs. Midwinter, without any acknowledgment that Jacques might have been attempting a pleasantry, "it is only the white hairs that molt. Most inconvenient."

Jacques stood with his back to the fireplace, trapped in an enfilade of polite inquiry: journey, family, home, work. . . . He turned to left and right and knew, like a St. Cyr infantry subaltern, that it was a matter of standing firm and soaking up the fire. He felt the affectionate eyes of Thomas and—he thought—Sonia on him as he held his position until relief came with a knock at the door: "Dinner is served," said Violet, giving a small curtsy, blushing and disappearing swiftly back into the hall.

The French doors of the dining room were open onto the terrace, and a light breeze cooled the overdressed company as they took their seats. Jacques found himself between Mrs. Midwinter and Mrs. Meadowes, wife of the local doctor; he disguised the weakness of his English by asking numerous questions of the ladies and obliging them to talk. Opposite him was Dr. Meadowes, who had a swollen foot and walked with a stick; his ailment seemed to make him short-tempered and disapproving. Thomas was two seats to the left, out of range for Jacques, unless he were to crane rudely in front of Mrs. Meadowes's bosom or sneak behind her back; but diagonally across from him was Sonia, who was doing her best to humor Dr. Meadowes.

Jacques found his eyes aching to return to Sonia's face, but forced them to remain on the plump and powdered cheeks of Mrs. Midwinter, as she explained the expense of keeping horses. When she looked down for a moment to her soup, he let his glance flick once across the table and found that Sonia was looking steadily at him. She smiled at him in an unembarrassed, sisterly way without breaking off her attempts to be pleasant to Dr. Meadowes. She had no need actually to look at Meadowes, because he did not raise his face from the soup plate.

Sisterly, thought Jacques. Of course: I am her little brother's friend. Why would she not be cordial and unembarrassed? Nevertheless, he felt inexplica-bly deflated by Sonia's friendliness as he turned to find out more about Mrs. Meadowes's herbaceous borders.

The English food was surprisingly palatable. After the soup, there was roast pork carved by Mr. Midwinter at the sideboard and taken round by Violet. Jacques noticed that her hand was shaking when she served him. He did not often eat so much or so well on his unforgiving budget and only wished they had not served vegetables at the same time as the meat.

"All our own, you know," said Mrs. Midwinter. "Jenkins has made rather a good job of the kitchen gardens this year."

Jacques noticed the enthusiastic helpings that she took for herself; he caught Sonia's eye again and thought he saw a light of amusement in it. His glass was filled with red wine from Bordeaux; his plate was cleared and another, with cold fowl, was placed in front of him. Perhaps he had imagined Sonia's look.

After a peculiar milk dessert, Jacques was surprised when Mrs. Midwinter abruptly stood up in mid-conversation, put her napkin on the table and made to leave the room. He hurried from his chair, presuming that dinner was over, hoping to be in time to open the door for her. Sonia and Mrs. Meadowes followed Mrs. Midwinter out, and Jacques stood by the door, waiting for the men. Thomas, still seated, shook his head and pointed Jacques back to his seat. Mr. Midwinter fetched a decanter of port from the sideboard and motioned the others to move up to his end of the table. The sweet wine was unfamiliar to Jacques, but he found it pleasant enough and pushed the decanter across the table into Thomas's waiting hand.

"So, Midwinter," said Dr. Meadowes. "Are you pleased to have your daughter back? What sort of fellow did he turn out to be, this Prendergast?"

"A rascal," said Mr. Midwinter, sitting back in his chair. "Not a rogue, not a cheat, but a man of straw. Couldn't keep the girl in a respectable way. Built up huge debts and had no chance of getting out of them. There were no children, so we did well to cut our losses."

"It must be disappointing for you."

"A little. But she is still young. The divorce settlement has been agreed. I still have hopes for her future, though of course she will be seen as tarnished goods, so one's hopes are modest."

"It is difficult to see how she is tarnished, Father," said Thomas, "when she acted in such good faith."

Mr. Midwinter chuckled. "That was the damn funny thing about it, Meadowes. When I had negotiated her release from this fellow—this impecunious rascal she wasn't even fond of—then blow me down she says she wants to stay!"

Dr. Meadowes coughed into his glass. "Why? In God's name, why? Frightened of being an old maid?"

"No," said Mr. Midwinter. "It was a sense of duty, I think. She said a lot of things I didn't understand. About how being his wife was what she did for a living, or some such thing, and she couldn't change that any sooner than she could change her parents. It was a rum thing, I can tell you. I would have been out of there like a shot."

"Hmm," said Meadowes. "Queer cattle, women."

"Exceedingly queer. But she seems all right. She's a little quiet, but I think in a way she's glad to be home. I know we're pleased to have her back. She's a good girl at heart."

Thomas put down his glass. "Papa, I think you might try a little harder to understand Sonia's position. I am sure you acted in her best interests, but can you not see how powerless and forlorn she must have felt to see her life decided for her, wondering about the lack of children, too, and whose fault that was? And then for you to call her 'tarnished,' as though—"

"It's just a word, Thomas, just a blasted word. And what's more it is a word that will be used, whether we like it or not. You were always such a pedant, weren't you, as though the future of the world depended on the choice of a single word or a line of Shakespeare. It doesn't."

"But, Father—"

"Let it lie, Thomas."

Jacques watched as Thomas controlled himself, cleared his throat and reached for the decanter, from which he filled his glass, before passing it silently to Dr. Meadowes. Jacques felt sure the Thomas he had encountered on the beach at Deauville would have poured the contents on his father's head; perhaps his acquiescence showed that Thomas, like him, had moved on from the days of student self-assurance.

"So," said Mr. Midwinter, unable quite to keep a note of triumph from his voice, "how is your boy, Meadowes? Following in the family profession, I understand."

After the port, they rejoined the women in the morning room, though it was not long before Thomas, drawing on the privilege of youth, asked if he and Jacques might be allowed to walk in the garden.

"My God, this grass," said Jacques. "It is like velvet."

"But you have lawns in France, Jacques."

"My father had a stable yard with fields behind. But this is wonderful, it's like walking on cloth."

"In the morning I shall take you for a tour of the grounds. I have brought a cigar for you. Shall we sit beneath the cedar? Hello? Who's that?"

Jacques turned round to see a female shape hurrying toward them in the darkness. "Do you mind if I join in your walk?" said Sonia, a little breathless. "I could not bear another of Dr. Meadowes's case histories."

"Come and sit down," said Thomas.

"'Have I told you about the old farmer's deaf wife who fell downstairs?' he asks. And you say, 'Yes, you told me earlier.' But then he just carries on and tells you again anyway."

"Ah, but we like case histories out here," said Thomas. "It is part of what we need to talk about."

"I am sure that you will not repeat yourself so soon or so often."

"We will try," said Jacques, emboldened by Sonia's modest manner.

"Mama thinks I have a headache, so perhaps it would be best if she does not know I came to join you," said Sonia.

"It shall be our secret," said Thomas. "Now Jacques was about to tell me what he has discovered since I saw him last."

Jacques puffed at his cigar. Although he felt inhibited by Sonia, he thought he might as well be serious. "I think what I am finding," he said slowly, aware that he could not express himself in English as well as he would like, "is that there may be very little time left in the life of what one calls psychiatry. From what I have seen in the Salpêtrière and from the place where Olivier lives, most of the illnesses are of neurological origin. Neurology, as you know," he said to Sonia, "is the study of diseases of the nervous system which stem from some lesion in the brain or the spinal cord. Anyway, in Paris there are certain eminent men who are making progress in attributing to the different parts of the brain the functions of speech, movement and so on. I believe that soon we will be able to diagnose at postmortem the half-dozen most important diseases. Then we can set about finding cures."

"It is a shame you have to wait until they are dead," said Sonia. "I suppose there is no other way of inspecting someone's brain."

"Not yet. Though one day we may be able to take a photograph through the bone of the skull."

"Not with my Underwood," said Thomas.

"But when this task of nosology is complete," said Jacques, "the majority of mental patients will become neurological. The remainder, whose damage is incurable, can only be nursed, but they may be looked after in hospital with the limbless or the blind. No more asylums."

"My dear Jacques, we have barely begun our lives as alienists and already you are declaring the profession moribund."

"All this is happening very quickly," said Jacques. "It is time for us to move, or we shall be overtaken."

Thomas sighed. "I agree with you that there is no time to waste. From my point of view the urgency is to discover treatments before all lunatics are classified as incurable and fit only to be managed. For you, the urgency seems to be to make our contribution before all the answers are discovered!"

Jacques laughed. "It is good that we have different views. As long as we agree that speed is essential."

Sonia coughed. "May I ask a small question? What exactly is this thing that you are going to do?"

"We are going to set up in private practice," said Thomas.

"Where?"

"Not in Lincoln. The competition from Dr. Meadowes would be too fierce."

"Don't mock, Thomas. He told me his son is to become a doctor as well."

"We will have to follow money, to some extent," said Thomas. "You cannot be a specialist without clients."

"Suppose we go to Paris," said Jacques. "That is where the best research is. And there is money."

"Suppose we go to Heidelberg or Munich," said Thomas. "I think the Germans have a broader outlook."

"Suppose we go to Vienna," said Sonia. "The music and the—"

"No, it must be Paris," said Jacques. "At the Salpêtrière, the senior neurologist, Professor Charcot, gives public lectures which have changed the face of medicine. He uses hypnotism to demonstrate the nature of hysteria. He is able to induce bodily changes in the patients. These lectures are open to the public. Anyone can go."

"It sounds a little cruel," said Sonia.

"No, the completion of the grand mal is good for them. The convulsion itself brings relief."

"I have another small question," said Sonia. "Do you not believe that talking to people and treating them kindly might have a beneficial effect?"

Thomas laughed. "You must not start us off on the psychological question. We are not yet at one on that."

"You don't appear to be at one on very much."

"Thank you, Sonia," said Thomas. "I believe that moral treatment, concern and so on may well help sick people; even if it does not, it is still kind to ask them about their thoughts and feelings. It is clear to me that many of my patients are suffering from organic illness of the brain that no amount of goodwill can reach. Jacques, on the other hand, I think, is skeptical about the achievements of his own countrymen in this field. He thinks—"

"I think," said Jacques, "that some of those apparently cured in small and wealthy asylums are not suffering from mental illness as you and I understand it. But what most persuades me is my own case." He turned to Sonia. "My brother has been in an asylum for ten years. Before that, he lived in the stable at home. When I go to see him, it is like talking to someone who lives in a world close to our own, but divided from it by an impenetrable barrier. I wonder if he inherited some abnormality of the brain. But I do not have it and neither does my father. As for my mother, I do not know because she died when giving birth . . . to me."

"I am sorry," said Sonia.

"So perhaps Olivier's illness is the result of what Pasteur would call a 'germ' that he breathed in somewhere. Or maybe he has been driven to behave like this by the circumstances of his life. Yet these were not so different from my own, or from those of most of the young men in our village. And until a certain age he seemed happy."

"Also," said Thomas, "we have noticed, and so have other alienists, that Olivier's symptoms are similar in pattern to those of many others. You feel there is a recurring shape to them. A large number of the people in my asylum have it, and it is hard to believe that so many disparate individual lives could produce such a similar pattern of symptoms, unless there were a common physical base, something they have inherited."

"And how are things inherited?" said Sonia. "In the blood, somehow?"

"The precise mechanism is still, alas, unknown. But it would be similar to whatever transmits family resemblances, color of eyes and so forth."

"I see," said Sonia.

"But the interesting thing," said Jacques, "is whether there could be some process by which the patient's experience can somehow release an inherited organic illness that until that moment was lying dormant."

Sonia and Thomas looked at one another and then at Jacques in the shaded darkness of the cedar. Neither of them spoke for a few moments.

"So something could . . . jump, as it were," said Thomas, "from the realm of the abstract—idea, experience—into the physical chemistry of the brain and release a reaction there?"

"I believe it is possible," said Jacques. He had not framed this thought clearly before, and he felt elated that he had so dumbfounded his friends.

"And that reaction," said Sonia, "would cause the patient to behave in the way you describe in your brother."

"It might," said Jacques. "I think it is conceivable that the physiological changes in the brain that follow on a sensation of fear or anxiety might cause a chemical reaction which might in itself precipitate the entire collapse. It might be like the straw that breaks the camel's back, or the first domino to fall in a line. The rest becomes inevitable because of what has been inherited."

"But without that straw, that domino, the inheritance might never be activated?" said Sonia. "It might just lie dormant?"

"I don't know," said Jacques. "But I think it is worth considering."

"There is a man who brings my coal," said Thomas. "He is called Stevens, and he is melancholic with some chorea. He may be afflicted by a sort of illness—a pneumonia, as it were, of the cerebral tissue—or he may still be mourning the death of his wife. But he cannot really be both, can he?"

"I cannot speak for your coal man," said Jacques, "but I believe we are on the verge of understanding this question and that when we do we shall be able to offer an almost complete explanation of human behavior. This is the most exciting time there has ever been in human science. Imagine. A theory that explains it all."

"They are certainly the profoundest questions," said Thomas, sounding unhappy.

"And that," said Jacques, leaping to his feet, "is why you must come to Paris."

JACQUES WAS awoken the following morning by a soft knock at his door. It was Violet, who had brought him a cup of tea with, to his surprise, milk in it. She kept her head averted as she placed it on the chest of drawers, and made her way back without having met his eye. "Your shaving water will be up in a moment, sir," she said, closing the door softly behind her.

He fetched the cup and took it back to bed, where he propped himself up on two pillows. He could see a fine morning through the window and could hear the sound of wood pigeons and blackbirds from the garden. He smiled as he felt the cool air drift through the open window; it was the dependably false chill that foretold heat; he knew it from many early judgments made before setting off into his father's woods. This England was a surprisingly agreeable place, he thought, with its plates full of succulent meat, its balmy weather, its pretty maids and French wine. He went over the previous evening in his mind. Nothing had been quite as enjoyable as arriving, when every sight and sensation was new, when all was promise; but it was the conversation after dinner in the garden that he dwelt on, as he sipped the tea.

After a time beneath the cedar he had ceased to be inhibited by Sonia's presence. In fact, there was something he took from her that he found also in her brother: a sense of uncritical encouragement. With them both, he felt wiser and less prone to fall; it seemed that he could be thrilled by her presence but that his brain could still work when she was there.

He smiled at this recognition as he replaced the cup on the bedside table. Some verbal peculiarity had been nagging at him, something that had not seemed right the night before, and now he remembered what it was. When he and Thomas had discussed the location of their future practice, they had said, "Suppose we go to Munich?" or, "Suppose we go to Paris?" Then Sonia had joined in, but she had not said, "Will you go to Vienna?" but "Suppose we go to Vienna?" "We." He was almost certain she had said "we." There was, alas, no way that he could relive the exchange, no method by which it might be recaptured.

Breakfast offered Jacques another chance to sample Lincolnshire meat—sausages, lambs' kidneys and bacon—to which Thomas, reading a newspaper by the open window, invited him to help himself.

"Normally," said Jacques, "I dip last night's bread in a bowl of tea."

"It is a miracle that you are still alive," said Thomas. "Please do not feel obliged to eat everything you see. I think my parents are trying to impress you. When you have fueled yourself, we are going for a ride. I have asked Jenkins to saddle Achilles. I think you will find him entertaining. He's a bay hunter, who used to belong to Edgar. Since my mother has had rheumatism, she can't manage him anymore. He needs exercise."

"Getting a bit fat, aren't you, old boy?" said Sonia in the stable yard, stroking the big beast's nose as she held his bridle while Jacques mounted. "Thomas, you will have to take Elektra because Jenkins has put the sidesaddle on Hector."

The three horses clunked over the cobbles of the yard, and Jacques felt the power of his mount's neck as he shortened the reins.

Thomas brought his horse alongside. "I am sorry there is no hunting at this time of year," he said, "but we can still have some good exercise. If you find him too mettlesome, you can have Elektra. She is a gentle creature. Achilles looks a little out of condition, so I expect you'll be all right."

Jacques had never ridden for pleasure before, only to reach outlying properties more quickly on his father's business. He settled in behind Sonia, who wore a long beige skirt over her boots and a hard black hat secured by a scarf; her mount, Hector, was a gray with powerful quarters who kicked his back legs out when he felt Achilles come too close.

Behind the yard was a paddock that overlooked the house; as Thomas held the gate open, the three Dalmatians ran through ahead of them. Thomas stood in his stirrups to canter up the hill and Jacques cautiously gave Achilles his head. He needed no urging, only stopping when they reached the copse at the edge of the paddock; Jacques wrestled his mouth back and felt the muscles in his forearms stand out as he regained control.

The sun was already high over the woods as Thomas led the way beneath the beech canopy, over dappled paths on which last autumn's leaves were still dry beneath the horses' hooves. The narrow tracks kept them in single file, so there was no conversation beyond the occasional inquiry or call of reassurance. Jacques found it hard to believe that an entire day stretched ahead in which nothing was required of him except to ride a horse, eat, and make himself pleasant to his friends.

On the far side of the small wood, they emerged onto a planted field. "This land all belongs to my father's farm," said Thomas. "On the other side of the valley, at the top there, we can go flat-out along the ridge and then down to the river. Come on."

They rode as fast as they could down to the road below them and paused as Thomas leaned down to unlatch another gate.

"Listen," said Sonia, "can you hear that? A skylark."

The horses were breathing hard as the riders listened intently for a sound from high in the blue above them. When they reached the top of the slope, they could see the spire of St. Mary's, the village church, and the west wing of Torrington Manor, half hidden by an avenue of limes. Thomas, panting a little, pointed out the sights to Jacques. "The Laceys, the people who own the manor, wanted to plant the avenue as far as the sea—it's all their land. But that was a hundred years ago and I see no sign of it."

Jacques looked across at Sonia, whose eyes followed the sweep of Thomas's arm. Her face was a little pink from the exertion and there was a single clear drop of moisture on her upper lip; riding sidesaddle did not apparently slow her down at all. Jacques, who was sweating hard beneath his jacket, wondered how uncomfortable it must be for a woman in her extra layers; she must have wanted to shed her long skirt and petticoats, the worsted jacket and black hat, and ride in thin, simple clothes with her hair flying in the wind like an Indian brave. He kept the image in his mind as they began to gallop along the ridge.

However hard he pulled at the reins he could not prevent himself from passing Sonia's mount, then Thomas's quick mare, as Achilles filled his lungs with the burning June air and stretched the muscles of his chest and mountainous bay quarters, pounding the grassy path. Jacques saw the foam of sweat creep out beneath the saddle and caught the stertorous breathing of the horse as he plunged on; there was still at least a minute's gallop before the wood, so he decided to let the animal run free and tire himself.

"You have a fine seat," said Sonia, eventually pulling Hector up alongside.

"I had no seat. I just held on."

"It's a phrase. It means you ride well."

"Thank you. So do you."

"I am out of practice. My husband kept a horse in London for a time and I used to ride in Hyde Park. But then . . ."

"Then?"

"Economies." Sonia smiled.

"I am sorry to hear about your husband. And that you . . . no longer."

"Thank you. I expect I shall survive."

"It must be wonderful for your parents to have you at home."

Sonia laughed. "Wonderful! Oh, I doubt that. Look. Here's Thomas. Let's go down to the river."

At the bank, they descended gently and allowed their horses to walk through the water, a sensation Jacques loved, as though his mount was moving through thicker, cushioned air. The horses plainly liked it too, dropping their heads to drink from the slow current. Thomas reached into his saddlebag.

"Are you hungry, Jacques?"

"Of course."

"I've brought you an English delicacy. A pork pie. Here."

He threw it over and Jacques had to lean forward to scoop the catch off the surface of the river. He bit into the fatty pastry and the clear salt jelly beneath.

"It needs mustard," said Thomas. "And beer, but that would have been too shaken up. You can drink from the river."

Jacques's teeth reached the packed, mild meat in the middle of the pie and hungrily chewed on. He could feel sweat running down his throat into the open neck of his shirt.

"I am going to swim," said Thomas. "Queenie, will you hold Elektra? Come on, Jacques, the water's quite warm. Sonia will look the other way, or maybe she will join us, as she did in Deauville."

"Thomas! You were never to refer to that. I shall lead the horses to the shade and wait till you have finished."

Jacques and Thomas dismounted, pulled off their outer clothes and plunged in. "You liar," spluttered Jacques. "You lied about the water. It's like ice."

"He always lies," Sonia called out from behind an oak.

When they were decent, they rejoined Sonia, leaving their shirts off for the sun to dry their backs.

"So," said Thomas, lying on his front and pulling a piece of grass from the earth, "did we decide? Is it to be Vienna or Munich?"

"I think we decided on Paris," said Sonia. "Jacques was so passionate."

"And shall you be coming too?" said Thomas.

"Dear Thomas, I so wish that I could." Sonia was standing above the two reclining men, holding the horses. "But you know that I cannot."

"Why not? You could be the practice manager, or the bookkeeper."

Sonia sighed. "It would not be respectable. Papa would not permit it."

"My dear Sonia, it is nothing to do with Papa. And there is nothing that is not respectable in what we have in mind. We are not quacks or charlatans but qualified physicians."

"But Paris . . . And I shall by then be unmarried again. Let us not talk about it. It makes me too sad to think what I am missing."

"All right," said Thomas. "What do you think, Jacques?"

Jacques was thinking how sincere Sonia appeared in her desire to be with them; he was also thinking that she was finding it difficult to keep her eyes from him when she was talking to her brother. He sat up on the grass, so she was compelled to look at him. He said, "I think that eventually we will need to establish a sanatorium or a hydro somewhere in the mountains, probably the Alps. But if we go now and find a large building before we have any patients, then . . . we shall starve. We must begin to make ourselves known in a city. We must first find our patients, and Paris is the place to be. Thomas, are you all right?"

Thomas nodded. "I was just thinking of my poor lunatics and how I shall miss them. I cannot begin at once."

"Nor I," said Jacques. "I have to complete my time as intern. Next year."

"Next year," said Thomas. "Paris it shall be. I shall work to make Sonia change her mind. Perhaps she will be married again by then. Perhaps to young Dr. Meadowes."

"Be quiet," said Sonia. "Put your shirt on and help me with the horses. Elektra is growing frisky again."

"Yes, I can see. Give her to me," said Thomas. "Poor Achilles, on the other hand, looks quite exhausted. Come on. If we go along the river, then loop up through the old bluebell woods, we should be back by one o'clock. Sonia, use my hands as a block."

Sonia sprang from his joined hands into the saddle.

"You remind me of Daisy, climbing the wall."

"Who is Daisy?"

"My other sister. In another world."

The Dalmatians scented home when they emerged from the woods, and ran ahead through the paddock, barking their pleasure and wriggling with impatience as they had to wait for Jenkins to come up from the stable and open the gates. By the time the riders had unsaddled and changed, the gong was sounding for lunch. Cold salmon, lettuces and ham were laid out on a trestle beneath a cedar close to the terrace.

Jacques found himself being introduced to more Midwinters: Edgar, who was a shorter, less intense version of Thomas; his wife, Lucy, pale and fair beneath a bonnet; a boy called Henry, and the twins, Lydia and Emily.

"Take a plate," said Thomas, "and help yourself. There are seats on the terrace, or you can sit on the lawn. Don't take your eye off your plate, though, or Gordon will have it."

Jacques did as he was told, taking rather less than he really wanted, and found a chair beneath a sunshade on the terrace, next to Sonia, who had bathed and changed into a white cotton dress. Violet offered lemonade or hock, and, while he hesitated, Sonia laid her hand lightly on his wrist. "Have both," she said. "One for your thirst and the other to go with the salmon."

"What was it like to live in London?" he asked.

"It was . . . very agreeable. You need money, though. Big cities are expensive. You will need money for your work in Paris."

"I already know that."

"But tell me about your home, Jacques. And your family."

Jacques felt euphorically relaxed after his exercise and was able to give a picture of old Rebière's smoky parlor, the unlit staircase, Grand-mère's room at the back, the fields and woods of his boyhood. He felt Sonia's rapt gaze on him as he spoke, but it did not inhibit him; he was expansive in his description of Olivier and then of the part that Abbé Henri had played in educating him. The more he talked, the more he felt Sonia's sympathetic interest pouring into him; he felt drunk on her attention.

The children ran in and out of the tables, halfheartedly rebuked or taken onto a knee, according to whim.

"Put on your bonnet, Emily. You will have sunstroke."

Mr. Midwinter was chuckling in his throat: "How goes the world with my favorite daughter-in-law? Come here, Lucy, come and sit next to a poor old man."

Violet was offering more hock, and Jacques found he had accepted, without losing his place in the story of his life: ". . . the first part of my exams. But then Olivier . . ."

"The strawberries are early this year," said Mrs. Midwinter.

Jacques was aware of the heat of the afternoon, the clink of dishes being cleared by Violet and May, the murmur of speech interrupted by occasional cries from the children. Someone had brought him strawberries. Thomas was calling to Henry, the little boy, "Bring the racquet in the hall. I have one for you." He was enveloped by Sonia's concern, swaddled by her fascination; he was only half-aware that they were no longer part of a throng, a concert of voices, but were in fact alone beneath the sunshade on the stone terrace with only two empty green hock glasses on the table in front of them. ". . . and take Olivier with me to our new clinic," concluded Jacques.

"So," said Mrs. Midwinter, coming through the French doors behind them, "if you two have quite set the world to rights, I need you, Sonia, to help me with some roses."

"Oh, I think we have," said Sonia, rising in a movement of rustling white cotton.

"Have what?" said her mother.

"Set the world to rights."

"Perhaps Mr. Rebbier would like to join the others for lawn-tennis."

"Thank you," said Jacques. "With pleasure. First, I must do some reading." He had a sudden need to be alone.

"There will be tea on the rose lawn at five."

The house inside was cool, and heavy with scents. From the warmed floorboards, Jacques could still catch traces of sap, memory of tree-life preserved under decades of polish; through the swing door to the kitchen came an aroma of steamed late asparagus; even the tapestries and chair upholstery released a dusty, fabric smell of summer. There were many corners of the house that invited him to sit and read, breathing the heavy scent of roses, blown through the open door of the library. He walked through the drawing room before settling on a windowseat on the half-landing that led up to his bedroom. He folded one shutter to block the direct heat of the sun; through the other he could see down to the lawn, where Sonia, carrying a weather-beaten trug, accompanied her mother among the blooms.

He remembered looking down at her once before, in the garden of the Pension des Dunes with her husband. Then, he had felt uneasy, like a spy, because she belonged to someone else, to whom she talked in a dutiful and animated way. Now she was alone, inexplicably alone, and he had no misgivings about looking at her. What had not changed through the years was what she represented to him: an embodiment of the qualities he most longed for, all of which had been absent from his life. Because he had not known the touch of his mother or the presence of young women in a house, he felt he was forbidden even to desire them. Foolish, he thought, to disqualify himself on the grounds that he did not already own what he most wanted. What kind of reasoning was that?

After tea, he went to join in the game of lawn-tennis. Thomas had marked off a rectangle with white lime on the grass and Edgar had brought a net which had been stretched between two sticks. Thomas handed him a racquet and explained the rudiments of the game.

"You will find young Henry rather fierce, so perhaps he had better play with you. I shall play with my sister-in-law. Lucy!"

Lucy, who had already played, was able to launch the ball over the net, and Jacques watched while Henry scurried after it and sent it looping back, the ball having come off the edge of the wooden frame. Thomas hit it back over the net and, as the ball approached him, Jacques swung at it.

"Good hit!" said Lucy.

"It went up against the net. Does that matter?"

"Perhaps. I am not entirely certain of the rules, but it is a marvelous game, is it not?"

Sonia and Mrs. Midwinter sat beneath the shade of a large chestnut tree.

"Marvelous," said Jacques. "I like it very much."

Thomas threw him the ball. "Jacques, it is your turn to have the first hit."

"I fear the honor is too great for me. Madame." He bowed and passed

the ball to Lucy, who hit it far over the end line and into the long grass of
a ditch.

"Dido! Fetch!"

Others came and went, as the heat of the sun began to diminish.
Edgar hit the ball firmly into the net; Sonia approached it on pointed
toes, then thrust the racquet beneath it. "Queenie, you look as though
you are serving a fried egg!" said Thomas. The twins could not manage
to hit the ball, which was growing heavy from repeated contact with
Dido's mouth. Mrs. Midwinter was the only one who did not play,
remaining seated beneath the chestnut tree and dispensing lemonade to
those who came off the court, until she declared it was time for her to
speak to Miss Brigstocke about dinner. "Mr. Rebbier," she said, "we shall
gather in the library at seven."

"Thank you. I will go and prepare myself," said Jacques, panting,
aware of the grass stains on his bare feet and the sweat on his forehead.

SONIA LAY back in the cast-iron bathtub, and pushed the window open
next to her; the casement caught on the growth of creeper outside, but
she managed to admit a whisper of breeze. The sun struck lily patterns
in the steaming water. She could hear a thrush repeat itself in the elm.

I must borrow that rustic calm, she thought. I must behave properly.

She did not know how to manage her emotions, because they were
unlike any she had known before. She remembered Jacques clearly
enough from Deauville, his dark and worried eyes, his defensive, slightly
wounded manner. Somehow he had not registered deeply with her at
the time, nor had she thought much about him when Thomas intermittently mentioned their continuing friendship. She had presumed that
this was because she was otherwise preoccupied, but now it seemed to
her that her indifference could, on the contrary, have been nothing less
than a perverse and deliberate flight from something she felt frightened
to confront.

Nothing else could explain how she had forgotten the passion with
which he spoke—of Paris, of Charcot—which seemed to suck the oxy-
gen from the air about her head. Or the even more obvious matter of the
way he looked. She had noticed Violet's jaw falling almost to her

pinafore and heard her frantic whispering to May, had seen the blushing and the giggling with which they served him. Sonia could not help smiling as she remembered. Yet he himself had clearly never thought of it; and now that she knew more about his life, she could understand why. No one at his home, or at the church, at school or in the hospital clinics where he had studied would have mentioned it, because they were all men, and all had other more important things to distract them. Yet merely looking at him was to her a furtive ecstasy; and the passions that seemed to follow from that looking left her feeling uneasy.

Sonia splashed water on her face. Not everything she felt for him was regrettable. The truer urge she had was to provide for him what his life had lacked; there was an area of experience, of laughter and domestic pleasure, which was apparently unknown to him; and the shape of that absence seemed to be the shape of her own self.

Out of the water, she raised one foot after the other to the rim of the iron bath, dried her feet and legs carefully, put on her dressing gown and walked back to her bedroom, where she stood in front of the window, gazing through the leaded lights over the pond toward the church.

There was nothing she could do about her feeling because it had come too soon. Even when the divorce was final, she would need to allow a proper interval. Her parents would not approve, because Jacques had even less money than Richard Prendergast; they would probably cast her off completely. She could not trust her own feelings, anyway, because they were so unfamiliar to her, and seemed so threatening. And what was there to suggest that Jacques felt anything for her?

He was so solitary and so self-sufficient that he needed no one else: everything necessary to him was in nature and in books. And in any case, she was what she had overheard her father call "soiled goods." As a wife, she had failed: her husband had not even wished to continue with her, so she could offer no bright example of previous success in the role.

She chose, after some thought, a light, cream-colored dress with short sleeves. She stared at herself for a long time in the glass on her dressing table, adjusting her hair this way and that. There remained the immediate prospect of seeing him, just being in the atmosphere he made, and that was going to happen: that experience at least was legitimately hers to enjoy. But beyond the evening ahead she could not look.

To be Jacques's wife, to be part of his living and breathing; to have his children, as she still believed she might; to be with Thomas, too, her steadiest friend . . . it was not decent for any person to desire so much, and the losing of it was too terrible to contemplate.

As she opened the door of the crowded drawing room, Sonia found Jacques was the first person to meet her eye. He was talking to Henry and smiled at her above the boy's head—so she was at once plunged in.

"Are you staying up for dinner, Henry?" she said.

"I hope so, Aunt Sonia."

"He is going to sit next to me," said Jacques. "He has promised to explain to me the rules of lawn-tennis."

"I thought you had picked it up rather well."

"And you. I admired your style."

"The fried egg?" Sonia smiled.

"I saw no suggestion of the kitchen, though many people consider cooking to be a form of art, so—"

"Aunt Sonia is a good cook. When Mama was nursing the twins, she came to stay with us and she cooked the best meals we ever had. You must ask her to make her chocolate cakes and cheese and bacon pie."

"I would like that very much indeed."

"Does your wife cook for you in France?"

"I am not married, alas, so I—"

"I thought all grown-ups were married."

"Most of them marry in the end, but you have to find the right person."

Sonia could see that Jacques was making an effort to be what he presumably considered jolly and sociable; though whether it was for her benefit or out of kindness to the child, she was not sure.

"Not like Aunt Sonia," said Henry. "Her husband—"

"Thank you, young man," said Sonia. "No more chocolate cake for you."

"What do frogs' legs taste like?" said Henry.

"I have never eaten frogs," said Jacques. "But I have dissected them. Hundreds of them. Shall I show you tomorrow? If we can find one in the garden?"

"Then Aunt Sonia can cook it. She could even make a frog taste nice."

"Your aunt is a woman of many talents."

"She can play the piano. She can make costumes for plays. She can do any sum you give her in her head. Go on, try."

"All right. One add one," said Jacques.

"That's too easy!"

"Then you tell me."

"One add one is two!"

"Sometimes it can still be one. One squared is one."

"We haven't done squares yet."

"Sometimes it can be both. Two can be one and one can be two."

"You're funny! Isn't he funny, Aunt Sonia?"

"I think so, Henry. Sometimes you cannot tell if people are being funny on purpose."

"Shall I tell you something else Aunt Sonia does? She tells stories with her hands. She pretends they are a family of spiders. In the morning, before breakfast, the twins and I get into bed with her and she makes them walk along the top of the sheets, then they make a hole under the blanket and she tickles us. My favorite spider is Augustus."

"I have always enjoyed stories," said Jacques.

"And I have always enjoyed telling them," said Sonia, "though only to children."

"Do you mean that when children grow older they no longer believe in such things?" said Jacques.

"No, that is not what I meant. But I think it becomes harder for the person who is telling the story to have faith in it herself."

"But we must continue to believe," said Jacques. "Even in the most unlikely of stories. Without that hope, without that willingness to hope, then what are we? Am I not right, Henry?"

"I don't know what you mean, sir. Is he being funny again, Aunt Sonia?"

"I cannot be sure, Henry. Perhaps not this time." She felt embarrassed by the falsity of the conversation and the way that she was sheltering behind the child's innocence.

"What I mean," said Jacques, "is that when you are young you may have a great dream or ambition, which appears to you like a story—the story of your own future. When you grow older you understand that it is not just difficult to achieve, but that it is full of risk and pain that you knew nothing of when you were a child."

"But you must still believe in it?"

"I know that I do. I always shall. I am like a man playing cards. When the banker asks me if I want to carry on, I always say yes, and increase my stake."

"Isn't that dangerous?" said Henry.

"On the contrary," said Jacques. "It is the only way to live."

It was time for dinner and Thomas was told to organize their going in. "Are you all right, Queenie?" he said. "Are these young men bothering you? You look hot."

"I feel a little out of breath."

"It's cooler in the dining room. We are going through now. Jacques, would you mind taking my mother in? You hold your arm out like that, and in principle keep the other hand free for your sword to fight off attackers. Henry, you come with me."

"Are we likely to be assaulted?"

"Could be. Appleton looks frisky."

The doors of the dining room were entirely open to the night, and the flames of the candelabra flickered in the evening breeze; it was light outside and they could still see across the velvet lawn, down to the shade of the cedar tree and the grass bank beyond.

Sonia drank the cold hock her father poured for her and tried to calm her flying thoughts by occupying herself with the needs of her neighbors, Edgar on one side, and, on the other, a stout gentleman new to the village whose name she had been too preoccupied to catch. Miss Brigstocke had sent through a dish of sweetbreads and a roast capon with tarragon stuffing and bread sauce. There was burgundy to go with it.

Something peculiar seemed to be happening to the passage of time, so that when Sonia looked down into the deep red of her wine she seemed to be lost in the infinitely slow process of the grapes, picked years ago from French hills on which Roman legions had once tramped; then when she glanced up, she could find no way into the numerous conversations around her, where the faces, in the treacherous candlelight, seemed to be accelerating, reckless, toward some headlong destiny, and she saw that piles of fruit were already on the table, and that her mother was pointedly pushing back her chair and inviting the women to follow her out.

It was not so easy for Sonia to escape from the company that night. When her mother took the women downstairs again, there was something close to rebuke in her voice as she asked Sonia to pay more attention to the new guest from the village, Mr. Appleton, who was allegedly a man of property. "You seem quite distracted, dear. Take him some coffee, will you, and make a fuss of him."

For a quarter of an hour, Sonia hovered over Mr. Appleton, until she noticed Thomas slip out through an open door. Jacques caught her eye when he followed a few minutes later, but was gone before she could read his expression.

". . . with at least a thousand acres," said Mr. Appleton. "Are you quite well, Mrs. Prendergast?"

"Yes, thank you. Well, no. Not really. I have a slight ringing in the ears. If you would excuse me, I think some fresh air might help."

Mouthing the word "air" to her mother, Sonia went out onto the terrace and over the dark lawn, down to the cedar tree, where she could see the glow of two cigars. She ran the last twenty yards or so.

"We were wondering," said Thomas, "whether Switzerland might be a better final destination than Austria. There is a sanatorium near Davos of which I have heard good things. What do you think?"

Sonia blessed him for easing her so smoothly into their thoughts. "Are they not mainly for patients with tuberculosis?" she said.

"Not always. The Alpine air is good for all manner of illnesses, including those of the nerves."

Sonia let out a deep laugh of relief at being outside. "I shall allow the gentleman of science to choose. Can you hear that nightingale?"

"Skylarks, nightingales . . . You have a very good ear," said Jacques.

"You should hear her play the piano."

"Henry was telling me of her talents."

"But the half was not told to you. That is why we call her the Queen of Sheba, though to be literal, it was of course she who—"

"Do be quiet, Thomas. There is no need to laugh, Jacques."

"I beg your pardon. I was laughing because I am so happy."

"You have enjoyed your day?" said Sonia.

"I think it is the best day I have ever lived."

"There it is again," said Thomas. "No, that was a thrush. The day does seem to have lasted a long time. Breakfast seems a month ago."

"A year," said Jacques.

"I promised Mama I would do some duty with the Appletons," said Thomas. "You two have done yours. I shall come back when the coast is clear." He vanished into the darkness.

After a moment, Sonia said, "I am so pleased you feel at home here." She could see Jacques's sudden, huge smile in the night. "Yes," he said, "I think it is the first day of my life that I have not worked."

"Not even Sundays?" Sonia was appalled.

"There was always work to do at home, or I did some study in my room. Now I have tasted idleness." He appeared to be trying to lighten the tone of the conversation. Sonia was relieved that this meant she was less likely to embarrass herself, but reluctant to let the moment pass too quickly.

"It is a good house, is it not?" she said. "It needs attention. And so perhaps do those who live in it! But I think it is possible for people to be happy there."

"I think so," said Jacques. "I imagine that your mother must have worked to make it so."

"Yes." Sonia was puzzled by his direction; she had thought of the house as possessing a more spontaneous power.

"I see that the girls are happy," said Jacques. "The ones who bring the food. Someone must make this atmosphere. And the man with the horses."

"Jenkins. Yes. I think he has a good life."

"So what is this gift your mother has, do you think? This gift to be a good wife?"

Now, Sonia thought, she could see where he was heading; but she could not presume.

"I am not sure," she said.

"But you must have considered it."

"I considered it a great deal when I was myself married, but evidently without success."

Jacques coughed and stopped. Sonia saw that, by being too effectively self-effacing, she had silenced him. She saw her future in the vanishing moment, and moved without hesitation. "But you, Jacques, when we were talking with little Henry before dinner, you said that most people do get married but that it was important to find the right person. What would the right person be like in your case?"

There was a silence while Jacques inhaled on his cigar, and Sonia watched the tip glowing in the night. She felt her life hanging in the balance.

"For me," he said, "knowing what I am like, the right person would certainly be someone who was a very good cook." He paused. "Someone who could cook a chocolate cake. And a bacon and cheese pie."

"You mean—"

"Sonia, from the day I saw you in the hot dining room of that pension in Deauville . . . Oh, I used to watch you in the garden. Then I felt it was not right, so . . . I can hardly hope that you might ever think of me in that way. And then because of Thomas . . . But for nearly ten years you have been in my heart and the reason I have not admitted it to myself before is that I could not bear the thought that you would laugh at me, or feel ashamed."

He held out his arms and Sonia clung to him, amazed at the idea that her life could yet be rescued, daunted by the prospect of happiness that he had held out to her.

"But we must not—"

"Not yet," he said. "Next year when we go to Paris. It is our secret. But do you . . . do you honestly love me? Can you?"

"My dearest, dearest boy, I adore you. I will make your life for you. I want no other destiny, just to be with you. Don't talk anymore. Just hold me tighter. Tighter. Always."

Jacques did as he was told, turning his face up to the sky above the cedar branches. Then he kissed Sonia's forehead and her lips.

She smiled. "You look . . . I can't describe it."

"I feel perplexed. I cannot believe that I should be so fortunate."

"It is real, Jacques. I promise you it is real. Will you sit out here a little with me now?"

"I will sit out with you all night, my love."

"Good. But do not be disappointed if you hear no more nightingales."

"Why?"

"I think that may have been a fancy of my overheated heart. I do not think we have nightingales in Lincolnshire. I am so sorry."

VII

JACQUES WAS RUNNING UP THE RUE DE L'ECOLE DE MÉDECINE WITH
the taste of Madame Maurel's stew reheated for breakfast still in his
mouth. He dodged across the traffic of the Boulevard St. Michel and into
the straight line of the rue des Ecoles. He had fourteen minutes in which
to make it to the amphitheater for Professor Charcot's lecture at the
Salpêtrière, and he knew that the professor started on time whether the
audience was assembled or not. The distinguished neurologist had left
the church at a wedding because the bride—the daughter of a close
friend—was late; he once closed the door to his private consulting room
in the Boulevard St. Germain and went to bed when his last patient had
not arrived at the appointed time, even though the man had crossed the
Atlantic for the appointment. Jacques jumped down into the horse drop-
pings and the swill of gray water in the runnel that edged the pavement,
as he dodged between the students, the idling matrons and the broad-
shouldered tradesmen who blocked the way ahead. He had the whole
flank of the Jardin des Plantes to negotiate before the great dome of the
church of the Salpêtrière, gunmetal gray and glistening in the morning
light, at last came into view.

He sprinted through the arch and over the graveled walkways,
where a few unfortunate women lolled on wooden benches beneath the
plane trees. They were the jetsam. Up around him, behind the high windows of the long stone wards, was the ocean: the waves of gibbering
infirmity, of twisted limbs and howling voices that had driven all before

Charcot to despair. Successive doc-tors had called it an inferno, pande-monium, a Babel: an epitome of human wretchedness, after seeing which no one could talk again of God's plan or man's purpose. Here were people twisted into bodily contortions which, however outlandish they appeared, remained regrettably human, so that they could not be dismissed as an irrelevance. Over the centuries, it had been poorhouse, prison and asylum for the broke, the broken and the irredeemable, who were swept in off the streets as young women and discharged, at their affliction's end, in a pauper's coffin. Only Charcot had seen that, far from being God's joke at the expense of mankind's pathetic hope of dignity, the women represented a resource of medical study with no equal in the world, because nowhere else was it possible to scrutinize a disease throughout its length and then, on the postmortem table, marry it to its precipitating lesion. So useless in their lives, the women were at last able, in the cross sections of their brain and spinal cord, to donate something of interest to the existence that had failed them.

Jacques elbowed his way through the sightseers, journalists and hangers-on who lined the amphitheater. He scrambled onto the raised benches and tried to still his noisy breathing as the audience of four hundred went quiet when, on the stroke of the clock, Charcot's favored assistants, led by his chief of clinic, Pierre Marie, then Joseph Babinski and Georges Gilles de la Tourette, walked silently onto the stage in their long white aprons. After a momentary pause, Charcot himself emerged, wearing a black frock coat and top hat, which he removed and placed carefully on a table behind him. He turned to look at his audience, unsmiling, unspeaking; his pale, clean-shaved face caught the light beneath the lank gray hair, swept back and hanging in a straight line over his collar, almost touching his shoulders. He looked for a moment like an older version of Abbé Henri, Jacques thought, then, when he stuck one hand between the buttons of his coat, like Napoleon. Jacques felt a shudder of excitement go through him: to be in the presence of genius was a transcendent experience, in the light of which the other moments of his life might be reviewed. He thought of his first frog.

Charcot spoke without rhetorical flourish, though this merely inten-sified the drama. "Ladies and gentlemen, I intend first to take some cases from the outpatients' department that I have not seen before and to examine them. I shall share my thoughts with you as I do so. My purpose is threefold. I wish you to understand the difficulties that beset any 'blind' diagnosis of a neurologic kind. Next, I want it to be clear to you that close visual scrutiny and steady observation are the keys to making a successful diagnosis. Finally, I want you to remember that it is the continuing contact with the patient and his symptoms that allows us to learn—much more than theories dreamed up in universities whose professors are far from the bedside of the unfortunate. In this respect I am a practical man, one might almost say Anglo-Saxon. Bring in the first patient, please."

An old woman, trembling in her rags and shawls, was brought on, held at the elbow by Babinski and an elderly nurse, Mademoiselle Cottard. Charcot asked her to stretch out her hand, which had a tremor visible even to Jacques, who was close to the back of the raked seating on the ramp. Charcot asked questions about the duration of the symptoms and attached a metal clamp called a sphygmograph to the woman's hand to measure the rate of the tremor. He asked her to undress so that the audience could see the extent to which her limbs were deformed; and in her gray under-linen, she made her way unsteadily to and fro across the stage. Jacques noticed the loss of flexion in the left ankle. A dialogue between doctor and patient ensued, though neither seemed to relish it, the woman reluctant to project her tremulous voice and Charcot preferring the evidence of his eyes: he stuck his face up close to hers, but refrained from touching her. Eventually, he asked her to replace her clothes and take a seat at the back of the stage for comparison with subsequent patients.

"You will have noticed that the patient walks in a way wholly characteristic of her disease," said Charcot. "Like this." Carefully, but with precise mimicry, he walked back and forth across the stage; in his progress was exactly the mixture of spastic hesitancy and dragging determination shown by the old woman, who now sat quite still, apart from the trembling in her hands. One or two of the audience giggled at the niceness of the impersonation.

"Listen," said Charcot. "You must listen as well as watch. The sound of the footsteps is important. The ataxic throws her legs and feet forward. The alcoholic bends his knees like a circus horse. If the ankle flexors are affected, as is the case with this patient, the foot is flaccid. As she walks, she bends the knee too much to compensate—like this. The thigh lifts more than it should, so that when she drops it, the toes hit the ground before the heel. So her step makes two sounds. Listen carefully. There. The ataxic, by contrast, has almost no flexion at the knee. He thrusts out his leg like this and his foot therefore makes only one sound. Look behind me."

Electric lights in metal shades hung at intervals from the ceiling of the lecture hall, and there were brighter spotlights on the stage which illuminated charts and illustrations held on stands to which Charcot now pointed. "Some of my students will be familiar with the pattern of these footprints," he said. "Over the months, we have asked patients to dip their feet in ink, then walk on paper. My staff have drawn up these scale representations of the results." He took a long wooden pointer from the table next to his top hat and walked along the half dozen stands, pointing to the different patterns of footprints.

"Parkinson's," he said. "Locomotor ataxia. This is Sydenham's chorea, something we encounter very often in the outpatients' clinic. This is a rather unusual pattern. If Doctor Marie would just . . . Thank you. The larger pattern. That's it."

The assistants replaced all the different charts with a single sequence. From left to right, the blackened footprints of a human being trailed life-size across the lit stage, their image preserved in ink and lit by the spotlights that Charcot's white-aproned men trained on them. While Jacques was thrilled by the diagnostic brilliance of his older colleagues and the way that the described patterns repeated themselves so unfailingly in character, he was moved by the sense of something more profound. In the clangorous wards around them the epileptics frothed and screamed, thrashing their heads on the soiled floor; the hysterics mounted their bizarre performances, bending their bodies into rigid hoops while torrents of verbal filth poured from their mouth; but there in the quiet of the amphitheater, the footprints of the wretched beings, abandoned by life and the world, left traces of their passage—a claim in ink that they had been something more than transients—and with it some fragile plea that those who followed after them were bound to try to understand their compromised existence.

Charcot resumed his position beneath the spotlight while two of his pupils set up a projector to show slides of examinations done in the pathology laboratory. It was whispered by critics among the sandy pathways of the Salpêtrière that Charcot's ability in the lab (a dingy little room at the end of the cancer ward) was limited, and that most of the work was done by his intern Victor Cornil, who had studied in Berlin. However, Charcot was generous in acknowledging his assistant, while his own early drawings of the spinal cord in multiple sclerosis remained, in the eyes of Jacques and many other pupils, articles of absolute beauty. To the less knowledgeable of his amphitheater audience, the very function of the new slide projector was a source of quite sufficient wonder.

In any event, the proof of the teacher's greatness lay, beyond debate, in his siting of the lesions he now demonstrated. Whatever his shortcomings in histology, it was he who had unriddled the mysteries of multiple sclerosis, amyotrophic sclerosis (now, indeed, known as Charcot's disease) and other complicated afflictions, images of whose actual seat in the brain or spinal cord were projected onto a screen behind him.

There was nothing triumphant in Charcot's manner of speaking, which remained clipped, reluctant and packed with meaning. No word escaped him that did not bend each syllable to work. "In Parkinson's disease, long-established," he said, "we have a complete clinical picture of the symptom, but our microscopes and our best endeavors have yet to locate its lesion. Other conditions in this pregnant state include Huntington's disease, epilepsy and hysteria. I have no doubt that in time we shall discover the lesion that initially affects the nerves in all these conditions. Science will provide more powerful means. Young men will supply a keener gaze. For the moment they remain what we might call a bridesmaid illness, one looking for a husband. This is not in any sense a less severe or less organic condition—a morning walk through the epileptic or hysteric ward will leave you in no doubt as to that. My procedure in this hospital, as most of you will know, is the clinical-anatomical method. The clinical part is provided by close observation of the patient's symptoms, the anatomical by the subsequent inspection at postmortem. Bridesmaid conditions, such as Parkinson's and hysteria, are as yet lacking anatomical completion—though that completion is imminent."

After Charcot had compared the symptoms of his outpatients and dismissed them, he progressed to the second part of the lecture, in which a variety of inpatients, previously selected by his heads of clinic and senior interns, were produced for the audience's edification. Doctors Bournville and Richer left the stage to bring them in one by one, with the help of the faithful Mademoiselle Cottard, who had been at the Salpêtrière, it was said, since she was sixteen.

The patients came and went, Charcot demonstrating with their help the difference between pure and partial forms of a disease. Jacques settled himself on the hard bench and turned the pages of his notebook. The final patient to sidle into the spotlight was a woman unfamiliar to him. Since there were more than five thousand in the hospital, this was not in itself surprising; yet there were some patients who were known to offer such pure forms of their particular ailments that it made them ideal for repeated teaching purposes. They tended to be younger, because older women developed complications from germs, habit and degeneration.

"And finally," said Charcot, "we examine a case of one of the most commonly encountered diseases at the hospital: hysteria."

The patient chosen to demonstrate hysteria was often a young woman with tumbling brown hair and large eyes called Blanche Wittmann; this patient was skinnier and paler than Blanche, with a focused, narrow gaze. Jacques felt a slight disappointment.

"Hysteria, as you know," said Charcot, "was once thought of as an ailment only of the uterus. Indeed, that is how it gained its name, from the Greek word for the womb. I am not going to detain you with a history of the illness, however. Let us be content to state where our understanding currently sits. Hysteria is a bridesmaid, like Parkinson's, though one of my distinguished colleagues will doubtless find its lesion within the next few years—or months. Hysterics suffer from fits similar to, but less severe than, those endured by epileptics. The classic attack has four parts which we shall shortly demonstrate to you. A predisposition to hysteria is inherited. In this respect, as in almost all the others, it is a standard neurological disorder. The fascination of hysteria, the aspect that makes it sui generis, is the way that it offers a bridge between the physical and mental functions of the patient.

"Let me recap: a standard neurological illness. Lesion, nervous malfunction, motor disorder with hereditary predisposition. Yet we note also the persistence of some ovarian element. An hysterical attack can be arrested by a doctor applying pressure to the ovaries. An epileptic seizure cannot." Charcot held up his wooden pointer in a rare flourish. "Second distinction. In mid-seizure, many of these women appear to relive a traumatic event from their past. Third distinction: I believe it is possible that such a mental element may be not only retrospective but causal. It may in fact be a precipitating factor in the unlocking of the hereditary neural disposition."

There was silence in the amphitheater. Charcot spoke softly, yet abruptly. "Not quite such a standard illness, then. But we have more. In the course of an experiment with metallotherapy on hysterical patients, I became aware that the sites of pain and contracture could be moved about the body. This led me to experiment with hypnosis, from which I discovered that all hysterical patients can be hypnotized, whereas those who do not suffer from this condition can under no circumstances be hypnotized. When hysterics are under the influence of hypnosis, they can be made to act out a full and pure form of the hysterical attack, as my staff will now demonstrate."

Charcot nodded to one of the aproned interns, who approached the hysterical woman and laid his hands on her eyes. A gong was sounded a few inches from her ear, and she quickly began to show signs of distress, clutching her throat, as though something was choking her. Dr. Gilles de la Tourette stood to one side of her and Mlle. Cottard to the other.

"After the aura," said Charcot, "the premonition of the rising attack, comes the *globus hystericus,* the patient's sensation that her uterus has risen in her abdomen and threatens to choke her. Next will come a subepileptic seizure. This is the first phase proper."

The woman fell to the stage, tearing her blouse as she did so and beating her head on the boards. The doctors watched over her intently as she writhed and thrashed. Jacques noticed Richer, an artist as well as a neurologist, making rapid sketches. The woman stopped her writhing and raised herself on her back, supporting her weight on her feet and hands only.

"The second phase," said Charcot. The woman held the position, her body in an arc with her belly thrust up at the peak of the semicircle, her breasts moving backward and sideways over her thorax.

"This acrobatic clownism," said Charcot, "requires considerable strength of the wrists and feet, far more than she would normally have. It will be followed by the striking of impassioned poses, as though the patient has seen someone she fears or hates. I should warn you that this is sometimes accompanied by profane language."

At once the woman stood up, and held her arm over her eyes, as though scanning the horizon in terror. Then she rushed from one side of the stage to the other, pausing to hold a position of horror and dismay. Jacques was aware of a burbling vocalization as she moved, which eventually became audible in a sort of masochism of the gutter, using language familiar to Jacques from his ward rounds but causing gasps from the audience. This finally gave way to a protracted delirium in which meaning was lost and the woman reverted to thrashing back and forth on the floor.

"The final stage," said Charcot. He nodded to two of the interns who awoke the woman from hypnosis by rubbing her eyes and banging the gong loudly again in her ear. They then guided her to a chair, where she sat looking quietly bewildered.

"And what do we deduce from this?" said Charcot. "That this illness not only has a mental element, as I described before, but also an auto-suggestive element, as we have seen. Yet this woman is not mentally unwell; on the contrary, hysteria remains a classic neurological illness with a somatic base. Our main task is to locate its cerebrospinal lesion, but I may say to you that the auxiliary task may turn out to be more challenging. And it is this: to determine the neural mechanisms by which trauma, thought and memory take over the motor functions of a patient to produce such symptoms of ataxia, contractures and so on. Hypnosis allows us to examine the course of an hystero-epileptic attack with the clarity normally reserved to the other end of our work— beneath the lights of the postmortem laboratory. However, let us not forget that hysteria remains also an affliction of the ovaries."

Charcot nodded to Richer and Bournville. "An attack may be triggered without hypnosis by a neurologist who knows the hysterogenic points." Bournville placed his hand on the woman's naked ribs below her left breast and squeezed. At once, she began the first part of the cycle again, going into subepileptic seizure.

"Equally," said Charcot, "it can thus be halted by pressure to the ovaries." He nodded again. A bearded intern stepped forward and, while Mlle. Cottard and Dr. Gilles de la Tourette pinioned the woman's flailing arms, pushed his hand down the waistband of her skirt. After a few moments of the intern's manual pressure, she relaxed, her seizure left her and she was once more escorted to her chair, where she sat, panting, with her sweat-drenched hair hanging down over her face and breasts.

There was no smile or look of triumph on Charcot's face as he checked his watch and turned in conclusion to the audience. "So there, ladies and gentlemen, we have been able to watch an hysterical attack— not in a partial or bastard form, but in a pure and classic form, fulfilling each of the four defining phases of its nosology. You may have found the pathology confusing, particularly my description of the effects of mental activity, autosuggestion and remembered experience in such a somatic complaint as this. I propose, however, that the explanation is available to us if we are to consider the as-yet unfound lesion of hysteria to be not a static but a dynamic lesion, caused by an alteration in the tissue of the brain brought on by metabolic or chemical change. Such process is quite consonant with our understanding of hereditary disease. I propose to you that although the lesion is imperceptible to present-day science, this will not be the case for long. I am a practical man and I do not like, as my students know, to theorize. However, I am prepared to offer an hypothesis that the lesion will be found in the gray matter on the side opposite to the hemiplegia, which you saw begin during that attack, probably in the motor zone of the arm."

Charcot began to gather the notes from the table behind him. "As to the connection with what I have called the mental side, I do not see an insurmountable problem there; I do not see anything in that complication that need remove hysteria from the domain of neurology and hand it to the alienists. One need only view the problem this way. As one may describe the physiology of the lungs as breathing or the physiology of the colon as the evacuation of waste matter, then one need merely envisage what we call 'psychology,' or thought, as the physiology of the cortex. In that way," he said, leveling off the edges of his gathered notes, "the entire process falls within the map of human neurology as we have it."

He thrust his notes at the chest of his chief assistant, Pierre Marie, said, "Arrange all this for publication," and strode from the stage.

THAT AFTERNOON, as Jacques was walking in a delirium of excitement across the Promenade de la Hauteur toward the chapel, Mlle. Cottard came hurrying toward him. "I have a note for you, young man," she said. "From Dr. Babinski."

"For me?" Jacques felt honored that Babinski, one of Charcot's favored sons, should even know who he was, and Mlle. Cottard's raised eyebrows suggested that she agreed.

"Monsieur," said Babinski's note, "I have heard good reports of the freelance teaching work you have done with the first-year students. I know that you are close to the end of your time with us and I believe that your defense of your thesis before the examining board will be a formality. I wonder therefore if, in the name of our common search for knowledge, you would care to offer a second opinion on a private patient, a young woman with a mild nervous affliction. Since you are not yet formally qualified, this must of course be viewed as an intellectual exercise only.

"However, the young woman's family is extremely wealthy and will continue to require medical services. Doubtless you are aware that our great professor himself enjoyed such patronage at the start of his career, traveling abroad as physician to an entire family, and that that aspect of his work continues to flourish. Please call in after my clinic tomorrow at five if the idea interests you. Yours truly, Joseph Babinski."

Jacques began to run back to Madame Maurel's boardinghouse. He was not late, but there was no other way in which he could express his happiness. In the morning he had witnessed human beings at the edge of greatness, men standing on top of the mountain that only they, by virtue of their genius and determination, had known how to scale, and looking for the first time into a promised land the other side. These great explorers peering narrow-eyed into the mist . . . he had seen them, been with them in the room, and he knew, as they knew, that when their gaze became accustomed to the view and the mist began to clear, the vista that emerged was little less than a complete landscape of what it meant to be a human—body, mind and soul—the geography of being, revealed in all its beautiful simplicity by the pure light of science. As if that exhilaration were not enough, one of the expedition leaders had now singled him out by name to join them—to be an associate in that enterprise.

The classes were coming out as he ran down the Ecole de Médecine. From the Ecole Pratique, the weary students issued onto the cobbles, cigars clenched between their teeth, and, just like the fastidious ladies who had once so irritated him, he held his breath as he went past them. He stopped to buy a bag of roast chestnuts on the corner of the Boulevard St. Germain, then, in a moment of exhilarated self-indulgence, went into a café and drank a glass of hot rum at the counter. He smacked the empty tumbler down on the zinc, wiped his mustache on his sleeve, and went on his way, down into the dingiest streets of the Latin Quarter, where the students and the prostitutes lived, where the artists' models and the provincial boys from Angoulême and Aurillac who had to find their fortune coexisted with widows of dwindling income, powdery dotards and sharp-featured men with bad clothes looking for investors in their fail-safe business schemes.

Representatives of all such people dined at Madame Maurel's at seven in the evening. The paneled parlor was filled with the vapor of their failing aspirations; it hung like fog above the pewter candlesticks, with the smell of tallow, boiled vegetable and Madame Maurel's tomcat. Jacques took his napkin from its place in a wooden box on the sideboard, reserved to the dozen full-time residents of the boardinghouse. This inner core was joined at dinner by half a dozen others, drawn to Madame Maurel's table by the modest rate the old widow charged them for their mutton and potatoes with mealy white bread. When the "externs," as Jacques thought of them, had gone home, the residents felt free to comment on their pretensions, hygiene and appearance. Between themselves the "interns" kept a semblance of civility, though Madame Tavernier and her round-faced daughter, who had the second largest suite of rooms on the first floor, found it hard to conceal their distaste for Pivot, the lank-haired traveling salesman in the single above them, who disturbed their sleep by walking up and down on the bare boards to ease the torment of his psoriasis. He in turn referred to them as Marie Antoinette and her little pug bitch and relished the way they wiped the rims of the greasy wineglasses before deigning to touch them with their lips. "Mend those lace cuffs one more time," he said, "and there'll be no lace left." "Do not answer the gentleman," said Madame Tavernier with a sniff.

After dinner, the guests who could afford it took a cup of coffee in the drawing room, a place furnished with the pieces of furniture that other houses had rejected; Jacques thought they were like the women of the Salpêtrière, given asylum by Madame Maurel because no one else would have them. There were indestructible sideboards, tastelessly carved, a table with an oilcloth and a wooden clock with copper inlay, greened with verdigris. The room was cold because its fire was never lit; even when Pivot took a glass of cheap cognac, it seemed to bring no warmth to him, because the air had the same saturated quality as that of the parlor, as though it had been too often exhaled from damp lungs.

Jacques's was one of four attic rooms, next to that of a law student from Tours who played the violin. These were the cheapest lodgings, uncleaned, unvisited by the handyman; they were the rooms whose occupants Carine was last to call in the mornings, and then only if her legs were not too swollen to permit her to climb the final flight.

He lit a candle, pulled his chair up to the table and began to write:

My dearest Sonia,

May I call you that? To me you are most dear—the most dear person in the world, dearer even than your brother—dearer even than my own brother, whom I love without reservation! I think of you in your lovely room, looking over at the church. No—it is nine in the evening, so you are still downstairs. You have dined in one of your fine dresses and entertained whatever dull merchant your parents wish you to impress. You have been loving and dutiful; but is there that look—what is the English word?—playful, perhaps, a little humorous, in your eye, as though you wished that there was somebody else there, whose eye you could catch? And could that somebody be me? You seem

so far away that sometimes I wonder if I can still exist in your
heart, or in your memory.

Now you are reading your book, wondering when it might be
time for you to leave and go upstairs. My heart hurts with your
absence. Yes, I feel it there against my ribs. I do not care what
modern science says; that is the organ of my emotions!

But today, dear Sonia, has been a great day. We are on the
edge of making such discoveries here as will change the
treatment of the sick, but more than this it will change what we
understand it means to be a human being (I have not expressed
that well). And today one of the most distinguished doctors
offered me one of his private patients! I shall see this young lady

Jacques dropped his pen with a cry. Where would he see this young lady?
Charcot had a palace on the Boulevard St. Germain, Babinski had a
respectable consulting room at the hospital, no doubt; but he, he could
not invite a society lady into the tubercular stew of Madame Maurel's
parlor, invite her to disrobe and leave her silk dress—where, next to
Pivot's soiled napkin on the sideboard, out behind the kitchen door on
top of the suspended meat safe? God. He picked up his pen again.

Tell Thomas that when you both come to join me in the
summer he must take decent rooms from which we can both
consult. I know he has saved some money from his pay at the
asylum. If I can find somewhere to do my first consultations, I
too should be able to save something to contribute. Once we have
a little practice running it will pay for itself, but these landlords
are cruel about wanting a deposit, so we must have something to
offer.

Sonia, I cannot wait for you to come. I can arrange for
Thomas to walk the wards at the Salpêtrière for a time; most
important is that he comes to Charcot's lectures, which are
changing the course of medicine.

Thank you for your last letter. I love reading about
Torrington. It feels almost like a home to me—more like a home
than my own in Saint Agnès, where I shall never return.

I do not believe that Violet still talks of me. I think you are
flattering. I can write no more. I am too happy and too full of
plans. Until the morning!

When the letter was delivered to Torrington House, Sonia was not there
to receive it; she was sitting in Dr. Faverill's office at the asylum, where
she had gone to visit Thomas.

"I am most disappointed, Mrs. Prendergast, that your brother has
given notice that he intends to quit his position here," said Faverill. "He
will have been with us less than two years, and I can say without fear of
contradiction that he has a greater flair for mad-doctoring than any
man I have yet worked with."

"I am sure he would be delighted to hear that."

"No, no," said Faverill, twisting the beard beneath his jaw, "I am sincere. He is so modest, so inquiring. *Nihil humanum sibi puto alienum esse,*
if you take my meaning. And he has such joyous optimism, the ebullience of youth."

Sonia smiled. "He is not moody, not rash?"

Faverill looked surprised. "No. Neither of those things. I have never
seen a man more dedicated to his work. And the hours he labors! He has
tried to conceal it from me, but no. I suffer from an inability to sleep, and
frequently I walk about the asylum in the night. Occasionally I have
come across him in the wards, but more often I have seen the candle
burning in his window."

"Ah yes. Thomas has always read a great many books. Even as a boy."

Faverill nodded his head several times and pursed his lips. "Well, it is
a great shame, is it not, Matilda?"

Sonia looked across the fireplace to where Matilda sat opposite
her; but she did not answer Faverill, appearing to be lost in thoughts of
her own.

"Has Miss Whitman found you a satisfactory bedroom?" said Faverill.

"It is very pleasant, thank you. Are you sure it is not irregular for me
to stay?"

"Not at all. Perhaps the commissioners might find it so, but the consolation for being superintendent here is that I can do whatever I wish. I
am the emperor of this small realm. It is a pleasure for us—we have very

few voluntary visitors. . . . And in any event, I understand the experience
may be useful to you in your new life."

"In what way?"

"Your brother tells me that you plan to join him and your husband in
a medical venture overseas."

Sonia found herself blushing. "I—he is not yet my husband." She
had a superstitious dread of anticipating the longed-for event.

"I beg your pardon."

"No, but you are correct. We are to go to Paris and then, I think, to
Germany. It is a great adventure."

"Indeed. Indeed." Faverill tapped his lip with a lead pencil he had
taken from the desk.

Sonia looked about his book-lined room and had the sense, as her
brother had before her, of some unspoken agitation in Faverill. Men of
his age, she thought, eminent in their work, surrounded by the calfskin
and vellum of their elders, should be sage and bonhomous; Faverill,
though kindly, seemed distraught.

"May I ask you something?" she said. "When you spoke a moment
ago, you said that being emperor here was a consolation. For what are
you to be consoled?"

Faverill shot a look across the room at Matilda. "It was a figure of
speech. A philosophical one. I was thinking of Boethius and the *De Con-
solatione.*" He smiled. "No, that is not altogether true. I suppose I had a
homelier thought in mind. When I was a young doctor, there was much
optimism in the air. The new asylums were embodiments of our hope. I
believed—as did my colleagues—that we could not merely care for mad
people, we could cure them. That was our article of faith. Now, thirty
years later, I have cured almost no one. The most common ailments in
this asylum are idiocy, which is inherited and incurable, and epilepsy,
which may have some source in the activity of the brain, though we
know not where. Then there is general paralysis of the insane, the
results of which I have observed postmortem when the brain is horribly
damaged. But we have no idea what causes it. My own suspicion is that
it is somehow connected with syphilis, but we have no way of demonstrating this. And finally there is a kind of dementia, hearing voices and
so on, which appears to begin in young people and to intensify. We are

far from agreeing even a description, let alone a cure for that. Some forms of mania and melancholia do seem to improve, but whether that is because of hot baths and cascarilla or whether they have just run their course, I could not say. It is a damnable state of affairs."

"But we will understand madness, will we not?" said Sonia. She was thinking of Jacques's poor brother. "We will cure it."

Faverill stood up. "That is why I admire your brother, Mrs. Prendergast, and am so loath to see him go. He too believes there will be cures. And unlike me, he has the energy and the will to find them."

"Do you no longer believe we will discover remedies?"

"Not until we understand what makes us who we are. My instinct, though I am pitifully far from being able to prove it true, is that what makes us mad is almost the same thing as that which makes us human."

Sonia frowned. "You mean that we are fallen? Imperfect? That God gave us the capacity to suffer more than other animals?"

"Yes," said Faverill. "That is one way of explaining it. It is the price we pay for being favored by the Almighty. Mr. Darwin might prefer to put it differently. If we were to borrow his language, we could say that when the brain one day developed the capacity that made the species *Homo sapiens*, it developed simultaneously a predisposition to kinds of insanity. Though since we are the only animals to have madness, you may regard what I have just said as no more than a simple tautology."

"I see," said Sonia, not quite certainly.

"Whether you choose to explain it in the terms of the Bible or Mr. Darwin seems to me to make almost no difference," said Faverill.

There was a knock at the door. "Ah, Midwinter," said Faverill warmly. "I was explaining to your sister how much we are going to miss you."

"Thank you," said Thomas. "And I shall miss you, and some of the patients."

"Not all?"

Thomas laughed. "By no means all. Now, Sonia, I promised you a tour of the asylum. I am going to show you some of the improvements we are making. May I, sir?"

"You may take the lady where you wish, Midwinter. Though there are perhaps one or two wards which might . . . The gentler sex, you understand . . ."

"Of course."

As she followed Thomas out, Sonia felt a little chastened by her interview with Faverill. She did not understand what he had meant about Mr. Darwin, whose book she had only ever heard spoken of with derision. Faverill seemed to suggest that human beings were not an absolute thing, but could easily have developed into something similar but slightly different. The "variation" that transformed them from pre-human into human entailed weaknesses that made them mad. If that tiny change had gone another way, they would not have been mad, but presumably they would not have been quite human either . . .

Thomas led her to a small brick outbuilding.

"I am going to show you my secret project," he said. "Shut the door and make sure you pull that black curtain across. Now follow me."

The building was divided into two parts, the second of which they now entered. The brick walls were painted black, the floor was made of earth, but there were two electric lights, one white, one red, which Thomas switched on. "You never expected to find such modern equipment at our asylum, did you, Sonia? Electricity! Only for the darkroom, I am afraid, not yet for the poor patients. I had to spend some time persuading Dr. Faverill."

"I think you are quite the teacher's pet, Thomas."

"Ssh. This is my beloved Underwood. Reliable, portable, and with beautiful tapering bellows. You see? If they did not taper it would be twice the size. The real joy of it is that it takes dry plates. I put one in here like this. Shall I take a picture of you? Come outside for a moment."

He posed her against the brick wall of the shed. "Smile, Sonia. Think of the great adventure you are about to begin."

Sonia looked at Thomas and the expanse of the lunatic asylum behind him. He uncovered the lens and she smiled shyly into it.

"Perfect! Now I just slide the cover onto the plate again, take the plate holder out of the camera and I can develop it any time I like."

"Will you develop it now?"

"Come on."

Back inside, Sonia looked round the first room of the shed and saw that the walls were covered with photographs of the insane. Some of them looked bedraggled and retarded, some vacant and some quite rational. Sonia felt a faintly demeaning curiosity to know more about each one, and what their problem was, but Thomas called her in to watch him at work.

He turned off the white light and lowered the red one, so that the square space took on an unreal glow. There were a dozen brown pharmaceutical bottles on a shelf in front of him from which he poured quantities into three dishes. "I am hopeless at all this," he said. "Pass me that book, will you? Mr. W. K. Burton. He tells me how to do it."

Sonia watched in amusement as Thomas bent over one dish, then the next, the chestnut hair falling over his forehead as he occasionally reconsulted Burton, before lifting the plate up to the red light, where he held it for a second. He rinsed it beneath a tap and moved it on.

"This is taking a long time," said Sonia.

"Sometimes I am in here half the night."

"And what exactly is the point?"

"I am making a reference library of the patients, so we know which one is which. They are stored in McLeish's office with their names on the back. All right, now I have to leave it under running water. Come and have a look in the other room while we wait."

He pointed out various patients to her on the wall. "This is Daisy. She is a very nice girl."

"And what is the matter with her?"

"Nothing very much. She has spent too much time in an asylum. This poor lady on the other hand is as mad as a March hare."

"Is that the diagnosis you offer to the commissioners?"

"No. I make up something more sonorous to impress them. Let's walk in the fresh air while we wait."

As they made their way slowly toward the icehouse, Thomas said, "There is a famous man called Galton who takes photographs of mad people and then lays the images one on top of the other. He is trying to show that all murderers have the same shaped head, or that if you have a long jaw you are likely to be melancholic."

"And that is not what you do?"

"No. I do just the opposite. I use them to make the patients look like less of a type and more of an individual. When I see them in their wards, I see a sort of undifferentiated mass. But when I take a picture, I see each man and woman. And each one is in fact a human with a story. In some ways the insanity is the least important thing about them. In a photograph they are still complete, so one is not tempted to see them so much as something broken."

"I see."

"Though of course that makes it in some ways even worse. If each is not just an example of an illness but a man or woman, then in each one you are trying to restore something like the fullness of being human when in every case this means something slightly different. And all that without having any real cures, even for their symptoms."

"No wonder Dr. Faverill seems sad."

Thomas glanced at her. "Yes. Yes, I suppose he does. I do not always think of them in that individual, photographic way. It is too much to bear. When a general orders a column to attack, he does not think of each man in it. If he did, he would be lost."

Sonia, put her arm through his. "If we walk back slowly, will the photograph be ready?"

"Just about. The other thing I do with these pictures is show them to the patients. They are very interested in them. Some keep them by their beds. They find it comforting to think that they exist."

"What do you mean?"

"If you live in a world that is full of delusion, it is novel to be confronted with evidence of your existence in a solid place. Some of them do not recognize themselves. Some look as though they cannot quite place the face they are looking at. But some of them are really heartened by the evidence that they have solidly gone on, grown older, that they are still someone. They deduce that their existence must seem real to others."

Back in the darkroom, Thomas turned off the running water and lifted the plate from the sink onto a towel; he then leaned it against the wall to dry.

"There you are," he said. "One half-plate portrait fit to hang in any lunatic asylum in England."

Sonia peered at the image. "It is horrible," she said.

"No, it's not. You are beautiful. You look eighteen years old. Your eyes are full of kindness."

"My dress is full of creases."

"I think we should send it to Jacques."

"Oh no! You must take a better one. Not with that cameo brooch Mama gave me. I had no idea how ugly it looked. And my eyes have lines at the corner!"

"Nonsense. You have the skin of a child. My dearest Queenie, if you truly imagine you are more beautiful than . . ."

Thomas tailed off because there was a hammering at the outer door of the hut.

"Dr. Midwinter!" It was Miss Whitman.

"Come quickly," she said. "There has been some trouble. In Room Fifty-two. Mr. Tyson is hurt and Dr. Stimpson ain't here." In the panic of the moment, her genteel speech was overwhelmed by the local idiom.

They ran across the grass toward the asylum. Inside the long corridor, Miss Whitman unlocked a gate and led them down a spiral staircase into the basement. She ran ahead in the gloom and paused outside a barred iron door where she fumbled with her bunch of keys. They could hear the sound of shouting from the other side. Miss Whitman pushed open the door.

Inside were about a dozen men, mostly without clothes, chained to the unplastered brick. A little light came through a half-window at the end of the room. One of the men, naked and streaked with blood, was holding a manacle, which he appeared to have wrenched from the wall, aloft in his hand. Tyson was sitting on the floor, leaning against an iron cot; he had a wound in his cheek, which was bleeding onto his uniform jacket, and his lower jaw hung down on his shoulder.

Thomas turned to Miss Whitman. "Go at once to the pharmacy. Find a dressing and something to bathe the wounds. I need also some tincture of opium. Go to Dr. Faverill's office. Tell him to send three male attendants as fast as possible. Sonia! Why on earth have you followed us? Go up with Miss Whitman at once. Stay in Faverill's office."

Thomas was left alone, like Daniel, though most of his lions were chained. He stared at the blood-streaked patient and began to speak calmly to him. "I am a doctor. I do not know your name but we are going to help you. Please be calm."

He could not think of anything helpful to say, but he wanted his voice to soothe the other patients, all of whom were moaning and distressed. Some were pulling at their restraints. He repeated quiet platitudes while he looked about the room. The resemblance to a feral den was increased by the scattering of straw on the stone floor and the smell it gave off. As Thomas bent over to examine Tyson's injury, he looked up to the mattress, on which lay a creature, barely man, no threat to anyone because so much of him was missing—limbs, hands, half a face—so that he was not much more than a trunk with most of a head, breathing, alas; scraps of human matter cohering sufficiently to live.

Thomas held the flesh of Tyson's cheek together as they waited. The instigator of the trouble began to turn his violence on himself, hammering his head against the rim of a bedstead. Thomas knew he should intervene to prevent self-harm, but hoped the man would stun himself sufficiently to become more docile.

There were running footsteps at last, and Miss Whitman returned with two attendants. "Morphia," she said, holding out a bottle to Thomas. "That's what they give me for him."

"That's all right," said Thomas. "You dress Mr. Tyson's wound, you two help me."

The attendants reluctantly approached the naked man, who now stood up and turned to face them. He was well-made, muscular, the torso part-covered in curling black hairs, but his eyes seemed disconnected from the activity behind them; looking into them, Thomas understood why people in earlier times had spoken of possession: some other force did seem to own him. He made little effort to resist, until they had him sitting on the floor and Thomas uncorked the bottle; then he began to escape their grip. Neither attendant was strong or particularly willing, but eventually they managed to sit one on each arm and to hold his head.

"I need him to open his mouth," said Thomas.

The attendants glanced at one another.

"You do it," said one.

The man selected punched the patient hard in the solar plexus. He gasped, and Thomas poured the medicine into his open mouth, then clamped his hand over the man's lips. The three of them held him till they saw his Adam's apple drag reluctantly upward in his throat and heard him swallow.

"Miss Whitman, please take Mr. Tyson up to Dr. Faverill to be examined. I shall stay with the patient until he is calm. Then we will take him to a padded room upstairs until whoever runs this ward arranges for his safety."

"We are not allowed to use the padded—"

"Please do what you are told. It is only for a short time and it is a better place for him than . . ." Thomas looked round about them, "than this."

DR. FAVERILL invited Thomas and Sonia into his private rooms for dinner that night. He had a paneled apartment on the second floor, high enough to give him a view above the brick wall and over the Downs to the south. The food was not from the asylum kitchen but was prepared by Matilda, who joined them at the table. There was soup and lamb cutlets, then pigeon with bread sauce and leeks from the kitchen gardens. Faverill poured wine from an old ship's decanter he told them had belonged to his father, who worked for the East India Company.

"I should like to apologize to you, Mrs. Prendergast," he said, filling her glass, "for the distressing scenes I understand you witnessed today."

"It was my fault," said Sonia. "I ran after Thomas without thinking whether it was proper for me to be there or not."

"I should not wish you take away a poor impression of our asylum. The patients in Ward Fifty-two are those who have proved beyond our capabilities. The man in question is someone who was sent to us from prison. We have repeatedly asked for him to be transferred to Broadmoor, but so far without success. The communication between hospitals, the county councils and the Home Office is not as it should be. There is another poor wretch there who should not be with us, but in some hospice or house of God."

"I understand," said Sonia.

"That is very gracious of you. I wish I could say that I also understood. I believe your brother dealt with the situation very well. We shall miss him."

Thomas put down his knife and fork. "Why don't you come?" he said.

Faverill spluttered over his wine. "What?"

"Give notice in writing to the Committee of Visitors, saying that in one year you wish to retire. By that time we shall have finished our work in Paris and shall be installed in a fine clinic somewhere in the Alps. The medical staff will consist of myself and another young doctor. It would be wonderful for our venture if we were able to boast also a senior consultant, an éminence grise. You could decide how much work you would like to do, how many hours. The air will be pure, the surroundings congenial. Our patients will represent a mixture of fascinating ailments, and some of them," said Thomas, leaning forward to engage Faverill's gaze more closely, "we expect to cure."

Faverill leaned back in his chair and laughed, not bitterly, thought Sonia, but with a richly sardonic enjoyment. "Cure! My dear Midwinter, I believe you may have found a marketplace. All of Europe is crying out for a cure for its madness. The doctors of my generation have failed. By bringing so many lunatics into one place we have merely demonstrated how numerous they are. But you . . . Ah yes, you must find the solutions. When the snake-oil salesmen sold their bottles from the back of their wagons in Colorado it was to a population crying out for medicine. You have the demand, you have the need. Now indeed is the time to supply the cure." His renewed laughter gurgled in his throat.

Thomas was flushed with indignation. Sonia was ready to lay her hand on his sleeve, but she watched with relief as he controlled himself. "The knowledge of science does go forward," he said quietly. "It does not go back. My generation will do more than yours. And my children's will do more than ours. We will never end our work because new illnesses will arise to test us. Occasionally in history, however, there are leaps. Progress is not smooth. I believe we are on the verge of such a leap, but even if not, I would be happy to contribute to a steady accumulation of knowledge. I am sincere in asking you to join us."

Sonia saw tears gather at the rim of Faverill's eyes and wondered how much of his previous mirth had been genuine. "My dear Mid—"

"Just let me make it clear, sir. A place in which we would take some wealthy clients, whose fees would fund the enterprise, but poorhouse patients too, whom we would treat pro bono. A private clinic with a proper research facility, set in beautiful surroundings. And Dr. Faverill, the senior consultant, with the room of his choice, an Alpine view, working the hours that he chose, lending the luster of his experience to two young men's endeavor. And the literature we should send out for our clinic, our hydro, whatever we should call it, decorated with your name and the initials of your many honors."

Faverill resumed his humorous manner. "Now you flatter me too much, though I am indeed honored by your words. Deeply honored, sir." He raised his wineglass toward Thomas and inclined his head. "However, I must make it plain to you that I shall not be tempted into leaving England. I doubt whether I shall leave the grounds of this asylum."

"Why?" said Thomas.

Faverill breathed in deeply. "Love," he said.

"Love?" said Thomas. "Of country? Of place?"

"Oh no." Faverill sighed and bowed his head in the direction of the fourth person at the table. "Of Matilda."

"In-deed."

Sonia noticed how Thomas managed to control the degree of surprise with which he had begun the word.

"Indeed," said Faverill. "We cannot be wed because she is married to another, but I have pledged my life to her, most excellent woman."

Sonia looked at Matilda, who smiled back at her beneath her white bonnet, and ground her fingers into the palm of her hand with unusual force. She spoke, and her voice was thin and high, with a hard edge to the brogue of the county. "Good Billy," she said. "Good boy, Billy."

"Yes," said Faverill. "Thank you. It would take me a long time to explain the circumstances and I do not wish to breach any confidences. I hope it is enough to say that I admire Matilda more than any woman alive. I have the very highest opinion of her character, formed from a long and intimate acquaintance. She was once, as you may have surmised, a patient in this asylum. The county council records still have her as such. She was never my patient, but was treated by my predecessor. All I have shown toward her is concern. She is a lovely creature, I think, quick as a little thrush on the lawn, lively as a sparrow. She has shown me great kindness, for which I shall be forever grateful. As for love . . . we know it comes unbidden, blind. So it was for me. A day without Matilda is for me a day not worth living."

Thomas opened his mouth to speak, but no words came. Sonia, feeling one of them should respond, said, "What a charming story, Dr. Faverill. I am so pleased for you . . . both." She smiled at Matilda, but what she said did not sound adequate to her ears.

"Alas," said Faverill, "my devotion to Matilda prevents me from traveling. She is the most intelligent of women, thoughtful and percipient, but she is sensitive to change. Her life before she came here was one of extreme difficulty. She has found her sanctuary here, inside these walls. She has her own room in the tower, a little boxroom with a view, nothing more, but it is a world to her."

Matilda nodded vigorously. "That's my home," she said.

Faverill smiled at Thomas, who was still speechless. "We all acknowledge the random power of love," he said, "but we do not quite believe it, do we? Men and women are drawn to those of their own age and station. Their marriages are negotiations. Even in the poets we see no more than lip service paid to the idea. Ophelia is in love with . . . not the grave digger, nor even Fortinbras, but of course with Prince Hamlet. Romeo's love may be star-crossed but it is inevitable, is it not? The family feud only makes it more so. And as for Miranda . . . had she fallen in love with Trinculo—no, had she fallen in love with Caliban—ah, what a play that might have been!"

Even on the subject of his favorite playwright, Thomas could find no words to contribute and Faverill looked amused by his discomfort. "Come, Midwinter," he said, "you look as though you had seen a ghost. You look like Marcellus on the night watch. Have another glass of wine. At least it will bring some color back to your cheeks. Is that not right, Matilda?"

IN HER room that night, Sonia sat down to write to Jacques. This was something she enjoyed because it allowed her legitimately to indulge herself in thinking about him. At other times she tried to stop herself from picturing the dark brows, the anxious eyes with the sudden dilatation she had taken for evidence of steel but knew now was no more than a reflex of self-defense that covered his gentler feelings—the emotions that now included love for her. Several months had passed since his visit to Torrington and she had no photograph of him, no sure way of knowing that she had not imagined the episode beneath the cedar tree, except on the rare days in between that she had spent with Thomas, who, she and Jacques agreed, must be included in the secret. The plan was that Jacques should return in the summer and that they should have a marriage ceremony in England before returning to Paris. Thomas had been thrilled by the news of his sister's engagement to his best friend; he told her it was the happiest day of his life and served to underline the fact that their joint venture (what he now called their *"folie à trois"*) was predestined. Sonia was touched that Thomas was so unaffectedly pleased, but a little put out that he was not more surprised; she did not altogether enjoy the feeling that a passion which had crept up behind her in the dark and filled her with joy and awe at the mysterious movement of providence should, to her younger brother, have been obvious all along.

She kept a ring that Jacques had sent her in a small velvet purse. She took it out and slipped it on her finger as she wrote to him, but even the unbroken circle did not quite convince her that she was truly loved—that she existed permanently and luminously in the mind of a young French doctor in the Latin Quarter. She did not feel she had the right to presume such a thing; it was a phenomenon for which she daily needed new evidence, even though his letters were as frequent and disbelieving as her own. She wondered if she should tell Jacques about her glimpse into Ward Fifty-two, but decided that it might worry him, that he might think she had been needlessly upset and blame Thomas for it. She felt a churning of fear and pity when she thought of the iron stable in the basement; it was worse than anything she had seen or imagined, but she presumed that Jacques and Thomas understood the philosophical and religious questions it provoked; indeed, that understanding must be the source of the urgency behind their medical ambition. It was not just scientific curiosity that drove them on, there was a deeper philanthropic motive, and therefore it was unnecessary for her to share her thoughts or to tell her story to Jacques.

Instead, she told him how Thomas had offered Faverill a position at their new clinic, and how he had already mentioned one or two patients he would like to take. "Are you quite sure, my dear, that Thomas is allowed to hire all your staff in this way? Are there not one or two brilliant young men at the Salpêtrière? And what about me? As the partnership manager—was that my title?—surely I should have a stake in these matters. There is a girl here called Daisy, a patient, whom Thomas seems keen for us to take (I think perhaps he is a little sweet on her). She has not been able to convince the Committee of Visitors that she is sane enough to be released, so Thomas is proposing that she escape! If a lunatic stays at large for more than fourteen days, she is deemed to be free. Thomas tells me that he and this girl have escaped before and that she intends to follow him when he leaves. He is still not quite the responsible man of science that he would have us take him for; a little of the night reveler persists . . ."

IN MAY, a few days before he was due to depart from the asylum, Thomas asked Faverill if he could take one of the many days of leave that were owing to him, so that he could make his farewells.

He put on his strongest shoes and went to the farm to watch the lunatics milking the cows and hoeing the rows of vegetables in the kitchen gardens. The spring breeze brought the smell of malt and hops drifting down from the brewery on the hill, and he glanced up to see the chimney of the laundry puffing away behind it, like the funnel of a stalled brick engine.

Thomas was surprised by how much he had come to tolerate, even to like, the asylum. The vast lateral folly was hidden from his view by the elms at the edge of the cow pastures, and he could briefly view it with detachment. The things he had seen inside the walls had seared his soul. But "sear" was perhaps the word, he thought, like "cauterize": he was burned, but he did not bleed. He dreaded becoming "a doctor," like old Meadowes, someone who examined a patient and diagnosed by elimination, checking symptoms against the remembered student textbook, then, knowing the rudiments of pharmaceutical science, prescribed. Or—in so many cases—said there was yet no cure. He passionately hoped that he had not become such a mechanical practitioner, such a clockmaker, such a cobbler of the human.

It was time for him to go, and his mind was full of Paris. He had estimated, before Tyson gave him the exact figure, that in the male wing of
the asylum there were ten thousand epileptic fits a year. Most of these
people were not even mentally unwell, but their tendency to choke at
dinnertime meant that the piece of medical equipment he had used
most was not a stethoscope or a thermometer but a probang, an instrument for pushing stuck food down the esophagus, something he had
been instructed to carry at all times.

He sucked deeply on the fresh May morning and sighed. He had
solved nothing by his stay at the asylum; all he had done was shine a
clear light on his ignorance. The trials of tube-feeding, the stench in
"dirty school" where the negligent were drilled, the candlelit struggle to
bring the casebooks up to date . . . how glad he would be to leave those all
behind, to enter into private practice with a chance of making someone
well. And in case he should become detached from the scale of the task,
there were still the wards of the Salpêtrière to visit, notebook and stethoscope in hand.

He began to loop back toward the circular icehouse, which made
him think of Daisy. He had agreed to meet her at an inn outside the town
in three weeks' time. Her appeals to the Committee of Visitors had been
rejected, and his word alone was not enough to have her discharged. He
told her he would help her find a job in a factory or farm (perhaps even in
a countinghouse now that she could read), until he had set up his clinic
with Jacques, when she could come and work for them. Daisy was confident she could escape by the brewery gate, as they had done before.
Thomas had also entered into negotiation about the case of the blind
girl, Mary, and had successfully persuaded the committee that in the
absence of any symptom of lunacy she could be released when he found
accommodation for her. He decided that he would not tell Mary until he
was ready to look after her; he feared that she might otherwise prefer
to stay.

As he made his way back to the building, he hoped that his time
at the asylum would be thought worthwhile by the patients. He
had cured not a single soul, but he had laid kind hands on them. He had
been compelled to protect himself from looking too long into the gulf,
because to do so, he feared, would make him lose his own mind. He

remembered God's visitation to King Solomon, and His offer to grant any wish the king might have. Solomon had asked for "an understanding heart." When he read the story as a boy, Thomas had been disappointed and indignant. Solomon, having already made a dutiful marriage to the Pharaoh's daughter, had surely merited some self-indulgence— castles, gold and dancing girls. Now, as he plodded back toward the asylum, he found that he could not recall the story without tears flooding his eyes.

Being a man who liked, where possible, to see things through to their natural end, Thomas decided he would visit the only part of the building he had not seen in his time there. Nodding to Grogan in his glass-paneled box in the main hall, he began to mount the main staircase. Lesser corridors, higher and lighter than the one on the ground floor, led off to wards on the right and left; but a narrower staircase led up, into the heart of the Tuscan bell tower. And here, he had never before had cause to go.

Through windows on the top landing he was able to look north toward the main gates and Patterson's lodge, or south over the Downs toward the river. A spiral staircase led up to a locked trapdoor, beyond which was presumably the bell itself. To the east and west sides were green wooden doors, on one of which was stenciled the word "ARCHIVE." Thomas tried the brass handle and found that the door opened easily.

He felt unaccountably frightened when he stepped inside. The room was a library, with freestanding bookshelves, a metal door into what appeared to be a strong room, and many rows of boxes, books and files. Seated at a table in the western window was an elderly man in a dark velvet jacket and a smoking cap; he had a reddish-gray beard and reading glasses, which he removed as Thomas approached him.

"I am sorry to disturb you. I am Dr. Midwinter. I do not believe that we have met."

"Indeed not," said the man, standing up and offering his hand. "You are not disturbing me. I have all the time in the world."

"I was just looking round. I am to leave the asylum shortly and I was just . . ." How odd it was, thought Thomas, that Faverill had never mentioned that they had an archivist.

"Saying goodbye?"

"Exactly. Saying goodbye." Thomas coughed. "And these are all the records of the asylum?"

"Since it began. The building was opened in 1851. Here we have all the casebooks, the daybooks, the minutes of the meetings of the committee, the reports of the Commissioners in Lunacy and so on."

The man stood up and walked to a shelf. He was about Thomas's height. "This one is signed by Lord Shaftesbury himself. Do you see?"

His voice was educated and kindly; there was something of the scholar in it, Thomas thought.

"On these shelves we have the farm records, all beautifully done. Until a few years ago, at least. Food is so important for lunatics, is it not? Do you see this? 'Provisions consumed during the Year ending Dec 31st 1858. Beef and mutton, 198,285 lbs. For the Sick: Porter and Ale, 34,400 pints.' Goodness, they were well looked after. It was quite a different place in those days."

"Did you know it then?" said Thomas.

"Oh yes," said the man. "I have been here since the first day. The building was opened by the mayor, of course. It was a fine occasion. The local press was well represented. Everything in the building was quite new."

"And were you . . . What was your . . ." Thomas found it difficult to phrase the question.

"A resident," said the man in his fussy voice. "I have always been a resident."

"I imagine the asylum must have been very different then," said Thomas, anxious to move the conversation onward.

"Yes, Dr. Midwinter. Yes, indeed. Those were the days of hope." He walked back to his table.

Thomas, for no reason he could explain, affected a rather languid manner. "I have been concerned with the casebooks myself. It is a little like the Augean Stables—no, like Sisyphus, I should say. I am forever rolling my stone to the top of the hill. But the next day . . ."

"I am aware of your work. Some of the books have already been sent up and stored here. You have an elegant hand. Not a doctor's hand, I should say."

"Thank you."

"Perhaps I should continue with my work."

"I am sorry. I had not meant to—"

"Do stay. But forgive me if I write."

He took his place at the table again and bent over the open volume, in which were pasted case notes written on individual pieces of paper. He appeared to be copying them out into a different book on his right hand.

"From what year are these?" said Thomas.

"These are from 1860."

Thomas smiled. "The year of my birth."

"Is that so?"

The western light was strong behind the man's head, and lit the wisps of reddish-gray hair above his ears. Thomas tried to read upside down what he was writing; it appeared that he was merely copying out the doctor's original notes into a more legible copperplate.

"Are you . . . transcribing? Or . . ."

"These words are so bare. 'Believes the devil is in his abdomen. Says voices come to him through the walls of the church.' I try not merely to transcribe, but to redeem. Is that not the duty of the man with the pen?"

"Perhaps."

Thomas looked once more round the room, then began to take his leave, seeing that the man was bent to his work.

"I have enjoyed talking to you," he said.

The man stood up. "It has been a profound pleasure to meet you," he said. "I seldom have visitors up here. I have admired your work and I did hope that one day I should have the pleasure of meeting you face-to-face. It is a remarkable coincidence. My name, too, you see, is Midwinter."

VIII

THERE WAS A TIMID KNOCK ON THE DOOR, AND THOMAS, WHO HAD been looking out over the chestnut trees and daydreaming, leapt to his feet.

"My receptionist," he said, "is absent. Please excuse me."

A note on the desk from Jacques told him to expect Madame Lafond. A Parisian woman of about thirty stepped into the room. She was wearing a burgundy silk dress with black gloves that she twisted in her hands; she had golden hair swept up and pinned beneath a black velvet hat.

"Please do sit down, Madame."

The woman spoke rapidly and nervously. "I have previously consulted your colleague, Dr. Rebière."

"So I understand." He picked up some notes from the desk. "And how are you feeling, Madame?"

Madame Lafond passed a hand across her forehead. "Not well, Doctor."

"You seem a little short of breath."

"Well, naturally. The stairs . . ."

"Forgive me. I am so used to them that I sometimes forget. And what difficulties are you having?"

"I have headaches. I do not sleep well. And I have a pain here." She held her hand to an area above the waist.

"Is this the same pain for which you originally consulted Dr. Rebière?"

"Not exactly the same. It is a little more severe. I first consulted Dr. Charcot. Then Dr. Babinski. Then Dr. Rebière for a second opinion. I am beginning to feel a little like a parcel no one wishes to unpack. But my husband . . ."

"Yes, Madame?"

"He insists that I must be cured. I took the waters at Aix last spring. And then we went to Vittel. I was bored."

"And I see that Dr. Rebière diagnosed exhaustion. Have you been able to rest?"

"It is difficult to find the time. My husband is a financier and he is obliged to entertain a great deal. Naturally he wishes me to act as hostess when his guests come to dine."

"Naturally. And how often would you have to preside at such a dinner?"

"Perhaps twice a week. Then we are also obliged to dine out frequently."

"I see," said Thomas. "And these dinners. Do they consist of many courses? Are they rich?"

"I eat so little I could not really tell you. I suppose they are sometimes lavish."

"What was the dinner the last time you entertained?"

"Some foie gras. Oysters. My husband is very fond of oysters. Some sole perhaps. A side of beef. Champagne. I forget."

"And wines?"

"Of course. You are English, I believe, Doctor."

"I am indeed. I am familiar with French wine, however. One of the glories of the world."

"I suppose so." Madame Lafond looked distracted. "I drink only water. Sometimes a little brandy. Tell me, what do you think the matter is?"

"I shall need to examine you before I can be sure. If you would care to step behind that screen and take off your clothes."

Madame Lafond obeyed with the docility of the chronic patient. Thomas went over to the window and looked down onto the traffic of the rue des Saints Pères. He had found the attic room in his first week in Paris and hastily arranged a brass plate; it was an unfashionable street and its three flights of stairs made it impossible for elderly patients. Most of his clientele, however, seemed to be young women, impressed by its proximity to the Boulevard St. Germain and strong enough to make the climb.

Madame Lafond was sitting on the edge of the couch in her under-clothes, staring stoically ahead; her narrow blue eyes had a look of weary patience as Thomas rubbed his hands together.

He touched her arm. "Please tell me if my hands are too cold."

"All right."

"Please lie down. I am going to examine your abdomen."

As he lifted the silk chemise and laid his fingers on the skin of her belly, Thomas had a picture in his mind of the first female corpse he had seen in "Meaters," as the Cambridge undergraduates had called the dis-secting room or meat-shop, a shanty with a tin roof and an overpower-ing atmosphere of formalin and pipe smoke. He often brought to mind the billowing stoves, the tallow soap and clammy towels by the sink when he was examining a female patient; it helped him concentrate. Madame Lafond's skin was soft, and the flesh beneath it felt normal to his touch. He pushed down the ivory drawers a little, and pressed over the appendix.

"Do you have children, Madame?"

"I have one son."

"And is everything regular? Your monthly period? May I touch here? I am looking for any sign of ovarian disorder. Has there been any swelling? Any pain? Good."

With some relief, he moved up to the area beneath the ribs, where he did elicit a small cry when he pushed firmly against the stomach.

"Nothing to worry about," he said. "A little air, I think. Now the liver. Is that tender? No? Very well. If you sit on the edge of the couch again and lift up your slip. I am going to test your knee reflexes. No need to roll down your stockings. Just sit on the edge. Very good. You may get dressed now."

He asked her some more questions about her diet, her habits and whether she took exercise. He checked her pulse and examined her eyes.

He looked at his watch: patients usually wanted a consultation to last for at least half an hour.

"And your relations with your husband, Madame. Are they quite normal?"

Madame Lafond looked a little uneasy. "Yes. He is a . . . demanding man. He likes to . . . I don't know what is normal, but I imagine so, yes. Listen, Doctor, there is a Swedish doctor I have heard of who diagnosed a friend of mine. He said she had colitis. It seems to be a very common ailment in Paris at the moment."

"Yes," said Thomas. "So I believe. Very fashionable."

Madame Lafond flushed. "And do I have colitis?"

"I think not. I could detect no problem with the colon."

She looked disappointed. "So what is the matter with me?"

Thomas licked his lips. This was the moment he found most difficult. "I naturally agree with my colleague, Dr. Rebière, that you are tired. However," he said quickly as her face clouded further, "I think there is a secondary problem."

"And what is that, Doctor?"

"I diagnose a mild gastritis."

A look of wonder came into Madame Lafond's face. "Is it serious?"

"In its chronic form it can be very serious. In its acute form, less so. It may cause vomiting. In the form that you have . . . it is unlikely to be too debilitating."

"And how did I catch this disease?"

"I should say it was probably . . . idiopathic."

"Idiopathic gastritis." She repeated the phrase slowly. She seemed to enjoy it. "They told me you were a good doctor. You have a reputation already, you know."

Madame Lafond's cheeks, flushed with excitement, made her look the embodiment of youthful well-being.

"And what should I take for it?"

"Quite a strict regime, I am afraid."

"So much the better."

"Take these pills, twice a day. You must walk briskly for an hour each morning. Avoid alcohol, and rest for half an hour on your bed after lunch. No longer, mind, or it will spoil your sleep at night."

Madame Lafond stood up, holding the bottle of pills in her gloved hand. "And shall I come and see you again?"

"Undoubtedly," said Thomas. "A week today at the same time."

"Goodbye, Doctor. Thank you so much."

Thomas heard her staccato steps dancing down the wooden stairs. I have cured her, he thought.

SONIA ARRANGED a small jar of flowers in Jacques's room and tidied the papers on his table. "Traumatic Hysteria," she read in Jacques's increasingly untidy writing. "Case study Four. Henri R——: coachman involved in traffic accident, Pont Neuf, July 5, 1887. Note particularly: memory of trauma retained in part of brain outside normal consciousness." In the margin of the page, he had scribbled, "This mechanism potentially universal?"

She smiled as she organized the papers, being careful not to alter the order in which they had been left; she had no wish to see again the look of amazed sadness in Jacques's eyes that had followed her first attempt at tidying his work. It had been the only uneasy moment in their infant marriage. Her parents' displeasure at her marrying again so soon, to a poor foreigner, had expedited the journey to Paris and made her blind to the less attractive aspects of Madame Maurel's boardinghouse. While Jacques put the last touches to his thesis, she bought flowers, mended his clothes and repainted the room.

The days were long without him. She visited the Louvre and stood before the paintings of Poussin and Ingres; her favorite was *The Raft of the Medusa*, by Géricault, where the figures seemed to ascend the scale of human happiness, from the mournful foot of the canvas to the top, where the bent-backed African sailor flourished his scarlet banner of hope. She had time to explore the Latin Quarter and the whole stretch of the Left Bank as far as the Gare d'Austerlitz and the Salpêtrière itself, where she sometimes took a sandwich to Jacques for his lunch and ate with him on one of the benches of the Promenade de la Hauteur, with a few patients for company. Sometimes she could meet Thomas as well, and would return to his attic in the rue des Saints-Pères because the bathroom arrangements were preferable to those of Madame Maurel and she could act as an unpaid receptionist when Thomas had a patient.

Sonia could not recall a time when she had felt happier. The boardinghouse did not repel her, it charmed her. Madame Tavernier and her daughter did not irritate her, they made her laugh, though not as much as Pivot, the psoriatic salesman, or the perpetually reluctant Carine. To supplement the cooking, Sonia baked small flans or tarts when Carine was out of the kitchen and sent them off to work with Jacques the next day. The narrow bed in his room was barely large enough for both of them, but Sonia slept in his arms each night, motionless with joy. Jacques admitted that he had at first surreptitiously checked her pulse, amazed at the depth of her unconsciousness, but then thanked providence for a tranquil wife, and wrapped himself tight around her. With some of the small amount of money she had been able to bring, Sonia bought a wardrobe for her clothes and had it installed in a corner of the room; she found a laundry that was reasonably priced, at least by the standards of Paris if not by those of Lincoln, and took it on herself to turn the cuffs of Jacques's shirts.

She felt it was important that she provide some comfort and stability for him, because he and Thomas were in a state of perpetual agitation. The final stage of Jacques's qualification was the defense of his thesis in front of the examiners at the Salpêtrière, and although he had been given to understand, by no less a figure than Dr. Babinski, that this would be straightforward, the writing of the thesis was still not complete. Sonia occasionally reminded him, but did not wish to nag when he seemed preoccupied. The trouble, she thought, was that he and Thomas were so enthralled by Charcot's lectures that Jacques had no time left; day after day, he would come pounding up the stairs of Madame Maurel's house with news of the professor's latest revelation.

Sonia had to try to understand; it was part of her love for Jacques that she simply must understand. He marveled at how well she could follow, with no medical education; he told her she was a doctor manquée and thanked his good fortune in having married such a paragon; yet she saw how he had to struggle to be patient when she had missed an important link in the chain of his reasoning, and she knew how hard she was fighting to hold her mind to the point. He assured her that there were no

more than a dozen words—two dozen at most—that she needed to
know in order to be able to follow, in broad terms, what he was doing. On
the back of an old Comédie Française playbill, he even wrote some of
them down, and she studied and learned them in his absence. "*Neurology:* the study of diseases of the nervous system, typically caused by
'lesion' (think of a tiny cut or blister) in the brain or spinal cord which
causes problems in the nerves that stem from that point, typically disorders of the muscles, thus odd movements. *Morbid:* diseased, unwell.
Somatic: of the body, physical. *Psychic:* of the mind, opposite of somatic
(but I generally say *mental* because *psychic* looks too like *physic* or *physical* on the page). *Innervation:* the fact of having, or the process of acquiring, nerves (for instance, the arm is innervated, but the colon or the
brain itself, oddly enough, are not; if someone stabbed a knife into your
brain, you would not feel it). *Neurasthenic:* suffering from a mild nervous
exhaustion of undefined cause and varied symptoms, including insomnia, mild phobias and so on. Usually responsive to rest and dietary
change. *Nosology:* the process of defining a disease by grouping symptoms together as a named entity. *Organic:* having an observable physical
existence. *Dynamic:* moving, therefore not observable in the same way.
Physiology: the study of how bodily systems work and what they do.
Neurophysiology: the study of what the nervous system does and how it
works. *Brain:* organ in the skull responsible for control of the body (via
the nerves), emotion, sensation, reason and thought (all via its own cells
in different areas). *Mind:* cognitive function of brain (*cognitive:* to do
with reason, memory and the connections they make). *Consciousness:*
human self-awareness, probably a function of mind but possibly of
brain; we do not know. *Psychology:* the study of how the mind works.
Psychiatry: the diagnosis and treatment of illnesses of the brain and
mind. *Neuron:* basic unit of nervous system with ability to transmit electrical impulses in chains. *Hemiplegia:* paralysis affecting one side of the
body. *Epilepsy:* a malfunction of the brain (probably caused by a lesion,
see above, possibly resulting from birth *trauma* [wound or injury] or from
infection) that causes an electrical discharge in the brain, like a small
thunderstorm, that spreads down various pathways. Its final destination, often in some center controlling movement, determines its effect on

the body, for instance in convulsions or spasms of the relevantly controlled part."

They invented a game in which Jacques played the part of a grand examiner and Sonia the role of a nervous student just up from the Auvergne. Jacques clearly enjoyed swaggering about the low-ceilinged room while she sat demurely on the rush-seated chair.

"All right, young man," he said in his professorial voice. "That's enough about Parkinson's. Now hysteria, please."

"Also a standard neurological illness. Lesion in brain or spinal cord, precise location yet to be confirmed, causing damage to nerves at the site and consequently shaking or paralysis at the end of the pathway where the nerve meets the muscle."

"And?"

"Inherited, though we do not yet know quite how that works. Also influenced by the patient's womb or ovaries."

"Yes, though that aspect is no longer considered fundamental. What particularly distinguishes hysteria from other standard neurological illnesses?"

"It has a mental element."

"Explain, please."

"Patients undergoing hysterical attacks appear to be reliving horrible things—"

"'Horrible things'? Hardly a scientific term."

"Traumatic events, sir. Things which happened a long time ago."

"And, most important?"

"It seems that such horri—traumatic events may actually set off the illness. They unlock the door onto it."

"Very good."

"We do not yet know how."

"But we will find out?"

"We are close to finding out."

"One last detail on the mental side?"

"All hysterics can be hypnotized. Under hypnosis they can be made to live out the classic hysterical attack which—"

"Which has how many phases?"

"Four."

"Correct. And what most crucially does this tell us?"

"That the mental element in the disease may also work through the process of 'autosuggestion.'"

"Young man, you are a scholar. May I embrace you?"

"You may, sir."

"Thank you. You are now ready to move on to the question of traumatic hysteria."

"Am I? Am I really?"

"I believe so. I promise you that it is the very last thing I shall ask of you, but understanding it is the key to the work on which we are about to embark. It may well be the key to understanding how the human mind works."

"My dear Jacques," Sonia laughed. "How right Thomas was. He told me that if I married you I should never be bored. Penniless, he said, exasperated, exhausted, uplifted, but never bored."

Jacques smiled. "All right. I think you should come with us one morning soon to hear Professor Charcot."

"But I am not—"

"Half the audience are not medical people. We shall need to be there in good time, to be sure of our seats."

THEY ARRIVED shortly after nine, an hour early, and made their way to the amphitheater where they were able to find places in the front row. As Sonia settled herself between her husband and her brother, she found herself reminded of the last time she had been taken to Drury Lane by Richard Prendergast. She looked up at the stage, which was set with a double row of chairs for the assistants and, at the front, an armchair and table for Charcot. On the other side of the stage was a platform with a blackboard on which were written the words: "Traumatic Hysteria. Three cases."

Behind the platform was a large oil painting of Pinel striking the chains from the lunatics of the Salpêtrière. Sonia's eye was drawn to the central figure, a young woman with waving auburn tresses, on the point of liberation by the father of French psychiatry. Pinel was just in time,

Sonia thought; a moment later and her extreme décolletage would have led to indecency: it was certainly too late for the young lady writhing on the ground, the upstanding firmness of whose naked breasts defied the gravity of her situation. Neither patient looked one bit like the gibbering crones with whom she ate lunch beneath the plane trees.

In the hour before the lecture was due, the auditorium began to fill with medical students, many of them wearing top hats, which looked peculiar, Sonia thought, with their unshaven faces, tired linen and greasy neckties. There was an unmistakable smell of stale alcohol, an odor she associated with Fisher, the occasional butler at Torrington; some students were humming tunes they might have picked up the night before in a café, some rustled newspapers and scratched their heads. There were a few older men with notebooks whom Sonia took to be reporters and others, better dressed, who, Jacques explained, were simply interested members of the public.

The lights above the raked seats went down, and the spotlights rose on the stage. All was quiet for a moment; then the audience rose and applauded as Pierre Marie, in faultless morning dress, with a scarlet buttonhole, led the assistants to their place, followed, after a momentary pause, by Charcot himself. Sonia looked about, smiling, amazed by the fervor that greeted the little man. He wore a short coat and peculiar black skullcap over his long, gray hair.

A builder's laborer was ushered onto the stage by one of the interns. He had been at a site near the Tuileries Gardens when a passing wagon, driven at some speed, had knocked him from the scaffold where he was working down onto the pavement. He lost consciousness, having taken a blow to the head, but suffered no physical injury. After some time (Charcot did not say how long) at the Hôtel-Dieu, he regained consciousness and returned to his wife and family. He appeared to recover fully, but following another interval, whose exact length was again not specified, he began to experience headaches, trembling, episodes of amnesia, and part-paralysis in the lower half of his body. He could not feel it when a flame was held to his left leg.

"Before we discuss this most interesting case," said Charcot, "I wish to establish the patient's heredity."

An intern read out details of the life of the man, whom he referred to as "Paul B." He lived near the Barbès-Rochechouart intersection in a slum house beside the railway bridge. His family, as far as could be determined, was a Sodom of idiocy, drink and syphilis; he himself liked nothing more than to reduce himself to insensibility on absinthe or cheap wine. He was sexually incontinent and had fathered children by several women.

"Degeneration," said Charcot, "has him in its grip, but that is not the intriguing feature of Monsieur Paul B. This patient is suffering from traumatic hysteria. Some of you will be surprised that a man can suffer from what used to be a woman's ailment, especially a man who is not in himself effeminate. In this instance, the hysterogenic action of the womb itself is absent, though we may surmise that there has been some testicular influence in its place. Dr. Gilles de la Tourette will now show the map of the male body with its hysterogenic areas marked. The shaded parts, here, here and here. Thank you, Doctor.

"None of this need detain us. What is of interest both in this case and in the treatment of traumatic hysteria in general, is the part played by the patient's mind, and in particular his memory of the accident that threw him from his scaffold. He was taken, uninjured, to the Hôtel-Dieu. There he lay, until such time as he was apparently well enough to go home. During that period, however, the trauma he had sustained was held outside the normal activity of his mind, outside the physiology of the cortex. It existed in a state of latency from which it eventually emerged, a considerable time later, to activate the hysterical disposition that is his sad neurological inheritance."

Charcot paused for a moment in the rapt silence of the auditorium and drank from a glass of water on the table. "The trembling, the hemiplegia and the headaches, even the sense of choking the patient has described, we recognize as classic symptoms of hysteria. What is most interesting about the nature of traumatic hysteria is the way in which somatic paralysis has been activated by trauma, or the memory of trauma. This is an example of what an English colleague, Mr. Reynolds, referred to as "paralysis by idea"—not imagined paralysis, for this man is as physically afflicted as any of my multiple sclerosis patients—no, paralysis *by* idea. An experience has been held out of conscious thought in such a way that it has been able to exert its influence directly upon the nervous system and thus upon the muscles of the patient. And that, ladies and gentlemen, is the peculiar interest of this condition."

Sonia felt Jacques rise beside her and break into spontaneous applause. She blushed for his rapture, but not for long, as the rows behind them followed suit, with many students stamping their feet on the wooden floor and hammering the desks.

Charcot was obliged to hold up his hand for silence, so that he could conclude. "When Paul B undergoes an hysterical attack or when his lower left side is paralyzed, it is because the trauma of his accident has exacted its delayed toll on a system predisposed by his inheritance to hysteria. The physiopathological pathways by which it does so can be shown in operation if the patient is hypnotized. Exactly the same mechanism will produce exactly the same result. Please watch."

As Paul B was hypnotized, Sonia whispered into Thomas's ear, "Could it not be that the poor man suffered some damage to his brain when he fell off his scaffold? Would that not be a simpler explanation?"

"Well, yes, but when they examined the brain of a traumatic hysteric who had died they could see no changes."

"Perhaps he just needs a better microscope."

"Please, Sonia. Hush."

Afterward, they went to have lunch in a jostling brasserie on the Boulevard de l'Hôpital where the waiters carried plates at shoulder height and shouted back their orders to the bar. They found a stall near the misty window and Thomas produced the banknote with which Madame Lafond had paid for his services. They ordered champagne to celebrate the formation of the new partnership. An impatient waiter in a white apron stood drumming his fingers on the edge of the table while they deliberated; when he brought the champagne he poured it clumsily, so their fingers were wet when they raised the glasses.

"To what are we drinking?" said Sonia.

"Marriage," said Thomas.

"Thank you," said Sonia. "And to a month of medical partnership. No creditors, no debtors, and a small profit even after the rent is paid. Jacques?"

"To new horizons. To the view we shall have from the shoulders of Charcot."

"Yes," said Thomas. "That view. Queenie, did you understand the significance of what he said?"

"It was hard enough to understand the words."

"Omelet," said the waiter.

"The most important part was when he made it clear that emotions and memories can lodge in a part of the mind outside the usual mental processes—as it were in a vacuum, a sort of psychic Deauville. Here, they can actually be transformed into bodily symptoms which—"

"Herring and potatoes in oil?"

"When they are ready, can be expressed as tics, or pains or partial paralysis or—"

"And this," interrupted Jacques, "is the kind of authority we have long been looking for."

"Exactly. Charcot's early discoveries more or less invented neurology. He is an authority, yet now also an adventurer."

"But how exactly—"

"You must understand the principle of the dynamic lesion, which . . ."

Sonia sat back and smiled as Thomas and Jacques waved their knives and forks at one another. What was apparent to her was that Thomas and Jacques were so in love with their master's mind that they had no time for less elevated thoughts. It did not really matter that she herself had not quite followed all Charcot had said; when he had a spare moment, Jacques would take her through the morning's lecture in his role of examining professor. What was important was that he and Thomas fully understood, and felt confident that they could build on what Charcot was suggesting.

"You have not forgotten your thesis, have you?" she said, caught by a mundane thought.

"No. Thursday week is the last day. My oral test is a month later. I have shown the first half to my director already. He has recommended a new patient to me for a second opinion."

"I too have a new patient," said Thomas. "After Madame Lafond's visit, a gentleman called and left his card. The concierge described him as looking like a Middle Eastern prince."

While the waiter cleared their plates and laid a cheese board on the table, Thomas found the card in a waistcoat pocket and placed it in front of them. Above an address in the Faubourg St. Honoré was the name: Monsieur Naim Munzar Kalaji.

"I have been to visit him," said Thomas. "He is a wealthy merchant and philanthropist from—I forget which country. Arabia somewhere. He has a fine collection of art, a Poussin, an Ingres, a landscape by le Lorrain. There is a family with a sick boy and a neurasthenic sister. They are to go on a tour of Europe in the spring. He wants a doctor to accompany them. He will pay for the entire tour and the medical services himself. The father of the family is a painter, and Monsieur Kalaji wants him to be inspired by his travels. I think I let slip to Madame Lafond in our second appointment that I had been on such a tour as a student and she told this Kalaji."

"And will you go?" said Sonia.

"When I tell you how much money he is offering, I think you will no longer need to ask that question." Thomas looked about the brasserie full of scruffy students, their textbooks and their stethoscopes bagging out the pockets of their worn coats; he felt suddenly diffident, and scribbled the figure on the back of Kalaji's card.

Jacques rolled his eyes.

"But it means you will have to leave Paris," said Sonia, "and we are so happy here."

"It is not until the end of March, when the weather begins to be warmer. We have plenty of time together. With this much money, taken with what I have saved from England, with what you have brought, and with whatever we can persuade other investors in Paris to give us, we will have enough to buy a lease on our clinic."

Thomas's face shone with confidence, and Sonia shook her head, a little sadly, but with resignation. He had already decided. Paris did not mean as much to him as it did to her, and perhaps that was not unreasonable: he did not lie down each night in a dream of earthly love; he did not pass his days in the reverie of hope regained.

"Perhaps you two could move into my room in the rue des Saints-Pères," Thomas said.

"And leave Madame Maurel?" said Sonia. "Certainly not! I love it there. And Jacques and I must make our contribution while you are amusing yourself in the Mediterranean. We shall sublet your room for a little profit, and Jacques, once his thesis is done, will take on all the fashionable ladies of Paris. Don't look so despondent, my dearest! You can still spend the morning with the old biddies at the Salpêtrière and your evenings in the laboratory. Four appointments a day will suffice. Two will cover our costs and the other two will be pure profit, which shall be our contribution."

Jacques's face finally gashed open in a reluctant smile. "What one must do for science."

BEING MARRIED was not how Jacques had imagined it would be. He had pictured a house in a village with a pet dog and himself feeling unaccountably dignified as he presided at a dinner table of children and servants. What happened, in fact, was that there was a woman in his room. He was the same man, with the same early start and late bedtime he had had since boyhood, but his dissecting knives were sometimes hidden under pages of a half-written letter to England; there were silk stockings draped over the back of the desk chair at night; there were small ceramic pots and mysterious floral pillboxes on the mantel; on a sidetable, there was a framed photograph of someone's mother, not his: in the bed linen and the chairs and the fabric of the room, Sonia had left a trail of minute prints, like spoors of femininity. It was intoxicating, such physical closeness, it was suffocating, yet he found himself hungry for more of it at nighttime in the narrow bed, when he melted into her.

He was disappointed that Thomas was to leave Paris after such a short stay, but did not try to dissuade him. They urgently needed money, and there was a sense in which he might breathe more easily without him. Jacques, to his shame, found himself irritated by the way Thomas had managed to qualify before him. The reason was simple enough: Thomas had gone young to Cambridge University while he himself was still struggling to acquire a belated baccalauréat through the lycée in Rennes; then he had chosen to prolong his student days by acquiring clinical experience as an intern. His years on the wards of the Salpêtrière weighed as heavily in the scale as Thomas's in the English asylum; his access to Charcot and the school of neurology was worth infinitely more than Thomas's course in despair from Faverill and McLeish; yet still he

felt he must pass the time when Thomas was away in profitable study if
he was to catch up and begin their true partnership as equals.

He enjoyed Thomas's company as much as ever. He had only to begin
to phrase a thought for Thomas to have anticipated its completion—not
in a way that deflated him, but with a sympathy that inspired him to
move on; yet when he was with Sonia and Thomas at the same time, he
sometimes felt uneasy. He did not wish to exclude Sonia from their talk,
but resented Thomas for distracting his attention from his wife; at other
times, he wished Sonia had not been there because he loved her so much
that he found his eyes and his thoughts always drawn first to her face;
and what now was left to prove by gazing at her? Occasionally, he suspected that the brother and sister enjoyed a subtle intimacy, something
historic, which for all his superior closeness—intellectually to one and
sensually to the other—he could never share. He loved them both, but it
became clear to him that he had not thought through all the implications of the "folie à trois."

He thanked God for the Salpêtrière. Their tactical decision to study
and work apart until they felt ready to unite had been vindicated by the
good fortune of his being present in a hospital making history. For all the
renown brought to it by Charcot, the Salpêtrière was still viewed by
many students as eccentrically placed, away from the main buildings of
the Ecole de Médecine, and dealing only with chronic incurables from
whom nothing could be learned. Most students completed the Ecole de
Médecine course in four or five years and barely set foot in a ward; when
they rushed back to Bergerac or Bourges they sometimes found their
first client was also their first patient.

Jacques, on the other hand, felt drenched in clinical experience, as he
had felt saturated in his years of anatomy by the effluent of the dead. His
manner of examination was based on that of Charcot: rigorous optical
scrutiny and minimal touch. He knew the human frame so well already
that every tremor, every tic and follicle was a clue to his eye; his waking
gaze was forever filled with skin, and his mind with rapid speculation as
to what lay beneath.

When, on a chilly October evening, he went to be examined on his
thesis, he found it difficult for a moment to focus his mind on physiology
in the abstract, with no swollen joints or mottled dermis to inspect. He

climbed the familiar external stone steps of the gray building that housed the amphitheater, and then the internal stairs to the numbered room. Of the five examiners waiting inside, two, Pierre Marie and Georges Gilles de la Tourette, were known to him. A copy of his thesis on gout and rheumatism of the joints, printed at appalling expense by Ecole de Médecine printers, lay before them on a long oak table. The lit gas lamps gave the room an ecclesiastical glow.

Jacques licked his lips and thought of Abbé Henri. His mind was for a moment filled with a view of the wind-whipped larch above the beach at home and the calls of the seabirds over the heaving waves. He thought of his mother.

"You have completed four years as an intern, Monsieur?" said the chairman of the examiners, a gray-bearded professor from the Ecole de Médecine, unknown to Jacques.

"Yes, Professor."

"And I see that you completed the final four medical examinations in the space of the last eighteen months."

"That is correct."

"And you are now twenty-seven years old? So it has taken you, I think, nine years to reach this point. After a somewhat . . . unconventional beginning. Do you regret that you have protracted your studies by working as in intern here?"

"On the contrary, the clinical experience has been invaluable. And to have studied here at such a time, with Professor Charcot, has been a privilege."

"I understand you have taught some first-year students. Has that been satisfactory?"

"I believe so. My motives for undertaking the work were not entirely selfless."

The chairman smiled. "I think we all understand why interns have to teach a little. Especially as you are a married man, I believe?"

"Recently, Professor, yes. My wife is English."

"And do you speak English fluently?"

"I do. I am also learning German."

"Commendable. I understand that you have undertaken some private consultations under the guidance of Dr. Babinski."

"Yes, though of course I have not been able to charge, so they have been merely educative."

"Indeed, Monsieur. But soon. Now to your thesis." The chairman picked up the printed papers from the table. "Most student theses are a formality—or worse. They are copied from some more or less reputable textbook and are no more than a rite of passage before the wretched youth hurries back to his hometown. You, sir, as befits an intern, have presented us with a serious piece of work."

There was silence in the examining room. Jacques, who had until that point felt nothing but a desire to behave in a correct, professional way, now felt the squeeze of panic in his gut. Two of the other examiners cleared their throats and moved their chairs closer to the table.

They began to question him on the causes of gout.

"You have read Charcot on the subject?"

"Indeed, Professor."

"You also make considerable play of an English physician called . . . let me see, Garrod. Though I am not sure if he is translated."

"I read him in English."

The examiner raised an eyebrow in what looked like skepticism, and Jacques rushed to justify himself. "Less than ten years ago he wrote a paper suggesting the precipitation of sodium urate in or near the joint is the principal cause. We have not yet found a way of verifying the thesis. No test yet appears sensitive enough. In this respect, I suppose one might call it a bridesmaid illness, like Parkinson's or hysteria."

All this information was already in the thesis, he suddenly remembered; but the examiners smiled a little and he gave himself room to hope that they would pardon his repetition.

They asked him to differentiate in detail between gout and rheumatoid arthritis and questioned whether there was any real distinction. He had been so involved in hysteria that it was a long time since he had thought clearly about his thesis; he began to talk more rapidly than he intended: he could hear the Breton accent of his childhood hammering the words "hyperextension deformity of the interphalangeal joints of the fingers."

He saw Babinski smile. He felt a thread of sweat on his spine. He was going to fail. After nine years, he was going to fail at the last.

"You have entertained us with your thesis, Monsieur," said the chairman eventually. "Your way of speaking has—if you will permit me to say so—something of the autodidact. The way that you pronounce certain medical terms and the passionate desire to persuade . . ."

"Forgive me. I do not come from Paris. I speak like that because—"

"No, no." The chairman waved his hand. "I did not mean to criticize. Your written work shows no such traces. This, my dear sir," he said, picking up the thesis in his hand and shaking it toward Jacques's face, "is a piece of utterly first-rate scholarship, one of the most interesting works on this subject that I have ever read. You may now stand up because the committee wishes to shake you by the hand."

Jacques made an effort to close his mouth as he pushed himself up out of the hard chair and moved down the line of doctors with his hand extended.

"My fellow-examiners and I congratulate you. Our official verdict is one of 'extremely satisfied.'"

"Thank you, Professor."

"Young man, you may now allow yourself to smile."

"Thank you," said Jacques again, making his way to the door of the interview room, where he turned and bowed. "Thank you."

He groped his way down the staircase, still unsmiling, too dumbfounded to think. Then, once he was out in the open air, he began to run.

He ran across the huge open courtyard of the Salpêtrière with his coat flapping behind him and the tears flying backward from his eyes. His heart was filled with Saint Agnès. "Oh, Olivier," he said out loud, "oh, my dear brother, I am coming for you. I am coming to get you."

THOMAS WAS standing in front of the Riemenschneider altarpiece of *The Last Supper* in St. Jakob's Church in Rothenburg when he heard his voice. It was fainter than ever, little more than a whisper. It had the sleepy, reassuring tone that was so familiar. "Giving him the bread . . . You are watching him . . . Good boy, good boy . . ."

Although it was still in external space, it was no longer on the other side of the room; it was in his ear, it was almost back inside his skull, and he felt certain that this would be the last time he was ever to hear it;

indeed, it whispered to him: "Adieu, Thomas, goodbye, God be with you, goodbye." So intent was he to catch its dying words that he did not hear a real voice, that of Nadine Valade, his sixteen-year-old charge, who was calling up to him.

He turned from the Altar of the Holy Blood, and saw a figure at the top of the stairs to the gallery. It was a girl of about Nadine's age, but, unlike Nadine, quick and slender, wrapped in a long coat with a high fur collar that hid all of her face except for her dark, glowing eyes, that looked at him for a moment. Thomas felt himself pierced by them.

The voice was gone. He turned back toward the altarpiece, in the hope of recapturing it. There was no sound; and when he looked back to the stairs, the girl too had vanished.

He felt weak. Something seemed to have been taken from him, some vital force. This was what Jesus must have sensed, when the woman with an issue of blood touched his garment, unseen, in the crowd. He gazed back at Riemenschneider's carving. Christ, with a pitying expression, held out the piece of bread to Judas, thus marking him as the one who would betray him. Thomas tried to identify the other apostles, with their curly wooden beards and long, carved hair. John, "he whom Jesus loved," was presumably closest to him, and his brother James, perhaps, on the bench alongside. The floorboards of the upstairs room were cut in section to allow a view into the three-dimensional carving. Was that Peter, with the bulging eyes and the clutched wineglass? In the panel on the left, Christ rode a tiny donkey into Jerusalem; on the right, with mountains in the background, he prayed in the Garden of Gethsemane.

Who were these primitive Galileans in their stiff robes? What had they to do with a church in Germany almost two thousand years later and with himself, living in the newest second of the present? They had doubtless imagined themselves to be the final word in humanity, as, at the moment they sat down to their supper, they were: like him, they rode the front edge of time into the darkness of the future. What he knew, and they could not have known, was that their species would change and that he, a modern man, would have developed in such a way that he was not human in quite the same way as they had been.

Looking at them, he saw beings in transition. One of them was endowed with a valued gift, which the others revered; but as he gazed at the muddled passions of the work of art, it seemed suddenly clear to Thomas what Christ's gift was. It was not that he was more developed or refined than the fishermen who were his Apostles; it was that he was less so. He alone possessed something their ancestors had lost: the power to hear voices and thus to commune with the unseen.

He looked again. What was so pathetic in the faces of Christ and of all the carved figures was their sense of absence. God was not there. Christ's eyes raked across the timber sky above Gethsemane, but he did not see Him. None of them had seen their god, and only one had heard him.

The physical absence of the god was the precondition of all religious faith. If the deity was there, self-evident, there would be no need for faith. But why was this the arrangement, thought Thomas; why should "faith" be necessary? The obvious course for a thinking god would have been to make himself observable, not to make his power dependent on belief in the unverifiable. The hypothesis that underlay religion was merely an argument from necessity, because there was no need for faith unless there was absence. The interesting question, then, was whether that "absence" was a caprice of an all-powerful deity or a real vacuum that followed a real presence: had someone or something actually vanished?

To put it another way, he thought: the situation that confronted him at that instant in Rothenburg was of a world in which millions of people worshipped something they could neither see nor hear. The explanation traditionally offered was that this not-being-there was central to the divine plan for human existence; that the world had either been created or had evolved with this childish paradox at its core. But suppose, he thought, that there was a simpler and more credible explanation: that the absence was real; that the conditions of life did not comprise some infantile test of "faith," but that something once present had genuinely disappeared.

Suppose that what had disappeared was the capacity to hear the voice or voices of the god. Once, all those fishermen would have heard a god; now only Christ could. For early humans separated from their group—the young man, for instance, dispatched to fish upstream—the ability to hear instructions, to produce under the influence of stress or fear the voice of the absent leader or god, had once been a necessary tool of survival; but as the capacity to remember and communicate through words had slowly developed, humans had lost the need for heard instruction and comment. The ability to do so had long since ceased to be important and was in fact now like the sightless eyes of bats—a vestigial ability. In this way the Bible all made sense, not as a ragbag of metaphor and myth, but as the literal story of a people crying in the wilderness for what once had been theirs. "I will lift up mine eyes unto the hills, from whence cometh my help." What was that if not the forlorn and agonized call of the solitary human whose once ever-present, helping voice had left him? He could picture the terrified, lone man, bent over his little bit of agriculture, looking up, craving a voice from the silent hillside.

Thomas felt quite calm as he gazed into the carving. At the beginning of the Bible, everyone—Noah, Abraham, Moses—seemed to hear God's voice externally; then it was heard only by a minority, who became priests; then the gift became rarer, so the infant Samuel could hear but the old priest Eli could not; and then by the time of the New Testament, Christ alone—and perhaps Paul—could hear voices.

Similarly, in the *Iliad* the heroes received their instructions direct from their many deities, from their individual and distinct voices; in the *Odyssey*, centuries later, the talking gods were in retreat: feeble, bickering and mocked by humans now capable of self-willed action. Penelope was faithful because she could choose to keep the idea of her absent husband alive in her "good" heart, not because she was thus vocally commanded by her goddess; and although Odysseus still listened to Athena, he had taken her inside himself as part of his own mental function; he could even—something impossible in the *Iliad*—outwit and deceive her. Indeed, deception, the very theme of the poem, was the hallmark of a developed being, able to make hypotheses of himself in different times and places. There were, it now seemed to Thomas, two interpretations of this development.

The first one, which he and the whole world had been taught, held that the bards whose accounts comprised the *Iliad* had used a literary device, a sort of metaphor, by which the dictates of conscience and will were personified into vocal debate and instruction from the audible gods. Their later followers in the *Odyssey* had lost faith in the multiplicity of gods, had grown tired of the poetic fancy of their elders and had opted for a more straightforward account of how the minds of human beings worked.

The second and simpler interpretation was that all the bards, old and young, told the stories as they happened. Achilles did hear Thetis. Moses heard Jehovah. Primitive men heard voices all the time and their ability to do so was critical to their success. Then, as they developed, they lost the need, and then the capacity, to do so. The change between the *Iliad* and the *Odyssey*, between aurally received instruction and greater independence of action, was not the result of a literary decision mysteriously communicated and agreed between illiterate bards over thousands of years. It was the story of what happened. Men of the *Iliad* era heard voices; those of the *Odyssey* could not.

If you looked at the two theories and balanced the probabilities, Thomas thought, there was no question as to which was more likely to be true.

THOMAS WALKED up into the main square of Rothenburg to look for Nadine Valade. His mind, as he walked over the cobbles and glanced around the half-timbered buildings with their red-tiled roofs, was elsewhere. He was thinking of his departed voice and of those less benign that afflicted Olivier and others like him.

He saw Nadine sitting at a café table beneath a colonnade, next to an expensive goldsmith's. She was drinking chocolate and swinging her plump leg back and forth over the arm of the chair, revealing her red-stockinged calf.

"You were ages in the church," she said. "It was so boring. All those wooden carvings. They are . . . macabre."

"That's an interesting word." Thomas sat down at the table and ordered coffee. "Who was that girl?"

"Which girl?"

"The girl in the church. About your age, wearing a fur coat. Dark eyes. Perhaps foreign."

"Has Monsieur the doctor taken a little fancy?"

"Don't be ridiculous, Nadine. She was a child."

"But she's lovely, is she not?"

"Who is she?"

Nadine's eyes sparkled in her round cheeks. "Buy me another chocolate and I will tell you."

When the waiter had obliged, Nadine leaned forward at the table and wiped some cream from her lips. "Well," she said, and Thomas smiled. She swallowed. "Well," she said again, "you remember that day we went down the river so Papa could do his painting? We met a Russian man in the restaurant where we had lunch and when he saw Papa's sketches, he wanted him to paint his portrait. He is very rich." Nadine's eyes widened. "He has a palace in St. Petersburg and a country estate."

"So we shall be staying in Rothenburg a little longer?"

"I think so. I like it here. Don't you?"

"Yes. But who is the girl?"

"When Papa went to the Russian's house, he met his wife and his daughter. The wife is from Persia. I think they met in Constantinople." Nadine rolled her eyes. "Can you imagine how romantic it must have been? The Russian prince and the beautiful lady from—"

"But who is the girl?"

"She is their daughter of course, you big silly! Her name is Roya. Roya Mihalova. Or Mikhailova. Or something Russian, I can't remember. They seem to have so many names."

Thomas looked at Nadine's happy face. Her mood would last for another hour or so, until after lunch, when she would be brought low by guilt about all that she had consumed; then she would either retire to her room and sulk or go quietly to the bathroom and try to make herself vomit.

"Is Roya your friend?"

"I have only met her twice. I went to visit them this morning, before church, with Papa. She is nice, but she is . . . strange. A bit frightening." Nadine giggled. "Where are we having lunch?"

"Back at the house. I have to give Gérard his massage. I told your mother we would be back by twelve thirty."

Nadine pulled a face. "I don't like the food there."

"So much the better. Come on."

PIERRE VALADE, Nadine's father, was an irascible man of whom
Thomas had become peculiarly fond. Valade slept badly and could not
bear to speak for the first hour of the day, while he drank cup after cup of
viscous coffee. He liked to go off alone into the open air with his easel
and paints, though Thomas suspected this was partly to escape the irri-
tations of family life, principally Madame Valade's incessant talking. At
lunchtime, when he usually returned to the family lodging, he often
painted over the canvas on which he had been working, returning it to
its blank state. He drank too much wine and slept in the afternoon, then
rose, ill-tempered, at five to work in his studio until eight. Then at last he
would commune with his family. He stroked Gérard's legs and massaged
his back; he teased Nadine about her playing of the piano and, emboldened by more wine, managed to still his wife's torrential conversation to
a manageable stream.

The Valade caravan had traveled through Heidelberg and Wiesbaden
before diverting to Rothenburg. Thomas protested that there were scores
of such picturesque towns in Germany, but Valade insisted that he wanted
to renew an acquaintance there. Although Thomas had been able to
attend lectures at the psychiatric clinic in Heidelberg, he worried that he
was not keeping up to date; at the university, they spoke with reverence of
a psychiatrist called Emil Kraepelin, a young man only a few years older
than Thomas himself, who was sure to rock the world on its axis, though
for some reason he had accepted a chair in Estonia. Thomas wrote to
Jacques, urging him to press on with his research while he carried out the
mundane job of filling their coffers with Kalaji's gold sovereigns, quantities of which awaited them by wire at every town they visited.

Jacques replied that he had been obliged, following his unforeseen
success with his thesis, to accept a position at the Salpêtrière. He had no
choice but to repay the investment of the hospital in his studies; as soon
as he could honorably extract himself, he would do so. He had spent the
three weeks before his appointment began in Nancy, where he had studied hypnotism under Bernheim. He had not told the staff at the
Salpêtrière about his visit, because Bernheim's view of hypnotism was
in direct and noisy contention with that of Charcot.

"As you know," Jacques concluded, "Charcot believes that only hysterics can be hypnotized. There are valuable lessons to be learned about the mechanism of hysteria from that of hypnosis. Bernheim, on the other hand, assures us that all people can be hypnotized and he is certainly impressive in being able to induce the state in people chosen at random, none of whom has any history of hysteria or any other neurological disorder. I have learned a lot here in Nancy. However, I think that Bernheim's view can be married to that of Charcot in an important way, which I shall not bother you with now, my dear friend!

"Sonia is very well and sends her love. Do not worry that you are turning into a 'money-machine.' We need every sou and I am doing enough research for two. Last night I had the strangest dream . . ."

THOMAS, TOO, was troubled by strange dreams, most of them concerning Roya Mikhailova, if that was her name. He dreamed he was in Torrington and had gone for a walk to the village duck pond on a hard-frozen day. As he stood among the weeds and looked down at the glassy surface, he glimpsed two dark eyes beneath the ice; he knelt down and tried to break the surface, to follow her, but with a flash of dark hair, she was gone. On another occasion, he was working in a field in Russia, mowing hay; he was exhausted and his back ached from the work. When he stopped for a moment to stretch, a carriage went rushing past, drawn by four galloping horses. He had a glimpse of a face at the carriage window, but he already knew whose it would be.

Night after night he went to sleep in his clean bedroom in the pink-distempered house in a backstreet of Rothenburg, knowing that soon he would see those dark eyes and that girlish figure with its redolence of Petersburg and Persia, of sherbet and frost, rubies and minarets, and sense beneath his fingers the feel of bare skin beneath fur in an open sleigh with horses stamping impatiently by torchlight for the order to depart.

When he awoke, he felt as though he had been touched by something immortal. It was frustrating because the condition of her presence was her evanescence, and it was shaming, because although the dreams were pure, there was something sinful tugging at their edge.

Thomas wondered if this image of Roya had lodged in his mind because he had seen her at the moment when he believed he had had, for the first time, a valuable thought of his own about the nature of the human mind. After years of plodding nowhere down the fetid corridor of the asylum, he had suddenly, when least looking for it, found illumination. In which case, there was nothing particular about the girl, it was merely the coincidence of timing which made the sight of her—the thought of her—a way of bringing his mind back to that moment when it had at last yielded a truth to him. So Roya was like the jan-gle of the horses' harnesses that, while meaningless in itself, roused the dogs to frenzy; or the taste of gooseberries, whose woolly tartness could transport him whole to childhood at the kitchen table at Torrington. The girl was no more than a trigger, or a password.

But it did not feel like that, however much his reason told him so. It felt as though she represented something universal; that she belonged to a world that existed beside his own, a place whose natural laws were transparent and where there was no yearning, only tranquillity and fulfillment. The curse of being human was to be granted glimpses of this place, in music, in dreams and through the power of imagination—but only glimpses because the reality, like the Promised Land from Moses, was forever withheld.

In the waking life of the family Valade, Thomas contrived to see Roya once, when he made an excuse to accompany Nadine to her friend's house. Their lodging was a good deal grander even than that provided by the Prince for the Valades: two footmen stood at the door, and there was no trace of either parent, a sure sign in Thomas's experience of unusual wealth. A German housekeeper accepted Nadine's coat and asked Thomas if he wished to take a cup of chocolate.

From upstairs, there was the sound of a violin, quite skillfully played, without the groaning scrape and wail of the beginner.

"That's Miss Roya," said the housekeeper, following his upward look.

"She plays well, doesn't she?"

"Very well. This way to the morning room, please, I shall bring the chocolate through presently."

"Goodbye, Thomas," said Nadine. She waved coquettishly as she made her way upstairs, presumably toward Roya's apartments, and he was certain that in her eye there was a teasing look: she was taunting him with her easy access to what he desired.

It was drafty and uncomfortable in the morning room and Thomas wished he had not chosen to stay. Eventually, he heard footsteps and the housekeeper entered with a cup of chocolate.

"Is there anything else I can fetch for you, Doctor? A newspaper?"

There was a note of concern in her voice, which could have been construed as insolence, he thought.

"No. No, thank you," he answered with the airiest charm he could conjure. "I shall just finish this, then I must be on my way."

The housekeeper withdrew, though he thought he saw a smirk on her face as she inclined her head.

Suddenly, there was a clatter on the ceramic tiles of the hallway and a sharp female cry. Thomas put down his cup and went outside.

Nadine and Roya were kneeling by a table which held an ormolu clock in a glass case. They were both laughing, but nervously. Nadine looked up, flushed.

"The cat . . ." she started to explain, then gave up because she was laughing. "It's . . . stuck!"

They were both kneeling on all fours by the table, and Thomas saw that a fat marmalade cat was attached to the collar of Roya's coat.

"We were dressing up the cat in doll's clothes and she got frightened. Her claws are caught. We were going to take her out for a walk."

"Would you like me to help?"

Nadine began to laugh again. "Are you frightened of cats?"

Thomas shook his head. "No, I think it's the cat who's frightened."

Roya was facing away from him toward the table; her green velvet dress was pulled up a little over the hips, so he could see the fine black stocking at her ankles above her buttoned boots. He knelt down and reached up to the cat, whose long claws were sunk into Roya's fur collar and hood.

"Keep still," he said, as he aligned himself behind her and took one of the cat's paws. He squeezed it to release the claws and told Nadine to hold the animal's leg away from the coat so it could not reengage its grip. Then he leaned across Roya's back and released the other claw; with no grip in its rear feet the cat was easily removed.

Thomas stood up and moved back with the cat in his arms.

"Let's go," said Nadine, helping Roya to her feet.

By the time she turned to face him, Roya had pulled the rest of her coat on and raised the hood, so he saw little more than the flash of her eyes and the trace of blood subsiding beneath the skin of her cheek as she disappeared onto the street.

THE VALADES' journey was extended to a full year and Thomas drifted to Vienna with them. At the poste restante, there was a letter from Sonia.

Dearest Thomas,

We read your last letter with interest. Jacques was very excited from the beginning by your idea of the voices, so it was good to read more about it. Of course, it has a poignancy for him because of his brother. How you set about demonstrating the truth of your theory and quite what it means, if anything, for us today, I do not quite know. But I expect you do!

We are still living at Madame Maurel's, very frugally, so Jacques is saving money from his private practice, which is going very well. His patients seem to be nervous young women for the most part, rather well-off and beautiful, but I try not to mind. Jacques is happy, I think, but to tell the truth I am a little worried about him.

He works all the hours of the day in a kind of frenzy. He is still the same lovely kind man, of course, and he is faultlessly tender and solicitous toward his wife. I look forward to our evenings together—or to be more accurate, I look forward to our nights together, because that is almost the only time he can spare me. In return for giving private lessons in anatomy, he receives four hours' tuition a week in German from a young student in the rue d'Assas. I go as well for the conversational practice on Wednesday, but Jacques is doing it properly with grammars and textbooks—and with remarkable results. In the evening, after

bolting down Madame Maurel's dinner, he reads in German
until the early hours, when he comes to bed at last. (I sometimes
pass the hours playing the piano with little Mademoiselle
Tavernier.) J assures me that what he has read is opening up
whole new worlds for him. He is still, I know, a disciple of the
blessed Charcot at heart, but he says that German is the
language of the new sciences.

Naturally, he wants to join you in Germany or Austria and he
now feels that another twelve months is all he need spend at the
Salpêtrière to repay what he calls their investment in his
education. He walks with a great spring in his step these days. I
think that his successes mean that at last he feels accepted by the
academic and medical world from which he previously felt
excluded. He told me he always expected to be "found out," as
though he were some kind of impostor, but now I think he feels
that his own thoughts and experiences are as valid as anyone's.
It is not that he is arrogant or ever could be, but he seems to live
in a state of constant euphoria—his feet hardly touch the
ground—as though the excitement of the ideas in his head
makes him float or exist on a higher plane than the rest of the
world.

I feel proud to be married to such a man and I love him more
than ever, though I do feel anxious for him. At the very least, I
wish he would get a little more sleep. I also wish he would see
you again, as I think you are a good influence. I never thought I
would write those words about my wild young brother, but I
suppose these things—self-restraint, moderation and so forth—
are comparative!

Paris is enchanting as ever and the French as mysterious as
always: private, discreet, and entirely uninterested in the world
beyond Alsace-Lorraine or the Pyrenees. Their country is a
universe to them, and those who would have it otherwise are
met not with argument or rebuttal but only with a long, pitying
stare. I love it here, though; I love the streets, the buildings, the
paintings in the museums; and I have learned many delicious

new receipts which I hope to practice on you when we meet
again. Let it be soon, dear Thomas.

      Your affectionate sister, Sonia

The following spring, Jacques received a letter from Abbé Henri to say
that his father was dying and was not expected to last the month.
Jacques made the necessary arrangements with the Salpêtrière and set
off in the train with Sonia for Brittany. They stopped on the way to collect Olivier from his asylum, but by the time the three of them arrived at
Saint Agnès it was too late: the cancer had moved rapidly through old
Rebière's body and he had died in his bed two days earlier, his passing
somewhat eased by the quantities of morphia Abbé Henri had been able
to procure for him.

    The body was still lying in the upstairs room on a fragile catafalque,
and Tante Mathilde sat on a rush-seated chair beside it, a handkerchief
clasped in her fist.

    Old Rebière's face was strained by death, and the flesh was reduced
by its long struggle; with his black necktie and hanging jaw, he looked
like one of the men in the back wards of Olivier's asylum, Jacques
thought. The father he remembered was not there in the coffin and he
found it irritating that this corpse should guy him so foolishly.

    Nevertheless, he felt reluctant to see him lowered into the grave.
Even an empty body was a kind of presence, and what he wanted was
more certainty. They could bury him, and in three days' time he could
come and dig him up; he could prop him up again in his bed as primitive
civilizations did with their dead leaders, unable to comprehend that
something vital was missing.

    In any case, what exactly had gone? When he was alive and Jacques
was in Paris, he was not there. When they were both in Saint Agnès, but
Jacques was out in the fields, he was equally missing. Most of the days
and hours of Jacques's life had been spent away from him, so in what
significant sense had death made his father more absent than before?

    Olivier seemed quite calm at the sight of his dead father. He stroked
the hair back from his waxy forehead, then lifted up the right arm and

examined the hand with fierce attentiveness. When he had seen all he needed to see, he walked over to the window.

Abbé Henri officiated at the mass the next morning. A handful of villagers were gathered, rubbing their hands together for warmth in the icy church. There were one or two old people Jacques recognized from childhood but whose names he could not remember; his father's employer had not made the journey from Lorient. Abbé Henri spoke of Rebière's lifelong connection with the landscape; he extolled his love of the country and his understanding of traditional ways. "His thrift and patriotism placed him in a noble tradition of French countrymen, though I know the accolade he would have sought, and which I think he deserved, was to be considered a true Breton. He was not a demonstrative man, but he had his passions and his beliefs. I know that he feared God and that in the end, when he made his last confession to me, he placed his trust in the Almighty."

What choice did he have? thought Jacques. His father was a man who had not lifted his gaze from the landscape of his birth; his existence had been that of the crab under the rock, while before him the sea lay unregarded. He might as well submit to the idea of a divine purpose now—now that he was to go beneath the sod, back into the land, because, at this moment, as they filed slowly from the church, there was no better explanation available to human thought. A sense of purpose was what he and the other mourners craved, faced with this block, this meaty absence, that weighed on his and Oliver's shoulders as they carried the coffin out into the churchyard. If God could provide purpose, then they had better turn to Him.

They stood by the grave, the wet grass lapping over their polished shoes. The church was on top of the hill, and in the distance Jacques could make out the gray, mist-covered sea. As Abbé Henri read the final prayers, Jacques put his arm round Sonia's shoulder to his right and, to his left, round Olivier's. He pulled them to him with the strength of his grasp, so that they might make a common bulwark of their energies against the void, and he felt the squeeze of their returned embrace. The gulls let out their indifferent cries, and Jacques found his eyes boring into a small knot of wood in the fence post at the edge of the graveyard. He pictured its tiny molecules in ceaseless agitation while his father's life had stopped. He could not believe that, God's purpose having been fulfilled, He had gathered His faithful servant to His bosom again, but he had no better explanation to offer and could only stare ahead, at the knot in the wood, with a sense of numb ignorance.

He noticed afterward what guilty pleasure he took in being alive. Something had happened which none of the mourners could explain, and when the funeral was over, they all became conspirators. They had gone through the rituals with due formality; they had been kinder about the dead man than he deserved; they had done everything they could to speed him on his way to some sort of afterlife that lay beyond their powers of conjecture. Then, shuddering with relief, like guilty children, they acted as though it had never happened; they pretended that it had no bearing at all on their own lives or on their ability to carry on. Because they could not understand death, they shoveled the responsibility for grappling with it onto others—poor widow, bereaved child, chastened old people closer now to death themselves—anyone at all, so long as they could put it out of their own minds. What frauds they all were, he thought.

Jacques watched Sonia making lunch for his family and the villagers who had come to join them. He loved the practical way that she took control of the kitchen, deferring to Tante Mathilde, but organizing it herself; he saw how her fascinated eyes took in all the details of his childhood home, and it made him feel happier than he could easily explain. He heard her laugh and then he heard the same sound coming from his own throat. They were laughing behind his father's back, he thought, but he could not see what else he was to do.

After they had been back in Paris for about two weeks, he found that he began to dream about his father almost every night, and in his dreams it transpired that there had been a mistake. Old Rebière was not dead; he had somehow survived the cancer and was still alive, albeit in a precarious state. There was something a little suspicious about these dreams, something unreliable that Jacques could sense even as he dreamed; but the central fact, though surprising, was irrefutable: there he was, alive.

During the day he could easily hear his father speaking inside his head, any time he chose to imagine him. He was alive in his memory and in his inner ear; he knew what his father would say or do in any situation. He had never been more present than now that he was dead, and Jacques wanted there to be a clearer distinction. This was not the dramatic decease he had imagined death to be, and it was for that reason unsatisfactory and hard to bear.

Come back to me, father, he muttered to himself; come back and put your arms round me as you never did in my life; take me to your heart—or else go away and let me go forward with my life alone.

THOMAS AWOKE one morning in May in a guesthouse in Carinthia, a mountain-locked province of Austria-Hungary, to which Monsieur Valade had been drawn by an idea of lakes and mountain views. There were white rolls and jam for breakfast, laid out on a table in the deserted dining room, where Thomas ate alone. There was no sign of the Valade family until ten, when Monsieur Valade arrived in a pony and trap with two bicycles.

It transpired that Madame Valade had risen early to take the children boating on the Wörther See, and Valade had decided to explore the countryside and take Thomas with him. They rode off a few minutes later, with painting materials stuffed into rucksacks on their backs. In the afternoon, they stopped to drink from a narrow stream that ran down the pine-covered hillside.

Valade looked about him with a quizzical eye. "It is too picturesque," he said. "Too many ravines and yellow cottages with irritating coils of smoke. Let us go on."

It was growing dark, and Thomas was exhausted from the unaccustomed pedaling.

"Where is the map?" said Valade. "May I see it?"

"You have it," said Thomas. "After we stopped by the stream, you put it in your pocket."

Each searched his belongings, looking disbelievingly at the other, but between them they could find no map.

"It makes no difference," said Thomas. "It is easy enough to orientate ourselves from the sun and the mountains. We started in the valley over—"

"We were not in the valley. The guesthouse was halfway up a hill."

"Perhaps. But not as high as we are now. The sun is going down to the west."

"Surprise me, Doctor."

"So Vienna is to the northeast, which is . . . that way. And that means Bad Ischl, where we all drank that unpleasant water, is over there."

"And where did we start from this morning?"

"I have not the faintest idea. We are in Carinthia somewhere. There are mountains. Lower down, there are lakes. I have money in my pocket."

"So do I. We should find somewhere to spend the night. We could have dinner. A quiet dinner, with little conversation."

"I understand what you mean," said Thomas. "Let us go . . . Let us go west, toward the setting sun."

"Why?"

"Because it is downhill."

After an hour of pedaling, they came to a run of rustic houses which thickened into a village; at the center was a triangle of grass. They went down one of the roads that led from it, and on the rising ground they saw the sign of a guesthouse, attached to a timber-framed building with magenta-painted walls.

Valade's face lit up with an unaccustomed smile. "It is exactly like the one we left this morning."

They leaned their bicycles against the wall and went inside. There was no one in the small wood-paneled hall, and Thomas called out to attract attention. Eventually, a young woman dressed in the full, pleated skirt and embroidered sleeveless jacket of the region emerged through a swing-door. She seemed slightly puzzled that any travelers might want to spend the night in the guesthouse, but willing enough to oblige; she showed them upstairs to a plain room with starchily clean sheets and red geraniums in its window boxes.

"We would also like to eat," said Thomas, taking charge, since Valade spoke no German.

"Of course. Maybe you would care to take a drink in the garden before dinner." The girl curtsyed and left them.

"What did she say?" asked Valade.

"She said she will serve dinner, but not to a Frenchman, only to her friend the Englishman. The only good thing the French have ever done, she said, was to surrender to the Prussians at Sedan."

"What an uncommonly well-educated woman," said Valade.

Thomas led the way into the garden, where beer was brought to them by a second girl, dark-haired, but dressed in the same way as the other.

"Now this is something I could paint," said Valade, pointing to the view over a narrow valley.

"Why this?" said Thomas.

"You would never be able to find this place again. It is entirely individual, yet at the same time it seems to represent or suggest the countryside we have been traveling through all day. It is one thing and everything." He drank from his glass of beer. "Perhaps that is what art is, Doctor."

Thomas looked ahead, over the grass and a chicken run behind, to the obtuse triangle of pine forest, some meadows with a dozen or so cows motion-less in the dusk and beyond them, an ascent into hills with a gray line of water going over sharp rocks. There was only one building in the entire view: an ocher-painted schloss, half-hidden on the horizon.

"I shall stay for three days until I have it right," said Valade.

"What about Madame Valade?"

"Sophie? She will not worry. I left her for a week once and I am not sure she even noticed I had gone. She knows there is money in the drawer."

The dark-haired waitress returned and told them what was for dinner. Thomas translated. "You can start with sheep's lung soup or clear soup with liver-dumplings. Then it is something that translates as 'battle-plate.' I believe it a mixture of grilled meats. 'Slaughter-plate' might be a better translation."

"Which animal? The pig?"

"The cow, I imagine. Perhaps a little of each."

"What a poetic country. 'The slaughter-plate.' Tell the young lady— no, tell 'the flesh-thing' I shall be delighted. And bring their best red wine. The prince would have us drink nothing less."

They were alone in the dining room, the dim candles making it hard to see which part of the animal they were devouring: sausage, liver or rump. The wine was elegant but rich. "This is how burgundy tasted when I was a child," said Valade.

Afterward, there was a thick pancake with dried fruit, of a kind loved by the kaiser. The two waitresses watched them as they ate, their eyes running up and down in candid appraisal.

"Do you think they like what they see?" said Thomas.

Valade snorted. "I had girls like that every night when I was a student. They just wanted someone to pay their rent and take them dancing."

"But why are they staring?"

"I could not say, Doctor. Perhaps they are intimating that they would like to share your bed. They would like you to take them both, then watch while they amuse each other. Or perhaps they are just curious about two strangers. But you will never know, will you? So many women . . ."

Thomas felt melancholy when he went upstairs to the bedroom. He was kept awake first by the coffee he had drunk to settle the huge dinner, then by Valade's snoring. There was light coming through the rustic shutters when he finally fell asleep and dreamed of Roya Mikhailova, dressed in riding clothes, being stolen from him by Valade and driven into the night while he ran after them through glue, shouting silently.

In the morning, Valade set up his easel in the garden. He told Thomas he wanted to attempt something in the style of Corot. He was much taken by the Barbizon school, but disliked the Impressionists, whom he blamed for having created an appetite for instant sensation in landscape which his own work was not equipped to satisfy. "I shall see you at dinner," he said meaningfully.

Thomas took a bottle of water and put some bread rolls and ham from breakfast in his jacket pocket. Then he set off on his bicycle, heading toward the ocher-colored schloss he had seen on the horizon. It was late afternoon by the time he found it. The road through the trees suddenly cleared and he found himself looking down on an extraordinary building.

To the traditional Carinthian country house or schloss was attached a newer part, an enormous rectangular courtyard, with a smaller court at one end and what appeared to be a kind of hall or meeting room at the other; it was joined to the old house by a covered cloister. The windows were shuttered and barred; the grass of the substantial gardens had long been left uncut. Attached to the chain that guarded the double front doors was a notice with the address of a lawyer in the nearest large town.

The dilapidation, the scale and the neglect suggested the place was without prospect of an owner; its enchanted position, its peace and grandeur made Thomas certain that he had found the site of his life's work.

IX

JACQUES AWOKE ONE MORNING IN SONIA'S EMBRACE. THE RAIN was pattering on the glass of Madame Maurel's dormer window, and beyond it he had a view of the glistening slate mansards of the Latin Quarter. For once, he took no pleasure in the feeling of Sonia's warm flanks beneath her nightdress nor in the black roofscape with its jutting angles and wisps of tired chimney smoke.

His mind was occupied by the dream that had ended a few moments earlier. The narrative was clear, the emotions complex and, for the most part, delightful. He went back to the start and let it rerun through his waking mind. In his father's house in Saint Agnès, he was lying wrapped in the embrace of a young, strange and exotically beautiful woman. They were not making love, but their embrace was sensual and possessive; it was certain that they were destined to be together. As they lay entwined—in Grand-mère's room, for some reason—the door opened and Sonia came in. Jacques felt confused. He was right to be with the strange young woman, yet here was his wife—to whom he was unequivocally devoted. How could this be?

He ran down the village street to the blacksmith's, where he found Olivier lying in a pool of blood on the ground, surrounded by a ghoulish crowd. Charcot stood above the dead body with the smith's hammer in his hand, proclaiming his responsibility for the murder. At his feet were the remains of several glass test tubes which he said he had found in

Jacques's room. "It's better this way," said Charcot. "Now go back to school, Jacques."

In the schoolroom, Sonia kissed him, and he awoke with an immense feeling of forgiveness and with tears of relief on his cheeks, feeling that something had been completed and resolved.

This dream, he felt sure, was not just a random assembly of images. Without knowing it, he had been profoundly anxious about something and his dream had removed that troubled knot. Could you be relieved of a distress of which you had been unconscious? Everything he had understood in his studies under Charcot told him that you could. The chances of such a cogent and beautifully therapeutic dream having arisen at random seemed absurdly slight, while the arguments to the contrary, though hypothetical, were compelling. In an essay he had just finished reading, Schopenhauer argued that the intellect organizes sense impressions it receives during the day in the only way it knows how: by time and space and cause. So many are the external stimuli of the busy day, however, that the mind has no time for the murmurings of the sympathetic nervous system. With the body asleep, however, and no news coming in from outside, this internal information at last gains access to the intellect, which organizes what it receives as best it can, along its same limited lines. In a development of this idea, Hildebrandt, a writer he also found convincing, argued that one of the main side effects of sleep was to remove a daytime censor who prevented immoral thoughts from reaching consciousness; and the Frenchman Maury had agreed that once a man's waking will was removed he became, in dreams, the plaything of the thoughts and desires he could only suppress by day.

This, Jacques thought, made fair physiological sense; more difficult to resolve was the question of why and how dreams disguised what they were trying to say. Did they always have an exact language or code? Perhaps not all dreams were meaningful; perhaps the messages of the nervous system were unclear and the poor brain could only do its best with the rough material it was offered.

The simplest fact, however, was to him the most convincing. In a hypothetical model of a human, you would expect the brain to sleep along with the rest of the body; for it to work away all night was bizarre. Because we dream from infancy, he thought, we accept the function as axiomatic, but in fact it is against objective probability. And mechanisms which survived millions of years against logical expectation did so for only one reason that he knew: they were favored by natural selection because they served a purpose. Non-dreamers had become extinct.

So he placed the dream at the side of his mind, where the functions of interpretation could do their slow work over the coming days, while he got out of bed, dressed and went out to his work at the hospital. If he might one day use dreams as a route into the unconscious minds of his patients, it would be a good idea if he began by analyzing his own, and a week later, he felt he had finally understood what the dream was telling him. The beautiful young woman—so strange to him yet so at home in the house—was his mother. He had until now felt unworthy of Sonia and unsure of her deep affection because Sonia had never met his mother. Equally, his mother had never blessed the match. He had wondered guiltily whether his physical desire for Sonia was based on some ideal of womanhood represented by his mother. In the dream, Sonia had told him that even if this were the case, it was permissible, and that tender feelings for two women could exist together.

The second part of the dream was more perplexing, until he saw that Charcot, the older man of authority, resident in Saint Agnès, was not himself but a representation of the true father-figure, old Rebière. Presumably the test tubes served some crude symbolic purpose, and Charcot/Rebière's smashing of the tools of Jacques's trade showed his resentment of the way his son had abandoned him and tried to assert his superior virility by moving up in the social hierarchy. More particularly, it illustrated Jacques's guilt at having done so. This guilt was connected to Olivier, and this was the tightest knot to untangle. Jacques eventually concluded that, however much his daytime censor had stamped out the thought, he must at some time have wished Olivier dead, because he blamed him for the death of their mother; or at least if he did not actually blame him, he was murderously jealous of Olivier for having known her. In this light, he could see that his own overpowering ambitions as a doctor sprang not so much from his professed desire to find a cure for Olivier and his like, but from a determination to show to both his father and his brother that he had no need of them, and in fact was better off with both of them dead.

If this was true, he unhappily concluded, then it must follow that his discoveries and the fame that followed them would be a kind of revenge on the two of them for having enjoyed the privilege that he himself had most desired—that of knowing his mother.

WHEN JACQUES said goodbye to the Salpêtrière in the spring of 1890, there were motorcars on the streets of Paris and he was thirty years old. He felt as though he needed to run faster each day to keep ahead of the changes he saw about him. No sooner had the German sage Wilhelm Wundt declared that "psychology" was to be a new discipline, not merely an offshoot of philosophy, than an American called William James was said already to have published the definitive book on it. Jacques cabled the publisher in New York for a copy and left instructions with Madame Maurel that she was to send it on to him in Carinthia as soon as it arrived.

Although she had been impatient to leave, Sonia found herself reluctant, at the last moment, to say goodbye to the boardinghouse in whose attic rooms her life had been refound. She shook hands with Madame Tavernier and her pug-faced daughter and wished them well; she felt Pivot's scaly hands grip her wrists as he kissed her on both cheeks. For Carine, who was nowhere to be seen, she left an envelope with a small sum of money.

The contents of their room were squeezed into a trunk and three suitcases, which were piled onto the back of the cab that took them to the Gare de l'Est; Sonia intended to have more clothes and some furniture sent out from Torrington when they arrived. When they finally settled onto the train, she sat back with a sigh that was too full of anticipation to be called contented. From a handbag, she took the photographs of the schloss that Thomas had sent her from Carinthia. She was excited by the possibilities they offered, and anxious to make her mark on the place as soon as possible. Thomas had negotiated the terms of the lease and instructed some builders in structural repair work, but she did not trust him with the interior; if it were left to him, he would simply

have the patients' rooms whitewashed and some cheap brass numbers
nailed to the doors.

"He has taken a lot of photographs, hasn't he?" said Jacques.

"Yes. He has a new camera. It has a hundred pictures on a roll and
apparently when you've finished you just send the whole thing back to
them to develop."

"I like the building. It looks beautiful."

"It has possibilities." Sonia smiled.

The train rattled on toward Alsace; the landscape through the flashing window became hilly, then covered with pine trees as France began
to roll out into Germany, while Sonia closed her eyes against the gentle
rocking of the carriage. There was another, more profound, more fragile
reason for her joy, but she did not feel she could yet tell Jacques: a providence that had appeared first cruel, then contrary, should not be provoked. She crossed her fingers, nevertheless, over her lower abdomen,
and as night began to fall over the Vosges mountains she could not help
but picture the life that she believed was stirring beneath her hands. She
felt her womb lift up and flood with love toward the being who was growing unbidden, all unseen inside her.

THE JOURNEY took them three days, traveling far to the east because
the Alps barred their straighter route into Carinthia. They left Munich
after dinner on the second day and arrived early the next morning in
Vienna, tired and rattled by the ceaseless jarring of the train. They wired
ahead from the post office to warn Thomas of their arrival; Sonia imagined him airing the beds and instructing the housekeeper to prepare her
best supper, though she had little idea what the cooking would be like.
She studied the map in Baedeker and ticked off the names as the local
train crawled through the rustic stations, puffing idly while the Carinthi-
ans piled on board with their baskets of eggs and string-wrapped parcels
of ham and cheese, pushing Jacques and her, exhausted, into the corner
of the carriage. She had a moment of anxiety: they seemed to be traveling away from Paris, discovery, Pasteur and the first nights of Debussy,
into an autochthonous peasant world ringed by mountains, drenched in
ignorance. She glanced anxiously at Jacques and hoped he was not

regretting the move, but he was gazing from the window, apparently fascinated by what he saw, and she recognized that, however he had been changed by the intellectual blizzard he had weathered in Paris, he was still faithful to the vision he had shared with Thomas that night on the beach at Deauville—a vision that was now only a few minutes away from becoming real.

At the busy mainline station, they were met by a tall, cadaverous man who introduced himself as Josef, the lampman at the schloss; he wore a black felt hat with a curling brim and a dented crown. He brought apologies from Dr. Midwinter, who had been called to see a patient in the village, but would be back in time for dinner. "The Executioner," Sonia silently christened Josef, as he loaded their baggage onto the roof of the closed trap and invited them to climb inside. It took another hour and a half before at last, as the dusk was throwing shadows at their feet, they had their first glimpse of the schloss.

Sonia gripped Jacques's arm; only a grim effort of self-control prevented her from telling him that it was in this ocher-painted house with its white plaster decorations and red tile roof, with its comfortable evocation of Torrington but its own distinct and foreign character—that it was here that she would bear his child. She ran into the large hall and called out for Thomas. He emerged from behind a plain oak door, the last on the right, and came striding over the stone flags, gathering her in his arms and lifting her off her feet.

"Let me show you upstairs," he said when the greetings were over. "I have made arrangements for you and Jacques to have the rooms on this side, so you will have a view toward the mountains from your sitting room."

"Is that a gray hair?" said Sonia, running up the broad staircase to keep up with him.

"I hope not," said Thomas, reaching to the side of his head. "I instructed the barber to get rid of any. Here. This is your apartment. Do you like it?"

Sonia walked up and down, through the four connected rooms which ran from east to west across one half of the house. The polished wooden boards needed more rugs and some of the fruitwood furniture was not to her taste, yet the suite as a whole, light and touched by a resigned, family elegance, filled her with such joy that she could not answer. In her mind, she had made the east room into a nursery, had repainted it and installed a rocking horse; she wondered if she would be close enough to hear the baby when he cried at night.

"Well?" said Thomas. "Queenie, I am going to expire if you will not tell me. I have taken such a risk for all our sakes. I have spent so much money too. And you trusted me to do it. Please tell me if I have made a terrible mistake."

Still Sonia could not speak, so she laid her head on Thomas's chest and held him tightly to her. Small tears were squeezed from her closed eyes and she wondered if it was wise to be this happy. Thomas stroked her hair and smiled; he pressed her no further about what she thought.

When they went downstairs, Sonia was surprised to find that they were not alone for dinner. Thomas's most recent letter had told them about the people he had engaged to help at the schloss, but it had not arrived by the time they left Paris, so he was obliged to explain their function as well as introduce them.

In addition to Josef, who was in charge of the horses, the grounds and the outside buildings, there was a scarlet-faced woman called Frau Egger, who was the housekeeper, and a young man called Hans on whose employment Frau Egger's appeared to be conditional.

"I would also like you to meet two friends of mine who arrived from England last week. This is Daisy, who is going to start off as a maid, at least until we have engaged some more people. And this is Mary, who came with her. Mary is blind, but she is anxious to be of service and I have started to train her in the art of massage, at which she shows considerable aptitude."

Daisy shook hands with Sonia. "I have heard so much about you, Miss, when I was in . . . that place."

"Indeed," said Sonia remembering Daisy's photograph. "It is extremely good to meet you also."

Frau Egger brought in a tureen of soup and they began to eat. The dining room took up two thirds of one side of the house, the remaining third being given to the kitchens and scullery.

"Everyone could eat in here," said Thomas. "I think we can sit sixty with ease and I doubt whether we will have more than fifty patients."

"How many more staff shall we need?" said Sonia.

"A great deal," said Thomas. "We shall probably need a nurse to every two patients and many more domestic staff. It is a very large establishment, as you will see in the morning. The courtyard has twenty-two rooms on the higher level and fourteen on the ground floor. I wanted Jacques to be here, though, before I took on any medical people and, Sonia, if you still agree then you shall be in charge of the domestic side."

"She talked of nothing else all the way from Paris," said Jacques fondly. "Now let us drink a toast to the schloss and to its success. To the health of our patients and the prosperity of our venture."

"Hans," said Thomas. "Will you please bring more wine?"

Sonia had a slight headache the next morning, but it did not stop her being down to breakfast at eight and then beginning her inspection.

The schloss had originally been built, Thomas explained, two hundred years earlier, as an abbey. The main house was built in a traditional style to house the abbot, clearly a man of self-importance. A chapel with a rectangular courtyard, about seventy meters long and thirty across, and two smaller courts had been attached to the house by a covered cloister, but a hundred years later a fire had destroyed the chapel and damaged other buildings. The property, after being deconsecrated, had passed through two families before being bought by a coffee merchant from Trieste in 1862; he had repaired and rebuilt the principal courtyard and restored such of the smaller ones as had been damaged. He had envisaged turning part of it into a concert hall and theater, but had died before he was able to begin the work. Thomas had bought a lease of ten years from his heir, a nephew, at advantageous terms dependent on their paying for repairs and improvements themselves.

The main house revolved about the great, stone-flagged hall. On the north side of it, opposite the dining room, were four rooms of approximately equal size which would act as waiting room, office and two consulting rooms; the broad, uncarpeted stairs swept up to a landing that ran the width of the building in each direction: Jacques and Sonia's apartment was to the south; the rooms on the north could be allotted to Thomas and to various staff. The walls were painted in white distemper and many had waist-high oak paneling; despite the simplicity of design, there were unexpected turns in the corridors and half-flights of stairs, where among the Biedermeier furnishings a wooden calvary might suddenly appear framed in a recess, or an old wine press would be serving as an ornamental table. Downstairs, double doors opened out from beneath the main staircase onto the cloister behind.

"It is peculiar," said Sonia, running her hand over the wainscot. "Despite the size, it feels like a family house. How long had it been empty?"

"About five years. They were relieved to find a taker. The only other possibility was to turn it into a hotel. Beneath the cloister here are enormous wine cellars which I thought we could make into laboratories. Now we come through this gate here into the main courtyard. The grass needs cutting and the fountain has stopped, but the buildings are in good repair."

This part of the schloss, it seemed to Sonia, was like a large house that had been unfolded and turned inside out, so that instead of the rooms being joined together, back-to-back and looking out, they were only half-attached to one another and could therefore look in over the central lawn as well as out toward the lake on one side or the mountains in the west.

"Obviously the rooms on the first floor have a much better view," said Thomas, "but that is an advantage because we can charge more for them. And it is ideal to have all this space on the ground floor for people who cannot climb stairs. We want to let some of these rooms go free to cases we take from the asylums."

"Will your rich ladies mind eating with the lunatics?"

"Tact, my dear Sonia. We shall find a way. We cannot just serve what you call rich ladies. Nor is it merely Christian charity to take on others; it is scientific, because among the poor we may find more interesting cases. Come this way. Here is one of my favorite parts."

A smaller courtyard opened from the southern end of the main one, its white walls covered in creeper and its inward-looking wooden shutters splattered crimson with geraniums growing from the window boxes. In the center was a small square of grass with a stone fountain.

"Peaceful, is it not?" said Thomas.

"Very calming. I feel my health improving just by being here."

"I have called it South Court on the plan I gave the builder. Prosaic, I know, but I wanted no mistakes. And this even smaller one here, which has only six rooms around it, with that lovely iron wall-lamp in the corner, I called it—"

"Did you call it Lamp Court?"

"I did, Sonia, I did. And that is how the builder knew to leave it all alone because it was quite untouched by the fire."

"Thomas, you have done very well."

"There is more to show you."

"That is all I can take in for the time being."

"Does Jacques like it?"

"I have never seen him so happy. He cannot wait for his first patients."

"There is no need for him to wait. The sooner we begin, the sooner our fame will spread. We will hire more staff as the need arises. I have taken on a clinic at the town hospital each Tuesday. Perhaps Jacques should too—it is a way of meeting people, and I know that the hospital would be happy to have another doctor, particularly one so distinguished."

They walked back together over the cobbled yard, down the cloister and back into the main house, where they found Jacques installing his books in one of the consulting rooms.

"I have had a letter already," he said, grinning as he held up a blue envelope from the pile on the circular table in the hall. "A colleague at the Salpêtrière has referred two private patients who need rest and quiet. He asks if we have room."

"I think we might," said Thomas. "And I have a referral in three weeks' time from the hospital in town. They could become a good supply for us, though we need also to make a connection with Vienna. When you are settled, Jacques, you and I must go and try to make our mark there."

"Yes," said Jacques. "I have been thinking about that. I feel certain that the quickest way to reach people is to give a paper to a medical society."

"And you have just such a paper in your jacket pocket?"

"It is not finished yet, but I have a draft. It contains the fruits of all my reading and research in Paris."

"More Charcot, then?"

"No, not really. It is based on what I have read in German. And on a remarkable French doctor who arrived in Paris last year from Le Havre. A man called Janet."

"But you are not forsaking our old master?"

"Oh no. On the contrary. It all fits together. That is what is so exciting about it. Will you pass me that box of books over there?"

"Are you happy with this room?" said Thomas, handing up some tattered calf-bound volumes to Jacques, who stood on a small stepladder. "You can have the end room if you prefer it."

"They are identical," said Jacques. "So far as I can see. So you and I are side by side, looking north. Is that north?"

"Yes it is. The steady north light that my Monsieur Valade always required. I think he will bring his family in the summer, too."

"What? All of them? Are they all sick?"

"Yes." Thomas laughed. "The girl has an eating disorder, the boy infantile paralysis and the wife is the worst afflicted. She has chronic logorrhea."

"And the father?"

"He is just angry."

"We must not become a hotel, Thomas."

"I know. But a clinic for people with nervous disorders must be flexible in whom it admits. At least until we are full up and profitable. Anyway, I like Valade."

"I understand. And we must make sure they eat well. Food is vital for nervous patients."

"Of course. That is where your wife will play her part. I saw her talking to Frau Egger this morning. I am not sure she understood much of Sonia's schoolroom German, but it was a start."

"I need a desk," said Jacques. "I have a chair but nothing to put my feet up on when I am making a wise diagnosis."

"There is more furniture at the far end of the main courtyard. I suppose we shall have to buy some at auction in town. Sonia may have an opinion."

"I think she will."

The echoing spaces of the main house began to fill with the sound of movement. Josef hired men from the village to fetch the furniture that had been stored in the North Hall; beds, armchairs and tables were redistributed among the empty rooms to the background noise of hammering and castors running over floorboards. The big range in the kitchen was riddled, fired and set to work, while the huge cylindrical heaters in their painted ceramic jackets were readied for the cool evenings. Boys were brought in to scythe the long grass, and after every hour of work they lined up outside the kitchen in the stable yard for drinks to be handed through the window; the lawns in the courtyards were mown and rolled; with long coaxing, the main fountain was made to throw up a spout of rusty water, which, after several noisy eructations, eventually calmed itself and ran clear into its carved stone basin. Water hoses were trained on the inside of the stable block, while the mare and the gelding stood outside and stamped on the cobbles, cropping hay from the iron manger. When the men had finished with the furniture, they were handed paint and brushes and sent to work on the stable doors; many of them were accompanied by their wives and daughters, who brought down cobwebs from the high ceiling of the hall, polished the wide expanse of wooden flooring and threw open the windows of the bedrooms to air the mattresses, while others washed and dried the sheets in the scullery below. In the kitchen, Frau Egger set her largest pots on the stove, from which, with Daisy's help, she was able to keep a running table of bread, soup and sausage available to the workers as they passed the dining room or sat down in the hall to rest.

For two weeks, the house and grounds, supervised by Sonia, were on the move; the company of helpers ran through the arteries of the extended body like red cells in a convalescent patient. Color and function began to return; the old courtyards stirred themselves and the shuttered windows opened their eyes onto the lake and the cold mountains. Meanwhile Thomas and Jacques each morning took the horse and trap into the city, where they set about trying to find patients. At the hospital, they arranged for Jacques to run a free clinic specializing in neurological cases; if the demand was low, he was to act also as consultant physician. They went to see the editor of the local newspaper and organized for him to send a reporter to the schloss to write an article about their renovation of the house and their projected clinic. For many hours they sat in a coffeehouse, writing drafts of their prospectus. When Thomas had visited his English asylum to collect Daisy and Mary (overcrowding meant the committee had, in the event, been pleased to see them go, so, slightly to Daisy's disappointment, no escape had been necessary), he had been given permission by Faverill to appoint him consultant emeritus; he knew Faverill's name would mean nothing in a province of Austria-Hungary, but he thought it a good idea to load the official documents with as many doctors and qualifications as they could. Jacques wrote to three colleagues at the Salpêtrière asking if they, too, might lend their luster from afar.

Their next visit was to the bank, where they found a florid, genial man called Leopold in a small office overlooking the town hall. He sat back in his chair and looked at the pair of them with something close to amazement.

"We do not have many . . . visitors in our town," he said. "I wonder what made you choose this region for your venture."

Pure chance and instinct, Thomas wanted to say, but felt he should provide a more businesslike reason, so talked of the relative proximity to Vienna, the climate and the mountains.

"And doubtless you would like me to lend you some money," said Herr Leopold.

Thomas explained that he had paid for two years of the lease in advance, using money he had saved from his private practice. The renovation works had been paid for by Monsieur Kalaji, Valade's princely patron in Paris, who had been so pleased by the paintings that had resulted from their European tour that he had asked to take a stake in Thomas's new enterprise. With what Jacques had also contributed from teaching and private practice in Paris, they had thus been able to meet all their costs to date and came to him therefore ready to start business without being a schilling in debt. Such happy circumstances were unusual, he imagined.

The bank manager smiled again. Thomas noticed that he was inspecting Jacques's boots, which were of an ordinary French design, but one obviously unknown in Carinthia.

Until they had a regular income from patient fees, however, Thomas continued, they would need a facility to borrow. They needed to acquire some electrical apparatus and to convert two of the downstairs rooms in the main courtyard into a water treatment center. Jacques began to explain the great hydrotherapy room that had been planned for the Salpêtrière, with showers as powerful as fire brigade hoses, but Thomas interrupted to say that their own plan was more modest.

"I see," said Herr Leopold. "And how many staff do you intend to employ?"

"We intend to build up slowly as the number of patients rises," said Jacques. "By the time we reach fifty patients, we shall need twenty or more nurses, an electrician to work the faradic and galvanic apparatus, a hydrotherapist, a masseur for the male patients and a masseuse for the women."

"The electrician is a specialized job, quite skillful," said Thomas. "So is the massage, but it need not cost us a great deal. We have a masseuse in training already and if I did not insist on paying her she would do it for nothing."

He still had the impression that the manager was not fully listening; but that might be a good thing, he thought: the rising number of employees was beginning to worry him.

"And what about other staff?"

"We have a lampman, who will have a boy to help him. A housekeeper and a maid. We probably need a cook, four or five other maids and half a dozen cleaners."

"And what about yourselves?"

Thomas and Jacques looked at one another; they had not considered the question.

"I strongly recommend that in the early days you do not draw too heavily against the profits," said Herr Leopold. "There is always that temptation in a partnership, particularly when you are working hard and feel as though you have earned your reward. Try to think ahead."

"Very well," said Jacques.

Herr Leopold stood up. "What I require from you," he said, "is a list of salaries and wages for the first two years. I also need a good estimate of how much you will spend on the further equipment you mentioned and an accurate projection of the costs of medicines and of the domestic and catering expenses. When we have those figures, then you must organize a structure of fees that shows a healthy profit. If you can show me that by running on an average of two-thirds capacity your business makes a profit, then I shall be prepared to make you a loan over a period of three years at the bank's current rate of interest. That will doubtless be less favorable than the terms of your Parisian gentleman, but I am obliged to make a small profit for my employers as well."

"Of course," said Jacques. "We understand." Sonia can do the figures, he was thinking.

"I suggest we meet again a week from today at the same time. Might I ask one last question? I know that these places are fashionable at the moment, especially in the mountains. Is there something particular about yours?"

"Oh yes," said Jacques. "We aim to cure the patients who put their trust in us and to run a profitable clinic. But we hope to do much more than that. We intend to establish beyond doubt how the mind works. We are going to show what makes us human. That is why your bank must not miss this chance to help."

Herr Leopold, more puzzled than ever, showed them to the door. "Cows!" he called after them as they retreated down the cobbled street. "Keep some cows!"

In the course of the next week, over many cream-topped cups of coffee and slices of apple and cherry cake, Jacques and Thomas debated the name they should give to the clinic. Jacques wanted to call it Schloss Seeblick, but Thomas objected that no one ever called a castle after its view. "Lake View Castle is absurd," he said, "and anyway you can only see the lake from half a dozen rooms." Jacques countered that "schloss" did not really mean "castle" anyway, but "country house." The alternative name, "Mountain View," would have applied to more rooms, but made it sound as though they were in a stagnant valley looking up, while Seeblick or Lake View, they agreed, suggested elevation, pure air and optimism. Haus Seeblick, Thomas said, sounded like a boardinghouse at Bridlington, and after trying out Seeschlössl and Seeburg, they settled on the original Schloss Seeblick. If there was an element of nonsense in it, they agreed, it was not inappropriate.

"In due course," said Jacques. "We will need to move to a mountain home. All the best sanatoriums are up in the hills."

"Do you mind if we make this one work first?" said Thomas. "We are above sea level anyway."

"We are in the foothills."

"In more ways than one."

Thomas wiped some cream from his lips. "So, Schloss Seeblick, sanatorium for nervous diseases . . . hospital, hydro, spa?"

"We do not have baths."

"We shall have water treatments."

"That does not make us a spa," said Jacques. "And I am not sure about 'nervous diseases.' The word 'disease' makes it sound as though all our patients will have organic illnesses."

"All right," said Thomas. "Disorders."

"That is a fine word. Congratulations."

"You don't think we should use the word 'psychiatric'?"

"No," said Jacques. "The word 'nerves' is the accepted euphemism. Everyone knows what it means. And in fact not all our patients will be psychiatric cases."

"We could call it the Mountain View Private Madhouse."

"We could, Thomas, but we will not. We will call it the Schloss See-blick, then in smaller print on the next line, 'sanatorium and clinic for nervous disorders.' 'Sanatorium' suggests that people can stay for a year, and 'clinic' will encourage those who just want to look in for a con-sultation. Then in the text we shall make it clear that we cater for every-thing from the most intractable dementia to the mildest exhaustion. And we should say that we have a speciality in neurological illness."

"Is that not covered by 'nervous disorders'?"

"No. To them that means madness. Neurology means trembling and paralysis."

"All right. Pass me the pen and start dictating."

When at last they had something that was both definite and vague, specific but inclusive, they wrote it out again neatly (Thomas's hand-writing, admired by his namesake at the asylum, was preferred) and took it to a printer recommended by the newspaper editor. They ordered a thousand copies and employed two clerks to send them to registered physicians far and wide, whose names they found in a directory in the town library. They took out advertisements in the local newspaper, in periodicals in Munich and Vienna and, ruing the expense, in the *Frank-furter Zeitung*. On their return to the bank, they found that Herr Leopold had scrutinized the figures and calculations done by Sonia and had authorized a loan. The following week, at the end of May, their first patients arrived.

SONIA FOUND that her presence was needed most in the kitchens. Thomas had written into the prospectus an undertaking that the schloss could administer the "rest cure" made popular in America, and to fulfill this undertaking they were required to offer not only intensive nursing, baths, massage and electrical treatments but a diet on which the patients, most of them slender neurasthenic young women, were expected to eat prodigiously. They were deemed cured and ready to leave when all their bodily functions, particularly the reproductive, were working regularly, and when they had grown by up to half their initial body weight.

Neither Thomas nor Jacques was much interested in the physiology of the patients or of the cure, but in the early days it brought them half their custom, and if the process told them little of medical interest, all the women did leave looking healthier and more content, so they felt nothing with which to reproach themselves.

Although Frau Egger's father was Carinthian, her mother was Vien-nese, and her repertoire in the kitchen included dishes from far beyond the mountains, rich and unstinting; sometimes Sonia felt she and Frau Egger were like foie gras farmers fattening geese. The young women arrived at Schloss Seeblick looking pale and undernourished; many of them had nursed parents or other members of their family on their deathbeds, then, when the strain was over, had fallen ill themselves. They had been too long in stuffy invalid rooms; their eyes were tired from reading in the twilight. Sonia wondered whether some of them had not become infected by the medical procedures they had attended; none had heard of the new germ theory of disease, the work of Koch and Pasteur, which, Jacques had explained to her, was changing the hygiene of hospi-tals in Europe (he grimaced already to remember the unswabbed wards of the Salpêtrière). One young woman called Bertha had sat for days by her father's bedside while a drain was inserted into a pleuritic abscess in his lung; sometimes her dress was soaked in his pus, but neither she nor the physician had thought of this as dangerous.

For the first few days at the schloss the rest-cure patients lay immobile in their rooms while one of the nurses attended to every need: they cut up their food and spooned it into their mouths while the women lay prone; they brought them bedpans and gave them daily sponge baths; they fetched cups of hot milk and read books out loud to give their patients' weary eyes the chance to rest. Daisy had been rapidly trained in nursing by Thomas and was efficient at what she did, though she was restricted to those who spoke English, and even there Thomas made sure the literary expectations were not high. As he walked down the courtyard he would occasionally hear her voice, loud and insistent, hammering out the words of a sentence to her prone charge and it made him smile with a deep, subversive pleasure as he hurried on.

After the patient had been immobile for a week, Mary would be sent in to start the massage. At first, Thomas or Daisy had to take her everywhere in the schloss, but she slowly began to find her way, feeling along the wall of the cloister, then stabbing at the cobbles with her stick and counting off the doorways as she went by. She had learned her craft on Daisy's body, its modesty preserved in cotton camiknickers, as Thomas explained the rudiments of anatomy. They began with the small bones of the feet and toes and worked their way up, with special attention to the joints, which were rotated through every position. A slight young woman, Mary developed strong muscles in the forearms as she grasped the areolar tissue, sometimes making Daisy squeal, rolled the large muscles of the calf and thigh firmly both ways and kneaded the belly with the heel of her hand. By the end of the treatment, Daisy was so relaxed that her initial self-consciousness had left her and she begged to be left to sleep.

Once it had been explained to them that Mary was blind, most of the patients allowed themselves to be massaged naked, and this allowed her to develop a sensitivity to match her strength; she could feel where their bodies needed help to heal, relax or break down the deposits of fat and salt from the large amount of food they were consuming. The young women sat up with a smile when they heard the tapping of her stick approach their door: they were allowed no visitors apart from the doctor and the electrician, and many of them were lonely; they talked to Mary as she worked, telling her the stories of their lives, though not sure that she could understand. She sensed their pleasure in the way they let fall their heavy limbs at the wordless instruction of her hands and in their dreamy gratitude when she had finished.

Each day her consciousness of what it meant to be alive was growing. There was the realm of speech, to which, after years of silence in the workhouse and the asylum, she was a newcomer. Neglect had made her own voice low and quiet, and it took many weeks before she could converse confidently even with Daisy, in English; no sooner was she there, than another language began to form in her brain and by simple repetition come to mean something. With no distraction from the seen world, she could concentrate on the sounds, remember and repeat them, wishing sometimes she had the courage to ask Thomas what some of the phrases really meant; she grew fluent in the idiom of tired young women, picking up their tics and idiosyncrasies as her own.

A physical world, not bound by chains or locks, was opened up to her in the extensive grounds of the schloss, somewhere she could move at will, encountering different sounds and surfaces and densities of air. Josef held her hand and made her stroke the gelding's nose, then compare it to the mare's. On the other side of the stables was a small pasture where, following Herr Leopold's suggestion, they had put two cows, which Mary's educated hands learned how to milk. Beyond all these new perspectives—greater than all the new worlds of language and sensation—was her discovery of what it meant to feature in the thoughts of other living beings. They knew her name; they asked her questions; she became a part of their routines; she believed that to a small extent they even needed her. Sometimes she wondered if there was any level at which this ascent into awareness might end. It was like climbing from the center of a set of Chinese boxes: how many new worlds can I discover, she asked herself, and still be looking at the same old life?

SONIA HAD been at the schloss six weeks and was dreaming one night of a meadow near Torrington where she had often played as a child; she was running up the hill, scattering a flock of sheep, when she developed a stitch that made her gasp for breath. She awoke, sweating, in the warm May night to find that the pain was real—not in her ribs but in her lower abdomen. She lit a candle, checked that Jacques was sleeping undisturbed, and made her way to the bathroom. As she walked, she found that she was bleeding. She locked the door and drew a warm bath, holding a towel between her legs. She placed the candle on the shelf beside the tub and climbed into the water, which she could see, by the light of the flickering flame, was blooming with the blood that poured from her. For a few minutes she lay still, rigid with the spasms and her fear of what they meant. Then the contractions and the cramps grew less frequent; the pain receded, but was replaced by an overpowering fatigue. Somewhere swirling in the candlelight, somewhere in the blood and water, the life of her son had been lost—a mess of red cells she washed away, down through the drains and out beneath the dark fields of Carinthia— no spirit, no laughter, no breath, just red human matter.

I have failed, she thought: I have failed a second husband. When she had cleaned the bath and the tile floor, she clamped a fresh towel between her legs and pulled her nightdress on again. She did not want to disturb Jacques, who slept far too little, and whom, for superstitious reasons, she had not yet told of her pregnancy. The night was warm and the ceramic surface of the floor was cool against her cheek as she lay down, wrapping her arms round her belly, covering over the pain, squeezing away the absence. The little boy was so real to her that she could almost hear his voice. "My little one," she whispered. "Oh my darling boy." She felt the uprushing love toward him fill her soul, then hang, until she crushed it back inside herself with the strength of her arms.

In the morning, she told Jacques she had bled more heavily than usual. She noticed the flicker of disappointment in his eyes before he offered sympathy; he examined her, palpating gently. She had no fever and he was sure that she was well, but told her she must go to see the gynecologist in the city hospital, to be certain.

"I shall ask the Executioner to take you in this afternoon," he said. "I can come with you if you like. It is probably nothing, but to me it suggests something positive. Activity of any kind is a good omen for . . ." He trailed off with a gesture; the subject was delicate, and they had never voiced their hopes.

The gynecologist confirmed that she had lost a fetus. After examination, he "tidied up," as he put it, and assured Sonia that he saw no reason why she should not conceive again; it was only if she miscarried three times consecutively at less than twenty weeks that there was deemed to be a functional problem.

"Nature generally aborts for a reason," he said, drying his hands on a towel by the basin. "You have lost a good deal of blood. Rest for two days, then be of good cheer. You are a healthy woman."

"I shall try," said Sonia. "In return, please do not tell my husband that I was pregnant."

"Entirely as you wish."

Back at the schloss, Sonia ignored the doctor's order and returned at once to work.

By the end of the summer, she produced accounts for Herr Leopold at the bank that showed they were already making a small profit; there were several bookings for the autumn, and although the world of human sickness was not predictable, it did look as though the economy of the schloss could be made to work. Heartened by this news, Jacques told her that the time had now come for him to go and fetch Olivier from his asylum. He had not wanted to uproot him until he was certain he could offer him a lasting home, but now, with the good financial news, he felt confident; Thomas would take over his patients while he was away and he expected the return journey to Brittany to take him no more than ten days.

X

AS THE TRAIN TRAVELED WEST FROM PARIS, JACQUES HAD LEISURE, for the first time since he had made his visit to Torrington four summers earlier, to look back at the period of furious passion through which he had lived. Beyond the shuddering glass, he could see the landscape reel out continuously, sliced into rectangles by the rapid return of his eye. His own life sometimes seemed to him to have that quality of being made up of a series of separate phases, barely understood at the time, for all that they formed part of an unwinding whole. The moment of his appearance before the examiners to defend his thesis had marked the dramatic end of one such section. He had prepared very little for the interview—dangerously little, when he came to think of it. It was as though he could not bring himself to imagine it in advance because too much depended on it; yet he could not have foreseen what really resulted, which was not just the ending of the student years or the acquisition of a license to practice, but the sense that he had become someone else: for a moment in the churchy upstairs room where the test took place, he had seen himself from the outside, as the examiners saw him, and he no longer felt provisional or disqualified, but filled with power and confidence. If they believed in this strange Dr. Rebière, then why should he not do so too? And then, why not send the fellow out to do his lifework for him—this awe-inspiring doctor whose work of "first-rate scholarship" had brought his superiors—no, his equals—to their feet?

After all, he was inventing other aspects of his life as he went along. The role of husband, for instance, was not how he had pictured it, this one-room urban penury with a divorced foreigner—no solid house, no servants or children—yet Sonia seemed content when all that he had brought was himself and what he carried in his head. So he turned his mind to his work and found that he could manage German as well as English and that much of what he read among the Germans seemed to fit in with his own preconceptions and interests. Was he allowed to take other men's ideas, pick them up like a jackdaw and carry them back to his nest? Was this thievery, or was it scholarship? The further he continued, the more he had the feeling that his work was blessed: almost everything seemed to relate to his central concern, to the working of the mind and to the subtle way that thought crossed into flesh. The evidence seemed to lie all about him, yet no one else had bothered to look down and pick it up. That did not matter: for millions of years the leaves had fallen from the trees before Newton described the simple force that made them do so; it was less than a hundred years since the brain had been identified as the organ of thought, relegating other favored contenders, such as heart, stomach and pineal gland, to their more mundane work. And as for the fact that he had not traveled an orthodox academic road, that might be an advantage. Who had discovered more: overeducated graduates of the finest schools who cautiously added a new level of research to the best that had been bought for them, or men inflamed by a sense of being excluded, driven by their own desire to labor onward, ragged, blind, into the night? Perhaps a little ignorance was a helpful and a necessary thing; it prevented him from feeling it had all been done before, while the blind spots in his vision helped him see other parts of the picture with burning insight.

And Sonia . . . He had learned to think of himself as she viewed him, everything reflected back from her, so that he became the man she saw. He knew her perspective was only partial, that everyone had a different picture of him, but Sonia was no fool, her gaze was steady and her interpretation sound; and if she was a little too forbearing, more indulgent than he deserved, then he could privately supply the corrections. Sometimes he did yearn for a different idea of what he was; he felt restricted within the role she had assigned him—not that there was anything wrong with it, just that it was singular and he wanted to exist in more than one pair of eyes.

At Nantes railway station, he caught a branch line to the small town that was nearest to Olivier's country seclusion, and from the station took a cab across the pale, flat countryside, through the forest roads and the planted acres of gnarled and stunted vines that produced the acidic wine of the region, then across the village itself and onward to his remote destination.

Night had fallen when he climbed down from the carriage at the gates of the asylum and pulled the bell. A nun came hurrying up the path from the main doors of the building, her habit flapping about her in the gathering wind. She scanned his face anxiously through the gate.

"Come inside quickly," she said when he had explained his business. There was a solitary gas bracket in the main hall of the building beneath which he stood while the nun vanished into the darkness. There was nothing to see in the old building and no sound came to him, so he began to think about other things: he pictured Sonia at the schloss; he thought of her in the bright family rooms, so different from the dank lowland where he found himself.

"Come this way," said the nun.

She led him down a stone corridor with a vaulted ceiling, then showed him into a room and indicated a chair at the plain, scrubbed table. She left him again, without explanation, and he heard her wooden clogs going over the floor. He was in what appeared to be a kind of parlor, lit by two small candles in holders on the table; behind him was a sink with a dripping brass tap. His mind began to move on again, and he was aware of disregarding his odd surroundings, because the thoughts in his head were more alive to him. Perhaps soldiers in a cavalry charge were thinking about something other than the guns. With their thighs they could contain the swell and thunder of the horse, guide the sword with a young man's eyesight, all muscles tensed to kill or die, but could also be pondering the growth of a wisteria above the lintel of an aunt's front door. Did they deserve to be called brave? He remembered once performing an emergency tracheotomy on an epileptic woman in the Salpêtrière, and—at the moment his dexterity opened up the airway and saved her life—he was thinking about lunch. How seldom it was that you fully inhabited your surroundings, engaging not only your senses but your awareness. On the occasions that you did so, time had a way of slowing, or appearing even to stop. So did we hurry on with other thoughts because we were preoccupied, so well adjusted to the world that it was scarcely worth our attention? Or would committing ourselves to it more fully involve experiences of time or doubt or fear that we did not really wish to have? Had the ability to escape into abstraction, to live outside our surroundings, been favored by natural selection? It certainly appeared to be an ability lacked by the mentally ill, who were engaged so fully with their reality that they were stuck in it. There was some problem with time here, he felt sure: a healthy mind needed a proper relationship with time, which was clearly no linear given, but something more mysterious, and could be experienced in various ways.

"Come this way," said the nun, and her voice caused Jacques to jump back into the candlelit room.

Although he had visited the asylum before, it had been by day, and he rapidly became disorientated in the darkness, following the nun's candle down a twisting corridor. A cat swerved between his feet, causing him to stumble and put out his hand: the wall was damp beneath his fingers.

"Can I take him tonight, Sister? The superintendent wrote to me and said that if I countersigned his report to the department, then—"

"I am instructed to show you to a room where you can sleep. The lunatics cannot be awakened after darkness. They rise soon after daybreak. I will bring you food in the morning. In here, please."

The nun lit a candle in whose light Jacques could see a narrow bed with a crucifix hanging from the wall above it, a table with a jug, a glass and a cloth-covered plate, a washstand and, beside it, a metal bucket.

"Good night," said the nun, handing him the second candle, which she had fixed in a china holder. "God be with you."

"And with you, Sister."

She backed into the shadows and closed the door. Jacques was certain that he heard her turn a key, and looked at the door for a moment in disbelief; by the time he had tried it and found that it would not open, it was too late to remonstrate.

He carried the candle to the table and found that beneath the cloth on the plate were two slices of dark, mealy bread and a piece of meat. The water in the jug was so cold that it must have been drawn from a well deep below any living earth; it sent jagged nerve pains through his teeth.

He sat down on the bed and opened the leather bag Sonia had packed for him. His eyesight was not what it had been when he worked upstairs in his father's house, and the light from the candle was too dim for him to read by, so he resigned himself to sleep, removing his boots and his outer clothes, then pulling up the covers.

He smiled to himself, not the full simian gash that had charmed Thomas in the Pension des Dunes, but a small, solitary grimace: it was an adventure, and in the morning he would take his brother back to human company.

JACQUES WAS in a narrow tunnel, crawling on his elbows; too late, he felt that his shoulders were too wide: he had reached the point where he could not turn round and he was now trapped. His lumpish heart was rising from his ribs and he could hear the noise of chains, metal grinding on metal, which slowly emerged as the sound of his shutter grating on its hinge, turning slowly in the wind from the Atlantic as he awoke. For a moment he could not pull himself free from the dream: he was exhausted by the struggle, but knew that if he gave in to fatigue and closed his eyes he would be back in the tunnel. He swung his feet down onto the cold floor. The room had the rare and utter darkness of the cave, of a time before fire. He walked forward, holding out his arms ahead of him to protect his eyes. He felt the iron lozenge of the espagnolette and twisted it, pulling the halves of the casement inward. He pushed his fingers into the blackness, but could feel nothing; he worried at the darkness with his eyes until the cornea stung, but there were no shapes and no light. He did not want to return to sleep, so groped his way back across the room, took his trousers from the bedpost and went down on his hands and knees to search for his boots. The second time at the window, his hand encountered the wayward shutter, and he pushed it back on its unoiled hinge. Then he climbed out into the night. He tried to orientate himself by keeping the outside wall under his left hand, though soon there was a narrow ditch alongside the building that made it impossible.

Through the blackness of the air he tried to picture the deciduous wood he had noticed by moonlight when he arrived; he imagined the high walls about the grounds, the ditches and lanes beyond, but it was no good: he was giddy and lost in the dark with no idea of his way back or forward; even the vast walls of the asylum were not there for his questing fingers.

He was not frightened; he had seen nights like this as a child, and had found his way back from the woods to his unlit home. Something at last reached his senses, and so concentrated was he on his denied sight that it took a moment before he registered that it was not vision but a sound—and it was that of a human voice. He tilted his head from side to side, trying to catch its direction, and moved uncertainly toward it. Despite the protective outreach of his hands, his head collided with sharp masonry; he closed his hands and found that he was embracing a corner of the asylum. There was no ditch at this part of the wall, and he was able to feel his way along again until the stonework gave way to the wood of closed shutters.

The sound was coming from inside, and it had a plangent, other-worldly quality, yet at the same time seemed familiar. As he gently pulled back the shutters, which were better oiled than those on his own window, a mist of gray light at last reached him. It came from a single candle, obscured by the cloudy glass, and as he peered at it, he saw it bow and stretch in a draft, and at the edge of its penumbra he caught sight of a dark, shaggy head, quite still, the features rapt. It was his brother. Beneath the beard, Jacques could just see the lips moving, then he heard the sound, a sort of incantation, and although he could not make out the words, he was certain from the tone of his voice that Olivier was in some act of supplication, and that if it was not exactly a prayer he was at least addressing himself to a higher being. His face, covered by the uncombed beard, came into view only when the candle flame bent his way; then Jacques could see his earnestly closed eyes and his passionate engagement with whatever reality he inhabited.

Jacques had a sudden picture of their shared bedroom as children and of his ten-year-old brother, still at that age blond-haired, his skinny body shaking with laughter as he climbed into Jacques's bed to escape from the flood they had been imagining downstairs. He could recall the distinctive sweet smell of Olivier's skin as they lay holding on to each other, trying to stifle their laughter in the darkness.

Gently closing the shutters, he wandered back from the building and found a dry piece of earth where he could sit and wait for the dawn.

HE WAS back in his bedroom by the time a nun, a younger one than the night before, unlocked the door and brought in a tray with a piece of bread and a bowl of tea. Jacques gave her his largest smile, but she appeared not to notice as she turned in silence to leave. He shaved in the cold water of the washstand and changed his linen; as he pulled a clean shirt from his bag, a small photograph fell from the folds: it was of Sonia, taken by Thomas outside the darkroom at the county asylum. Jacques smiled: he knew she disliked it, but it was the only photograph of herself she had and she must have debated hard before slipping it in.

The nun returned and conducted him in silence to the medical superintendent's office where he signed several forms asserting that he had examined the patient and took full responsibility for him. The asylum's own diagnosis of Olivier, he noticed, was "dementia"; he did not demur in countersigning it, though the bluntness of the term affronted him. He felt happier to complete the section headed "Hospital or institution to which Patient is to be transferred," writing "Schloss Seeblick Sanatorium and Clinic for Nervous Disorders" with a flourish. It made it look as though Olivier had been singled out for special treatment, or promotion.

The superintendent, a severe, dark-haired man in a frock coat, apologized for the fact that his door had been locked; they had had some trouble with a previous visitor who had come under a false identity and had upset the patients at night by his wandering. He then escorted Jacques to a locked double door which he opened with some keys attached to his waistcoat. It was a large, light room, with pleasantly high ceilings and long barred windows overlooking the grounds. There were perhaps a hundred men in it, and when the superintendent walked down the middle, toward a long refectory table at which some were finishing breakfast from wooden bowls, there was a rustle of interest.

"They do not see people from outside very often," the superintendent said from the corner of his mouth. "Which one is your brother?"

Jacques's eye ran through the assortment of idiots, neurological cases and madmen; he was reluctant to engage too many of the hopeful eyes that were fixed on him. He saw Olivier by the window, standing alone, and his heart was twisted by the sight because Olivier was a man, his loved brother, and did not fall into the categories in which the others could be placed. It was an error. Every time he saw him in the asylum, Jacques had the same feeling: this was a real person, a man with a name, not, like the others, a patient, a mere example of an illness, but Olivier still. You could not allow the man to be swallowed by the illness, thought Jacques: surely the human soul was more robust.

"How are you?" He held Olivier's hands between his own. Olivier said nothing.

"I am going to take you with me and look after you myself. I have a beautiful house near the mountains. You are going to live with me and Sonia. Do you remember I told you about Sonia? And her brother Thomas, who is my friend." He looked deep into his brother's face: he had aged in the last couple of years, grown fatter; there were gray hairs in his beard and lines about his eyes. The years of delusion and being shut away were wearing him down, and life had gone on elsewhere, without him.

The clutch of papers in the superintendent's hand, together with the appearance in their midst of an outsider, was exciting the patients, who smelled the possibility of escape. They began to shuffle toward Jacques and Olivier.

"It is not safe for me to go," said Olivier.

Jacques knew that anxiety of any kind seemed to intensify Olivier's symptoms and was prepared. He took a twist of paper from his bag, emptied the powder from inside it into a clean cup on the table and filled it with milk.

"Drink this," he said. "It will make you feel better. Then we need to find your belongings. Look, my dear Olivier. All your friends here would love to leave. They would give anything to be in your shoes. You will be with your family and we are going to make you better."

"Last night I was talking to the Sovereign. He warned me."

"Do you know who I am?"

Olivier nodded. "They told me you would come."

Jacques turned to the superintendent. "Does he have belongings? I think we should leave as soon as possible."

The superintendent spoke to an attendant, who returned with a small canvas bag containing a toothbrush, a shirt and a notebook full of intricate architectural drawings.

"Is that all?"

"Yes. I think you should leave. Some of the men are under the impression that you have an official function, that you are from the town hall or some such thing, and that you may be in a position to discharge them. Your carriage is waiting at the front gate."

"All right. Are you ready, Olivier?"

"I am not coming. They want to kill me, I know."

"Olivier, it is natural for you to feel anxious."

Two attendants were looming.

"Please drink the milk," said Jacques. "It will make you feel better. When you move home, it is a big change and everyone feels uneasy. But we are going to a beautiful place overlooking a lake, where I will make you happy."

Olivier began to back away, looking for the refuge of his solitary corner. The attendants took his arms; one of them raised the enameled cup of milk to his lips. The other punched him in the belly, and when he gasped they were able to pour most of the milk into his mouth. They held their hands across his lips until he swallowed.

Olivier began to struggle and swear, though Jacques could still recognize the sound of his brother's voice and detect the true cause of his raving and his violence, which was fear. As the two attendants began to force him toward the door, a wave of activity ran through the other patients. Some were so upset by the sight of Olivier's anger that they went into their rituals of self-protection, wrapping their arms about their heads, rocking, thrusting their hands inside their clothes to take comfort from their own bodies. Others saw in Olivier's departure a chance of release for themselves and came to plead their case with Jacques. "Monsieur, Monsieur, for several years I have been kept here, but there is nothing wrong with me . . . My sister's husband has had me

Sebastian Faulks

confined. . . ." There were hands clutching at his elbows, there were men placing their faces close to his, bodies barring his way to the door. "I beg you take a message to the Quai d'Orsay, they will know who sent you. . . ." There were hands about his ankles and he struggled to keep walking. With the help of a third attendant they fought their way through the rising clamor; Jacques was compelled to use his arms and elbows to keep the supplicants at bay; he tried not to listen to the specific agony of each tale for fear of weakening. It seemed that scores of men had surrounded them and were placing their hopes of life and freedom on his shoulders; the room had turned from a place of quiet despair into a riot of shouting and pushing, as he squeezed between the double doors where the attendants cleared a passage with their fists. The superintendent slammed the door on the tumult and turned the keys in the heavy lock. Jacques leaned back, struggling for breath; Olivier was next to him, still held by the two attendants. After the sound of the lock turning, there was suddenly a pause in the commotion from inside, an utter, bottomless silence; and in that quiet, Jacques felt he had heard the sound of hope lost.

THE RETURN to the schloss took them four days, during much of which Jacques had to keep Olivier sedated. Even slumped silent against the corner of the train compartment, he aroused inquisitive and disapproving looks. In Paris, Jacques called in at Madame Maurel's to see if there were any letters and because he knew that in such a household Olivier could spend the night without incurring anything worse than the odd disdainful glance from Madame Tavernier. In his torpid state, Olivier allowed Jacques to bathe him thoroughly, to cut his hair a little and to dress him in new clothes from a draper in the rue Christine. (He paid proudly in cash; for the first time he did not have to beg credit.) He offered to lend him his own razor, but Olivier's reaction was such that he did not pursue the matter. Then came the wearisome journey from the Gare de l'Est, food and drink bought from small wagons on the platforms as they crossed the border. After they had changed trains at Vienna, Jacques found his spirits starting to lift. Soon he would be able to share responsibility for Olivier with Sonia and Thomas; soon the change of atmosphere, the diet and the loving care would start to make his brother well. They could not cure him, but surely they could ease his pain.

Sonia had made the best spare room ready for Olivier in the main house, not far from Thomas's, at the front, with a view over the lake. Although it was late in October, she had found enough blooms in the recultivated garden to fill two vases in the room, where she had lit the fire and made up the bed with new sheets. She had some trepidation about the safety of the fire, not knowing Olivier, but she thought it best to treat him normally and leave any special adjustments to Jacques. She was waiting at the front door when Josef, who had been despatched to the station, came back with his two exhausted travelers.

The nine days of his absence were by far the longest period that Sonia had been apart from Jacques, and her joy at seeing him helped her to overlook the strange appearance of his brother; to her shame, she found herself reminded of an illustration from her childhood Bible showing the fettered Gadarene demoniac, whose many tormenting spirits ("My name is Legion. For we are many") Christ cast out of him and into a herd of swine. Thomas emerged from a consultation in his room at the end of the hall and summoned Hans to bring up wine from the cellars. Sonia had taken charge sufficiently of the kitchen to be able to insist on a plain leg of lamb with garlic for dinner, but compromised with Frau Egger by permitting fried veal brains with egg, one of her specialities, as a savory to follow the dessert. They had set the circular table in the waiting room so they could for once not eat in with the patients, and Thomas poured red wine for them all from misty decanters he had found in the cellar. Sonia felt light-headed from the wine and from her joy at seeing Jacques again; a slight apprehension about Olivier only made her dizzier, but she thought their idyll needed something rougher in its texture to make it more likely to endure.

For some days after his return, Jacques continued to give Olivier acetate of morphia, gradually decreasing the dose and switching to hyoscine, which Thomas told him was recommended by Bucknill and Tuke, his dependable English authority. Olivier seemed calm, though completely unresponsive. Thomas slept nearby and listened out for him; Jacques also quietly locked his brother's bedroom door each night from the outside, worried that his apparent docility might be covering an emotional response to his change of home that was taking time to develop.

It was decided that Olivier should be treated by Thomas. Jacques did not feel able to view his brother dispassionately, and Thomas was excited to feel that, after the years of warehousing in the asylum, he could at last spend time with someone suffering from what appeared to him a classic dementia. They had taken a dozen similarly afflicted patients from the regional asylum and housed them on the ground floor of the main courtyard. Their fees were met in part by the local authorities who had transferred them; the patients' families contributed what they could and the remainder was waived. The "public" patients ate in the large North Hall rather than in the house dining room and were asked not to use the main courtyard; in most respects they were treated in the same way as the others, and were free to wander in the grounds or help with maintenance under Josef's eye.

There was no official division of responsibility between Jacques and Thomas, but it began to happen, partly through the treatment of Olivier, that Thomas took more of the severe psychiatric cases and Jacques more of the neurasthenic. Every evening at six o'clock, they met in Thomas's consulting room to compare their clinical notes; each morning at eight fifteen they met in Jacques's room for half an hour with Sonia, Frau Egger and Josef to discuss the administration of the day ahead. Sonia would then repair to the narrow office, which lay between Jacques's consulting room and the main waiting room at the front of the house. They ate lunch and dinner with the patients, except at the weekend when Sonia insisted they dine privately in the waiting room, laid up with flowers and candles for the occasion, and all talk of medicine was forbidden.

In the spring of the following year, they were visited by Abbé Henri, whom they at once appointed ex officio chaplain to the sanatorium. On the day after his arrival, Thomas decided that they should have a photograph of the staff, both for the sanatorium archive and for possible use in future prospectuses; he thought the presence of a man of the cloth would lend a certain tone. His own Kodak he thought inadequate to the task, so a photographer was summoned from the city, a man with enormous mustaches who hid his head beneath a black cloth while he adjusted the focus of the camera on its tripod. He positioned them between the pillars outside the double front door, with Thomas and Jacques seated in the middle, Sonia to Jacques's left and Abbé Henri in full clerical costume on Thomas's right. Standing behind them were Hans, Mary, Daisy, Josef, Frau Egger and Olivier, who insisted on being included.

"It is a pity Dr. Faverill cannot be here," said Thomas. "He is on our writing paper and that would make us a full eleven. A cricket team."

The exposure time chosen by the photographer was so long, however, that Hans had time to run along the back row and appear twice, substantially at one end, a ghostly presence at the other, in the resulting photograph that was framed and hung in the office.

"WE ARE a real concern," said Sonia, when she completed the accounts for the first year, ending in May 1891, and handed them to her husband.

"Why not?" said Jacques.

"I never thought we could truly make it work. It was just something we . . . invented."

"All the practical side has been much easier than I thought. Mostly thanks to you, my love. No, really. Of course, the scientific side, our research and so on . . . we are still in the foothills."

"But you are climbing."

"I am definitely climbing."

"Alone?"

"At the moment Thomas and I are taking separate paths. We shall meet at the next plateau."

"Are you going to share your thoughts with us?"

"When I am ready. It is important to try to publish. It would also be good for the schloss. Provided people think my ideas make sense."

"Are you worried that they may not understand?"

"I need to go back to Paris at some stage to speak further with Pierre Janet. And before I read my paper in Vienna, I should like to try it out. I think I could perhaps read a short version to an invited audience here."

"You could do it in the North Hall. In fact, we ought to have regular lectures and entertainments there."

When Jacques left the office to go on his rounds, Sonia tidied the papers and went up to their private rooms. Truly, she was surprised by how straightforward it had been. She herself had no training in any more than simple arithmetic, learned at dame school, then from a governess at Torrington; yet the bank seemed happy to accept her copperplate accounts, to set one of their clerks to make two transcripts, one for the tax collector and one which they returned, signed and franked with a scarlet seal, for her to put proudly in her desk drawer. They even showed a small profit. She had not been brought up to work; girls of her background were not expected to do more than supervise a house, though in a sense, she supposed, that was all she did. It was a large house, however, and a thriving one.

It surprised her that a place of sickness could provide an atmosphere of such content. She was careful to keep their private rooms separate from the life of the clinic, but even in the main house and the courtyard there was an atmosphere of something purposeful, something worthwhile being driven through by force of will and character. Sonia walked across the great flagged hall in the late morning and glanced at the closed doors of the twin consulting rooms, behind which the two men bent their minds to the great task they had set themselves; then she pushed open the door of the kitchen, to be greeted by a rush of steam as Frau Egger and her maids were working scarlet-faced among the clashing lids and cauldrons they were heaving from the range. Then she went beneath the stairs, through the rear doors, out along the cloister and into the tranquillity of the main courtyard, where one or two of the patients might be reading on the benches, sewing or walking up and down. She would make sure the early lunch was on time for the public patients in the North Hall, then circle the far end of the building and come round into the gardens in the west, where her favorite seat gave her a view up to the mountains. It was an old bench beneath a cedar, and the tree reminded her of Torrington, though the vista could not have been more different. At first the ground gave way, going down to meadows dotted with cows, then it rose and she could see yellow and pink wildflowers in the fields as they edged into spinneys and pale woods, then into evergreen forests that went up steeply toward the tops of the mountains with their permanently white peaks. She allowed herself twenty minutes with her book before returning to her duties, but some-times, particularly in April and May, the prospect was so beguiling that she simply sat and stared. "I will lift up mine eyes unto the hills," she thought, settling back with a sigh of incredulity. She sometimes thought of Richard Prendergast, but it seemed long, long ago, and to have hap-pened to someone strangely different from herself.

Sonia measured time in spans of twenty-eight days. Most of the women patients, she knew, had irregularities, some of which Jacques appeared to be able to cure by placing the patient under hypnosis and suggesting to her that the next period would follow at the appointed time. Although she did not envy the women's unpredictable cycles, nor the deeper illnesses of which they might be a symptom, she did resent the clockwork arrival of her own pains, followed exactly thirty-six hours later by bleeding. She tried everything she could think of to become pregnant, once waking Jacques from a deep slumber when she thought she felt the egg drop inside the fallopian tube; but whether she tried at the most propitious time, a little before it, a little after it, once or many times, or even, perversely, when it seemed impossible, it made no differ-ence: after twenty-eight days came bright, healthy blood as punctual and predictable as the postman who bicycled up the drive at precisely five to eight each morning.

ELEVEN MORE such intervals, an autumn and a winter, went by before Jacques declared that he was ready to read his paper, which he had enti-tled "Psychophysical Resolution: A Proposed Cure for Hysteria and the Neuroses. A Paper read by Dr. Jacques Rebière to a Select Audience at the Schloss Seeblick, Carinthia, April 18, 1892." He had not had time to visit Paris, but had sent a draft of his paper to his former colleague Pierre Janet at the Salpêtrière, who had responded in encouraging terms.

They sent out invitations to the local newspapers and to medical col-leagues at the hospital and in the surrounding area; they asked all the professionals and tradesmen with whom they had done business and representatives of all the institutions who had sent them patients or whom they had first approached through the register in the city public library. The patients were asked if they would like to invite members of their family and it was hinted to them that their own attendance was expected; at least, dinner would be late that night and there would be nothing else to do until the talk was given.

Jacques spent the days before it going over his notes again and again, practicing his delivery. He tried to model himself on Charcot, but found that his own voice was more expressive, with natural rhetorical emphases and changes of pace. He justified this to himself by thinking that his audience, unlike Charcot's, would not be comprised of medical people, but largely of laymen and their wives who would need all the help he could give them.

It was a warm spring day, and at half past five he went up to his apartment to change into his best suit. Sonia looked flushed and excited when he emerged from his dressing room. She handed him a glass of water and straightened his tie. "Are you all right, my love?"

He smiled. "I think so. I feel . . . quite detached. I have put so much work and thought into this that now I feel resigned. It is like a bird, and either it will fly or it will not. It really needs no more help from me now. The time when I could affect it is past."

She looked into his dark eyes and she saw that what he said was not true; they were filled with effortful hope and anxiety. In the bright light of the upstairs sitting room, she felt time stop for a moment to draw breath: Jacques glanced at his watch, she heard the front door open to more visitors and the crunch of horses' hooves on the gravel outside. The comic busyness of their lives rushed on all about them, but in the eyes of her husband she saw that this was the moment: there, behind the irises, was all that ambition and desire that had kept him reading through the night and now, on this soft spring evening, there could be no avoiding the fact that this was the hour on which his life's work hitherto depended and that—whatever the distracting domestic details, however much they each pretended otherwise—such moments in a man's life were few.

Jacques poured two glasses of Madeira from a decanter on the sideboard. He raised his own glass to Sonia, drank it off in one gulp and said, "It is time to go." They walked downstairs and Sonia took his arm as they went down the cloister, across the courtyard and into the North Hall. He had the look of a condemned man, she thought, as she released him to take her own place.

There were a hundred and fifty people in the hall, perhaps two dozen with a knowledge of medicine, the rest with little more to guide them than a high school education, and some with less than that.

Jacques caught Thomas's encouraging and humorous look as he showed the last of the visitors to their seats. He climbed onto a small platform that Josef had put together that morning and poured a glass of water from the jug that stood on a little table alongside. He coughed once, and began.

"Ladies and gentlemen, I have a new theory to put to you tonight. It concerns the way the mind functions. I believe that by studying certain illnesses and their treatments I have been able to deduce something that may be of universal relevance to mankind and to our understanding of what it is to be human. It is the dream of all scientists to stand up and proclaim a great discovery; the greatest dream of all is to say: 'I have a unified theory which explains everything, a single key that can unlock all the mysteries of being.'

"How do I dare make such a claim? I explain what must look like immodesty by saying that I have contributed almost nothing of originality to this discovery myself. All I have done is look at the work of others and put it together in a new way. I have read some books—many books—and I have observed some patients, alive and dead. That is all.

"The greatest doctor of our time is Professor Charcot of the Salpêtrière hospital in Paris. As you will doubtless know, he described many complex illnesses which had previously defeated his colleagues, such as multiple sclerosis, for instance. Rightly is he viewed as the Napoleon of the medical sciences, the preeminent doctor of Europe. When I and my colleague Dr. Midwinter had the fortune to study under Professor Charcot some years ago, he was engaged in unraveling the mysteries of a most prevalent and distressing condition: hysteria. I do not intend to recapitulate Charcot's findings tonight. You may well look them up for yourselves; a series of his famous Tuesday Lessons was recently translated into German. I wish to concentrate on one aspect only of what Charcot discovered.

"The classic symptoms of hysteria are of a fourfold seizure. This is seldom seen. All medical students are familiar with the problem of finding 'pure' examples of diseases: even a simple affliction such as pneumonia rarely presents in a pure form because it is usually complicated, especially in elderly patients, by other ailments of the lung. This need not detain us. Symptoms of hysteria such as we generally encounter it may include paralysis, usually 'hemiplegia,' which is paralysis of one side of the body; 'contractures,' in which a limb or joint becomes rigid; assorted abdominal or other muscular pains; tremors and standard neurological signs such as speech and ocular disturbance; amenorrhoea and related menstrual problems—as well as headache, anxiety, sleeplessness and symptoms of what one might term a more psychological nature.

"A woman is predisposed to be an hysteric by inheritance; the physiological disturbance is often activated by a malfunction of the womb or ovaries. In all these ways it is a standard neurological illness, in which a lesion—which you may wish to imagine as a minute wound or blister caused by the localized death or infection of a small number of cells—in the brain or spinal cord affects the nerves that radiate from that point. Thus a lesion in the part of the brain responsible for the movement of the right foot would affect that remote organ. The site of the lesion in hysteria has not yet been found, and in this case it is like Parkinson's disease, awaiting a complete description from what we might call both ends of the process: basic cause and outlying effect.

"However, Charcot has proposed that the lesion in hysteria may be what is called a 'dynamic' lesion. I think that some people would understand by that word that it moves; that (as in edema, commonly known as dropsy, or in anemia) it is an organic, or physical, lesion that proves transitory.

"However, my former colleague Pierre Janet, of whom I shall speak more in a minute, a doctor at the Salpêtrière, has pointed out that hysterical paralyses do not follow the proper paths of innervation. Experiments at that hospital showed that there is a fundamental difference between organic and hysterical paralyses. An hysterical paralysis of the arm is not only more acute, it is more confined; it does not spread through the connective nerve pathways. A complete organic paralysis of the arm is rare, but when a paralysis reaches that stage of severity it will naturally spread to a greater or lesser extent through the adjacent systems.

"It is as though hysteria does not recognize how the body's nervous system is connected. That is why Monsieur Janet believes—and so do I— that the hysterical lesion exists completely independent of the standard anatomy of the nervous system.

"Where? This is one of the key questions. Janet argues, and I am with him, that hysteria's apparent 'ignorance' of the nervous system is not a problem but is in fact the clue to the nature of the dynamic lesion. The lesion in fact consists of a loss of the idea, of the very conception of the affected part of the body. A woman with hysterical paralysis of the arm has, at some level of her brain's consciousness, lost her idea of the arm as an integrated part of her anatomy. The reason she has done so is because of the severity of the associated trauma or memory: the greater the emotional content, the more completely will the affected part of the anatomy be removed from the normal sense of the body's integrity. And whilst in organic paralysis you would look for a lesion in the corresponding motor zone of the brain responsible for the arm, in hysterical paralysis you might look for an event whose traumatic impact was not through the complex innervation of the system but on the very arm itself.

"Professor Charcot discovered that hysteria was not confined to women, but that men could suffer from it too. In their case, of course, the ovarian influence was absent, though the male body may have zones equally 'hysterogenic' or capable of activating the hysterical inheritance. The English neurologists Brodie and Reynolds had written about 'paralysis by idea,' often following an accident and hence termed 'railway spine,' but were not able to show how such a process worked. That discovery was left to Charcot. Most male hysterics suffer from an accident or trauma, the impact of which they did not fully assimilate at the time. As a consequence, it was held out of the normal mental processes and lay dormant, stored as a latent energy in the brain. Eventually, when it reached a certain stage of what one might call toxicity, it released its noxious effect into the physiology of the patient's nervous system, causing contractures and paralyses of the kind so typical of the hysteric. Again, I refer you to Professor Charcot for case studies of such men.

"The influence of the womb is no longer considered as important as it once was; the influence of mental or emotional events, however, is now thought to be central in both female and male hysterics. Many doctors noticed that hysterics appeared to relive at some stage in their fits traumatic events from their past; Charcot was the first to suggest that such events might also have been the trigger in releasing their neuropathic heredity. He proved by experiments using hypnosis that there is a strong mental element in hysteria; he showed that physical paralysis or contracture can be induced by mental suggestion—either that of the doctor, or, even more interestingly, that of the patient. Thus he proved conclusively that there exists a bridge between what used, in Descartes's day, to be thought of as the immaterial, thinking side of human life and the organic, physical side of it.

"Charcot, however, did not conceive of it as a bridge because he did not accept Descartes's division; his explanation was to describe thought and emotion as the 'physiology of the cortex,' or to put it in layman's terms, the active, chemical employment of the brain. In that way, we do not need to see these two functions, the mental and the physical, as separated by a gulf. There exist neurophysiological mechanisms by which a memory or a trauma may be held out of the normal functioning of the brain. These mechanisms prevent it from being positively remembered, dealt with, laughed at or wept over. As such, it exists as an undischarged energy which may wreak havoc with the economy of the nervous system.

"Charcot described it thus: 'An idea, a coherent group of associated ideas, settle themselves in the fashion of parasites, remaining isolated from the rest of the mind and expressing themselves outwardly through corresponding motor phenomena . . .' Only three years ago, in 1889, Pierre Janet echoed him: 'The idea, like a virus, develops in a corner of the personality inaccessible to the subject, works subconsciously, and brings about all disorders of hysteria and mental disease.'

"We do not have as yet either the chemical knowledge or the optical instruments sufficient to describe these neurophysiological mechanisms, but that is no reason to suppose that they do not exist. When

William Harvey first described the circulation of the blood, he could not identify the vessels which carried it from artery to vein and was consequently mocked by some of his contemporaries; shortly after his death, the capillaries were observed by the Italian anatomist Malpighi, and Harvey was vindicated.

"Now, the precise nature of this dynamic lesion may as yet be unclear to us, but we may without fear of accident adopt the phrase used by Janet for its location: the 'subconscious.' That is where this bundle of unassimilated energy is held, at first dormant, then morbidly active. Some of you may be aware of the existence of something called 'brain mythology,' a doubtful procedure, I think, in which certain doctors have tried to explain brain functions by inventing psychological analogies of how the brain might work, then searching for such actual systems under the microscope. I do not believe this is scientific. It is one thing to say as Harvey did, 'This is how the blood circulates, and a stronger lens will find the missing connection,' because he started with arteries and veins and a knowledge of how they functioned. It is quite another thing to begin with nothing verifiable at all, then create hypothetical structures in one discipline and search hopefully for them in another. The reason that Monsieur Janet's idea of the subconscious is acceptable is that it is happily understood by Charcot's notion of thought as the physiology of the cortex. We are crossing no anatomical, let alone Cartesian, divide.

"If Monsieur Janet is right, and I am certain that he is, then my proposition is this: that we may extrapolate from the physiology of these unfortunate hysterics the existence of certain mechanisms which may ultimately explain the way that all human minds work—not just the minds of those afflicted by this hereditary disease, but the minds of all of us, every man and woman in this hall. That is the nature of my discovery, ladies and gentlemen; that is what I wish to share with you tonight."

Jacques stopped for some water, and looked over the row of faces in front of him. Because the progress of his logic was so familiar to him he had been able to spare some concentration to gauge his effect, and he had noticed the gratifying silence while he spoke. However, as he looked over the rim of his glass, his eye was caught by a matron, stout and flushed in a high-necked cream dress. She could not possibly have understood, he thought, and he decided to improvise a paragraph that would reengage her attention.

He smiled at her, and at those behind her, as he put down his notes for a moment. "Sometimes patients say to me, 'Doctor, is my illness real or is it all in the mind?' And do you know how I respond? I laugh. I cannot answer the question because its premises are false. It is like being asked, 'Is cheese more ambitious than brick?' The fact that a question can be phrased grammatically does not mean that it can be truthfully answered.

"Things which exist in the mind are real and their very existence makes them so. The love we feel for our parents and our friends is real; the grief we feel if someone dies is real. The fact that we cannot see or touch it does not make it less real. The opposite of real is not 'in the mind'; the opposite of 'real' is 'not real.'

"The opposite of 'in the mind' is 'in the body'—up to a point. This boy has a broken arm; this boy has lost his parents. Both have 'real' problems, one somatic and one mental. This third boy has dementia. His symptoms are mental, but their cause is somatic: a fault in the neurones of his brain, we believe, makes him hear voices; his illness is real enough—you might say it is doubly real. To take the complete opposite: this man has suffered a coronary seizure, brought on in part by overwork. Our demented patient has mental symptoms of somatic origin; our coronary patient has somatic symptoms of mental origin. Both illnesses are only too 'real.'

"So the opposite of 'all in the mind' is not quite 'all in the body,' is it? Because the mind is the function of the brain, a bodily organ. In fact you could say, truthfully, 'the mind is all in the body!' If this all seems a little too abstract for you, let me just remind you of some homely sights with which you are familiar. When your child is nervous, she may stammer; when she is ashamed, she blushes; when she is frightened, she trembles and her hands perspire. How easily the abstract emerges in the physical! From idea, through mind, into brain, into the nervous system, through a gland and out through the skin—a thought made water! A pure idea—that of fear—produces liquid on the child's hands that you can lick or drink. We have heard of water into wine, but idea into water . . .

well, is that 'real,' or is that 'all in the mind'? Do you now see that the question is false?"

Jacques smiled and picked up his notes again. He would not repeat his little diversion when he read his paper to the psychiatrists of Vienna, but he hoped it had served to rekindle the interest of the stout lady to whom he had been speaking.

"Before I share with you, ladies and gentlemen, the nature of my discovery, I would like to show you that what I am proposing is in medical terms not at all revolutionary. You may think it strange for a scientist who is claiming a new theory to say that it is not particularly original, but I believe my work has a better chance of being appreciated if I show how naturally it arises as a synthesis of the innovations and discoveries already in the public domain.

"Let us take the hypnotists. The function of hypnosis in this century has been far greater than merely to illustrate the mental component in hysteria. You will be familiar with the name of Franz Anton Mesmer, who proposed that humans were joined to one another and to the heavens by an invisible fluid. Good health depended on the individual's having the right balance of this fluid, which could, by magnetism, be redistributed between different people. Mesmer's successor, the Marquis de Puységur, was able by magnetism to introduce 'artificial somnambulism' in patients, with good therapeutic results. The relevant state of mind was subsequently christened 'hypnotism' by a physician from England called James Braid. Well, we know that there was no Mesmeric fluid as such and we no longer think magnets are of much use; but these people had discovered something important, and that was that the certain rapport which existed between magnetizer or hypnotist on one side and patient on the other could provide a path into the patient's unconscious mind. And all this is quite old history, as you see.

"Hypnotism fell into disrepute until rescued by a doctor called Hippolyte Bernheim, who worked at Nancy, developing the techniques of his master, the physician Liébeault. I have studied under Bernheim myself and have witnessed at first hand his ability to hypnotize all but the most recalcitrant of subjects and have seen the therapeutic benefits that result. Patients have been able to disclose the root causes of their symptoms, to partake in their cure and even to foretell the day of its completion.

"I have touched on Charcot's immense contribution already, particularly his distinction between, on the one hand, 'dynamic' paralysis— caused by hysteria, trauma or hypnotism—and, on the other hand, 'organic' paralyses caused by a static lesion of the nervous system. Charcot also distinguished organic from dynamic amnesia. In the first, memory is utterly lost; in the second, it can be recovered under hypnosis. The mechanism of this recovery is a serious consideration for us. In his famous lecture of 1882, Charcot reestablished the respectability of hypnotism, but he went further: he showed how 'fixed ideas,' held outside normal mental function, could be the base of certain neuroses.

"All hypnotizers have been struck by what their process reveals about the working of the human mind in general. Two years ago, in Leipzig, Max Dessoir published a book called *The Double Ego*, which reflected the feeling that the mind appeared to be divided into conscious and unconscious parts. The latter was accessible only under hypnosis. Others believed the split went many ways and that we are all an assemblage, or chorus, of personalities. However, it is the split into two which intrigues Janet, and on which I am relying. A long time ago, in 1846, the leading psychologist Carl Gustav Carus wrote: 'The key to the knowledge of the soul's conscious life lies in the realm of the unconscious.' In Carus's view, psychology is the science of the soul's development from the unconscious to the conscious. Truly, ladies and gentlemen, I offer you nothing new: Carus wrote almost half a century ago. In 1869, Eduard von Hartmann's celebrated book *Philosophy of the Unconscious* saw a kind of universal unconscious as the lowest stratum, then a physiological unconscious, which is at work in the evolution of all beings, and last, at the highest level, a psychological unconscious, which underlies your mental life and mine.

"For decades the truth has been all about us. The work of such men as Fechner and Bachofen is in the library in the town. You may go and read it. Even the great Wilhelm Griesinger, who is known as the 'somatic' psychiatrist because he insisted that mental illness is a bodily disease of the brain, was aware of the role of the unconscious. He wrote:

'Almost all fixed ideas are essentially expressions of a frustration or a gratification of one's own emotional interest.' And if Griesinger is not famous enough for you, there is always Nietzsche, who wrote about the mind's quantities of dynamic energy, and how the conflicting drives within it can inhibit or suppress desires, driving them down into what Janet calls the 'subconscious.'

"The name of Janet comes happily at this point. He is not yet as famous as I am sure he will become, but I had the pleasure of knowing him when he began his work at the Salpêtrière in 1889. Before that time he had practiced as a doctor at Le Havre, and it was here that he made some astounding discoveries, the details of which were published by him three years ago in Paris. A nineteen-year-old girl called Marie was brought to him, apparently raving mad. She had hysteria with severe menstrual complications. Every month, she had contractures of the arms and the muscles between the ribs; she had partial loss of feeling; she went blind in one eye and she vomited blood. Janet discovered that on the occasion of Marie's first menstruation at the age of thirteen, she had been so ashamed that she had plunged herself into a large barrel of freezing water to stop the bleeding. She did arrest the flow, but contracted a violent fever. Under hypnosis, Janet took Marie back to the age of thirteen, convinced her by suggestion that her menstruation had not been interrupted by the cold immersion but had painlessly completed its natural course. As for the blindness in Marie's left eye, this had arisen at the age of six, when she slept with a girl who had impetigo and subsequently contracted a partial anesthesia of the left side of her own face. Janet took her back through hypnosis to the night in question, suggested that the other girl was quite well, without infection, and that Marie had passed a pleasant night asleep close to her. All of Marie's symptoms disappeared and her menstruation returned to normal.

"Janet had further successes of this kind at the Salpêtrière with a young woman called Marcelle, whom he helped to walk again by removing in reverse order the fixed ideas that had lodged hysterically in her mind and, only last year, with a patient of Charcot's called Madame D, whose complete amnesia he cured by making her relive the trauma that had caused it. Janet used Madame D's dreams to unearth her hidden memories; he also asked her to indulge in 'automatic talking,' whereby she said anything that came into her head. This is a development of 'automatic writing' done by those under hypnosis and by spirit mediums.

"Janet has many other compelling cases, but my time is short tonight. The important conclusion he drew is that 'in the human mind nothing ever gets lost.' A subconsciously fixed idea persists because it is a kind of congealed emotion of which the patient remains unaware, but which may lead to physical symptoms as extreme as paralysis. It is our task to find what has been mislaid, or hidden. The ways of finding it are many. Some of the symptoms—one thinks of the girl Marie, with the arrested menstruation, vomiting blood—appear to be symbolic. In the case of Madame D, it was her dreams that allowed Janet a window onto her unconscious.

"In Vienna, the great neurologist Moritz Benedikt has recently described what he calls the 'second life,' by which he means the important existence of a secret life in many unwell people, which contains a 'pathogenic secret,' almost invariably of a sexual nature. He has given many examples of patients with hysterical symptoms, almost all of them women, who have been rapidly cured by confessing their secrets. The interesting point about Benedikt is that he has always claimed, since 1864, that hysteria does not depend on organic disorders. He has presented four cases of male hysterics with no heredity and no physical trauma or accident. He contends that the root of their problem is mistreatment in childhood. This is very important.

"Do you see where we are going, ladies and gentlemen? I hope so, because we have almost arrived. I hope also that I have not wearied you with the mention of so many names and the descriptions of what these men discovered or believed. They may sound strange to you, but to me they are as well-known as the names of my old classmates at school; their work is as familiar to me as the unformed handwriting of those little boys long ago. I have mentioned so many only to assure you that what I am proposing is firmly based on work already published.

"Before I conclude, I would like to tell you very briefly why I believe the study and interpretation of dreams may be one of the most powerful weapons in our new cures of madness and distress. First, I must make a small confession. It was a dream of my own, a remarkable one, that first led me to wonder whether there might be some therapeutic value in the analysis of dreams. I shall of course not share that dream with you; it would be both unscientific and tedious—there being perhaps no worse manners on earth than telling others of your dreams. My analysis of my own dream, however, gave me a much fuller understanding than I would otherwise have had of the state of my affections and profoundly relieved a distress of which I had been only half aware.

"I was wary at first of this line of thought, because it seemed to be medieval, or older, in its assumptions; there was something of the shaman about it. However, it was not long before a search of the relevant libraries in Paris led me to a different view. Now it is true that many great German psychologists have seen dreams as little more than the side effects of chemical activity in the brain—a sort of neural waste matter. But there exists a large and equally respectable school of thought to the contrary.

"In my own language there is the example of the Marquis Hervey de Saint-Denys, whose rare book *Dreams and the Means to Direct Them* I was fortunate enough to be lent by a benefactor in Paris. This charming work is mostly about the author's attempts to direct his own dreams, but part of his analysis was suggestive to me. He showed that many apparently novel or unexplained images that occurred in dreams turned out, on closer inspection, to be enactments of things he had forgotten. Our compatriot Alfred Maury's book *Sleep and Dreams* confirmed this phenomenon. Saint-Denys also showed how one quality could be abstracted from an image in a dream and projected onto another. He had no theory to expound; this was simple autobiography.

"In Germany, in 1861, Karl Albert Scherner's book *The Life of the Dream* did have a thesis to propose: that dreams are a language of symbols, which can be interpreted. He showed that the symbolism was mostly related to the physical condition of the patient, so that dreams of flying, for instance, occurred to those with temporarily increased lung function. However, he also maintained that some symbols existed regardless of the patient's health. A house always represents the human body. Over the space of ten or more pages, Scherner listed such things as pipes, towers and clarinets as emblems of the male, while the female is represented by staircases or narrow courtyards.

"A few years later, another highly respected German philosopher, F. W. Hildebrandt, wrote of how dreams could be the materialization of a suppressed immoral thought. I think we can perhaps all think of an instance in our own lives where this may have been the case. Then, just three years ago, under the nom de plume Lynkeus, the German Josef Popper developed this idea to the crucial point by suggesting that unresolved conflict in the dreamer, between conscious and unconscious levels, finds expression in puzzling or coded dreams.

"From the basis of what all these scholars have written, it is not difficult for us to move one step further and suppose that dreams are a necessary mental function; that far from being mere 'neural waste,' these images are those thoughts with which the conscious mind has not been able to deal. In dreams they come to us, these troubling ideas, sometimes in heavy disguise. They come as beggars, mendicants to our door, asking either to be understood or else discharged for ever. They constitute our best guides into the unconscious; they are Virgil to our Dante, as we descend into that dark region.

"Ladies and gentlemen, I must now draw to a close. It is probably clear to you that I have devoted many hundreds of hours to this subject. I began with an orthodox study of an apparently orthodox neurological illness, hysteria. It proved a hard nut to crack, or, as people in the village where I was brought up used to say, 'a hard oyster to open.' The fault line or crack in the closed shell, however, was clearly the mental element. By following Professor Charcot's preliminary examinations and Monsieur Janet's subsequent remarkable case studies, I have been driven into an extremely delicate area of neurophysiology.

"From there, I widened my researches, particularly in the German psychological literature, a glimpse of which I have given you in the last few minutes. The important ideas and phrases often seemed to lie, oddly enough, in the footnotes or the obiter dicta. I remind you of Janet's words: 'The idea, like a virus, develops in a corner of the personality inaccessible to the subject, works subconsciously, and brings about all disorders of hysteria and mental disease.' Not just hysteria in his view, you will note, but *all* mental disease.

"I kept returning in my mind to Charcot's concept of 'dynamic amnesia.' It was not something he had time to investigate fully himself; it was by way of something thrown out by the continuous activity of that great brain. Surely, however, the idea that some amnesia could be unlocked by suggestion was highly significant.

"And then there was Moritz Benedikt, a neurologist second in renown perhaps only to the great Charcot, who pointed out almost in passing that the mechanism for forming a pathogenic secret might exist universally, independent of any specific pathology. It might exist in healthy people too.

"Benedikt also gave me leave to explore the possibility that hysteria might not depend on an organic neurological pathology. I am not ready to abandon Charcot's elegant description of the disease; nor should any doctor do so while hysterical patients present themselves by the score in his consulting rooms. However, Benedikt's suggestion prompted me to examine the way in which an entire psychology might be based on some of the key principles we developed in studying one complex hereditary disease.

"I have not reached my destination yet, but I am well on the way, I believe, in a personal journey which began some years ago in the dissection of eels and crayfish, and has moved on, step by scientific step, to the threshold of something of rather greater importance: the meeting point between thought and flesh.

"I have yet to find an entirely satisfactory name for the new therapeutic technique that attaches to these discoveries. I had wanted to call it 'psychosomatic resolution,' but it has been pointed out to me that many people do not understand the meaning of the word 'psychosomatic.' It truly means 'existing in mind and body,' and is often used of physical symptoms whose cause is in the mind; it suggests a double existence. I believe that a common misunderstanding of the word, however, has it as little more than a synonym for 'imagined'; that in many people's minds, far from meaning dually existent or doubly real, it means unreal or nonexistent! Well, alas, one cannot deal only with what words truly mean, one must deal also with words as they are used or abused. For the time being, I am calling the process 'psychophysical resolution,' and I hope in due course, little by little, we may shed the ugly adjective and call it simply by the more attractive noun, with all its beautiful connotations of healing and calm: resolution.

"Enough of philology. Ladies and gentlemen, I leave you with the firm hope and the modest belief that my discovery, when it is complete, should be nothing less than—and here I permit myself to borrow a phrase once used by my colleague Dr. Midwinter, though it may have lost a little of its elegance in translation from his original, indeed highly original, French—'the way in which functions the mind of the human.'"

JACQUES SWEPT up his notes and leveled off their edges; he had no chief of clinic to hand them to, no one to instruct to prepare them for publication, but there was in his manner something of the Napoleon of the neuroses, of Charcot himself, as he strode from the stage.

XI

ONE OF SONIA'S RESPONSIBILITIES AT THE SCHLOSS WAS OVERSEE-
ing the diet of those patients undergoing the rest cure, and the cornerstone of it was raw beef soup. The prescription was strict: to one pound
of chopped beef she was to add a pint of water and five drops of
hydrochloric acid; the mixture was left in a bottle on ice overnight, then,
in the morning, boiled for two hours at 110 degrees. The warm filtrate
was given to the patients in three portions daily in addition to their regular meals.

In the first week of their confinement, the rest-cure patients took all
meals in their room, beginning at eight o'clock with a plate of oatmeal
porridge and cream, followed by dried ham, white rolls, scrambled eggs
and cheese. This was preceded by the beef soup and followed by a pear
and half an ounce of cod-liver oil; cascara was prescribed for those who
needed it.

Lunch might be a leg and loin of venison, one of Frau Egger's staples,
finished with red wine and half a pint of sour cream and served on a
hillock of buttered noodles. This was preceded by the beef soup and
might be followed by fruit loaf, chocolate sausage or cream cheese pastries with a pint of milk.

The number of patients and the volume of food required meant that
Sonia and Frau Egger had to decide on the menus a week in advance so
that the tradesmen knew what to deliver and on which day. In the summer, when the kitchen gardens of the schloss were at their most fruitful,

rumors began to circulate among the patients that tonight would see one of Frau Egger's strawberry soufflés. These could be served only in the main dining room, not in the patients' bedrooms, but Frau Egger never failed to make them rise, the secret, apparently, being a refusal to inspect them until some native instinct told her they were ready, at which moment they would be carried through in triumph.

Sonia tried to work some lighter English dishes into the repertoire. For every pike with anchovies, she would counter with boiled beef, and fresh carrots from the garden; after liver dumplings and trout in aspic jelly, she would propose gammon hock and sauce infused with parsley that grew in the sunny beds beneath the scullery windows. Frau Egger was in command, but Sonia felt she had established her right to contribute when her other duties left her time to spare.

One day, she was working on the accounts in the office next to the waiting room, where a mother and her teenage daughter sat anxiously awaiting their appointment, when she heard the front-door bell being vigorously pulled. Since she heard no responding footsteps on the stone flags of the hall, she went herself to open it.

A gray-haired man, bearded, travel-weary, dressed in a cape, was standing on the step. "Forgive me, Madame," he said in French. "I believe this is the famous sanatorium of Dr. Midwinter and his partner?"

"Yes, indeed."

"Good. I remember the building, though I see you have done a considerable amount of work to it. You do not know who I am, do you? I visited you briefly in the summer that you opened. Pierre Valade."

He held out his hand and Sonia shook it. "Yes, I do remember," she said. "You have . . . you have lost a little weight, I think. And the beard. That is why I did not recognize you at first. Please excuse me."

"Not at all. You, Madame, on the contrary, are as lovely as ever. Scandal that an ugly villain like Midwinter should have such a beautiful sister."

Coloring a little, despite the obvious insincerity of Valade's bluster, Sonia invited him in. "Perhaps you would care to sit in the garden until Thomas has finished his consultation."

"That would be splendid. Shall I ask your man to bring in my trunk? He is awaiting instructions."

"Yes . . . I mean, yes, I expect we can find a room. We are full up, but . . .

Daisy! Ask one of the girls to make up the green bedroom at the front, will you? Thank you. This way, Monsieur. I shall bring Thomas out to you as soon as he is finished."

Valade sat in the main courtyard on a bench near the fountain, reading a newspaper and smoking a cigar until Thomas appeared at the end of the cloister and strode over the grass to greet him.

"Good heavens," he said. "What on earth has brought you here?"

"My health, of course," said Valade. "Why else would a man go to a sanatorium? It is not for the company, I assure you." He nodded his head toward one of the patients referred from the public hospital, who was tracing a pattern of steps on the cobbles at the edge of the grass and talking animatedly to someone invisible.

"Yes," said Thomas. "He is not strictly speaking meant to be in this courtyard. Never mind. You had better come and join us for lunch. How is Nadine?"

"Vast."

"And Gérard?"

"A little better, thank you, Doctor. He is quite mobile."

As they entered the cloister, Thomas said, "I dare hardly inquire about Madame Valade . . ."

"Sophie has left me," said Valade. "She said that she was lonely."

"Lonely? But surely—"

"I know," said Valade. "A husband, two children at home, friends to visit every day. She said there is nothing so lonely as being unable to communicate."

"But surely she has no difficulty with—"

"Apparently she does. I did not listen. I was too self-absorbed. She felt like a prisoner, she told me. Now she has gone to live with a Russian financier in St. Petersburg, though not as his wife, since he is already married. The children spend six months with her and six with me. At the moment I am unencumbered."

Valade invited himself to stay at the schloss, insisting that it be as a patient. "Melancholy" was his self-diagnosis, though there was little sign of it in his behavior, and he resisted Thomas's offer of a consultation.

"Perhaps you should see my colleague, Dr. Rebière, if you would find it awkward to speak to me."

"I have no desire to talk about my private thoughts to a man I barely know," said Valade. "To tell a stranger my inner feelings! It is a barbaric idea. I ask only to be allowed the peace and quiet of the sanatorium and to feed myself on its excellent cooking."

At dinner that night, he placed himself at the only spare place, which was at a table with two neurasthenic young women, Fräulein Fuchs and Fräulein Wolf, and an elderly German lawyer, Herr Hassler, who suffered bouts of mania in which he believed himself to be the king of Prussia.

"Boy!" called Valade to the startled Hans, who was helping as a waiter. "Bring me a bottle of the best red burgundy in the house. Ladies, will you do me the honor of taking wine with me?"

Valade spoke an inelegant, accented German, quite comprehensible, if hard on the ear. The two girls laughed uncertainly. They were known to Thomas as Miss Fox and Miss Wolf, and he had taken some pleasure in arranging for them to share a table, regretting only the departure—though not the cure—of Miss Hare, Fräulein Haas, the previous month.

"Thank you," said Fräulein Wolf, "I still have a little Riesling left from last night."

"Please do not trifle with me. A half of a half-bottle of German grape cordial is not going to restore you to health, Fräulein. You need red wine from France. Bring a second bottle, young man, and put it on my bill."

Hans had anticipated Valade's needs and had brought up a number of bottles from the cellar. Valade took the first one from him and emptied it into the four glasses on the table. "Ladies and gentleman, to your renewed good health."

Fräulein Fuchs, who seldom drank wine, raised the brimming glass nervously to her lips and inclined her head in thanks.

"Not bad," said Valade, draining his glass, "though it could do with another year or two. I understand that Dr. Midwinter plans to convert the wine cellar into a laboratory, but I suspect he will find more meaning in the bottom of a glass of Nuits St. Georges than beneath the lens of his wretched microscope. Ladies, would you now like to propose a toast of your own? More wine please, boy."

Fräulein Wolf, who had enjoyed her first glass of burgundy, said, "To our kind benefactor. Your good health, Monsieur."

"Thank you. And you, Fräulein?"

Emboldened, Fräulein Fuchs said, "To the good doctors and the wonderful cooks."

In French, Valade replied, "And which of you two ladies will eat me up for dinner? Miss Wolf or Miss Fox?"

The women, both of whom understood Valade's French, laughed, as though the coincidence of their surnames had not occurred to them; and it had certainly never been referred to in such a way. "And Herr Hassler," said Fräulein Fuchs. "To what will you drink?"

"To Germany," said Herr Hassler. "United and strong."

Valade's merriment faltered for a moment, but he managed to drain his glass another time. "To Germany. United and strong," he said. "And on this side of the Rhine."

Sonia, Jacques and Thomas dined at a separate table, to which they usually invited one of the women patients, but Valade spoke so loudly that all the room was included in his conversation, whether they liked it or not. After some breaded carp with cucumber sauce, the waitresses brought in plates of Tyrolean liver, fried with onions and sour cream, with sage dumplings and a lettuce salad, the sight of which encouraged Valade to venture further into the schloss's cellar.

"I think we need something more broad-shouldered to carry the weight of this dish," he said. "A Châteauneuf du Pape, perhaps." Hans obliged with two bottles, and Valade poured for other patients what his own table could not manage.

"Doctor Midwinter," he called across the room, "I would like to congratulate you on your cellar, your kitchen and your altogether excellent establishment. I have only one suggestion. You need to move into the mountains. Who ever heard of a sanatorium in the valley?"

There was a murmur of embarrassment among the patients, who were accustomed to a degree of formality at dinner. Although the public patients ate in the North Hall and those on the rest cure stayed in their rooms, there were still enough in the dining room to give it the feeling of a medium-sized, and respectable, hotel.

Thomas was not put out by Valade, however. "We are not quite in the valley, we are on a hill. But I do agree with you. There is a mountain, my dear friend, called the Wilhelmskogel, whose summit is about one thousand meters above sea level," he said, projecting his voice a little so that it would reach Valade's table. "It is a short distance from here and commands a wonderful view. It is popular with visitors and has a number of tracks for climbers and mules. At present there is a refuge at the top and some unused houses. I have long thought that we should move there when the lease on this place expires, but one cannot ask sick people to undertake such a climb, even on horseback."

"Then you must build a railway," said Valade. "Or a cable car. A funicular, perhaps, the system of weights and pulleys that has become popular. There are any number of ways that such a thing can be done."

"I am sure it could be done, but the expense would prohibit it."

"Then you must find outside investment. 'Ye are the light of the world. A city that is set on a hill cannot be hid.' So our Lord told the multitude on the Mount. 'Let your light so shine before men, that they may see your good works and glorify your Father which is in heaven.'"

"It is a thrilling idea," said Thomas. "From tomorrow I shall start to organize the investment."

"Begin with the mayor," said Valade. "Explain that it would help his city. Boy! We need champagne to go with the dessert."

Valade asked Hans to deliver champagne to all the tables in the dining room, to go with the black cherry cake and apricot Ischl tarts that the girls were bringing in from the kitchen. After dinner, he persuaded Fräulein Wolf to play the piano in the hall, while he commanded Hans to bring more champagne for those who stayed to listen. The party went on till midnight, when Sonia was persuaded to play "The Lincolnshire Poacher" and Jacques sang a song in French: "There was a little ship . . ."

THE NEXT day, Valade cornered Thomas as he was smoking a cigar in the courtyard between consultations.

"I hope the patients were not disturbed last night," he said.

"Not in the least," said Thomas. "It is good for them to have their routine broken a little. They enjoyed themselves."

Valade looked down at the ground. "I was thinking of Sophie," he said. "The woman drove me mad with her incessant chatter. Yet without her, I feel . . . bereft."

"I understand."

"One's own company," said Valade, "is pretty thin stuff."

"You have friends in Paris. And here, of course."

"Yes, but I live my days in my own head. I no longer live through the eyes and thoughts of another. When I was a child I was certain that I was unique. Then as a young man I became convinced that I was, if not unique, then of a complexity and fascination previously unknown." Valade levered a loose cobble up with the toe of his boot. "But over the years I came to understand about half of the paradoxes that made up my complexity. The remainder, it transpired, were either insoluble by me, or, more likely, had no solution. They were simply dead ends of no significance. So you see, Doctor," he said, replacing the cobble and firming it back in place with his foot, "that at the age of fifty-five I have essentially ceased to be of interest to myself."

Thomas smiled. He never knew how serious Valade was being, because he wore the same quizzical, slightly bad-tempered face for humor and solemnity.

"I suppose you still have your painting," Thomas said. "Presumably that provides some consolation."

"I did not turn to art for consolation," said Valade fiercely. "I turned to it in the hope that I could use it to push back the edges of experience. I hoped that I could use it to reset reality."

"That was ambitious."

"It was. But I could see no other point in it."

"And did you come close?"

"I came close in my head. In my head, I even succeeded. But as soon as the wretched hand was involved, I became trapped by the poverty of my talent. Each brushstroke was a smear, a defacement. Each time I touched the canvas, a shadow fell across the purity of the idea and took it further from what I had envisaged. Every painting ended up as an advertisement of my limitations. Only I could see through it to the glorious thing that it was meant to be."

"They looked pretty good to me."

"Pretty good is what they were, Doctor. I aimed for transcendence and I ended with some 'pretty good' paintings."

They walked over the courtyard to the North Hall, which was being prepared for a lecture that evening by a visiting speaker from Vienna.

"Ah, Sophie, Sophie . . . And, Doctor, have you never thought of marrying?"

"I have thought of it. I am not against it. But I would feel sorry for the woman in question. I am still in love with the work I do. I still have great ambitions for it."

"Did you have many loves as a young man?"

"I was in love with someone I met years ago in Heidelberg. She was a nurse at the hospital. She was a very mysterious young woman and in the end I ran away from her rather than be ensnared."

"I did not have you marked down as a coward."

"She would have derailed my life. She had already awoken in me emotions I did not wish to see through."

"I have heard many reports of the morality of young nurses. Something about their daily closeness to death makes them eager to seize the minute."

Thomas laughed. "The study was exhausting. I dare say that for some there were consolations."

"It would suit you to have a wife now, would it not?"

"Perhaps. I seldom think of it. Young women come and go here all the time. Some of them are my patients. Many of them are insane. So in either case, I remain detached."

Thomas felt Valade looking at him curiously.

"And are you happy here, Doctor?"

THOMAS LOVED the Schloss Seeblick and he loved his work there. At the age of thirty-three, he had become, he supposed, a rather serious man, aware through the lives of those he treated how capricious—to put it no more strongly—human life could be, and unwilling to risk his own contentment. He looked at Sonia and how she had blossomed in the Carinthian air, at Daisy and Mary, his cuttings from foreign rootstock, who were unrecognizable as the sad creatures he had first encountered in the asylum. He had reason to be pleased with them and with the way the schloss was going. At the same time as watching over them and treating his patients, he worked hard to develop his own concerns, aware that his interests were diverging from Jacques's and anxious that he himself seemed so far from being able to produce anything original or worth publishing.

He was stuck with the alienist's perennial problem: human mind-sickness was impossible to understand. They converted the cellars into laboratories with overhead electric light (keeping back one room for wine) and hired a third psychiatrist to help them with the growing number of patients. He was a young man from the local district called Franz Bernthaler, whose intellect had made him precociously famous as a prize-winning student. He had recently returned from studying at the asylum in Frankfurt, where he had been taught new ways of looking at cell layers of the cerebral cortex by two eccentrically industrious men, Franz Nissl and Alois Alzheimer. Sections of brain tissue were taken from patients who had died or were brought in from local hospitals; Franz instructed Thomas in the newest histology and staining techniques and together they bent over the microscope until their backs and eyes ached, when Thomas would go through to the end room of the cellar to select a bottle, over which they then discussed what they had seen.

Thomas liked Franz, though he felt a little daunted by the younger man's expertise at the microscope. "I am not at root a scientist, you see, Franz," he said one evening, sipping a glass of hock. "My first interest was in poetry and drama and I have this weakness that makes me always want to see things in large human terms rather than through a magnifying lens. I want great theories and connections, though I know perfectly well that that is not how real scientific progress is made."

"I think that is a preference you may share with Dr. Rebière, if I may say so," said Franz. He was sometimes critical of his employers, but always spoke respectfully, aware that they had dealt with far more patients than he had.

"Oh, no, Jacques is a proper scientist," said Thomas. "The gentlemen of the Salpêtrière rose to applaud him. He is entitled now to talk in larger abstract terms because he has mastered the chemistry. I began with . . .

Oh God, I can barely remember where I began. With some poetic abstract. Humanity. Hope. Some such thing."

"Did you see the obituary of Professor Charcot in the newspaper?"

"Yes, I did. It was very florid, I thought. It had little understanding of his important early work. It was all about his later fame."

"Indeed," said Franz, removing his spectacles and holding them up to the electric light to polish them. "It will be interesting to see what happens to his disciples now that the master is dead."

"I count myself a disciple," said Thomas. "His legacy is secure, I would have thought. Though I suppose you mean the way in which others have developed his work."

"Yes. In Vienna," said Franz. "And Dr. Rebière himself."

"The evil that men do . . ."

"What do you mean?"

"I think that Charcot's best work may be overlooked, 'interréd with his bones,' as Shakespeare might have said. I have doubts about his legacy. I think perhaps it is as well that he died when he did and I suspect that after a respectful pause, some of the avenues he opened will be . . . I have lost my figure of speech here . . . abandoned. I am not sure they lead anywhere."

"A mercy, then," said Franz, resettling his glasses. "How will Dr. Rebière proceed?"

"He was thinking of returning to Paris for the funeral, but I dissuaded him. Jacques's work has its own momentum now. He read a paper in Vienna last winter which was a development of one he read to us here in the spring. It was well received. There are a number of people in Vienna who are thinking in the same way, but they do not all have his authority as a clinical neurologist. That is why people respect him, not as a psychologist, where it is so hard to establish a position, but because he can explain in detail the love life of the eel. And because he is so eloquent, damn it!"

Franz laughed. "And German is not even his native language. Imagine what he must be like in French."

"Not nearly so persuasive, oddly enough," said Thomas. "I think he feels that French was the language of his restricted childhood, English for romance and happiness—but German for science and intellectual freedom."

"Do you have misgivings about his ideas?"

"Misgivings, yes. I would put it no more strongly than that. I would not wish to see him develop a complete psychological theory on the basis of what he learned from one neurological illness—a mysterious and not fully understood one, at that. And I think he would find it extremely difficult to move outward from that base into psychiatry, where the different illnesses may have their own singular organic nature. I think what he has done is wonderful, and I do see why he wants to learn from it and extend it. It looks like a cure and a breakthrough and it is so philanthropic in its application. A cure! Happiness! And yet . . ."

"You have doubts?"

"Yes. I do not believe you will ever cure severe psychiatric illness by the application of psychological theory and what at the Salpêtrière they now call 'psychotherapy'—talking to the patient—however complete your model and whatever your gifts of understanding. He has not yet established the physiology of this process either—how an idea becomes a seizure. He cannot say in exact terms how it works."

Franz smiled. "When I was in Frankfurt, a visiting professor told me the story of a man he knew whose wife had endured an agonizing labor. The husband was present throughout, greatly anguished by what his wife went through. At the end she was delivered of a healthy boy and suffered no after-effects. After two days at the hospital, the father went home elated. Two days later, when his wife and child had returned home, he went to open his bowels, something he had done every day of his life after breakfast. On this occasion, however, something went wrong. The matter he was trying to evacuate got stuck. His sphincter kept contracting, but what it was trying to expel was too big. It was enormous. He began to cry out in pain. 'I can't bear it, I can't bear it.' His wife heard him and came to help. Somewhat shamefaced, he explained the problem. He was in agony, pouring sweat. She went to fetch him a suppository her doctor had given her for the likelihood of constipation in late pregnancy. He inserted it, the contractions increased and eventually this enormous thing was expelled. He expected there to be damage and bleeding to the rectum, but in fact, as soon as it was done, he felt completely normal. He inspected this freak of nature in the water, shook his head in wonder, then disposed of it. It was only a week or so later when he heard his wife describing her childbirth to her sister that he suddenly remembered the words of hers that had so upset him at the time. 'I can't bear it,' she had screamed. 'I can't bear it.' But now it appeared that he had taken over a part of her pain, he had done the proper thing and experienced a version of it for himself."

Thomas laughed. "Did he weigh it?"

"I think he was pleased to see it go! But although there is a practice in certain primitive tribes—it is called *couvade*, I believe—when the men go through rituals of shutting themselves away in sympathy or strapping weights to their bellies, that is all a conscious performance. They feel no pain. But this man . . . Something happened. The idea of sympathy was converted by his brain, through the operation of his nervous system into a somatic offering."

"Unarguably somatic by the sound of it," said Thomas. "But you might suggest a quite prosaic explanation. He had late nights at the hospital, he did not have his normal diet. In his care to bring water to his wife he probably neglected to drink enough himself. All available energy was diverted into remaining alert; little was left over for the normal process of digestion."

"Is that what you think?" said Franz.

"It seems probable. At any rate, it provides a plausible account of how the body worked, even if there was also an emotional motivation."

"That is not how our professor interpreted it," said Franz. "His view was that either it happened as you describe or as I describe. There can be no mixture. Either it was a simple change of dietary habit and it was an utter coincidence that his cri de coeur used the same words as his wife's; or—his subconscious mind entirely took over the working of his body for its own ends."

Thomas smiled. "It need not be a choice. Take the phenomenon of temporary impotence. A man is ready to perform, then lacks confidence, and suddenly the blood drains away. The draining mechanism can be activated chemically, by the effects of alcohol, for instance, or simply by an idea: I am not worthy. So, you would say, this collapse might be caused by the chemical content of wine or the mental content of a man's timidity: either, or. Yet in fact I would suggest the mechanism is the same. Increased blood flow depends on a degree of relaxation. Both alcohol and fear can affect that degree of relaxation through their own separate accesses to the operation of the central nervous system. A room with two doors, but the same room."

Franz put his wineglass down beside the microscope. "Dr. Rebière tells me you are much interested in your fellow-countryman Mr. Darwin. What would he have to say about this mechanism of temporary impotence, do you suppose?"

"I think he might argue that it is an advantage for the less self-confident male not to reproduce. By revealing his lack of fitness at the vital moment, he demonstrates to the female that he is to some extent an impostor and she had better mate elsewhere. Though I must say I do not personally believe that every embarrassment, every tiny experience in life is the selected best outcome of a billion previous experiments. There is still chance. As for the drunkard . . . I am not sure he serves a high purpose in the process of 'descent with modification.'"

"And what about your demented patients? What would he say about them?"

Thomas sighed. "You may say that they are misfits who should be bred out of the human strain. That is the dominant view of European psychiatry, that they are degenerate and part of a doomed process. Yet I cannot accept that. My instincts tell me it cannot be so, partly because they are so numerous. I believe as many as one man in a hundred may have this disease—Dr. Rebière's own brother, for instance. My feeling is that the root of this illness lies very close to the mental faculty that first made us human. It is a relatively new ability, and as a wonderful doctor called Hughlings Jackson—the English Charcot, you might call him—has pointed out, those neural circuits which have most recently evolved are those which are most likely to go wrong. I do not see men like Olivier as degenerates, as simple idiots but with more florid symptoms. I think what they suffer from is a problem in awareness and making connections in the brain. Mr. Darwin's great collaborator Alfred Russel Wallace believes that God has been present at various moments in human development, principally the one at which we gained this consciousness of being alive. I strongly sense that at that crucial chemical moment, when one mutation was 'selected' and the first *Homo sapiens* was born, a certain instability came into the neuronal circuits of the brain. If God was present, you might argue that He was also for a moment absent. Homer nods. One day, this instability may regulate itself through successful transmutation. Until then, I do not see men like Olivier as being degenerate or retarded; I see them rather as at the forefront, in the vanguard of what it means to be a human."

"But they suffer," said Franz.

"My God, they suffer. I think they suffer for all of us. It is almost as though they bear the burden of our sins. It is scarcely too much to say that they pay the price for the rest of us to be human."

"And how do you treat them?"

"I talk to them," said Thomas. "I listen and I try to learn. It is how I treat Dr. Rebière's own brother, though I am aware that I probably take more from it than he does. But, frankly, I have little else to offer him."

Franz smiled. "It is an adventure."

"Yes," said Thomas. "One must always see it in that way. Sometimes I feel such a fool. How can I possibly know these things which are of their nature unknowable? What mad arrogance keeps me hitting my skull against the wall? These are mysteries which no man can know. But there is something of Don Quixote in me, I suppose. Where I see a windmill, I will take my lance and saddle up. I dread growing older because one day I will think that I can no longer be bothered."

Franz took the glasses to the sink to wash.

"We must all try to keep the quixotic element," said Thomas. "Throw the old knight a pie. Give oats to Rosinante."

LATER THAT year Thomas read the new edition of Emil Kraepelin's *Handbook of Psychiatry*. Kraepelin had suffered a frustrating exile in Estonia, where his inability to speak the language had prevented him from making progress; on his return to Germany, however, he had gone to Heidelberg, where he continued to study the long-term course of severe illness. With the help of an enormous card index, he had begun to identify two repeating patterns of psychosis. The first had been baptized "circular insanity" by doctors at the Salpêtrière, because periods of high elation and mania alternated with passages of profound depression; Kraepelin developed the idea and went on to call it "manic-depressive illness." The second category of psychosis he called "premature dementia" or dementia praecox.

Reading the definition in Kraepelin, Thomas recognized it immediately as Olivier's disease. Its basis, Kraepelin stated, was a "psychopathic predisposition"; in other words, it was a biological brain disease. Thomas was moved by the intentions that lay behind the monumental industry of Kraepelin's research: he wanted to be able, as a doctor, to help the woman who asked, "Will my husband recover from his illness? What will happen to him now?" About three quarters of those suffering from dementia praecox grew steadily worse, Kraepelin concluded; but the remainder might grow well again.

Thomas enthusiastically pointed out the passage in Kraepelin to Jacques, thinking he would be encouraged to know that his brother's illness finally had a name; but Jacques said the term had been coined by a Frenchman called Morel some years before, and did not seem able to share Thomas's enthusiasm. To Thomas, it did look like progress. He remembered the ledgers in the asylum, and the multiplicity of colorful and unscientific diagnoses: old maid's insanity, honeymoon psychosis, moon madness. In the older books, causes of insanity were divided into moral and physical, the former including "loss of several cows" and "overexcitement at the Great Exhibition." He saw the faces, gray and dirty, of the urban poor who came to stand in front of his trestle table in the hall, waiting to be assigned a ward number, waiting for an instant name for their distress, then set to vanish down the shrinking corridor.

Kraepelin had divided psychoses into those with violent swings of mood and those without. From the former, patients tended to emerge, from the latter they were unlikely to. He had established patterns, something close to a nosology, and surely this progress at least gave grounds for hope?

What he described to Franz as the "quixotic" element survived in Thomas because he found there were still enough things for him to despise or rebel against. In the summer of the following year, his father died and he returned to Torrington with Sonia for the funeral. His brother, Edgar, told him he would be moving into the house with Lucy and their five children; he asked if Thomas would like to join him in the family grain business and promised him a farmhouse. Edgar seemed bemused when Thomas explained that he had a profession and a life in Carinthia; it was as though, Thomas thought, Edgar believed that he was in some obscure way joking. "Write and let me know if you change your mind," Edgar said, his hand on Thomas's shoulder when the time came to say goodbye. "I will always try to keep a place open for you." Thomas wondered if it was just that Edgar felt he had taken Sonia away from England and that if he returned, she might follow. It was certainly true that without her Torrington was not the same. His mother was bewildered by her husband's death, was herself growing old and had lost some of the self-belief necessary to make such a household seem worthwhile; Lucy was a kind enough girl, he thought, but overwhelmed by children. At least their noise made the old house feel inhabited, and Sonia could not be in two places at once.

Back at the schloss, he learned that Olivier had been found one night in the city, hiding naked in an alleyway. No one was certain how he had got into town in the first place—presumably he had gone with one of the tradesmen who came to deliver each day—but it had been difficult to reassure the police who took him into a cell that he posed no danger to the public or to himself. Jacques enlisted colleagues from the hospital, where he and Thomas still had a clinic, to vouch for their qualifications and good standing. He undertook to make certain there would be no recurrence of the incident, and Olivier was released into his care. The policeman's major concern, it appeared to them, had been that Olivier's nakedness might have affronted people who happened to be walking by.

The next morning, Olivier came down to Thomas's consulting room as usual. He had been at the schloss for four years, and they had grown close to one another. The warmth was manifest in an exasperated affection on Thomas's side, a sort of habitual and frustrated brotherly love, and, on Olivier's, by a manifest anxiety and bizarre behavior if ever Thomas went away.

Thomas always spoke gently, but he had learned that he could also be direct and that, provided he was not alarmed, Olivier often responded well to a kind of bluntness.

"Would you like some of the drink that makes you feel drowsy?"

Olivier did not answer. He touched each arm of the chair, then put his fingers soundlessly together, then each hand back to the chair arm, back together and so on without interruption. This was a sequence of movements he seemed frightened to abandon at any time.

"How do you feel, Olivier? Do you feel better today? Do you feel better now that we are all back?"

Olivier glanced up over his left shoulder. His lips moved, though as far as Thomas was aware he did not speak, at least not to him. It would be one of those days on which it was going to be difficult to engage his attention, but this was often the case.

"Olivier, do you remember what happened? Do you remember being taken into a cell by the police?"

Still there was no answer, though Thomas was not surprised, since this was not something Olivier would wish to confront.

"Who told you to take your clothes off?"

"What did you say?"

"Who told you to take your clothes off?"

"The Sovereign."

Thomas leaned forward; at last he had Olivier's attention.

"The Sovereign? You've told me about him before, haven't you? But he doesn't speak to you often himself, does he?"

Olivier shrugged. "Sometimes. There are a number of people. The Carver comes. Or the Seamstress. Sometimes there are more."

"What determines if there is to be more than one?"

Olivier shrugged, not really interested by the question. "It depends if the message is important."

"And are they here now? Is the Seamstress here now?"

Olivier looked up over his left shoulder. "Yes, she's here now. I won't go to market, I won't go back there. They are all foreigners and they have read the books. So why should I lend them to—"

"Olivier." Thomas regretted mentioning the Seamstress, because now Olivier was talking to her instead of him. He stood up. "Talk to me."

He felt himself appraised by Olivier's gaze; it was clearly a reasonable choice for him—which one to address.

"Last time we met," said Thomas, "you told me something of your thoughts, how they are shared with other people. Do you remember?"

"Yes, of course. What I think can be seen by the Sovereign and by the President of the Republic. I have no need to write to him."

"Which Republic?"

"The Republic of France."

"What is the president's name?"

"The president."

"Do you live in France?"

"Of course." Olivier was unruffled by the question. "There are five or six people who have a list of traitors. They have a list of all the illnesses in the world and they have the cures. It is a very well kept secret."

"How do you know about it?"

"I just know. I receive messages. Sometimes the Carver tells me. Or I can read it in books, you see. It is not in the lines, not in the printed lines. No, no, you would not open the book and just see it there. It is between the lines, that is where I can see it. The monarchy will return. I have been informed."

"But how?"

Olivier gave him a curious look. Thomas was sometimes reminded of one of the fellows of his old college at Cambridge, a man so secure in his superior knowledge that he seemed reluctant to impart it to anyone of lesser intellectual standing; he responded to questions with the same slightly pitying expression that Olivier now directed at him.

Then Olivier spoke quite calmly, something which Thomas always took to be a good sign. He liked watching him, this handsome man of thirty-eight; his graying hair was trimmer these days, as was his beard. There was something oddly cogent in his understanding of the world; the scheme had a completeness, almost a beauty, and in his better moments Olivier achieved a measure of serenity. His voice was gentle and explanatory, and at such moments Thomas felt overcome by love for him.

It was clear to Thomas that Olivier had put a vast amount of emotional energy into understanding the world as it appeared to him; not

only energy, but reason and creative intellect as well. These mental faculties were clearly separate from the perceptual area of his brain which
told him that there was a woman at his shoulder and a creature on his
thigh, where he occasionally made dismissive, brushing movements.

". . . and I can understand the contents of books I have not read,
because I have been chosen," Olivier was saying.

"Do you know by whom you have been chosen?"

Olivier considered. "Do you know that the fire in the sky is how God
cleansed the world of sin?"

"No, I did not know that."

"Really? It's quite simple. I have the powers of blessing, they were
given to me."

"By whom?"

"By God. You see, when a cloud forms, there is a slow increase of
pressure from the vapor gathering inside. If this bears down too hard,
you will have thunder. That is how mankind first came down from
heaven."

"In a cloud?"

"Yes."

"Have you been to heaven?"

Olivier's fingers were moving very rapidly through their rhythm.
"Yes, I have been to heaven."

"What happened there?"

"Jesus held me."

"Jesus held you?"

"Yes. In his arms."

Thomas said nothing, hoping Olivier would continue, but then saw
him glance up, as though listening to another voice.

"What else happened in heaven?"

"What?"

"You were telling me about heaven. How Jesus took you in his arms.
What else happened there?"

Olivier rocked slowly backward and forward on his chair. When
Thomas had first begun his conversations with him (he hesitated to call it
"treatment"), Olivier had been tirelessly expository, extremely patient in his
explanations of the universe he inhabited; often he seemed enthusiastic

about it, eager to share with Thomas its wonders and its laws. No one
had ever taken the time to ask him before, and he seemed to enjoy talking about it. These days, he was a little less lively, Thomas noticed, and
that was something he had observed with patients suffering from the
same disease in the county asylum. By the time they reached the age of
about forty, they began to lose the fight to make a cogent world; they
seemed less able to make even workaday connections. Sometimes
Thomas pictured the inside of their brains as being something like the
network of twigs and branches in an oak tree, though perhaps a million
times more dense. He watched them when their faces grew puzzled and
their speech slowed down; the logic became tenuous; the content of the
sentences began to loop, repeat and trail off into non sequiturs. He pictured the misrouting of electrical impulses over all those years, the auditory area chronically aflame with nonexistent voices; he imagined the
damage done by years of short-circuit in the brain, the buildup and
overspill of chemicals at the point of electrical exchange; and in his
mind's eye he saw not local "lesions" but entire pathways burned away,
like the landscape after the scorched-earth retreat of a vandal army.

"Olivier?"

"Yes."

"What else happened in heaven?"

Olivier brushed vigorously at his trouser legs. "I was given the powers of speaking languages, the gift of tongues."

"And do you speak other languages?"

"Yes, I do."

"Which languages?"

"I speak German. I speak the High German, the proper German. It is
called Royal German, not the other one, which is the Nasal German. You
know, because that is spoken through the nose. It's a different language.
I learned that from my mother."

"Your mother?"

"Yes. My real mother is Joan of Arc. We are descended from Jesus
Christ. The Sovereign has given me the genealogy, I have it all written
down."

"So are you also related to the Virgin Mary?"

"No, no. She was not his mother. No, no. Elisabeth was his real mother, the mother of John the Baptist. Mary was not Jesus's real mother. I can trace my lineage back to Adam."

"Have you ever been to the Garden of Eden?"

"Eden, eaten. Not eaten."

"Would you like to? Is there anything we can do to make you feel happier? Do you like your room in the schloss? It is a good view, isn't it? Across the lake?"

Olivier looked puzzled.

"Why are you here, Olivier? What are you doing here?"

"I have been sent here for some reason." He seemed to regain some of the old enthusiasm, and a little of the donnish quality returned. "You see, there is a formula by which I have worked out the number of cells in my brain and in this way I am unique. My thoughts are in fact recorded for posterity. And I think that is why I am here."

"I meant here, in this building, in this part of Austria-Hungary."

Olivier said nothing. He was lost again.

"How old are you, Olivier?"

"I am twenty. I am twenty years old."

Thomas knew that this was the age at which he had been removed from home and sent to the asylum by old Rebière.

"And do you have any brothers and sisters?"

"Yes, I have a brother."

"How old is he?"

"He is . . . he is . . . I don't know how old he is."

"Where is he now?"

"He is . . . he is at school."

Thomas stood up. "I have spoken to you enough this morning." He laid his hand on Olivier's arm. "I think you should go for a walk in the sunshine and then have something nice to eat at lunch."

He escorted Olivier to the door and watched as Daisy took him out beneath the stairs into the cloister, his fingers still fluttering in their rapid pattern of touch.

XII

IN THE SPRING OF THE NEW YEAR THOMAS BECAME UNEASILY
aware of one of Jacques's patients, a fair-haired young woman, fashion-
ably dressed, with a healthy, trim physique but a weary, troubled manner. He saw her walk rapidly from her room on the first floor above the
courtyard through the cloister to the dining room and exchanged pleasantries with her as she passed by; she smiled and returned his greetings
in a clear, soft voice, but there was something about her demeanor that
troubled him. She appeared feverish, he thought; there were sometimes
spots of color in her cheeks. He noticed these when he saw her emerging
from Jacques's room after a protracted consultation, but he was inclined
to ascribe it to the rigors of the interview: hysterical or neurotic patients
were frequently embarrassed or upset by the content of what they had
revealed.

Thomas's misgivings, however, would not leave him. He found himself fascinated by this woman, with her agile movements that seemed to
mask pain, her loose fair curls neatly held back from the skin of her face
and the reading glasses she removed if she felt she was being watched in
the courtyard or in the dining room; he was intrigued by the way her
expensive clothes seemed at odds with a rather studious manner. He was
also anxious that she might be seriously unwell, and one morning
brought up her case with Jacques.

"Ah yes," he said. "Fräulein Katharina. She is a very fascinating
problem, I think. She has made good progress and she will shortly be

leaving us. I am writing up her case notes because I am hoping to read a paper to the autumn meeting of the Psychiatric Association in Vienna. I shall have to ask her permission, of course, and find another name for her. Why do you want to know?"

"She intrigues me."

"She is an intriguing woman. In some ways a textbook case of hysteria, I think, but with interesting complications."

"I don't suppose you would allow me to read your case history?"

"I was trying to pluck up the courage to ask you to do just that. I would value your opinion very much indeed. As soon as I have finished it, I shall pass it over."

Thomas decided to ask Sonia if she knew any more about this Fräulein Katharina, but when he went up to her apartment he could find no trace of her.

Sonia was sitting in her favorite seat beneath the cedar tree, looking up to the mountains. The previous afternoon, she had gone into town on the pretext of visiting some tradesmen, but had made a secret visit to the gynecologist, who had confirmed what she believed: that she was three months pregnant.

At the age of thirty-seven, she felt it might be her last chance. The doctor assured her that he could see no reason why she should miscarry a second time, but did urge her to rest each morning for as long as she could. Sheepishly, because she was worried that Jacques might think her idle, she explained to him what the gynecologist had said.

"And the reason I must rest, my love," she said, "is that I am expecting a child."

She watched his dark eyes carefully as she broke the news, and she saw tears rise up the iris, tremble on the lower lid, then run in two unchecked lines down his cheeks. He reached out his arms and held her close to his chest, with a comically exaggerated care, as though already aware of a third person between them. He made her undress and lie down on the bed, so that he could run his hand over her belly and kiss it.

Sonia looked down from the pillows. "How big is he now, do you think?"

Jacques bent his thumb in half and pointed to the top joint. "About this long, I think. He has a head and limbs. A large head, small arms and legs."

"Does he have a brain?"

"Not much yet."

"Oh dear, do you think he is a simpleton?"

"No, I think he will take after his mother."

"Stop it. What else can you tell me about him?"

"He is sleeping a lot. He is very warm and happy in there."

"Oh, I love him so much, don't you?"

Jacques laughed.

"I mean it," said Sonia. "He is a perfect sweetheart."

"Will he be English or French?"

"I don't know. Ask him."

Jacques placed his lips on Sonia's belly and spoke in German, then French, then English; then he put his ear to the skin, where a thin brown pigmentation was already starting to make a line.

"He says he is an Englishman because he loves his mother best."

"Good boy. What a charmer. And what does he like doing?"

"He likes sleeping. Wait a minute. I'll ask him. He says he would like to play cricket."

"I feel I know him already," said Sonia. She grew suddenly serious. "I have known him all my life, since I was a child. He has been there since before I was born."

She began at once to cry, the sobs taking over her body, as she came to see the enormity of what she said, of this life about to happen, something eternal, returning from a land unknown.

THOMAS HAD to be told the news, so that he would know why Sonia was resting on her bed in the morning rather than working in the office. He was moved by her happiness, and his own; he felt that Sonia's life might now move on toward its appointed purpose and fulfillment.

That evening, when his last consultation was over, he swiveled his desk chair round and put his feet up on the windowsill, so that he could look out over the lawn. It was a pity his father was not alive to see Sonia's child, he thought, to see how she had redeemed her fortunes.

There was a knock on the door. "There you are, Thomas," said Jacques. "I have been looking for you. My paper on Fräulein Katharina. I finished it last night and I need to send it off before the end of the week. Do you think you might have ten minutes to glance through it?"

"I shall do it now."

"Bear in mind that it's only a draft. I have written it in German and have tried to give it a fairly authoritative tone for the benefit of the audience."

"I understand," said Thomas. "I shall not expect to hear your own Breton voice in it."

"No. Though the science and the resolution are certainly mine. It's on the blotter on my desk. It is held together with a pin."

Jacques's consulting room had a faint odor of cigars from the indulgence he allowed himself each evening when the last patient had gone. There was a large blue-and-white pot full of hydrangeas on a windowsill and a vase of cut flowers on the desk. The bookshelves were lined with the astonishing extent of his German and French reading, much of it in cheap or secondhand editions, but the shredding rug on the oak boards managed to give the room a homely rather than intimidating feel.

Thomas took the pinned papers from the desk, went over to the window and pushed back the folded wooden shutter so the light fell across his shoulder as he began to read.

FRÄULEIN KATHARINA VON A

In the early summer of 189–, a patient was referred to me by a physician in private practice in Vienna. A young woman, aged twenty-five years, Fräulein Katharina von A had been complaining for some time of severe lower abdominal pain, accompanied by infrequent vomiting. She had been wrongly diagnosed by a doctor in Vienna as suffering from uterine fibroids, when she was too young for such a condition typically to have developed and had experienced no increase in menstrual flow; in fact, as later became apparent under more careful examination, she had suffered an intermittent amenorrhea.

Fräulein Katharina gave the impression on first meeting of being a young person of outstanding character. Her father was a businessman of considerable means, and Katharina had passed an apparently uneventful childhood in the company of her younger brother and sister, to whom she appeared tenderly devoted; indeed, in speaking of her family, and in particular of her father, she invariably displayed a most natural and pleasing affection. Her mother was English, though had spent a great deal of her own youth in Ceylon, where her father worked as a tea planter; she had met and married Herr von A in London in 1869, and Katharina was born the following year in Vienna, where the family retained a house even when the father's work necessitated their temporary removal to Hanover and to the Baltic states.

Of a little above average height and with a fair coloring characteristic of her Prussian and English descent, on her first visit to my consulting rooms Fräulein Katharina in many ways presented a picture of youthful vigor. On a close visual examination, I found the epidermis to be fine, with a scattering of reddish-brown maculae on legs, arms and lower back, typical in one of such coloring; the areolae were unusually thin, barely discrete in texture from the surrounding skin. She informed me that she had practiced archery as a hobby, and the effects of the sport were visible in a somewhat enlarged brachialis of the right arm and a firmness of the extensor and flexor muscles. She had recently been on a walking holiday in the Eastern Alps, where she had climbed in the Hohe Tauern range, at heights of more than two thousand meters. There was a minor development in the adductor and quadriceps; the pelvis appeared fairly narrow and there was no excess tissue on the gluteus maximus.

The patient spoke with a soft but clear voice; it was apparent from the first consultation that she was a person of considerable education and self-possession. However, in addition to lower abdominal pain, she reported chronic joint pain in the shoulders, elbows and fingers. She had also suffered a form of spasm in the shoulders, and, on infrequent occasions, in the hips and face: the symptoms she described were similar to those found in Sydenham's chorea, though she said they recurred less and less often and was inclined to treat them as a closed episode.

The pains in her joints had been attributed by her family physician to an excess of secretarial work undertaken for her father, whose failing health had obliged him to work more and more from the family house in an affluent part of Vienna instead of going into his company's office. I was not initially in a position to confirm or reject this diagnosis, but I did note that she reported that the pains recurred regardless of whether or not she had been working at her desk; and that the amount of secretarial work she was obliged to do had dramatically diminished, for the simple reason that her father had recently died of an infection of the heart.

Since the age of seventeen, Fräulein Katharina had suffered from right-sided occipital headaches, though she had been largely cured of these by an oculist in Vienna, who diagnosed a moderately severe astigmatism, a common abnormality of vision from which her father also suffered. Katharina wore small, silver-rimmed glasses for close work of any kind. She assured me that she only needed them if she was required to concentrate her eyesight for any length of time; indeed, she exhibited some aversion to wearing them, but I attributed this to feminine vanity, she being in other respects a manifestly modest and serious-minded young woman. She still suffered from stinging in the eyes if she was tired or upset, regardless of whether or not she had been using her reading glasses. Her eyes in other respects appeared normal when I tested for diplopia and the Argyll Robertson sign.

Her health as a child had generally been good, though she had had a tendency to infections of the throat, which had caused her to lose many weeks at school. At the time of our first consultation, she had a minor irregularity of the pulse and her temperature was elevated a degree above normal. This she attributed to a mild chill she had caught in the coach on the way to the sanatorium, and since the pyrexia was absent on our second meeting, I was inclined to accept her own diagnosis.

The patient seemed bemused by her symptoms, particularly the degree and variety of abdominal and joint pain from which she was suffering. I have frequently observed that patients with organic illness are able to give, according to their powers of self-expression, a more or less coherent and consistent account of the sensation of pain they are experiencing; they can say, for instance, whether it is throbbing or stabbing, twisting or dull. Neur-asthenic patients, on the other hand, often devote many minutes to trying to describe the discomfort and generally seem dissatis-fied with their own efforts, even when they are people of superior lucidity. The present patient fell into neither category, but, while clearly distressed by her pain, spoke of it in a detached and cool manner which made me suspect that her atten-tion was in fact more passionately engaged elsewhere, on issues of which the pains in her joints and lower abdomen might be little more than representations.

There was no obvious neuropathic heredity in Fräulein Katharina's family, though she seemed to know little about her mother's English relations beyond her maternal grandmother, a healthy old woman who had occasionally traveled from her home in London to visit them. Though German was her first lan-guage, Katharina spoke fluent English, with no accent, so far as I could judge; she also demonstrated competence in French when I asked her to speak in that language. The reason for my doing so was that she had complained of complete aphonia on two occa-sions in the last two years, the first time when she was visiting her brother in Paris, and I was interested in establishing whether her temporary loss of speech might have had some connection with a lack of confidence in a foreign language.

The most intriguing aspect of Fräulein Katharina was the contrast between, on the one hand, the range of symptoms she presented and the very real distress that they occasioned her and, on the other, a kind of rational detachment. It was becoming clear to me that the initial impression that this evidently thoughtful young woman gave to the world concealed an extremely troubled interior life, and I was inclined to attribute the stoical air with which she bore her considerable troubles to what Charcot called the *belle indifférence* of the hysteric.

The clinical picture was further complicated by what one might term superficial anxiety states, expressed in a chronic insomnia, a tendency to low spirits, and a somewhat morbid fear of animals.[1] It was, at our first consultation, impossible for me to investigate fully these symptoms or to assign them their proper places in the hierarchy of her illness. My initial reaction was to see these relatively common and not particularly severe symptoms as—with one exception—a kind of diversion or displacement of more serious concerns and not in themselves particularly significant; and I am happy to say that my subsequent investigations were to prove me right.

Having arranged for Fräulein Katharina's admission to the sanatorium, I concluded our first consultation by assuring her I was confident we should shortly get to the root of her troubles. Privately, I was inclining to a mixed diagnosis, in which it was possible that while some organic disorder might originally have been present, it was hysteria that was now, as it were, conducting the orchestra.[2] I told her that we would begin with some massage and electrotherapy and that her diet and exercise regimen would be closely supervised by the staff between her consultations with me.

She appeared happy to think that positive steps were being taken and made no resistance when I told her that, in addition to these measures, I might wish to inquire into her personal history in considerably more depth in the course of the following days. To tell the truth, I was somewhat daunted by the thought of how the techniques of psychophysical resolution might be applied to such a wide variety of symptoms in the case of a patient with an

[1] I had a most arresting example of this zöophobia when one of the stray cats occasionally found in the gardens pressed itself against the windowpane of the consulting room, causing Katharina to jump in exaggerated fright. She explained that as the creature turned sideways to rub itself against the glass, she felt as though a single eye was watching her.

[2] Hysterical symptoms regularly become attached to what were originally manifestations of an organic disorder. Neck and arm cramps, for instance, can be employed for the purpose of hysterical attacks, where the patient does not have the typical symptomatology of hysteria at her disposal.

apparently well developed self-understanding. It was difficult, on the other hand, not to feel sympathy for the evident suffering of a transparently affectionate and well-meaning young woman, so the prospect of resolution also held out considerable therapeutic allure.

April 19 [morning]

Fräulein Katharina said she had passed a very disturbed night. She was at pains to stress that the fault did not lie with her accommodation, which evidently pleased her and which she was quick to praise, but with the acute discomfort from her joints.

I examined her again and applied the faradic brush to a part of her arm she reported as having lost sensation; I then massaged her back and shoulders and told her she could expect a consequent relief in the pains of the joints. She appeared to enjoy the experience and was happy for me to stroke the parts of the lower abdomen that had most troubled her, though I applied only a limited pressure. I said I would arrange for twice-daily massage to become part of her regime, but she seemed alarmed that it might not be I who administered it on each occasion, so I agreed to postpone any firm decision.

By now I had decided to try to hypnotize the patient to see if somnambulism could provide a route into her unconscious, there being in my view a degree of urgency about the case. She readily agreed to the procedure and, when she was fully dressed again, lay down on the couch. After several attempts to put her into a hypnotic sleep, I had to confess that she was an extremely resistant subject; for all that I have studied Bernheim's methods at close quarters, I have concluded that his own skill with hypnosis is as much responsible for his remarkable results as the innate suggestibility of his patients. With Fräulein Katharina, I had to be content with a state of cooperative relaxation, from which, I told her, she would be able to remember more at key moments suggested by the pressure of my hand on her forehead.

Using this technique, I was soon able to establish the moment at which she had first been aware of her abdominal troubles.

Her father had first fallen ill when Katharina—or Kitty, as she was known to her family—was twenty-one years old. They had enjoyed a relationship of unusual closeness throughout her life; he treated her more as a sister than a daughter and appeared to rely on her for a levelheadedness and equanimity sometimes absent in the mother. He used to take Katharina to the theater and discussed his work with her in detail, sometimes joking with her that he wished he could take her into the gentlemen's clubs he frequented for supper, since she was "as good as any man." He was a generous and loyal father; he enjoyed buying her dresses and small pieces of jewelry. On many occasions he told her how much he loved her and that she was a "blessing sent to him as a sign of love from God."

By her own account, Katharina had been a tomboy, who much enjoyed playing with the local youths on a farm near Hanover where they had passed the summers of her early childhood. In the course of these she had become acquainted with the rudiments of animal reproduction; she had watched a bull being put to the cows and one spring had helped with lambing. Her mother appeared to have been an indolent and rather foolish woman who, while remaining undoubtedly good-looking and possessed of considerable charm, had not made the most of her gifts.

Katharina had a brother called Gustav, two years younger than herself, and a sister called Anna, three years younger than Gustav. It naturally fell to Kitty to help nurse them, particularly when her mother was going out for the evening. These tasks she performed with good grace and devotion, dressing up dolls for Anna and allowing Gustav to share her room and even her bed when he was frightened of the dark. The ebullience of her temperament doubtless made such duties easy for her to perform, but at the same time she told me she was anxious that she was likely to be used both as a substitute mother for her siblings and to some extent as a surrogate wife by her father; she was clearly a high-spirited and determined girl who felt there was a possibility that she would be denied the time to develop her own talents, which her father had convinced her were the "equal of any boy's."

At the age of fifteen, Fräulein Katharina was sent to a girls' boarding school near Wolfsburg and for a time felt extremely disconsolate about being parted from her family, particularly from her father and from little Gustav, with whom she had been accustomed to share her secrets. At school, her anxieties about being used by the needs of others, and thus somehow finding herself overlooked, began to take a sexual form. As I applied mild pressure to her forehead, she confessed that she craved attention and had enjoyed sapphic fantasies about the older girls at school and had occasionally masturbated at night in her bed. She further volunteered that when she was about twelve, she and her friend Maria had been playing in the woods when both found it necessary to hoist up their skirts to squat down and micturate; they discovered later that Gustav had been spying on them, and Kitty confessed that she had enjoyed being exposed to her brother's gaze in this way and had wanted to touch Maria's genitals while they were wet, "to lure something warm out of her," as she put it. She had, at this time, an irrational fear that she would die virgo intacta and felt she could not rest easy until she had experienced the sexual act, though her modesty and upbringing of course made such a thing impossible.

When she returned home for the holidays, she found that her father had hired a secretary, Frau E, a commanding character who had to some extent taken over Kitty's role in the house. A domestic war seemed to break out between this woman and Katharina, who not only resented the way that Frau E had usurped her place but found, to her alarm, that she felt physically fascinated by her. Things came to a head about a year later when Katharina was seventeen, when, after they had drunk some of her father's wine, the secretary seduced her and apparently showed her how to masturbate to orgasm, something Katharina had never achieved before.

The important events of the next few years can be briefly summarized: on leaving school, Katharina resumed her position as her father's principal helpmeet and secretary; Frau E parted from the family on good terms, and wrote frequently to Kitty, whom she called "my little weasel." Their secret was not discovered by either parent and the incident itself was apparently not repeated.

Soon afterward, Katharina's father fell seriously ill with a heart complaint and was obliged to retire from work; the task of nursing him fell to Kitty, since her mother declared herself too distraught and was not in good health herself. During this time, the house in Vienna was frequently visited by Herr P, a lawyer of about thirty-five who was a junior partner in Herr von A's company and his confidant in business matters. Kitty would be obliged to leave the sickroom when Herr P came to visit so that the men could conduct their business in private. On such occasions, she would either repair to the kitchen to instruct the maid to make some refreshment for the visitor or would go to her own bedroom until such time as her father should need her again. She would also, quite naturally, follow the same course of action when the doctor came to see her father. On one such occasion the regular doctor could not come but sent some sort of locum tenens in his place, a young man less well-mannered than the regular physician, who, after his consultation with Herr von A came into Katharina's room without knocking to tell her he was leaving. She had felt irrationally furious and embarrassed by this intrusion, she said; she felt powerless, "as though my hands were tied," and she thought it typical of this young man's presumptuous yet stealthy manner in her father's house.

For almost two years Fräulein Katharina nursed her dying father, with little help from her mother, who was suffering from chronic anemia, and none at all from her younger brother and sister, who were respectively at university in Heidelberg and at Kitty's old school near Wolfsburg. She was doubtless lonely and vulnerable at this time, though was still able to leave the house occasionally and to see friends of her own age, and usually of her own sex. She said that she "fell in love easily" with young men, but distrusted her emotions and had never had any sort of sexual relations with a man; her mother told her she was "too affection-ate" and she was inclined to agree. During all the time of her father's illness, Herr P was the most regular visitor, though vari-ous family friends called for half an hour or so in the evening and Frau E remained a regular correspondent.

One day at lunchtime, Kitty left her father with the doctor and went down to the kitchen where she made a tray for herself and took it back to her room so she could be near at hand if he should call. While she was drinking some courgette soup and eating a bread roll, the door swung open after a single knock, and the doc-tor came in to tell her that the worst had happened: her father was dead. Kitty, overcome by grief at the loss of this most loving and gentle of fathers and distraught that after a vigil of almost two years she should not be present at his bedside when it hap-pened, was violently sick, vomiting her lunch back over the tray.

After persistent questioning on my part, she confirmed that she had no recollection of abdominal pain before this moment, but that it had been intermittently with her ever since.

Fräulein Katharina had been extremely cooperative during the preceding ninety minutes; she had evinced some surprise at the intimacy of some of the inquiries, but had done her best to respond, even when evidently embarrassed by the memories that I had unearthed. I judged it prudent to terminate the consulta-tion at this point.

April 20 [evening]

Katharina was in much better spirits this evening. She had had a bran bath in the morning and ate well at lunchtime; she had had some galvanic treatment on her shoulders and arms and then a warm bath before coming to see me. Her menstrual period had started today after an interval of only two and a half weeks; although she seemed pleased by this, I promised her that if she

were fully hypnotized, I could reset the interval, using suggestion, at twenty-eight days.

We began by bringing the story of her life up to date, and this
was easily accomplished. Her mother had recovered her health
quite quickly after her father's death and within the year was
engaged to be married again—to Herr P, her father's young colleague whose visits to the house had been a regular but, she
claimed, to Katharina a less than welcome feature of life during
her father's illness. The newly married couple would move to a
house in the outskirts of Vienna and the family home would be
sold; Katharina expected to set up house in an apartment in town
with her younger sister, Anna, since her brother, Gustav, was
now working in Paris. In the time immediately preceding our first
appointment, she had been searching for a suitable place and
helping to pack up her parents' old house.

I had spent many hours reflecting on what Fräulein Katharina had told me in the course of our previous meeting. I felt that
a fairly clear picture of the trauma that had precipitated her hysteria was now available to me (and must by now also be taking
shape in the mind of anyone to whom the outline of the case has
been related), yet I was puzzled by the fact that the patient had
found access to the relevant memories without being in a state of
hypnosis, since it is a principle of resolution that pathogenic
memories are not present in the conscious mind, or at least only
in summary form. I continued my questioning, therefore, on the
assumption that a part of what Fräulein Katharina had told
me was the result of what I shall call a "delegate" or "proxy"
memory—that is to say a recollection which, while not in itself
mendacious or incomplete, is of interest to us chiefly for what it
tells us of something more important which is absent or withheld.

With this thought in mind, I decided to see if I could find a
more direct road into her unconscious by asking her about her
dreams. She affected to find this amusing at first, assuring me
that her dreams were commonplace and lacking significance,
but I emphasized that, on the contrary, as Maury had explained

so well, the commonplace is the one thing that is never present in
our dreams.

Eventually, she was able to tell me of a dream that she could
clearly remember after some months, aspects of which still
troubled her. She was in a large street in Vienna, probably the
Kärntnerstrasse, and running up the stairs to a set of rooms in
an office building where her mother lay dead. She was in a panic
because she had to make the arrangements for the burial as soon
as possible, yet she felt that someone very important was missing.
"I felt it was imperative that I take matters into my own hands,"
she said, "yet I felt paralyzed from doing so." It was this haunting
or double sense of absence, not only of her mother but of someone else, that made the dream so memorable. She was also worried about her clothes, which had become mud-spattered as she
ran down the Kärntnerstrasse; there was a more suitable dress in
a wardrobe in the corner of the room where her mother's body
lay, but she feared to open it because there was a mouse hole in
the adjacent wainscoting and she had seen a single eye glinting
out at her from inside.

April 25 [EVENING]

I had seen Fräulein Katharina on a number of occasions
since she revealed to me the content of her troubling dream,
though without feeling that she had subsequently disclosed
anything of a great significance so far as the resolution was concerned.

I felt that the preconditions for the onset of her hysteria were
now established beyond doubt: namely that a traumatic incident
had been deliberately suppressed by her conscious mind because
she found the implications of it intolerable. This sum of psychological excitation, being denied proper release, had converted
itself easily through the pathways of somatic innervation into
the distressing symptoms—the abdominal discomfort, the joint
pains in arms and fingers—from which she now suffered. The

basis of her decision to suppress the memory of the incident could quite easily be seen to spring from an unendurable conflict between the thoughts and desires it gave rise to on the one hand and, on the other, the entity of her social personality, composed of the duties and affections that had been expected of her. The last laugh, as it were, had remained with the suppressed ideas, however, which had turned pathogenic.

I was now ready to reveal to the patient my understanding of the pathological process that had taken place—and indeed I was eager to do so, since it must be remembered that it was distressing to see the anguish of a young woman of such principled and gentle character.

Before proceeding, I asked her to recall the occasions on which she had suffered her aphonia and found that the first instance had followed swiftly on the incident in which the young doctor so suddenly interrupted her reverie in her bedroom. She could not place the second incidence with any degree of certainty.

I began my resolution of Fräulein Katharina's difficulties by asking her to reexamine the dream she had described to me. Who was it that she believed to be bafflingly absent from the scene? "Why, my father, of course!" she responded in a lighthearted way. I explained to her that the interpretation of dreams depended on their being understood essentially as the fulfillment of a frustrated wish—a longing which the censor who watched her thoughts by day had compelled her to displace. The release of such a wish in her dream, albeit disguised and clothed in paradox, was the parallel process to that of resolution with which we had been engaged: her dream offered a semaphore version of a displacement that we should more surely establish in waking hours; we might pore over it, I suggested, as over a pictographic script.

Since she was unable to identify the desire of which her dream was a fulfillment, I was obliged to do so for her. "You wish your mother dead," I explained. She cried out in remonstrance that she had no such desire, though this was of course entirely to be expected since, had she been conscious of her true feelings, they would not have been suppressed. "The reason you wish your mother dead," I continued, "is to leave you free to marry Herr P, with whom you have been in love for more than two years." Fräulein Katharina, as I anticipated, indignantly denied that she had had any amorous feelings toward Herr P, whom she described as "ingratiating" and "irritating." She did concede, however, that she felt her mother's remarriage followed with indecent haste on the death of her father.

When she had calmed herself, I continued therefore to explain the resolution. The person whose absence so distressed her was, as we have seen, Herr P. Her mother's death ought to have freed him to marry Kitty, so it was to be expected that the lawyer would at least be present in what sounded like his own office. Her anxiety over her clothes (the funeral dress, the mud-spattered skirt) could be explained, as so often, by the reverse: she was anxious about her clothing precisely because she wished to be naked, as she had many times imagined herself with Herr P. The most conclusive detail of the dream, however, was the mouse hole in the wainscoting and her fear of the little animal which prevented her from arranging her dress or undress as she desired. Was it not true that Frau E had called her "little weasel"? She herself had volunteered the fact that in the scene of childhood exposure, when she had enjoyed showing herself to her brother in the woods, she had also wanted to touch the genitals of her little friend Maria, while they were still wet, "to lure something warm out of her." In Katharina's unconscious, the act of mastur-bating had become associated with the idea of small animals in their holes or burrows; doubtless Frau E's successful manipula-tion had involved the appearance of the clitoris from within its pro-tective hood, like a timid animal that subsequently withdrew.

At the moment she felt she had triumphed over her mother and secured the love of Herr P, she feared that Herr P knew both of her connection with Frau E and of her solitary habits which disqualified her from possessing that which she most desired. Even at that moment she had felt a need to "take things into her own hands"—as though the frustrated part of her perversely still wished to demonstrate to Herr P that she was unworthy of him.

I then asked Katharina to return to the moment when her abdominal pains first started. The doctor came into her room to tell her that her father had died; she vomited her lunch back onto the tray: from that moment, she had not been free from pain. Naturally, she ascribed her reaction to grief: shock at the loss of her adored father, and chagrin at being absent from his bedside when it happened. However, it was clear that the emotion that she truly felt, in order to become pathogenic, must have been otherwise. What her vomiting in fact revealed was her revulsion at what the future now held in store for her: the death of the father had released her mother to marry Herr P—an idea she literally rejected or threw out. The intermittent pains in her lower abdomen were a mnemic symbol or aide-mémoire of that distressing emotion, which had been at once held outside the normal physiology of her consciousness.

Since her father's death, she had been without a confidante: Frau E was gone, her brother and sister were away, and her mother's fondness for Herr P had ruled her out as a friend. The scope of Katharina's duties was wide, and she performed the whole of the mental work that was placed on her, in the winding-up of her father's estate, the organization of his papers, and the emotional support she gave to other members of the family with her usual conscientiousness. In addition to the loss of her father and all that it entailed, she suffered, in losing Herr P, a severe blow to her self-confidence as a woman and, in short, the conditions could not have been more disposed to the retention in her nervous system of large amounts of undischarged mental excitation.

The irregularity of her menstrual periods, dating also from about this time, was evidently caused by her desire that she should in fact by now have been carrying Herr P's child. Masturbation to orgasm is also known to precipitate amenorrhea, and it was indeed my suspicion that such a practice had taken place which led me to the heart of Fräulein Katharina's trauma, as we shall shortly see.

The pains in her arms and fingers had initially been caused by the excessive amount of work demanded of her by her father; I had no doubt that this trouble had begun as little more than writer's cramp, an organic, secretarial version of "housemaid's knee" or some such trifling ailment. However, it had become complicated by two further factors. To begin with, she had been in competition with her mother for the attention of Herr P, and had tried to demonstrate to him how much more assiduous and reliable she was than the listless Frau von A; diligence in office work naturally occurred to her as the obvious way of impressing a serious young lawyer. I doubt whether even this aspect of the strain, however, would have survived the effective discontinuation of the manual work after her father's death, because Katharina was sufficiently conscious of the competition.

No: the crucial development as far as suppression was concerned was the digito-manual nature of the pain and the fact that such activity had already become symbolically associated in her unconscious with the private habits that had disqualified her from becoming Herr P's wife. It was this unacknowledged guilt which enabled the symptoms to persist in her shoulders, elbows and finger joints; indeed, as time went by and Herr P and her mother became overtly attached, then engaged to be married, the situation worsened: the painful region was extended by the addition of adjacent areas; every fresh event in her life which had a pathogenic effect cathected a new region in her arms. She had signaled desperately to herself, and to me, with her repeated phrases such as "I really must get to grips with this," or "I must take things into my own hands," but it was only now that the connection was established that the business of resolution could take place.

I felt that, having laid out the groundwork of the resolution in the course of this consultation, I should leave the patient time to reflect on what we had discovered before I moved on to what one might call the dénouement. I therefore concluded the session and arranged to see the patient the following day.

APRIL 26 [MORNING]

Fräulein Katharina appeared in a subdued mood. The skin of her face was slightly flushed. She told me she had slept badly, though admitted to a complete absence of pain in the lower abdomen and a considerable improvement in the joints of the arms and fingers. One might describe her demeanor as chastened, though she continued to be as obliging as before in her dealings with me.

I began by tidying up, as I put it, a few of the lesser symptoms with which she had presented me. Her low spirits, her insomnia and minor anxiety states were no more than the reaction of a young woman of unusual sensibility to the experiences she had gone through. The zöophobia, on the other hand, which I had at first been inclined to put into the same category, could now be seen in fact to be somewhat more significant.

While it seems beyond dispute that Fräulein Katharina's heredity included a predisposition to hysteria, it would be unfair to describe her, as the diagnosis of that disease strictly requires, as degenerate. On the contrary, the moral seriousness with which she viewed her duties, the compassion and energy she displayed were the equal of a man's—and in this respect her father's words to her were touchingly vindicated. Kitty's degree of education, regard for truth and tender feelings for others drove me to conclude that, despite what we have learned, a predisposition to hysteria may be compatible with a fine character and a well-governed mode of life.

I tried to reassure Fräulein Katharina of this paradox, as I persuaded her to confront the central moment of her story: the moment at which the young locum tenens came into her room without knocking. I suggested that it was this incident, more even than the death of her father, which had been most difficult for her to deal with in conscious life. It was not, in fact, the young doctor who had surprised her. In her story, as in real life, he was a delegate or proxy standing in for someone more important: Herr P. It was the man she loved who had in fact entered her room without knocking and had caught her "red-handed." In the

moment of her shame, when she felt that her "hands were tied"
she became aware that, having seen her engaged in this private
act, he would never be able to view her as a future wife. It was not
surprising that, with everything else going on in her life, this disappointment had proved too crushing for her to assimilate.

We moved then to the question of how her aphonia, which I
had wrongly thought at first to be connected to her anxiety about
speaking a foreign language[3] while temporarily removed from
the company of the man she loved. I suggested that a more likely
explanation was that at the moment she had been interrupted in
her room she had in fact been fantasizing about the act of fellatio
with Herr P, and that it had been the pain of her absence from
him while in Paris that caused this somatic representation of
what she had lost. I did not doubt that the circumstances of the
other instance of her aphonia, which she claimed not to remember, had also involved a separation.

Fräulein Katharina was reluctant to concede the truth of my
interpretation of events. She was adamant that it was the young
doctor, the locum, who had burst into her room without knocking and she had been engaged in no indecent action at the time.
She admitted it was possible that she had become confused about
the details and that there had certainly been more than one incident in which Herr P had himself knocked at her door. Although
she would not concede that the incident I had interpolated into
her story was necessarily true, she was not in a position to recognize it as something she had actually experienced: I believed it
would have taken hypnosis to achieve that.

Having explained to Fräulein Katharina the genesis of all her
symptoms, I warned her that it might be some time before she felt
a full remission from them. Just as it took some time for the conversion of trauma to manifest itself in the production of hysterical phenomena (Charcot called this the "period of working out,"

[3] It will be remembered that the first instance came when she went to visit her brother, Gustav, in Paris.

or "elaboration," and one thinks of the case of the coachman Henri R), so the reverse was also true: some time was required for the catharsis to work through her system.

In fact, Katharina reported a considerable improvement in her symptoms over the next few days, and when I last saw her appeared to be well on the way to making a full recovery.

Thomas carefully replaced the papers on the desk. His astonished eyes were dry and stinging because he had barely allowed himself to blink in the time his gaze raked down the pages.

"Jesus suffering God," he said, and steadied himself against the edge of Jacques's desk.

He looked up to the sky outside the window, exhaled deeply, then set himself in motion.

He ran into the hall and shouted, "Sonia! Sonia!"

She appeared upstairs and looked down at him from the galleried landing. "What on earth is the matter? Why are you shouting like that?"

"What room is Katharina in? That young fair-haired woman, a patient of Jacques's."

"Eighteen, I think. Why? What is it?"

"Tell Josef to get the trap ready at once. We may have to go to the surgeon in town."

"Why? Why? What's the matter?"

But Thomas was already gone, his running footsteps echoing in the cloister as he made for Katharina's room.

He hammered at the door. "Fräulein, forgive me. May I take your temperature?"

Ten minutes later, a startled and reexamined Katharina was ready in the hall of the main house, her scarlet overcoat belted at the waist, a hat pinned over her fair hair, her reading glasses folded away in her pocket, while Josef brought the covered trap to the front door. Sonia stood watching anxiously.

"Where is Jacques?" said Thomas.

"I think he is in the laboratory with Franz."

"Please tell him nothing about this. I will not be back for dinner, so please tell him I was called away to see a patient at the hospital. Or some such thing. Come, Fräulein."

In the hour or so it took them to reach the town, Thomas discovered that a great deal of what Jacques had written about Kitty was accurate. She was a young woman of composure and clear thinking who seemed embarrassed to have so disturbed the routine of the sanatorium and quizzical about the need for a further medical opinion; she also, to Thomas, appeared to be someone who was acutely ill and whose stoical self-control had not been in her own interest.

To pass the time as the trap bounced along, Thomas talked to her about his life. This was not his normal conversational procedure, but he felt that the one thing Kitty had talked enough about was herself. He liked her shy, slightly skeptical response to his narrative ("Really?" she said. "Another brush with the authorities?"); it drove him to greater candor than he intended. They talked in English, which Kitty spoke as a native, though with a faint accent that Thomas could not place.

It was dark by the time they reached the hospital lodge and descended from the trap. Thomas gave Josef some money to go and buy supper for himself and told him to return in two hours. In the hospital, he was able to find Herr Obmann, the surgeon, and to explain the situation to him. Obmann sent for an anesthetist, Herr Aichwalder, who had to be fetched from his dinner at home. Kitty, by now candidly alarmed, was taken to a private room, undressed and given a sedative.

Thomas told her that the operation was a minor one and that she must not worry herself. It was possible that he and Herr Obmann were in any case incorrect in their diagnosis, in which case they would make sure any scar was all but invisible. A nurse came in to shave her, and Thomas left the hospital.

He went to a small tavern, but found that he was too agitated to eat. If his suspicions were correct, the consequences for him and Jacques were appalling; he was not sure the schloss could survive them. There was another factor in his anxiety that he could not yet identify, but it made him push back his plate and return to the hospital, where he paced up and down the dimly lit brick corridors, waiting for any word from the operating theater.

Toward eleven o'clock, a weary-looking Herr Obmann emerged

from the theater with traces of blood on his apron. He sighed as he approached Thomas.

"Let us go outside," he said.

In the hospital forecourt, Thomas gestured to the waiting Josef to be patient, while Obmann sat down heavily on a bench and lit a cigar.

"Quite a battle," he said.

"For God's sake, man," said Thomas. "Tell me!"

Obmann looked at him curiously. "Calm yourself, Doctor. It was a straightforward procedure. I removed two cysts from the same ovary. One was the size of a hen's egg, the other about as large as a Seville orange. The larger one had twisted on its pedicle, cutting off its own blood supply, and had also twisted the fallopian tube. It was exerting considerable pressure on the neighboring organs. I imagine it must have been extremely uncomfortable."

"Nothing else?"

"No . . . that was it. A nasty thing, but a straightforward one."

"And will she be fertile still?"

"I see no reason why not. The other ovary was healthy."

"Thank God."

"You were right to bring her to me."

"How has she put up with the pain for so long?"

"I imagine it was intermittent. It all depends on the degree of twisting. Sometimes by twisting they can free themselves. And the smaller one she would not have felt at all."

"But there was no suggestion of cancer?"

"I have taken a biopsy, but it is unlikely. Nine out of ten are harmless. We will keep her here for the time being."

"Certainly," said Thomas. "I believe that she also has rheumatic fever."

"It is no use asking a butcher like me about that."

"I know. But I should like a second opinion from Maierbrugger."

"He is coming the day after tomorrow."

"Perfect. May I see her?"

Obmann shrugged. "She's asleep, but you know where she is. You know your way around."

"Thank you, Obmann." Thomas held out his hand. "Thank you very much."

Back in the darkened hospital, he went up to Kitty's room on the first floor and knocked gently. The nurse opened the door and Thomas went in. By the light of the candle next to the bed, he could see Kitty's pale face, flushed with a slight fever, the hair a little damp at the temples where a strand of it lay over the tiny freckles on her forehead.

"Look after her, won't you?" he said.

"Yes, Doctor. Of course."

"Don't leave her bedside. I will make sure you are . . . rewarded."

The nurse nodded. "I shall not move."

Thomas leaned over the bed and stroked the hair back from Kitty's forehead. He felt his heart seethe behind his ribs.

XIII

"GOOD MORNING, FRÄULEIN. I AM DOCTOR MAIERBRUGGER. HOW are you feeling?"

"Much better, thank you." Kitty levered herself up on the pillows and tried to remember if she had seen this gray-haired gentleman in his silver spectacles before; the last two days had passed in a haze of morphia and men's faces bent over her bed.

"The surgeon, Herr Obmann, is extremely pleased with the outcome of his operation. I believe he paid you a visit this morning."

"Yes. He came when the nurse changed the dressing. He did seem pleased with . . ." She tailed off.

"With himself?" Maierbrugger raised his eyebrows. "It is a characteristic of the profession."

Kitty smiled. "And when may I go home?"

"Not yet, alas. We need to observe you a little longer. To begin with, I would like to look at your throat, if I may. Open your mouth wide. Thank you. Now I am going to listen to your heart, if you would care to open your nightdress a little. There. I hope it is not too cold."

Kitty looked down at the crown of Maierbrugger's head, red flaky scalp through a gash of gray hair, as he moved the diaphragm of his stethoscope over her skin. Free from pain, she felt happier than she had for some time and was beginning to be impatient with the exaggerated care to which she was being subject.

"Are your parents alive, Fräulein?"

"My mother is alive. My father died a few years ago. Of a heart complaint."

Maierbrugger nodded. "Did you nurse him? Were you in proximity?"

"Yes."

"But you also have a history, I understand from Doctor Midwinter, of throat infections."

Kitty pursed her lips. "Not a history exactly. I suppose I was sometimes sick as a child."

"Did it cause you to miss school?" His voice was rasping.

"On occasions, yes."

Maierbrugger tapped a pen against the clipboard he had taken from the end of her bed. "I understand that at one point you had some involuntary movements of the shoulders and the face. Is that correct?"

"Yes. At one time the muscles seemed to have a life of their own. This shoulder particularly. It was a little alarming. But it stopped. I have not been troubled by it for a considerable time."

"Did you have movements in the hips as well?"

"No."

"Not the entire St. Vitus in that case. However, Fräulein, I have little doubt that you have been suffering from rheumatic fever. It is a distressingly common ailment, which varies a great deal in severity. Its early symptoms can include the spasms you have described, particularly in children and young people. The main symptoms, however, are pains in the joint, such as you have suffered in your fingers and wrists, and an intermittent fever, which I understand you have also had."

Kitty said, "But I do not really feel unwell anymore."

"Good. I suspect you have had a number of attacks and that your most recent and most acute one is now receding. If you rest, you can expect to return to full health."

"Is that all?"

"Not quite," said Maierbrugger. "The disease can damage the heart valves. We have little way of knowing whether or not it has done so. Your throat problems suggest you may have contracted it as a child, and if in its various recurrences it has so far caused no problems then you are probably safe. If, however, you caught it from your father and the heart problem that killed him was caused by a weakness of the valves, then the outlook is somewhat less good. However, I must say that I could hear no irregularities when I listened to your heart just now."

"And is there any treatment?"

"Nothing yet, alas. We believe it to be caused by a bacterium, but we have no means of suppressing it."

"So what do you recommend?"

"Take precautions to avoid throat infections. And lead a well-governed life that does not place undue stress on the heart. That does not mean lying down all day; it means moderation in all things. And then we hope for the best."

"I see."

"You should rest for at least a fortnight, however, to recover from the operation as well as from the illness."

Kitty inhaled. "So you do not believe that any of my illness has been caused by . . . by the circumstances of my life. By emotion or bereavement."

"I think it extremely unlikely that a personal feeling might influence the activity of the microbe we believe to be responsible for streptococcal infection."

"Thank you."

When Dr. Maierbrugger had left the room, Kitty sank back onto the pillows and closed her eyes. She felt exhausted, yet dizzily relieved. Although she had been an active girl, a tomboy, as she had told Dr. Rebière, the prospect of a quiet life without undue exertion seemed, in her weakened state, attractive; it would make her begin her life again, away from her family. She had no wish to return to her mother's house now that her irritating stepfather was resident there; her indifference to him had, after all Dr. Rebière suggested, turned to revulsion and distrust. Perhaps she would go to Paris, where her brother was working and, until she found employment of her own, she could be the housekeeper in his apartment near the Place des Vosges.

She longed for normality again, to know that all the thoughts and hopes she had had, and all the private desires, were merely human and forgivable. She blushed when she remembered some of the confessions she had made to Dr. Rebière; the hot blood in her face made her eyes sting for a moment and she moved her head uneasily on the pillow. At the time, she had experienced remarkably little shame. His manner was so correct, so scientifically inquiring, that she had felt like a peculiarly fascinating and complex musical instrument, not like a woman at all.

Her embarrassment subsided and gave way to a smile. She ought perhaps to feel angry with Dr. Rebière for misleading and exposing her; but her relief at the absence of pain in her womb and at the knowledge that her other ailments had a simple cause was now so overwhelming that there was no room for harsh emotion.

In fact, she would probably return to the schloss for the two weeks' recommended rest. There was something powerfully attractive about the place, something she had loved even when in distress; and now that the causes of all her pain had been removed, there was nothing to prevent her from enjoying the scenery, the company, the sumptuous cooking and the play of sunlight on the bricks of the small, hidden south courtyard where she would read her book in peace.

There was a knock on the door, and the nurse's head appeared. "Another visitor for you, Fräulein." It was Sonia.

WHEN HE returned from the hospital, Thomas knew he would be unable to sleep, so went outside for a walk; he prowled the furthest reaches of the grounds, then walked all the way down to the lake itself and sat on the wooden jetty. He imagined Fräulein Katharina von A bringing a legal action against the schloss, though it would admittedly be hard for her to prove that she had suffered material harm as a result of their misdiagnosis. He pictured critical reports in the newspapers that would relate how a young woman of impeccable character had been subject to intense and lewd speculation which had transpired to have no basis in reality. Against these charges they could argue that they were not alone among neurologists and psychologists in making such psychosomatic connections; they could point to a small but growing literature in Vienna and Paris. No matter what defense they raised, however, the reputation of the sanatorium would be undermined; it would never again be looked upon as what Valade had called the city on a hill: it would be tainted forever by a suspicion of bad science, credulity and a sort of brutal opportunism, a desire to supply a sensational cure for an ailment it had partially invented. He remembered something troubling that Faverill had once said to him about the snake-oil salesmen of Colorado whose potions met a crying need. Jacques and he had not been able to cure madness, so they had fabricated something that they could cure; and whatever happened now, the burnish of their great enterprise, its innocent luster, was gone.

In the morning, he took Sonia to one side after breakfast and asked her to cancel his first consultation, then come to his room.

"Does Jacques know anything?"

"No," said Sonia, closing the door behind her.

He explained to her what had happened. "It is good news for the patient, whose pains have been cured by Obmann's knife, but for us . . ." He opened his hands wide. "It is ruin. Disaster."

Sonia's thoughts were for Jacques, and what this reverse might mean to him, but she tried to see the consequences for them all.

"Thomas, before you become too despondent, let us just think for a moment. It appears that Jacques has made a misdiagnosis. This often happens in difficult areas of medicine, does it not? It was made in good faith and no harm has resulted. On the contrary, a second opinion was promptly provided by a fellow-doctor—you—and it now appears that the patient is cured, or soon will be. She may not be so much angry with Jacques as grateful to you. Don't forget, she was simply a sick girl and now she is well."

"It is possible."

"I shall go and see her in the hospital. If she has been shamed by what has taken place, why should she seek to broadcast that shame? I suspect she may be so relieved to be well again that all other thoughts will be secondary."

"And what shall we do about poor Jacques?"

"We must break it to him slowly," said Sonia. "I suggest we use some slight subterfuge. We could say that Katharina developed sudden pains, nothing to do with what she had before. . . . I don't know, but surely you could think of something."

"I think we can delay the full impact, but eventually he will need to know because otherwise . . . otherwise, he may persist in error. It could lead to worse things. Suppose he were to miss an instance of cancer. A doctor in Vienna recently diagnosed a patient suffering gastric pains with hysteria. Two months later, she died of cancer of the stomach and he merely commented that hysteria had used the symptoms of the cancer to disguise itself."

Sonia's lip began to tremble because she knew how many thousand hours Jacques had worked and with what ardent philanthropic motive.

"Don't worry, Queenie," said Thomas, seeing her distress. "We will manage. I think I must tell him about the cysts. I see no way out of that, and it is an easy mistake to make when you consider how much time he and I have both spent on the pains of hysterical women and the fact that most cysts give no symptoms at all. Hysteria was a fair deduction. I think we can deal with that. As for the rheumatic fever, perhaps we should keep that to ourselves for the time being."

"All right," said Sonia quietly.

"Tomorrow, you go into town to visit Katharina. Under no circumstances should she know that Jacques had written anything of her history down, let alone in a paper that he hoped to publish—though I know he would have disguised her identity. She must not know that anyone else is privy to her story. Meanwhile, I shall talk to Jacques."

"Very well. But Thomas, will you explain where he went wrong? Perhaps you could put it in a letter. I wouldn't show it to him, but I should like to understand."

"I shall. It is easy for me to do with hindsight. But he was the adventurer. He was the pioneer. We must not forget that." Sonia squeezed his hand and went out.

A WEEK after the operation, Kitty returned to the schloss and resumed occupancy of her old room. In the afternoon, Thomas came to see her. He heard a scurrying when he knocked and wondered if she was taking off and concealing her reading glasses before calling out for him to enter. He discovered her sitting on a small balcony with a view down to the lake; she poured some iced lemon from a jug and invited him to join her in the unusually warm spring sunshine.

"How are you feeling, Fräulein?"

"Entirely well, thank you. I am very grateful for your intervention."

"Thank you. What are your plans now?"

"I am advised to rest for two weeks, and if you still have room for me, then—"

"Of course. With pleasure. But I would prefer it if you would be our guest. In view of the time it took us to diagnose you correctly."

"That is most generous."

Thomas looked across at her arms, which were partly bare beneath a sleeveless blouse; the muscle was youthfully firm beneath the pale, teeming freckles. He wondered if she had them also on her legs and at what point they might fade out, because presumably the skin of . . . He remembered himself in time, and coughed; she was looking at him, a little quizzically.

"I have spoken to Maierbrugger, and it seems that you will need no further treatment. However, you must nominally be under the care of a physician here. We should at least take your temperature twice daily. However, Dr. Rebière himself would perhaps no longer . . . I imagine I could ask the nurse, but in view of, in view of . . ."

"Would you be able to take me on to your own books, Doctor?"

"That is exactly what I was proposing," said Thomas in a rush of relief. "In view of what transpired with—"

"Please do not concern yourself with what happened in my earlier treatment. Dr. Rebière was extremely civil and professional. I also found what he had to say extraordinarily interesting. I read a copy of his introductory lecture on the subject of resolution and found it fascinating."

"Yes, indeed," said Thomas, feeling an unaccountable squeeze of jealousy, "it is a fascinating subject." He heard his voice—emollient, repetitive—and felt ashamed of it.

"What a wonderful life you have here," said Kitty, smiling. "A beautiful house, your sister to look after you and, as I understand it from Daisy, your best friend to work with. No man could ask for more."

Thomas felt a drop of sweat at the top of his spine. This woman was a saint—no, not a saint, there was nothing worthy or dull about her: she was a goddess. She had forgiven them, she had redeemed their life's work from destruction; the clarity of her thought was such that she had welcomed the surgeon's knife, bore no grudge and was able to make herself pleasant to him—intimate almost—with her bare arms and guileless blue eyes. Dear God.

He breathed in. He had better start behaving like the man of science to whom she wanted to entrust herself. "Yes," he said. "I am very happy here. Happiness creeps up on you, does it not? You never see it arrive, but one day you hesitate and you are aware that there is something . . . additional. I noticed it this morning when I came up from the lake. It was the smell of the hawthorn blossom along the path—not really a beautiful scent in itself, not like a rose—a faint something of the cat about it I always think, but it seems to me the smell of England, of childhood summers—evenings in the woods, walking over dry lanes, when time was endless. To be transported back, you must be open to suggestion, you must already be a little happy, perhaps."

Kitty laughed. "And when you were a child, was your sister there all the time?"

"Yes. That was one reason I was so content, I suppose. She was no angel, of course, Sonia. She did many spiteful, elder-sisterly things, but I must have been a profoundly irritating child and it was no more than I deserved. I was a boy running round in a small village and no one really took control of me. Sonia was my only confidante."

"And she, too, is happy?"

"Yes, indeed. Sublimely so, I think. She is expecting a child in the autumn. Please do not tell anyone. I should perhaps not have told you."

Kitty laid her hand for a moment on his arm. "I promise. But what can have made a wild young boy from a remote English village into a man trying to establish cures for insanity? That is your aim, is it not?"

"Yes, it is. One must say that for me to end up here is an unlikely story. But all men come from somewhere."

"You had no personal interest, no members of your family who were afflicted in some way?"

"No, not like Jacques, whose brother, as you probably know, is a patient here. And that has always been his driving force and ambition, to find a cure for Olivier's illness."

"But you? You speak so well, if you will forgive me saying so, about feelings. Did you never experience anything unusual yourself?"

Thomas thought. "Periodically, I have had spells of what psychiatrists call melancholy or depression, but not severe. Sometimes so slight, in fact, that it was only when it left me that I recognized that I had been suffering from it. I noticed that the trivial aspects of a day—the arrival of the postman, sunlight, food, the company of a friend—were bringing me pleasure and for how long it had not been so—when the sound of the letters on the mat was simply the start of more oppressive debt and toil."

He wanted to ask Kitty about her own feelings, but did not wish to reveal how much he knew of her history, and felt sure that she would welcome a rest from questioning.

"But you have never experienced any of the more remarkable symptoms of some of the poor people here?" said Kitty.

"I have never believed that I am the king of Prussia, no."

Kitty poured some more lemon. "And while Dr. Rebière pursues his theory of resolution, where is your work taking you?"

"I think we are in the same room, but we are looking out of different windows."

"Thank you, Doctor." Kitty laughed. "That is quite clear now. Are you plasterers or decorators?"

Thomas turned his gaze on her—the long, unsmiling, weighing-up scrutiny that Sonia had once found so intimidating. "A little of each. The room is where the mind and body meet. Jacques is working, as you know, on a particular affliction and on what of general application can be extracted from that. I am looking at other forms of illness, generally more severe, and seeing if they are like rheumatic fever—a germ—or like bereavement, an idea. Or perhaps they are both. I am particularly interested in the way in which one such severe illness, a psychosis as we people call it, may have entered the human animal—how it came in, why it seems so unhelpfully prevalent, why there seems to be no equivalent in other animals, whether it is in fact related to a particularly significant moment of human development."

"I see. Those are your two windows."

"Yes. I suppose, for simplicity's sake, you might say that his guiding light is Charcot and mine is Darwin. For the rest we share a vast amount. I hope that our paths will fully converge again at the next stage."

"Does Dr. Rebière not have the same reverence for Mr. Darwin?"

"Respect, but not reverence. One of his reservations, I think, but you must please not repeat this, is that Darwin suffers from a fatal disability in Dr. Rebière's eyes."

"What is that?"

"He is not French."

"Would that make a difference?"

"It might. But it is better this way. If Jacques took on any more theories his head might explode."

"Do you not think you have set yourself an impossible task? Can you really hope to discover all these things in your lifetime?"

Thomas listened but could not hear any mocking edge to Kitty's voice. He ran his hand back swiftly through his hair. "Yes and no. In some ways, it does seem impossible. We need much better equipment in the laboratory, lenses a thousand times stronger, new inventions to help us look at microscopic matter. We do not yet even understand how heredity works. I imagine that your parents both had blue eyes, but the precise process by which you have inherited them is still a mystery. Mr. Darwin talked about 'pangenesis' and 'gemmules,' but they don't really make sense; in fact, his theory can be quite easily disproved. So we are in the foothills. Yet I think we shall find answers. Never have we been closer. There are these sudden jumps and revelations in history. Take Shakespeare, for instance. He not only wrote the finest plays, but he described human motivation and behavior in a way that had never been done before. You could say that his analysis did more than describe; it actually defined what humans were. From that moment on, the idea was born that each man and woman, instead of being a bundle of primitive desires and unreliable memories, had a consistently motivated psychology. They believed they might make something of themselves and change; they discovered a 'self.' Perhaps it was not until Shakespeare that humans really began to behave like humans."

"Or like characters from Shakespeare, I suppose," said Kitty.

"Well, it came to be the same thing. Of course, there are some drawbacks to this model. Some people do act inconsistently, they just do. And our brain cells die at such a rate, Franz Bernthaler assures me, that people do become literally someone else as they age, so in some ways it is not wise to expect them to preserve the same 'character.' But it was nevertheless a breakthrough in the sixteenth century, to imagine people to have a consistent and explicable responsibility for their actions. And I do believe that again, now, we stand on the edge of a full explanation of what it means to be human. It is a great moment."

Kitty said nothing, but looked out toward the lake, which glimmered flatly in the late afternoon sun. A small village of white- and ocher-washed houses was beginning to grow on its far bank. She turned back to Thomas. "Will you be able to do all this without recourse to God? Is He not more likely to provide the answers than hereditary processes we cannot understand and instruments that have not been invented?"

"That has traditionally been His role—the guardian of mysteries. But He is a costive and niggardly keeper. He does not give up any secrets. Humans unriddle them all for themselves. When we have answered the last question, we will have no more need to dignify our ignorance with the name of 'God.'"

"My word, you are a true scientist, are you not?" she said gently. "I have never previously met anyone who would give Mr. Darwin the time of day."

"His reputation has fallen because there are some gaps in his theory. The machinery of heredity in particular. But I believe they will be filled. And the process of natural selection, which is the center of his work— that has been established beyond reasonable doubt."

There was a silence, and Thomas thought he had perhaps offended or bored Kitty with the intimate detail of his speculations; but when he turned his head to look at her, he found that her eyes were fixed on him in a kind, almost indulgent gaze.

"I have a favor to ask you," he said. "I shall tell Dr. Rebière that you are becoming my patient and I am certain that he will happily agree. However, if you should happen to run into him and he inquires about your health, as he is certain to do, could you perhaps not tell him about the rheumatic fever?"

"If you say so."

"I feel a little . . . protective. We do share all our discoveries, but it is sometimes a question of timing."

"I understand. May I ask you something in return?" said Kitty.

"Of course."

"Are you absolutely certain that you have never experienced any of the same symptoms as the patients that you treat? The more seriously ill ones, I mean."

Thomas stood up and walked from the balcony into the room. Kitty's large brass bed was made up with a quilted cover and two large pillows trimmed with white *broderie anglaise*; it reminded him obliquely of his room in Torrington, of Sonia sitting on the edge of the bed many years ago, on the day when he feared that he had broken his arm. Something stirred in his mind; he felt the idea move—from one part of his awareness into another, just as he himself had walked from the balcony into the bedroom.

"Yes," he said. "I have never recognized it before, I have never allowed it out of the place where it lived. I used to hear a voice. But it was not real. I mean, it was real, but it was not attached to a body. It used to talk to me regularly in a slow, stuporific way. Then it stopped. It went away. I have not heard it for some years now and I feel sure that I never will again. It even said a kind of goodbye."

Kitty had come into the room and stood beside him nodding her head gently. "And you have never told anyone about this?"

"I have never even told myself about it," said Thomas. "I have never let it into my conscious mind. It just moved in at that moment, when you asked me."

"But you were aware of it?"

"I was aware of it very clearly, but only at a certain level of awareness, not at all levels."

"And you did not question yourself about it?"

"No. It felt like everything that happens to you: it felt like nothing. I discounted it because it had happened to me personally and was therefore valueless. Of no interest."

Thomas put his face between his hands. He felt overcome by fatigue, as though some mortal weight, under which he had long been laboring, had been removed; now he barely knew how to stand.

Kitty laid her fingers on his arm. "If you would like to," she said, "you may put your head on my shoulder."

He wrapped his arms round her waist, gently; and as he did so, she ran her fingers up through his hair. "I wanted to do that," she said, "when I saw you doing it to yourself just now."

Thomas lifted his head and looked at her. Kitty saw that there were tears on his cheeks.

She said, "It is a hard life, Thomas."

He felt himself in pieces before her. "Yes, Kitty. Yes it is. But it has its moments of transcendence." He took the bare freckled skin of her upper arms, feeling its softness beneath his large hands, and gazed into her eyes.

THE NEXT day, after lunch, Valade approached Thomas in the hall and gave him a picture magazine.

"I found this in town when I went in yesterday. It is a little out of date, but I think you'll find it interesting. It's about Mount Lowe in California. They have built a railway up into the Sierra Madre mountains near a little town called Pasadena. It runs to a height of about a thousand meters already and they are going to take it on further. Isn't that the height of the place you have your eye on?"

"Mount Low," said Thomas, smiling. "That is a curious name for a mountain."

"Lowe with an 'e.' It is named after the proprietor of the railway, a Professor Thaddeus Lowe. It was previously called Oak Mountain. Though perhaps you also find that amusing."

"Less so," said Thomas.

"In any case," said Valade, "you will see that they were able to build an electrical railway with an overhead trolley cable up the gentle incline, then when it comes to a steep lift, the passengers get out of the train and into a cable car on an incline of roughly one in two."

"Remarkable," said Thomas. "I shall read it this evening."

"You should do so, Doctor," said Valade. "You will also find the details of the finance instructive. Perhaps we can talk about it further tomorrow."

"Indeed. I am unusually busy at the moment and I need to talk to my colleague Dr. Rebière, but I shall make time for this. Perhaps you would care to come to our table for dinner tomorrow night."

"Delighted. I shall speak to your cellar boy straight away."

Thomas spent the afternoon with his patients and it was not until the evening that he finally saw Jacques, when they met in his consulting room to discuss the day. Thomas feared that Jacques would be humiliated and in despair, even though they had kept from him the diagnosis of Kitty's rheumatic fever. He tried not to meet his eye too directly when he went in, yet Jacques seemed strangely unruffled, Thomas thought, as he lit a cigar and looked out over the lawns of the schloss.

After an exchange of minor news, Thomas said, "I saw your former patient yesterday. Katharina."

"Yes," said Jacques. "So did I. She seemed well."

"I have taken her on for the remainder of her stay. Merely a formality. Temperature, pulse and so on. I am not trying to—"

"Yes, she told me."

"Is that all right?"

"It seems . . . appropriate in the circumstances."

There was a pause. Thomas coughed. "Jacques, I—"

"Thomas, I am not going to be cast down by a single clinical error— the failure to diagnose an asymptomatic condition. I am not going to abandon or alter the course of my work because one girl's womb had an impalpable cyst. And we are not going to lose face or lose heart as an enterprise because there was a slight delay in the treatment of a patient before the second opinion of such a highly astute doctor was able to set things right."

Jacques's eyes were glowing, but his manner remained calm. Thomas found his mouth open, then close. This was not the response he had expected and he felt a clutch of panic. Was it possible that all along Jacques had been a fanatic? Perhaps when he was working all night in Paris, while Sonia looked on lonely and anxious, he had not been in a state of scholarly open-mindedness, but had really been driven by a desire to find a closed theory that would be the cornerstone of some personal church.

Thomas said, "I think it is important that we do not panic. Naturally one case proves very little, and I am not suggesting we abandon all we learned at the Salpêtrière in those great days. But we must understand what we can learn from this setback. If we do not examine it properly and—"

"I do not see it as a setback. Fräulein Katharina presented a case of hysteria which has been cured by the techniques of psychophysical resolution. I told you at the outset that I believed it was not quite a classic case and that there were some complications. And so there were. You discovered them. Well done. But it takes more than two invisible sacs full of benign fluid to destroy the work of a decade. I dare say she had corns as well."

Thomas found his anger rising, and held hard to the edge of Jacques's desk. "I am not trying to destroy anything. I want to build and progress. Before we can do that, you have to admit something. In the case of Fräulein Katharina, you were wrong, Jacques, and you were dangerously wrong."

"I was not wrong. She suffered from hysteria, which—"

"She does not suffer from hysteria, and she never has. Furthermore, I sincerely doubt that the disease entity of hysteria will continue to be recognized in ten years' time."

"That is an absurd thing to say. It is one of the most completely described neurological—"

"For God's sake, Jacques, do you not read the papers and journals? Do you not see how Charcot's heirs are respectfully trying to distance themselves from him?"

"Then they are wrong. Hysteria is a protean disease which can imitate—"

"It cannot imitate every damned thing. I read a paper the other day in which the patient was diagnosed with hysteria, caused by some emotional stress that made her stammer. It was quite clear to any disinterested doctor that she had Tourette's syndrome, first identified by our old friend and colleague Georges Gilles of that name at the Salpêtrière."

"Explain to me the pains in Katharina's wrists and fingers," said Jacques.

"I . . . I will in due course," said Thomas. "But, please, my dear Jacques, please consider that in this instance you may have made a mistake."

He saw Jacques struggling with himself. "I will consider it," he said eventually, "but I do not expect to change my mind."

Thomas sighed. "Let us say no more about it for the time being. We both need time to reflect. Tomorrow night, by the way, Valade is dining with us and we are going to talk about railways. I shall see you in half an hour."

He did not trust himself to say any more to Jacques, so left the room and ran upstairs to change. He was sure that the schloss could not proceed and flourish until Jacques admitted his error and examined all the consequences that flowed from it. Thomas knew this process was essential for the well-being of the joint venture; but how pure, he wondered, were his motives in thinking so? Perhaps there had always been a rivalry between him and Jacques and this was his chance to assert himself as the senior partner. Maybe he was anxious, too, that there be no taint of mental illness, hereditary or otherwise, in the woman with whom he was now so abjectly yet exhilaratingly in love.

He straightened his tie in the mirror. At least he was going to see her in a few minutes; presumably she would come in to dinner. Whatever happened to their life's work, there was the consolation of seeing her across the room. It seemed at that moment, as he stared into his own face in the looking glass, to be enough; and perhaps, he thought, it really was enough.

HE WENT to examine Kitty the next morning after breakfast. He took her temperature and felt her pulse. She let her arm rest on his thigh, and he dug down between the veins and sinews to feel the small throb through his finger. He let his watch run a full minute to be quite sure.

"You are definitely alive," he said.

"I have seldom felt better."

Thomas smiled. "It took humans a very long time to understand that not being alive was a single thing. They saw people losing blood in battle, or losing breath or losing weight, losing their minds or falling asleep, but they had different words for each cessation. The idea that all these calamities were versions of the same thing—being dead—took them millions of years to understand. That is why they propped them up in tombs and expected them to come back or carry on, depending on what kind of interruption they had had."

Kitty smiled. "Why not?"

"Exactly. The only thing common to all these deaths was loss of conscious thought. But since they did not know what conscious thought was, how could they possibly be aware of its absence—least of all in others?"

Kitty stood up. She wore a long beige skirt, tight at the hip and broad at the hem over buttoned brown boots; on top she had a high-necked blouse with a silver brooch beneath a green woolen jacket.

"Quite soon I shall be ready to leave," she said.

"Yes." Thomas tried to sound casual. "And where shall you go?"

"I thought I might go to England for a time. My mother's family is in London. And you?"

"Me? I have an enormous amount of work to do here. Your case has precipitated a certain . . . crisis of confidence which we have not yet overcome. In fact, we have not even confronted it."

"In view of that," said Kitty, "perhaps we should both forget anything which passed between us yesterday."

Thomas could feel her steady gaze on him. He looked up from where he was sitting on the edge of the bed. "I could never forget what happened," he said. "It was the most extraordinary moment of my life."

"But since I have been passed from the care of one doctor to another then it would not do—"

"It would not do for you to be passed on so quickly to Dr. Bernthaler like—"

"Like a hot potato?"

"Like a parcel." Thomas smiled. "It has its comic side."

"It does, Thomas."

He stood up, went over to where she stood and took both her hands in his. "I have fallen in love with you," he said. "It is better to say it."

There was a slight flush in Kitty's cheeks, but not the feverish discoloration of the preceding days.

"Be careful, Thomas. You have worked so hard and for so long. I cannot be responsible for some calamity that would affect all of you—Sonia as well, and her child."

"I would not allow that to happen."

"I am perfectly prepared to allow any minor indiscretion that may
have happened yesterday to be forgotten, and never to make reference to
it again."

"I'm afraid that is entirely impossible."

"Please be serious. For the pleasure of indulging some whim, you
must not risk everything you have dedicated your life to achieving."

"I would not do that. This is no whim, I assure you."

"Are you certain?"

Thomas felt Kitty's eyes searching his own, trying to see through
them.

"I could not be more certain of anything," he said.

She held his gaze for a moment longer. "In that case," she said, "you
may kiss me."

She threw her arms round his neck and turned her face up toward
his. He kept his eyes open as he touched her pale lips with his, and as he
pulled her closer to him, the tip of his tongue accidentally touched the
tip of hers. He stroked the fair hair back from her forehead. She looked to
him so charged with beauty, so complete and ready for whatever life lay
ahead of her, that he could not believe the good fortune of his timing.
Why had no one else come before him and carried this woman away?

"What will we do now?" she said.

Thomas held her at the elbows. "I am ready to be bad in a good
cause," he said.

"Very bad?"

She sat down on the bed and it seemed natural for him to sit next to
her; he placed his hand on the beige skirt, where it was stretched across
her thigh. Since she made no protest, he left it there.

"In ten days' time," he said, "when you leave my care, I shall have no
conflict of interest."

"Can you wait ten days to kiss me again?"

"Of course I can." He laughed. "What sort of libertine do you take
me for?"

"One who leaves his hand on a woman's thigh when he is talking
to her."

"I cannot help my hand." Thomas was so disturbed by her proximity
that he did not know what he was saying.

"Tell me something," said Kitty. "Those English girls you brought over with you. Did you ever . . . with either of them?"

"You really must have a very low opinion of me," he said.

"No, no." She sounded truly alarmed, he thought, no longer playing with him. "I do not have a low opinion of you. Quite the contrary. It was just a silly jealousy on my part. I am ashamed of it already. But I wanted it to be me who first discovered what a wonderful man you are. And you are, you are. You do not know it, but that in itself is wonderful."

Thomas was touched by her words, though he did not want to think about their implications. "So there we are, Kitty," he said. "I shall wait ten days, and in that time I shall visit you once a day, or maybe twice if your temperature is elevated in the morning or if either of us is aware of any change in your condition."

"And can you wait?"

"I can wait." He looked at her face, which was smiling and anxious— eager, he thought, to please him. "But would you grant me one favor?"

"What is it?"

"Do you have freckles on your legs like those on your arms?"

"Yes, though less dense. I hate them."

"I love them. And where do they finish? Do they cover all your skin? Or do they stop?"

"They stop," she said, taking his hand and replacing it a little higher up her thigh, "about here."

Thomas stood up. "You would not, I suppose, dear Kitty, if I promised to ask no more favors, allow me just to see?"

Kitty blushed. "Good heavens, I—"

"Just to see. It is no more than the nurse saw, or old Obmann or—"

"All right. Just for a moment."

She went over and locked the door, then came back and undid the waistband of her skirt. She lowered it to the ground and lifted up the pet-ticoat beneath; it was an armful for her to hold above the top of the silk stocking, so he could see the golden skin of her thigh as it paled into white near the top. There was something childish, tomboyish in the slimness of the thigh and the sharp patella; Thomas was moved by a vision of the active girlhood it suggested to him. She looked down at him, her face burning. Despite what he had promised, he held out his hand and touched her thigh at the point where the pigmentation changed, as though he expected the texture to be different where the freckles ended; the petticoats let out a gasping rustle as she quickly lowered them.

THREE DAYS later, Thomas went to Trieste to visit the lawyers acting on behalf of the owner of the schloss to see if they would agree an extension to the lease, which would otherwise expire at the turn of the century. The lawyers were discouraging. Although the original agreement was thought to contain an option to renew at the same terms for a further five years, it turned out that this was not binding. Thomas was given to understand that the owner would wish to repossess the schloss and that they would do well to consider looking for a new home. However, he reflected as he sat on the train going home, they still had more than four years to run, and by then their lives might be very different.

Soon after his return, Kitty prepared to leave.

"I wish you would stay," he said, when he went to her room on the day of her departure.

"I cannot," she said, folding some clothes into a trunk. "I am quite well now and if I eat any more of Frau Egger's food I shall not be able to fit into any of my skirts. Look how tight this one is at the waist already. I cannot face the thought of my mother's house in Vienna just at the moment. So if I spend a week in Paris with Gustav on the way back, then perhaps a month in London, I shall be back in Vienna by the end of June at the latest."

"Where will you live?"

"I shall find an apartment to rent and begin to do some work."

Thomas was aware that there was only one way that he could make her stay, one question he could put to her; but he sensed that she wanted to be alone, not fussed over, that she needed time to clear her head after all she had been through and that for him to pose any question to her now would be tactless.

He understood how she felt, but could not stop himself from saying, "Carinthia is beautiful in June. The wildflowers . . ."

Kitty looked up from the trunk. "I know."

At the main railway station, he put his arms round her when he heard the whistle of the arriving train. He did not care if any of the other passengers might recognize him.

"You will come back, won't you?"

She kissed him lightly on the lips. Her face was anxious. "If you want me to."

"Dear God, I do."

He paid the porter to help with her luggage, then walked quickly down the platform without looking back, out through the ticket hall and on to the forecourt, where Josef was waiting.

The succeeding weeks went by slowly. Sonia grew larger and slower, but was said by the gynecologist to have passed the most dangerous stage of her pregnancy; she found it difficult, however, to deal with all the paperwork of the schloss if, as was recommended, she did no work before lunch. A girl called Lisl was hired to help in the mornings, but seemed unable to spell.

Thomas found himself restless. He went for long walks down to the lake and excursions round its five-mile shore. He thought about Kitty, and feared that she had been driven away by a combination of his ardor and Jacques's preposterous misdiagnosis. However much he tried to put it to one side of his mind, he found himself increasingly angry with Jacques for his refusal to accept responsibility for his failings.

One evening, he went into the office, unlocked the cabinet and took the paper Jacques had written about Kitty from her file. He then shut himself in his own consulting room and wrote a response to it, as Sonia had requested. He need not necessarily hand it over to Jacques, he thought; he would give him time to change his mind spontaneously; but at least the expression of his dismay might help him concentrate again on his own work.

He wrote:

FRÄULEIN KATHARINA VON A

A young woman with lower abdominal pain and occasional vomiting. Intermittent amenorrhea.

Previously diagnosed by the family physician with uterine fibroids. You dismiss this diagnosis because she is too young and has had no increased menstrual flow. You at once give up on any organic cause when even a student would suspect ovarian trouble of some kind: if not fibroids, cysts.

Her skin and muscle tone are normal.

She has chronic joint pain in shoulders, elbows, wrists and fingers; also a temperature; irregular pulse; tendency to infections of the throat; and—at an earlier date—tics and spasms that look like Sydenham's chorea.

Instead of seeing these symptoms as a whole, you separate them and dismiss those that do not interest you. So her raised temperature is a chill, she says, and this you accept without question. You have nothing to say about the pulse. The family physician—brusquely rejected in the matter of the fibroids—is now welcome: the pains are indeed caused by too much typing and secretarial work. The chorea, although a closed episode, is treated by you as though active—presumably because it gives you an entry into neurology. The temperature, the pulse, the aches, the history of throat trouble and the chorea are given five separate authorities—respectively: hers, none, the physician's, none again, and yours. Had you looked at the symptoms taken together, you would have seen a classic case of rheumatic fever.

It was not difficult to see. I saw it. Maierbrugger saw it. In fact, he rejoiced in such an astonishingly complete and uncomplicated presentation.

Her eyes were normal, save for astigmatism, which the oculist had correctly diagnosed. You were prepared to accept this.

Aspects of her case did trouble you. You stress that she was an affectionate character, well-meaning, dutiful, principled, gentle, a person of high moral seriousness and so forth. You emphasize that she spoke of her own sufferings in a detached way.

One would naturally conclude from this information that she was not a neurasthenic person, but was someone strong-minded and self-possessed, suffering from an acute organic illness. But no: you conclude that her apparent sanity is a symptom of her insanity; it is no less than the *belle indifférence* of the hysteric. She is trapped either way.

You cannot immediately find access to her unconscious because you cannot hypnotize her. According to Charcot—and to you—if people cannot be hypnotized, they are not hysterical. But you do not follow this to its conclusion (viz., that she is not hysterical); you modestly blame your own lack of skill as hypnotist.

One of the other diagnostic cornerstones for hysteria is heredity. You can find none. Instead of again concluding that she is not hysterical, you conclude that hysteria is a mysterious disease.

On two occasions she has lost her voice. What could be more usual in someone chronically prone to throat infections? Your first diagnosis, however, is that it is caused by a lack of confidence in a foreign language. When, as you admit, this turns out to be mistaken, you do not return to the sore throat; you suggest that the aphonia is caused by a suppressed memory—acting psychosomatically we know not how—of an act of unremembered fellatio. You do not examine her throat at any stage.

Her minor anxiety symptoms—low spirits, tendency to insomnia—you diagnose as the natural response of a healthy woman to her medical condition. But how can she be both a psychologically healthy woman and a neuropath? Elsewhere, her pathology is such that she is, according to you, incapable of any honest coordination between any mental and physical process whatever. But where it suits you, she makes healthy and discriminating responses.

She suffers from a mild fear of animals, like the majority of women—mice and suchlike. This, too, you see as morbid; and this—unlike her fevers, for instance—you do not disregard but wish to make central. So instead of being a characteristic shared with most of her sex, it becomes a symptom of anxiety at remembered—or perhaps not remembered—acts of masturbation.

Her adolescent sexual feelings at boarding school are slightly more intense than those of most girls. They should be examined

in the context of her life. She had been a tomboy; she had spent
time on a farm; she knew about copulation of animals and so on;
she had moved among older people in her father's company. In
the context of this childhood and the reserved and proper young
adult before you, the adolescent period seems a normal bridging
phase. But you do not take it in context, you see it in isolation.
The episode with Frau E can also be explained as a transition;
though to this too you give a weight it cannot really have had—
despite admitting that it was a single event and that the two
women corresponded as friends happily afterward.

The core of your resolution depends on your belief that K was
in love with Herr P, her father's business associate. When she
denies it, you merely conclude that that is further proof of how
strongly she has buried the idea. If she could ever be aware of it,
you suggest, then the secret would not have turned morbid inside
her. This is an example of a logic known in my country as Mor-
ton's Fork. Damned if you do, damned if you don't. If what she
says fits your theory, it is the truth; if not, it is an evasion or an
inversion. In your "pictographic script," a thing may represent
itself, or something else, or its opposite. Such a protean script or
alphabet can have no literary meaning, still less a medical application.

If you throw all this paper in the bin, Jacques, just answer me
this one question. <u>Why did you not ask to speak to Herr P</u>? He was
not a remote character from a fictional story. He is Kitty's stepfather! He could have told you almost everything you needed to
know. And what about her mother, who brought her to the
schloss? Why did you not recall her? Or go to Vienna to visit her?
Reading the paper, one has the impression that you prefer to treat
these people as characters in a short story rather than as human
beings. <u>You prefer to solve the puzzle with limited information</u>;
that is the challenge you have set yourself. There are moments—
such as the one when you speak of the case's "considerable therapeutic allure"—when you appear to put your own intellectual
self-gratification above the well-being of the patient.

The bewildering thing is that you lay out with such clarity all the details you needed to solve the case. You return time and time again to her studious good character and the naturalness of her heart's affections. You report that she says of herself that she "fell in love too easily" but that she had never had sexual relations with a man and distrusted her emotions. Her mother agreed that she was inclined to be "too affectionate." Yet she was *virgo intacta*. If there is a sexual/mental conflict, it is there—open and acknowledged, and it is the most natural tension that a healthy young woman could have, between affectionate exuberance and the need to be proper.

And if you accept this part of her self-diagnosis, why can she not acknowledge that she has fallen in love with Herr P? After all, she has the habits of emotional honesty and intellectual self-criticism. Why on earth would they fail her in the case of the visiting lawyer?

The vomiting of her lunch when she hears of her father's death is taken by you to be a symbolic rejection of her future life—without Herr P. We can now see that it may have been caused—as vomiting can be—by the ovarian cyst. My guess is that it was a simple shock reaction. To be more sure about this, of course, we need to know whether the soup just "came up," or whether there was paroxysmal vomiting. But you do not ask.

Talking of not asking, I would mention here also the renewed menstrual period after two and a half weeks. You note this, but attach no importance to it. It does not occur to you to palpate the ovary or reexamine that part of the abdomen. If you can hypnotize her (though you know you have so far failed) that will provide an easier way of sorting out this problem. You prefer to retry autosuggestion, rather than simply examining her body.

The locum tenens who knocks at her door is diagnosed by you as a "delegate" memory, standing in for Herr P. But why? Again, you could have asked Herr P himself if ever he broke in on K! No delegates, surrogates, inversions or pictographic symbolism. Just: did you or did you not?

We come to the dream, which provides much of the fabric of
your resolution. In it, she is haunted by a sense of absence. She
believes the missing person is her father, who has recently died.
No, you conclude, it is Herr P, the irritating lawyer. Do you not
remember the dreams you had when your own father died? Time
and again, you movingly told me, you had this feeling of something not satisfactorily completed. Yet to K you deny the possibility of a puzzling absence/sense of presence. What has happened
to your dream theories? In the lecture you gave us in the North
Hall, you were circumspect and scholarly about how they might
help. Now you are doctrinaire. A dream is <u>always</u> an expression
of a suppressed wish. Everything is the opposite of what it
seems—unless it is not, when it may be itself again. Anything
can represent anything else—or its opposite!

When you run into problems, you resort to a sleight-of-hand.
In the matter of K's lost voice, for instance, when you can find no
conclusion, you escape thus: "I did not doubt that the circumstances of the other instance of her aphonia, which she claimed
not to remember, had also involved a separation." But why did
you "not doubt"? When K firmly rejects your interpretation, your
narrative continues with a conjunction such as "as we have
seen" or "now that it was established" when nothing has been
"seen," still less "established." When you stub your toe on a large
"but," you simply gloss it to an "and"; if a daunting "however"
blocks your path, you hurry through by calling it "moreover."
Your story flows, but it does not connect.

I think your analysis of the words she used—"my hands were
tied" and so on—is ingenious, but I do not think it is conclusive.
"Suggestive" is about as far as one might reasonably take it. Incidentally, two can play at that game. You yourself use the word
"interpolated": "Although she would not concede that the incident I had interpolated into her story was necessarily true, she
was not in a position to recognize it as something she had actually experienced: I believed it would have taken hypnosis to
achieve that." Is the word "interpolated" there to give unwitting

encouragement to the skeptical reader? Or is it, like her hand
metaphors, a betrayal of an "unconscious" fear?

The sentence above is, alas, characteristic of the circular logic
that underlies your resolution. Paradox offers you a permanent
escape, as in this sentence: "She cried out in remonstrance that
she had no such desire, though this was of course entirely to be
expected since, had she been conscious of her true feelings, they
would not have been suppressed." There is a tenet of science that
no truth can be established unless its hypothesis contains the
possibility within itself of being disproved. Your theory of resolution fails that test, because its <u>selective</u> recourse to paradox
makes it intrinsically and permanently self-verifying.

(Incidentally, it is not "known" that masturbation to orgasm
precipitates amenorrhea; it has merely been asserted by various

There was a knock at the door, and Thomas put his pen down. It was
Hans.

"You are late for dinner, Doctor."

XIV

AT THE END OF JUNE, THOMAS RECEIVED A TELEGRAM. "AM BACK in Vienna. K." He wired a reply at once, inviting her to come to the schloss. He might even offer her work there, he thought, but wanted to see how Jacques would respond to her presence. He had a delicate course to steer: he did not wish to humiliate or enrage Jacques, but he did want him to understand the gravity of his error. Meanwhile, there was a shadow between them; there was something that needed to be resolved; and when he was certain that Jacques was in a sufficiently robust frame of mind, he told him about the diagnosis of rheumatic fever.

Jacques became agitated and pale as Thomas went over the steps by which he and Maierbrugger had arrived at their conclusion. He nodded gravely, and Thomas, like a doubtful assassin, felt pity and embarrassment as he watched.

"I see," said Jacques finally. "So when I asked you for an explanation of her joint pains you already had this one."

"Yes. I did not say so at the time because—"

"I understand why."

They were in Jacques's consulting room. He got up from where he had been sitting at the desk and walked to the window. He looked out over the gardens, but he said nothing.

Thomas said, "Of course, we shall probably never know the exact diagnosis. Perhaps none of us is right."

"Perhaps."

"But I knew that you would want to be aware of this severe compli-cation, if only so that you can develop your theory in the light of it."

"Yes," said Jacques. "Yes indeed." He seemed far, far away.

When Jacques turned at last to face him, Thomas found it hard to meet his eye. He thought of the sands at Deauville and he felt weary, as though he had heard the first call of middle-age, inviting him to subside into comfortable self-mockery, recognize the embrace of defeat and to indulge his own—after all, only human—failings. But he had seen men like Faverill go that way, and the outlines of their modesty and good humor were in fact a deception because they were etched with the acid of regret. He himself would never give up.

"We may have lost a battle," he said.

"Perhaps only a skirmish," said Jacques. "But the war, you were doubtless going to say, is not over."

"Of course not. I wanted to ask you something, while we are on this subject. Katharina may come back to the schloss to stay for a little while, just a holiday. Or I might ask her to do some of Sonia's work while she is pregnant. She is evidently rather good at that sort of thing."

"Evidently."

"But would you mind?"

"Do you think that every time I saw her in the cloister I would doubt my own abilities?"

"I don't know."

"Would she be like a raven on the battlement? A bird of ill omen always in the courtyard?"

Thomas laughed. "I very much hope not. She is a very . . . fine woman, as you yourself pointed out—most eloquently—in your case history."

"I remember. She made a good impression."

"So what do you think?"

"I think that you have presented me with a choice. Either I recognize Katharina's qualities and humbly see what I can learn in retrospect from her ailments or I allow myself to withdraw into some kind of unscientific isolation with a closed mind and an embittered heart."

"That is putting it a little starkly."

"A little. But it is a stark choice. And quite an easy one."

"You mean—"

"She is undoubtedly a person of superior gifts, Thomas. Ask her to do whatever you like, provided you consult Sonia. Now please leave me for a moment."

SONIA WAS reading on her bed, with the shutters and windows open, giving her a view down toward the lake. She was wearing a white cotton shift and held the book on top of her distended abdomen. Occasionally, she put it down, lifted the shift and ran her fingers over the skin, stretched to near-transparency, beneath which the veins ran like the streams of a blue delta. She seldom felt the baby move, but it seemed to be growing at a vigorous rate and she was anxious about how much bigger she would have to grow before October. Already she had started to shuffle a little when she walked, while her feet turned outward and her hand reflexively went to the small of her back for extra support when she hauled herself out of a chair. The heat of the summer made her feel that she would like to lie all day in the shallows of the lake, like a basking porpoise.

Despite these discomforts, she had seldom felt more purposeful. She ate amply of Frau Egger's cooking, though could not bear the taste of wine and used her condition as an excuse to turn down the bony river fishes that were otherwise destined for the lunchtime tray. In the afternoon, she went down into the office next to the waiting room, where she corrected Lisl's spelling and brought the accounts up to date. In the evenings, she sat with Jacques and Thomas and caught up with news of the schloss; she sensed the strain between them and was able to lighten it by appealing to shared memories of Torrington or Madame Maurel's boardinghouse.

But in the mornings, she was alone with the unborn child. She lay on the bed and heard the bellpull being answered by Lisl or Daisy, and the clatter from the nursery, where Hans was putting up new curtains and repainting the room. Josef had found a wooden crib among the furniture stored in the old stables and Sonia had had a new cot with elephants painted on the headboard made by a craftsman in the village. As she lay back, she thought of the millions of women in the world, in

Africa and China and England, who were like her at that moment, absorbed by their bodies' invisible toil, which took from her all it needed to sustain the life of something that had started as a mere idea in the nursery at Torrington ("When I grow up I am going to have . . .") yet now was daily turning into flesh. The size and weight, the specificity, were miraculous to her; he was not just a child, but her child, this very one; and how could you love so much a being you had never met?

She smiled briefly because these fancies did not really puzzle her; in fact, she was assailed all the time by a sense of rightness. What was happening beneath her hands seemed bizarre and in some way unexpected, yet the more she marveled at it, the more it felt inexorable. She sighed and closed her eyes as a slight breeze came up from the lake and through the open window. This is being alive, she thought; this is what it feels like.

WHEN THOMAS knocked at the door, she quickly covered herself with a sheet. "Come in."

Thomas sat at the end of the bed. "I wanted you to know that I have told Jacques about Katharina's rheumatic fever."

"How did he take it?"

"Philosophically. He did not like it, but he accepted it. I think there is no need to do any more. He will work out his own response, though I think he will need time."

"So you are not going to show him your notes on the case history?"

"No. That would be unnecessary now. I want him to come to his own conclusions and they may be quite different from mine. The only important thing is that he understands the dangers to the patient of a theory that is too rigid. We must never forget the simple things—fevers, sore throats and so on."

Sonia sighed. "I do hope he will find a way forward again. All his hopes rode on this theory."

"I think he will need some looking after."

"We will manage. The baby will be a distraction. It will occupy his mind."

"It will occupy all of us. There is another thing I needed to tell you,

Sonia. Or to ask you, I should say. I have invited Katharina back to the schloss to stay for a week or so. I wondered whether it might make sense for her to do something to help us. She could do your morning's work, for instance."

Sonia squinted down the bed at her brother. "Is that all you wanted to tell me—or to ask me? Is there something else?"

"I . . . No. That was it."

"Thomas, you are blushing."

"Don't be ridiculous."

Sonia laughed. "It is all right, you know, Thomas. It is allowed. You are a man of thirty-six years old who—"

"Thirty-five, in fact."

"Who has never had so much as a dalliance or—"

"Not recently, but—"

"And Kitty is a considerable prospect."

"Prospect! You sound like Father discussing things with Mr. Prendergast!"

"I did not mean financial, I just meant that she holds out promise for the future. She is on the threshold of her life. And she seems such a studious girl as well as being—"

"Exactly! That's exactly what I love about her. I—" He stopped short, hearing what he had said.

Sonia said nothing, but smiled at him. It was a long time since she had felt older, more advanced in her experience, than her younger brother.

"So," he said. "Congratulations. You have found me out. Can you understand why I love her so much?"

"Of course, Thomas. Have I not just said?"

"Yes, I know, but do you really understand? It means a good deal to me that you should like her."

"I do not know her well, but I think that if I were a man, she is the kind of woman I should fall in love with and want to marry."

"You are very kind."

"No, I am not. I am quite selfish and hard-hearted."

Thomas looked at her to see how serious she was. "Of course it is difficult with Jacques. I do not want him to be embarrassed or to see her as some kind of permanent rebuke."

"That is what made me suspicious," said Sonia. "I knew you would not have asked her back unless there was some particular reason."

Thomas nodded glumly. "It is awkward. If I were to propose marriage and she were to accept, then presumably we should all have to have dinner together every night. And . . . did you ever read the case history?"

"No."

"Good. Do not ever be tempted to read it. But it went into detail that he may find difficult to forget."

"But doctors can manage these things," said Sonia. "You are capable of seeing someone in the morning, inspecting their most intimate functions, then seeing them again in the evening as a social being in a white tie. That is what doctors do. That is why we admire you. I think you will find that Jacques will manage. He is a man of great imagination. He has a creative soul."

"You mean he will be able to imagine that he has never met her before?"

"It would not surprise me. If that is what he has to do. To him she was a patient, Thomas. That is all."

Thomas stood up. "I must go and get a room made ready for her."

"Yes," said Sonia. "But before you go, I must say that I am not sure about her working here. She may do some office work eventually, if everything goes to plan, but I don't want to give up all I have done. The accounts, for instance."

"We will tread gently."

WHEN KITTY arrived at the mainline station, Thomas was waiting. He had forgotten, when he held her in his arms, how slight she was: even in her traveling cloak and jacket, he felt he could have crushed her. On the other hand, the set of her blue eyes was precisely as he remembered, and so was the scent of her skin. She had brought only two suitcases and no trunk, as though not wishing to presume anything about the length of her stay, but in the trap on the way back to the schloss, her eyes were large with questions.

"We have put you in a bedroom in the main house," said Thomas, "on the same side as me. My room is at the front, yours is right at the back, overlooking the cloister and the South Court."

"I love that little courtyard."

"So your room faces west, and you have a view of the mountains as well."

"It sounds perfect."

"We can move you if—"

"Don't fret, Thomas."

Josef whipped the horses on as they began to climb from the valley. Thomas tried to explain what had passed between Jacques, Sonia and himself regarding Kitty's visit; he told her of the delicate negotiation and of how Sonia felt sure that Jacques would be able to forget what had gone before.

Kitty looked amused. "My dear Thomas, you are making a fuss about this. For myself, I have already forgotten almost all the details of my previous consultations. I have no more interest in them than in records of my childhood dentistry."

Thomas laughed. Mind you, he thought to himself, she has never read the case history; in fact, she does not even know of its existence. "So what are you interested in?" he said.

"The future. A healthy future without pains and fevers. You forget that for a former invalid it is wonderful just to be cantering up a hill with the summer breeze blowing through the window."

"Dear God, Kitty. I love you so much it makes me want to burst out laughing. I feel that if you are here, nothing can go wrong."

"Nothing will go wrong, Thomas. Why should it?"

"Because . . ." He was about to say, "because that is the way life is designed," but did not want to appear gloomy. "Nothing."

Kitty dined with the three of them that evening, and Thomas felt surprisingly little awkwardness. Jacques asked Kitty about her mother's family in London and told her about his one visit to England; Kitty asked Sonia about her plans for the baby and what names she had considered for it. The chestnut gâteau had already been cleared by the time Thomas managed to make any contribution of his own to their exchange. Afterward, he took Kitty outside into the gardens, where they walked down over the sloping lawns toward the mountains in the west.

Eventually the grass gave way and rolled down into a kind of ditch that formed a natural boundary; beyond it was a paddock, and after that some dark green cow pastures before the land began to rise again up into the foothills of the mountains. Thomas took off his jacket and spread it on the ground for Kitty to sit on; then he placed himself next to her and she leaned her head on his shoulder.

"Did you find a job in Vienna?" he said.

"No, I . . . I hardly had time."

"And an apartment?"

"I did look in the paper. I have brought it with me. But I can stay at my mother's house for the time being."

"How long were you in Vienna?"

"Three days. Two days."

"Not long, then."

"No. I was in a hurry to come back here."

"Why?"

"To see if things were as I remembered them."

"And are they?"

"Yes. Exactly so."

Thomas looked down and pulled a stalk of grass out of the ground.

"Do you find my work interesting, Kitty?"

"Very much. And your partner's work. I told you that I read his lecture."

"Yes."

"I may have been lucky. A surgeon's knife removed my minor problem. But I think there is a great deal in his psychophysical resolution."

Thomas smiled. Her perversity was liberating. "But," he said, "do you not think it faintly ridiculous that the two of us should be beating our heads against a rock?"

"What do you mean?"

"We are trying to answer questions which, at heart, we suspect we cannot answer."

Kitty put her hand on his arm. "You might, Thomas, you might. As you explained to me, there are moments when truths are revealed— sudden leaps forward. I expect they come when people have for a long time been beating their heads on a rock."

"But you would not think me ridiculous?"

"I would not think you ridiculous, no. I should probably need to read Mr. Darwin's books, but I would happily do that."

"You would do that just for me?"

"Of course."

Relief made Thomas pause. To think that someone would share his boneheaded convictions and his peculiar, blind ideas. . . . He saw that he had been half in love with Kitty from reading her case history, and that being close to her in person had inflamed the feeling; but the decisive moment came when she showed such interest in his work. She had questioned him and pushed him until that strange release had come, and he had told her of his now-silent voice: only Katharina had been able to connect the different parts of him.

"But," said Kitty, standing up, "you did not say if what."

"What do you mean, 'if what'?"

"You said, 'You would not think me ridiculous?' 'Would' is a conditional, and I wondered what the other part of the sentence was, the 'if' part."

"You are quite a grammarian," said Thomas.

"So, what was it?"

"I feel an idiot. It is too soon, much too soon, and you have been through so much that you need time to recuperate. In fact, as your doctor, I insist that you—"

"You are not my doctor. You have kissed me. I am asking to be transferred to Dr. Bernthaler's list. I am perfectly well. I have had several weeks' rest and I am now ready to work."

Thomas pushed himself up into a kneeling position and took her hand. "In that case, may I . . . Would you think me absurd if . . ."

Kitty shook her head, her eyes stinging. "Not at all."

"Will you marry me?"

"I would be honored," she said. "So very honored."

Thomas stood up and wrapped his arms round her. As she laid her head on his chest, he lifted up his eyes to the hills, but, despite all he believed, he could see no end to this happiness.

———

THEY AGREED that the wedding should take place in December, when Sonia would be recovered from the birth. The difficulty was in telling the others. It would not seem right for Kitty to remain at the schloss unless she was either engaged to be married or was employed there. However, Thomas did not want to push her into Sonia's place, nor did he yet want to break the news of his coming marriage to Jacques. It seemed precipitate, and he wanted nothing to deflect their energies and attention from the birth. Eventually, he and Kitty agreed, with reluctance, that she should go back to Vienna until after the baby was safely born, returning only for the occasional visit to make Sonia and Jacques aware that she was someone who would be part of their future. Thomas stilled Sonia's questioning by telling her that everything was well between him and Kitty, but that she still had personal matters to attend to; he assured Sonia that she would be the first to know of any development, and she was satisfied with his promise.

In the middle of October, Frau Holzer, a midwife from the city hospital, took up residence in one of the ground-floor rooms of the lower courtyard; and on a rainy Tuesday evening, two days later than predicted by the obstetrician, Sonia went into labor. Daisy volunteered to help Frau Holzer and was sent running up and down the corridor with towels and pans of water. Mary took up a position at the head of the stairs, her refined hearing giving her a good idea of the progress of the delivery, as she wound the hem of her apron convulsively in her fingers.

Jacques stayed in his consulting room and tried to read. He had developed a picture of what the child would be like, based on the idea that it would be a fusion of himself and his wife. The exact process of heredity was a mystery, but anyone could see the work of parentage: the ovum and the seed guaranteed half shares, and while the boy—like Sonia, he was certain it would be a boy—might have his dark eyes or Sonia's lighter ones, the details hardly mattered because he would be an intermingling of their blood and, it seemed to him, the baby was sure to represent not just a fusion but in some way an improvement. Sonia would die of no childbed fever, and in her continued life his own mother's death would be redeemed. The boy, meanwhile, would have all of the good and none of the bad: he would be the best of them all.

In the bedroom, Sonia braced herself and bore down as Daisy

mopped her forehead with a wet cloth. Frau Holzer spoke to her rather as she remembered Jenkins the stableman talking to the horses at Torrington. Having at first told her not to push, she was now urging her onward. "You are not trying, Frau Rebière. Take my hand and squeeze it. I want you to *push*."

Dear God, thought Sonia, I am pleased Jacques is not here to see this mess and strain. She felt the sweat cold on her shoulders and chest as a draft came through the window in the warm night. The pain was greater than she had expected and beyond her control, as though she were caught in a wave that would break only when gravity dictated; yet she did not panic or regret the pass in which she found herself. Though she was surprised at the animal in her, she let it have full rein, she howled, as everything she was—the memories, the instincts and desires—drove her on to break her body's limitations.

Daisy screamed. She was standing by the side of the bed. "Its head! I seen its head!"

Frau Holzer stood opposite, the sleeves rolled up on her brawny, bloody arms. "Wait for it," she said. "Wait one more moment."

"It's coming," Sonia gasped. "It's coming."

"Go on then, my love. Go on. One more time. Go on!"

At the stairhead, tears came from Mary's blind eyes.

Jacques stood still, craning his head toward the ceiling.

The shoulders of the baby extruded far enough for Frau Holzer to take them in her hands. She pushed her finger in and round the neck to see if the cord was wrapped there. It was free. As Sonia bore down one final time, Frau Holzer gently pulled the shoulders between her fingers and, with a sound like a huge cork being drawn, the baby, gray-purple, waxed and bloody, slid out into her attentive hands. It was a boy.

She blew on him, and the child screwed his features into a scarlet howl; she passed him up to his mother and went to wash her hands before she cut the cord. Sonia lay back on the stacked pillows with the boy at her breast and closed her eyes. Daisy wept noisily by the bed; she had never seen such a thing in all her life.

When Frau Holzer had cut the umbilicus, she examined Sonia to make sure that there was no tearing, then set about cleaning up.

"Stop sniveling," she said to Daisy, "and get some fresh cloths. Then bring a nice bowl of hot water so we can tidy her up for when Father comes to call."

Daisy went out onto the landing, but she did not really know what she was doing. She saw Mary and ran toward her. "It's a boy," she said. "He's such a little treasure. He's so perfect. Oh, Mary, you can't believe it." The two girls clung on to each other, weeping and laughing.

When all the sheets had been changed, the towels and cloths cleared and Sonia bathed and put into a fresh nightdress, Frau Holzer went downstairs and knocked on Jacques's door.

"Herr Doktor," she said, as the door opened. "You have a son. Congratulations. The mother and the boy are both well."

Jacques gazed at her, openmouthed. It was the news that Sonia was well that struck him to the soul: the mother would live, and the son would know her.

He ran up the stairs and down to the bedroom. Sonia looked up at him, pale, but full of shy pride. He kissed her, but could not find the words to speak. She offered the child up to him and he held it in his arms. Then he laid him on the bed and unwound the simple cloth in which he was wrapped so that he could see the whole body.

And he saw that it was not a fusion, after all. It was a separate being, like the first man born. You are on your own, thought Jacques: I will do everything I can for you, but in truth, little boy, you are on your own.

THE CHILD was baptized Daniel Thomas on November 25, 1895, in the local Protestant church of St. Luke, his father yielding to his mother's denomination, and his baptismal certificate showed that his godparents were Dr. Thomas Midwinter, Dr. Franz Bernthaler, Fräulein Daisy Wilkins and Fräulein Mary, who signed her name with a cross. There was a party afterward at the schloss, where many people from the local villages came to see the baby and to stare at the lunatics in the courtyard. Kitty had come from Vienna to stay the weekend, and the next day, in the afterglow of family pride, they told Jacques and Sonia that they were to be married.

The wedding itself took place in Vienna in the week before Christmas; there was snow on the streets and candles inside the church, where the bridesmaids (two young cousins of Kitty's on her father's side) wore green velvet dresses trimmed with white lace and decorated with sprigs of scarlet-berried holly. None of Thomas's family could come from England, but Pierre Valade traveled from Paris, and Dr. Faverill, who had seen an announcement in the London *Times,* sent a letter of congratulation. Kitty was given away by her stepfather, "Herr P.," a gray-haired man with a face like a deep-sea fish, whose name, it transpired, was Julius Bittmann; she wore a dress of ivory satin that had been her mother's. When they left the church to go to the wedding breakfast at her mother's house she put on a long cream coat with a fur-trimmed hood, and in her clear skin and bright eyes there was no sign of the invalid who had arrived at the Schloss Seeblick nine months earlier. Jacques proposed the health of the bridesmaids, having first briefly spoken of his friendship with Thomas. He said how much Kitty had impressed people at the schloss with her quiet stoicism, but did not say how she had been treated, or by whom. Thomas thanked Kitty's mother and regretted her father's absence, though his words were not heard by everyone over the sound of Daniel's fit of crying. A string quartet began to play waltzes and polkas, and Thomas was prompted into asking Kitty to dance. He looked down into her flashing blue eyes as he guided her round the shiny parquet beneath the skeptical gaze of various elderly Prussians. He wanted the day to be over, so that he could be alone with her; but he could see that she was enjoying it and did his best not to tread on her feet as they circled among the trays full of pastries and mulled wine, of champagne and jellies.

He was reminded of the asylum ball; and for a moment felt himself back on the scrubbed boards of the dining hall, among the meat pies and glasses of ale, while Brissenden tried to slow down Mary Ann Parker's piano and the old lady danced alone with her arms held out in front of her. When the polka was over, he yielded Kitty to her stepfather's request and went to find Mary.

He led her out amid the politely circling couples and felt less stricken by grief and guilt than on the last occasion they had danced together; Mary did not cling to him like a limp doll, but held herself upright, smiled, and, so far as she was able, danced. The movement of her pink pumps made its individual pattern of footprints on the floor.

Kitty and Thomas had agreed that there would be no honeymoon until the spring, when the weather would be better and, after the Christmas and New Year celebrations, there would be less to do at the schloss. Kitty was eager to begin decorating the rooms that had been set aside for them on the first floor of the South Court.

For the wedding night, however, Thomas had booked a room in a mighty hotel on the Kärntnerstrasse with fiery torches burning either side of the front doors, and Josef delivered them there shortly after ten o'clock. When the bellboy who brought up their cases had been tipped and despatched, Thomas built up the fire and drew the heavy velvet curtains, while Kitty turned down the gas in the lamp and lit the candles by the bed.

She hung her wedding dress in the wardrobe, but then found herself unsure how to proceed. Her fantasies of making love had generally involved some shameful candor or exposure of herself to rapacious eyes and hands; but now that the moment was there, she found that she was merely worried about doing her duty and not disappointing the man she so loved and admired. When he ran his hands over her shoulders and gently pulled down the straps of her underclothes, she was not able to be the abandoned woman of her imagination. He whispered reassurance, and the sound of his affectionate voice was helpful; there was light enough for her to see his expression and there was an earnestness there that showed he too was anxious. She allowed him to undress her, so that in the end she stood naked in front of the fire, which sent flickering shadows up and down her legs, while he knelt down and kissed her skin, murmuring to himself, as she looked down and stroked his hair. Eventually, he lifted her up in his arms and carried her to the bed, stepping through the tangle of her dropped clothes. The evidence that Kitty had from the words that Thomas whispered, from his sighs and the hunching of his bare shoulders, suggested to her that she did not altogether displease him.

BY THE time spring came, Daniel could often sleep an entire night without waking and Sonia was able to feed him without difficulty. Kitty set about furnishing and decorating the five rooms allotted to her and

Thomas in a previously unoccupied part of the South courtyard; once she had had the chimneys swept and had installed one of the large cylinder heaters in the sitting room, it became more homely. Thomas spent many evenings in the cellars with Franz Bernthaler, hunched over their histology slides, searching for the bloom and stain of madness.

One night, in idle and tired curiosity after two hours at the microscope, he tried a barred door at the end of the cellar. He found to his surprise that it opened outward into a dark passage. He took a candle from the shelf and walked about twenty paces on an earth floor between brick walls; at the end were some steps going up to another door. It was unlocked, though stiff, and when Thomas put his shoulder to it he found that he had emerged at the back of a larder in a scullery in the corner of the South Court. He smiled; it was nothing less than a secret passage, installed goodness knows why, by a previous owner, perhaps even the abbot himself.

He went up the internal stairs to tell Kitty about it while they had dinner. He had suggested to Sonia that it might be better if they did not all dine together every night, so they took it in turns to be with the patients during the week, all four going to the dining room together only on Friday.

Thomas was enchanted by his new life. The private world of his intimacy with Kitty was the most thrilling part of it, yet it did not seem to distract his energy from the communal life of the schloss, where he was the sanatorium's most public face. If at any point during the day his strength or interest flagged, he had only to go down the cloister and double back through the gates into the South Court or, as he now preferred, to take the secret passage underground, to find himself once more in his private world, where Kitty was always willing to stop whatever task she was engaged on, however much she might at first protest. He liked to whisper in her ear as he stroked her hair, to lift her skirt and run his hands up her leg, to touch her while she still had on her reading glasses. As in time she became more confident, and was reassured that she was pleasing to him, she came closer to enacting the fantasies of her adolescence; and once she was inflamed, she wanted him to go through to the conclusion. Thomas was not sure what he had done to deserve the indulgence of his private desires, but presumed that everything was ratified by the sacrament of marriage. He looked at Kitty at dinner on Friday nights, her head tilted to one side as she listened to Sonia or Jacques, and remembered what she had done to him an hour before; he looked at the fuchsia coloring on her lips and wondered which parts of his skin might bear a trace of it. Marriage, he was inclined to think, was a bountiful and surprising invention.

THE ONLY person in the schloss not flourishing was Jacques. He went for long walks round the lake and cried into hands clamped across his face.

The birth of Daniel had delayed the need for him to face his humiliation and he had thought it better for the practice to behave outwardly in a calm and organized way. Inside, he felt like a child, back in the upstairs room at his father's house, fiddling with a dead frog. He could only dream of greatness because real achievements belonged to other people, to his betters—people with a proper education. What pathetic self-delusion had allowed him to believe the words of flattery that had come his way? Intern! Doctor! The applause of the examiners, the patronage of Babinski, the encouragement of Janet . . . how vainly he had taken them, allowed them to insinuate themselves into his own picture of himself. But he was just a peasant boy, he was a child and always would be; he was good at mending roofs and trapping rabbits, but as far as science was concerned, his level was teaching at the village school. He had given himself airs, strode about the sanatorium with a grave and masterful demeanor, as though he understood the mysteries of the human mind and body. He knew nothing; he had read some books, that was all. Franz Bernthaler knew more than he did. Thomas Midwinter knew more than he did. In a way, it was a relief that the reverie, the trance of self-importance, was at an end. He had climbed one rung at a time, daring himself to fall, not seeing that the fall would be complete; now he wanted only that people should know that he recognized exactly who he was and would never again have thoughts above his natural station.

He could not bear to look at Sonia. She had married him on false pretenses, taking him at his estimation of himself when he was really her inferior, not worthy of the delicacy of her nature. She had indulged his frenzied working, had not complained when he ignored her in the early years of their marriage, preferring the company of some German book. He had behaved like a boor, and he could never recapture those times or relive them with more grace.

As he looked over the still waters of the lake, he seemed to understand for the first time the limits of what he might achieve. He could take some comfort from the fact that all ambition, all desire must have an element of delusion. After all, people talked of the necessity of self-belief, of having faith in one's own abilities, which implied that such capacities were always open to doubt and that it was the act of believing, the leap of faith itself, which somehow made them greater. The degree of comfort that he found was very small, however.

Sonia did her best to reassure him, telling him that nothing could change her passion for him and that all pioneers faced setbacks on uncharted roads. She said she was proud of the honesty with which he had admitted his errors, but that he must retain a sense of scale: his life's work was not over, his skill as a doctor was still urgently required. Privately, she welcomed the fact that he seemed so reliant on her and put her feelings first, before his books, but she also felt that this was not the natural order of things for them. She had learned to stand a half-pace behind him as he looked forward into the future; she had become content in that role and she did not now want a husband whose imploring gaze was turned sideways onto her, because such a man was not the one she had married or first loved.

During the spring of the new year, 1896, Jacques fell into a lethargy, which he ascribed to lack of sleep. He had begun to wake at four every morning and found it impossible to fall asleep again. He prescribed himself strong medicines in various doses, but although he could in this way achieve unconsciousness, he never felt rested. He had to be roused from such drugged slumber by Sonia shaking his shoulder, and he felt stunned or stupefied throughout the day; although the clock told him he had been asleep for eight hours, he did not feel renewed by it: there was no sense of replenishment, no appetite for work, merely a feeling of exhaustion, a dryness exacerbated by the strong coffee he drank and a mind going through superficial exercises without the ability to reach down to any worthwhile depth of wisdom, insight or enthusiasm.

In March, Thomas established that the widow in Salzburg who owned the land and decrepit buildings at the top of the Wilhelmskogel would be prepared to sell them; the news from Trieste was that there was still no chance that the lease on the schloss could be extended. One evening, as he was explaining the situation to Kitty over dinner in their upstairs rooms, Thomas suddenly stopped and banged the table with his fist.

"Of course," he said. "That's it. Jacques must go to America. Two birds with one stone. Three birds, perhaps."

"Thomas, what are you talking about?"

"Wilhelmskogel, the site of our new sanatorium. A fashionable perch up in the mountains. But we need some sort of funicular or cable car to get the patients and supplies up there. You can't put a madman on a mule track. There is this place in California which Valade was telling us about. They have built a railway and a cable car, I think, and people go up from the valley for the day. It all works very well, apparently, with New World engineering and enthusiasm."

"And?"

"Well, don't you see? We should send Jacques to investigate. It would give him a holiday, it would clear his mind. He has never traveled before, he has just worked and worked and worked. It would be a marvelous adventure for him. An Atlantic steamship. Dinner at the captain's table. Can you imagine? We have been running now for nearly six years and it is time he took sabbatical leave. We can manage without him for a little while and it would show that we have confidence in the future of the enterprise if one of the cofounders goes off across the world to look at new ways of expanding."

"He won't want to leave little Daniel. And Sonia."

"I think he will. And I think it would be a good thing if he does."

Kitty looked unconvinced. "What about the cost and all that time away?"

"The railways are not expensive. In that article Valade showed me, there was a story of the different railroads competing for custom. You could get from Chicago to the Pacific for a dollar. The voyage would cost a good deal, I imagine, but we have a surplus at the bank. As for the time, I think if it could be done in three months, we could manage. Also, it is not as if he would not be working. He would have nothing else to do but read—though I think we should give him some Walter Scott or Dickens rather than Emil Kraepelin."

Thomas mentioned the idea to Sonia, diffidently, in case she might think he was trying to interfere; to his surprise, she did not resist.

"I should miss him most dreadfully, but it is not as though I do not have family and friends around me. I am certain that Jacques would benefit from such a venture. It is not just that he needs a rest, it is that he needs to gather himself to go further."

"Exactly," said Thomas, looking a little curiously at his sister.

Jacques was more difficult to persuade. He argued that he had work which no one else could do and that Sonia needed his presence, particularly now that she had a child. She gently pointed out to him that, fond though he was, he took no care of the infant, seeing him only for a few minutes in the evening, while as for her own needs, she alone was in a position to judge them. Thomas assured him that they could cover his absence, and proposed to offer part-time work to someone he had met in Vienna, Peter Andritsch, a bearlike, bearded man in his thirties who had studied under Janet at the Salpêtrière before setting up as a nerve specialist in Vienna, where he had found the competition intense.

With all his arguments benevolently forestalled, Jacques had no choice but to acquiesce, though he felt wounded by Sonia's easy compliance and suspicious of Thomas's motives. He felt as though he had been banished, sent into exile for his failures, by the two people he had most loved.

The person most sympathetic, oddly enough, was his former patient, Katharina. She occupied herself with planning a route for him and investigating how long it would take. The fastest Atlantic crossing, she established, was by the White Star steamships *Teutonic* and *Majestic*, which could make the crossing from Cobh, in Ireland, to New York in five and a half days. She showed him a picture of the *Teutonic* leaving Liverpool, with her twin yellow funnels and triple mast with the company flag showing its white star on a beautiful scarlet background.

"I wish I was coming myself," she said. "I have always wanted to go on a beautiful ship like that. Think of the romance."

"Think of the hundreds of Irish emigrants in steerage," said Jacques. "I suppose there is little romance for them."

"One of my great-grandfathers was Irish," said Kitty.

"Indeed, I meant only that it is a harrowing journey for them—to leave their home for a new life."

Kitty laughed. "I did not take offense. I have found another possibility. The *City of New York,* a similar ship, leaves from Southampton for the American Line. I can book you a single ticket from Paris by way of Le Havre and your baggage is transferred. You do not need to go to Liverpool or Ireland. She will take you to New York in six days. She looks even more elegant than the *Teutonic,* a little longer and with three funnels."

"I think the extra funnel must decide it," said Jacques. "I shall go and pack my bags."

"She sails on a Saturday."

Ten days later, he had said goodbye to Sonia and to Daniel, and found he was halfway to Paris. Le Havre and Southampton passed him by, and he was two days out to sea before he allowed himself to stop and think. While the cabin had its own mahogany washstand and mirrored wardrobe, the steel bulkhead above his face when he lay down left him in no doubt that he was at sea, belowdecks. He took meals in the saloon and walked about the deck when the weather was fine; he said good-morning to his fellow passengers, but all the time the great steamer lumbered through the gray waves of the Atlantic, he felt that he was being sundered from his past. At night he heard the rumbling of the twin propellers as they screwed the water out beneath the waves; he thought he could hear the steam bubbling up in its gigantic boilers as it drove the cylinders; he pictured the half-naked men hurling wood and coal into the furnaces, and the thought of that slippery-backed toil helped him at last to fall asleep. The past went down beneath the waves, to be forgotten, as the ship pushed forward into the night, thoughtless, blind, like time.

IT WAS somewhere beside the Ohio river—New York a dream and Pittsburgh far behind—that Jacques began to feel a change in himself. He had switched to the Fort Wayne and Chicago line and perhaps there was something about the transfer that made him feel he was now embarked beyond a chance of turn-ing back. He thought of Daniel, as though he had never truly thought about him before. The baby was strong enough to support his own weight when he sat, but was still so small that Jacques could balance him on the palm of his right hand with his fingers bracing his back. Sometimes he would lift Daniel up to the light, and turn his wrist so that Sonia could look at her son from all angles, like a jeweler examining a remarkable piece. The boy himself stared back placidly with large eyes given a curious look by the way he sometimes cocked his head to one side, as though he were a bird perching on a branch. My God, thought Jacques, staring at the flashing fields of Indiana, he is my bone and blood, a thought made flesh, and I have barely stopped to ponder it.

In truth, he found it difficult to feel deeply for his son. He watched Sonia with him and her attitude seemed sentimental, and at times affected. How could she be experiencing all those emotions for a creature that she barely knew, that no one knew? He supposed his own responses were shaped by his never having known his mother and by a fear that if Olivier's disease was in part hereditary, then he himself, though without symptoms, might be a carrier of it. He did not wish to become too fond.

He was told at the Union Pacific Depot in Omaha that for an extra eight dollars he could secure himself a Palace sleeping car all the way to San Francisco, and as the booking clerk pointed out, this was really an economy when you considered that a stopover at even a modest hotel could be four dollars, while the Dellone, where he had stayed the night before, had doubtless cost him . . . But Jacques had already pushed the extra cash through the window and went off to have his spare bag checked through to the coast.

My Dearest Dearest Wife,

I shall write in English because you have so Anglicized me.
What happened to the Breton child? He is in a "sleeping" car in
California, traveling alone between the Rocky Mts. & the Sierra
Nevada, though little sleeping. I hope you are; and that the boy
allows you to. Are you both well? You may telegraph to the
station in any large town; I shall check in Omaha and New

York on my return, though perhaps I shall be home before this letter.

The train journey will take in all ten days, so with the sea crossing (six), the various stops and the journey from Carinthia, it will have taken me 21 days from my first pace out of the schloss into Josef's carriage to my first footstep on Mt. Lowe, God willing.

On Wednesday, we made a brief stop at a place called Sherman. This is bad-weather country, as you can tell by the number of "snow sheds," which are like wooden tunnels to keep the snow off the most exposed parts of the track. We were urged to step down from the train for a little while. It was hard to breathe. This is landscape of enormous grandeur. Surely believers feel the hand of Him who made them among these desolate peaks.

Thursday, we were in the mountains all day. I was filled with an odd sense of having lived before. This place seems so wild and terrifying. My heart melts when I think of the men and women and their children who had to cross this terrible landscape. Legends of how some never made it, fell ill or died in the mountain passes, starved, ate one another. Unimaginable—yet familiar. And I somehow feel I know what it was to be a rider for the Pony Express, going on and on through all weathers, attacks from Indians, sunburned, snow-drenched, over prairie and mountain, terrible pain and lungs burning, but having to do it— no alternative or your wife and child will starve, & at last seeing the light ahead of the station where you hand over the mail and fall exhausted into sleep. Two thousand miles coast to coast in nine days! Would there be food and drink? Would you make love to the stablemaster's daughter, knowing that there are no normal rules in this wilderness? How do I know so much what it felt like? Have I lived it? Am I a reincarnated man? Is there some sort of universal human memory available to all? Or are all our little minds just aspects of one great consciousness?

I do not like these thoughts. They make human life seem perpetual, with no escape from self-awareness, even through death . . .

Oh, Sonia, reading this back, I see how little I have conveyed what I have really felt in my travels—the utter loneliness, as though I knew not one soul in the whole wide world, had never seen your dear face; I sometimes wonder if you really still exist. The appalling strangeness of being entirely alone in this enormous world, a little collection of cells hurried west in clanking wagons. Above all this pointless sense of being alive, or being a soul—a self—perhaps for ever.

If the soul is not distinct enough to die, then what one wants is utter extinction of <u>all</u> consciousness—because there is no rest in individual death. Do you see what I mean? The belief of the Buddhists that one's soul returns again and again on its climb to perfection is surely absurd. But what we can manifestly see is just as terrifying—as one is extinguished, another, near-identical, reaches self-awareness, and all the old intractable problems begin again. It is intolerable. The human mind has evolved in a way that makes it unable to deal with the pain and mystery of its own existence. No other creature is like this.

Whether this thing I call myself is real or not, whether it is the flickering wave of some electromagnetic field, or exists only as a whirlpool—as a dynamic movement made of other particles—please, God, let it be real: because a self that does not exist cannot be extinguished.

And if my consciousness is not sufficiently differentiated from those of all mankind, then something so close as to be indistinguishable from it is born again each moment in some poor city or village on earth; and I, or a being so like me as to make no difference, is bound to live again, forever, caught up in some loop of eternal return. Dear God, may my consciousness be real, so that it may die at last . . .

Later:—

That night we made Promontory, elevation 4,905 feet, so we were into our descent. Ghost town. It was just near here, I was told by the attendant who comes to bring me fresh water, that the East and West of America became one country when the

rails of the Central Pacific Rail Road were joined to those of the
Union Pacific. Men from Maine and Florida shook hands with
men from California. Flags, drums and muskets. The final tie in
the track was silver-plated. As the last spikes were driven and the
telegraph lines were connected—"like chained lightning," he
said—all work was suspended in San Francisco and New York.
Bells rang out.

The attendant had tears in his eyes as he recounted this story.

Then Friday: the palisades of the Humbolt River. Sheer rock
with our "cowcatcher" nose a chisel through the narrow gap.

Finally, the Truckee division. We arrived at Reno in the
evening, about nine. This was the last stop in Nevada. It was
dark and I could not see outside, but there was the sound of a
lone banjo and a man with an English voice singing—

Then I felt the train began a steep descent into the promised
land.

I awoke in sunshine which penetrated the lowered blind of
the compartment, but it was not the usual four a.m., it was 7.15!
Heavenly repose, rest, God be praised.

I was in the station at Sacramento. I had just time to buy
coffee and a bag of oranges on the platform.

Oakland Wharf late morning. Across the Bay and disembark
at ferry-slip in the city of San Francisco. A morning of
transfixing beauty. Explored the city, much of it rebuilt after fires
and now home to some 300,000 people, many in the hills, of
which some streets served by new cable cars. Dined at hotel on
oysters and American wine!

I walked at night into a place frequented only by Chinamen.
Was advised to avoid the area known as the "Barbary Coast,"
haunt of pickpockets and villains. San Francisco is an
enchantment, it seems to me, but it is also a port; & like all ports
draws drifters, misfits—or simply those who have fled the
Puritan pioneer towns of Nebraska or Indiana. It is the end of
the world. Nothing lies beyond, except what Cortez saw from
Mexico—and in the eyes of some of the men at night there is a
kind of desperation.

I spent a day in SF, then took a train to Los Angeles: a small town, population about 20,000, I would guess, though much older than San F—it has been settled for more than a century, a garden city of groves and parks with tropical fruits—orange, lemon, lime, banana, eucalyptus. Connected by train to Santa Monica, bathing resort of about a thousand residents, but I had no time for the seaside waters. What if Santa Monica should precipitate a change as great as that wrought in my life by Deauville?

No: it is on to Pasadena, the end of my voyage. I am on the new train that since only last year has connected the two towns, and as the warm sun floods the carriage, I have only one thought:—

It is for you, my dearest Sonia. May God or Providence be thanked that I found you and was not displeasing to you. I love you. I shall always love you, the thought of you, the soul of you, what lived before in your name and whatever shall survive of you. May it prove to be when I return home that you were not the product of my imagination, but exist in reality, my true and breathing wife.

XV

PASADENA WAS A LITTLE TOWN WHICH AT FIRST SIGHT LOOKED abandoned in its orange groves at the foot of the mountains, like a piece of sleeping Eden unaccountably spared by the Gold Rush. Inside, however, there were signs that the settlers had ambitions, and as he stood looking up Fair Oaks Avenue, Jacques could see several stately buildings already in place. Most were formed from cast-iron frames and traditional brickwork, but many also had stone balconies, painted clapboard sides and towers with colored tiles and flags. The rails of a horsecar line were embedded in the center of the road, while small carriages waited by the sidewalk as their owners ducked under striped awnings into shops and offices. All around, the workmen drilled and hammered in the even light of sunshine, with palm trees to shade them and hummingbirds darting among the lemons and hibiscus.

The Grand Opera House had onion-dome towers, pierced metal decorations and Moorish window arches; on its ground floor, beneath a steep white sun canopy, were the offices of the Mount Lowe Railway.

"You need to speak to the Professor," said the clerk, a small man in shirtsleeves and an eyeshade, when Jacques went in to ask for help.

"Professor Lowe?"

"No. Professor James, the director of publicity for the railway."

"I only want to ask some questions, I am not offering to—"

"I understand," said the clerk. "The Professor would be mighty pleased to help. He's from England. You from England, sir?"

"No, I am from France, but my wife is English."

"I thought you spoke funny, if you'll pardon me saying so. Now, the Professor, you might find him taking his dinner in the Green or the Raymond. I do believe he's going to show some of his magic lantern slides there this evening. But if you want to be sure to catch him, you just stop by here at nine tomorrow morning. That's when he's always at his desk."

"I'll come back," said Jacques.

"And if you want somewhere good and homely to eat tonight, can I recommend you try the Acme? It's right next to the Fire Station on the corner of Dayton and Fair Oaks."

"Thank you," said Jacques, a little uneasy at what this American's idea of a good dinner might be. "Until tomorrow."

At nine the next day, he found a large man with dense eyebrows and a thick graying beard sitting at his desk, as advertised, behind a wooden sign that read: Professor George Wharton James, Mount Lowe Railway Co. He stood up and enthusiastically greeted Jacques, pumping his hand as he did so.

"We welcome all kinds to Paradise, sir," he said. "But a French nerve specialist . . . well, darn me, that really is something. I shall take you up the mountain myself this afternoon. Perhaps you would care to join me for dinner at Echo Mountain House? I guarantee you will have some travelers' tales to pass on to your friends back home. Let us meet here at four, when I shall have done my business at the Raymond. We take the railway to Altadena before we embark on our journey. Does that suit you, my friend?"

"Very well," said Jacques.

"Bring a stick if you care to do some walking in the mountains, and a coat. It will be cool tonight."

"Thank you, Professor."

"There is no need to call me Professor. Call me George. I shall call you Jack."

In the train on the short trip to Altadena, Professor James told Jacques that Pasadena had been a settlement for little more than thirty years; it was only in the last decade, when the little town had grown to around ten thousand, that the inhabitants had started to lift their eyes up to the mountains and consider what they offered. The more athletic plain dwellers had made a trail to the summit of Mount Wilson, named after an early settler; but the hike was far too arduous for the majority, who contented themselves with a short climb into the foothills, where they walked among the fields of golden poppies.

"So this paradise was unexplored. It needed vision. It needed daring. Then," said Professor James, as they stepped down from the train and crossed the platform, "from New Hampshire by way of Cincinnati, came a genius—Thaddeus S. C. Lowe. You are now climbing onto one of his railroad cars for the journey of your lifetime. All aboard!"

Jacques was struck by the similarity of the terrain to that in Carinthia; although what was proposed at home was more modest, many of the difficulties appeared to be the same. Lowe's engineer had devised a mixed system: an electric trolley for the gentle ascent through the first canyon, which was called Rubio; then, when the gulf ahead had proved impossible to span, the railroad was temporarily abandoned and the passengers were asked to switch to a cable car, which hauled them to the summit of Echo Mountain, and a sumptuous hotel. Thence the electric railway resumed its more gradual ascent to the peaks of Mount Lowe.

There were two other passengers in the carriage with Jacques and the bombastic Professor, as it made its way up into the canyon, grabbing power from the line above; it snaked around the poppy fields and through the hills with their covering of chaparral and cactus. Jacques tried to picture the journey as it might be experienced by some patient in the Alps, and the first thing they would need against the European chill, he thought, was wooden sides and windows rather than roll-down canvas. The ride itself, however, would pose no problem to an invalid; one had only to sit back on the wooden bench and admire the cities of the plain. Jacques glanced across at the flushed face of his companion, which was full of the joys of the ride, and at that moment they rounded a sharp bend, the track straightened and James let out a throaty cry. "There she is! The Rubio Hotel. Isn't she a beauty?"

Jacques smiled. To the right of the track was a large building that seemed to be floating in the void above a narrow gorge, in a green mist of sycamore and fern. The pavilion-hotel was made more remarkable by the fact that two further floors were hanging from its underside, one with its own pitched roof beneath the terrace of the upper building. As the trolley car stopped alongside, Jacques saw that this was an illusion and that the lower floors in fact spanned the narrow ravine and took their footing from its sides; but the appearance of a three-story pleasure palace somehow suspended in the gulf was enough to make anyone smile.

"Let's have a look-see, shall we?" said Professor James, pulling his hat down firmly as he stepped onto the platform. They crossed over to the terrace of the hotel, where several brakemen and drivers were taking a rest, and the Professor led the way down wooden steps to the middle floor, from which walkways departed above the ravine. Jacques followed him at a brisk pace until they came to a waterfall, which the Professor invited him to stop and admire.

"Did you ever see a prettier cascade? Look at those great boulders. Listen to the crash! We have to give folk something to do once they are up here. Most of our visitors are local people who first came out here from the Middle West. The Indiana Colony they used to call it. But since we had our rail connection to Los Angeles last year, we can expect tourists from all over America. Let's go and take tea at the Rubio, then we can go up the cable car to Echo Mountain itself. You are in for a treat, Jack!"

Jacques found himself warming a little to the Professor, and as they drank tea in the dining room of the Rubio Hotel, he politely asked him about his title.

"At which seat of learning are you a professor?"

"Retired now," said James with a wave of his hand. "It is a courtesy more honored in the breach than the observance. Have some cake."

"And of what subject? Engineering?"

"No, we have an engineer, Macpherson, none better. My qualifications are in people. Yes, Jack. People and their minds, that's my special subject."

"Like me. Though I am only a doctor, not a professor."

"Yes. Just like you. I used to run a correspondence school here in California. It was for memory training. The human mind is a very wonderful organ."

"So I believe," said Jacques.

"It never forgets. It's all in here, you know. It's just a question of knowing how to find it."

Jacques nodded, thinking of Janet's statement that in the human mind "nothing ever gets lost," which sounded more persuasive, but perhaps was no different in essence from what the old salesman was telling him.

"I was born in England," James was saying, "came out West as a Methodist missionary—what they called a 'circuit rider.' Can you believe that? John Wesley was my hero. I used to love to preach and lead the people in singing. Proper hymns for devout people. Now, if you're ready, Jack, we shall go up into the clouds."

Jacques followed his guide out onto the wooden platform and over to the foot of the incline, where an open white cable car was waiting for them. It had three separate parts, each at an angle to the gradient, so their floors were parallel to the ground far beneath; the lowest section had gilded decorations on the bow, which made the whole contraption look like a three-tiered opera box going up into the unknown.

The cable gripped and shuddered, the brakeman whistled and the car began its electrically driven ascent, noiseless but for the drag of wheels on the new rail. In a minute, they were looking down steeply onto the roof of the Rubio Hotel; a few seconds later they were lost in low cloud. Jacques felt a roar of childlike exhilaration building up in him. Halfway up the incline, they slowed as the downward car approached, then passed, as the track briefly widened for the purpose. Shortly afterward, the upward car lipped over the top at Echo Mountain and drew silently to a halt. It was cold.

"Hop out, Jack, there's plenty to see up here."

Echo Mountain House was a three-storied building with a dome, much larger than the Rubio Hotel below, and with a smaller companion chalet built off the edge of the hill. Both were painted bright white. In the palatial lobby of the main building, the Professor asked the housekeeper to reserve him a table for dinner—"Keep me back some oysters," he called after her—then took Jacques outside again.

"This is our zoo," he said. "We have to keep them interested while they wait for the car to go down. We got raccoons, an eagle. Watch this. Hold my hat."

He pulled open a cage door and jumped down into a pit, where, to Jacques's astonishment, he began to wrestle with a black bear. "Don't worry," he called up. "She likes a roughhouse. Ursa Minor, we call her. She's a little character, she is. Here, give me a hand up."

When he had dusted himself down and consulted his watch, Professor James said, "We have just about time to go on up to the Alpine Tavern. I guess that might be of interest to you, coming from Europe. We call these here the American Alps. Sure sounds better than the Sierra Madre."

"And where is the Alpine Tavern?"

"It's on the side of Mount Lowe, which is halfway to our final destination at Mount Wilson. After you, now."

They were just in time to catch a trolley car, like the first one that had taken them up into Rubio Canyon. The ride was up a similar gradient, slow but not particularly steep, as the carriage snaked round the mountains and the rails rattled on their granite bed.

"You could do this back in Europe," the Professor said. "You could surely do it. But you need a first-class engineer and it could be expensive. What costs you is all the clearance. On this section alone we rolled enough rock into the canyons to build a city the size of Pasadena."

"But not on the incline, where the cable car is?"

"Not so much there. It depends on the landscape and what your surveyor says. The engineering is simple enough. It's just a thick wire that goes round a wheel! You might have trouble finding a manufacturer in Europe, but you could buy the wire and the wheel in San Francisco. It's the terrain that holds the key. Just ask the good Lord for a nice even run so you don't have to blow up half the mountain."

After they had negotiated two hairpins, the car stopped to allow them to enjoy the view. Jacques looked down through the evening air from which the earlier cloud had lifted. They could see the dome of the observatory and across to Echo Mountain House, shining white on its green promontory. The streets of Pasadena were so few and so spread, that the Professor was able to point out to him Fair Oaks and Lake Avenue, like straight scratches made with a burned match in the surrounding green scrub.

Although it was evening, they could see the ridges of the hills in the plain, and the towns they enclosed: Glendale to the right, Los Angeles in the center, and beyond it, the undeveloped land that ran down to the little bathing resort of Santa Monica; and still just visible through the thin air, as the sun began to fade, was the island of Catalina, dimly sparkling in the aptly named Pacific.

Jacques sighed, loosened his tie and pushed his hat back on his head. What a country, he thought. What a place, where everything was still to do. He decided that in the morning he would make an appointment to see Macpherson, "the finest mathematician ever to come out of Cornell," according to the Professor, and ask his advice about the feasibility of a cable car in Europe; then he might take the train up to San Francisco to see the wire rope manufacturers. How expensive could it be, he thought—a wheel, a wire and a rail?

"This is our terminus," said Professor James. "For the time being at least. We call it Ye Alpine Tavern because it looks so old. In fact it's been open just six months, but it does look European, does it not?"

It looked like a version of Europe, Jacques thought: to be precise, it looked like the baroque dream of a homesick European exiled in California. The tavern was in the style of a Swiss chalet, cross-timbered, with a stone foundation that rose to the sills of the ground-floor windows. The tall pines and bare-faced granite outcrop behind gave it a slightly melancholy air, though even in June, Jacques noticed, a mountain spring was running nearby.

They went inside to a wooden lobby, where three women were sitting at a round table playing cards. One of them looked familiar to Jacques, though he could not quite place her. Paris . . . Vienna . . . Saint Agnès . . . Where? It was quite impossible that he would happen on someone he knew at the top of a mountain on the other side of the world, so he thought no more about it as he pulled up a chair near the door.

They had been there only a few minutes when one of the three women came over to their table. She was young, plump and confident; she spoke in French.

"Please excuse me for interrupting, but I heard you mention your sanatorium in the Alps. I didn't mean to listen, but I couldn't help hearing. It sounded very like a place my father has been to visit. Are you by any chance Dr. Rebière?"

"Yes, I am."

The young woman let a cry of delight and called out to the two other women at her table. "Roya! Mama! I told you so! This is the most extraordinary coincidence, is it not? My father is Pierre Valade. Do you know him?"

"Yes, of course. He is a memorable gentleman." Jacques could not help smiling at this exuberant young woman.

"I was a patient of your colleague Dr. Midwinter some years ago," she said. "He traveled round Europe with us. That was before you had set up the sanatorium. Now my father says you are both famous."

"Hardly. I think—"

"Please come and meet my mother."

Jacques bowed his head as he was introduced to Madame Valade. "And this is Roya Mikhailova. She is my sister. No, no, not really! But she is like a sister to me."

There was a gloved hand offered to Jacques; as he took it, he looked up into violet eyes in a pale skin. It was hard to put an age to this second young woman—twenty or nineteen, perhaps—but there was something neither American nor French about her, Jacques thought, as the hand was rapidly withdrawn from his; the name Scheherazade came briefly to mind.

Nadine was explaining in English to Jacques and to Professor James, who had come across to join them. "Mama and I have rooms in Roya's father's house in St. Petersburg. He is a very wealthy man—stop it, please, Mama, I am allowed to say that. Roya has not been well, but now that she is better, her father thought it would be good for her to travel. California was where she had always dreamed of going. Then my father told me about this mountain railway. I think he had seen an article in a magazine."

"And does the mountain please you?" said Professor James.

"Very much," said Nadine, "though we have been in the Alpine Tavern for three days and we are starting to be bored. We have done all the walks and we want to go down now."

"Tomorrow, dear," said Madame Valade in French.

"So," said Nadine, "you gentlemen must stay and have dinner with us and then at last we can have a fourth at cards."

"Alas," said Jacques, "I must decline. We are returning to dine at Echo Mountain House."

"My visitor must sample the delights of the dining room at Echo Mountain," said the Professor. "The table here is a little more modest."

"If it is good enough for us, surely it is good enough for Dr. Rebière," said Nadine.

"As you know," said the Professor, "in the evening they cook only to order for those staying over, so I doubt whether they have food enough in any event."

"Oh, please, please stay."

"Really, Nadine," said her mother, "you should not press the gentleman in that way."

Professor James seemed to be weakening, as he considered how all his clients could best be pleased.

"If I can get a message down to Echo Mountain, I could ask them to send up some dinner on the next car," he said. "But we would not eat before seven. Would that be too late?"

"That would be fine," said Jacques. "We cannot in all conscience refuse the ladies' request." The higher up the mountain he ascended, the greater his euphoria became.

The Professor looked across at Jacques. "All right," he said. "Leave it to me."

An hour later they sat down at a long table to begin their dinner with a plate of oysters packed in ice. The staff of Ye Alpine Tavern, excited by the presence of the Professor and his guest, did their best to make an occasion of it, opening bottles of wine that had been ferried up from below to go with the beefsteaks that they grilled in one of the large open fireplaces that dominated the downstairs room.

Jacques found himself placed between Madame Valade on one side and Roya Mikhailova on the other. The ladies had been upstairs to change from their walking clothes and Roya now wore a dress of dark purple with a black shawl over the shoulders. The violet of her eyes was echoed in the color of the dress, but Jacques found it frustrating that so little of her skin was visible in the low light of the tavern.

He checked himself in the middle of his speculation and forced himself to listen instead to Madame Valade, who was talking about . . . What was she talking about? It began as one thing, then, just when he was about to grasp it, transformed itself into another. There were many names of people no one knew and what they had said and how others were right to be outraged, or disappointed, or indifferent because . . . But they never found out why, because Madame Valade was—not sidetracked exactly, because that implied that there was a path from which she had been diverted—"inspired" was perhaps the word, to continue with a new narrative that was contained within the first one, like a kangaroo in the pouch of its mother. Jacques presumed there was one main idea that she was trying to impart and he nodded in sympathy when he thought he saw it, but Madame Valade looked at him in surprise and waited for his brief interruption to finish before she resumed. It occurred to him that although she had been speaking for about fifteen minutes, he now knew less about what she meant than when she had begun.

He tried to catch the eye of Nadine, but she was telling Professor James about their time in the mountains; Roya Mikhailova was making contributions to this conversation also, and had turned half away from him, so Jacques was unable to engage her attention. Finally, in desperation, he stood up from the table and asked to be excused.

It had grown dark outside, though beneath him he could see white Echo Mountain House and the nearby chalet brightly illuminated by electric lamps. He breathed in the cold, thin air and sighed with the relief of silence. He would take home to the Alps, he thought, some of this exhilaration and, above all, some of the feeling he had here that all things were yet possible. At the schloss, he had undoubtedly become too absorbed by the scientific detail of his theory and by the excitement of the paradoxical connections he had made. He had lost sight of the grand design. He would have to make his peace with Thomas—not from a practical point of view, because they had retained their day-to-day civility, but at a deeper level, where they would need to redefine their aims and work more closely together. He had been too much alone, he now saw, while Thomas had been a source of knowledge and invention he had not used; and Thomas himself had not moved onward as he should have done.

He was aware of a footfall beside him, and a woman's voice said in French, "Are you all right?" It was Roya.

"Yes, thank you," he said. "It was a little hot in there. The fire in mid-summer, even at this altitude . . ."

"Were you admiring the view?"

"Very much so. One feels . . . enlivened. It is inspiring."

"It reminds me of the Elburz Mountains in Persia, above the Caspian Sea," said Roya. "I have been there only once." Her French was lightly accented, though fluent.

"But you live in St. Petersburg, I understand," said Jacques.

"That is correct, though my father wishes me to travel. He says the great days of Russia are over and I need to prepare for a new world. Europe is the place, he says."

"And Mademoiselle Valade said you had been unwell."

"It was nothing. There was a young man in St. Petersburg whom my parents wanted me to marry. I was in love with another. It was painful. I disobeyed them."

"And what happened?"

"I was diagnosed as suffering some mild exhaustion. It was nothing more than you would expect."

"I mean, what happened to the man you were in love with?"

"He was sent to a garrison in another town. He was a cavalry officer."

"You speak of him in the past tense."

"That is where he lives. In the past. And you, Doctor. What is the matter with you?"

"The matter?" He was surprised by the assured way this girl spoke.

"Yes. You have an attitude of great weariness and frustration. As though you are fighting some long battle."

Jacques looked down into the darkness below their feet. In the canyon above Rubio Hotel, hundreds of Japanese lanterns were sparkling, like fireflies.

"I am suffering from the limits of my mind," he said. "There is a simple enough problem that I have set out to solve. How our minds work. How sickness enters in. Why the limits of what we can under-stand seem so narrow. As humans, we have a gift of self-awareness, but it seems to lead us to no explanation. Of what use is consciousness if all that one is conscious of is ignorance?"

Roya laughed lightly. "Sometimes one does see through the veil of that unknowing, does one not? At moments of higher awareness?"

Jacques looked across at her, but could barely make out her features in the darkness.

"In a few days," he said, "I shall take the train back to San Francisco and investigate the purchase of some wire rope and a wheel. That is all I am good for. To be a workman with a pick and shovel on a railway line."

"It is a noble ambition, Doctor. At least you will be lifting your endeavors to a higher plane."

She laughed, and he felt her hand lightly touch his arm in consolation.

JACQUES'S LETTER did reach Sonia before he returned, on account of the two weeks he spent in California, a day of which he passed with Macpherson, the engineer, and two more at the California Wire Rope Works in San Francisco. Sonia read it with fascination but a faint unease at the tone of her husband's voice. He sounded overexcited, and although such passion was not uncharacteristic, there was something worrying about the agitation of his tone.

She was sitting in the office next to the two consulting rooms, deep in her thoughts about Jacques, when there was a knock at the door and Kitty asked if she could come in for a moment. This was unusual, as Kitty was particular about keeping out of Sonia's way and, under instruction from Thomas, made sure never to ask about the accounts or finances of the schloss.

"Come and sit down," said Sonia. "What is it, my dear? Are you all right? You look a little flushed." She had grown fond of Kitty, but— whatever the evidence to the contrary—could not stop thinking of her as an invalid.

"I have wonderful news," said Kitty, who, in her excitement, had forgotten to take off her reading glasses, "and I wanted you to be the first to know. You are going to be an aunt. Thomas is going to be a father."

"Oh, my dear girl." Sonia stood up and embraced her. She was winded by the suddenness of the announcement. Thomas a father . . . There was something comical about it—yet apt; she wished their own father had been alive. And how much it would connect Thomas to the world, she thought: it would be the making of him.

When they had finished tearfully exclaiming and embracing one another, Sonia said, "I am not sure I like the sound of 'Aunt Sonia.' She sounds rather strict, doesn't she?"

"Dear Sonia. I think you will be the best aunt a child could hope for. If my children grow up half as well as Daniel, I shall be happy."

"That is enough, Kitty. You will make me cry again. Am I allowed to tell Jacques?"

"Of course. It is due at the end of February. We had better ask Frau Holzer if she is free."

"I shall write to her at once."

THE END of Pier 14 was so crowded that Jacques had to fight his way through the press of people standing, gazing at the *City of New York*, which rode like a tethered Gulliver, straining at her moorings among the tugs, barges and tenders that huffed in her shadow. On the wharf were lines of passengers waiting to embark, anxiously trying to ensure their baggage was correctly loaded, impeded by the groups of sightseers—idling ladies in bonnets with parasols, small boys in flat caps who stared up in awe to the decks above them. Tiny men were in the rigging of the three inclined black funnels with their single white stripes; far below them on the deck were cranes which lowered roped parcels on creaking pallets into the hold, and animals, some butchered, some alive in cages, were winched aboard as though for a carnivorous ark. In all the tumult, Jacques was sure he glimpsed a familiar female face, but by the time he was on board, greeted by a smiling officer at the head of the gangway and reunited with his bags, it was too late for anything but to push his way once more through the crowd.

He found his own cabin, after asking directions from a steward. The stipulations of the line were strict: trunks not to exceed three feet six inches in length or fifteen inches in height, and it might further have laid down a limit on the size of passenger, he thought: a man any larger than he was would have found it hard to squeeze into the space between the

mattress and the bulkhead; even as it was, he had to post himself in, like
a packed envelope in a narrow letterbox.

These discomforts he remembered from the outward passage, so
spent most of the time in the sumptuous public rooms. On the first
night, as the *New York* pitched bow-first into the Atlantic swell, he forti-
fied himself with brandy before sitting down to dinner at a long table in
the saloon, in a chair that was screwed to the floor. The ceiling was a
glass dome, like the Crystal Palace in miniature, and somewhere hidden
up there an organist, invisible like a phantom of the opera in a short
story he had read, was playing melodies to soothe the travelers. The
lurching waiters splashed quantities of hot consommé over their wrists
as they swayed up and down between the fixed seats; when they brought
out the main course, Jacques noticed one of them holding the lamb cutlets in place with a determined thumb; as they set fire to the dessert he
had to look away for fear the whole ship would go up in flames. Afterward, he went to the smoking room, which was paneled in black walnut
and furnished with scarlet leather armchairs, but found that the atmosphere of cigar smoke was undoing all the good of the brandy, so took
one of the ascending "electric chambers" and went out on deck.

It was late July, still light, and he breathed deeply on the sea air as he
looked astern toward the receding coastline of America. He wished that
he had felt wise or wistful, able to summarize what he had learned from
traveling the width of the country; but he did not: he felt confused and
nervous, unenlightened; he felt disorientated and subtly changed. From
the short raised deck where he stood, he could see a broad surface on
each side of the deckhouse stretching back to the stern, a distance
roughly as far as the length of the main street at Saint Agnès; it was
crossed at intervals by passageways from port to starboard, down one of
which he saw the quick movement of that same familiar figure he had
glimpsed on the pier in New York. He followed quickly, and found her still
wrestling with the key to a first-class suite that opened from the gangway.

"Mademoiselle. Good evening. I thought I saw you at the pier. Are
you enjoying the voyage?"

"Yes, thank you, Monsieur. It is kind of you to ask. Nadine and
Madame Valade are both unwell, but I have barely noticed the movement."

"Perhaps you would care to walk about the deck a little."

"I cannot, alas," said Roya. "I must look after the invalids. Perhaps tomorrow, or when it is calmer."

"Of course. Good night, Mademoiselle."

"Good night." She lingered for a moment, he thought, as though on the point of changing her mind; then she was gone and the door to the suite had closed. He went down to the library, where the stained-glass windows, inscribed with quotations from poems about the sea, threw a strange purple light across the dozing readers. He pulled out a volume with its title embossed in gold lettering—*Quentin Durward* by Walter Scott—and sat down to tackle it.

For two more days the ocean heaved, and to find himself air, Jacques explored the ship. On the third evening, when the wind had dropped, there was a knock at his door and a steward held out a salver with a folded note on the ship's paper. "We should be delighted if you would take dinner in our apartments. S. Valade. 7 p.m. Do not dress."

Do not dress, he thought, as he took out a clean shirt from his bag and struggled with the collar; although the wind had dropped, the occasional swell lifted the ship at the moment he was about to secure the stud. Do not dress. . . . As though he had worn a white tie every night on the train in the backwoods of Wyoming. He brushed his hair carefully in the mirror, deciding it would be dishonest to try to conceal where it had receded from the temples: as well cover the gray above the ears with boot polish. . . . His skin was clean and smooth from the razor, and, except for the odd white hair that Sonia assured him added dignity, the mustache at least had remained for the most part bravely black.

The steward knocked at the door with brandy and water at six thirty, and soon afterward he took the electric chamber up to the main deck. Madame Valade's suite of rooms was like the apartment of a wealthy widow in one of the stuffier blocks near the Place des Vosges. From its cluttered sitting room, full of velvet cushions and fixed occasional tables, a door opened into a separate bedroom where Jacques could see the outline of a large brass bed anchored to the floor.

"Awful people in the saloon for dinner," said Madame Valade. "Groups of shrieking young women calling themselves 'Kansas Belles' or some such thing. I have seldom seen anything less 'belle' in my life. They are serving our dinner up here."

"You are absurd, Mama," said Nadine. "It is very lively in there, is it not, Roya?"

Roya smiled. "Very lively."

"All those handsome young men from Yale going over to some rowing match. What was it called?"

"The name was not familiar to me," said Roya.

"Henley, I think," said Nadine. "Does that mean anything to you, Doctor?"

Jacques shook his head. "The English and their games. It is a mystery to the rest of us. Though I did enjoy playing lawn-tennis once."

"What is that?" said Roya.

"Not something you will play in the Elburz Mountains, I think."

"You do not know what happens in the Elburz Mountains, Doctor."

Dinner was brought by a perspiring steward and accompanied, to Jacques's delight, by French wines, which Madame Valade invited him to pour. As her guest, he felt obliged to absorb the greater part of her talk with an appearance of understanding or of interest, but she was low-spirited by comparison with the night in the Alpine Tavern and he was able to talk also to Roya and Nadine. The wine made them all nostalgic for France; they talked of Paris, Burgundy, the Auvergne; Nadine insisted that Jacques ring the bell to order more.

Afterward, they played whist, while Nadine poured brandy and water until her mother told her to stop. Nadine seemed incapable of following suit even at the beginning of a hand and talked loudly throughout the game. Roya looked distracted, Jacques thought, as though her mind was on St. Petersburg or Persia; her movements, normally so swift and contained, had become slow. Her fingertips brushed his hand when she picked up her cards, and beneath the table he could feel the light pressure of her relaxed leg against his own. He presumed that both girls had drunk more wine than they were used to.

When Madame Valade began to yawn, he stood up, rocked for a moment in what he took to be the swell of the Atlantic and thanked his hostess for a delightful evening.

"I shall come as well," said Roya.

"I thought you . . ." Jacques could not conceal his surprise.

"No, it is just Mama and I who share this little apartment," said Nadine. "Good night, Doctor. Thank you for letting me win at cards."

"Good night, Mademoiselle. Madame."

He held the door open for Roya and bowed, partly to avoid hitting his head on the door frame, and stepped out into the gangway.

"I am going to walk round the deck once," she said. "It is such a beautiful night."

"May I?"

"Of course."

It was late, and there was no one else on the first-class deck. They leaned over the rail and watched the black sea far below them.

It was very strange, thought Jacques. He felt like a child, as though nothing had ever really happened to him before in his life. This, he thought, must mean he was happy.

Roya turned round, so that her back was against the rail. Her eyes had narrowed and her lips had taken on a sharper outline, as if slightly stiffened or swollen. Without speaking, she placed her hands on Jacques's shoulders and kissed him on the mouth.

He put his hands on her waist and held her, but was too surprised to do more.

"That is what you wanted, isn't it?" said Roya.

Jacques said nothing for a long time. "I suppose it must have been," he said at last.

She smiled. "Good. I am tired. I am going to bed."

"I thought you were with . . . Where are your quarters?"

By the time he had framed the question, she had already slipped from view.

XVI

IN OCTOBER, DANIEL HAD HIS FIRST BIRTHDAY. WHEN THE DAY'S work was over, a dozen adults gathered in the waiting room, where the circular table held a cake that Sonia had made for the occasion. She carried Daniel from the nursery in his best short trousers and woolen jacket; he was a compact armful, solid but not heavy, resting comfortably on her braced forearm, while her other hand gripped beneath his armpit to secure him to the front of her dress. When he was being carried by either parent, he had a habit of patting them lightly on the shoulder, as though in consolation. Sonia leaned down and inhaled the smell of his washed hair and the aroma of his skin beneath: it was like warm biscuits and honey, and the loose curls brushed her cheek, fleeting, like his life's breath.

She set him down on the floor at the entrance to the waiting room, squeezing his rib cage one last time, reluctant to let him go.

"Cake," he said, and set off across the room, shuttling from side to side in sudden spurts, then stopping, swaying like a sailor as he searched for balance, then plunging off again diagonally. Eventually, he made it to the table, where Jacques lifted him into his high chair and pushed it up close so that he could admire the cake as they sang to him. He held both small arms straight up above his head in amazement as his father cut the first deep slice, then settled down to eat, with his ankles crossed, as was his habit, on the footrest of the high chair.

Sonia looked on from the doorway, happy to be apart and to observe the way in which her child was starting to acquire characteristics of his own: the crossed ankles, the precocious drunken walk, the head held to one side, the eyes wide in wonder as some everyday object was pointed out to him; the voice like a treble bell that sounded out each new word with tentative clarity as though his was the first human mouth in which it had found utterance.

Children from the village came to the schloss to play with Daniel, and sometimes Sonia would take him back to their houses. She talked for hours with these young mothers about their children and their husbands and their lives; they were not conversations she felt she could relay to Jacques and they were not women she thought might otherwise have been her friends, but the intensity of what they shared was such that it dwarfed all differences. It was such a common human experience, thought Sonia—by definition, perhaps, the commonest of all; yet to each of them, she could see, it was a private rapture so intoxicating that they were forced sometimes to play at being blasé, to complain about the work, the sleepless nights, the loss of time alone, when she could see that all they really felt was incredulity that something so mechanically natural was in truth so sublime.

They were changed forever, these women—changed by the everyday transcendence they had lived through. She saw them stealing glances at their children on the grass or in the hall, rationing their gaze, hoping not to wear away the miracle by too much looking; but she did not mind that her own exultation was not unique; it reassured her to think that anyone might feel as she did—because if the commonplace was miraculous, then it was possible, after all, to take an optimistic view of human life.

In return for Jacques's sabbatical leave in California, it had meanwhile been agreed that Thomas should also be permitted to travel or explore outside the schloss. Much though he loved it there—the geraniums in the window boxes, the playful water in the fountain, the secret passage that took him back to Kitty—he accepted the point that Jacques made on his return, that he needed to develop his own theoretical interests. While Jacques himself was in a position of retrenchment from which to leap forward better, at least he had leapt.

Thomas was pushing forward slowly on two fronts, but there was no breakthrough. With Franz Bernthaler's help, he had become a keen-eyed pathologist; he was adept at the postmortem table and had, with Franz, noted abnormalities in the brains of those who had suffered from general paralysis of the insane and, less marked but still significant, in those who had had dementia praecox, or what they had formerly called Olivier's disease. Even in their most optimistic moments, however, they could not present their findings as anything more than work in progress—a promising start on a road that would take many years to travel and one which really needed better instruments.

The second advance was on what he called to himself the Rothenburg Front, after the town in whose church he had first been struck by the idea that hearing voices must once have been a common experience. If his work with Franz was stains and slides, biochemistry, notes and observation, the Rothenburg Front was ostensibly the opposite: speculation verging on the metaphysical.

He was not alone in sensing that he had come to a temporary halt. Much of what he felt by intuition—and he had to confess that it was little more than that—depended on the theories of what Mr. Darwin called "descent with modification" (he did not seem to use the word "evolution" until *The Descent of Man*) being more fully explained. Until someone could fill in the details of how heredity worked, then it seemed to him that there was little chance that they could understand, let alone cure, the forms of madness that had an hereditary taint. His own thinking had been influenced by what Faverill called his "mad-doctor's hunch," something he had mentioned to Sonia: the idea that if humans were the only creatures to be mad, then perhaps it was the very thing that differentiated them from the apes that predisposed them to mental illness. Thomas believed it was possible that the illness had indeed entered into mankind at the moment he evolved into *Homo sapiens;* it might have been the very price he paid for the acquisition of higher consciousness. But Faverill had never dreamed of trying to prove his theory; it remained for both of them a "hunch"; and what good were hunches in the world of factual science?

He took the train to Vienna one freezing Thursday in December to attend the meeting of a learned society. The gathering was in a lecture hall attached to the university medical school, and because it was open only to members of the society and their guests it was not fully attended.

There were few women and no students; it was quite unlike the circus atmosphere of Charcot's lectures at the Salpêtrière, Thomas thought, but presumably that was the idea. These distinguished medical men did not want members of the public or students reeking of last night's debauch; they wanted like-minded colleagues who would listen in respectful silence.

An air of self-congratulation hung over the audience as the speaker, a man of about Thomas's age, with a black curly beard that reached up almost to his eyes, climbed onto the stage. Dr. Wilhelm Fliess, an ear, nose and throat specialist with psychological ambitions, outlined some theories concerning the relations between the nose and the female sexual organs. He had published a monograph three years earlier on the "nasal reflex neurosis," in which he cited the case of 130 patients whose various physical pains had been cured by application of cocaine to the inside of the nose. Since the treatment had been especially effective in the treatment of menstrual pains, Fliess maintained that there were "genital spots" inside the nose that were associated with some neuroses and which influenced the menstrual cycle. He was almost ready, he said, to publish a new book: *The Relations Between the Nose and the Female Sexual Organs from the Biological Aspect.* The periodicity of the menstrual cycle suggested that two numbers, 23 and 28, might unlock all mysteries of human biology, including unknown dates of birth, onset of illness and death. Furthermore, Fliess maintained, his numerical pattern underlay the workings of the entire cosmos: all natural laws were obedient to these two numbers, their sum, their difference and, probably, their square and their cube.

Thomas listened in some disbelief, and was surprised that the audience was not hostile. The Viennese world clearly believed itself to be so close to discovering a universal key that it must listen carefully to every offering: no one wished to risk having laughed at the new Galileo.

Afterward, the audience repaired to a sitting room where coffee and wine were served in a dense atmosphere of cigar and pipe smoke. Thomas, who knew none of the others, introduced himself to a friendly seeming man who stood nearby.

"Did you enjoy the talk?"

"Not at all. I know nothing of medicine."

"Why are you here?"

"I am the guest of one of the committee."

"And what is your area of interest?"

"I am a cartographer. My name is Hannes Regensburger." He held out his hand and Thomas introduced himself.

"Where do you make your maps?"

"My next venture is to Africa. Although maps are my profession, I am an amateur of paleontology and in Africa I hope to be able to combine the two interests."

They talked for half an hour about the descent of man and the few fossil clues he had left behind; it was a relief to Thomas to speak of things other than the sufferings of contemporary lunatics, and he warmed to Regensburger's dry style of conversation, which did little to conceal his enthusiasm for the subject. He asked if, since it was still early, he would care to join him for dinner afterward, and Regensburger agreed; they fetched their coats and thanked the secretary of the society.

"Did you enjoy the paper?" said the secretary.

"Yes," said Thomas. "Though Dr. Fliess might benefit from knowing something of the nervous system. The cocaine clearly enters the patients' bloodstream, thence the brain, where it has an anesthetic effect. It makes no difference where it gets in. If I make a patient calm by giving him morphia by mouth, I do not look for areas of neurosis on his gums."

But the secretary had turned to speak to another member, and Thomas was obliged to finish the explanation to Regensburger, who said, "I have no idea about such things, but I do remember elementary mathematics from the gymnasium. If you take two positive integers with no common factors you can combine them to make any other number that you wish. Particularly if you also throw in the difference, the sum and the square!"

He laughed as they walked down the frosty street together. In the distance, Thomas could see the two braziers burning outside the front door of the hotel where he had spent his honeymoon night. He shivered—in recollection, in cold, in anticipation of fatherhood: he felt irrationally happy as Regensburger pushed open the door of a restaurant and stood aside for him to go in.

Regensburger told Thomas of his planned visit to German East

Africa. "I expect you have heard of Oscar Baumann," he said. "He has made two expeditions to the area for the German Anti-Slavery Committee, and a map of his journey was published in Berlin three years ago. It is a beautiful piece of work in its way, but it lacks detail. He was unable to survey the land that was not on his route, and in any event cartography was not his principal purpose."

The waiter brought their food and drew the cork on a bottle of red wine. "Do you have a particular interest in the area?" said Thomas.

"There is commercial interest from numerous European concerns who hope to exploit the natural resources, to build further railways and so on. We shall solicit contributions to the expense of the expedition from such people. For myself, it is a journey I very much hope to make on account of something Baumann himself told me."

Regensburger helped himself from the dishes on the table with the heedless appetite of the thin man. He had glasses rimmed in gold and hollow cheeks; the skin was tight over his forehead and scalp, where the hair was sparse. There was a slight swelling in the finger joints that made Thomas suspect arthritis; he wondered whether Regensburger's dry manner had developed partly as a result of dealing with pain.

"The area close to the great Ngorongoro Crater," he said, "is rich in fossil remains—animals, plants, all sorts of things. Baumann told me of a particular place known to the Masai, though I believe they have little interest in it themselves. They do not understand the significance of such things."

"What is particular about this place?"

Regensburger carved himself a slice of calf's brain roulade, a speciality of the restaurant, in which the offal was baked in a Swiss roll of sieved potato and flour. "There are footprints preserved in ash," said Regensburger. "They appear to be human, I am told by Baumann, yet the layer in which they are fossilized seems to belong to a period before any human record we have."

Thomas found his interest quickening. "Did he take photographs?"

"No," said Regensburger. "Sumptuous roulade, is it not? Such a mild taste, and the parsley adds just a little freshness. Baumann has Christian beliefs of an old-fashioned variety. He is a very good man, but he is not happy with new theories about the descent of mankind."

"Why might these prints alarm him?" said Thomas. "Unless some-one was proposing that they belonged to Adam and Eve themselves and that the Garden of Eden was in German East Africa."

"I am not sure," said Regensburger. "To a believer in the literal truth of the Bible, many natural phenomena pose awkward questions. To live in an age of such scientific progress makes them unhappy. It is not every generation which is alive at a time when we are on the brink of explain-ing creation. Do you have difficulties, Doctor? Or are you one of us?"

Thomas felt as though he was being tested for entrance to a Masonic lodge. "I believe that all species originated in a process of descent with modification, as Mr. Darwin calls it, and that natural selection was the agency of change. I believe that man is no exception." It sounded as though he was reciting a creed. He coughed. "But there is still mystery, of course. Maybe Alfred Russel Wallace is right and human evolution needed the presence of God at certain moments. It would be vain, in all senses, to suppose that I know the exact truth of our history."

"I see," said Regensburger. "But to suppose that we shared a com-mon ancestor with the apes—that does not disturb you."

"I accept that it has been scientifically established."

"Good." Regensburger seemed satisfied, though Thomas was not sure whether it was the roulade or his own answers that had so pleased him. "We hope to leave in the spring of '99. I shall be gone for two years. I shall see the new century dawn somewhere to the west of Mount Kilimanjaro." He wiped his mouth with his napkin and pushed away his plate. "Perhaps you would care to join me. We shall need a medical officer."

Thomas laughed. "It is an intriguing idea, but I could not possibly be away for that length of time. We have discovered that my wife is expect-ing twins next year and I have a very busy sanatorium to run in Carinthia."

"As you wish," said Regensburger. "When we part company, I shall leave you my card. Then you may write to me if you change your mind. I suppose it would be possible for you to come only for a part of the expedi-tion. There is a railway proposed from the interior which could take you back to the coast. Otherwise, with sufficient guides, you could retrace your steps on horseback, the way we came. In a man's life, such oppor-tunities are few."

JACQUES COULD not settle to his work when he returned to Carinthia. He felt as though he had joined the roll of ordinary doctors, the pessimists content to manage rather than cure—the carpenters and plumbers of the human who did repairs only; he felt he had been forced to sign his name to the doctors' universal declaration of impotence, which said: We Do Not Know. We can cure neither your cancer nor your cold. We do not know what causes dementia praecox or how to alleviate its horror. We wait for better instruments. We hope for a change in the weather. Meanwhile, here is a box of small red pills.

He developed a kind of therapy by which he listened intently to the stories of unhappy people and made modest suggestions about how they might improve their outlook. He continued to examine how trauma and high emotion, when denied expression, might subsequently affect the well-being of the person, but gave up seeking to apply a universal formula, or trying to derive from it a psychology that might apply to all.

In Vienna, a form of therapy that bore a close kinship to his own theory of psychophysical resolution had made an impact in scientific circles. Although many people scoffed at psychoanalysis and called it an expensively protracted cure for Jewish girls nervous about sex, Jacques had no doubt that therapies based on the interpretation of dreams and the function of the unconscious were more than the fashion of the day; they seemed to offer the best hope of therapeutic advance in all manner of conditions, ranging from psychosis to everyday symptoms of a mildly psychosomatic nature. Such treatments, in addition, represented the first real advance in the treatment of the mentally afflicted in his lifetime.

Yet Jacques felt what the lawyers would have called "estopped"; because of a clinical error that in the end had turned out to have no serious ill effects, he was barred from publicly pursuing the line of inquiry that he felt was most congenial to him and most likely to be medically fruitful. He was limited to reading about psychoanalytic activity at a distance, the country cousin in Carinthia to the metropolis of Viennese discovery.

The irony of the case of Katharina von A was acute for him. While his own hope of glory had been dashed, the fame of the Schloss Seeblick began to spread, and Katharina was herself a dynamic proselytizer, spreading word of the sanatorium among her old friends in Vienna. To deal with the increase in outpatients and short-term residents they were forced to open rooms in the small Lamp Court and, in the new year, to find a permanent place on the staff for Peter Andritsch, the doctor who had covered Jacques's absence. There was hardly ever a spare room, and in January Sonia was able to present accounts to Herr Leopold at the bank that showed a steady profit.

What worried Jacques was that it was earned by conventional means; they were becoming like numerous other well-run hydros and sanatoriums in the Alps. It was true that they still took and cared for public cases from the asylums, but few of these improved or were willing to leave, so the number of new patients from such places was small. The arrival of Peter Andritsch did allow him some freedom, however. Together with Franz Bernthaler, Andritsch could take the majority of the nervous cases, and Jacques was able to spend more time with the psychotics. Here, like Thomas, he found that his work was largely one of observation and note-taking—of scrutiny over a long period. There remained the hope, a little forlorn at times, that some insight might be gained by merely looking.

To prevent himself from becoming downcast, Jacques also took charge of the question of where the sanatorium should be rehoused when its lease on the schloss expired on the first day of the twentieth century. He had convinced Thomas by his enthusiasm for the Mount Lowe solution and together they set off once more to see Herr Leopold at the bank.

"Gentlemen," said Leopold, "you have reserves and a facility to borrow. You do not need my permission to spend your own money. Clearly the first thing that you need to know is whether the land on top of Wilhelmskogel is for sale and how much rebuilding you would need to do."

"We have already established that," said Jacques. "It belongs to a widow in Salzburg. She has no interest in the land, but she is short of funds and is ready to accept a reasonable offer. I have obtained an estimate from a builder in town for the cost of repairing the main house and for building further accommodation for the patients. Although it is considerable, you can see that it is still cheaper than buying an existing sanatorium or hotel of that size."

Herr Leopold agreed to look at Jacques's preliminary figures, while Jacques and Thomas examined the possibility of taking a spur from the existing valley branch line into the foothills of the mountains—a ride of a few minutes only—before a cable car would take traffic to the summit. After some inquiries, they were recommended an engineer in Salzburg called Tobias Geissler, who had wide experience of Austrian railways, both passenger lines and narrow gauge in mining, but had long wanted a project of his own. He was currently engaged in advising on the works at the lead mines near Villach, but it was said that his heart was not in it, and the alacrity with which he agreed to meet them was encouraging.

Thomas and Jacques went to Villach on the last Sunday in January, with Sonia and Daniel, leaving Franz Bernthaler in charge of the sanatorium for the first time. Kitty had been advised by the obstetrician at the hospital to spend the last month of her pregnancy resting in bed. Twins, he told her, should not be taken lightly, particularly when the mother had not always enjoyed good health.

Herr Geissler was waiting for them at the hotel, a newspaper spread across his knees and a clay pipe in his mouth.

He sprang up when he saw them. "I am delighted to make your acquaintance."

The skin on his bald head was tanned a smooth, woody brown; he reminded Thomas a little of McLeish, though his attitude could hardly have been more different: for every problem they raised, he had a number of urgent solutions.

"First of all, we will need an excellent surveyor. I have just the man. We worked together on several projects and he owes me a favor. A completed survey will give us an idea of cost. But I am more or less certain that—unless there is much more money in mad-doctoring than I have been led to believe—you will need to form a company in which you sell stocks. That is how these projects are normally financed. It is quite straightforward."

Jacques told him about the design of the Echo Mountain cable car.

"Excellent," said Geissler. He had a ringing bass voice and thick, powerful hands that continually opened and closed, as though itching for a jack or spanner to hold. "But do not contemplate, even for a moment, importing the wheel or the wire from San Francisco. I know of several railway engineering works where such things can be made to my design for a fraction of the cost. We also need to see how the descent of one car might power the ascent of the other. We could make it almost self-sufficient. On second thoughts, why do we need two cars? The traffic will be much lighter than on your Mount Lowe. We can have one line with just two rails—no double track, no run-out. And we can store the energy of the descent in a battery to power the next lift!"

As the waiter brought the food, Sonia said, "But will it not all be terribly expensive?"

"It should not be beyond the reach of a modestly sized company. The rail itself is not expensive, nor is the timber. As for the labor, I have found the best men are Slovenes, and they, poor fellows, will work all day for a bed and a hot meal at night. Which of you is to be my point of reference?"

There was a brief consultation between the three of them. They had not expected Geissler to move so quickly.

"We can discuss my fee later," he said, laughing deeply. "In case that is why you are hesitating."

It was finally agreed that Jacques would be in charge. Sonia would have control over the finances while Thomas for the time being would continue to devote his energies only to medicine. Kitty might help Jacques with the paperwork at a later stage, if she had time to spare after the birth of the twins, though there would be nothing for anyone to do until a thorough survey was completed, which could take until April.

Thomas could see the light coming back into Jacques's eyes as they discussed the schedule; he thought it was a good way for his partner to rekindle his passion. It amused him to think that Jacques might eventually spend time with Kitty once again, and wondered how he would square the real woman he came to know with the Katharina von A of his imagination. He hoped, or so he muttered disloyally to himself, that the clerical work would not make her arms hurt.

KITTY WAS restless, stuck in her bedroom, feeling once more like a neurasthenic patient. Mary came to talk to her and massage her back and legs in the morning, not because Kitty really needed it, but because she enjoyed the company.

"Tell me the news from the other girls," said Kitty.

"Well," said Mary. "I shouldn't tell you, Miss, but I know as you are very dependable."

"You can count on me, Mary," said Kitty, who was leaning over the bed while Mary worked the lower spine with her strong thumbs. "That's lovely."

"I think that Hans is a little sweet on Daisy," said Mary.

"Hans? Josef's little helper? But isn't he too young?"

"A little bit, Miss. But Daisy, she's coming on thirty-seven—though she doesn't know exactly, and . . . you know. If she wants to have children and that."

"My goodness. I do see, Mary. And how old are you?"

"I'm a year younger than Daisy, Miss. But no one's going to marry me."

"But you're a lovely—"

"No, Miss. I don't want to get married. Honest. I'm very happy as I am. Just so long as you and Dr. Thomas is happy with me. I'm already happier than I ever thought I might be."

"Of course we are happy. You are an important part of the schloss. We need you. I am going to lie on my back so you can do my legs. But tell me, is Hans a good prospect for Daisy?"

"I know she's thinking about it. Josef will retire one day, then Hans can be in charge of all the buildings. And he already does a lot of work in the labs, looking after things for Dr. Bernthaler."

"He looks like a naughty boy, Mary, that's the thing. He has a face like a little monkey."

"Daisy says he's clever, Miss. Maybe he doesn't look it. But he can write and read and he's good with figures."

"Perhaps we should give him something to do with the new buildings on the Wilhelmskogel, see what he can manage. I shall speak to my sister-in-law about it."

"Thank you, Miss. Shall I stop now?"

"Yes, Mary. Thank you. But will you come tomorrow?"

Kitty's bedroom looked onto the lawn of the South Court, beneath whose chestnut tree she had often sat to read her book when she was a patient. Her old seat was these days frequently occupied by one of those referred from the asylum, a powerful-looking red-haired man who talked earnestly to himself, or to someone unseen.

"'Under the spreading chestnut tree,'" remarked Thomas one afternoon, standing at the window and looking down, "'The village madman stands./The voices in his fevered head/Are loud as marching bands./We don't know if he's made that way/Or has infected glands.' Longfellow."

"Thank you, my darling. That was enlightening."

"I have been working on it. Now listen, Kitty. I have a little thought that you might want to turn around in your head as you have your rest this afternoon."

"Very well, Thomas."

"You have read Mr. Darwin's book, have you not?"

"Which one?"

"The Origin of Species."

"Yes. I hurried through some of it, but I did finish it."

"Good. Well, let us suppose that humans have developed with modification in the same way as other species."

"Very well. This is what Mr. Darwin calls 'transmutation.'"

"It is indeed. It was another English writer, called Herbert Spencer, who was I think the first to use the word 'evolution' in this context. He also gave us the phrase 'survival of the fittest.'"

"It sounds unpleasant. Do I need to read Mr. Spencer too?"

"He is influential, but for the moment you merely need to understand those words."

"Not very difficult."

"Not at all. But suppose that the gentleman beneath the chestnut tree, who has Olivier's disease, or what we are now obliged to call 'dementia praecox'—suppose that people like him have been around for millions of years. And suppose that the incidence of this illness was roughly the same in all populations, despite differences in climate, conditions of life, diet and so on."

"The very things that influence the outcome of Mr. Darwin's 'natural selection.'"

"Precisely. Suppose this illness had remained at a stable level in all populations, even though it appears to have no natural advantages. Quite the opposite, in fact. What does that suggest to you, Kitty?"

"How do you know that it has stayed stable?"

"We can come back to that. But just suppose we could demonstrate it. What would that suggest to you?"

"Well," said Kitty slowly. "It suggests that this characteristic has not been lost, but has somehow been passed on . . . despite its disadvantages."

"Indeed. Now consider the extent of those disadvantages. People with dementia praecox are irrational. They die young. They frequently kill themselves. Sexual selection works against them because they are an unattractive mating proposition. They have fewer children than ordinary people. Yet, relatively speaking, they have flourished."

"But that seems to contradict the theory. I thought only characteristics useful in the battle for life are naturally 'selected.'"

Thomas smiled. "Exactly. So just take the reasoning one step further."

"I suppose that, if Mr. Darwin is right, then there must be advantages in this condition. But we cannot see them."

"You are a remarkable woman, Katharina. That is exactly what it tells us. But we can go further. We can refine the basic logic a little and still be strictly and simply Darwinian."

"Which we want to be?"

"I think we do. He may be out of fashion, but I feel sure the theory of natural selection is correct in its fundamentals."

"So?"

"Well, I think we must say that dementia praecox itself confers no advantage, but its survival against all its apparent disadvantages suggests to me that a hereditary predisposition to the disease must be closely allied—in whatever microscopic way these things are transmitted from one generation to the next—to something that is advantageous, connected in fact to something which by definition must be overwhelmingly advantageous to the development of the human. The more terrible the drawback, the more important must be the related advantage for the disease to have survived at that consistent level."

"That is certainly logical."

"What I am saying is that it is like a misprint. It is a mistake which serves no purpose. But the capacity to misprint is the minor price you pay for literature."

"I don't quite follow."

"It doesn't mean that there is something fundamentally wrong with the process of thinking, writing, printing or reading—the sequence that com-prises literature. It is a sequence so magnificent that misprints have been perpetuated—tolerated. Because they are an organic and insepara-ble part of the greater good. Because you simply cannot have literature without misprints. And it is still a price worth paying. If misprints were somehow taken out of the mixture, you would risk losing literature too. You might throw out the baby, humanity, with the bathwater, dementia."

"A very unfortunate choice of words in the circumstances," said Kitty with her hand on her belly.

"I am sorry."

"So what you are saying is that the capacity to be mad in this way is somehow close to the very thing that made us human in the first place."

"Exactly. It is something my old employer Dr. Faverill first mentioned to me. But of course I should have to be able to prove that the incidence of the illness really is stable throughout the world and has survived the selective pressure of all different environments. And that I cannot do—though oddly enough it would not present any great scientific difficulty. It is just that the task of organizing and collecting the data would take so long. And people would have to agree a precise diagnosis of the illness—which, knowing doctors, would be difficult."

"But how would that prove that it is as fundamental as you say? If there are as many people with it in Japan as in Brazil?"

"Because if it was both universally spread and indifferent to the pres-sures of natural selection then it must have been endemic in the first humans who came out of Africa. It would suggest that it was related to whatever transmutation took place in Africa that first turned pre-humans into *Homo sapiens.*"

"But you cannot prove it, Thomas."

Thomas laughed. "No. I cannot. At heart, I am only a scholar of

Shakespeare, though I am perfectly sure, as a matter of fact, that Shake-speare recognized and described this illness in several characters. You see it also in the Bible. Think of John the Baptist—naked, raving, hear-ing voices, eating insects. I have treated a hundred such men. You could argue that in the times referred to by Homer it was in fact more wide-spread, because almost everyone seemed to hear voices. But we don't know when that time was, and the voice-hearing could be a literary invention rather than a literal fact."

"But what does this mean for your work now?"

Thomas sighed. "You are very practical, Kitty. It means that Franz and I will go on looking at pieces of brain tissue beneath our microscope in the hope of finding something. We shall try to find out more about the mechanics of heredity, the nature of which eluded even Mr. Darwin."

"I thought we believed in him," said Kitty.

"We think he was right about natural selection as the engine of evo-lution. But he thought that the characteristics of the offspring were transmitted by a 'blending' of the characteristics of the parents, and he was wrong about that."

"How do we know?"

"Because if you fully transfuse the blood of a white rabbit into that of a brown rabbit, it still has brown offspring. A man called Galton did it. So the nature of the brown rabbit's offspring is not altered by anything that happens to it. If you cut off its tail, its offspring will still be born with tails—unless it mated with a naturally tailless species, of course. And then you would not get half-tails. You would get either one or the other."

"And what then does determine exactly what the offspring inherits?"

"Nobody knows. Though gardeners and livestock breeders have always had their theories."

"So Mr. Darwin was right about one thing and wrong about another."

"Yes. That is the nature of science. Mr. Galton is right about this, but he was wrong in thinking that all murderers have square jaws or that adulterers have high foreheads. Though that theory was quite popular when I worked in the asylum."

"And does that apply to you as well, my love? That you will not get everything right?"

"Yes. The two-steps-forward-one-step-back law of scientific discovery will take care of that. And the limits of the human mind."

"And are you right about your theory of the man beneath the chestnut tree?"

"I am probably right about some parts and wrong about others. But I will persist in thinking in this way, because even if Franz and I don't find the lesion or the particle beneath the stain, even if we don't find a medicine that soothes these patients, it may be helpful to think about them in this way, to see their illness in the longest human perspective. It might help us, at the very least, in our efforts to be kind to them."

KITTY'S TWINS were born on February 24. A girl arrived at nine in the morning—purple, slight, with dark hair and swollen genitals; then half an hour later, distressed by the umbilicus tight round the neck, quickly freed by Frau Holzer, a second girl. Thomas had given Kitty a powder to dull the pain at the onset, but she waved him away as the labor progressed and he left her with the midwife while he went for a walk by the lake. He knelt down by the small landing stage, concealing himself from any inquisitive eyes that might be turned on him from the schloss, and offered an awkward prayer to whatever deity might be allowed to exist in the interstices of Mr. Darwin's theory, Mr. Wallace's more theistical variations and in his own child-memory of the Bible and its literary grandeur. He began with many scientific qualifications and apologies to the divinity whose existence he could not logically concede, but ended with a tearful plea to the God of his fathers: please spare my wife and our children and I will always believe in You.

He was anxious that, if Kitty's heart had been weakened by rheumatic fever, the birth of twins might strain it, but when he returned in mid-morning, he found her sitting up in bed, washed, tidy and smiling, with a twin at each breast. He sat with her until noon, when Sonia and Daniel came to visit. Thomas felt as though he had been singled out among all men for some enormous, inexplicable and undeserved good fortune; as though after almost forty years of unrequited prayers, each of his desires, including many of which he was unaware, had been granted all at once. Why me? he thought as wandered in a daze through the main hall of the schloss. The fountain sang to him in the courtyard. The snow on the distant peaks flashed messages in the winter sun. The madmen in the gardens muttered and gamboled to a tune whose unheard melody was surely part of a benign universal harmony. Daisy came running up from the North Hall, her wooden shoes sounding on the cobbles, and threw herself onto him. The wind whipped the snow-drops on the bank into a flurry of white felicitation. He heard Mary's stick tap-tapping at an urgent pace over the terra-cotta floors of the open section of the first-floor gallery; and in a minute she too was hugging him. He walked on toward the stables, Daisy on one arm and Mary on the other, to tell Josef and Hans of his astonishing fortune, readying his modesty for the onslaught of their congratulations.

In the afternoon, Pierre Valade arrived for one of his twice-yearly but still unannounced visits.

"It could not be better timing," said Thomas. "I shall put you in the green room."

"Tonight," said Valade, "we shall celebrate. I suppose you would have preferred boys, but never mind. Nature cannot be helped. We can still have champagne."

"I can," said Thomas. "But you can only have some if you concede that my daughters are not only far better than any boys but also the most beautiful children ever born."

"I shall go at once to your wife's room to see for myself."

Thomas spent the afternoon with Kitty, in the course of which they discussed names. They began with the idea of something Carinthian, and tried out Andrea, Ilse, Fanny, Ulrike and Claudia, but could not agree on any of them; in the end they settled on Martha, which was almost the local Marta, and—since the girls were in any case three-quarters English—Charlotte. Martha was the firstborn and Charlotte the younger; they appeared to be identical, but Thomas pointed out that all babies look much the same. Kitty, though tired and with a spot of fever in her cheeks, had suffered no ill effects.

That evening, Thomas ate in the main dining room with Sonia, Jacques and Pierre Valade. He distributed champagne to all the patients so they could drink to the health of his daughters, and after dinner Valade insisted on bringing brandy and more champagne to his rooms in the South Court, where they closed all the intervening doors for fear of waking the girls.

Thomas went to bed at last in a spare room not far from where Kitty was sleeping with the twins.

In the middle of the night he was awoken by a terrible screaming. "Thomas!" It was Kitty's voice. "Thomas! *Thomas!*"

He threw himself out of bed and ran down the corridor. She had rolled over and suffocated one of the twins. . . . He had never heard panic like this before. They had been savaged by a wolf. . . . Both were dead. . . .

The bedroom door rebounded against the wall as he burst into her room.

"What is it? What is it?"

Kitty stirred sleepily in the depths of their large bed. "What?"

"What is it? Why were you screaming?"

"I didn't scream, I was asleep."

"What?"

"I was asleep until you came in."

"And the girls? Are they all right?"

"Look."

They were both asleep, wrapped tight and peaceful, lying in wicker baskets by the side of the bed.

"But . . . but you called."

"No, I didn't. Everything is fine, my love. Now go back to bed."

"All right." He leaned over the bed to kiss her. "But I did hear you."

VALADE WAS thrilled by the proposed railway, for which he took the credit, since it was he who had first seen the magazine article about Mount Lowe, and he appointed himself draftsman to the project. He and Thomas went by mule to the summit of the Wilhelmskogel and inspected the widow's buildings. They had clearly once comprised a tiny village, from which a church with double bell tower and onion-dome spire survived. On its west wall were faded outdoor frescoes, punished by the wind and altitude, but still with recognizable biblical figures in sandy orange and blue.

The main house was in the local style, dilapidated despite its extra wooden weatherboarding; there were two farms and a dozen smaller dwellings, some of which had collapsed beyond repair.

Valade sat down and took out his sketchpad. Within an hour he had produced an impression of what the new schloss might look like: half a dozen satellite buildings ranged about the main house, which he had extended to include a walled courtyard and a shallow stream. He had notionally laid down a large area to grass among the existing trees, with walkways, pergolas and secret gardens.

"You should have roses here, though of course I don't know what will survive this high up," he said. "And your kitchen gardens will need sun, so they had better be on the south side, down a little and out of the wind. You should keep the structure of the main house if you can. It is rather fine—if you like Carinthian vernacular."

"A complete world," said Thomas. "And the wonderful thing is that when the cable car is built and the railway spur is running, you could be in the middle of town in little more than half an hour. So we would be apart and above, but not isolated. I shall show your sketch to the architect."

"You have an architect?"

"Well . . . he hasn't done anything yet, but in theory we do."

"Could it not be me?" said Valade.

"But you are not trained as an architect, are you?"

"No, but as far as any calculations of weight or stress are concerned, your little engineer could do them, couldn't he? What was his name?"

"Geissler. I suppose he could. What about supervising the builders?"

"I don't imagine that with you and your sister and your brother-in-law they will be short of instruction. And your wife told me that the stable boy wants to oversee it as well."

"Yes. She mentioned that to me. In fact, it might work quite well. Hans could live up here during the week and make sure they do what they are meant to. He has become quite bossy lately. He is a nuisance at the schloss. I imagine most of the builders will live up here as well rather than go up and down by mule, and he could keep an eye on them."

"May I make a suggestion?"

"Of course."

"The sooner you get the cable car installed, the easier it will be. Then you can bring the building supplies up on it."

During March and April, Jacques and Sonia, with the help of Herr Leopold and a lawyer called Kalman, set about forming a small company to finance the building of the railway and the cable car. Jacques talked to the mayor and persuaded him that the new schloss would bring renown to the district; he persuaded him to invest some money from the city reserves on financing the rail extension. In return, he conceded that for the first five years passengers would not be charged for this part of the journey, which took them about a third of the way up the mountain, to a place from which there were many walks to be enjoyed. They would build a refuge here, a modest version of the Rubio pavilion in Echo Mountain, with food and drink, lavatories and first aid for blisters, heatstroke and such things. The mayor agreed, knowing that his city's wealth depended on attracting summer visitors. Jacques also went to the physics and astronomy department of the university and explained that the Wilhelmskogel would offer an excellent site for the telescope which he knew they had not been allowed to situate on the nearby Magdalensberg; in return for funds for the building of the cable car, he proposed that all members of the university department should receive free transport to the telescope at the summit, an arrangement to be reviewed after ten years. It happened that the university's endowment exceeded the requirements of the modest number of students it attracted and its treasurer was eager to invest. Thomas then wrote to their old patron Monsieur Kalaji in Paris; he received a reply from the secretary of his foundation saying that Kalaji was abroad and could not be reached for several months, but in view of the success of his investment in the schloss, the secretary was authorized to make another advance up to a certain figure; further funds would have to await Kalaji's return. The balance of money they needed was raised by a stock issue for the Wilhelmskogel Railway and Cable Car Company supervised by Herr Leopold's head office in Vienna, and by the time the surveyor's full report arrived in late April they had funds enough to start the work.

The existing branch line in the valley was served by small steam engines, but Geissler had determined that the Wilhelmskogel line should run on electric traction, and although it was referred to as a "spur," the rails did not actually join those of the steam line. Passengers were to dismount and cross a sturdy wooden platform to join the mountain railway; at one end of the platform was an engine shed and at the other the electric power house. The first spike was driven by Daniel Rebière at noon on May 30, 1897, his mother holding the hammer in his hands, the moment repeated several times for the benefit of his uncle Thomas's Kodak camera. Sonia was appalled to see how gray her hair was growing when the picture was eventually printed.

A photographer from the local newspaper was also present, and his picture appeared on the front page under the headline: "All Aboard for the Madhouse! Doctor's wife inaugurates new railway to proposed mountaintop sanatorium." The article went on:

Work has begun on a new private railway line under the direction of Herr Tobias Geissler, the well-known Villach engineer. More than forty laborers, mostly Slovene-speakers from Karfreit in the Julian Alps, are working night and day to lay two kilometers of track up a slope in the foothills of the Wilhelmskogel.

At the narrow-gauge railway terminus, passengers may transfer to an electric cable car that will take them on a gradient of almost one-in-two, up to the top of the mountain. Here, local alienists Dr. Thomas Midwinter, aged 37, from England, and Dr. Jacques Rebière, also 37, from France, are to move their existing Schloss Seeblick sanatorium for nervous disorders.

Work is going on simultaneously on "grading" the slope for the cable car lift. Herr Geissler assured reporters that there would be no repeat of the loud explosions which alarmed local residents throughout last week.

"It was necessary to lay sizable dynamite charges to clear the rocks at the foot of the cableway," Herr Geissler explained. "Men were lowered on ropes to drill holes in the rock for the placing of the charges. But I believe the rest of it can be cleared by hand. We apologize for any disturbance caused by the explosions."

The electric railway will span minor gulfs and ravines in the foothills by means of large wooden trestles which are already under construction. The design of the two electric railway cars is based by Herr Geissler on that of a Viennese tram; it takes power from 600-volt conventional overhead cables, many of which are already in place. The cars are being built by the Neubauer-Hebenstreit ironworks in Villach, under Herr Geissler's supervision.

The most unusual aspect of the work, however, is the steep cable car lift to the summit. Dr. Rebière traveled to California in the United States of America to inspect a similar system last year, and is collaborating closely with Herr Geissler on the construction. The main wheels and cables are being made in Bavaria, but the car itself will be manufactured locally by Blatnik and Sons in Graz.

Use of the cable car will at first be restricted to patients and staff of the sanatorium, though it is hoped that it will be opened to the public when the summit has been sufficiently developed to afford privacy to the patients and recreational facilities for the paying public. Viewing platforms, a restaurant and a small zoo are envisaged.

"It is important to get the cable car running as soon as possible," said Dr. Rebière. "Then we can use it to take building materials to the summit."

The famous Parisian architect Monsieur Pierre Valade is a consultant to the building work, which is being overseen by Schloss Seeblick employee and local man Hans Eckert, aged 29. It is expected that the work will take eighteen months to complete.

As the laborers cleared and smoothed the cableway, they discovered they could not dispose of the debris without blocking the run below, so had to drag it fifty meters up the hill and tip it down a side canyon, a vertical gash that ran all the way to the top, parallel to the gentler incline up which the cable car would run.

Progress through the summer was extremely slow.

"Do not worry, gentlemen," said Geissler. "It is always this way. Once the electric railway is complete, it will be much faster to take what we need to the foot of the cable car. Once the cable incline is graded, the rails are down and we can pull a wagon up, the work at the summit will rush ahead. At the moment, everything waits on everything else. It is just hard labor, hacking rock, night and day. Life is sometimes like that. There is a time to dance and a time to keep hacking rocks, but one must not lose the faith. When it lifts, it will all lift at once."

Geissler moved into the schloss and sat up late with Jacques in his consulting room, where the new electric lights illuminated the plans he spread across the desk. He stabbed his forefinger at the paper.

"The car will have the capacity to carry twelve people. To reduce the weight, I propose a tin roof, though of course we must have closed wood-and-glass sides in our climate. I calculate it will take ten horsepower to raise an empty car and thirty to raise a full one. Not that we can persuade a mule or horse up a sixty-degree gradient."

"A hypothetical horse," said Jacques.

"Precisely. I also calculate that perhaps a third of the necessary power can be generated and stored by the descent." Geissler laughed. "Not quite perpetual motion, but a damned good effort. The main power source, as you know, is a series of two hundred storage batteries."

Jacques had a sudden picture in his mind of old Signor Volta with two hundred batteries beneath his tongue. Suppressing a smile, he said, "How is the water supply?"

"Almost ready. The stream from the summit, which will provide your daily needs, has been diverted into a reservoir. A narrow pipe runs down to a seventy-five-horsepower waterwheel at the foot of the incline. The volume of water is small, but the pressure is intense."

The main cable was only four centimeters in diameter. It was spliced round grip wheels at the top and bottom of the incline; the lower wheel was placed below the platform with access for engineers to go in and adjust the tension. Geissler had it tested to twenty times its maximum load and specified a second, independent safety cable that could stop a full car in less than a meter. The car was to be detached each night and the cable wound on a fixed distance daily to prevent uneven wear.

"The main wheel is cast iron," said Geissler, "three meters in diameter, attached to an electric motor. If the wheel itself is geared to turn at twelve revolutions per minute, then the incline should, I calculate, take six minutes to ascend. How's that, Doctor?"

"I think anything faster would scare the patients, Tobias."

On through the summer, the autumn and deep into the winter, the Karfreit workers toiled. They moved into the buildings on the summit and at night made conflagrations in the huge stone fireplaces from spare railway sleepers.

Hans watched over them fiercely, excited by his first position of authority and determined to make sure his employers were not cheated by the workforce. Food still had to be brought up by mule, but they established a cook tent halfway up the mountain for the midday meal. The Slovenes were dark, lean men who liked eating, particularly when once a week they had breaded veal with cheese sauce; they also liked wine— and dancing if they were given a chance—but were prepared to work in all weathers and, so far as Hans could see, with minimal rest.

Jacques was taken in the coach by Josef to inspect the work once a week, but he seldom went to the top since it took a further hour by mule. He relied on daily despatches from Geissler and a weekly report from Hans when he came back for his day off at the schloss.

By the following summer, the railway was almost complete, but a fall of rock on the cableway took six weeks to clear and extra men had to be drafted in to try to complete the work by Christmas 1898. This would still allow a year for the work on the sanatorium itself to be completed in time for a move in the last days of the century.

Life in the Schloss Seeblick seemed to slow down, because everything—appointments, repairs, planning—became provisional.

Sonia watched Daniel wander round the garden with the handle of a wicker basket of toy animals digging into the flesh of his right arm. She regretted the imminent move, because, although she saw that it was inevitable, and a measure of their success and optimism, she did not see how they could be more happy than they were. Never mind, she thought; her husband had regained some of that imaginative fire that had first made her love him; she could see that the move would be good for him and so, in a way, it must be good for her and Daniel too. The unexpected bonus in her life was that she had come to love Kitty, who made her laugh immoderately, particularly when confiding in her about Thomas's peculiarities, though Sonia could never quite stop herself thinking of her as an invalid.

Jacques counted the days impatiently until he could make a new start and put behind him the irksome memories of his professional failures at the schloss. He liked the buildings well enough, but he had not cured his brother and he had not made his name. Thomas shared his excitement; he felt there was something propitious about their moving at the start of a new century. They had paused; but now they would move on with new heart to fulfill the youthful ambitions they had declared at Deauville.

Kitty loved her South Court home, the chestnut tree and the room where the girls had been born. When it was being cleaned for a new arrival, she went to visit Number 18, where she had lived as a patient. She remembered how Thomas had stepped in off the balcony, then seemed to unravel in front of her; how he had seen himself whole for the first time. It was a moment of privilege, and one on which she knew her own life had turned. She remembered, too, how he had gone down on his knee to propose to her, with the mountains behind him; and for these and many other reasons, she was sad to leave. Yet she had been the newcomer; she had tactfully restrained herself, particularly with Sonia who, while she could not imaginably have been more generous, sometimes spoke her mind with a directness that Kitty found unnerving. On the mountaintop they would all begin again as equal partners, and she shared Thomas's delight in the fact that while they would be removed from the world, high above the clamor of the cities of the plain, she could be in the best shopping street in town in half an hour.

THE WORK was not finished by Christmas, nor by February, when there was further delay while the workers celebrated the Slovene festival of Kurenti. Hans was informed by their foreman that no work would be done for a week because the men needed to drive out the "evil spirits of winter."

Extra consignments of wine were brought by mule; in the evening the men built a huge fire outside and dressed themselves in animal masks and old furs. They ran through the woods shouting and banging drums; they commanded the evil spirits to be gone, to throw themselves from the summit of the mountain and let the spring begin once more. Hans watched in trepidation, wondering if the exorcism really needed a whole week, and so much wine.

The railway was complete, though the car was not yet ready, and in April the cableway, too, was finished. Horses were led up the mule tracks to the top and attached to a wooden windlass, whose rope was in turn attached to the steel cable itself, which, under Herr Geissler's agitated supervision, was hauled up to the summit. It took two days to attach the cable at each end and to tension it to Geissler's satisfaction. The car itself was still being weatherproofed and painted in Graz, but it was possible to attach an open truck to the cable and it was proposed that this first ascent should be marked by a celebration. Although the mayor had agreed to officiate at the formal opening, whenever that should be, Sonia was selected to break a bottle of champagne on the top wheel at four o'clock on April 20, and so inaugurate the run.

XVII

"SO, YOU SEE, WE ARE ALL OF US HAPPY IN OUR DIFFERENT WAYS," said Thomas.

"As happy, at least, as we have any right to expect," said Kitty. "There are philosophers who tell us that happiness is not a proper goal for humans. They say it is infantile to expect to feel happy. It is just an emotion, a transitory feeling, not an adequate purpose for a life. They say you should make your life's work something more enduring."

"Yes, I think I have read some of those philosophers. What they say is logical, but it does not seem especially true. It is not how we experience life, is it, Kitten?"

"I try to think that way," said Kitty. "But I think being happy is one of the few things I am any good at, so I am reluctant to throw it away. Especially since I have known what it is to be unhappy."

"You hold fast to it, my love. We shall need it on the mountaintop." Thomas frowned. "Of course, the only person one cannot say is looking forward to the move, or to anything at all so far as we know, is Olivier."

"Do you think he is ever happy?"

"It is impossible to say. To hear those voices day and night would make you or me most desperately miserable, but with Olivier you cannot always be sure what he feels."

"WHY WON'T he get up? Why does he just lie in bed?"

"Lazy. Good for nothing."

"Today he must do it. He must end it."

"He is a sodomite. The world is better without him."

"They have made a railway for him."

"Look at him."

"Why doesn't he do what he is told and just put an end to it?"

"They let him have a razor now because they know he is too feeble to do any harm."

"Too much of a coward."

"He killed his mother. He split her cunt, so she died when the next baby came."

"They needed a proper child. The second time they got the one they wanted."

"But she couldn't survive. Not after what *he* had done to her."

"What is he doing here?"

"Why is he infecting the world? Look at all the people he has made ill with his thoughts."

"All he is good for is to lie and play with himself."

"Cunt-splitter."

"Ape."

"This railway. It's for him, isn't it?"

"They have given up hope that he will do the right thing."

"He doesn't even know what the right thing is anymore."

"Sodomite. He should have died when the cities of the plain were burned."

"How did he escape? He who dreams of fucking the young women and the boys? Fucking them in the shithole like an animal."

"The Englishwoman. He wants to fuck her, doesn't he? When he rubs himself?"

I must move, thought Olivier, I must get dressed. Here is a shirt on the chair. I must move ahead. I must not melt. I must find my edges.

I cannot concentrate on what the Seamstress is telling me because of the people I see. All these seen-people with their faint voices, too faint for me to catch.

Here is the seen-girl.

"Good morning, Olivier. It's just your old Daisy again. Nothing to fret about. It's time for breakfast."

"He wants to fuck her too, doesn't he? He's always thinking about it."

"He is a disgrace."

Follow the seen-girl with the soft voice. Move and keep ahead.

"You haven't got your trousers on, love. That's the way. Then we can go and have breakfast. Miss Sonia's made some nice eggs."

Legs? Why can't the seen-girl talk louder? The Carver. I can always hear the Carver. Or the Acrobat. Dear God, I can hear the Acrobat.

I do not want to eat their food because the Seamstress told me they are still trying to poison me. I will throw this food away from me.

"Oh well done! Now he's broken the plate. It's no wonder they won't let him eat with them."

"He is a savage."

"A dirty savage. He smells like an animal. See how they all back away from him."

"He stinks. He never washes."

There are too many seen-people in this room, this hall. There is all this noise of wooden spoons on bowls, the clattering, the shouting, hurling, banging, outdoors horses, spades on stone, the people asking me, asking me questions. I want the waterfall that will drown their noise. I want the quiet.

"Come on, Olivier. Do as Daisy says. Just eat a little bread and tea. Then it's time for your appointment with Dr. Midwinter. It's Wednesday. You like talking to him, don't you?"

They are always asking me these questions. The Sovereign has explained the answers and will not let them take my thoughts now. I am going to be enlisted into the German army. They know that I have the secrets of the king of France. They know I know the day of his return. They want me on their side and have sent me here so I can be watched while my thoughts are taken from me. I do not want this. I am an architect, not a soldier.

"Do sit down, Olivier. How are you feeling today?"

"He shouldn't answer him. He knows he's a spy for the Germans."

"He's not a real doctor."

"He knows about Olivier. He knows that he plays with himself when he thinks about the doctor's wife."

I must try to hear what the Englishman is asking me. I will read his lips.

"Read his lips? He thinks he can hear him above our voices!"

"He killed his mother! Mother-killer, mother-killer!"

"Why don't you answer me, Olivier? I am trying to help you."

"What?"

"I am asking you some simple questions. Who is the president of the Republic?"

What in public? Something in public? Present? I must say something. Try an answer. "I have no present."

"He is useless!"

"He doesn't know anything!"

I must keep the walls away. If I touch the chair arms, touch my fingers—like this—I can hold them back.

". . . and so how old would that make you now, Olivier?"

Cold? Me? What I must make sure when I leave is that the man with the hat, the man who has the horse and carriage, does not get me alone because he will take me. He is one of the Germans. And the English-woman who has married my brother . . . But my brother is a boy. . . . He cannot be married. He is . . .

"Olivier? May I ask again?"

"His brother! Yes. He was the one they wanted, wasn't he? They always liked him more."

"What good was Olivier? Good enough to fuck pigs in the stable yard, that's all."

I must find the thread of myself again. I must breathe in and try not to dissolve in the world. I will breathe in.

"Olivier?"

He does not speak French properly, this seen-man. He is English. I cannot hear him. I must read his lips above the noise of the voices.

He is not important. He is not loud enough. I wish he would go away. "Go away!"

They are all like this, the seen-people. Not loud enough. They are not like the Acrobat or the Seamstress. I hate them, and the Carver and the others, but they are me. They are part of me. I did not choose them, but I deal with them because that is what I am given and I cannot choose anymore than I could pick the color of my hair. I do not like it, but that is the arrangement.

I will go to the place by the lake where the stream runs in and makes a noise. This will drown the voices for a time. I will watch water.

"Olivier, you are not speaking to me. I am your doctor. I am your friend—Thomas. You remember me. I am Jacques's partner. We used to be such friends, you and I. Do you remember? You were sad when I went away. These days you don't seem to talk to me anymore. Do you know how long you have been sitting there now without speaking? Do you know?"

Breathe in. Say *something*. All right. "I will watch water."

"I don't understand. Watch water? Why?"

"Daughter, no. No."

"He is such a clown, isn't he? What daughter does he mean?"

I didn't hear him right because you were talking so loud.

"Listen, Olivier. You have been sitting here for almost fifteen minutes without speaking. I want to help you, but you must talk to me."

I am trying to read his lips but the noise is too loud for me to concentrate. There are too many people here and the man in the garden outside with his rake on the gravel, and the birds in the trees and I hear them saddling up the horses so I cannot pick out my thought. There is a line in me, which is a thought. It runs like a thread from my feet up through my spine into my head. It is a true thought but I cannot grip it for all the distraction. Let me breathe, let me find it.

"Well, Olivier?"

I have found it. Here it is. "The Germans want me. They want to capture me because I know the movements of the French king. I know when he will return, when he will attack. So the Germans have sent their spies for me."

"Are the spies here in the schloss?"

"The man with the hat. With the horses."

"Josef? He is just the lampman. The groom."

What is the point of telling the Englishman? He never understands. He cannot see truth. He always contradicts.

"Olivier, do you remember last time, you told me that the Germans know you because your face is colored black? I took a photograph and sent my camera off for the film to be developed. Here is the photograph of you. And here is one of me and one of Jacques. And do you see how our skin is all the same color? You are no different from the rest of us. Look!"

Touch the chair and hands together fast to stop the walls. Touch, touch, touch.

"What do you say, Olivier?"

"My skin is black."

"Scared now, isn't he? Little coward."

"The mother-killer is frightened of the picture!"

Picture is a fake. It isn't me. They changed the color. The Englishman is one of them. Lots of reasons. Take your pick. Which is true? *It doesn't matter.* Show me a picture of a green sky and I still know the sky is blue!

"So, Olivier, tell me what you think."

All right. "I think the sky is never green."

"Thank you, my dear Olivier. Our time is up. I don't wish to tire you. Perhaps you would like to go out into the grounds. Shall I ask a nurse to go with you? You can do some work in the kitchen garden if you want. Whatever you would like, my old friend. Come along now. Let's find Daisy."

"Follow the little bitch out then. Think about how you want to fuck her. In the mouth, is it?"

"You made the doctor sad. Don't you see his face?"

"He wants to help you. But you're no good."

"Why can't you talk sense to him, pig-fucker?"

"Shall we go to the lake, dear? Take my arm if you like."

"Why do you talk such shit to the doctor?"

"He had tears in his eyes."

"You are a bad man. You cause such pain in other people."

"Don't you see that pain?"

"Didn't you see that poor doctor?"

I am tired by all this. All this trying to find a thread. I am like some sea creature that can still just live on land. But it is too hard. It is easier to be back under the water, back with the voices, back in the hell-world.

"Is this the place you like, dearie? Just here under the tree? I've brought your special book. The one you did the drawings and the coloring in. Here it is. If you need me, just call out my name. Call out 'Daisy.' I shall be up in the flower gardens with some of the ladies. You can call me if you need. Goodbye for the minute, dear."

"'Some of the ladies.' He would like that, wouldn't he?"

"They know that. That's why they don't let him near them!"

Let me see the water now, where it comes down. I want to wash myself in it. I want to take some of my filth away.

"He looks at their dresses but he's thinking of their breasts."

"They know that. They know he wants to put his fingers in them. His dirty fingers."

"They would not allow his dirty fingers near their cunts!"

"Don't say those vile words. Don't *say* that!"

"He talks to us, now, does he? Talk to the air, pig-fucker. Talk to the Carver. He always listens."

"I do not think that way of the women. Once there was a girl in Vannes, that is all."

"Of course he doesn't. He prefers boys."

"Sodomite. Why don't you end it? You never get it right, do you?"

"Kill yourself."

"No, no, no! It is a sin."

"He is in hell already. He is dead and gone to hell."

Watch the water, listen to the streaming, white bubbles, gray bubbles, jets beneath the surface, eddies, surge and currents. See it settle, see the surface of the lake is always flat. Why does it never slope? In lakes there are no valleys. What is a water hill? Where are the landscapes of my lake? By the rivers of Babylon, we sat down and wept when we remembered thee, O Zion. Even where it runs at a steady pace, the shape of the flow is always changing. The trees cover me with their shadow and the willows of the brook compass me about. Behold I drink the river and I haste not. I pour tears into the sea. O hadst thou hearkened to my commandments! Then had my peace been as a river and my righteousness as the waves of the sea . . .

But I did hearken to your commandments, Sovereign. I heard your voice when I was alone. I thought everyone heard your voice. I heard you speak to me loud and clear and I did what you told me. Break his collection of little animals. Smash his room. Break his heart. I did what you told me, but you did not bring me peace.

"... and end it now, you coward ..."

"... and thinking of their bodies underneath ..."

"Be quiet! I shall lift up mine eyes unto the hills from whence cometh my help."

For my help cometh even from the Lord. . . . I see his miracle of water foam and white splitting. Does it never end? Does the rock throw out water from inside the earth and does the earth suck it back from the clouds? Never ending, never end. What lies inside a drop? A million smaller drops. And what lies inside each one of those? There is peace in them because they join. They make softness flow.

God speaks his thoughts through me because I am His son. And I once could read His will in the paper of the book, between the printed lines. I can make sense of this world because I use my brain. Why then do others always tell me it is not so? Your hand is not black, they say, but I knew that it was. I could see it! Just as I know the sky is blue. Why pretend? It is so tiring, so wearing, all this nonsense they talk in their soft voices.

"A great war is coming to the world."

"And it is his fault. It is Olivier's fault."

"The mother-killer carries the sins of the world."

"In his name ten million will die."

I will take the special book and stop the war if I can shade the letters of my name again and again. Take my pen here and shade out the *o*, every time I see it in every line of the book and the top of the *e*, like this, and that will save the world from this catastrophe. But my name has too many straight lines, like the *l* and the *v*. I can cover in the valley of the *v*, but that still leaves the *i* and the *l*. My name has too many straight letters, but if I can keep going with all the spaces I may spare the world this tragedy.

Once I wrote a book, didn't I? I wrote the Bible. I wrote a book, I drew a book—drew a book that showed how people like me might be housed better. I did draw that book. I have good writing. I can draw. I made beautiful pictures in it of many rooms with plumbing and electrical lights and I showed how all the pipes connected to carry out the filth below the buildings. I made that book in another place. In a big house which had nuns in it . . . Why did I live with nuns? With nuns and madmen in cages . . . I . . .

I like to write books, so then I wrote the Bible because the Sovereign explained it to me. But I do not like the way he shows my thoughts around. I see them laughing because he had showed them the inside of my head and what I am thinking, and it is true that I am thinking of the women and I know that they can see that I am thinking about fucking her, the one with the little reading glasses and the freckles, I am thinking about her cunt, it is true and I can picture its color, the soft blond hairs and the pinkishness of it all puckered on itself and I wish the Sovereign would not show my thoughts abroad, like the finger writing on the wall for all to see.

I must keep moving, try to drag the true thought up through me like the line they drop for building—the plumb line for the bricks.

It is too hard to think one of those thoughts. I would have to close down everything else to give myself the peace to think it. Like a householder at night, I would go into many rooms and close the shutters, blow out the lamps, lock the doors, close down everything, one by one by one, stop the shouting and the talking in every single room until at last I had the peace to think my one clear thought—a thought like those that are thought by the seen-people, like the Englishman or the girl called Daisy. It would be a simple thought, a quiet thought, full of reason, spoken softly, not against the clamor of competing voices, but spoken into silence.

But I cannot get into all the rooms at once to close them down. I cannot be upstairs, downstairs, in the cellar, in the courtyard all at once with my keys and breath to blow out lamps and my gags to shut the voices down. How can a man be in fifty places all at once?

So it is easier to be in pieces, in the Babel. It is easier to live in fragments. So long as I keep some edges, do not lose the edges of myself.

I will lie beneath the tree and listen to the wind in the leaves. What kind of tree is this? Is it a poplar? Or a willow? By the side of the water here. Not an oak or a pine, but a tree with little leaves of gray that rustle in the wind.

So let me hear the wind.

"It is his fault. Ten million men will die."

I will listen to the wind.

"Stable boy. Pig-fucker. Why won't he kill himself?"

One leaf rustles on another.

"He is too much of a coward."

It is like the faintness of cymbals.

"It all adds up. It all makes sense. His evil has caused it."

I will not hear you in the wind. Cannot hear you, I am lost in the leaves, in the hiss, in the sound, in the green and the gray in the big perfection because the wind is perfect, as the water is perfect, you could not make it better, it could not be more beautiful or more watery, not like the things men make, which could always be better, you could not improve the wind, this sound that rings and whistles softly in my head; and all the other voices, all the sounds are mingled in me and I am the center, chosen, center of the world through which the harmony is made and in the gray whisper and soft clatter of the leaves I hear the mountains of the east, the sands of Arabia, brown-skinned men playing music, girls dancing with clinking cymbals in their fingers, carrying me and my million thoughts and pictures each one of which carries a million more I do not have the time to catch or see as they ride by in the branches over me, a shadow on a brick wall in a garden, splash of silver fish on the quay in Vannes, wail of women, thrust of green and smell of grass, root and finger, bone and blood, and all in me spinning and whistling, blown and hissing in the wind.

"Why is he denying it? It is his fault. A child can see that."

Your voices will fade in the rippling leaves.

"Kill yourself. Only that can save the world."

I can hear the colors of the leaves, the green on gray, the gray on green, the smooth metallic rustle, each sound distinct, each part of a greater whole we cannot see. Cannot see the wind. Cannot see the wind, they say! But I have always seen the wind. When I was a child I saw the wind. I saw it in the apple trees. It was not difficult! Like water made into air, that's all. But lovely in its sound, like Saul and Jonathan, they were lovely and pleasant in their lives and in their death they were not divided.

"Kill yourself."

The leaves weigh on the twigs and the twigs lift the branches and the sounds are all around me as I lie here on the grass beneath the tree . . .

"Kill yourself, coward. That will save the world."

I am very sorrowful for the pain I see in the madmen where I live. It tears at my heart. I know it is my fault.

. . . as though the leaves are tiny cymbals being kissed by the wind . . .

"Kill yourself."

. . . am submerged in this heavenly sound that whistles and rustles and beats like my heart, like butterfly kisses on my face that no one has kissed since . . . I do not know when someone kissed me last.

"Kill yourself, you coward."

"Kill yourself."

"OLIVIER? WHERE are you? It's me, Daisy. Where are you? We are going to see the railway. Olivier! There you are, you funny boy. You've been out here for hours. I thought we'd lost you. You are to put on your coat and come with me and Miss Sonia and Miss Kitty in the trap to Wilhelmsko-gel. Dr. Rebière and Dr. Midwinter went ahead and they are having a little ceremony at the top to mark the first truck going up, or some such thing. Come along now, Olivier. It's going to be such a lark."

I do not want to go with the man in the hat. The horse-man. He is working for the Germans.

"Now is the time to do it. To end it."

"It is the perfect opportunity."

I must find my coat and go. I must pretend to be normal. Pretend I do not know about the horse-man. There he is. He is looking at me. He can see my thoughts. Why does the Sovereign let him see them?

"Now then. Kitty, why don't you sit here on this side, and Daisy you sit next to Kitty and I'll sit next to Olivier. There we are. Everybody happy. Off we go, Josef!"

"So he's got himself opposite the fair-haired one. She's not wearing her glasses, though, is she?"

"He likes her in her glasses. He likes to think of her naked with just the little reading glasses on."

"He likes to fuck her from behind, like a dog. In his mind. In his imagination!"

"She wouldn't really let him. Only pigs let him."

"I brought some cakes, Sonia."

"Thank you, Kitty. I think Jacques said it's about an hour. Josef has arranged to change horses at the stables in town."

He will take instructions from the ostler. I have seen him before. He is a Bavarian. He wants to kill me before the Monarchy returns. I must keep touching my fingers, keep touching the door of the carriage.

"Daisy, would you like some cake, or shall we wait until we stop? We can have a cup of chocolate while Josef changes the horses."

An hour. An hour with the horse-man. What is an hour to me? I have no idea of time. Sometimes time laughs at me. I saw a clock laugh at me once.

"What exactly is this ceremony, Sonia?"

"Well, you know that the track for the cable car is ready? They are going to try it with an open truck. With just some old railway sleepers on it."

"When they first talked about this cable car I somehow pictured it being up in the air, suspended on the wire."

"No, no, you silly girl! It is just pulled up on rails. The cable is attached to the underneath of the car. It is terribly simple. It is like one of Daniel's toys. But don't tell Herr Geissler I said that."

"And how do we get up to the top?"

"Josef takes us as far as he can up the track, then we change to mules for the steep bit. It takes another hour from there, I think."

We are changing horses already. That was not enough time. We are in town, and there are too many people here.

"Do you want to get down and stretch your legs, Olivier?"

I must stay in the carriage, don't let the Bavarian see me. My thoughts are being shown. Keep inside. Keep my head low.

"He is too scared to get down."

"Even though the fair girl's got down and he wants to watch her."

"Wants to see her hips in the tight skirt and think . . ."

"Too frightened even to want her."

"Come on then, Josef. Let's get moving, shall we? I told my husband we would be there by four. Come on, Kitty."

I am not managing well. This man Josef. I fear today is the day he has chosen. I saw his face in the horse's face, when it whinnied and stamped its hoof on the cobble. It was his devilish features beneath that mane. It was like the face of the old mare. . . . God, I remember the old mare in the stable where I lived. Why did I live in the stable? In the name of God, why there? Perhaps I do not remember it right. Or the nuns.

". . . so bossy, Sonia!"

"Katharina, I can assure you I am not bossy. I have to organize a household full of . . . eccentrics, shall we say. And none more eccentric than your husband, I might add. Someone has to be in charge."

"Let us ask Daisy for her impartial judgment. Don't giggle, Daisy. Tell me, do you think Miss Sonia is bossy or not?"

"Miss Sonia is . . . Miss Sonia is ever so well organized."

"There you are, Kitty! Look. There is the beginning of our railway line, our own 'spur,' as the men like to call it, leading up into the foothills."

"Why don't we take the train, Miss?"

"Because there isn't one yet. There is only a line."

This journey is over too soon. These seen-women with their silly chatter have made it pass quickly. We are stopping too soon. Josef will hand me over now to the Germans. Touch my fingers, touch the door, touch my fingers, touch the door.

"Of course I can ride a mule, Sonia! I am not just a Viennese flibberti-gibbet, you know. I was more or less brought up on a farm."

"Daisy, you take that one, he looks friendly. Olivier, you get on this one, because I know for sure that you were brought up in the country-side with horses and dogs. Josef will lead the way."

We are in beech woods and they are very dense. I like beech trees, but the forests are easy to hide in. Higher up there will be larch and pine. And there will be bears and wolves. These stupid people do not under-stand how dangerous these mountains are. They eat wild boar but do not ask themselves where it comes from. From the beech woods. I am tired of this riding. This stony track. I am so very very tired.

"He is frightened of the lampman."

"He knows today is the day. There is no time left."

"He is not worth killing. He will have to kill himself."

The forest is getting thicker. I want to be above the tree line, where the Germans cannot hide, but maybe this mountain is not high enough. The Sovereign must stop showing my thoughts to the man in the hat. I am worn down by the ceaseless, ceaseless voices.

"Getting colder, isn't it, Daisy? Do you feel it?"

"Yes, Miss. I can see the buildings at the top. Is that Dr. Rebière waving?"

"Yes! Come on. Let's hurry up to the top."

"My donkey won't go no faster!"

"Kitty, you go first through this little bit, then it's round to the right, past the old chapel. You'll see them waiting."

Who is this man talking? He is like my brother, but my brother is . . . is a child. I am so tired.

"Hello, everyone. You made it. Come and see our wonderful cable track. Thomas is waiting with a bottle of champagne. This way, my love. Come, Olivier. Over here. Isn't it a wonderful view? The whole of Carinthia, almost. See those mountains? The Schladminger Tauern. And down in the valley over here is Wolfsberg and right up there are the Fischbacher Alps. Thomas!"

"Come and see our wheel. Jacques, bring them over. See this, Queenie? This mighty wheel will pull the car up the sheer side of the mountains. The truck is waiting at the bottom. Look."

"No! It makes me feel sick."

"Don't be silly! Can't you see how beautifully smooth it is? That's why we chose this incline, because there was so little grading for them to do. I do hope it's going to work. I am feeling a little apprehensive, though not as much as Geissler. Kitty, my love, come and look."

"It is magnificent, I must admit. It would be hard to feel melancholy with such a glorious view."

"Exactly. And you can see how the builders are progressing with the main house? It should be ready by October. Just in time."

"Kill yourself. This is a good place."

"He could throw himself off. But he's too scared."

"Olivier, hold the champagne a moment. I want to show Sonia something. Here, take it. Thank you. Now look, my love, this is where the cable comes up and this is where the safety cable runs and this is where the platform will be where the passengers will step down."

"It is wonderful, Jacques."

"We will lift the poor creatures up. We will raise them above suffering, will we not, Thomas?"

"I do hope so, Jacques. We have worked hard enough to build our promontory—it is the height of our ambition."

"The peak of enlightenment."

"Josef, can you fetch the champagne from Olivier? Then, Sonia, would you break it on the wheel?"

He is coming for me, the hat-man is coming for me. . . . He is coming.

"Kill yourself. Kill yourself."

"Just run and throw yourself."

"Too cowardly to do the right thing."

He is coming for me, he is coming!

"Run and kill yourself. Just run."

I will, I will, I *will*, I am running, I am running, I am running, I am . . .

"Stop him! Thomas! Stop! *Stop!*"

. . . I am running, I am running, I am

IT TOOK them two days to recover Olivier's body, which lay among the rocks that had been tipped down the sharpest fall, next to the cable car incline. Men were lowered on ropes, as they had been when laying the dynamite charges, but Olivier's body was hard to reach and harder still to raise. Eventually, two workmen managed to secure ropes beneath his armpits and tie a sort of noose round his back; three mules at the summit turned the windlass and began to drag him to the top. Olivier arrived at last, over the lip of the mountain, his clothes shredded by the friction, but otherwise oddly unmarked by his fall. It appeared that his neck and left leg had broken; there was some blood that had clotted and stained the white of his beard around the mouth. His eyes were open but their gaze was empty. Under Hans's instructions, the body was then taken down by mule to where Thomas waited with Josef's horse and trap to take it back to the schloss.

It was the practice that any psychotic patients who died at the clinic should undergo postmortem, to see what Thomas and Franz Bernthaler could learn, but Thomas presumed Jacques would rather his brother was not subject to this indignity and had the body despatched to the morgue at the city hospital while they made arrangements for the funeral.

Jacques sat quietly in the drawing room of his and Sonia's apartment. The shock of the incident, its brutal surprise, at first made it impossible for him to think deeply about it. When at last he could do so, he found that he felt a most peculiar sensation of solitude.

His father was long dead, his mother he had never known; and though he had "lost" his brother years ago, when he drifted into madness, Olivier had remained his only link to the family of his birth, to that small group of humans that had been his first and irreducible unit of allegiance in the world. Now he was like the last survivor of a platoon. It had a name, a number and a history, but no existence: what had seemed indestructible, his base and point of deepest loyalty, had been dissolved before anyone had made out what it was for; suddenly it was too late, and there was something unsatisfactory about it that left him utterly alone.

Sonia comforted him, wept with him and watched carefully over him; but, much though he loved her, she was not of his flesh and blood. In Olivier's skin and veins had been particles of inheritance that they shared with no one else, and that had been the nature of their existence and its challenge: to make of their lives whatever they could, beginning in their narrow Breton world. That challenge now was ended; there was no one left for him to report back to on his progress; and without that narrative, the game, whatever might happen to him in the future, was barely worth the playing, because no one else, however much they loved him, really cared.

"We should have a postmortem," he told Thomas. "I remember asking myself once what Olivier's brain might look like. If he can tell us anything that might help others, then we should certainly look."

"Are you sure?"

"Yes. I should like to be there. I would like to see this story through to its end."

"As you wish. I shall send Josef to the hospital to tell them. I will make arrangements for the funeral the day after."

Thomas meanwhile looked back at his record of the last conversation he had had with Olivier to see if they could illuminate his sudden leap to death. Were there signs a better doctor would have seen?

What Olivier appeared from his hasty notes to have said was, roughly:

—I have no present.

—Go away!

—I will watch water.

—Daughter, no daughter.

—The Germans want me. . . . I know the movements of the French king. . . . They have sent their spies for me.

—The man with the hat is a spy.

—My skin is black.

—I think the sky is never green.

And that seemed to be all. There was an emphasis on color, on spying and . . . and nothing else at all that Thomas could see. Olivier's mind had long since been unable to make sense, so surely these ramblings were nothing more than the obiter dicta of a broken mind? Yet Thomas could not quite believe it. He felt there was more to his friend than that, and he felt that he should have found it.

IT WAS seven in the evening, the appointed time, and the small, bad-tempered servant manhandled the body from its refrigerated bed, banging the head as he did so, laboring beneath the weight before he finally wrestled it into place on the marble slab. Jacques, Thomas and Franz Bernthaler looked on, their faces concealed behind white masks.

Around the walls of the dissecting room were specimens in glass jars: livers, aortas, larynxes. At the far end was a wooden board on which were hung saws, chisels, knives and other banausic instruments of the trade.

The prosector was the senior pathologist at the hospital, a man called Holzbauer. He approached the table briskly, rubbing cream he had taken from a tub into his hands. When the corpse had been arranged in the anatomical position and he had checked the identity, he began to examine the surface, dictating notes to his student as he did so. The skin was covered with abrasions from the fall and the ascent. Then it was time for the incision. Although Jacques had seen it countless times before, he found his fingernails deep in his palms as Holzbauer took the large scalpel to each shoulder and cut a "V," meeting at the breastbone;

without pausing, he carved straight down to the pubic bone, perhaps three millimeters deep, diverting a fraction as he went past the navel. Working with a smaller scalpel, he began to ease the V-shaped section of skin from the chest wall. He held the first triangular corner of skin taut between forceps, from which it occasionally slipped, and used stroking motions of the knife to separate it from the cutaneous layer. Bits of fat or waste were occasionally deposited with the forceps in a metal mixing bowl near the cadaver's head. As the section of lifted skin grew larger, he was able to grip it in his hand, dispensing with the forceps; and when he had cut both sides clear he folded the flap up over Olivier's face, so the hairs of his chest pressed those of his beard. Jacques was glad not to have to look at his brother's features anymore. Poor boy, he thought. He had a desire to embrace him, before he became no more than separate pieces it would be absurd to kiss. He reached out and briefly held the cold thick hand.

There was a slight smell, not unlike that inside Meissner and Trattnig, the expensive butcher behind the market square in town. With what looked like a pair of secateurs such as Sonia carried in the garden, the prosector cut the sternum and front ribs away, revealing Olivier's heart and lungs. With a scalpel, he cut delicately through the sac round the heart, reported no blockage in the pulmonary artery, then went down to the tail of his "Y," slicing back the muscle from the abdomen till it fell away on either side, so that all the inner organs from neck to groin were exposed. Jacques felt that he was looking at what he himself was made of, and noticed that the mixing bowl was gradually filling up with waste, with the detritus of his brother.

The next stage was the most difficult, and reminded him of what Olivier himself, at a time when he was first starting to go mad, had shown him when they went hunting with guns and killed a roe deer. After some ritual marking of his virgin younger brother with blood from the testes, Olivier had taken out the guts entire and thrown them to the dogs.

Holzbauer glanced toward Jacques as he detached the larynx and esophagus, then went into the cavity to free the remainder of the chest organs from the spine. He left them in place while he detached the diaphragm and freed the abdominal organs. The contents of the upper body were now held in place only at the pelvis. Holzbauer looked over once more before slicing through this last tie. He stood back for the servant, who mounted a dissecting table over Olivier's legs, then removed the entire bloc of organs en masse and placed them on it.

His brother was in pieces and Jacques could see through the empty body cavity to the spine. And this was all, this was all, he thought, as he gazed at the innards on the tray: the great delusion of the human being that he might himself be something more than matter.

The prosector continued with impressive legerdemain to separate the organs. He withdrew from a leather sheath beneath his gown something that looked like a carving knife, which he used in single, deft slices. Only the adrenal glands above the kidneys gave him pause for a moment. Franz Bernthaler went to work on the liver and spleen, while the servant opened the intestines over a stone sink, beneath a running tap.

Jacques found himself stifling a protest. Surely this invasion of his brother's privacy was too much. It was a moment before he could name the emotion that gripped him at the sight of the servant rinsing Olivier's intestines: it was, to his great surprise, embarrassment.

Since Olivier had eaten nothing on his last day, having hurled his breakfast plate from him, the stench of gastric acid, when Holzbauer opened the stomach, was less than Jacques had known it, though still enough to make his own stomach turn beneath his gown. Franz was busy weighing and slicing the pancreas and the kidneys; he took samples to be examined microscopically and placed them in small glass jars.

Thomas whispered in Jacques's ear, "Are you all right? Do you want to stay for the brain? You can always look at it later, back at the schloss."

It was such a forlorn sight, thought Jacques. Though Holzbauer had been as neat a performer as he had seen, there was blood on the floor beneath them, blood in the gutters of the slab, and small pieces of flesh stuck on the hooks of the scales. Even the chalk that the student had used to write up the measurements on the blackboard was red-tinged, while some of the statistics themselves were pink and smudged on the black background.

There was no escaping the matter of his brother, the red and stinking material of his being. The hulk of his body now was like a half-built fishing vessel in the boatyards at Vannes: though beautiful, it was desolate, and already spoke of shipwreck.

The servant poured the organs back into the cavity, where they made undignified slippery noises, as when Herr Trattnig heaved a large order of lights from a tray onto the scale, while the servant packed them irritably with his hands and replaced the chest plate over them. The prosector nodded to the student, who leaned over the body and began to sew up the Y with thick stitches, like those on a canvas sail.

Holzbauer turned his attention to the head, instructing the servant to take the block out from under the body and place it beneath the neck.

For the first time since Olivier had died, Jacques felt the desolation rise up in him. The prosector took a scalpel to begin the cut behind the left ear, and the annihilation of Olivier was suddenly too much for him to bear. He found himself back in the bedroom of his childhood, back in a broken past, with the mother he did not know, in a dark room with just his childish hope of what life might bring, his boy's bravery and determination, where the only connection to the past he longed for, and to the future to which he would blindly burrow on, lay in the shape of his elder brother: Olivier alone had held the key, and Jacques could feel him now, ten years old, come to his younger brother's bed, healthy and alive, and lying there next to him, shaking with laughter as they listened to the grown-ups downstairs, wrapping his arm round Jacques and holding him against his chest, where Jacques first noticed that special clean, sweet smell of his, so that the recollection of it as they took Olivier to pieces made him suddenly gasp with the appalling grief that came up like a wave in him—death, his own death too and the inevitable loss of all the vain hopes of life—howling and breaking in the darkness.

Thomas helped him from the room and took him upstairs to a bench in a gaslit corridor, the seat where he himself had briefly sat while waiting for Herr Obmann to operate on Fräulein Katharina.

The two men sat side by side in the murky light, as once they had stood gazing from France at the English Channel; now they leaned forward, heads held in their hands in the silent moment of defeat.

"WOULD YOU like to see your brother's brain?" said Franz Bernthaler three days later. "It has been well fixed in formalin and you might find it instructive."

"All right. I always said that I should like to see what it looks like, so I suppose I had better do so."

Jacques followed Franz reluctantly to the cellar. Olivier's brain was in a bucket of fluid on the workbench, from which Franz lifted it and held it beneath the electric light.

"They are always a little smaller than one expects, are they not?" he said. "So much of the skull area is taken up by the jaw, the eye socket and so on. Then the protection given by the skull restricts the brain space. Anyway, do you want to hold it?"

"No."

Looking at the organ, Jacques was thinking of Olivier's astral diagrams and of the stable; but he was also thinking of the little boy who had once healthily been governed by this beige and silent piece of matter, from which had sprung inexplicable games and fancies and laughter.

"Grossly visible," said Franz, "is a degree of cortical atrophy in the frontal and temporal lobes, here and here. I see a slight thinning of the surface brain tissue and a generalized shrinkage."

"Are these not normal postmortem changes?"

"No. And you see here, the sulci are slightly enlarged. The gray matter seems to ripple slightly more than normal because of the depth of the sulci."

"And how do you account for these changes?"

"Rather mechanically," said Franz. "I suspect that we shall find that the ventricles are enlarged and that as they have pushed up and outward, other things have had to make way."

It did not seem enough, somehow, thought Jacques, as Franz took a large knife and made a sagittal cut, down through the center of the two hemispheres. In section, Olivier's brain had the look of a squashed boiled cauliflower, in which the gray matter replicated the shape of the rippled florets, and the white that of the solid inside of the vegetable below. In the heart of the white area was the opening of the ventricle.

"I have the brain of a patient without mental illness for comparison," said Franz. "Even in gross appearance you can see the disparity in size in the openings here."

Jacques nodded. It was true; though he could not see that an increased capacity for the generation of cerebrospinal fluid told him much about the metaphysical enigma of his brother's madness.

"I shall now take some smaller sections to examine beneath the microscope," said Franz. "Would you like to stay and look?"

"No, thank you. Tell me if you find anything unusual."

"Of course."

"And Franz."

"Yes."

"Do you normally incinerate the brains when you have finished with them?"

"Yes."

"Do you think you might arrange with the priest to have it interred with his body in the graveyard?"

"I will ask him."

"Thank you."

Jacques was pleased to be back on the stone flags of the hallway; he felt the absurdity of the countless living functions his own brain performed each second without his even feeling them. You could not properly value such a thing; you could only laugh at it.

IN THE autumn, they began to move to the Wilhelmskogel. None of them gave voice to what they all felt: that Olivier's death had blighted the place; that it had taken the joy from it. At a practical level, it had drawn their attention to how unsafe the situation was for lunatics, and new plans were drawn up to keep those most seriously unstable from having access to the drop. There was no alternative to the move, however; the lease on the Schloss Seeblick could not be extended and the stockholders in the railway company had legally protected expectations of the new venture.

Geissler's transport system worked well, and throughout the summer large numbers of visitors were taken up on the railway and transferred into the cable car for their ride to the top, where they were offered refreshments and directed on various walks. The local newspaper carried letters from one or two people complaining that their fellow-citizens had become lazy and instead of taking this newfangled apparatus should be made to hike to the top of the mountain, but the populace thought otherwise and bought tickets in large numbers.

Jacques could not contemplate the move, in fact could concentrate on very little, tormented as he was by insomnia. He dragged himself through the days, dry-mouthed, dry-eyed, though he knew that his inability to sleep was the result of his mind trying to digest his loss, of the grief and the loneliness that he could not face by day.

When September came, Sonia organized the carriages to start moving furniture, while Thomas went twice weekly to the top of the mountain to oversee the final stage of the building works. The laborers had been discharged, back to Karfreit, and the plumbing, electrical works and decoration were in the hands of a building company from Villach. Hans had proved himself a worthy foreman, but was anxious to return to the schloss to see Daisy.

The only person truly enthusiastic for the relocation was Daniel, who was allowed to celebrate his fifth birthday in October by taking six friends from the village up to the summit to play hide-and-seek in the building site. A place was found for him in the village school near the foot of the mountain, beginning in the New Year, and the thought of traveling to and from school each day in a cable car filled him with delight.

In December, Thomas received a letter from Hannes Regensburger, asking if he could pay a visit. His expedition to Africa had been delayed, he said, but he was more than ever certain that Thomas would benefit from accompanying him; he would not be leaving for another two years, so there would be time to make arrangements at home.

Regensburger was the last visitor to the old Schloss Seeblick, arriving a few days before Christmas. He took dinner with Thomas and Kitty in their apartment in the South Court.

"I am proposing to steal your husband away, Frau Midwinter," he said.

"So I understand. But I shall fight you for his company."

"If I promise to bring him back safely, would that make a difference?"

"Certainly. I do not want him to be eaten by crocodiles."

"I give you my word. We would be traveling a well-beaten path in open country and in cool weather. Some of the German government guesthouses have running water and electric light."

Kitty handed Regensburger a dish of vegetables. "What concerns me more," she said, "is what possible use an English mad-doctor could be to a cartographical expedition. Are you all expecting to go insane?"

Regensburger gave a deep laugh. "No—though in fact it has been known to happen. No. I was impressed by your husband when we met. It is really as simple as that. Of course, it is a good idea to have a doctor in a large party and I am presuming he has not forgotten the elementary skills—cuts and stings and bruises and so forth. I understand that he is also a good photographer, which is not a claim I could make either for myself or for Lukas, my assistant. But we have managed the pictures before and we could do so again."

"So, what is it about Thomas?" said Kitty.

"It is a question of spirit," said Regensburger after a pause in which he drank from his wineglass. "There are one or two archaeological questions on which I have been doing some preliminary work at the university. These concern the dating of fossil remains. While I shall continue to be responsible for the homework, I know that your husband will share my intellectual interest and that he is a keen amateur of Darwin. But it is more even than that. Africa is a large country and it calls for a large response. When one sits by the campfire at night, it is better to be in the company of a man who has risen to the occasion. I feel confident that your husband is such a man."

"And your assistant, Lukas?"

"He is a very good cartographer."

"I see. Well . . . I think I do."

"I have been to see Oscar Baumann twice more and have talked to him about the archaeological sites he found. Although he was not personally interested, he did make maps and keep a good diary, so I think that we should be able to locate one or two of them."

"And how long would you take my husband for?"

"I shall be away for more than a year, perhaps nearer two, but I have worked out a different itinerary for him that would have him safely back to you in three months."

"Do you think he is strong enough for such an undertaking?"

"I believe he is stronger than I am. Look at him. Hardly a gray hair. No excess weight. You see, my dear Frau Midwinter, there is a fine adventuring tradition among British doctors. They have always been mountaineers and explorers. All I ask of your husband is to sit on a mule, take the occasional photograph and keep me company."

"We will think about it," said Thomas. "There is presumably no hurry to decide."

"Indeed not," said Regensburger. "You have at least a year to settle into your new home before I start to look elsewhere for my companion."

AS THE builders neared the end of their task, Sonia inspected the main house on the Wilhelmskogel and marked out which rooms might be used for what. Frau Egger had already visited, somewhat apprehensive of the machinery that whisked her up, and given her approval to an enlarged kitchen, while Jacques and Thomas had chosen their consulting rooms. Neither family would live in the main house, it was decided, which was to be given over entirely to the patients and their welfare. The Rebières and the Midwinters had a small house each, a minute's walk apart, both with a fine view of the valley.

At the age of forty-two, Sonia felt she had it in her to make only one more family home and hoped that this would be the last. She sighed at the prospect of more builders, leaking roofs, upheaval, unsatisfactory finishes; nevertheless, as she walked through her new house, assigned a room to Daniel, selected in her mind the curtains she had seen for it in the draper behind the church in town, it was hard not to admit a small quickening of pleasure, like an old war horse, she thought ruefully, roused one last time by the sound of the trumpet.

XVIII

THE WORLD LOOKED BEAUTIFUL TO DANIEL REBIÈRE. EVERY MORNING his mother came to dress him in front of the fire in his room. He could dress himself, but liked the fuss she made of him, stealing kisses when she buttoned up his woolen jacket, calling him odd names and telling him how much she loved him, squeezing his ribs till they hurt. There was no one but them, and although he never thought as much, he had the joy of sensing that she was quietly obsessed by him.

After porridge, bacon, white rolls and hot chocolate, he was packed off in the cable car with either his mother or Daisy or Hans to accompany him to the school in the village where the railway spur ended. His best friend in the class was a boy called Freddy, and when they had not seen each other for a while, they trembled with excitement. Not wanting to embrace, they hammered one another on the shoulders with their fists. Sometimes Freddy was allowed to come home with Daniel and stay the night in the spare bed in his room, where they lay whispering into the small hours.

Daniel's father always came upstairs to say good night; he read to him and stroked his hair. He taught him French songs and sometimes spoke to him in French, though Daniel resisted it, since speaking German at school and English at home was work enough. His father was always kind to him, never raised his voice, but he was a little frightening.

Daisy was ridiculously kind, even more indulgent than his mother, feeding him chocolates and desserts left over from the patients' dinner.

Hans called him "Little Soldier," though Daniel did not know why, and gave him rides round the top of the mountain on the pony.

Then there were his cousins. He was fascinated that there could be two identical girls. One minute he might be helping Charlotte in her red woolen dress to set out some dolls at the tea table in her nursery—not a task he relished, but stuck at for the sake of looking at her. The next minute he would be pulling Martha, in her green woolen dress, on a wooden cart. But she was essentially Charlotte. There was no difference—and he should know: he had studied them extensively. He discussed the matter tirelessly with his mother. "I think maybe Charlotte is a bit more boyish, Mummy." "Do you, darling? In what way?" He pondered deeply. "Hmm. I don't know," he said mysteriously.

He was one and a half years older than the girls, and understood it was his duty to be kind to them, to encourage them in their childish games. When they reached the age of three in February, they were old enough to play satisfactorily together; so Daniel could sit on the floor, no longer needed, and just indulge himself by watching them, and laugh and laugh inside at this preposterous thing: these pretty girls with blond hair and brown eyes, so snugly dressed, so individual, so unlike any of the girls at school, yet doubled. He loved them each, but liked them especially for being two.

"You are a spoiled little boy, aren't you?" said his mother, when she put him into his pajamas. "All these people fawning on you."

"Who is falling on me?"

"Not falling, you silly boy, fawning. Doting."

The other person he particularly liked was his aunt Kitty. Unlike the other grown-ups, she talked to him rather seriously, as though he were himself an adult; he felt thrilled by her confidence and tried to be worthy of it. He was invited to have a picnic lunch with her on his own one day, and took a sandwich in a box from his own mother's kitchen. Kitty found him a chair in her main room and prepared a picnic for herself; she poured them both some apple juice, then sat down and asked him for his opinion of their new home, listening to him carefully over the top of her reading glasses.

Daniel's brows came close together as he pondered his answer, but he was delayed by his sandwich of butter and cheese, which he was finding irresistible. He didn't really want to talk; he just liked being with Aunt Kitty. He liked looking at her, in the same way that he liked looking at her daughters.

He finished too soon, but Kitty pretended she had also finished and went to fetch some fruit tarts from the kitchen. She played songs to him on a gramophone that her mother had sent from Vienna, the needle thumping and hissing through the brilliant black grooves as it conjured pictures of a band, a ballroom, men and women dancing in smart clothes and a world awaiting him.

He noticed that she was looking sad.

Kitty smiled. "I was just remembering. The songs remind me of when I was sixteen or so. Not an old lady, as I am now."

"But you are not old." Daniel was appalled.

"No," said Kitty. "You are quite right. I am not that old."

"You are pretty."

"And you are a flatterer. Have another tart."

Daniel's room had a sleigh bed and a long view toward the Karawanken and the Carnian Alps, and the white tops of the distant mountains were the last things he saw at night before his mother pulled the curtains. His toys lived in boxes arranged beneath the big window. He liked soldiers, though there was one that had always repelled him: a clockwork drummer with an alarm bell that went off in its head. He tried to interest Charlotte in swapping it for a knitted monkey he had coveted, but she hysterically refused.

Having all his life been surrounded by lunatics, Daniel thought nothing of the oddity of their behavior. Some of them befriended him, as though they sensed in him a fellow-oddball, this only child wandering over the great mountaintop retreat with his wicker basket of toys digging into his arm, his head forever cocked to one side in curiosity: wide-eyed, but not to be taken lightly; quietly spoken, but clearly possessed of will and determination, not someone they would trifle with.

When he was six, he was taught at school about Saint Valentine and, under the mistress's instruction, made a colored card for his love. He drew on it a picture of flowers in a bunch, and inside, again with the teacher's help, wrote: "Dear Mummy, Be My Valentine, Love ?"

He watched intently as Sonia opened it that evening and feigned amazement, delight, then utter bafflement as to the identity of her admirer.

"Have you any idea who it might be, Daniel?"

He pursed his lips and shrugged with his palms turned outward at the bottom of his skinny arms, trying not to smile.

For weeks Sonia kept the card on the mantelpiece in her bedroom; it was the question mark that made her laugh every time she looked at it. When Jacques came back from work, he took to asking her, "How are you, my love? And how is Mr. Question Mark? How is little Herr Fragezeichen?"

As for Sonia, what she felt for the child was beyond words and she did not really care to examine it. When he had saved with his own money to buy her a present, a useless embroidered purse, the pleasure of receiving it was so shot through with a sort of anguish at what it told of Daniel and of his view of her that the pleasure lasted only for an instant, and she experienced the charming gesture as a sort of memento mori. Likewise, when she went to kiss him good night, the last thing before she herself went to bed, she murmured words of utter devotion as she leaned over; as she kissed him and inhaled the smell of him, she felt her whole being shift in her guts and knew that this vertiginous lurch of feeling came about in her because she was really thinking what a short time he would remain a child—the nights could be numbered—and what a short life would be his on earth. In truth, it occurred to her, she was not kissing her child a happy good night, she was thinking of his death.

Seeing this, and feeling shocked by it, Sonia decided she would not be maudlin anymore. Just because these thoughts sprang naturally, from an excess of love, did not mean they were healthy. She would banish them, she decided, and look at the world through his eyes only, because his view was assuredly a happy and a healthy one. Daniel saw delight in everything. His day was love and food and cable cars and Freddy and the bewitchingly comic twins; it was Hans and the pony and Aunt Kitty and the majestic view from his warm bedroom. This was human joy; it was his birthright; and it was Sonia's privilege and duty to share in it, simply, without morbid or excessive underthoughts.

So she looked at the clock to see how soon he would be home from school.

VISITORS TO the Wilhelmskogel were looked after by Hans, who had built and now administered a refuge, to which they were directed from the top of the cable car. It was some distance from the clinic and offered food, drink and a simple washroom. Hans was also able to give advice on the walks available at the summit, of which the most popular was a two-hour ramble back to the foot of the cable incline. Neither Jacques nor Thomas cared much for the inflow of visitors, but the provision of some tourist services had been a condition of the public funding, so they had no choice and offered Hans a share in the visitor profits. The clinic itself was full. The publicity that surrounded the building of the transport system had proved an effective advertisement, and in the following summer Pierre Valade, in the course of an extended visit, drew up plans for a further building, safely walled, far from the edge, but with walkways under wrought-iron decorations.

When the work had started, Thomas told Jacques that since his American venture had paid off so profitably it was time for him now, after twelve years in partnership and seventeen with his shoulder to the wheel of lunacy, to take sabbatical leave. He wrote to Hannes Regensburger to tell him that his business partner and his wife had consented to a three-month absence; and in the summer of the following year he departed.

My Dearest Little Kitty,

This is the most wonderful experience I have had—or perhaps the second most wonderful, because nothing could better my discovery of the secret passage that led me straight to you . . .

However, this is different. The voyage itself was extremely dull and I had run out of books by Suez. It was easy enough to complete the rail journey to Brindisi, where we (Hannes R, his assistant Lukas, and yr husband) took a ship to Piraeus, through the Suez Canal and down the Red Sea to Aden. Hannes is a poor sailor and spent much of the time in his cabin. There was little for me to see except the picturesque Arab dhows sailing back and

forth. From Aden there is a monthly mail service that runs down
to Zanzibar, where we were to meet an Englishman called
Crocker who has "experience of the Interior."

The island of Zanzibar, Hannes told me, was once famous for
its evil smells and I had read Burton on this subject (he called it
"Stinkybar"); but I thought it was beautiful. It was early
morning when we arrived. The sea was deep blue save for the
occasional flash of white sail; and beyond it the continent was
invisible under dark cloud. As we docked, though, and as the
small boats came alongside, the mists began to lift; the sun came
through; and suddenly I could see the dark outline, the
mountains and shapes of Africa. Oh, Kitty, I cannot describe the
thrill it struck to my soul. From here, from somewhere just
beyond those lifting mists, human beings had first walked—and
no one who calls himself human can fail to be moved by his first
sight of our long home.

The small boys on the boats were diving in the water, hoping
we would throw them money; tradesmen tried to sell us skins
and ivory, spices and bananas, calling up from their craft. We
ignored them and made for the beach—at the far end of which
was a sturdy white building with a Union flag: the British
consulate.

Here we were to meet Crocker, the big white hunter who was
to make up our number. The staff of the consulate were thrilled
to have visitors and by noon we had already drunk the King's
health in a variety of gin cocktails. Crocker turned out to be
rather small, with spectacles, but extremely loquacious and
knowledgeable. He talked about Stanley's journey from here to
Ujiji on Lake Tanganyika to find Livingstone—and rather gave
the impression that he had been on it, though he can only have
been about twelve years old at the time.

We stayed two days, then sailed for Tanga. Here the
expedition began in earnest. Hannes and Crocker set about
hiring porters; Crocker assured us we should need ten natives to
each white man, which seemed excessive to me, but I let them
get on with it. The first hired were then set to make packsaddles

for the donkeys and I noticed that most of Crocker's baggage seemed to consist of weapons and ammunition. I have promised to do my share of game shooting, but since I could seldom hit a rabbit at Torrington, I am not too hopeful.

My darling Kitty, I am writing this to you on the evening of July 1. Tomorrow we set off for the Interior. I am sitting in my bedroom in a small hotel in Tanga, all alone, because the others have moved to a campsite out of town, where, once I had run my eye over the native porters (I rejected two—one rickety, one clearly feverish), I was deemed surplus to requirements. The consulate in Zanzibar, <u>and</u> Crocker <u>and</u> the Germans in Tanga <u>all</u> assure us that the journey is safe and straightforward, so you are not to worry about me, my dearest one. For most of the way, we can apparently stop at Government rest houses with clean water and good food.

I must post this letter tomorrow, but I shall write a diary every day, in the form of a letter to you, so you shall have it handed to you on my return. Please kiss the girls good night every day from me. Say to Martha, "Papa loves you"; and to Charlotte, "Dada loves you." The difference may seem nugatory to you, but I assure you it is <u>vital</u>. I embrace you, Kitten, with all my heart. Auf Wiedersehen.

Your ever-loving husband,
Thomas

Kitty—

We set off early, in the cold misty morning. The Government rest houses are a day's march apart and German E. Africa is well provided for in this respect. Our caravan consists of thirty-eight porters, about forty-five donkeys, four mules (for the white men, though I prefer to walk as much as I can), Hannes, Lukas, Crocker and your husband. It is frankly a ridiculous sight, like a gaudy Chaucerian pilgrimage, but with Crocker the only tale-teller. On the first day, we made fourteen miles and could have done more if the packsaddles had not kept slipping.

Crocker told the boys to look lively or he would take them to the government station, about fifteen miles away in Wilhelmstal, where they would receive a good thrashing from a powerful Nubian the Germans keep for the purpose. There was much muttering and rolling eyes, but it seemed to work, as they set to with a will in the morning.

This is a beautiful country and the climate is heavenly. I had imagined equatorial conditions—torturing heat, thirst, humidity—but by day it is warm, growing hot but seldom unpleasant; by night it is cool enough to sleep easily, growing cold later, so that I take a woolen blanket or two to bed. When we pass a native, he stands aside deferentially, imagining, I suppose, that we are his colonial masters—and at least we all do speak German, except Crocker; though fortunately he is fluent in Swahili. Or so he assures us; and he certainly made himself understood over the thrashing business. He is in the trade of buying and selling cattle, and we now have half a dozen emaciated cows tagging along with us. Rinderpest and other diseases have decimated the cattle population, apparently, but a few can still be traded for cloth, trinkets or money and Crocker is certain they will fetch high prices at market.

Everything was perfect until we reached the Wagogo River, bound for the "boma," or government station at Kilimanjaro. Some of the porters did not like the look of the swamp; neither did the donkeys; and neither, to be frank, did I. The donkeys were off-saddled and this was a mistake as we did not all make it through before dark, and some spent a miserable night on the far side waiting for dawn. However, the "boma" was a fine place, with three Germans in charge of about a hundred natives. There was also a very boring Hungarian count, full of stories of his travels through Arabia; I managed to settle him with Crocker and a bottle of whisky and left them to it. It was cold, and I slept like a child in a wooden Bavarian bed.

Our next stop is Arusha, a few days away, still on a
northwesterly line, after which we head due west toward
Ngorongoro. After Arusha, the country, though open, is much
less known and the going will be slower, partly because this is
where the business of cartography will begin in earnest (the
environs of Tanga, Moshi and Arusha already being quite well
surveyed). Mt. Kilimanjaro itself is a lonely beast, awkward,
unattached, not like an Alp, thickly covered in green at its base,
then rising steeply to—I think—about six thousand meters (six
little Wilhelmskogels on top of one another!). Its peaks are snow-
white, which is not at all what one expects to see in Africa; and
above the snow is a kind of golden band of reflected light. It
makes one's heart soar to look on it.

In addition to being the medical officer, I have been
appointed official photographer to the expedition and I have
brought my faithful old Underwood as well as a Kodak. I have to
develop at night, in a makeshift hut-darkroom, without electric
light, and this is hazardous, since you do not know what your
hand is going to alight on. It is not always a chemical bottle; last
night it was a snake.

On our third and final night at Arusha, Hannes was excited
that his work was about to start and Crocker, who had so far shot
little but wildebeest, had the scent of bigger game in his nostrils.
One or two of the natives seemed anxious about going into
territory they knew less well, but Crocker (so he reported) told
them it was just a large plain, so provided they kept their wits about
them, they could not go wrong. I have noticed that he talks to them
as though they were children and he a rather fierce schoolmaster;
when he rebukes them they look at their feet like naughty boys—
but they do not seem to mind, provided they are paid. We give them
pieces of calico, to make clothes, meat from game we have killed
with our rifles and in some cases rupees, though these are of no
use to them outside large towns. It is not much, but the
alternative for them is nothing but hunting with spears.

Then we set off to the west, and the succeeding days have
become a little blurred in my memory:—

I wake in an African sunrise. It is cold. I go outside the tent and see some of the natives sleeping, some tending the fire. The donkeys snort; occasionally, one of them brays loudly, like a creaky old windlass at the end of its rope. The smoke from the little fire rises straight over the windless plain. I hear Hannes snoring in his tent. There are distant volcanoes over the grassland. I feel close to the beginning of life. Here are animals, humans; nothing has changed for millions of years. It is simple, it is harmonious, but it is also magnificent.

I go back into the tent and pull more crimson and purple blankets over me. I feel light—insignificant—yet profoundly happy and at ease. I am woken later by a boy with tea.

We have hard-boiled eggs left over from the last rest station, with bread made from something called "matesi"; cold roasted meat (eland for preference, but we are not fussy; they are all quite good with a little salt). Then we plod off before it grows too warm. After an hour or so Hannes and Lukas stop and set to work with theodolites; they take notes, write down angles, compute distances. Lukas also sketches rapidly and well. They compare their findings with the rudimentary charts that have been made before—often the occasion of hilarity. I am required to take photographs, which I am to number carefully so that they tally with a particular piece of triangulation. It is enjoyable work.

The villages we pass through are generally dirty; the natives have little idea of hygiene, and all the filth runs down an open gutter. George, the chief bearer, told Crocker that when the whole place becomes too disgusting they simply abandon it and move on. The people generally run away at the sight of us. George said they believe our skin color is due to the fact that we come from the coast; they do not think of us as a different race, but as a sort of coastal Negro.

One night we pitch camp above Lake Manyara on a magnificent plateau, giving views over what feels almost like an entire continent. The whole lake was visible, with a dark, forested mountain range beyond it to the north. Clear streams

run at this altitude. We bathe and drink as much as we like. I feel
we should play cricket or football, but, unlike the Indians we
have met, the Africans are not a playful people. They are solemn
and watchful.

They frequently stop by the wayside to leave a stone or a
piece of wood at the foot of a tree or on a rock where others have
done the same; this is a votive offering to some Supreme Being.
These spirits are quite easily propitiated; I have seen them offered
nothing more than a tuft of grass!

We make slow progress because of the stops for
cartography—perhaps ten or twelve miles a day. At night we
build a great fire, pitch the tents and have a feast. We carry
plenty of water, but there is always anxiety about where the next
supply will be. The natives drink recklessly, but Crocker told me
that weak tea is the best thing to drink during the day and
provided me with a bottle. He was right, and one of the boys
makes me one up each morning. We have a case of whisky and I
like to sit on a rock with Hannes and watch the sun go down to
the taste of Scottish peat.

It is a dream, Kitty. Time has stopped and there seems
nothing in existence but this endless plain. I lie down tired to
sleep and I am happy.

For the first time in my life, I feel that all the small insights,
intuitions and flashes of knowledge I have had are beginning to
make sense and to cohere. Those years as a child reading the
Bible, for instance, so that I had most of the prophets by heart;
and then the school years with my head between my fists as I
took in Homer and Hesiod, Thucydides and Herodotus. I think I
am beginning to see what their stories mean. And then my
manhood with the lunatics, when my reading changed to
Darwin, Maudsley, Hughlings Jackson—the great English strain of
thought and medicine. I am starting to see patterns there as well.

I often think of you and the girls, of course, and I wish that
you were here. I also think of the lunatics in my old asylum in
their locked wards. How very very far away they seem, in the
deep darkness of the African night.

Ten days from Arusha, the party began to climb up a steep but well-used track over reddish earth. After two hours, there was a cry from the front, and Thomas and Hannes, who were at the rear, ran up to see what it was. From a small clearing in the vegetation at the side of the track, the porters were looking down into the crater, jabbering excitedly to one another. Thomas could pick out the word "Ngorongoro."

For some minutes they stood in silence, looking down into the immense caldera created by the eruption of a volcano, the remaining outer rim of which formed the steep sides of the crater. The floor was green with pale grasses and patches of darker forests; toward one end was a soda lake that appeared to be steaming in the sunlight.

Thomas saw Hannes fighting his emotions.

"We may be the first Europeans since Baumann to see this sight," he said at last. "And he was the first ever."

It was difficult to know what to say; Thomas had seen nothing like it in his life, but whatever it meant to him, he felt sure it meant more to his friend. He knew that Hannes would be computing distances: thirty kilometers, fifty . . .

"When it was a volcano," Thomas said, "it must—"

"Yes," said Hannes, "it must have been as tall as Kilimanjaro. I am glad I have lived to see this sight, Thomas. If I died tomorrow I should have no grounds for complaint."

Thomas put his arm round Hannes's shoulder. "I shall set an extra guard against roaming buffalo tonight."

Soon after midday, they found a site toward the western end of the crater to pitch camp; Hannes wanted to spend three days at Ngorongoro because its elevation at about 2,500 meters gave him a good vantage point, and Crocker decided to lead an overnight expedition down to the floor of the crater to shoot game.

Thomas felt a little breathless, but presumed it was the altitude. What was so beautiful to him was that the floor of the crater, with its lakes, forests and rivers, with its hillocks and pale green grasses, its mass of intimately cohabiting wildlife, had obviously been that way for thousands of years; yet the rim provided by the remnant of the giant volcano was a reminder of a previous reality that was just as solid. Time in effect was laid bare before them in its almost incalculable length; little, therefore, either human or animal, seemed important because in the length of that perspective nothing amounted to more than a handful of grass.

"Come on, Midwinter, we are going down into the crater to bag some rhino," said Crocker. "I hear they have some splendid whites down there. Damnably dangerous, you know, but we shall survive if we stand our ground."

Reluctantly, Thomas set off with Crocker and about half the party with their donkeys. The porters were given a choice of resting at the top, while Hannes and Lukas did their map work, or of going hunting with Crocker and Thomas. Some were anxious about encountering the Masai, who grazed their cattle on the crater floor, but the extra pay persuaded them.

Thomas took his notebook and camera. He had promised Jacques that he would try to keep a full account of the flora, even though his own interests were much more for the animals and humans. At the previous rest station, they had acquired a Masai guide—essential for interpretation, George told them, and for smoothing the way, as they would in due course have a long march across Masai country to the site of the fossilized footprints that Hannes had been told about by Baumann.

"African teak," Thomas wrote dutifully in his notebook. "Is this the same as euphorbia?" The commonest tree was the shortish, scrubby acacia; many had long trailing creepers hanging off them and thick lichen which were testament to the purity of the air. Their descent was slow, there being no clear paths down to the crater floor, and the donkeys were refractory on the steep incline, stepping awkwardly through the volcanic boulders that lay where they had been thrown out on the rusty soil. Thomas felt the heat through his tropical clothes, and his hands were scratched as he pushed through aspilia and morning glory. How was he ever going to remember all these plants for Jacques? He took as many photographs as he could, but did not want to lag behind the group.

On the crater floor, the hunting was easy. Zebra roamed in trusting herds that gave an easy shot to his and Crocker's rifles; wildebeest were profuse, and advertised their presence with odd nasal grunts, like old clubmen snoozing after lunch. Eventually, Crocker called a halt to the slaughter and said that from now on they would go only after rhino; such of the remaining kill as they could carry up they would eat or trade for grain; the rest they would leave for the Masai. The bearers pitched camp in a small forest whose broken trees showed evidence of recent ele-phant passage; when they had all eaten as much meat as they could, they lay down to rest.

Thomas fell asleep and dreamed of Dr. Faverill's Matilda and her pet gnu. He was awoken by a commotion in the small camp, where bearers were running back and forth and shouting. Half a dozen had just arrived back from the grassland where there had been some frightening incident; George was among those absent, so Thomas had no way of knowing what had happened until an hour later, when Crocker returned with a satisfied expression, flung himself down in the shade of a tree and demanded water.

"White rhino," he said. "I stalked him for a half an hour up wind. He was a huge beast. I hit him in the chest, but it didn't stop him. Con-founded animal charged me. I could feel the whole crater shaking. Natives all ran away, shrieking, of course, leaving me on my own. I man-aged to step to one side at the last minute and got him through the head before he could gore me. He fell to his knees and rolled over. Fine animal. But your expedition was very nearly one man down."

"What will you do with the carcass?"

"Leave it for the Masai. And the vultures. And all the rest of them. I took its horns with my trusty little saw. They should pay for my expedition."

When they arrived back at the main camp on the crater rim the next evening, Thomas told Hannes the story of Crocker's rhinoceros, but he was not as impressed as Thomas had expected.

"You do know, my dear Thomas, that the beast is almost blind? A half-step to one side when it charges is enough to disorientate it com-pletely, and while it is looking round for you, like a shortsighted gov-erness looking for her thimble, you have time to amble up and shoot it through the head."

"I see."

"Which is more than you can say for the poor rhino. Anyway, Lukas and I are well ahead with our maps, so tomorrow we leave for the site of the footprints. We now have four Masai among the guides. It is apparently two days' journey, so I suggest we take half a dozen other men. Then, when we reassemble here, we can push on with a full complement toward the Serengeti. You take two Masai and the Wanderobo guides and head north toward the railway—and back to your madhouse."

Kitty:—

We rose soon after dawn so that we could make good progress before the heat of the day. Hannes and I took a dozen of the best porters, including George, half a dozen donkeys and two mules. We had plenty of water from the streams near the Crater, guns and ammunition, medical supplies and—most important—two Masai, one of whom went with Baumann ten years ago.

By the time the sun was high, we were up on a plateau, still heading west, and we had our first sight of giraffe gliding over the deep green ground, like great tall-masted ships in the production of whose forward motion little effort is visible. They are extreme examples of Mr. Darwin's theories of natural selection—"adapted" to the point of *grotesquerie*—yet they do have a sort of elegance, and such beauty in that long-lashed eye that, were you so inclined, you might yet imagine a Creator.

There was rain later in the day, but we made our objective, and well was it worth the long's day travel. The plain on which we had been walking ended suddenly. At our feet was an enormous cleft in the earth, as though part of the plateau had slipped and fallen. The obvious result of this collapsed valley is that many layers of earth and rock are revealed, each belonging to a different geological period; between them, they constitute a mine—almost literally—of information waiting to be excavated.

Hannes was very excited by the "rift valley," by the sparkling blue lake within and the mountains rising on the far shores to form the Serengeti plateau. It is the landscape of dream, of something indescribably ancient; you sense the sound of the first human footfall, of a fish pulled from that lake by the first being who learned to bait a hook. Even the natives, who have lived their lives hereabouts, seemed not to know quite what to say. They smiled a little and shifted from foot to foot; they looked at us questioningly, as though we might explain it all to them. We looked back into their eyes, equally children, all of us, in the fading summer light, in the great mystery of our existence.

I do not think, dearest Kitty, that I have explained to you what a capital fellow Regensburger is. He is, as I suspected from the first, in pain for much of the time (from arthritis), but he makes no complaint. Occasionally he asks if I can help, and I administer such limited medicines as I have. He is a man of science, who is capable of looking the discoveries of the last century in the eye without flinching; yet there is no triumphalism in his manner. He does not exult in the absence of a Creator; I think he regrets it, but he does what he can to lead a life of dignity notwithstanding. The natives all respect him and he has no need of beating or bullying, which is what they expect from the white man.

"All I seek to do," he told me, "is to understand, as best I can, what is in the world—and to pass my understanding on, entire and without compromise, to those who follow. If I am reduced to mere mapping, so be it."

We rose early, as ever, and with a feeling of great excitement. Hannes was pacing up and down the camp, drinking tea, urging the bearers to saddle up quickly.

It was a cool morning, and we made good progress. There were no roads, no tracks, not even any paths, but the Masai guide led us from the front with calmness and certainty. It was often easy to orientate ourselves from the disposition of the old volcanoes, but then we might find ourselves in a declivity in the plain, and I soon lost all sense of direction. We crossed numerous cracked and rock-hard riverbeds, and the going became more difficult. At first there were numerous cattle tracks, but these soon died out. I do not know if disease had killed the cattle or if even the Masai themselves never penetrated this far into the endless plain.

By noon, it was very hot and some of the porters were fractious, demanding rest and more water, but George, taking instructions from the Masai guide, pacified them. We did stop briefly in some shade, ate some meat and bananas, which had gone brown and soft, then pressed on. I had some of the weak tea which has served me so well.

Hannes was determined to match the nimble Masai stride for stride, though I know how much his joints were aching. I walked with them, disdaining the mule, which was anyway uncomfortable. George walked beside me. The four of us left our dusty footprints on the plain for just a moment till they were turned over by the donkeys and the bearers. To walk with three such men made me feel alive in a strangely elated way.

It was late afternoon, we were exhausted, and I had long since lost all sense of direction or of time. My darling Kitty, we were in a wilderness. . . . We had reached the end of the world.

As we came over a low grass ridge, the Masai pointed to a spot in the dale a hundred yards or so away. He instructed the natives to rest under George's supervision and gestured to me and Hannes to descend with him to the place.

What did we find? Among the short brown grasses was a gray layer that looked almost powdery, but was quite hard. It was a wide, flat expanse, covered with patches of gray soil and tufts of yellow and white grasses. In it we could see numerous fossilized imprints, both plant and animal. By far the most notable of these was a trail of what appeared at first sight to be human footprints. The Masai pointed to the volcano in the east, indicating the probable source of the ash in which the feet had left their mark, then withdrew and allowed Hannes and me to get down on our knees and inspect our find.

It took a day of patient toil: stripping off the soil, sweeping loose material gently from the surface with soft brushes, marking out the area with squares of string. I set up my camera on a tripod to record the resulting "map" of our find.

"This is Baumann's trail," said Hannes eventually. "It is exactly as he described it to me. These creatures were walking

through the volcanic dust after an eruption. It was probably
softened by rain, and that is why the footprints sank in so clearly.
The sodium carbonate in the ash then formed a cement with the
rain. Layers of further ash concealed them. Then, over millions
of years, the covering was eroded by wind and rain and a section
of this little journey was laid bare to our modern eyes."

"I see."

"Now you tell me, Doctor," said Hannes, his voice a little
shaky, "are these the footprints of human beings?"

I inspected the trail. There appeared to have been two, or
maybe three creatures—human, humanoid or "proto-human,"
whatever one might wish to call them. I will call them "people,"
because although they may not yet have been *Homo sapiens*,
their feet were—in all respects that I could see—human. The big
toe was in line with the rest of the foot, not at an angle like an
ape's. The foot itself was clearly arched—a uniquely human
feature. Everything in my instincts and my heart was telling me
that this was not only a human trail, but that of a family:
mother, father, child. I was feeling so overpowered by my
emotions that I decided I must be scientific and talk to Hannes of
anatomy. I took out a measuring tape.

"The medial margin here has a short pronounced convex
shape which reflects the size and shape of the
metatarsophalangeal joint. The toes have gripped the ash for
support and have driven back against the front of the ball of the
foot. The ridge they made—here—has retained the shape and
contours of the anterior margin of the ball of the foot. The toes
have human alignment with respect to relative length. The big
toe is roughly twice the mass of the next, which is typically
human."

We walked carefully along the length of the trail, keeping to
the side. There were some puzzling elements. For instance, the
smallest set of prints, presumably the child's, was irregular in its
pacing. A small-hoofed animal had crossed the track, its prints
impinging on those of the child. Hannes discovered the imprint
of a leaf, which he was easily able to show me was that of a

thornbush, it being identical to one that he plucked from a bush
about ten paces away. So while the fauna had evolved, the
vegetation had not changed in this incalculable time. Beneath
his magnifying glass he discovered something else. He handed
me the glass, and his eyes were shining.

"Look," he said.

I knelt down and looked very closely. It was a raindrop.

"Tell me more about the creatures who left these prints," he
said.

I struggled to remember my anatomy lessons in "Meaters,"
the awful dissecting shed in Cambridge. Had there not been a
ratio of footprint to height? I recalled a figure of 15 percent, by
which calculation I reckoned, after some measuring, that the
smallest creature was forty-six inches tall, and the largest maybe
five feet nine inches—exactly the same height as Hannes himself.

I carried on reporting what I found, like a pathologist
dictating to a student. "The big toe, as I remarked, is
nondivergent. The medial ball pad is under the first and second
metatarsophalangeal articulations with the lateral part of the
ball pad formed by the third, fourth and fifth joints. The lateral
pad gives stability and the medial pad gives propulsion. This is
characteristically human. The rear edge of the heel strikes first
and takes the full body weight, which is then shifted through the
heel center to the side of the arch, then to the ball and across to
the big toe. You can see the round impression where the big toe
pad was planted and pushed the ash back against the front edge
of the ball. The center of gravity is indistinguishable from that of
a human and I believe that the foot structure is morphologically
and skeletally human in all but name."

"So?" said Hannes, and his eyes scraped my face.

"These people walked like you and me, Hannes."

Yet the other fossils in the exposed layer, according to
Hannes, long predated *Homo sapiens;* they were comparable to
those found in Europe, in Spain and Italy, that had been
confidently assigned by geologists at home to the Pleistocene
epoch. Hannes was rather proud of his homework.

"We must take samples back with us," he said. "Not only of the rock, but of these animal prints, which I believe to come from some extinct creature whose dates may be known. Then we must cut out one of the human prints as well."

I was surprised at the casual way he spoke, with no sense of desecration of the site, but I suppose that is how science progresses. Alfred Russel Wallace did not merely observe the orangutans in the jungles of Borneo; he shot them and brought home the bodies to be studied properly.

I persuaded Hannes to let me finish my examination first, and we began by inspecting the rhythm and pacing of the trail. As I explained, there were probably three beings, whom we might call man, woman and child, though of course one could not be sure. The child's track was clear and separate; it remained at a fixed distance from that of the smaller adult, presumably the female. Yet each trail had inconsistencies. After an hour or so, I felt that I had found a solution to the puzzle they posed.

I believed that the man, or male "humanoid," walked first through the hot ash. The smaller adult, presumably the female, had deliberately placed her feet in his—perhaps to protect herself from the heat, though her placement was not always accurate. Most of the adult footprints were thus blurred or overlapping, though there were about a dozen quite distinct.

The most puzzling thing about the trail of small prints—the child's, as we assumed—was that the paces were of varied lengths. For a long time I puzzled over why there should be this irregularity; and then it came to me: the child was skipping.

Perhaps the child's skips helped him keep in step; they coincided with a heavier press from the "mother's" trail where she had slowed or waited. I thought of Sonia and Daniel crossing the main courtyard. I felt the holy bond of mother and child, and as I knelt beneath the African sun, I had the terrifying feeling of the gulf of past time opening up in front of me. I was almost scared to look back at what was there beneath my eyes.

Hannes had gone off to inspect the surrounding earth and rock to see what further it could tell him of the age of our find. I called him back and explained to him my theory, and he nodded, agreeing that it fitted the shape of the trail.

"But why, Thomas, is the child at such a fixed lateral distance from the one we are calling the mother?"

"I have thought about that too, long and hard, Hannes. I have looked at the track from both ends and tried to imagine the circumstances in which these beings walked, in the aftermath of eruption, in rain, among animals. And it seems to me that the only conclusion one can draw from the evidence here is that he was holding her hand."

Hannes blinked and looked away toward the distant mountains. I felt that he probably did not wish to speak for fear of betraying some unscientific feeling.

When we had thoroughly photographed the footprints, Hannes withdrew, with some rock samples he had taken, to join the rest of the party, leaving me alone. It was by now about five o'clock, and the sun had already started to weaken.

I sat down on the ground and lowered my head into my hands. A crested bird flew away from the end of the trail. From the corner of my eye I could see our bearers waiting patiently on the ridge. I heard what must have been an elephant snorting and—very faintly—the sound of a far distant Masai cowbell. There was a gentle breeze from the east that was coming through the whistling acacias and thorn-bushes.

Oh, Katharina. I was sitting at the end of the trail, as though waiting for the three to come and meet me. I picked a tiny white flower with a purple center which withered almost at once in my hand.

I thought of you, my love, and I thought of our children and what we have become. I thought of the demented wretches in the stinking wards of my old asylum. I remembered poor Olivier and his torments. I thought, too, of the sleepy voice that all my youth would speak to me . . . then slipped away. I thought of the terrible briefness of all our breathing lives.

And in the cool of the evening sun, I lay down and I placed my hand in the child's full and perfect footprint. And it was warm. Not hot—because the sun was fading fast, but it was warm with the stored heat of the day: it was, in fact, blood-heat.

And I am not ashamed to tell you that I lowered my face into the earth and howled.

THAT NIGHT, they pitched camp a short way from the site of the footprints. After they had eaten and the porters had gone to rest, Thomas and Hannes sat together over the remains of the fire, drinking whisky from their tin cups.

"Are you satisfied?" said Thomas.

"Yes. I feel it was worth the long trek. I doubt whether we have shed light on the origins of mankind, but we have perhaps gained a better sense of ourselves."

"Yes," said Thomas. "By seeing who went before. By offering our respects."

"Indeed—though it would be a fine thing if we could deduce something of more scientific value. I fear we lack as yet the tools to date such fossils accurately, but my suspicion is that one day these prints will show that man's predecessor walked upright earlier than had been thought."

"Yes," said Thomas, "which would be of interest, though surely it would not change our scheme of things. It would be a detail."

"On the contrary," said Hannes. "Most people believe that the size of our brain preceded our ability to walk upright. Evidence to the contrary would be radical."

"Well," said Thomas, "my strong feeling from the anatomy of these beings is that they were early men—*Homo*, if not yet *Homo sapiens*. I suppose you remember that lovely verbal picture in Darwin when he compares living things to a tree. The green and budding twigs represent the existing species, but of all the original buds, only two or three, grown into great boughs, have survived, and from them depend the groups and families. But the tree shows the history of all the twigs that tried to overcome the others in the fight for life, and failed."

"I do not quite follow you, Doctor."

"I mean that there were several kinds of man or 'proto-human' along the way to *Homo sapiens*—to us, the green buds. They lived side by side. They may have interbred, but probably, alas, we killed the others—the Neanderthals, the Java men. There was not a single, smooth development from the moment we split from the line of the apes; there were many kinds of pre-human species before *Homo sapiens* triumphed."

"And his triumph, according to Mr. Darwin, came at the moment when he walked upright and freed his hands for making tools and weapons."

"That was Darwin's suggestion, though he had no way of knowing if it was right. I expect that was a stage or step, though I do not really see why it should involve the creation of an actual species."

"Pass the whisky, Thomas. Your good health."

"And yours. Listen. My own understanding of Mr. Darwin's books is that a separate species can develop quite rapidly. It will then live alongside its predecessors, as the fossils show us. Eventually, the earlier species fails because it is less well adapted than the new in the competition for resources—or it is simply killed by the newcomer. But in my view the mutation that created *Homo sapiens* is less likely to have been in the gaining of an upright walk than in the chemistry of the brain. This is where Alfred Russel Wallace could not agree with Darwin's theory of blind variation—because mankind was in his brain and consciousness far more perfect than, from the point of view of survival, he had any need to be. Wallace therefore believed that there was a purpose, a sense of direction, involved—that *Homo sapiens* was the model of perfectibility which some outside force was, at various points in his otherwise blind evolution, continuing to shape. He believed that we were not an ape but an apex!"

"Yes," said Hannes, "but if we can show that today we are still in the process of evolving, then that argument must fail."

"Indeed. Though it is hard to prove these things in the short space of a man's life. . . . But, Hannes, what today has made me more than ever sure of, is that the mutation in man that made him human was in his brain. I cannot prove it, but I feel it. And I have always thought that whatever the change was, it involved a connected vulnerability. Psychosis is a human condition, as human as the straight toe or the arched foot we saw in the volcanic dust. No other species has it. Dogs do not hear voices. Cows do not imagine themselves pursued."

Hannes said nothing for a little, but watched Thomas sympatheti-
cally. In the African night, there was the sound of a large animal groaning, many miles away, its voice carried by the faint breeze over the long
empty plain.

"What you must understand, Hannes, is that one day, one very specific day, the first human was born, the first being with the entire collection of inherited material with which we have been dealing ever since."

"There was an Adam."

"Indeed there was. And I think he must have been a very lonely,
frightened creature. Somewhere not far from here, somewhere perhaps
just beyond those volcanoes, all the pieces came together, for the very
first time, in the brain of one being. And I see him hiding among reeds by
water, I see him walking alone, apart from the group in which he lives.
Perhaps he is shunned, outcast or put away."

Hannes got up and put another piece of wood on the fire.

"So," said Thomas, "what really differentiates you and me from our
volcanic little family of three?"

"Intelligence, I suppose," said Hannes.

"Not if you measure it by brain size, because the Neanderthals
appear to have had larger brains than we do. No, it is an awareness of
ourselves. You know you are a man. The creature who left those tracks
did not know he was a 'humanoid,' or whatever he was—anymore than
that mule over there knows he is a mule. It was the acquisition of the
ability to introspect that made a leap in our species, and that faculty
depended on our development of language."

"So this capacity of self-awareness was not in itself the result of a
mutation?"

"No, I think not. It was a cultural development that was passed on
and learned afresh in each generation. It depended on our having language. It may well be that that was the defining change in our species:
the ability to talk. Let me try to explain. One day, long ago, perhaps there
was a proto-human in whose brain, somewhere near Broca's or Wernicke's area, a mutation caused an extra neural connection that made
his grunts more like words attached to things. And we can see what
advantages that would give him, both through the number of descendants his superior ability would enable him to leave and through positive

sexual selection by his mates. He—if it was a man—must have been attractively different; and his or her heirs like Casanovas or Cleopatras, honeypots to the other sex. Quite soon the faculty would spread—though soon in this instance means thousands of years, I suppose. And with language came control. You give orders. People hear your voice. A society that lived by heard instruction could form larger groups. The success of all other mammals was restricted by their need to keep their group sizes small enough for eye or sound contact with the leader."

"But without writing," Hannes said, "the same restrictions must have applied to your early men. They must have been forever shouting."

"Not necessarily," said Thomas. "Once you have given someone a name, you can carry the idea of them in your head, even when they are not there. That was a huge advance in language. Then the evidence of the Bible and of Homer and of such archaeological remains as we have, is that these men—not yet conscious as you or I are conscious—were able to hear the voices of their leaders even when they were out of earshot. A report by my countryman Henry Sidgwick a few years ago found that nearly eight percent of people today hear voices. My belief is that the true figure is much higher than that because people today are ashamed to admit it, and that in early man the hearing of voices was almost universal. In fact, it is the only conceivable way in which early farming societies, in which herdsmen, fishermen and planters were dispatched long distances, can have held themselves together. I think we are all agreed that the major leap in civilization came when mankind stopped hunting and feeding ad hoc, and organized itself into farming groups. But how could men without consciousness—a modern sense of time, and cause and other people—have done this? Picture your shepherd far away in the hills with no sense that he is a man, no idea of time in which he can visualize himself and his situation. . . . How does he know he must keep tending his sheep? Why does he not forget what he is meant to do—as an ape would forget? Because under the anxiety of solitude, under the pressure of fear, he releases chemicals in the brain that cause not sweating palms, or racing heart, though perhaps those as well—but the voiced instructions of his king. He hallucinates a voice that tells him what to do. He uses the uniquely human gift of language to his own advantage. No other creature could do this."

"It sounds unlikely," said Hannes. "Such a pathological condition, so widespread."

"But it was not pathological. It caused no suffering; on the contrary, it was helpful and conferred huge advantages. But the difficulty with sound is that it is hard to shut off. You cannot block your inner ear in the way that you can close your eyes or hold your nose. It was therefore a delicate mechanism, which, like all the nervous reflexes, depends on a fine balance of glands and chemicals in the endocrine system and the brain. It would have been unstable, prone to break down; it might not come when you needed it, or it might come too much—so that you heard voices even when you were not under pressure of survival to do so. The prophet Amos was clearly afflicted by a barrage of voices. And it could be self-contradictory. Think of poor Abraham. A voice tells him to kill his son. Then, at the last minute, the voice contradicts itself. But it was overwhelmingly useful. And evolution, working blind, produces improbabilities—think of the peacock's tail, the camel's hump, the giraffe's neck. The point is, Hannes, that between our forefather in the volcanic ash and the first fully conscious human man we know of—say someone at the time of Aristotle—there must have been stages of development."

"Well, I suppose so," said Hannes. "But why must there have been this particular stage, the voice-hearing one?"

"It is the only one supported by literature. In the *Iliad*, the characters take instruction from the voices of the gods. Achilles is not a conscious man. He is a human at an intermediate stage. Achilles did not know he was a Greek. In all that poem there are no words of introspection; there is nothing to suggest that its heroes understand the idea of decision or free will. I am no classical scholar, Hannes, but I do recall that by the time of the *Odyssey* there is the idea of deceit—you might say that the poem is really a story *about* disguise and trickery, and that at once implies a modern consciousness, like ours, because you cannot falsify unless you can tell stories, picture yourself as a being and develop different versions of that story. Odysseus even tricks Athene. Unthinkable for Achilles, sulking in his tent, hoping to hallucinate the instructive voice."

"Yes, but what has caused the change?" Hannes did not sound convinced.

"Writing. Early forms of writing, like cuneiform, are pictures of things. Many depict instructions from the god-kings; when an early man looked at the marks, he may even have heard the voice. Later, you have letters that represent not the thing itself—the pot, the wheat—but the sounds of language. What an astonishing transformation that is! From that moment, the voice of the gods is not inescapable, in your inner ear, but controllable and portable. You are free—but you are also bereft. Then follows the terrible period of migrations, and famines and disasters. It is the story of a people crying in the wilderness—and what they are crying for is their lost gods. They lift up their eyes to the hills, from where their help once came. From page after page of the Old Testament comes this terrible, heartrending cry. It is the lamentation of a people who have been literally abandoned by their gods."

Hannes laughed richly, his rosy face illuminated by the fire. "I want to tell you something that I have often thought on my travels, Thomas. You know that I am an amateur of archaeology. I have read a great deal about ancient civilizations. I have visited Mesopotamia, Egypt and the Holy Land. I have a particular interest in burial sites. One of the things that has been drawn to my attention is the way that kings, pharaohs and so on were so often buried upright. I had assumed it was because the people did not understand that death was a termination. They thought it was just the breakdown of whatever faculty had proved fatal. So they continued to feed the dead king or god. They housed him in a temple, which they built tall so that workers in the distant fields could see its high point. Now from what you have been telling me, I suppose these buildings could also have inspired the workers to hear the king's voice."

"I don't see why not," said Thomas. "Ziggurats, pyramids, temples . . . these could all have been aids to hallucination for the worker toiling in silence."

"One still sees the pattern in Europe," said Hannes. "Even in Carinthia, the barley sugar spire with the onion dome—home of the absent god, from which the streets and houses radiate."

"Yes," said Thomas, "but then, you see, with writing, men acquired new ways of thinking—independent of these voices. The size of the cities made it hard for the people to be controlled. The great wars and migrations—the Dorian invasions and so forth—drove people to scatter, and further reduced the impact of the voices. And then, as they traveled, they met other peoples. Tentatively, they began to exchange goods, to trade. Perhaps what they saw in other people made them think about themselves. By observing that the stranger had some unpredictable mind area inside him they may have inferred that they too had such a space."

Hannes laughed again. "So a man may first have deduced the existence of his own consciousness by imagining it in another!"

"I think so."

"And has our story reached the time of the Bible yet?"

"Yes. I think one sure sign that the instructive voices have gone is when people start to cast lots, draw entrails, throw dice to try to guess the will of the absent gods. And since the notion of chance does not exist for these preconscious people, then the short straw or the chicken's twisted gizzard can *only* have divine meaning."

"But in the Old Testament, their god still often seems to be with them."

"Sometimes. The prophets are the chosen ones, because they can still hear the voice, but increasingly it is hard for them to do. Moses and Jeremiah are driven mad by the inconsistency of their instructions, and then it all begins to fade. The old prophet Eli latches on to the infant Samuel, who still has the gift. And poor Elijah, who sits through whirlwind and fire until at last he is able to hallucinate the still small voice of calm."

"You sound so sad. My dear Thomas."

"It is more than sad. There is the whole of humanity crying for what it has lost. The gods who tended us are gone; they are absent and offended. No longer is there that happy, day-to-day communication— like a farmer with his steward giving matter-of-fact instructions about tilling and harvesting. Now the gods are angry and absent; now we must get down on our knees and worship them. Now we must beg them to come back. When the gods were there, no one ever thought of 'worshipping' them; we just did as we were told by a friend."

"And Jesus?" said Hannes. "Was he a prophet too?"

"I suppose he could hear voices. Perhaps he and St. Paul were the last prophets to do so, but he was more conscious in our sense than any man before him. What he did was take the preconscious religion of Judaism and refashion it in a way that fitted it for modern human beings."

"So the Bible is not so sad in the end?"

"Yes, it the saddest book in the world. We are asked to believe that God has played an infantile trick on us: he has made himself unobservable, as an eternal test of 'faith.' What I read, though, is the story of a species cursed by gifts and delusions that it cannot understand. I read of exile, abandonment and the terrible grief of beings who have lost something real—not of a people being put to a childish test, but of those who have lost their guide and parent, friend and only governing instructor and are left to wander in the silent darkness for all eternity. Imagine. And that is why all religion is about absence. Because once, the gods *were* there. And that is why all poetry and music strike us with this awful longing for what once was ours—because it begins in regions of the brain where once the gods made themselves heard."

Hannes scratched his cheek. "What about our man in the ash this afternoon? He heard no voices, he had no gods, I presume."

"No. Because he had no language. My guess is that the order of events was this: first, a mutation that enabled the brain to develop language. Then the hearing of voices. Then, with writing, the loss of those voices and the slow development of modern self-awareness, the unique human quality."

"But surely that must mean that for many thousands of years you had beings who were by Darwin's definitions *Homo sapiens* yet who lacked consciousness as we know it."

"Oh yes," said Thomas, "I think so. Most of the things that humans do can be done without any consciousness at all. When you play the piano, your ten fingers perform intricate separate movements according to signals relayed to them by your nervous system, reacting to signs read from the sheet music and relayed via the optic nerve to your brain. And in all that complexity, there is no awareness at all. Indeed, it might be fatal for your playing if there were. Your conscious mind—insofar as it is active—is thinking of the vision of beauty the music produces, a waterfall perhaps, or whether it will impress the attractive young woman in the audience, or what is for dinner. You can be skillful to the highest human degree without being conscious at all."

"Are you saying our volcanic walker could have played the piano?"

"I am saying that we could have existed as humans and acted efficiently for a geological eternity without the faculty of consciousness— without knowing what we were. Think of the Garden of Eden. What happens, quite simply, is that Adam and Eve acquire self-awareness: 'Eureka,' they cry, as they are endowed with this gift—and with all that it entails, beginning, alas, with shame. I am suggesting that this is something that truly happened—but not until very recently in our history. Wallace was right in talking of these important leaps in human evolution, even if he was wrong to ascribe them to the sudden interference of the Creator's hand."

Thomas stood up. "What I believe consciousness to be," he said, "is the ability to tell a story to ourselves. To begin with, it enables us to see time—not as it really is, because we cannot do that—but in representation, at least, as a straight line. You cannot conceive of time in any other way—but the straight line is only a useful metaphor, or representation, not the reality. But once you have a grasp of time—even if it is essentially a misrepresentation—you can start to plan and visualize a past and future, and therefore causality. Likewise, consciousness enables us to make conjectures in which someone called 'I' can be seen in a hypothetical situation or a story; and from that flows the ability to make judgments, plans, decisions. In short, consciousness takes the vastness of the physical world, whose coordinates of time or space we cannot really grasp, and gives us a model, a working version—a simplified, toy version, if you prefer—in which we can more usefully and successfully operate."

"That is a fine story, Thomas. Though it seems to me that in some ways we might have been better off without this human consciousness."

Thomas smiled. "It is a problem, certainly. We are much more developed than we need to be. I think consciousness is like an extra sense— the equivalent of sight, perhaps. It gives us a way of reading the world. Sight uses light waves, hearing uses sound waves, consciousness uses language to help us construct a reduced model of the universe, in which we can picture ourselves as actors in a simplified version of time. But just as our eye does not give us all the light waves, so our consciousness gives only a sample of reality. It is our sixth sense and it is unique to humans, but it is no more complete or transcendent than a dog's sense of smell or a hawk's eyesight: it is good of its kind, but it is limited; it is just a sense. I would no more base a philosophical reading of reality on the evidence of my consciousness than on the evidence of a hound's nose. Furthermore, because it is the only 'sense' that deals in ideas, it is the only one to give us an idea of its restricted powers; it is consciousness itself that makes us aware of its own limitations. In reality, there are probably more than the three dimensions that our optic nerve can perceive, but only seeing three, we do not fret over what more is there. With consciousness, it is otherwise. We are frustrated by the limits of our capacity to answer what we think of as the big or important questions. But we should not be. The failure is not in the answers, but in the questions. We can only wonder at the tiny mysteries thrown up by this blindly evolved faculty. But these are not real mysteries; these have as much and as little to do with reality as the questions that remain unanswered by the limited range of the hawk's eye."

Hannes smiled. "And one day we will know the answers."

"Or perhaps one day," said Thomas, "we may know the questions."

"How?"

"When another faculty, as great as consciousness, has also evolved in us. This is how the great mysteries are solved, not by answers, but because the changes in the way we apprehend the world make the questions irrelevant."

"So there will be a seventh sense?"

"Indeed. Though it, too, will of course be limited."

"But it will be a step."

"Steps are all there can be, Hannes. That is how life evolves."

"Good night, dear doctor. I shall think about what you have told me. I shall think, too, about those footprints in the ash."

Hannes heaved himself up stiffly from the ground and straightened his knees; he laid his hand on Thomas's shoulder then moved off awkwardly.

Thomas went and lay down in his tent and listened to the night. He thought of the creature who had walked through the dust with his female and their child; he pictured his face, bewildered by the natural disasters all about him. He thought of his own girls asleep at home, Charlotte with the triangle of tiny moles beneath her left ear that he

kissed each night; Martha with the small birthmark on her forearm, like
the passport stamp from a previous world; he thought of modern men
and politics, Vienna, motor cars, the clamor of literature and science. He
trained his ear back again to the darkness, to the depth of it. What he
felt, when his mind had slowed sufficiently for him to find the words, was
the grandeur of human insignificance.

IN THE morning, Hannes set about cutting a footprint to take home. A
trench was dug around the end of the trail and its side wall consolidated
with burlap soaked in plaster; then the chosen print was cut round with
a trenching tool while pieces of wood were inserted on either side in further plaster mixture. Hannes covered the print surface itself with newspaper, then with burlap and more plaster; when all had set firm, he
knocked smartly at the base with a pick, and a six-inch-deep slab came
free, with the carrying timbers firmly embedded in it.

The return to the crater was accomplished without difficulty, and the
following day, when the entire party was reassembled, they prepared to
separate for the last time: Regensburger, Lukas and the bulk of the
porters were to go west across the Serengeti, along the line of the projected railway to Speke Gulf at the foot of Lake Victoria, while Thomas
was to head north toward Simba and take the train to the coast, before
embarking at Tanga for the return passage. At the last minute, Crocker,
initially bound for the interior, decided that he would accompany
Thomas, as he wanted to make a fast return on the cattle he had
acquired. Thomas was daunted at the thought of days, perhaps weeks,
of Crocker's conversation, but a little pleased, as well, to have the other
man's guns and confidence.

"You are a good man. You are a brave man and I thank you for coming with me," said Hannes, embracing Thomas at the crater. "I shall be
back within a year and I expect a proper welcome.".

"You shall have it, I promise you."

Thomas gave Hannes his Kodak camera and all the plates and films
connected to the map work; the Underwood and the rest of photographs
he packed to take with him back to Carinthia. He was also entrusted
with the excavated footprint in its careful wrappings.

With a smaller retinue and without the need to stop for cartography, Thomas and Crocker were able to make fast progress. The first night, they stopped at a Masai village where the headman welcomed them with warm milk from one of his cows, mixed with blood taken from the beast's artery. He was fond of his cattle, and was familiar with them, squeezing the testes of a bull, and rubbing his hand in the cleft beneath a cow's tail. In return for cloth and trinkets, he offered them fresh water and a place to sleep, though before the deal was done, he produced a document for them to read.

It was a twenty-year-old copy of *Frankfurter Zeitung*, much folded and yellowed by use. Thomas ran his eyes down its columns and opened its pages with the air of someone examining a legal document. At length, he nodded sagely, indicated all was well, refolded the paper and handed it back to his host, who appeared well satisfied. With the interpretative help of a Masai guide, the chief told them of a great famine in the Serengeti, of many of his people wandering the plains in desperate search of food; his was among the last well-stocked villages, he said, and further north it would be difficult. He also told them stories of his many wives and of his great prowess as a lover when he had been a young man. When he discovered that Thomas was a doctor, he took him to see one of his younger children, a woman in her twenties, who had been deaf since birth.

"He wants to know if you will cure her," said Crocker.

"Please tell him I cannot."

"He says, 'Why not? Surely if you are a doctor you can make her well?'"

"Please explain to him that medicine is not like that."

The chief looked bemused, and before they went to bed Thomas gave him an old toy of Daniel's he had brought for such a moment: it was a clockwork soldier with a drum on which he played a slow roll with stiff arms; at the end of it, a surprisingly loud bell rang inside his head. Thomas showed the chief how to wind it up, and the old man did so with rapturous enjoyment, then invited all the village in to see the toy. Each time the bell rang, they burst into delighted applause. The drummer boy was rewound time and time again, and each bell ring appeared to take the audience entirely by surprise.

Thomas and Crocker left them to it, and were escorted to a grass-roofed hut by one of the headman's wives. All night long, the bell rang at one-minute intervals, followed by sounds of delighted amazement. In the morning, the villagers were full of joy, but the white men were haggard with fatigue. "Fucking drummer boy," muttered Crocker, as he loaded his donkey.

The next day they traveled twenty miles, which took them to the edge of Wanderobo territory. A calculation was done of the likely distances and times, though since the natives could count no higher than seven, Crocker found this hard to follow. He was becoming an increasingly difficult companion, Thomas noticed: disease was causing his collection of cattle to dwindle by the day and he was desperate to bring them to a town where they could be sold; they had also lost two donkeys, which had died after being bitten in the anus by the ndorobo fly, and by the end of the third day morale among the bearers had noticeably fallen.

They passed through the foothills of some mountains and into thickly wooded country; the temperature began to rise and the supply of fresh water became precarious. Thomas tried to make the bearers ration what they drank, but with little success, as they guzzled it like children; and for the first time since stepping into Africa, he began to feel afraid.

XIX

KITTY READ THOMAS'S LETTER FROM TANGA WITH A WIDENING smile. A cautious, chastened Thomas, grieving for the loss of Olivier and doubtful about his new home, was no use to anyone, as she had told him with the candor that always marked their conversations. He had to be impulsive—reckless at times—because it was only in those moments, even when he failed or overreached himself, that he had his moments of inspiration. There was always blood and disappointment, but without them there was no gain; that was the nature of the man, and from his letter it seemed, to Kitty's relief and despite the misgivings she had had about his safety, that the African adventure was going to give him back his self-belief. She read parts of it to Charlotte and Martha, then showed it to Daisy, who, in her opinion, understood Thomas as well as anyone.

Flattered by Kitty's confidence, Daisy pored over the letter and was thrilled by the talk of porters, guns, gin cocktails, wild animals and the "Interior." She worried a good deal for the doctor's safety, but since her admiration of him was almost limitless, she knew he would triumph in the end.

Daisy had undergone a course in the administration of electrical treatments. One of Jacques's early heroes, Moritz Benedikt, had been an enthusiast and Jacques had retained some faith in the treatment for that reason; Thomas viewed it as old-fashioned but harmless. His lukewarm attitude did nothing to diminish Daisy's pride in the "electrical room" that had been handed over to her in the back of the main building. At the Schloss Seeblick they had had a galvanic machine that produced a powerful and continuous current, but they had given it to the public hospital in favor of two new faradic machines, which mildly stimulated all parts of the nervous system and whose electrodes did not have to be placed directly on a nerve or motor point. One was a machine which had been popular through the sanatoria of Europe for more than a decade, but Daisy's treasure was a mighty American continuous-coil apparatus, which bore the words "Dr. Jerome Kidder. Inventor. New York" on a smart brass plate.

The patient, stripped to the waist and barefooted, sat in a chair with her feet on a copper pedal. After Daisy had switched on the machine and made sure the current was at the correct setting, she attached her own right hand to a damp sponge electrode wired to the front of the machine, and took in her left hand the brass ball electrode and applied it to the patient's bare back. With the circuit complete, the patient reported a tingling sensation, not unpleasant, which could be intensified by an increase in amperage.

Most of them were happy to chat with their therapist as the treatment continued, though Daisy was careful not to instigate the conversations, seeing her role as the listener and questioner only. Silence was equally acceptable to her because she was delighted simply to have such modern equipment entrusted to her.

Mary was intrigued by Daisy's new responsibility and acted as a guinea pig when she was learning how to use the Kidder machine.

"It's like having lots of little spiders running all over you," she said. "It's nice, really."

Her own simple art of massage was not subject to changes of fashion and, after more than twelve years, Mary's skill was such that many new patients asked for her by name. She took on a full-time and a part-time assistant as the numbers grew.

In the summer, Mary was the first to be told that Daisy and Hans were to marry. She was to keep it a secret, however, until Thomas returned because Daisy wanted him to be the first to know. She also planned to ask him to give her away in church.

Kitty:—

We left the last government rest house two days ago. They told us there that there was cattle disease in all the towns and Crocker was frantic to take another path through the wilds that would avoid contact with infection. Our guide said he could manage this, but I thought it unwise, since he is one of those men who always agree to what you ask rather than risk displeasing you.

Our water supply is already uncomfortably low, and in this wild uninhabited country we are entirely dependent on the memory of two guides. Three of our original porters deserted the party at the rest house, and if any more go it will be quite impossible to drive Crocker's eighty head of cattle through the thick bush.

Yesterday afternoon, I went on a small scouting mission to climb a hill with one of the guides. I found pandemonium on my return. One of the porters had been shot through the chest, and was dying. Crocker told me that the fellow had been threatening to desert and take half a dozen others with him. He had meant to shoot above his head to frighten him, but had somehow misfired and caught him in the chest. I did what I could for the poor man with morphia and bandages, but it was not much, and he died soon after nightfall. I then had to sit up all night talking to the men, begging them to stay. I offered them the last of the rupees and paid them double wages of cloth; I also gave them some of the trinkets we had been reserving—a small mirror, a harmonica, one of Martha's old rag dolls—and by dawn had just about quelled the rebellion. The natives not engaged in negotiation with me howled all night for the departed. Crocker slept throughout.

The next day was taken up with the obsequies, with the dead man wound in a piece of cloth and carried slung on a pole, as though in a hammock. It was noisy and prolonged; it cost us a whole day and a great deal of water.

The following day we pressed on through dense scrub and growing heat. We made about twelve miles, but spirits are low.

Two days later:—

In the afternoon, we came to a feverish river, stagnant and hung about with old creepers hanging from dead trees. Mud-colored crocodiles basked by its edge, and at dusk I saw a giraffe come down to drink, slowly spreading out its legs one by one, like a tent being lowered at each corner, so that its neck could be brought down low enough to sip the brown water, as it looked round all the time for predators. This scene may not have changed for several million years. In any normal world, all these peculiar animals would long ago have been extinct—these freaks of nature. But here in Africa, time stopped and nothing changed.

There was a rope-and-wood bridge across the river, which Crocker urged his cattle over, before any of us could question him. He is quite fanatical about these wretched animals (which now number fewer than sixty). In my view, the bridge was not well made in the first place and was very much weakened by the passage of the cattle; I undertook the crossing with extreme trepidation. Sure enough, I found some of the wooden planks broken or missing; but mercifully I made it over, and so did our guide. The donkeys were not all so fortunate.

Two of them fell twenty feet into the river, and within seconds one saw little but churning hooves and bulging eyes as the brown water turned red to the sound of their terrified cries. The indolent crocodiles moved with appalling haste. I am very sorry to say that we lost one of the porters in the same way.

Loaded onto one of the donkeys were several calabashes of water and onto the other were all my photographic plates, films and my old Underwood—everything photographic not related to the map-making, including every single record of the trail of footprints. I am afraid that the footprint itself, safely wrapped and preserved as it was, went down too, and will remain on that prehistoric riverbed for the remainder of time.

It was growing dark, and we were forced to pitch camp not far from this evil place. A hippopotamus sniffed round my tent during the night, but Crocker assured me that the hippo is a harmless vegetarian and would only attack if I got into the river. I said that in the circumstances that was an unlikely move on my part. I was beginning to hate this man.

The next day Thomas found he had contracted a fever. There were so many flies and sources of infection that it was surprising only that he had been well for so long. He wanted to lie in the shade and do nothing. He had never known lassitude like it; it was as though he had smoked ten pipes of opium. However, the mood of the party was for moving on as fast as possible, so as soon as the funeral rites of the dead porter had been observed (more quickly this time, since the body could not be retrieved from the river), he was helped up onto a mule and strapped into the saddle.

The heat intensified in the closed scrub through which they were traveling. Toward noon, they saw a group of Masai, who had wandered many miles from the Serengeti in search of food; they were dying off each day, and a flock of vultures followed them, barely waiting for the corpse to stop moving. Thomas found it difficult to stay upright in the saddle, and was tormented by a desire to drink, but knew that he could not take more than his share of water.

"You are fortunate to be on the move," said Crocker. "There is nothing worse for fever than to be stuck in one place."

They were kept awake that night by lions roaring. Crocker sat up by the fire with his rifle to keep them off his cattle, four more of which had perished by day.

The next evening, just after they had pitched camp, the guide came to see Crocker and Thomas. He began to weep as he explained why he had come. Crocker struck him in the face, and he wept more bitterly.

"What is going on?" said Thomas.

"He says he is lost."

"But I thought he knew the way."

"He said he has made the journey before, but only once. When he was a child."

Thomas estimated that the man was now about fifty. "But we are in a plain," he said. "Once we get out of this bush, then surely we will see landmarks by which we can navigate. Anyway, we have a compass."

"He said there is only one path through the wilderness, and he cannot remember it."

Thomas did some calculations, though his fever rendered them approximate. The distance from the crater to the railway—the length of the entire journey—was not more than two hundred miles. In the early days they had made twenty miles a day and they had left the crater roughly eighteen days ago. Even if their average had fallen to only ten miles a day—quite possible with the deaths and the river crossing—they must be almost there. He was able to see the peak of Mount Kilimanjaro, and took a bearing northeast from it.

He turned to Crocker. "Tell the guide that we will travel by night when our thirst will be less tormenting. Meanwhile, we are going to kill one of your cows and drink its blood."

"You can't do that, you—"

"Yes, we can. If you had not shot one of the natives we would be a day closer to our destination. And the damage your wretched cattle did to that bridge has cost us another death and another day." He did not mention the photographs or the footprint.

"That is quite untrue. Without me, you—"

"From now on, you will do as I tell you." In a fever of irritation, Thomas ripped the spectacles from Crocker's face, threw them to the ground and stamped on them.

"Look what you have—"

"Listen to me, Crocker. I did not come to this beautiful country to die like a pathetic animal. I came here to discover and to understand—then take my knowledge home to my family and my colleagues. Tell the natives we will strike camp in half an hour and walk till dawn."

Crocker moved off, grumbling, and unsure where to place his feet. Some of the bearers came up to Thomas, grinning, to congratulate him; one offered him a handful of grass as a mark of his respect.

They had three calabashes of water left between twelve humans and all the animals. Early the next morning, they saw a large number of rhino tracks, which the guide thought might lead to water. They found a

place where once there might have been a pool, but the rhino had rolled
in it and reduced it to mud. The men got down and licked the puddles, or
picked up handfuls of mud and squeezed the moisture onto their
tongues.

By afternoon they had no water left at all, and one of the natives
looked close to death. Thomas bathed his forehead with the damp mud
and offered him some whisky, which he sucked at greedily; he knew the
alcohol would dehydrate him further, but the short-term relief improved
the man's morale. They found some shade and rested until the evening,
but Thomas felt they were now all so depleted that it was better to continue, however slowly, than to stay still.

"Crocker, tell them that the white man's compass said that we are
very nearly at the railway line and that they must not despair. Have you
got that? No despair."

They were prevented from moving off in the cool of the evening by
the death of one of the Masai bearers. His body was taken, in accor-
dance with tribal custom, to an open place where it was left for the hye-
nas and the vultures; but the other porters, from the Wanderobo and
Wachagga tribes, would not continue until a respectful time had passed.

Now that his fever had left him, Thomas felt elated and quite clear in
his thinking. There was no longer any reason to be angry with Crocker;
in fact, he felt sorry for a man who, for all his bombast, was a trader of
pathetically small ambition, trying to scratch a living in a hard place.

Late that night, over the remains of the fire, he apologized to him. "I
was not myself. I was feverish, and I am sorry for what I did. I think I was
also upset by the death of the bearer."

"When you have spent as long as I have in the dark continent,
Doctor, you will learn that the loss of a native life is not a cause for great
concern, even to the family. Look what they have done with the corpse—
thrown it to the jackals."

"I meant what I said, though, about not wanting to die. I have a scientific purpose. When I think of the dead warrior over there, behind the
trees, I am thinking of his mind, and what it looks like. Have you ever
seen a human brain?"

"No."

"But I sense that you are curious."

"I am a little tired. To put it mildly."

"I see no disrespect in a postmortem," said Thomas. "His tribe has finished with him. It is us or the vultures."

"No disrespect, perhaps," said Crocker, "but what would be the point?"

"I am here to learn and to make notes. That is the curse of scientific curiosity. It never leaves you. But there is an aesthetic pleasure also. The brain is a beautiful organ."

"Do you suppose the Masai brain is different from ours?"

"On the contrary, everything I have learned and everything I believe is predicated on its being identical, because we are one species. However, I cannot deny that I am curious to see. Indulge me, Crocker. We may die tomorrow. I should like to think that my last act on earth was an effort to understand or educate. I have humored you and your cows for long enough. Just keep me company for half an hour."

"I don't know where you find the strength." Crocker looked doubtful, but as though he felt obliged to do what was asked of him.

"The fever has left me light-headed," said Thomas. "I feel oddly vigorous. Bring that little saw you had in the crater."

Thomas took two torches from the fire, handed one to Crocker and led him away from the camp, across a clearing and over to the edge of the plain, where they had left the body of the Masai porter. It was certainly an eccentric venture, but in the African night, thought Thomas, the normal conventions did not apply. A vulture flew away as they approached the dead man, its huge wings battering the darkness.

"Not too bad," said Thomas, kneeling over the body. "They have had his nose and one eye, but what remains will be adequate for our purposes. Hold the torch. Pass me your hunting knife."

Thomas propped the corpse's head up on the side of a small mound in the grass so that it looked as though it was on a stiff pillow. He made an incision with Crocker's knife behind the left ear, cut down to the skull, then ran the knife up over the crown of the head, through the black shaved hair, down to the other ear.

"Sit on his chest," he said. "Keep him steady."

As Crocker did what he was told, Thomas pulled the front flap of the scalp forward and down over the man's face, grunting with exertion; the rear flap, which he pulled backward, down over the nape of the neck, came away more easily. The top of the skull was fully exposed; the warrior looked halfway between life and death.

"Now hold the torch steady and pass me the saw. Place your hand on his skull. Think of Yorick. Does that name mean anything to you? This is a good saw."

"I carry a whetstone."

"The trick is to cut right through the bone of the skull but not to damage the soft tissue of the brain beneath. I would prefer a stronger light. We take a line through the equator of the skull, roughly through the center of the forehead. Hold him steady now."

The saw grated through the bone, which made a sound like hard wood yielding, though Thomas could feel when he had cut deep enough. It was tougher work than he remembered, and he felt the drops of sweat running off his face and splashing onto the exposed whiteness of the bone beneath. He hoped to find . . . He could not say exactly what this man's brain would tell him that the others he had seen had not; but in some way he hoped to see, in flesh, a vindication of the theory he had outlined to Hannes.

"When I have completed the round," he gasped, "you can pull the top off. It is like pulling apart the two halves of a coconut. There, I have completed the circle. I may have damaged the brain a little, but the bone is fully cut through. Now lift off the top. Go on."

As Thomas held up the flaming torch, Crocker leaned forward and took the top of the skull in both hands.

"Just lift it. Go on."

"It's no good. It won't come off."

"Of course it will. Go on. Try again. Pull harder."

As Crocker placed his knee on the man's shoulder and pulled again, they heard the first sound of suction being released. A long hissing noise gathered into a plop that sounded like a horse's hoof on a hollow cobble; and at that moment the top half of the skull came away in Crocker's hands. He fell back on his haunches, clasping the almost-empty calvarium in his palms.

Thomas looked inside it. "Good," he said. "You have the meninges. The brain is now ready to be lifted out."

He straightened up the dead warrior and took Crocker's hunting knife. The brain was exposed and vulnerable; it had two small cuts from the saw, but in other respects was so flawlessly intact that it was almost as though its last thoughts might still be lingering.

"Now all I have to do is cut the spinal cord. I am going to leave as much brain stem as I can. I think it will be instructive to you. There. I have cut through the entire nervous system of this man. Millions of years to evolve, a moment to sever. Now I need to cut through these little bits—hold the light up, yes, that's better. . . . These are called dural reflections. And that is all there is to it. It is now ready to be lifted free. I am going to take it out, and then I shall instruct you on the greatest organ in existence."

Sliding his fingers between the edges of the gray matter and the bone of the lower skull, Thomas was able to lift the brain out whole, intact, with a stub of brain stem attached.

"Would you mind holding it for me? Hold it very carefully. It is soft and you might damage it. It feels like a rather firm blancmange, doesn't it? Normally we would fix it in formalin before examining it, to make it more robust and easy to cut."

Crocker's cupped hands held the dripping brain at arm's length. The torchlight flickered up from the dry grassland.

"So that is it. In your hands. All human life, its mystery, its thoughts. There is nothing more than what you hold, Mr. Crocker. That is what you are, that is what I am. This is a moment to be humble and to know yourself. Know yourself. That is what the Oracle commanded. And this, my dear Crocker, is the self that you must know."

"Yes, but it's rather dark." Crocker had adopted a casual manner, as though he had decided not to be impressed.

"This place here is called Broca's area." Thomas gestured with the tip of the knife. "If I were to damage it, the man could not speak. A little further back and lower down is Wernicke's area, also responsible to some extent for speech. And the curious thing is that there appear to be no equivalents of them on this, the right-hand side. Does that strike you as odd?"

"No."

"Well, look at it. What is the first thing you notice about the shape?"

"It is in two halves."

"Exactly. And do the halves look different or similar?"

"Similar. They look symmetrical."

"The very word. You are a better student than I expected. And if I told you that each part of the brain had a corresponding part on the other side, you would not be surprised?"

"No."

"And so it does, at least in mass and appearance. Only one part is not replicated—the pineal gland—but that is another matter. But for the rest, symmetry is the rule. And yet, and yet . . ."

"Yet what? When can I put this bloody thing down?"

"And yet," said Thomas, "there is no symmetry of function. This left half forms words and deals with information, it talks to us and organizes our intellects. And this half, the right side," he said, touching the temporal lobe with the tip of the knife, "is more brutish, yet sees larger pictures, feelings, meanings, poetry and who knows what else. Now, do you think that apes are arranged like that?"

"Very similar, I would guess."

"Have you ever seen a left-handed chimpanzee?"

"Not lately, Doctor."

"But this is the core of our lesson, Crocker. The ability to use the different halves of the brain for different functions may well be what enables humans to be superior. So my colleague Franz Bernthaler has convinced me, at any rate."

Blood and fluid were running from the brain stem down Crocker's upheld arms, mixing with the hairs on his wrists, going down to the rolled sleeve of his shirt. "Something else must strike you," said Thomas. "If you wanted to create a brain, is this what you would make? The cerebral cortex—this upper bit, the beautiful indentations of gyrus and sulcus, the huge intellectual power—yes, perhaps you would fashion that. But not this stuff. See here. These bits. The lower brain. The cerebellum. And in here, the limbic system. Remnants of our past, from when we walked on all fours or crawled in slime, yet still—after all these millions of years—faithfully reproduced each time according to the instructions that our bodies pass to one another when we mate."

He took the knife and poked it up beneath the middle of the brain.

"This is the limbic area," he said. "This is what we had as mammals. Here are your appetites, your base emotions, mammal urges—perhaps deep memories lie here as well. Down here is the brain stem itself, which probably developed when we were something more like fish, and does what you would need to lead a reptile life—it regulates your heartbeat and the pressure of your blood. And here, the cerebellum. Let me cut a section. Now. What does that remind you of? It is like the most beautiful fern, worthy of Kew Gardens. They call it the arbor vitae, the tree of life, and once it was the best that we had for a brain. What do you think of that?"

"It is certainly an intricate pattern. I can see what you mean."

"Thank you. But what do you think of the whole arrangement? All these different bits of our past still here? I mean, we don't still have tails from our monkey past, or gills, do we, from our days as fish? The truth is that for all the beauty of the cerebellum, the brain as a whole is a bit of a mess. If you were to design a man, you would not start with this. To put it more scientifically, it is an aggregate of chance and extremely bizarre mutations."

"What?"

"It is as peculiar as a giraffe. If you wanted to make an intelligent creature you would not design this. It is like a rift valley. You can see the strata of all the long eras of geological time that preceded *Homo sapiens*. The *Homo* bit is just the top—the cortex, the gray matter. And as to the *sapiens* part—the tiny thing that makes us human—you cannot see that at all. It consists in the invisible."

"What do you mean?"

"What made the species was the ability of this hemisphere to perform differently from this one. It is the asymmetry of function, and when you do not have it, or you have it insufficiently developed, you may be mad. Or to be more precise, you get functions working simultaneously from different times in our evolutionary history."

Thomas sank the tip of the knife into the upper cortex. "Do you remember what this bit was called?"

"Something German."

"Wernicke's area. Before the brain skewed, allowing us to develop into *Homo sapiens*, perhaps it had its symmetrical equivalent over here.

Perhaps this is where early men generated the sound of voices that passed through here, the anterior commissure, which is like a basement passage—a safe conduct of primitive emotion."

"I am losing you, Doctor. And I can't see without my glasses."

"The lesson is nearly over. Turn the brain upside down now. Hold it as far away as you can. I am going to cut it in half. Now, if I hold the torch you should be able to see the corpus callosum, this white band here that separates the hemispheres, but also joins them. It is through this intricate connection that they communicate. The work of this is not just to facilitate communication, but to edit it. Imagine a million, million signals each second firing through this meat."

"Do you mind? I am fed up with holding this thing."

Crocker handed the brain to Thomas and set off over the dusty ground until he came to the edge of the camp, where he paused and looked back. Thomas was silhouetted by the light of the torches, holding his brain, still talking in the endless African night.

Some of the words were audible to Crocker as he stepped carefully over a sleeping bearer. ". . . like a brand-new locomotive, coupled to ancient rolling stock and running on prehistoric track . . ."

When Crocker lay down to sleep, he could still hear snatches of what Thomas was saying. "Problems of compatibility. You would surely expect breakdown. . . . Unable to deal with the improper message, processes it not as a thought but as a voice . . . Connections for so doing lie deep, disused, but not quite extinct—dormant, ever ready to be reactivated . . ."

An hour or so later, when he had finally explained things to his own satisfaction, Thomas knelt down over the dead warrior and pushed the part-dissected brain back into the base of his skull.

Back at the camp, he lay down beneath a tree, took one sip of tea from his bottle and fell into a profound sleep.

Out on the plain, a jackal came up to the unburied corpse and, nosing round, detached the calvarium, exposing the manhandled cortex in the skull. Later, vultures descended and fed on the partly dissected brain, rising up into the night with bloodied beaks, carrying the dead man's memories away.

———————

THE FOLLOWING DAY, Thomas awoke feeling refreshed. He drank what remained of his tea, with a little whisky, while he urged the men to move off in what he still believed to be the right direction. The sun seemed to grow hotter as they plodded on. The animals, who had been denied water longest, suffered most, and several of Crocker's cows perished before night. The natives grumbled and made rebellious noises, but, as Thomas explained to them, it was their fault that they had drunk down their supplies too quickly and their only remaining hope was to keep going.

He found his own thoughts return again and again to Torrington, to the bedroom of his childhood with all the Greek and Latin texts ranged along the shelf below the window, with the Bible and the prayer book underneath. He thought of Sonia coming in and sitting on the side of his bed and how he told her stories of the deeds of Hector and Ajax and King Priam of Troy, having always for some reason wanted the Trojans to be successful in their defense of the city. He pictured the cedars overhanging the damp lawn and thought of the jugs of lemonade that the maids set out on the terrace. What was the name of that young maid who had been so taken by Jacques? His dry lips moved into a half smile, but it was painful, because it split the skin. His hair was long at the back of his head, hanging over his drenched shirt, and he could feel that his beard, unshaved since Tanga, had grown again, though this time he knew it must be gray.

The girl put little bits of ice in the lemonade. She used to go to the ice-house where a block was delivered in the spring and chip some pieces off for use in the house. Why had he so often disdained the drink? Just half a glass, just some moisture from it on a handkerchief with which to wet his lips . . . Or better still, to go to the river where they had gone that day on the horses, to lower his head beneath the surface of the stream and gulp. His tongue was like a piece of wood; it was like two tongues in his head. And the horse . . . Achilles. Did Achilles know he was a horse?

Or the fountain at the schloss. He could step over the stone rim and curl himself around the spout, allow the drops to splash down on his face, while Kitty stood beside him, naked on the grass, carrying stone pitchers of water on her head from the colonnade, then bending over him and pouring.

For three days they walked on without water until the evening, when even Thomas could take no more, and they fell down, ready to die, in the shade of some acacia trees. It grew dark. One of the hardiest of the Africans still had the wit to make a fire; most of them were prone and motionless. Crocker was muttering something as he lay with his mouth open. Thomas listened carefully until he was satisfied he had heard correctly: Crocker was praying for death.

Thomas was deeply asleep when he found himself being shaken by a terrified native, the man's wide eyes white against his dark skin. Thomas looked up. It was soon after dawn.

"Elephants," said Crocker at the man's shoulder. "He says there is the biggest herd of elephants he has ever heard in his life."

Thomas walked with both men to the top of the hill. It had been dark when they arrived the night before, and they had been too tired to explore.

When he looked down from the peak now, he could see that at its foot, less than a hundred yards distant, was a railway. The sound ascribed to the herd of elephants was in fact coming from a steam locomotive about a mile up the track. Thomas ran down to the rails and waved his arms. He took off his shirt and waved that too. Eventually, he could hear the driver start to apply the brakes and he sent the native back to bring the others down as fast as possible.

The driver, who was Indian and spoke English, agreed to hold the train while the bedraggled party climbed aboard. Thomas had a large bundle of rupees which he thrust into the man's hand. It took time to bring all the enfeebled members of the expedition down the slope, none more reluctantly than Crocker's cattle, which now numbered only eighteen specimens of hide and jutting bone. One or two passengers on the train had supplies of water that they shared with the most needy; half an hour later, they stopped at a small station, where there was tea.

KITTY RECEIVED a cable from the High Commission in Nairobi. "Dr. Thos. Midwinter boarded German steamer *Zanzibar* bound for Marseille, yesterday, September 18. In good health, to confirm arrival Europe shortly." She ran to find the girls, to share the news with them, and then to Sonia, who was sitting at the kitchen table, drawing pictures with Daniel.

"I never had the smallest doubt that he would come home safely," said Sonia.

"Neither did I," said Kitty, and both burst out laughing at their lies.

"We shall have to kill the fatted calf," said Sonia. "What is his favorite dinner?"

"Something cooked by you," said Kitty. "Not by me or by Frau Egger. Steak and kidney pudding. Or rib of beef. Oysters. Strawberry tart."

"We are too late for strawberries," said Sonia. "But we will manage something. You must help me. I am so happy for you, Kitty. And for myself."

"I know. It is not easy being married, is it?"

"No," said Sonia. "They need so much attention and encouragement—and indulgence."

Embarrassed for a moment, the two women stood opposite one another, Sonia with her brown hair flashed with gray, small pouches of flesh forming on her jaw and with deep lines running from the corners of her eyes; Kitty still with her athletic figure, but a little thinner than before, and prone to coughing.

"But I would not have it any other way," said Kitty. "I mean, one has to let them take chances because that is their nature."

"I suppose so," said Sonia. "But I don't imagine that all husbands are like that."

"I am quite sure of it. And I shall bear that in mind in my next life. Meanwhile, I shall go and find Daisy. She will be beside herself."

"Don't tire yourself, Kitty."

"What do you mean?"

"You look flushed."

"I am exhilarated, Sonia, that is all. Goodbye, Daniel. I like your picture. Is it a lion?"

Only as she ran across the mountaintop to the main house, only when the worry had been lifted, did Kitty see how anxious she had been. She would not let him go away again on one of these foolish adventures; from now on she would bind him to her.

AT TANGA, Thomas bought some new clothes, and on board ship he visited the barber and tried to fatten himself up. By the time he boarded the train in Marseille, he looked respectable again: trimmed, shaved and only a little underweight. He appeared to have no aftereffect from the fever, though what he was finding difficult was to digest the experience of Africa: to see how the thoughts he had had there might be incorporated into his work at home. There were moments as the ship puffed slowly up the coast and he looked back at the previous two months that it seemed to him he had taken leave of his senses. He was anxious to see Hannes again to discover what he remembered of his long speech by the campfire. Although he despised Crocker, who had cost them their most precious scientific evidence, he had undoubtedly bullied him in the end and he wondered if he should send a note of acknowledgment of that fact to the poste restante in Arusha. Then he thought of the bearer Crocker had carelessly shot and of how he had slept peacefully all night afterward, and he decided that a letter could wait; presumably Crocker would not be able to read it, in any event, until he had replaced his glasses. In his cabin, Thomas took out the pages on which he had written his narrative for Kitty and divided them in two. Those covering the days up to his departure from Hannes at the crater, he folded neatly and replaced in the lid of his case; those dealing with later events, he stuffed in a large envelope. He put in a bar of ship's carbolic soap for ballast, went up on deck and threw them over the stern into the Red Sea.

In Vienna, Thomas spent the night in his honeymoon hotel in an effort to reacclimatize himself and reconnect with the life he had left behind. What he had to do was somehow to find a synthesis—or at the very least a common thread that ran through the various areas of his clinical experience and his personal speculation. He knew the dangers of trying to present, as Jacques had done eleven years earlier, an all-encompassing theory based on the clinical examination of a single doubtful disease.

If he himself were to begin with another difficult condition—dementia praecox, something whose definition was still not universally accepted—and use his experience of treating it to bring in ideas of evolution, heredity, neuropsychology, literature and archaeology, then force them into some sort of unified theory of why madness was the defining human disease . . . how exactly would that be more scientific, more respectable

and less of a desperate grab for glory than Jacques's "psychophysical resolution"?

As he sat on the train the next day, he had an idea. He would return
to his old asylum in England, walk through the wards and talk to Faverill.
He would see whether the mass of lunatics looked any different to him
now. He would consult his old employer, talk things through with him
and measure himself against the young man who had first set out into
the difficult country of madness.

In the meantime, he would enjoy his home and his life. He had barely
allowed himself to look forward to the pleasure of his return until he
wired ahead from Vienna; but as the branch line left the local station
and the Wilhelmskogel came into view, he thought of Kitty in his arms,
of Charlotte and Martha running out to meet him, of Hans bringing old
wines up from the cellar, of Sonia's reproving smile and, perhaps, since
one never knew, of Pierre Valade on an unscheduled visit.

When the cable car lipped out at last over the summit, he clambered
out, straightened himself up, stiff from all the traveling, and walked to
the green front door of his house. He dropped his bags in the hall and
called out Kitty's name.

A door banged, there were running footsteps in the corridor and he
was submerged beneath his family. When the exclamations and
embraces had subsided, when the gifts had been handed round and tea
had been taken, Kitty said, "So, after you and Hannes separated at this
crater place, how did you find your way back to the railway?"

"We had a few adventures on the way."

"What, Papa? What happened?"

He looked at the three female faces gazing eagerly at him. "Nothing
really," he said. "It all went according to plan."

ONE NIGHT in the spring, Sonia and Jacques went to a concert in town.
An amateur orchestra gave a program of work by Beethoven, Mahler
and Brahms in order to raise money for an orphanage. Sonia settled happily in her seat, always pleased to be in a place of public entertainment.
Jacques slipped his watch from his waistcoat and calculated when they
would be home; if it ran late, they would have to spend the night in a

hotel because they would be unable to get back to the top of the Wil-helmskogel.

As the pianist was working his way through the Emperor Concerto, Jacques ran his eye along the musicians in the pit, over which their raised seats gave them a clear view. They were not the usual city orchestra, but competent amateurs, women as well as men, smartly dressed and diligent in the service of their charity. Of the three violins, one was a dark-haired woman in a black velvet dress, young, tensed, her face a little averted from Jacques as she turned the page on her music stand. Although he could see only a quarter of her profile, there was something familiar about her that made him start. She turned a little, to catch the eye of the first violin, at whom she nodded and smiled, as though perhaps remarking that they had completed a difficult passage. As she did so, Jacques saw enough of her face to be certain it was Roya Mikhailova.

His response was one of despair. He did not want her to be living in this town. When he had thought to himself how strange this reaction was, he experienced a more normal sequence of thoughts: surprise, curiosity, a frisson of guilt at the memory of her kiss.

He could not drag his eyes from her for the remainder of the program. She was engrossed in her playing and was clearly accomplished at what she did; at least, he heard no discordant strings, only a harmonious unison, so she must be at least as adept as the others. Yet while she concentrated, she was at the same time detached. When the violins rested, she laid down her bow and smiled at one or two of the other players; he saw her mouth a message to the cellist and put her hand across her lips to stifle a laugh. Yet as she turned the pages and saw where her entrance was marked, she resumed an attitude of obedience, raised the violin and settled it beneath her chin, flexed the bow and, at the instruction of the conductor, returned to her work, her naked shoulders, arms and hands moving with submissive concentration. For an hour, Jacques watched, his gaze never leaving her as she moved between engagement and detachment, entirely sufficient to herself. He felt a surge of infantile jealousy when she bowed meekly to the conductor's bidding or opened her eyes wide to a colleague in a silent pleasantry.

Afterward, there was a reception in an upstairs room of the concert hall where the chairman of the governors of the orphanage thanked his guests and urged them to make further donations. Waiters circulated with champagne and Jacques tried to edge Sonia toward the door so they could catch the last train back. She was engaged in conversation with the pianist, however, and he could not interrupt them. He felt his sleeve being lightly tugged. He breathed in deeply before he turned and found himself looking into a pair of deep, violet-colored eyes.

"Doctor . . . Rebière, is it not?"

"Yes."

"Do you remember me? We—"

"Yes, I remember very well. Roya Mikhailova." Belatedly, he took her hand. "Why . . . er, what brings you to Carinthia?"

"My husband."

"Your husband?"

Roya laughed. "You sound so surprised. Marriage is quite a common institution, dear doctor. Conventional, you might even say."

"Yes, I know. Is he here tonight?" He was not concentrating on what he was saying because he was looking at the color of her skin, noting that it was still unmarked. How young must she have been when first he met her—seven, eight years ago, perhaps.

". . . his political work. And his family was originally from Carinthia, so it all fell into place quite conveniently."

"His what? Political work?"

"Yes. Here he is. Let me introduce you. My husband, Hofrat Drobesch. Doctor Rebière, who runs a very famous sanatorium."

Jacques found himself shaking hands with a gray-haired man, with a public, smiling manner and a belly that made the tails of his white waistcoat stick out in front of him. He must, thought Jacques, have been twenty years older than his wife . . . thirty years . . . forty. It seemed impossible.

". . . I found myself most interested," Drobesch was saying.

He had used the word three or four times already, Jacques noticed.

"And as for the recent Serbian development," Drobesch said, "I found that I was very interested by my own reaction to it!"

"How very interesting," said Jacques, before he could stop himself.

Drobesch continued. "We must get you along one day to one of our summer symposia. I am not sure we have ever had a psychiatrist read a paper before. It's all most agreeable. We try to bring together people from all the different disciplines—not just boring old politicians like me. We do like to spread our net a little wider, do we not, my dear? Last year, we had the most interesting time."

"Indeed," said Roya. "Perhaps you would care to come and dine with us. We would be delighted to meet your wife."

Jacques wondered if he had imagined a sardonic sparkle in her eye.

"Thank you."

"Or perhaps you would care to call one day after you have completed your clinic."

"Most kind. I must be going now or we shall miss the last train and be stranded in the valley."

"I shall write to you with our address so you know where to come."

"Thank you. Good night, good night. Sonia! Come!"

AFTER DAISY and Hans's wedding in the summer, Thomas took his family to England for a holiday. They spent a week at the seaside, then went to stay with Edgar and Lucy at Torrington. Mrs. Midwinter was being nursed in her room and did not recognize Thomas when he went up to see her. She was seventy years old and was not expected to survive much longer. For almost ten years she had suffered from a form of premature senility; it had started as mere forgetfulness, but the symptoms had lately confined her to her bed. When Kitty and the girls were settled, Thomas traveled to his old asylum, where Faverill had said he would be pleased to see him; the distance was great, the train was slow and he spent a night on the way.

The cab set him down at the main gates, where he introduced himself to the porter and was directed to the main building. He walked slowly down the path, through the park. Nothing had changed. There was the line of elms away to the right, bordering the meadow; there were the workshops on the hill, the same gate that he and Daisy Wilkins (now Frau Eckert of Carinthia) had once climbed; and the aromatic, puffing brewery. He remembered the specimen trees—a yellowish catalpa, a copper beech—on the lawns as he passed and the great double doors of the asylum with their barred fanlight ahead of him.

This place had entered his memory at the lowest level. It was only when he saw again the angle of certain buildings and their brickwork corners, the alleyways, lawns and arches, that he recognized them as the settings of a thousand different dreams that he had dreamed in Paris, at the schloss, in Vienna and the African bush—dreams that had taken him from late boyhood deep into middle age. Few places in a man's life could enter so profoundly, he thought; it was almost as though the asylum had limned some earlier outline that had already been laid down in his unconscious mind.

He could not yet face going in, so walked along the flank of the asylum, on a graveled path; at his feet were half-windows from the basement, barred, their lower lights underground, and sometimes a ground-floor window with the same arched top as the others, but bricked in. He felt as though he was twenty-five again and might be told to book in the new arrivals; yet he also felt in some odd way an impostor who could at any moment be apprehended. He should not really be there, because he knew too much; he knew the secrets of the past. If the young staff of today could read his mind, they could not perform their jobs, because the ability to continue depended on a baseless optimism, on a willfully blind faith.

He turned and made his way back to the front door. The saliva began to leave his mouth as he approached; a knot began to twist slowly in his gut. Dear God, he thought as he mounted the step and pulled the bell: please let it not be Grogan. The spyhole swiveled, an eye peered out and there was the sound of bolts and chains. A burly, youngish man with a leather cap and a cigarette in his mouth asked him what he wanted; his manner was crude, but he had one great advantage in Thomas's eyes: he was not Grogan.

"Dr. Faverill's up in the West Tower. He told me you was coming. Third floor up. Down the corridor here, into the—"

"Yes, I remember the way. I shall need a master key, shan't I? Unless of course you have done away with all the locks."

"No fear. You can borrow this one."

As Thomas set off toward the corridor on the women's side, there was a throaty laugh behind him. "Mind where you step."

When he pulled the door closed behind him, Thomas felt the smell of

the asylum cover him in a wave: the rotting asphalt, feces and paraldehyde; the damp brick and unmopped waste that tacitly admitted that
humans were no better than the beasts and that any aspiration to be so
was a folly.

Electric lights had replaced the gas, though what it showed was better left unilluminated, Thomas thought, as he burrowed on down the
tunnel. The doors into the wards had also been renewed and now had
glass upper panels, reinforced with wire, through which he could
glimpse the lunatics as he walked. Doubtless he would already have
passed by some of the same patients who were there twenty years ago:
that Welsh woman, for instance, with the erotic mania—was her ardor
undiminished after all this time or had it burned away the brain all
round itself and left her senile?

Eventually he came to a gallery at the foot of a ventilation tower,
where he left the corridor by a small side door and emerged into a brighter
area, a hall where once a banner had been strung from the banisters, its
message picked out in winter flowers, white and pink: "WELLCOME."

Thomas climbed the stairs, and at once his spirits lifted. He quickened down a passage, turned and climbed again. He was not far from
where his own room had been, with its solitary bookcase on which he
had so proudly displayed the sum of human knowledge on insanity.
Faverill's name was written on a wooden plate beside his door.

"Come in. Ah, Midwinter. How extremely good to see you."

An old man Thomas barely recognized was starting to lever himself
up from a chair at the fireside.

"Do come and take a seat. We shall have some tea in a moment."

"It is very good of you to see me, sir. I was not sure you would remember me. I was not here for long."

"Remember you? Dear God, of course I remember you. I had never
had an assistant with more of a gift for mad-doctoring. I think I said so at
the time. I was sorry to see you go."

"Thank you, sir, I—"

"You had better not call me 'sir.' I am not your senior officer. You
could call me Faverill if you liked, though if that is too intimate for you,
my Christian name is William."

Faverill's fairish hair, such of it as was left, had turned white and he had lost his beard, though there were patches of white whisker that had escaped the razor. He wore a velvet jacket over a waistcoat and shirt that bore the marks of dropped food and drink. His eyes were rheumy, and there was a tremor in his hand as he filled a pipe with tobacco from a jar on the table.

"Tell me all you have done," he said. "I have few visitors. My sister occasionally, no one else. So tell me your story at length, Midwinter. I am all ears."

Thomas smiled and began. He stopped occasionally to ask Faverill about himself.

"I am seventy-five years old now, and am retired from work, though they allow me these rooms and a small pension. In theory I remain a 'consultant,' though the present superintendent has never in fact consulted me. He is a very rum fellow in my opinion. Name of Arrowsmith. Not disagreeable, but very decided in his opinions. Not a very scientific man, I fear. Now go on. You were in Paris, with Charcot and your French friend. He sounds a splendid man, I must say."

"He certainly is, though we have had our difficulties, I am afraid to say. Are you familiar with the Viennese School?"

"Indeed," said Faverill. "I read the early communications with enormous interest. These Viennese seemed to be the first people to be offering a cure of any description for mental distress. A cure! A remedy! Only people such as you and I who have labored in the mad-doctoring business could know the allure of those words. I read the case histories with great enjoyment. Are you familiar with the short stories of Harrison Lindsay? A little-known Scottish writer, rather splendid in his way. His stories are like intricate detective puzzles, full of clues. They all come out right in the end. Most satisfactory. Where was I?"

"The Viennese School."

"Ah yes. I found their stories equally entertaining. But when I read that it was proposed to apply their techniques not to the comfort of high-strung Viennese girls but to the treatment of psychosis . . ." Faverill spread his hands wide. "I confess that at that stage I lost interest. I despaired."

Thomas went on to describe his own work and his attempts to reconcile his beliefs in some sort of theory that even if it would not answer every question could at least provide a stepping-stone for others.

Faverill nodded as he listened and occasionally smiled, not unkindly. "Proof, my dear Midwinter. That is what you are going to lack for this great scheme of yours."

"I know. In the absence of molecular proof—something that will take a hundred years or maybe more—the best I can do is shore up my theories by quoting good authorities who have thought in similar ways."

"Yes. But if I were you, I should forget about the Europeans. Charcot's work in this area is discredited. The Germans, the Viennese . . . Hmm. You may find more sense in the West Riding Asylum. Or in Hughlings Jackson, a very fine neurologist—the English Charcot, you might almost say, though fortunately still with us."

There was a knock at the door and a woman in a green overall came in carrying a tea tray.

"Thank you, Susan," said Faverill, picking up the pot.

When the maid had left, Thomas said, "And may I ask, how is Matilda?"

"Alas, alas," said Faverill, putting down the pot again in a hand that shook. "I am sorry to say that she was taken from us—almost five years ago now. She did not enjoy good health—physically, I mean. She had had consumption as a child. A severe case of pneumonia carried her off one winter." He passed his hand across his forehead. "And, oh, the difference to me."

"I am very sorry to hear that."

"Indeed. I had the misfortune to choose a branch of medicine in which I have seen almost no one cured. It has been dispiriting. We have struggled on, giving what comfort we can. For myself, I found the company of Matilda gave me joy despite it all. She gave me leave to hope. I was devoted to the woman."

"I know. I am very sorry."

Faverill at last poured the tea. "I have arranged for you to stay in your old room," he said. "It was on the floor below, was it not?"

"Yes, directly under this one."

"I suggest you take dinner in town. There is a chophouse on the high street and they say the dining room at the Lamb and Flag is reliable. The food in the asylum has suffered somewhat. Then in the morning you can come back here and I shall accompany you on your visit to the wards, if that is still what you would like."

When he returned after dinner at the Lamb and Flag, Thomas found an old copy of the *British Medical Journal* from March 1884 on his bed. Pinned to it was a note in Faverill's hand that said, "I thought you might be interested by the passages I have marked on page 591."

Thomas turned to the page, which reprinted the Croonian Lectures on "Evolution and Dissolution of the Nervous System," delivered at the Royal College of Physicians, March 1884, by J. Hughlings Jackson M.D., F.R.S., F.R.C.P., Physician to the London Hospital.

Faverill's pencil had underlined with vigor.

1. Evolution is a passage from the most to the least organized; that is to say, from the lowest, well-organized, centers up to the highest, least organized, centers. . . . 2. Evolution is a passage from the most simple to the most complex. . . . There is no inconsistency in speaking of centers being at the same time most complex and least organized. Suppose a center to consist of but two sensory and two motor elements; if they be well joined, so that "currents flow" easily from the sensory into the motor elements, then that center, although a very simple one, is highly organized. On the other hand we can conceive a center consisting of four sensory and four motor elements in which the junctions are so imperfect that the nerve-currents meet with much resistance. Here is a center twice as complex . . . but only half as well organized. 3. Evolution is a passage from the most automatic to the most voluntary.

So far, Thomas thought, what he had read was unremarkable, though he had seldom seen the word "evolution" used so suggestively in a medical journal. It confirmed his own belief that the most highly evolved, most characteristically human systems were what Hughlings Jackson called the "least organized," or in other words most vulnerable.

Faverill's underlining pencil had wavered on.

Dissolution being the reverse process of evolution . . . is a process of undevelopment; it is a "taking to pieces." . . . Evolution not being entirely reversed, some level of evolution is left. To "undergo dissolution" is to be "reduced to a lower level of evolution." Disease is said to "cause" the symptoms of insanity. I submit that . . . all positive mental symptoms (illusions, hallucinations, delusions and extravagant conduct) are the activity of nervous elements untouched by any pathological process; that they arise during activity on the lower level of evolution remaining.

Under the closing phrase, Faverill's hand had doubled its emphasis. Thomas thought of Olivier; he thought of Achilles and the Psalmist, hearing voices. Now he was excited by what he read.

In health, each person's normal thought and conduct are . . . survivals of the fittest states of what we may call the topmost layer of his highest centers: the highest level of evolution. Now suppose that from disease . . . the topmost layer is rendered functionless. This is dissolution, from which arise the negative symptoms of the patient's insanity. I contend that his *positive* mental symptoms are the survivals of his fittest states—on the lower, though highest functioning, level of evolution. The most absurd mentation and most extravagant actions in insane people are the survivals of their fittest states. . . . We need not wonder that an insane man believes in what we call his illusions; they are his reality. His illusions, etc., are not caused by disease but are the outcome of what activity is left of him (of what disease has spared); his illusions *are* his mind.

In the morning, he received a telegram from Edgar telling him that their mother had died.

XX

IN THE FOLLOWING YEAR, A GERMAN-BORN PHYSICIST DECLARED
that there was no such thing as absolute time or absolute motion, but that
everything, even the order in which events happened, depended on the
observer. While his father and uncle debated these findings, the most significant event of the year for Daniel Rebière was that, on their eighth
birthday, his cousins were finally permitted to attend the village school
with him. Their mother had made a number of excuses about their
fragility and the length of the daily winter journey, but what really
alarmed her was how quickly they seemed to be growing up. Most
people with two children had a younger one to hold on to and to spoil;
they had a chance to catch and relish the fading days of innocence. But
both Kitty's children were her oldest; both galloped away from her; and
while the relativity of time was all very well in theory, not even Mr. Ein-
stein had devised a way that she could keep her girls forever young.

She waved them off sadly on the cable car, in Daniel's fierce custody,
wrapped her arms tight round her ribs and went back to her empty
house.

Daniel showed the girls off to Freddy and his other friends with silent
pride. They wore matching dresses of holly-leaf green wool with red
woolen stockings and buttoned boots; they had had their curly hair cut
just above the shoulder; Charlotte had a green ribbon in hers and
Martha a red, but at lunchtime they quietly exchanged them. They
traded on their similarity to give themselves double protection in the

new world of chalkboards, boys, wooden forms and spelling. Only Daniel could in fact see through their ribbon swaps and double bluffs: Charlotte was a fraction taller, Martha's eyes were a shade darker, though neither of these details was of any use unless they stood side by side. Daniel's way of knowing was instinctive and depended on the way they looked at him; there was just something more Martha-ish and less Charlotte-like about Martha. Perhaps it was the voice, perhaps only the way the light caught the eye.

Charlotte excelled at arithmetic, to Daniel's alarm, and was moved up to the class he was in, under Herr Baumgartner. In the summer, Martha was also promoted. The following year was Daniel's last at the village school before, at the age of eleven, he would move to the big school in town and he felt it was important that he should not be overtaken by his cousins before he left. He doubled his efforts in grammar and spelling and elementary Latin, but long division continued to trouble him unless Martha allowed him to look over at her slate, as she frequently did. In the rest period after lunch, Daniel sat next to one or other of the girls while the teacher read the class a story. Charlotte sometimes pretended to be Daisy with her electrical apparatus and ran the tips of her fingers over his bare thighs, between the bottom of his shorts and top of his socks. Or, if he asked her nicely and gave her some of the fruit pie his mother sent in with him, Martha would sit behind him and stroke the back of his neck and hair, so that he heard the folktales of Europe in a trance of delight.

Sonia underlined to Daniel that it was his duty to make sure his cousins were not bullied and that they returned home safe each day with the right books, with their clothes untorn and their hands and faces clean. Since the girls seemed rather better adapted than he was to the world of school, this was not a troublesome responsibility for him and he received his mother's praise with equanimity.

In fact, Sonia was less worried about her son or her nieces than about her husband. Since Olivier's death, Jacques had changed. He had become colder, and sometimes seemed dismissive of other people's feelings; on the days that he went to the hospital in town for his clinic, he was distracted on his return. He often came back late, and although she did not press him for a reason, she noticed that he offered none. He was going through another turbulent period in his life, it was clear to her, but her previous experience had taught her that it was best to leave him to it.

They frequently dined with Hofrat Drobesch and his wife, despite the fact that both of them thought him insufferable and Sonia thought Roya untrustworthy.

"Well, one meets other people there," said Jacques. "It's a way of getting off the confounded mountaintop and away from the society of lunatics. And the wine is good."

It was true that the evenings were enjoyable in their way. Sonia could still be excited by the process of dressing up and going out; she was still interested to hear the stories of the people she met and see how they managed to deal with the demands of their lives.

Jacques also sometimes called at the house in the afternoons, when only Roya was there. At first it was every three months or so; then every month.

She always expressed surprise and delight when he called in. She told him she was lonely by day, with little to do but practice her violin; the other wives in town were . . . well . . .

"I know," said Jacques. "You are an exotic flower to them. They do not understand strangers. They live where they were set down. They are autochthonous."

"Does that mean plump?"

"Invariably."

He persuaded himself that Roya benefited from his visits. When the clinic closed, he looked at his watch. I should hurry home, he thought, but on the other hand, the poor girl, alone in that big cold house . . . She needs a little conversation. It is not as though the slightest impropriety . . . Well, one quick kiss, but that was years ago, and we are friends, emancipated people of the twentieth century in which it appears that women will shortly have the vote. Our friendship is one of equals. We talk of the issues of the day—painting, Russia, the Balkan question, music; it is actually my duty to welcome the foreigner at the gate and to make her feel welcome.

Three years had passed since he had first seen her again at the concert, and Roya gave no sign that she looked for anything more than tea and conversation. Even when the frequency of his visits increased to once a week, and then were planned in advance; even when he found hand-delivered notes in his pigeonhole at the hospital hastily rearranging times ("Drobesch unexpectedly back from Vienna")—at no point did their exchanges move beyond the bounds of a sophisticated, modern friendship. Jacques was proud of his restraint and was able to remain unconscious of his deeper feelings; he saw no need for caution because he saw no danger.

THOMAS LABORED on. He was hurt by a teasing remark from Jacques about his lack of published work; he was almost fifty years old and he did not want to end his working days like one of those old Fellows of his college at Cambridge who had published nothing. Relations between him and Jacques were difficult again. Although Jacques did not blame him for his brother's death, Olivier had been Thomas's patient and Thomas did feel to some extent responsible. He had become openly hostile to the Viennese School, to Jacques's manifest irritation. After the case of Fräulein Katharina, Jacques had had no choice but to disavow his own similar line of inquiry, but Thomas knew that he secretly still had hopes for it.

There was also the question of Jacques's friendship with Hofrat Drobesch and his wife. The reappearance of Roya, the girl from St. Jakob's Church in Rothenburg, was troubling to Thomas. He remembered the disconcerting effect she had had on him at the time, more than twenty years ago. When he saw her now, as he occasionally did when he was in town, he did not think, from a close if covert examination of her skin and her physique, that she could possibly be more than thirty-five, so at the time that she had so disturbed him when he glimpsed her in the church, then later at her father's house with the cat on her shoulders, she might have been as little as fourteen years old. . . . As if this thought were not worrying enough, he suspected that Jacques had formed an improperly intimate friendship with her. He had once been in the same room, at a party after the theater, and he sensed a kind of thunderous closeness, a charged and crackling air between them. It aroused a primitive jealousy in him, which he tried to extinguish by concentrating on the question of his sister's welfare.

"What do you see in them?" he said innocently.

"They are Jacques's friends. You know how it is. I am not sure how fond you are of Kitty's old friend from Vienna, what's her name, and her husband—"

"Indeed. But I see them only once a year and Kitty admits that it is a duty even for her. But Frau Drobesch—"

"Roya. You knew her before, did you not?"

"Yes, a little. Many years ago. She was a friend of Valade's daughter. But Jacques does seem unusually . . . attentive."

"She is more lively than her husband."

"Indeed. He is certainly a man of astonishing self-importance. What exactly is a 'hofrat' anyway?"

"I think it is a sort of counselor or courtier," said Sonia. "He spends a good deal of time in Vienna offering his opinion on affairs of state."

"I think he is a man whom no one has ever told to pipe down. Brought up by adoring women, I suspect."

"Indeed. So naturally one gravitates toward the wife."

"And do you like her?"

"Oh, Thomas, don't be ridiculous. I am a doctor's wife. We must go out sometimes. I do not criticize each person I meet. We dress up and dine. And the wine is good." Sonia looked at her feet.

"And does it concern you at all that Jacques seems so rapt in her company? One would not have thought that intellectually—"

"How do you know what they talk about? She is quite a cultivated woman. She speaks many languages and reads the newspapers and—"

"But, Queenie, you know what I mean."

"This is quite improper, Thomas. I trust Jacques absolutely. He has never given me grounds to doubt him. I love him, you see. I love him without question."

"I know. But—"

"I believe that the friendships Jacques has with other people are not, ultimately, any of my concern. Jacques may talk to a beautiful woman without betrayal. I trust and believe that I am the only woman that he thinks of in an amorous way."

"And if you were wrong?"

"If I were wrong, Thomas, there would not be very much that I could do about it. In which case, it is better to retain one's belief and one's dignity."

Thomas was not reassured by this explanation, but if Sonia did not regard Jacques's friendship with Roya as her business, then it certainly was not his. He returned to his books and began to prepare a lecture to be delivered in the spring of the following year. He shortened the horizon by choosing the date of his mother's birthday.

He then wrote to the owner of the Schloss Seeblick, who was in the process of turning the buildings into a hotel for the increasing tourist trade, and booked the North Hall for his lecture on May 12, 1909. By this time he would have to have organized his life's thoughts on madness and humanity.

THE TALK was advertised throughout Carinthia, and a notice was placed in the Viennese press. It was entitled: "Why Are Humans Mad? Dr. Thomas Midwinter, cofounder of the celebrated Schloss Seeblick and Wilhelmskogel Clinic, reflects on 25 years in psychiatric practice. North Hall, old Schloss Seeblick, 7 p.m., May 12, 1909. Please be seated by 6:45 p.m. Proceeds from admission to the St. Ludovic's Public Hospital Psychiatric Research Department."

The audience began to arrive soon after six. Lemonade, cakes and coffee were served to them on the lawn of the main courtyard. They were much the same people as those who had gathered for the orphanage musical evening: the wealthy bourgeoisie, the most indefatigable local socialites and those who liked to be seen at events denoting "culture." For Thomas, there was also a representation from the university, the hospital, the local newspapers and the medical press. Hannes Regensburger had promised to come down from Vienna.

"You look absolutely beautiful," Thomas said to Kitty, who was organizing the refreshments.

"Thank you. I like it here. It always makes me feel happy. It is a beautiful evening and my favorite chestnut tree is in bloom."

"'Under the spreading chestnut tree, the village madman—'"

"The very one. And I have the prospect of listening to a thrilling lecture from my husband."

"It is not that thrilling, it—"

"My darling Thomas, I spent four nights typing it out for you. I even corrected your German in a couple of places. I ought to know how interesting it is."

"And do your shoulders and hands hurt now? Do you dream of—"

"Hush. Stop it."

"In any event, I may depart a little from that text."

"I have complete faith in you, Thomas. Oh look, there is Frau Drobesch."

"So she is. Talking to Dr. Rebière, I see."

"Thomas, if you are going to be mischievous, you had better go away."

"I am sorry, Kitty. I am a little apprehensive. I shall go and collect my thoughts."

"Good idea. Charlotte. Come here. I need you to take these round. Where is Martha?"

Without asking permission, Thomas went down the cloister to the main house.

He paused for a moment at the double doors that he had pushed open so many times. He knew that he was susceptible to the past and wondered if it was a good idea to revisit. He pushed the door gently and gasped. The smell of the polished wood, potpourri and old books was exactly as he remembered. All the years of hope came rushing up to meet him, and his heart turned over when he trod once more on the worn flags of the hall. His consulting room . . . and Jacques's, where he had incredulously read the case history of his future wife, standing motionless in the window. He pushed open the bare wooden door. The bookshelves were empty; the room had been half-repainted, then abandoned. He remembered Sonia arriving from Paris for the first time, the suppressed excitement in her step as she accompanied him upstairs to the room that would one day be Daniel's nursery.

Thomas found tears starting in his eyes. He went down to the cellars, where they had first daringly installed electric light. His and Franz's workbench was still there; there were even a couple of empty chemical bottles. He went to the end of the cellar and pushed softly at the door; he knew the twenty paces that would bring him up behind the cupboard in the South Court and had no need of a candle.

Once there, looking carefully about him, to make sure he was not disturbing anyone, he climbed the stairs to his and Kitty's old apartment. The bedroom was empty, but he could see her still, a twin at each breast, looking up at him defiantly, proudly, a fever spot on each cheek. There: I have done it now, her face seemed to say.

He sighed from the pit of his heart. He thought of the sands at Deauville. Oh Daisy, oh Mary, oh Faverill, Olivier. Oh dearest Katharina. And Charlotte, Martha . . . What a long, long road it has been. And now I must explain it all . . .

His courage was failing him. What on earth did he know? What could he ever know?

He looked at his face in the looking glass on top of the chest, the Biedermeier one that had always been there. He saw the same eyes, the same wide brow that he had seen each day since his mother first sat him on her lap one cold morning in Lincolnshire and pointed to his face in her dressing-table mirror.

You idiot, he thought. You fool.

He took a flask of brandy from inside his coat and drank it off. Now go on, he said out loud. Go on and tell them.

He went downstairs and walked briskly over to the main courtyard, where Kitty was waiting for him at the door into the North Hall.

"Are you all right?" She straightened his tie. "I love you," she said, kissing his cheek.

"Thank you."

"You smell of whisky."

"Brandy. Never mind. Are they all in?"

"Yes."

"Then let us proceed."

The chatter of the audience subsided to a respectful silence as Thomas walked up to the dais.

He put on the glasses that presbyopia had made him wear for reading, gripped the edges of the lectern, coughed once and began.

"Ladies and gentleman, when I first entered the profession of mad-doctoring, or alienism, as it was then called, I was asked to register the new arrivals at a large county asylum in England, my native country. They were all mad—demented, manic, deluded, nonsensical—and it was a question only of finding a bed in a numbered ward and forgetting all about them. Bang. Shut the door. Goodbye. There is an old English ballad of a woman doomed to try to keep the waves of the sea off a small rock by means only of a broom: one little brush against the rising tides. That was me, that was our asylum and there was nothing we could do to cause the seas to fall.

"Since that day twenty-three years ago I have given all my working life to treating the insane, and most of my resting hours to studying brain tissue beneath a microscope. I dream in histological patterns. I have read all the prominent work of my American and European colleagues, particularly the British, as they pushed forward their researches on different fronts; in this very place, the Schloss Seeblick, I have seen modest successes, some triumphs, few cures and several disasters.

"When I first became a doctor, I worked hard to distinguish what we call the organic element of madness—by which we mean the observable disease or malfunction of cells—from the psychological, by which we meant the effects of the events in the life of the patient on his thoughts, feelings and behavior.

"We still dispute these things, and perhaps we always shall—at least until such time as we develop a magical apparatus for peering into the brain with such clarity that the function of each 'neurone,' as Herr Waldeyer-Hartz has christened them, is apparent to us. Meanwhile, progress has been pitifully slow.

"The greatest advance in my life as an alienist came just three years ago, when a German zoologist called Fritz Schaudinn discovered the microbe for syphilis and thereby showed that a peculiar range of symptoms, from problems of the aorta to severe psychiatric delusion, were caused by a single germ. Some of the most floridly mad people in my English asylum—the kings and Bonapartes, the Virgin Marys and Boadiceas—were not really 'mad' at all; they had venereal disease. Goodbye, then, good people, goodbye to the lunatic asylum: you are not wanted here and—who knows—perhaps one day the physicians will find a cure for you.

"Quite early in my career as an alienist I became familiar with a pattern of symptoms that first showed in young people—slightly earlier in men than in women, for some reason—and usually involved the hearing of voices, among other delusions and behavioral abnormalities. This complex of symptoms had been christened 'hebephrenia,' was known to my partner and me as 'Olivier's disease,' then universally, following Emil Kraepelin, as 'dementia praecox.' Patients had a poor prospect of recovery; indeed, their symptoms generally grew worse over time. When they presented themselves to me at first—young, often intelligent, bright-eyed and scared by what had happened to them—I could believe them to be suffering a reaction to a terrible event. By the time they left me, most were like the chronic patients of the old Salpêtrière in Paris: shuffling, spastic, incoherent, their mental functions seemingly burned away. To put it in doctor's language: they came in psychological, and they went out neurological.

"Less than two years ago, in an article entitled 'Die Prognose der Dementia Praecox (Schizophreniegruppe)' published in a German psychiatric journal, the professor of psychiatry at Zürich University, Eugen Bleuler, proposed that this disease should be rechristened 'schizophrenia.' I think there is almost no chance that this confusing word will be widely adopted by the medical or the lay world; it seems to imply some sort of split or double personality, when in fact the 'personality' of the patient is more often than not tragically unified—straitjacketed, indeed, into its singular delusions. The last thing these poor people need is to have the nature of their suffering further mystified by a clumsy piece of nomenclature, as though they were suffering from nothing more than a nervous indecisiveness!

"However, it is not the word that worries me; it is the thrust of Professor Bleuler's argument, which is to suggest that his 'schizophrenia' is a psychological reaction to problems in the patient's life—to the same difficulties that you and I might have, though perhaps the patient's problems are a little more severe or he is a little less robust in dealing with them. The delusions, meanwhile—the cacophony of voices in his ears—not in his head, dear ladies and gentlemen, but sounding from external space on the drum of his ear and then in the auditory area of his brain—these voices, says Professor Bleuler, are no more than clues to the psychological basis of the distress. The inference we are to make is quite clear, I think, and it is this: that such people can be treated by psychotherapy—by talking, in other words—and in Professor Bleuler's eyes the best form of such talking cure is that which is at present fashionable with the Viennese School.

"Some years ago, I went to Vienna and was fortunate enough to hear a lecture by a doctor called Wilhelm Fliess, an ear, nose and throat specialist who had developed an interest in psychology and believed that parts of the nostril corresponded to parts of the female reproductive apparatus. To this end, he rubbed the inside of the nose with cocaine to relieve pain in the uterus. He also believed that two magic numbers—alas, I have forgotten which two—provided, in combination, in square or among their factors, a key to all mysteries of human biology, as well as to the workings of the cosmos. Goodness, how I do wish I could remember what those two numbers were.

"I corresponded with Dr. Fliess after his lecture and took the liberty of pointing out some of his simpler errors, particularly with regard to the entry of stimulants into the bloodstream via the mucous membrane. He was a game and combative correspondent, however, and while we seldom agreed and never formed a friendship, we did continue to write. Dr. Fliess became more than ever excited by the advance of the Viennese School. He felt that doctors who had started as physicians or, in one instance, as a neurologist, were now in a position to turn their back on such humble apprentice work. Instead, keen-eyed mountaineers upon Mount Darien, they were now ready to pronounce a Universal Theory of Human Behavior.

"Under my insistent teasing, Dr. Fliess showed me a letter he had received from one such practitioner, whose name I shall not repeat for fear of giving it further réclame. This doctor had formulated a general rule of human behavior, namely that all young male children must pass through a period of sexual desire for their mothers. Forgive me, ladies and gentlemen, it is indeed a bizarre thought—though the theory itself is nothing like as bizarre as its genesis, which the letter to Dr. Fliess, received by him on October 4, 1897, described thus:

> My libido toward *matrem* was awakened . . . on the occasion of a journey with her from Leipzig to Vienna, during which we must have spent the night together and there must have been an opportunity of seeing her *nudam*.

The doctor does not remember if he spent the night with his mother, but thinks he 'must have'; he does not remember if he saw her naked, but thinks there 'must have been an opportunity.' He certainly does not remember being aroused. Yet on the basis of three blanks of memory, he asserts that he was indeed stimulated; on the foundation of a trebly unremembered experience, he postulates a universal human axiom. To give the theory grandeur, it is, I believe, intended to name it after the mythical Greek character Oedipus. The crux of the Oedipus story—the whole narrative point of it, you might think: that the poor man had not the faintest idea who his parents were—would seem to me to disqualify him entirely from the question of a child's everyday struggles with the two people he knows best.

"I have never traveled by train from Leipzig to Vienna, though I am fairly certain that, had I done so, I should not have stripped naked in the carriage—whether I was accompanied by my daughters, by my wife or merely by Josef, the old lampman. It would be cold, inconvenient and unnecessary. I can assure you of one thing, though: that if I had no recollection of it, I would not base an argument about my own mind on it, let alone extrapolate from my forgetfulness a dogma for half humanity.

"There are two tragedies here. One is the failure of science in a medical man. It is more risible, perhaps, than tragic. But then, when you consider some aspects of what is suggested, it does become tragic—because anyone who has observed young boys will have noticed that there can, sometimes, be a tactile relationship with the mother at certain ages, and an amicable competition with the father for her attention. It is a sort of commonplace, a fireside truth, quite interesting in its way; but by no stretch of the imagination could it form part of the basis of a treatment for the biologically insane.

"And this is the site of the second tragedy: that this homespun insight, for what it was worth, has become degraded—as beliefs invariably are—by politics: in this case the politics of a 'school' of medicine that must have the universal key, the only answer. Small truths, homely facts, when they are applied to the world as representative of *all* the world, cease to be facts and become superstitions. Thus has this little thought become elevated, made sacrosanct and set to work as a dogma in a school of 'medicine,' which, so far as I know, will be the first such school since the time of Hippocrates to base its treatment of the sick on the withholding of medicine.

"For many years I treated a patient in this building, a gentle, tormented creature called Olivier, after whom, for a long time we named the disease that Professor Bleuler now proposes to call 'schizophrenia.' I cannot describe to you the torments of that man's life or the profundity of his illness. Sometimes I fancied I could hear his voices in my own head, so real were they to him, so attentive was he to their commands, even as I tried to reach him with my own voice, offering him . . . Well, what did I offer him—what could I?—beyond consolation, the occasional sedative, the hope of better things?

"I had no cure. I still have none, though I have some thoughts that I will come to in a minute. When Olivier and his kind are ministered to, one day, when we can make them well again, it will be one of the great moments in the history of medicine. In the meantime, I cannot quite describe to you the indignation that I feel at the Viennese proposition that the experience of Olivier—a man I saw cut the 'devils' from his forearm with a knife—was something caused by the behavior of his mother to her child and should be cured therefore not by medicine but only by a system based—among other scientific non sequiturs—upon what one small boy did not remember whether he had seen (or not seen), felt (or not felt) one night, on a train."

Thomas, shaking with indignation, sweating beneath his black coat, paused and drank some water. In the quiet, he heard a chair being pushed back, candid footsteps and the main door being noisily closed: it was more than an exit, it was a marked departure, though he did not see who had left.

Realigning the papers on the lectern, he coughed and gathered his thoughts.

"I need now to explain to you my interest in the disease which, out of respect for current usage, I am going to call 'schizophrenia.' My fundamental position can be put quite clearly. Schizophrenia is a disease unique to humans, neurological in its base; in other words it is like Parkinson's or Huntington's diseases, where a brain or spinal column lesion causes tremor in the dependent outlying area. A schizophrenic patient has a lesion in the part or parts of the brain that allow us to imagine. Its supreme interest is as follows: it is not just a human disease, it is *the* human disease."

Thomas paused and looked at the audience. He was aware that his style was much more polemical and informal than that of any of his mentors; it was not like the speech of John Hughlings Jackson with its stiff grammar; but he was a modern man of the twentieth century, speaking to laymen, and he must make himself clear.

"Let us look at what distinguishes *Homo sapiens* from other species. Some years ago, in Africa, I gave a rather excited speech to my colleague Herr Regensburger about what divided Mr. Darwin and Mr. Wallace, the codiscoverers of natural selection. It was the faculty of awareness, or consciousness."

Thomas then gave a shorter account of the theory he had offered Regensburger, of how man, after he had learned language, had been able to conjure instructive voices in his head; and of how, after the invention of writing and under the influence of huge population upheavals, the ability to summon such voices had become rarer.

"What it left," Thomas continued, "was this heartrending desire in humanity for something it has lost: its gods, its vanished Eden. Which of us can deny that at some level we are afflicted by a sense that our human lives are incomplete and that there lies, just beyond the reach of our perceptions, a paradise that once was ours?

"But that is not quite all that was left. The old mechanisms for hearing voices remained in some neural patterns; and these patterns continued to be transmitted through our breeding—like the bat's blind eye and the whale's vestigial arms—long after we had ceased to need them. The neurophysiology of our consciousness is by no means set for all time. It is forever developing. We are not, ladies and gentlemen, the finished article. I am going to support my opinion now by reading a short extract from the father of English neurology, John Hughlings Jackson."

Thomas then took the *British Medical Journal* and read the passages that Faverill had marked; and he seemed to feel his old employer's hand on his shoulder as he did so.

"So," he resumed, "I submit that in schizophrenia, the modern man or woman becomes something very like the earlier human I described to you. He hears external voices, and he loses the edges of himself because he cannot see his own identity and tell stories about it in the model version of the real world that normal people have—that which constitutes what I earlier called our 'sixth sense,' our self-awareness, the very thing that distinguishes us from the beasts. I watched Olivier, my friend and patient, try to conjure up this inner world, I saw him struggle with all the information that bombarded him, and he could not shut it out for long enough to see himself.

"Now, what else do we know of this condition? Well, we know that it appears to run in families. An American doctor called Isaac Ray, as long ago as 1863, noted that relatives of people with this ailment tended to display milder forms of it themselves; in 1878 the German psychiatrist Richard von Krafft-Ebing estimated that twelve out of nineteen such patients had family histories of the illness. Thomas Clouston, the great Edinburgh mad-doctor, assiduously documented family patterns more than ten years ago.

"And if it runs in families, what does that mean? Well, that a predisposition to it is inherited, of course. Another compatriot of mine, Henry Maudsley, wrote much of 'degeneration'—an idea he had borrowed from a Frenchman called Morel. The idea was that not only would an individual inherit the traits of insanity, but that the way he lived his own life—in drink and dissolution, for instance—would aggravate the characteristic when his children inherited it.

"This idea of accumulated inheritance was made popular by the French naturalist Jean-Baptiste Lamarck, and a version of it, alas, was accepted by Darwin. (I believe it even informs some of the novels of Monsieur Emile Zola.) However, we now know that this is not how inherited traits are passed on. Very simple experiments have proved that an individual's accumulated experience is not transmissible through breeding. To put it crudely, if you cut off a mouse's tail, its child is still born with one. The actual way in which characteristics are passed on is through units of inheritance. The mother donates half these units, the father half. Some American gentlemen named Sutton, Boveri and Morgan have recently established that these units are transmitted through the chromosomes. But they do not blend or mix: when the embryonic cell forms, either one unit is chosen, or the other. The one not chosen, however, is still carried by the child, but mute, as it were; and then it may be transmitted in the child's own breeding to take its chance of self-expression again, in the next generation. This process is absolutely vital, and, as I said, has only recently been explained. My own knowledge of these things is limited; I am not a botanist or a biologist, so, ladies and gentlemen, when I wanted to know a little more about the subject, I did what any good schoolboy would do: I looked up the *Encyclopaedia Britannica*. And there, under the entry for 'hybridisation,' in the 1881 edition, I found listed, among others, the name of Gregor Mendel, a Moravian monk, who discovered the principle of the 'either/or' in the units of inheritance. I read his papers, and was impressed by them. I am not going to explain to you now his work with garden peas; but I am going to introduce you to a new word for the units themselves. It is not a very good word: it is etymologically ill-bred (a nice irony) and, like 'schizophrenia,' I feel sure it will in due course be replaced by a better. But I do not wish to appear an old cuss, so I will go along with the Dane Wilhelm Johannsen, who has recently christened it a 'gene.'

"The point is, to recap for a moment, that the idea of inherited madness has been loud in psychiatry for more than fifty years. I am saying nothing very new here, I do assure you. It is just that now at last we may be in a position to understand better the mechanism of such inheritance.

"What else do we know of 'schizophrenia'? The second important thing is much harder for me to prove to you and I may as well be honest and say to you straight away that it is a speculation on my part—at this time. I believe that schizophrenia is found in all human populations, regardless of climate, race or nutrition; and I believe that it occurs at roughly the same level of incidence all over the world. In Europe it seems that we can estimate that perhaps one in a hundred people will develop the disease, and I believe that one day, when we deal more often and more constructively with doctors in other countries, we shall find a similar figure.

"I would like to quote Shakespeare to you now, but I fear my time is already running short. Suffice to say that Shakespeare has descriptions in his plays of such madness and many odd details that, it seems to me, can only have been drawn from his observation of people we would now call 'schizophrenic.' I profoundly believe that it is a universal condition.

"Now, if I am right that the capacity to pass on and inherit the gene, or, more likely, combination of genes, for this illness is steady throughout mankind, then it seems to me inevitable that it must have entered the human makeup before we spread ourselves around the world. Only if it existed before the great diaspora could it be constant; it could not have sprung up by simultaneous, identical mutation in different peoples—now in India, now in Peru. No, it must be fundamentally human and it must have arisen before the first *Homo sapiens* began to migrate from Africa, where Darwin and others better qualified than I believe us to have originated.

"In this context, what does 'originate' mean? Quite simply, a chance mutation in the inherited matter, probably brought about by the simple molecular inaccuracy in cell reproduction, will cause an individual to be born who differs from his parents in some respect. And that is usually the end of it. But very rarely, that difference is so helpful to him and to his children that they can outsurvive those who lack it; they dominate; they preponderate; they live alongside the less endowed until those forerunners, failing in the competition for resources, become extinct—or are killed off by the new mutants. This is what the fossil record clearly, unambiguously tells us.

"Homo sapiens 'originated,' like all the others, alongside his precursor species, cheek by jowl. Now, I want you to imagine a picture. We are somewhere in Africa, many tens of thousands of years ago. Here, beside a pleasant stream, are two primitives, or 'proto-humans' as some call them; let *us* call them He and She. For thousands, tens of thousands, perhaps hundreds of thousands of years they have not changed. Then suddenly, one day, a mutation occurs and out of nowhere He and She look up to see just there, on the other side of the stream . . . Adam and Eve. Let us leave the four of them there, just for the moment. But do not worry, we shall return to them.

"What I want to find out is what exactly was this tiny change that opened the door for Adam and Eve. What was in Adam that was not in He?

"I have cut up many brains to try and see, and, fortunately, I have not been alone. Many psychiatrists have noted something odd about the human brain. It looks symmetrical, but it is not. It is symmetrical in appearance, but not in function. Behind me—if Hans would be so kind as to switch on the projector. Thank you—is a large illustration of the human brain. All its parts, as you can see, are duplicated, mirror images, and for many years, that lovely duplication was taken as a sign of mankind's superiority—a sort of divine symmetry, one might almost say.

"Then, about forty years ago, a Frenchman called Paul Broca, when treating a patient who had lost the ability to speak—an 'aphasic' in doctor's terms—showed that the capacity for speech was located just here, on the left. The corresponding area on the right had no such function. Then a German called Carl Wernicke showed that another left-only area, further back and down, just here, was also implicated in speech and understanding. Again, the matching area on the right had no such function. It appeared that not only were the two halves of the brain not doing the same things, but that one faculty—language, the very thing that made us better than the apes and little lower than the angels—was resident exclusively on one side!

"This is how Broca himself put it more than thirty years ago: 'Man is, of all the animals, the one whose brain in the normal state is the most asymmetri-cal. He is also the one who possesses the most acquired faculties. Among these faculties—which experience and education developed in his ancestors and of which heredity hands him the instrument but which he does not succeed in exercising until after a long and difficult individual education—the faculty of articulate language holds pride of place. *It is this that distinguishes us most clearly from the animals.*'

"So, clearly in Monsieur Broca's view, this is what made Adam different from He. That is not to say that Adam spoke at once; on the contrary, I should say the all-important change between the two was an earlier mutation which enabled the hemispheres of Adam's brain to develop differentially; and it was that mutation that gave us essentially two brains, which can both complement and back up one another, whose sum is greater than their parts and led to the vastly increased intellectual capacity of *Homo sapiens* over his precursor being; and thence to language, which opened the door to the development of 'consciousness'—and to all that we now think of as characteristically human.

"Including, unfortunately, schizophrenia and the related psychoses.

"To recap once more. We have already seen that these illnesses are in some way heritable and therefore that they must be related to the 'genes' that we pass on. If the illness is evenly spread throughout the world, as we believe, then that gene or genes must have been acquired before the human diaspora from Africa. We know that the symptoms of the disease involve a loss of proper self-awareness or higher consciousness. It also seems likely that these symptoms are the result of improper communication between the left and right hemispheres: in other words, that in some way *thoughts* are being experienced as though they were external *voices*—the left hemisphere receiving too many signals in too crude a form from the right, and, in its typical anxiety to please, resorting to prehistoric methods of dealing with it. The only hypothesis that can make sense of all these data is this: that the key mutation that changed He to Adam was one that allowed him to become functionally lopsided in the brain; that that same mutation allowed him to develop language; that language enabled him to develop a primitive voice-hearing consciousness. When, however, he developed writing and so made his self-instructions portable and when, furthermore, his environment—and let us remember how the environment according to Darwin selects those best fitted to survive—made the voice-hearers less useful than the readers and the self-aware, they began to be selected against: to die out. From being the majority of the population, the voice-hearers dwindled down to about, in my estimate, fifteen percent. Most of these people hear voices only occasionally, and are not troubled by the experience. They are not sick. I myself had such a voice as an adolescent; many others are ashamed to admit to it, or in some way manage not even to admit it to themselves. In a small minority, however, the hearing of voices is part of a wider pathology, and these are the schizophrenic patients. But the important point is that the voice-hearers, whether healthy or psychotic, did not, as you might expect, become extinct. And why, ladies and gentlemen?

"Darwin published the *Origin of Species* fifty years ago; although his reputation fell toward the end of the last century, the argument for natural selection has long been won, and its basic tenet is that only that which confers an advantage on the species is continually selected by the environment and therefore, as we should presumably now say, perpetuated in the 'genes.' Nature never selects against the benefit of the species; it cannot. Furthermore, these poor schizophrenic people have self-inflicted losses in reproduction. They kill themselves; they are mad; they are unattractive to others; they are sexually selected against. Yet they survive at a constant level in the population. How can this be? It breaks the first law of Darwin! It can only be that a variant of that inheritance—the same units, but differently combined, so that they do not express themselves as illness—confers huge advantages. So huge that they compensate both for the misery of the illness, against the species's interest, and the reproductive failure of the afflicted! And what are the advantages? They are superior brain power, language, creative ability; and, consequently, divine dissatisfaction, a yearning for the absolute . . . the very things that distinguish us from the animals. The same 'genes' that drive us mad have made us human: in different combinations, I admit, but precisely, and in my view unarguably, the same particles of inheritance. You cannot have humanity without psychosis; they are indivisible. Both, ladies and gentlemen, stem from the same submicroscopic change that changed He to Adam."

Thomas stopped to drink some more water. There was utter silence in the hall, though it was not appreciably a friendly one, he thought. His throat felt lacerated and his temples were pounding; he wished he had not drunk the brandy. He breathed in hard.

"Before I go on to the concluding part of my talk," he said, "I want you to be clear about one more thing. Whatever that minute change was, from He to Adam, it could have been something else." He paused again. "As Darwin so memorably wrote: 'What a chance it has been . . . that has made a man—any monkey probably might with such chances be made intellectual, but almost certainly not made into a man.' It might not have led to me and you and Carinthia and Brahms and the hall of the Schloss Seeblick tonight. It could have been one of a million changes with a million, million different outcomes. That is how precarious we humans are, and that is why it fits us to be humble."

A man in the front row of the audience, known to Thomas as a lawyer in the local town, stood up noisily.

"Dr. Midwinter," he said. "I paid money at the door to hear a talk I was assured would be both enlightening and thought-provoking. Instead, you have told me in the last hour that there is no God, no Creator, that we are the result of some microscopic accident beside an African stream, that we might just as easily not have been human beings but something else, and then, for heaven's sake, that we are all insane! Well, I have had enough. Tomorrow I shall listen to a concert of Brahms, since you mention him, or Mahler or one of the others who has made a home in our beautiful province. I shall look at the stars in the sky and I shall read Goethe. I leave you to your 'genes' and your African watercourse. Good night, Doctor."

"Good night," said Thomas. "Your money is destined for the hospital, but my wife will refund it to you, if you prefer. She is the beautiful woman at the back, sitting by the door. To you, her beauty may be 'proof' of a divine hand; to me it demonstrates the astonishing good fortune entailed in the direction human evolution took. That we should end with this transcendent gift of self-awareness that has enabled us to live as moral beings, appreciating beauty, writing symphonies, pondering our own mortality . . . 'What a piece of work is a man! How noble in reason! how infinite in faculty! in form, in moving, how express and admirable!'" He found that he was hammering the lectern as he spoke, his raw voice in shreds. "Admire her as you pass, sir. 'In action how like an angel! in apprehension how like a god! the beauty of the world!' Each minute of our tiny lives we should give thanks for that providence—that molecular chance that proved more far-reaching, more beneficent, and—yes—far more improbable than the blessing of any god."

There was some mild applause, some embarrassed laughter and some further discreet deserters, but the body of the audience remained. Thomas gritted his teeth and drank more water. He looked up to the long row of electric lights suspended from the beam that spanned the ceiling of the hall. He felt his life's work hang in the balance, and he moved to shore it up.

"Some years ago," he said quietly, "in this very hall, my dear colleague Dr. Rebière read a most interesting paper on his theory of 'psychophysical resolution.' It sounded revolutionary at the time, and I remember well the trouble Dr. Rebière took to point out that all his conclusions were based on existing, published work; what he had effected was a new synthesis. The ability to see original patterns in a mass of data is one of the most characteristically human aspects of our intelligence, and draws, I believe, on the functions of both sides of the brain.

"I assure you that however bizarre some of what I have told you tonight may have sounded, I have done little more than add my own clinical observations to a synthesis of what is already known. If, in doing so, I have managed to make a new pattern, so be it. More than sixty years ago, a general practitioner from Brighton, in England, a man called Arthur Wigan, published a book called *The Duality of the Mind,* which noted that the brain's two hemispheres had separate, though to some extent interchangeable, functions. Numerous postmortem measurements—here I commend to you the work of another psychiatrist, Dr. Ernest Southard—have also noted different weights in the two hemispheres.

"Then came Broca's moment of 'eureka,' when he localized language on the left. At first, people mocked him, saying he was like Descartes, who superstitiously placed the 'soul' in the pineal gland; but the clinical evidence overwhelmingly supported Broca, especially when Wernicke's area was added and the situation was pleasingly complicated by the discovery that language could, in unusual circumstances—either in infant brain damage or in unusual left-handedness—be switched to the corresponding area on the right. These exceptions, to cut a long story short, gratifyingly proved Broca's rule.

"Sir James Crichton-Browne, a very brilliant Scottish mad-doctor on whose staff at the West Riding Asylum the great Hughlings Jackson once worked, put it strongly only two years ago in an address to the Royal Institution: 'It is by the superior skill of his right hand that man has gotten himself the victory. . . . To try to undo this dextral preeminence is to fly in the face of evolution.' I do not have time to go into the question of right- and left-handedness here, except to say that the apes perform any task with either hand; humans are the only hand-lopsided species, and this reflects the unique skewing of their brains that enabled them so greatly to increase their capacity, to generate language and, through language, self-awareness.

"Incidentally, what does it tell us that the location of language—the prime human attribute—is still so uncertainly moored, so that perhaps five or ten percent of people have it in a variant place? It is as remarkable, I submit, as discovering that one in ten eagles has an eye at the end of its beak. The answer, I am sure, is that it is the most recently evolved facet of humanity; and, as Dr. Hughlings Jackson has written so persuasively, it is the most recently acquired faculties which are under the greatest pressure, while those which have been with us since our mammalian past are the most firmly embedded. In 1879, Dr. Crichton-Browne echoed him when he wrote: 'It seemed not improbable that the cortical centers which are last organized, which are the most highly evolved and voluntary, and which are located on the left side of the brain, might suffer first in insanity.' To give a simple analogy: modern motorcars, for all their marvelous design, are forever steaming forlornly at the roadside with their bonnets raised; old horse carts hardly ever need attention.

"I could list the names of many others—Moxon, Bastian, Gaussin, Myers, even William James—who contributed to the literature of localization; but I am not going to detain you with a history lesson on a thesis that is already established. Instead, I am now going to speed ahead to the important question: what did establishing the brain's asymmetry tell us about human beings, and about madness?

"And I want to be quite clear that my mentor and source here is not Charcot and the French tradition, not German psychology and certainly not the Viennese School: it is still Dr. John Hughlings Jackson, the father of English neurology. My entire definition of 'consciousness,' or what I have called our 'sixth sense,' is based on Hughlings Jackson. His distinction between 'subject' and 'object' consciousness was a philosophical one, but he went on to place it in the functioning of the lopsided brain. To summarize very briefly, he believed that people became conscious of changes in themselves only by the agency of what he called 'symbol-images.' The words and pictures thrown up by left and right sides of the brain served to dramatize, in the mind's toy theater, thoughts or feelings that would otherwise be imperceptible. The task of Jackson's double brain was nothing less than to provide the self with a continuous and orderly, if somewhat simplified, commentary on its personal reality.

"All this, as I have said, was there to be read in the mainstream medical literature, available in any reputable library. Also there to be read, since the beginning of literary civilization, were the first stories of mankind, including Homer and the Bible, with their accounts of early humans receiving heard instructions from their gods. All I did with these books, ladies and gentlemen, was believe them. I did not reinterpret them, I just *believed* them.

"I started my life as an amateur of literature, devoted above all to

Shakespeare, whose plays show many examples of human beings aware dramatically of themselves and their ability to choose and change this still-new entity, this 'self.' Think of Hamlet, whom I just quoted. If, as I believe, this second level of consciousness, the one at which we now exist with our 'sixth sense,' was not caused by a change of 'genes' but flowed from the astonishing moment at which we developed writing not as pictogram but as sound representation, then it must by definition be a product of culture, not of biology, and must be learned by each infant. Shakespeare did more than anyone since Jesus Christ to spread that 'sixth sense,' to enshrine it; one might even argue that he changed our very idea of what humans were, and say that after Hamlet, introspection became universal.

"I took these literary readings and squared them with Hughlings Jackson's neurological idea of consciousness in the asymmetric brain. In my version, I have given more emphasis than he did to the verbal rather than the visual storytelling that makes up our metaphor of reality, for the simple reason that I believe language to be more important and that the model it offers us is, by definition, more exclusively human. A dog, after all, may have a picture-sample of reality, but, without language, it has no self-awareness."

Thomas paused to drink again, raising his eyes above the rim of the glass as he did so to survey his dwindling flock. He saw Kitty at the back, her gaze anxiously fixed on him, and for a moment felt a scalding flush of love for her. There was a temptation to weaken, to throw up this hard argument, and to retreat into her arms behind closed doors.

He tightened his jaw, coughed and drew himself up one last time.

"To conclude," he said. "The implication for certain kinds of psychosis is, as I think I have told you already, fairly straightforward. Quite minor neural malfunctions, caused by minute combinations of inherited matter, could cause grotesque distortions in the signals that go through the corpus callosum from one side of the brain to the other. There may be an abnormality in the neural impulse, but the greater error, I feel sure, is in the overeager responding of the left hemisphere, which must take action to avoid being overwhelmed by excitation. It is better to mishear a half-formed thought as a real voice and respond to what it says than to drown in a deluge of impulses; it is easier to deal with a pathological story than to have no story at all in the theater of your head. Any story is better than no story; and on that survival instinct, the brain will always come up with an interpretation, however illogical, harmful or frightening. All the accumulated aeons of natural selection, of the 'survival of the fittest,' are bearing down on it to do so. To fail would be, literally, inhuman—though the strain of not failing killed my friend Olivier.

"So, before I conclude, I would like to stress two final, minor but important things about Olivier's disease, or schizophrenia. First, while it is an awful and frightening condition, there is a sense in which the lesion may not be organically so very profound. Why? Because its patients almost always live to the age of about twenty in males, or a little older in females, without developing symptoms. They are healthy; they are fine; indeed often, as in the case of Olivier himself, rather more intelligent and self-aware than normal. From this, we deduce that the predisposition to the disease is activated only when the development of the cortex is complete. At that moment of maturity, alas, the malfunction fires—perhaps spontaneously; or perhaps the brain chemistry is excited by some external stress, as we believe to have been the case with our primitive ancestors, able to summon voices when the raised stress chemicals in their brains activated certain circuits. The difference in schizophrenic patients appears to be that once these circuits have been connected, they cannot be turned off.

"One last note on this illness. I said that it was terrible, yet that in some ways very little seemed to be wrong. Imagine a ship leaving West Africa for the New World. If the compass was set only one degree out— just one tiny degree out of three hundred and sixty—it could end up not in New York but in Mexico. That is what I mean by a tiny flaw and a catastrophic result.

"We stand now at a crossroads in the life of the mind. The gentlemen of the Viennese School tell us that their psychic apparatus of 'repression' and so forth is not just a metaphysical concept but a tangible entity. We cannot *yet* perceive it with our senses, even with the best microscope, but, they claim, it is a functional system whose diseases are emphatically its own and follow their own pathology, independent of any brain disease. The treatment, they say, lies in talking. The famous

American psychiatrist Adolf Meyer, who trained in Switzerland, wrote in *The Psychological Bulletin* five years ago that it is increasingly being understood that psychology, not neurology, must serve as the foundation for the study of mental illness.

"Well, it depends what you mean by psychology, dear doctor. If you mean Oedipus and dogma, unseen and unprovable mechanisms, a church of true believers in the great universal truth that will have no other, then you are wrong. And furthermore you will systematically withhold help from some of the most pitifully suffering people in the world. Pray God you fail.

"If, however, you mean that the biological illness of the psychotic mind finds shape and character in the individual life of the patient and is molded by it, as water flooding a plain will be diverted by the topography of the valley, then you speak true.

"But how are we going to cure these sick people? For all I have said, I do believe talk and kindness may have a part. Each of these patients is an individual, and each responds differently to the electrical short circuits in the brain. To me, this implies that each one, too, must be approachable and helpable according to his or her circumstances. I have had some very modest success from listening and advising, from offering consolation. I have also used the resources of the pharmacy in times of emergency and they have given some temporary respite, though in reality little more than the effects of a long sleep. However, chemists busy in their laboratories may one day synthesize some compound that addresses itself to this particular, invisible disease. We do not expect it to happen soon. After all, we have as yet no cure for the visible microbe of syphilis.

"If we are right about the hereditary nature of schizophrenia, then perhaps we can breed it out of the population, as we bred Jersey cows, tea roses or greyhounds. On the other hand, if it is as closely linked as we believe to the combination of genes that give us our human capacities, it can never be eradicated. You would have to annihilate the whole of humanity.

"I was shocked as a young man by the writing of Henry Maudsley, Britain's most fashionable psychiatrist, who preached 'degeneration' and advocated a sort of antibreeding program. He has now changed his mind. Last year, in his book *Heredity, Variation and Genius,* he wrote: 'To forbid the marriage of a person sprung from an insanely disposed family might be to deprive the world of a singular genius or talent, and so be an irreparable injury to the race of men. . . . If, then, one man of genius were produced at the cost of one thousand or fifty thousand insane persons, the result might be a compensation for the terrible cost.' I do not pretend to follow the reasoning behind his change of mind, but he has clearly seen how psychosis is indissolubly part of humanity.

"Indissoluble, did I say? Why? Why can we not dissolve it, separate it out? Because to do so we would need to know the chemical makeup and the physical function of all the units of inheritance in humanity—individually and in all possible combinations. And as yet we cannot even *see* them!

"I can offer very little to my psychotic patients—little but gestures of love and comfort. Their release may take thousands of years, because in my view the only certain cure is . . . evolution. If *Homo sapiens* were to mutate again and shake the kaleidoscope of particles that make him, it is possible he could retain his modern mind but lose his madness. Possible. But the truth is, we have always, from the moment of our origination, been a profoundly flawed species—mad in the basic particles of our being, radically insane—and the building of the great asylums only served to show us the magnitude of our madness, as the rural lunatics were gathered up and put beneath one roof with their urban cousins for the first time. Psychosis, ladies and gentlemen, is the price we pay for being what we are.

"And how unfair, how bitterly unfair it is that that price is not shared around but paid by one man in a hundred for the other ninety-nine. Think on that.

"And that minute, momentous change in Africa that made us men—was it really worth it? What it has enabled us to do is to understand that our brains are the result of physical processes as comprehensible to us as those which make the waves of the sea or the stamen of a flower; that we are part of a continuous physical universe and that there is no niche in it—not one crack—in which we can find any special dispensation for ourselves. One of the greatest achievements of the human intellect has been to show us precisely this deficiency: the fruits of our conscious brains have robbed us of any privileged place in creation. There is no God and there is no consolation for us, only death.

"And yet, and yet . . . I do see grounds for hope. It is possible that we will lose our 'sixth sense,' our human self-awareness, and with it our psychosis. Since we are, in Alfred Russel Wallace's belief—and mine, for what it matters—far more evolved than we have any need to be in the competition for resources, it could be that, with a change in environmental pressure, natural selection will favor a less developed brain. It is certainly possible. After all, the most miraculous organ, after the human brain, ever to have developed in nature is the eye. Even Darwin found it hard to explain this miracle. And yet, the bats in their caves, who once had sight, survive as well or better without their eyes. They ceased to use them or to need them; they are more 'successful' *without* eyesight and now they carry vestigial blind eyes. Perhaps one day human beings will carry only vestigial higher consciousness, a simpler version having been selected in the fight for survival.

"The second ground for hope is the exact opposite. We are continuing to evolve, perhaps more rapidly than ever. And just as we developed, first through mutation, then through culture, our 'sixth sense,' so we may go on to develop a seventh—*a new faculty, as great as self-awareness.* To me the benefits of such a development would be less medical than philosophical. But they would be productive of happiness, if that emotion survived the change. The beings we became would, of course, no longer, strictly speaking, be *Homo sapiens.*

"As things stand, we have a problem. To conceive of ourselves as fragmentary matter cohering for a millisecond between two eternities of darkness is very difficult, because our lives do not feel like that. Either, therefore, that is not the reality, or there is something wrong with the way that we register reality. That is why I am a psychiatrist, because the evident problems the insane encounter in dealing with the world should be instructive to us all. We who are well are straining very hard at this intermediate stage in our evolution, driving our reason to work, in an attempt to reconcile and make palatable all the contradictions, mysteries and non sequiturs we experience from day to day.

"To think of ourselves as atoms in an infinite universe is in fact not really possible; it is just not how we experience life—which we feel as something linear and driven to an end. So either we have the science wrong, or we are merely encountering the limits of our toy conscious- ness. I believe the latter, and I hope I have shown you what a small, sim- plified and metaphorical sample of reality our consciousness really offers us, with its one-dimensional time and shadow 'I' in its tiny inward theater.

"But we may evolve and we may change; and that, as I have said before, is how the insoluble knots and mysteries of life are eventually resolved, not by the finding of an 'answer,' but by the development of a perspective in which the problems no longer exist. We do not lose much sleep over the eternal conundra of the domestic cat. . . . It is not that we could not 'understand' them, I suppose, if they were described to us, it is more that they would seem beside the point.

"Yet, what glory is there in our very own cat's-eye view of the world, our one-degree peephole on the sphere of reality! As I remarked to the gentleman who left, the chances of such richness, of Shakespeare and Mozart, developing from a submicroscopic mutation are so great as to be beyond calculation. From that mathematical fact, you may deduce, like my critic who left the hall and like Alfred Russel Wallace before him, that such an improbable change must therefore necessarily have involved the interference of a higher outside force; or you may believe, like Charles Darwin and like me, that the biological laws of evolution cannot be *selec- tively* breached. Whatever you believe in your hearts, ladies and gentle- men, I ask you to believe with me that either conclusion must logically lead you to see that we are the most fortunate species ever to have lived or that it is possible to conceive of existing—ever, in this universe or in any other; and that it is our duty each day therefore to appreciate our astonishing good fortune by caring for the insane, who pay the price for all of us, and by turning our own healthy lives, so near as we can man- age it, day by day, into an extended rapture."

Thomas gathered his notes and descended stiffly from the podium, rubbing his hand over the small of his back, where the muscles had gone into spasm from his long standing. He walked down the aisle of the hall, gray-haired now in his fiftieth year, between the rows of silent people who averted their embarrassed eyes, until he reached his wife. She took his arm and led him out into the courtyard, where the fountain played. He slumped down onto the stone rim. Kitty sat down beside him and placed her arm round his shoulders.

"They did not believe me," he said.

"I believed you, Thomas."

"I know I am right, but I did not convince them."

"It was good, it was noble, it was very fine."

He did not reply.

"'O, young Lochinvar,'" she murmured. "It is a hard life, Thomas, as I think I told you once before." She stroked his hair. "'He rode all unarmed and he rode all alone . . .'"

XXI

JACQUES DID NOT SPEAK TO THOMAS FOR A YEAR AFTER HIS LECTURE, and nothing Sonia could say would persuade him otherwise.

She stood in for him at the morning meetings, while the informal exchanges at the end of the day, which had in any case become less regular, ceased altogether. He asked her to organize his diary so that while Thomas's consultations started on the hour, his own began at half past; he dined in his house and refused several invitations from Kitty to join her and Thomas. On the occasions when they saw one another in the course of their work, he merely nodded silently in Thomas's direction.

It had been his loud footsteps that Thomas had heard leaving the hall after his opening remarks about the Viennese School. What Jacques could not forgive was what he took to be a kind of gloating. Many years ago he had failed to diagnose a largely asymptomatic condition in one patient, believing some lower abdominal pain to be of mental rather than uterine origin. It was hardly a crime, and the cysts had proved harmless. For fifteen years he had lived with the daily reminder of his mistake; he had watched Katharina become one of the principal forces in the sanatorium that was his life's work. She had been meticulously friendly to him; indeed, he was actually prepared to believe what she had once told him—that her delight at being well again was such that she never gave a thought to the "little false start" in her treatment. Why would she care about that, when the schloss had successfully cured her in the end? The lightness of her spirit was a reproach to him, however;

and he could not help noticing that the winter months were a trial to her, bringing fevers and throat infections, even though, since there was no cure to offer, an earlier diagnosis of her rheumatic fever would not have helped.

Why then, with his healthy twins, his gaily ungrudging wife and the stimulus of his own theories to sustain him, had Thomas chosen to preface the presentation of his philosophical and medical position with an attack on a school of thought he knew had been both attractive and painful to his partner? It was not necessary for the explanation of his own thinking that other systems first be shown wanting or demolished. It was quite possible to have a biological view of Olivier's disease, and to link it—albeit speculatively—to questions of consciousness and evolution, while at the same time allowing room for a more psychological view of the basis of some nervous symptoms. Indeed, Jacques himself believed in the coexistence of the two schools of thought; the Holy Grail still remained to be found at the point where they intersected. He himself had so far failed, but so had Thomas.

The lecture had been reported in the local papers in quite sensational terms, as though Darwin had not published sixty years before, but its reception in the medical press had been quieter. Their reports pointed out the gaps in the hypothesis, chiefly the lack of evidence that schizophrenia was evenly spread through different populations; others questioned Darwin's belief that *Homo sapiens* had necessarily originated in Africa, close to his nearest obvious relatives. There was unhappiness about the extent to which it had been established that human inheritance followed the model of Mendel and his garden peas. Above all, Thomas's theory seemed to offer no therapeutic hope, since the particles of inheritance responsible for the condition could not be identified, let alone modified. His suggestion that evolution might be the best cure for psychosis was held to be frivolous. Although the learned journals declared themselves impressed by the range of connections he had made, and largely convinced on the question of brain asymmetry, they were concerned by the extent to which Thomas relied on British authorities, and none was sufficiently convinced by the underlying scientific argument to offer to reprint the lecture. A popular science magazine in London did run an edited version, but it seemed that, as far as the college of opinion that made up the European school was concerned, Thomas remained marginal and eccentric; it was as though after twenty-five years with a microscope he had emerged as he went in, as little more than an amateur of Shakespeare, with scientific longings.

Jacques took no pleasure in the relative failure of Thomas's venture; failure was a condition of being a mad-doctor, so he had expected little else. He could not lose the feeling, however, that Thomas had tried to trample on him, to use him as a step up for his own ambitions, and the feeling of betrayal was like an ulcer burning out his belly.

In his own life, he felt he had reached an impasse. The last survivor of his original family, he could now go quietly into the final decade of his working life, thence into comfortable old age; or he could survey the landscape and decide to move onward. He had withstood the worst that life could offer, death and humiliation, and although he could feel a coarsening in the texture of himself, he felt no diminution of energy or desire. If life, as it appeared, was only this vain struggle before the endless dark, then he might as well be bold.

For five years he had been friends with Roya and had checked his feelings for her by refusing to acknowledge them. It was not the kind of simple repression or displacement he had diagnosed in Katharina; it was more subtle than that, in that he was aware of the process of repression. He was conscious of what was unconscious, and when he allowed himself a glimpse, it was frighteningly primitive; but even at such rare moments of honesty, he never dignified the emotion with the name of "love." Sonia was the woman he loved; she was all he had ever wanted and he would no more forsake her than he would trade Daniel for a hypothetical daughter. The sensation of Roya's presence was something quite different: it played across his nerves in an exquisite way, the baseness of his half-acknowledged desires so at odds with, yet so complementary to, her youth and femininity.

Yet it seemed to him that it was more also than that: she was a fragment from another world, a glimpse of some paradise withheld, and if he did not somehow claim his kinship with her, then all his lives, in past and future time, would be forever disconnected. Once he had allowed this knowledge into his mind, it assumed command, and his normal thoughts became subordinate.

In the spring he had received a firmer invitation from Hofrat Drobesch to his "Modern World Colloquium, 1910," and in the second week of June he set out for the village near Bad Ischl where Drobesch had his summerhouse. His train arrived earlier than he had expected, and although he spent some time looking round the town, he found himself feeling agitated and furtive; he wanted to be at the lake house ahead of the others. He asked a cabdriver at the station how long it would take them, and decided to leave straight away.

As they bounced over the cobbles, then left the town on dry summer roads, Jacques found that his mind seemed empty. On long journeys he usually read medical books as part of his never-ending education; when his eyes grew tired, he would close them and try to piece together what he had learned, to see if it illuminated what he already knew. Then he spoke to himself, silently, explaining his knowledge, noting the gaps in his understanding, either mentally or in a small black notebook—like a constant, thinking engine.

On this warm evening, however, he seemed incapable of thought; he inhaled the smell of the unharvested fields, he sometimes heard the cattle and the birds over the rumble of the carriage, and was content to be borne along in this animal state. He felt helpless and impelled.

When the cab arrived at the top of a drive, the hedgerows heavy, the track overgrown, he climbed down and paid the driver. The name of the house was inscribed on a stone by the wayside, and he pushed open the gate. A minute's walk brought him to a courtyard with an arch covered in wisteria; through it was a large house on which the pink paint was peeling. He walked round the side and found himself looking down over sloping gardens to a huge lake, shimmering and empty in the evening sun. There was a boathouse and a wooden jetty; on the far side of the water, the woods grew down to the shore, with no sign of habitation. Returning to the house, he found a key beneath an old stone water trough in the courtyard and opened the side door. He was in a hall, leading to the kitchens, from which he walked across into the main part of the house. The air was trapped by the closed windows, and he could smell plaster, the wood of the floorboards and dried flowers. He called out, but it was clear from the silence and the feeling of the house that there was no one there.

He climbed the stairs and found himself on a wide landing with three different passageways opening from it. He took the one that he thought would lead to the bedrooms overlooking the lake, calculated which room would have the best view and knocked at the door. There was, as he expected, no answer, so he turned the handle and went in. A brass bed with a faded floral cover had been recently made up, to judge from the starched white linen he could see on the bolster. It was a large room with two painted wooden chests and a wardrobe; through its windows, the lake lay empty and glistening.

The cupboard door swung open easily. He had feared to find—he did not know what: men's clothes, suits, children's things; but the hung row of dresses and skirts reassured him. He pulled them out one by one until he had come across at least five or six he knew were hers. His heart was lumbering in his chest and his hand was shaking. He saw a corner of purple on white and pulled out a skirt. Before he could stop himself, he had wrenched it from its hanger and lifted the material to his face, where he inhaled a smell of cotton, soap and rosewater. He ran the fabric over his tongue, as though he might taste her. Then, in a panic of haste, he went to the chest and pulled open the top drawer. It was full of papers: bills and receipts from local tradesmen, some old photographs, a man— perhaps her father—with a white mustache standing in front of a build- ing with a minaret. He pushed the drawer shut and went to the other chest. He wrenched at the brass handle and thrust his hand inside, into softness. The clean underclothes were unsorted, as though the maid had merely thrown them in after they came back from the laundry. Jacques lifted a handful, soft straps and stockings trailing from between his fin- gers, and pressed a piece of lace to the skin of his lips. He breathed in and filled his lungs with her. He glanced round at the open doorway, but there was still no one there.

THE HOUSE party was under way by seven in the evening, as carriages dropped the visitors at the top of the drive. Hofrat Drobesch addressed his guests in what he called the "summer room," a conservatory that overlooked the lake.

"Dear colleagues and friends, you are most welcome to our Colloquium and I trust that your accommodation is comfortable. This is a most informal venture and we have a very limited staff, but I hope you will feel free to ask if we can make your stay more pleasant. Although our conversation will be serious, I would like you to view the weekend in other ways as a holiday—an outdoor holiday or a hike, if you will, in which you should feel free to make your own arrangements. Should you wish literally to go for a walk or an excursion, the kitchen can provide a modest picnic for you. My wife or I can advise you on the best paths and views."

Drobesch then began to outline what the themes of the weekend would be. He was a man who enjoyed talking; in fact, Jacques noticed, he actually listened to himself as he talked, and his speech was punctuated by notes of unconvincing modesty: "If you would not think it presumptuous . . ."; "if you would permit me to say . . ."; or on two or three occasions: "How shall I put this?"—a hesitation followed by a phrase he had clearly worked out before.

Roya sat beside him, her hands folded in the lap of her lilac dress, a pair of black slippers with pearl decorations occasionally visible when she shifted her weight on the wicker chair of the "summer room." Her black hair was loose to her bare shoulders.

Around him, Jacques saw assembled various men he knew by face or reputation: among them, two politicians, a diplomat, a newspaper editor, an astronomer from the university in Vienna, a banker and a playwright.

". . . at the start of this new century, a time, I feel confident, that will at last see an end to bloodshed in Europe," said Drobesch, "an end to the wars and squabbling which so disfigured our continent in the last hundred years. This is a time when, if I may say so, the work of scientists as much as of philosophers gives us leave to hope that we will shortly be in a position to give clear and certain answers to almost all the problems that have troubled us for so long. How did we get here and what makes us who we are? Of what is the universe made? How old is it? What is the future and how do we bend it to our civilized will? From the worlds of theoretical physics, biology, astronomy, psychology as well"—here he inclined his head graciously to the playwright—"as from literature, the answers are coming in an irresistible flow, so that soon, dear friends, I feel sure we shall be in a position to offer a unifying theory that will satisfy our deepest intellectual cravings and will be our legacy to future generations."

Jacques caught Roya's eye as the speech concluded; her expression remained one of impassive attention to her husband. She applauded briefly with the others when he finished. Jacques lit a cigar and went out onto the terrace, where a man in a short white coat was handing round drinks.

As he looked down at the view, he was aware of someone behind him, and knew, without needing to look, that it was she, though he did not at once turn round. He was surprised by how calm he felt: incapable of thought again, and relieved to be so.

"Are you settled in all right?"

There was a noncommittal hand on his sleeve, and he turned to smile at her.

"Yes. Thank you. A maid showed me to my room. It is a lovely house."

"It has been in my husband's family for a long time. I am afraid it is rather run-down and too cold to use in winter. But he and his brothers like it just as it is, and they refuse to do any work to it."

"It has charm. How are you, Roya?"

"I am very well. But how are you, dear doctor?"

He searched her face for some sign of humor or complicity, but the mask was impenetrable; he saw how young her skin was, still unlined, but with a slight flush in the neck above the collar of her dress—rose flooding gold.

"I am all right." His own voice sounded hoarse and abrupt.

"Have you had time to explore?"

"I . . . Yes, I got here a little early, as you know. I let myself in before the servants arrived. I hope that was all right."

"Of course. It is what I intended. And was everything to your liking?"

"I . . . Yes. Very much so."

"I think you are blushing, Doctor."

Jacques put his hand to his face. It was true. He coughed and tried to reassert his dignity. "I have not blushed since . . . not since I was a boy and was caught showing off to the local curé about how much I knew about biology. I was just making it up."

"And now?"

"I feel hot. It is a warm evening."

He smiled and, to his delight, she smiled back into his eyes. Could it be that she suspected, or knew what he had done?

"Perhaps tomorrow," she said.

"Tomorrow what?"

"Perhaps tomorrow," said Roya, mildly, but still looking into his eyes, "you may conclude your exploration."

"My . . ."

"Exploration. You may find what you are searching for."

Jacques wanted to say nothing, in case by speaking he might destroy the fragile suggestion that hung between them. He raised an eyebrow, but she did not look away.

When he had let the idea hang long enough, he said, "Indeed. The 'unifying theory.' The Holy Grail. Or what we scientists might more honestly call the great chimera."

"As you wish, Doctor. Dinner is in ten minutes."

Jacques walked down to the lake on his own, not wanting to join the professional banter of the guests. He thought of Daniel, who would be fifteen in October. They still sometimes called him Herr Frage, abbreviated from Fragezeichen, after his mysterious valentine; but he had suddenly grown tall, with a jawline forcing its way through his soft boy's features. Then he thought of his beloved Sonia, the only person in the world who had never disappointed him. He felt the anguish of his human love for them; it was the shape of himself, it made him who he was; yet both seemed absent, and he could not quite bring them into his living thoughts.

At dinner, he drank all the wine the butler offered and made reluctant conversation with those on either side, replying to inquiries about his work with a brevity that barely qualified as civil. There was an "informal gathering" in the main sitting room afterward in which one of the politicians was to "lead a conversation" about the rumbling Serbian quarrel with Austria-Hungary over the ownership of Bosnia-Herzegovina.

Of what possible interest could that be to anyone, thought Jacques as he went out on the terrace once more, stumbling for a moment as he caught his foot on the step. He took off his jacket and threw it over his shoulder; he still had a glass of wine in his hand as he walked alone over the lawn and down to the lake. There were stars all over the woods and the hills beyond. He sat on the jetty and leaned back against the wall of the boathouse, looking up to them, hearing the occasional lap of the tired water beneath him. There was depth in the heavens, there was the comfort of distance, yet looking at the sky always made him feel more than ever ignorant and boyish, as though he had never grown up since he first ran beneath the cold moon at Saint Agnès.

When there was a footfall behind him, a light step transferred to wooden boarding, he sighed and resigned himself. "Roya," he said, without turning round.

She came and sat beside him.

"I am going to put my feet in the water," she said. She raised her feet and pulled off her slippers, then lifted her skirt and rolled down her stockings. She leaned for balance on Jacques's shoulder as she did so. She kicked her bare feet in the water. Without speaking, he lifted her skirt, as she had herself done, and ran the palm of his hand up over her knee and onto her thigh. He left it there in case she should protest, but she said nothing. Instead, she kissed him, letting her tongue touch his lips, squeezing his rib cage with the force of her embrace. She remained with her mouth against his for a long time, while he ran his hand further up her thigh till he felt the risen junction of her legs beneath silk.

"I have thought about this for so many years," he said. "Just this part of you. I have pictured it so often." He was surprised by his own directness. His voice sounded rough; he could not force any tenderness into it.

"I love you so much," she said. "I love your voice, I love the way you talk to me, the quizzical way you look at me. I love your hands, your beautiful hands, I love your kindness, I love—"

He did not want to hear her protestations of love, so put his lips against her mouth to silence her. When he had finished, he whispered in her ear what he had imagined doing to her. He said things he had never said before, as though someone else were speaking through him. He could feel her breathing hard against his face, but she did not tell him to stop.

———————

THE NEXT morning at ten, the "colloquium" began in earnest with a paper on "Sutton, Boveri and the Function of the Chromosome." The theme of this was interesting to Jacques, though he found it hard to concentrate.

The weather was still fine, but the air had grown heavy, he noticed, when they went into the dining room for lunch. A cold collation had been set out on the main table, and they were invited to help themselves and take their plates outside or find seats with the neighbors of their choice.

Jacques took some cold meats and salad outside onto the terrace. He saw Roya standing on the grass, pouring wine for a couple sitting at one of the small white wrought-iron tables that had been set in the shade. She was wearing a long cream skirt and high-necked blouse, with a string of purple beads, he noticed, as she leaned forward to pour from the green bottle.

"Ah, Dr. Rebière. Why don't you come and sit here, at my table? I can tell Florian to take over my wine-pouring duties. Florian, ask Maria to bring me some salads, will you?"

She seemed to be in high spirits, he thought, unabashed by anything that might have taken place between them. For a few moments they were alone. He raised his glass to her and drank some cold hock. Then Hofrat Drobesch came to join them, bringing with him the diplomat who had spoken the night before.

The Hofrat settled him at the table with a good deal of insistence on how informal he was being; then he sat with his fingertips touching in a pensive steeple before his lips and asked Jacques's opinion of what he had heard that morning. Jacques shot a rapid glance at Roya, who raised her eyebrows, all attention.

"I . . . Well, we have known about the chromosome for ages, since before I was born. Sutton and Boveri seem to have established that each species has a set number of chromosomes and that when they split to form the sex cells you have a basis for a law of inheritance not by 'blending' but by a choice of units, as was argued by a Moravian monk called Mendel. Though he confined his researches to peas."

The diplomat laughed. "It sounds very old hat to me, suggesting all this stuff is predetermined. It sounds just like the idea of 'preformationism,' that every being carries all its descendants ready-made in a little bag! We had stopped believing in that when I was a schoolboy."

Jacques shrugged. "Perhaps." He looked at Roya, to see if she had followed.

"Come, come, dear doctor!" said Drobesch. "Do not be put off so easily. Defend your man—your Moravian kitchen-gardener!"

Jacques looked at Drobesch for a moment or two. The days when such men intimidated him had long gone. "He is not really my man," he said eventually, stirring himself. "What your lecturer seemed unaware of is the existence of something called a 'gene,' which is a tiny particle contained on the chromosome, like a pearl threaded on a string, that instructs the cell how to grow."

"Go on, Doctor."

"I suppose that in the course of division, errors can occur. After all, these are living, moving particles, not mathematical constants—or bricks."

He felt a stockinged foot run up the skin of his calf, beneath the leg of his trousers. "And what happens next?" said Roya, her head on one side, a schoolgirl attentive to the teacher.

"I . . . Well, I suppose a variant creature is born. A mutant, if you will."

"And does it then die out?"

"Yes. Unless its mutation gives it an advantage, in which case it will successfully breed and pass its variation on—and on and on. Till almost all the species has it."

"And what is that process called, Doctor?"

"Evolution by natural selection."

"Good heavens!" Drobesch smacked the table. "I knew we should return to dear old Monsieur Lamarck!"

"Mr. Darwin, in fact," said Jacques. "I regret to take the credit from my fellow-countryman, of course. He, among others, wrote about evolution before Darwin, but the discovery of the mechanism of natural selection and the beautiful description of its intricacy was Darwin's own."

The foot was removed from Jacques's leg. He felt a trickle of sweat at his temple. The conversation moved on to other matters, and when he shifted in his seat he found the shirt was damp on his back.

Fruit and coffee were brought out to them, and Drobesch eventually stood up to go inside. "I must make sure everything is set up for this afternoon," he said. "We have a fascinating program. Then time off till dinner at seven."

The diplomat excused himself and followed Drobesch into the house.

"It is very close, is it not?" said Roya, peeling a piece of apple. "I feel a slight headache coming on. I shall need to retire to my bedroom."

"You will be sorry to miss the lecture."

"It is my husband speaking. I can always catch up. Do you feel quite well, Doctor?"

Jacques paused. He recognized the moment. He had waited many years for it. "No, I also have a slight headache. It is probably only the heat."

"But you ought perhaps to take no chances."

"Yes. You may be right."

"Do knock on my door if you should need anything. I think you know which one it is."

He watched her go back over the grass onto the terrace and hold the doors open for the last of the guests as they returned to the main room. Then he walked down to the lake and gazed at the water for a long time. He kept looking at his watch, but the hand seemed not to move; he looked over the water and counted off the seconds. He could think of nothing—except what he had felt beneath his hand the night before. No other image could make itself present in his mind; his thoughts had stuck. When ten minutes had elapsed, he walked round to the far side of the house and let himself in at the side door, as he had done the previous afternoon. He went quietly up the servants' staircase and doubled back along the upstairs corridor to the front of the house. He paused outside Roya's room, looked both ways down the empty passage, and knocked. He heard her footfall inside.

"I thought you wouldn't come." She stood back to let him in, her face at first distraught, then loosening with relief.

"I didn't mean to, but I couldn't stop myself. I didn't know what I was doing."

"Kiss me. Touch me where you did last night."

"Oh, Roya, I have thought about it for so long."

"So have I. I have been obsessed."

"But what do we do if your husband comes back?"

"He won't. Nothing will tear him from his own lecture. But I shall lock the door. There. Tell me, Jacques, did you come here yesterday?"

He thought about denying it, but everything in her eyes suggested forgiveness and excitement. He said, "Yes. I am sorry, I—"

"What did you do?"

"I went over here, to the wardrobe. And I pulled out this skirt. And I held it like this. And I inhaled it. Like this."

"Did it make you feel excited?"

"Yes."

"Is that all?"

"Yes." Surely she could not want to know more.

"Are you certain? Did you not come to this drawer here?"

"I . . . Yes. I am afraid I did."

"And what did you do?"

"I took out these things and I kissed them."

"Show me."

"Like this."

"And what else?"

"I . . . touched . . ."

"What?"

"Here."

"With my things?"

"Yes."

"Show me."

"Just here."

"No, actually show me."

"Like . . . wait a minute . . . like this. I felt I was going to burst."

"And did you rub them on yourself?"

"Yes."

"Show me."

"Like this."

"Now let me do it. Was it like this?"

"Yes. Like that. And with the skirt."

"This one? The one with the purple flowers?"

"Yes."

"Is this what you did?"

"Yes."

"Anything else?"

"The cream blouse."

"This ruched one?"

"Yes."

"Like this? Faster?"

"Yes."

"And what were you thinking?"

"I was thinking of you. Of a particular part of you."

"And would you like to see it? Not just imagine it?"

"Yes. Lift up your skirt. Will you take these off? Now hold your skirt up so I can . . . this part . . . here."

"Does it feel as you imagined?"

He could not answer.

"And now?" Roya still seemed exhilaratingly detached.

"Now I want to . . . I can't allow myself to say it."

"Whisper it, Jacques. Lie on top of me and whisper in my ear what you would like to do to me."

He did as he was told.

"There. You said it. It was not so bad."

"And do you want me to do it?"

"Yes."

"Are you sure?"

"I want you to do it now."

"Are you ready?"

"Yes. Now."

"Then ask me."

"Please, Jacques."

"No. Beg me."

"I am begging you."

"Say what you want me to do. Whisper it in my ear. Say that word."

He lifted her up and moved her further back onto the bed and positioned himself so that he was ready to make love to her. His face was against the smooth skin of her cheek; his head was full of the smell of her hair and her skin. His whole body ached.

"Now," she said.

"Not until you ask me. Say it."

She put her arms round his neck and whispered the rough invitation he had craved, and when she said the word, he drove himself completely into her.

LATER, SHE said, "I have never behaved like this before."

"Neither have I."

"Did you like it?"

"Yes. But I feel ashamed. I did not know I was so coarse a man. And you?"

Roya sat up on the bed, her hair disheveled, her throat and cheeks flushed. "It was not me, it was some other girl."

"You are perfect. Your skin is so soft, and this part here. And here. You are unique."

Roya laughed and stood up, the skirt still caught up round her waist; then she took off all her clothes and stood naked in the slight breeze that came in from the window.

"Turn round," he said.

She twisted slowly, still smiling, shaking loose her black hair, allowing her lover to see every part of what he had taken.

"You are perfect," he said again.

Roya smiled.

"You look happy," he said.

"I feel happy. I feel free. As though from a long imprisonment. Now kiss me goodbye."

"Can I kiss you . . . there?"

"Yes." She closed her eyes. "Now goodbye. Go quickly."

Jacques went as if in a dream.

"Will I see you—"

"Go quickly!"

"I hope your headache improves," he remembered to say as he closed the door.

He stumbled down the back stairs in a panic of remorse and exhilaration; it was as though every part of him were both applauding and lamenting. He found a door into the garden and ran until he was in an orchard beneath some apple trees. He felt himself losing control of his bladder, fumbled at his buttons and released a stream onto the grass amid some prematurely fallen fruit. Such a thing had not happened to him since the age of three or four. Tears erupted from his eyes as he thought of Sonia; anguish and fear squeezed his belly when he pictured what might happen if his awful act was discovered. He walked up and down the orchard, twisting and turning as the waves of remorse and exultation alternated; but somewhere in the confusion he felt he could discern a hard, small voice that told him not to repine, to recognize what kind of being he was and to survive.

"DO YOU think," said Kitty one day, "that your brother is growing a little . . . how can I put it? Eccentric?"

"Thomas?" said Sonia. "Well, he has always been inclined that way. Why do you ask?"

"He seems a little forgetful at times. Distracted. When he shaves, he sometimes misses a patch on one cheek, but he doesn't seem to notice."

Sonia smiled. They were sitting in her office and both were tired of filing patients' reports. "As a boy he was very unpredictable, moody, rash, peculiar. But he had charm and he could be sensible if it was truly necessary. He was clever. He seemed to have his rashness under control."

"Yes," said Kitty. "I remember watching him once at dinner in the schloss, making himself pleasant to some of the patients. He was joining in their conversation and the two young women seemed rather flattered. Then I suddenly heard something in his voice which made me see he thought the whole thing was the most tremendous joke. He was playing with them."

"Oh dear, I know that feeling," said Sonia. "I remember when we were children. Sometimes when I had put my most heartfelt feelings into words I used to look in his eyes and see that all along he had been miles ahead of me and had just lingered, as it were, to humor me. It used to make me very cross."

"But he never said anything unkind?"

"No. No. Thomas has never been unkind. It was just that I felt a fool. And to be honest, I think I felt a little sorry for him. I wondered what he was finding so far out ahead there. I thought he must be lonely."

"Yet when I first met him," said Kitty, "he was not like that at all. He was very earnest."

"He changed," said Sonia. "It is as simple as that. People do change. I think that in mad-doctoring he found something commensurate with his capacity to keep ahead. Rather too much so, in a way."

"So he stopped playing with people."

"Yes. I mean, he would still tease Fräulein Fuchs or Fräulein Haas without them noticing it. Or me, sometimes. But I think that his sense of being superior or one step ahead was something he lost after being an undergraduate. It is the besetting sin of studenthood, after all. I think he left it in the county asylum. What he saw there changed him."

"You see," said Kitty, "what I so loved about him, what I love still, was that passion he had. There was no compromise. On the question of what makes us mad or how to cure these illnesses he was so earnest. He wanted to be the savior and believed he would be. He sincerely thought he would discover things that would change the way we see ourselves. And he saw nothing funny in that belief—that self-belief. Everything else was funny to him, though. Hans, Josef, Daisy. You and me. His world was quite divided."

Sonia sighed. "I know. For years I worried about him. I thought that his irresponsible side would surface and get us all into trouble. I remember he told me once how he had smuggled Daisy out from the asylum one night. It was a terrible thing to do. He risked his professional life—to say nothing of the consequences for her. Then when he was traveling round Europe with those rich families—he claimed he was learning languages, and indeed he was, but somehow I felt . . ."

"You felt he must be enjoying the Italian Riviera," said Kitty.

"Exactly. I am sure he did. But once we arrived in Carinthia, I saw the depth of his seriousness. He became admirably disciplined. The hours that he and Franz would work in that wretched cellar. I never dreamed he had it in him. It quite ruined his eyesight. About the time you met him, he had become . . . so admirable. A man so committed to his destiny."

Kitty smiled. "He was sublime."

"I suppose he was. He was so *kind*. I think of the hours he spent with Olivier. The patience with which he listened and searched for clues from a man who was clearly beyond help. The gentleness he showed toward him. It makes you want to weep."

Kitty coughed. "I suppose that each of us may have a great moment in our life—a month, a year—when we are most fully what we are meant to be."

"Yes," said Sonia. "I believe so. Mine is with Daniel."

"Of course. But now. Poor Thomas. He is frustrated. He is disappointed. If only he were ten years older, he could retire in the knowledge that he had done everything a man could do. But I fear he will find it hard to fill the time."

"Yes," said Sonia. "He may revert to his old ways. His old mischief."

"Out of boredom."

"Perhaps."

"And Jacques," said Kitty. "Has he changed much?"

Sonia sighed. "Well, of course. I am so unhappy that he cannot end this absurd feud with Thomas."

"I know. It is heartbreaking. Thomas was appalled at first. He tried everything to apologize and explain. But now I fear that his heart is hardening. He feels he has done all he can to make the peace."

"It is too sad. When you think how much they loved each other."

"Don't despair, Sonia. I can to some extent make Thomas do what I want. I will not allow him to neglect his duty to Jacques."

"But Jacques has changed," said Sonia. "That's the trouble. The years wear you down. It is like erosion. It is slow and invisible, but eventually the cliff will take on a new shape. Jacques was diffident when I first knew him. He told me he felt 'provisional' and dishonest in some way. But he was also very romantic, Kitty."

"I can believe it. He still is. I see the way the young female patients and the nurses look at him."

"I know. He became very confident. Suddenly. When we were in Paris. It was not just that he had faith in his own abilities, like Thomas. He believed his greatness was imminent. Any day! He was so happy. And then . . . and then it failed to happen. It was very difficult for him to settle just for being another 'nerve specialist,' as he sarcastically puts it."

"But you have reassured him."

"Of course. He became a very impressive man. His fluency in English and German, his appetite for work. The number of books he read. He, too, had a golden period and I have tried to tell him that all that work is not wasted, that he is a wonderful doctor."

"Does he believe you?"

"It is hard to say. He does not appreciate the success of the sanatorium. He sees such success as vulgar, merely 'fashionable.' The trouble is that I fear he has become dismissive of the thoughts and feelings of others."

"Don't be upset, Sonia. We will make them friends again."

"Oh, Kitty, if you only knew. When you have been as unhappy as he was in his childhood, you may never be whole. He made a wonderful life through the effort of his mind and will. But I know that in some way he still thinks the first experience he had of life is the true one—the one to which he is fated to return. Motherless, loveless, his brother mad, in a dark, dark world. I worry that in some way he must feel that that is what life is really like, and that all the years in between have been an illusion."

Kitty laid her hand on Sonia's arm. "We will make sure he is all right. We will do what we have to do to make certain that that view does not prevail."

"Of course," said Sonia, sniffing, "there is also this awful question of inheritance."

"What do you mean?"

"Olivier's disease. It is possible that Daniel may develop it."

"Surely the chances are against it, even if it is in the family."

"Yes, they are. I expect that Daniel will be all right. But do you know what haunts Jacques, what makes him lie awake at night?"

"What?"

"He thinks that perhaps his mother also suffered from it. That is why no one ever talked about her after she died. The only words he ever heard used to describe her were 'strange' and 'difficult.'"

"I am so sorry, Sonia. But we will never know, will we? And is it not better that way?"

"No, I think he would love to know. He cannot be at peace until he does."

A WEEK after the "Modern World Colloquium," Jacques and Sonia received an invitation to dine at the Drobesches'. Jacques had not seen Roya since he reeled from her bedroom, and it was with trepidation that he pulled the bell handle on the large town house. He had never lied and never been an actor in his life; he expected to stumble and be unmasked; he did not see how it could be otherwise.

They were, as usual, shown upstairs, to the large drawing room, where a dozen notables were standing round the fireplace listening to Drobesch. Roya stepped out of the circle to come and greet them; as she approached, the light from the candles in the chandelier caught the purple print flowers in her long skirt. Jacques shriveled as he watched Sonia's guilelessly polite greeting.

At dinner, the men, by Drobesch custom, were required to rotate two places clockwise after the soup, to avoid what the host referred to as the "municipal tram theory" of entertaining—a reference to the improbability of finding oneself entertained by being stuck between two strangers. The second rotation came with the dessert, and brought Jacques, by an inevitable arithmetic, next to Roya. The candlelight was reflected in the silver bracelet at the cuff of her ruched cream blouse.

Across the table was a man who did something important in a Viennese bank, though no one had been able to establish quite what, since his modesty was so grandly self-effacing that it conveyed no information at all. Jacques glanced up the table, where Sonia was listening attentively to an opposition politician expounding hotly on the Balkan issue.

As the banker turned aside, Jacques turned to his hostess.

"And how are you, Frau Drobesch?"

"Very well, Doctor."

"How elegant you look."

"Thank you. I have never worn this skirt in town before. It is more of an informal, country garment."

"But it is very charming. It complements the blouse." Jacques could not believe the serpentine duplicity with which he heard himself speak.

"Thank you. It is so warm at the moment that I thought a little infor-
mality would—"

"Indeed. Very warm."

"And how is your work progressing? Do you find yourself often in
town?"

The banker had now returned his attention to them, and Jacques
made some stiff reply about the local hospital. All the time he was thinking of Roya's bedroom, of her turning round naked in the afternoon
sun, a vision that occupied his waking and his sleeping thoughts.
Although he was intoxicated by desire, he was aware of the danger of
what he was doing and repelled by its dishonesty.

He could not stop himself, however. He admired Roya's calm men-
dacity; he was drawn, whether he liked it or not, into a conspiracy of
two, and since the happy continuance of his life depended on the success
of their deception, he was bound to feel more and more warmly toward
his fellow-conspirator. In a way, he admired her; and like Adam and Eve
exiled from the Garden, they were nothing if not a pair. He found that he
had quite properly received and accepted an offer to call in for tea the following Thursday after his clinic. He did not ask, because he already
knew, whether Drobesch would be there or absent in Vienna.

He was relieved to be outside again after dinner, back in the normal
nighttime street beneath the gas lamp; to be with Sonia again in the trap
going back to the station for the last train to the cable car. He held her
hand in the back, beneath a rug, and felt the sin of his betrayal.

YET ALL Thursday morning at the hospital he was in a state of anguished excitement. A scientific part of him was curious that a man of
his age could be so febrile; he would have thought such passionate feelings belonged to youth. At no point in his five hours at the hospital did
his desire slacken; he saw outpatients, visited inpatients, dictated notes,
had a meeting with resident physicians and at no moment was his mind
free of an image of Roya; at any time he would have been ready to make
love to her. He ached for her all morning.

Such ardor is exhausting, he thought, as he finally left the hospital
and began the walk across town. As a young man he had experienced

lust as an inconvenience. Some Paris students had little girlfriends who would sleep with them in return for having their rent paid and being taken dancing once a week, but although some of the girls were charming, some of the boys fell in love and the arrangement could be carried off with dignity, it was essentially a kind of prostitution that his Breton soul could not approve. When he himself had erotic feelings toward some girl, he merely sat up longer, read more, and arrived earlier at the dissecting room; he extirpated the impulses. Although there was a sweetness about such longings, a joyous urge selected by nature, he had come to hate them because they could never be satisfied, they must always be denied. The rich lady whose lower abdomen he palpated, running his hands over her soft skin, beneath her silk drawers, once feeling the curl of fine hair snag beneath his fingernails as his touch moved from the inguinal crease . . . He had thought of cadavers on the slab to distract himself; after all, that was how he had learned anatomy. One such lady even took his hand and rubbed his fingers through the hot, parted flesh, but he hated her for it. And other women, a nurse called Isabelle at the Salpêtrière, such a kind girl with dark brown eyes and a friendly manner who clearly liked him . . . But he must not kindle hope or desire in her, because he would never love her, could not marry her and his feelings for her were merely base. He was vigorous and alive, but circumstances had conspired to exclude him from this natural activity, which seemed reserved to other people—to married men, to those who visited whores or those who somehow could find a moral code in themselves and in their lovers that permitted it. Lust for him was frustration: they were coterminous.

Everything had changed with Sonia, when his desires were licensed by marriage, but above all by the respect he felt toward her and his sense that his instincts were pure and honorable. When he sometimes felt desire for other women, he had little difficulty in stifling it, because it seemed trivial. But in the long years of their marriage, he supposed, his amorous feelings had become respectable, bound up with childbirth and family, had turned into a token of his respectful affection; somehow they had moved over in his mind, and left vacant a plot where the old weeds of lust had taken root.

What he felt as he rang Roya's doorbell was the dark and furtive desire of the very young man he had once been; it was the lust of fantasies too shameful to name, which now appeared to be on the verge, at this late stage in his life, of being enacted.

So it proved, when Roya herself answered the door and within moments had let him know that there was no one else in the house. She took him to the drawing room where the guests had gathered before dinner and put her lips to his before she even had closed the door. He felt her fingers on the front of his trousers, then found his own hands beneath her skirt and in a few moments of undignified fumbling and tearing of clothes she was bending over the arm of the sofa and he had raised her long skirt as she reached her hand back between her legs and he gave himself to her, leaning back on his heels so he could see the detail of the junction where their flesh met. He dreaded that it would be done too soon, before he had seen her face, so pulled back to allow her to stand up. He then laid her gently down on the sofa and moved on top of her; he talked to her as he made love, telling her in the language of the peasant what he was doing, saying the words into her ear so she must hear them.

When they were finished, his shame at what he had done and said was mitigated by the fact that she could look him in the eye and tell him, as she did, that she loved him. His remorse became their shared secret, so that instead of bringing him back to normality, as he felt it should have done, it served only to bind him more tightly to her in their conspiracy.

For weeks they continued to meet at her house, and Jacques wondered if there was no act he could devise that she would not willingly indulge. She said that she had never done such things, in such a way, and he believed her. Nor had he. He was fascinated by her body, by its folds and textures, its colors and shapes. It was as though he had never examined the female form before, never anatomized, dissected or palpated. Each time he lifted her dress or parted her underclothes it was a revelation and he could sense how much she loved the effect she had on him, the way she could make him lose control.

"It is not me," she said again, still mystified. "It is some other girl who does these things."

"But it is you who enjoys them."

"I think it must be."

Her eyes grew narrow when she wanted him again and her lips, filling with blood, grew into a stiff pout. When they had finished making love and he lay tightly against her, there was sometimes a catch in her exhalation which told him that a small knot of desire was still not unraveled; he liked it best when her breath came clear, untroubled, and he knew that for the time being she was complete.

"You are so beautiful," he said. "Every little bit of you. And this part especially."

"I had never thought of it as possibly being—"

"Yes, it is. It is the color. It is like the color inside a shell. It is coral. I have never seen anything like it."

"You are absurd."

"I may be," he said. "But that is what I think."

Sometimes on a Thursday morning in the clinic, as his excitement mounted, Jacques wondered if he should not be feeling something more elevated, something more like "love"; but what he felt was too complex to be given a single name, and the vocabulary for emotion seemed to him in any case ridiculously small. It was like trying to describe the taste of asparagus or egg using only the words "sweet" or "bitter." Perhaps "love" was part of the distinctively flavored compound of a thousand feelings that made up his sense of Roya; perhaps not. He did not care. So long as he could see her again, feel himself rigid and bursting inside her, it did not seem to matter.

FOR THREE years they met weekly, and the indulgence of his habit only caused the desire to grow. Jacques remembered a sermon Abbé Henri had once given, in which he had warned his parishioners how the revisiting of a vice does not satisfy the craving but intensifies it. Perhaps he had been thinking of avarice or financial dishonesty in his flock, but the principle seemed to hold good for Jacques's sin too.

One day, without telling Sonia, he canceled his clinic so that he could spend the whole day at Roya's house. By the time he left in the evening he had lost count of the number of times he made love to her. Between each one, she changed clothes into outfits he had seen her wear in public on occasions when they had had to maintain a distance and had been left frustrated. He liked to reenact the occasion, only this time with the fantasy that at the theater or at the dinner where she had worn this dress he had found a chance, surprisingly, to . . . He avenged himself on all the days of frustrated longing—not just those occasions in the time that he had known Roya, but for all his life in which, as he tried to explain to her, frustration was the condition of being a man. And she insisted that he take her in every room of the house except the marital bedroom—where he had in any case no desire to go, the thought of Drobesch's long face and steepled fingers being the only thing he had discovered in three years that was sure to cool his passion; but in the bathroom and the music room, the drawing room and even, since the cook had been given the day off, in the kitchen she took him into herself again and again. Jacques was surprised that he could manage at her merest suggestion to be ready. It was not an area of physiology that he had studied, but folk wisdom had it that after the age of thirty a man needed longer to recover. It was as though each act, exciting as it was, had failed to kill the urge. A brash part of him was secretly proud of his vigor, but he wondered if there was something wrong in their ideas of one another that so much lovemaking seemed not to satisfy them.

On the final occasion, he did feel tired; they were both naked in the spare bedroom, sweat-streaked and without shame. He protested that he was done at last, but she would not let him be; she coaxed precarious life from him until to his astonishment he found that once more he was on top of her and from the depths of him she was somehow hauling up one last dying spasm of his great desire. And when she had squeezed it from him, when it was finally over, he lay across the foot of the bed, naked, in a slight warm breeze that came in through the open window from the garden, and he felt at last, for the first and only time in his life, that he was no longer frustrated by the eyes and looks and skin of women, but was drowned, dead and empty. He felt his jaw fall and his arms flop down, like the dead sailor on the raft of Géricault's *Medusa*.

IN THE same summer, speaking from his palace at St. Petersburg, the czar threatened that if the Slav cause was betrayed he would use Russia's military power in the Balkans. In the following spring, the English newspapers noted that Britain had by far the smallest standing army of any

European power, while Germany and Austria-Hungary were multiplying their arms to match the Russians.

Thomas told Kitty they should make plans to leave.

"It seems so unreasonable," she said, "that the quarrels of Bosnia should bring the whole continent to war."

"I think there is a desire to fight," said Thomas. "The desire is looking for a pretext. We will not be well placed here, my love, on our mountaintop. You could plead your German nationality—"

"Or my British."

"Yes. But I have no choice. I never saw a need to change and I felt a loyalty in any case. It is the same for Sonia. And Daniel."

"Oh my God. Daniel."

"Yes, indeed. France and Britain are still at some remove from the argument, but there seems . . . some sense of the inevitable."

"We cannot just leave our sanatorium and our patients."

"We could, in fact, quite easily. Franz is a partner in the business. We could promote Peter Andritsch. I don't think either of them would be required to fight if it came to it. And they could take on two more doctors for the duration."

"It is dreadfully sad," said Kitty. "To give up your life's work."

"We can return. When the war is over. It may not take long. And the girls would have a good education in England. We could be happy in London. Or I could take up my brother's offer of the farmhouse."

"What about Sonia and Jacques?"

"Their need to leave would be just as pressing—more so. I suppose they would go to Paris."

"Could we not persuade them to come to England with us?"

"I do not think Jacques would want to. Sonia might, but not Jacques. I think he would welcome the chance to start again elsewhere."

Kitty went over and took Thomas's hands in her own. "Perhaps it will be all right," she said. "No one can really want a war."

"I think they can."

"I am so sorry for you, Thomas. The schloss, the Wilhelmskogel. I know what they have meant to you. Your whole life."

"It is over, Kitty," said Thomas, standing up and walking toward the door. "In truth, it has been over for some time."

WHILE THOMAS spoke, Jacques was lying beside Roya, stroking back a strand of hair from her face.

"Why must you go to St. Petersburg?" he said.

"My father is ill. He has no one else. And he says a war is coming. He is scared."

"Will you come back?"

"Of course."

"Do you expect him to die?"

"I think so. That is why I must be there."

Jacques ran his hand over the skin of her back, over her haunches down to the thigh.

"Sometimes," he said, "I have the feeling that you are not real."

"What do you mean?"

"You are not real in the way that I am. Or my wife. Or my colleagues. You came from nowhere. Now you vanish."

She laughed. "I promise you that I am real enough. Touch me."

He smiled. "I am not convinced."

"All right," she said, leaning up on her elbow. "What is the most real thing you can think of?"

Jacques thought for a long time before answering; he tried to weigh up what was most vital and enduring in all that he had known. Eventually, no longer smiling, he said, "Memory."

"Very well, then," said Roya. "I am as real as memory."

WITH ROYA gone, Jacques became biddable in the question of moving. Like Thomas, he felt that their joint venture had ended some time ago, and while he had become fond enough of the Wilhelmskogel, he did not wish to spend the rest of his life there. The thought of going back to Paris was attractive to him and he reminded Sonia of how much she had liked the city.

"May I spend the summers in England?" she said.

"Of course, my love. You can travel to England as often as you choose."

So it was agreed that Franz Bernthaler and Peter Andritsch would take over the running of the clinic and would have financial control, with a right to hire and dismiss staff, for a period of twelve months, to be renewed at yearly intervals. If neither Thomas nor Jacques resumed his partnership within five years, they could be bought out and the entire business would be made over to Bernthaler and Andritsch.

In December, Sonia began to pack up their belongings. She told Daniel, who was just eighteen, that he would not be able to complete his last year at school but could finish his studies in Paris. "Then you should go to the university at Cambridge, like your uncle Thomas."

"Would they take me?"

"Of course they would. If nothing else, you could study languages. You already speak three—four if you count Italian. And so long as your father can take enough money out to pay the fees I am sure there would be no difficulty."

Jacques heard nothing from St. Petersburg. Perhaps Roya could not write for fear of Sonia seeing the Russian postmark, though she could always have sent it to him at the hospital; maybe she thought that even there some suspicious nurse or porter would see the stamp and start to gossip. Drobesch held no more dinner parties; the Modern World Colloquium for 1914 was postponed sine die and it was said that he planned to travel to Russia, to be with his wife. Jacques called at the house to wish him bon voyage, but found him gone. The butler told him that the house was up for sale and that he had been instructed to show it to prospective purchasers.

"Does he intend to stay in Russia? Why on earth would he want to be there?"

"I imagine he wants to be wherever Frau Drobesch is, sir."

Jacques thought he detected something facetious or suggestive in the man's tone, but he did not care. He walked away up the cobbled street and he knew that he would never see her again.

The Christmas festivities were a burden to him, with their social visiting and arduous bonhomie. He once more lost the ability to sleep and spent the days in a nervous coma of wakefulness. She had gone, she had never been his; she was vanished like a torn-off page in a book of hours. He felt the whole shape of himself collapse and fold inward, shrunken and desiccated; he could barely push his footsteps through the air. He longed to move, to be anywhere else.

Then in February, at the lowest time of the year, there came a cable to the hospital, addressed to him. The words were typed and pasted in strips on the flimsy paper from the regional post office: "CANNOT RETURN. P'BURG HOME INDEFINITE. D HERE. I LOVE YOU ALWAYS, BEYOND TIME AND PLACE. R."

XXII

DANIEL WAS NINETEEN YEARS OLD WHEN HE STARTED AS AN UNDER-graduate at the college next door to his uncle's at Cambridge in the Michaelmas term of 1915, but the place was already starting to seem empty. By the spring of the following year the undergraduate population had fallen from more than four thousand to less than six hundred, most of whom were either medical students or were unfit for service. The west court of Daniel's college had been taken over by the military, and on the lawns that adjoined the Fellows' rose garden, sheep had been put out to graze. Daniel wrote to his parents in Paris to tell them what was going on, but Sonia, who had heard the German guns on the Marne and seen the Gare de l'Est teeming with the maimed and wounded, replied that he should devote himself to his studies. It was a French war, she said, and Daniel was English. "Papa may disagree," she wrote, "but in my view, nationality, like religion, comes through the mother. Anyway, Herr Frage, you are as much Carinthian as French, so which side would you choose to fight for? Put your nose back in your books and do not listen to bloodthirsty boys who tell you otherwise."

In the summer, Daniel read of the British attack on the Somme and he saw the strained faces of his fellow-students and their teachers, who were missing brothers, pupils, friends; it seemed that a layer had been excised from British life. Young men who only months before had been a sixth form or a football team were now black-bordered notices in the columns of *The Times*, the subject of prayers and averted eyes, their college doors locked, their books unopened. In the small backstreets of the town, with their toylike cottages in tight brick terraces, Daniel sensed the loss in every family, in almost every face he passed. It was difficult to return to France in the summer, since all transport was required for troops; and in London, on a visit to his cousins, he was so moved by the sight of English soldiers at Victoria Station pushing to be let onto the trains for France, that he went to the first recruiting station he could find, which was in Battersea, and volunteered.

He did not at first write to tell his parents, fearing they might somehow contrive to have him discharged, but once he had passed the medical and been sent for training, he wrote, from deep within the protective walls of discipline and censorship, to break the news.

I had thought I was bilingual, but I could not at first understand anything the men were saying. The Londoners speak, so far as is possible, without consonants; and there are also men from Glasgow and Durham and Belfast, as I suppose you would expect in a capital city. My section is Alton, Jeavons, Kemp, Reader, Scott and Turney. My messmates or muckers (there are many odd words in the army) are Billy Reader (who <u>cannot</u> read; I have to do it for him), Jack Turney and Harry Scott.

Harry is known as "Mac" because he comes from Scotland. He is about thirty-five, I think, and has worked in shipyards for most of his life. He is married to a woman called Ellen, of whom he speaks very fondly, and they have two children, Dougal and Ailsa, whose photographs I have been shown many times. He is extremely strong and rather bad-tempered. His idea of the war is to save up his pay in a cushy billet and make sure that on no account does he get promoted. He assured me that whatever the casualty figures suggest, we are unlikely ever to have to go "over the top" and that half the army is "transport," a general term just meaning support and backup. He eats prodigious amounts of food in preparation for leaner times ahead. His favorite expression is "Sailor Vee, pal." You can probably work out what this means, though it took me several days.

Billy Reader and Jack Turney are about twenty-eight, but they seem much older. Both were unemployed, though Billy had worked as a signwriter and Jack in the docks. Billy looks like a ferret, with a sharp face and greasy brown hair. He has a surprisingly good singing voice and is a good artist, as you might expect—he does nice little sketches of the sergeant (of whom more below). He is only interested in one thing, and that is girls. He and Jack talk about almost nothing else and between them seem to have seduced (not their word) every female between the ages of fourteen and forty "from Hainault to Epping" as Billy puts it. All of these ladies seem to have been extremely grateful for his services and he clearly feels that he has done them a tremendous favor.

Jack Turney, who is short and bald, has a son from a liaison with a woman in Milwall, though he appears not to be married to her. Of the three, Jack is the most openly patriotic and believes it is our duty to "shut the Hun back in his **** sty and bolt the door." He believes the Germans have raped a lot of women in Belgium and northern France, though seems slightly resentful that they got there before he did. (I apologize, Ma, if some of this seems awfully coarse to you; believe me, I am keeping out the worst!) Jack is also aggrieved that we are having to help out "the **** French" and is anxious about how he will manage to "parley" with the local women.

We are all drilled into the ground by Sergeant Duncan, a small man with no chin but an unpleasant and aggressive attitude. He claims to have fought in Sudan with the regular army, but there is some skepticism about this. He seems a most bitter and vindictive person. "What that man needs," says Billy about five times a day, "is a good . . ." But I am sure you can imagine what Billy's prescription is.

There is one other thing that Jack and Billy will talk about and that is football. This does not always go well because they support different teams, and it is almost a relief to hear them get back to whether short girls are "more willing" than tall ones.

The barracks (I am in Surrey, but cannot say where) are not too bad. We have beds and blankets, which is good because it is already quite cold. The food is not as good as the food in college, but no worse than that in the average eating house. Stews, beans, jam, bacon, doughy bread, sweet tea; but there is enough and I don't mind. We are issued with as many cigarettes as you can smoke. In addition to drill, kit inspection, marching up and down and scrubbing the floor, there is a fair amount of bayonet practice. We have been taught how to clean the rifle, but very little about how to fire it; and of course there is far too little ammunition for live practice. I have a very nice soft khaki cap, tin helmet (recent addition, I gather) and a uniform which fits well with a very smart regimental badge (a species of Goat Rampant—very suitable, as Mac drily pointed out to Billy). Shirt and undergarments are just picked out of a pile and a lot of swapping has to go on later. Mess tin, ground sheet, field dressings etc., etc., and something called a "hussif," an all-in-one tool to open tins and "make yourself useful" as Sgt. Duncan puts it. When I am posted, you can send me other things, such as scarves. I am hoping to be issued with a leather waistcoat before winter.

And what do they make of me? I am sorry to say that they think I am a bit of a joke. Most of them have a nickname— "Barmy" Jeavons, "Gunner" Kemp and so on—and I am "Frenchie" because of my surname. They can't understand why I am not in the French army. I have explained everything but they can't seem to follow, while my being a student makes them very suspicious. At first they thought I might be some sort of spy or "MP" (military policeman), but now they accept that I am just an ordinary volunteer like them. English graduates become officers almost at once, and even at the age of eighteen well-educated boys can find themselves commanding a platoon of men twice their age. But I am only an undergraduate, they have no record of my schooling and I seem to have slipped through that net. I am very happy with this, as I would be hopeless at telling people what to do since I have no idea what to do myself. Also, I have become fond of Jack and Billy and Mac. Well, not "fond" perhaps; but I can get on with them all right. I just wish they would not tease me quite so much about being "sixteen" and inexperienced with women etc., etc. I think that Jack thinks it is worth keeping in with me, so that when the time comes I can translate for him to the local French girls; though whether they will be much interested in his assessment of his local team's center forward, I am not so sure.

My dear Ma and Pa, I know all this is a shock to you. But almost every family in Europe is going through this. I could not stand aside and watch every other French and English man go off to fight. And believe me, the best are already dead. We are already down to the second- and third-rate, men like Jack and Billy and your son; the next stop will be conscription—predicted for Christmas. I would be ashamed to wait till I was forced. And although I volunteered on impulse, I have read the newspapers carefully and have lived, as you know, on a mountain from which I had the best view in Europe of the quarreling nations. I have no doubt whatever that Germany must be stopped. Thank God your respective native countries are allies! What must it be like for Aunt Kitty—though I know she is only half-German? I hope Charlotte and Martha are not being teased or persecuted. I saw them only for a moment when I was passing through. Here is a photograph done in a little studio in Epsom High Street. Don't I look smart?

THE FIRST thing they had to do, once they had cleared out the bodies from the concrete pillbox they had captured, was put sandbags up the opening, because what had been a back door to the Germans was at the front for them, and invited a rude entry of explosive from the unmoved enemy guns. The brief telephone message from the support line told them that if they wanted sandbags they would have to come and get them.

"Me and Frenchie'll go, sir," said Billy Reader. "If you wants to keep Private Turney for company, sir."

"All right, Reader," said Captain Denniston. "Good luck, and see if you can get any cigarettes from the chaps back there. And Reader?"

"Yes, sir?"

"How long have you been in Belgium?"

"Come here first in November last year, after training at Etaples, then we was moved to the Salient before the attack on Passchendaele Ridge, sir, a few weeks ago, which—"

"I don't want the story of your life, man. I just wondered if you were going to take your helmet."

"Oh, yes. Thank you, sir."

"Honestly, I don't know how you have survived."

"Rabbit's foot, sir. Old lady give me it at Folkestone. Though more likely need a fucking rubber ring out there—"

"Get out."

Daniel followed Billy out of the pillbox into the twilight. It was raining, though they did not notice the rain anymore. Daniel shone his torch onto the duckboards which made a path across the liquid mud. They would have to make about three hundred yards back to the forward supply dump where they could load mules with the sandbags and bring them up to the pillbox. Daniel looked about to see if there were any aids to navigation, but the sky was clouded and the landscape had no features. The trees in the plain had been brought down or splintered; the knolls and hillocks had been flattened by weeks of artillery fire; the grass and earth had long been turned over, so that the grayish-brown mud stretched unrelieved by any change of shade or contour until it met the grayish-brown horizon. Even the shellholes, some of them twenty yards in diameter, quite soon lost definition in the rain, as their rims subsided and they joined hands with one another, first as craters in a planetary landscape, then mere dips in a quagmire whose marsh gas came from yellow lurking phosgene and in whose liquid slime the only solid mass was the disconnected limbs of horses and men.

"Why did you volunteer for this?" said Daniel, starting off with careful steps.

"Two-to-one on says I was going to get told to anyway, mate. Also, I can't stand the smell in that fucking pillbox. Like half the Hun army's used it as their private latrine."

At night the Engineers came out to mend the duckboard paths the German guns tore up by day, but the weeks of Passchendaele had thinned the sapper numbers, and gaps had started to appear in the walkways. Daniel was valued as someone with good balance and a steady nerve. "A level head," as Denniston had put it, "in both senses. Shame you have no initiative, Rebière, or we could have made an officer of you."

Daniel heard the rain dripping on the groundsheet he wore as a cape across his shoulders. A late German shell exploded some two hundred yards or so to his left, but he did not quiver at the sound; in fact, he found it helpful in orientating himself in the darkness. He felt his leading foot slip for a second on the slimy wood. At moments such as these he often thought of Charlotte and Martha, because the world they came from was so different in all its lineaments from the one that he inhabited; yet they wrote to him and he knew they cared; they seemed to represent to him everything that was worth fighting for. It was extraordinary, he thought, how insulated you could be from your surroundings; if there was one part of you that remained dry, as his torso still was for the time being, you could exist within a private cocoon; while you fumbled with your respirator as the stench of gas rose in the evening mist and seemed to seep into your skin and lungs, you could be holding the thought of two girls in a foreign capital far away, hanging up streamers for Christmas.

"We 'alfway yet, Frenchie?"

A British flare shone a brief yellow light in the gloom ahead of them and Daniel thought he could make out the section of reserve line where the supply dump was identifiable by the remains of a dry stone wall, which in the summer had been part of a trench system. The rain and the artillery, however, had obliterated all the trenches, so that the men in the line now lived like reptiles in the mud. Daniel had overheard Denniston saying to a fellow-officer that staff estimates put the British casualty figure in the battle so far at 300,000. "Not much of a loss, most of them," Denniston continued. "Conscripts. Men with rickets and short sight. A lot of them have just drowned."

They came to a section of better duckboarding and scrambled up the incline to the heap of white stones and down the other side. Behind it was a dugout made of timber and corrugated iron with a double gas curtain; it looked almost fussily correct, built by the book, in a landscape where nothing was solid anymore. Inside were a sergeant and two signalers who were trying to breathe life into a broken telephone system.

Daniel explained what he and Reader had come for and after initial reluctance owing to his lack of paperwork, the sergeant told him to take what he wanted. "And if you can get them mules back where you've come from you should be in Barnum and Bailey's bloody circus. Take all the sandbags you want, young man, but I can only let you have one packet of Woodbines. The stores haven't come up for days."

After they had had some tea, they went out to load the mules. Reader held the first animal's head while Daniel heaved the sodden sandbag onto its back.

"This is a mug's game if you ask me," said Billy.

"We don't have a choice," said Daniel. "We can't leave the front of our pillbox unprotected."

"We do have a choice, Frenchie. We could leg it. Denniston would never know. No one knows where anyone is anymore. They don't care, neither. Don't you see? It's just a shambles. Me and you, we could slip off in the dark and say we got lost. Join some unit in support, say, 'Ever so sorry, sir, and all that. We was heading in a westerly direction and must have lost our bearings and all ready and reporting for duty, sir'—but by that time our pillbox is blown to smithereens and our number's come up for leave."

"What about Jack? We can't leave him."

"You're a stubborn bastard, aren't you? You 'old the bloody animal, 'e's giving me the willies. That look in his eye. I'll load the bloody bags."

They took two laden mules and led them back round the dugout, down through the mud and onto the duckboards.

"Good luck, men," said the sergeant. "See you at the Theater Royal, Drury Lane. Top of the bill, I expect. Put that light out. I'll put up a flare for you in ten minutes if you like."

"No thank you, Sergeant," said Daniel. "I don't think the snipers have gone to bed yet."

They pulled the mules by a leading rein until they would go no further, then stuck their bayonets in the animals' rumps to move them on.

Soon Daniel found there was no part of him that was not wet: his puttees clamped the sodden trousers against his skin; his feet were cold and slipping inside his boots, and his face muscles ached from where he had screwed up his eyes against the rain. Artillery fire was increasing from the German line, as it usually did for an hour after darkness when they guessed the Engineers had come out. He pressed on, wondering why he did so. In the fifteen months that he had been in the army he had long since stopped being able to give himself a reason for anything he did. He was no longer motivated by a sense of patriotism or a certainty that his side was right; he kept going only because he could not stop.

He felt his right arm suddenly pulled, then a pain in his shoulder; his mule had slipped and fallen from the duckboards and was thrashing in the deep mud beside him. Daniel at once let go, for fear of being pulled under. They were at the edge of a shellhole, not large, but filled with liquid mud. The mule was drowning under the weight of its sandbags and could not find a footing; twice it seemed on the point of pulling itself clear, and twice it slipped, the frantic churning of its legs seeming to bog it further into the mire. Daniel briefly shone his torch to see what he could do, but the beam of it only caught the animal's eyes bulging in panic as it went under.

As he went to grab the leading rein once more, he felt his arm pulled back. "Leave 'im, Frenchie, or 'e'll pull you in with 'im."

It was too late, however, as the toss of the mule's head at the rein caused Daniel's feet to slip. His hip cracked on the duckboard and he slid down into the slime, feeling the ooze come over his head for a moment before he bobbed up. There was something unpleasant beneath his feet; there was something in his hand that felt like someone else's face. He scrabbled at the edge of the shellhole but could get no purchase. He was desperate not to go down beneath the surface, among the arms and legs of those who had gone before him.

"Billy!" he cried in the darkness, his throat full of mud and the fumes of mustard gas. "Billy!"

As he started to slip back again into the pit, he felt a hand flapping at his wrist, his arm, and finally succeeding in clinging on. "Hold this, mate." It was the rein of the second mule. "Don't pull. Just hold it. I'm going to back 'im up slow. Don't let go now."

Daniel had a terrible fear that the hands of the dead would clutch him and pull him down before he could be dragged clear. He heard Billy cursing the mule and heard the animal bray and squeal with pain, as Billy jabbed it with his bayonet; but slowly the creature did move back, and Daniel felt the suction of the mud start to slacken and release his legs. When he was halfway out, Billy took him under the arms and pulled him clear, cursing his stupidity all the time.

"You should have let the animal go straight off, never mind turning the fucking torch on him. Now Fritz has got a bearing on us and—"

"Not much of a bearing," coughed Daniel. "It was just for a moment. And anyway, thank you."

"Don't thank me, you daft French cunt, just get me out of here."

"Let me get my breath back."

They were a hundred yards short of the pillbox, with enough sand-bags on the surviving mule to have made the trip worthwhile, when Billy suggested they stop for a cigarette. "We want to smoke as many as we can before we 'ave to give 'em up to Denniston. Stick a couple inside your shirt for Jack."

They crouched behind the mule and Daniel struggled with a damp match; eventually it flared for long enough to allow Billy's desperate inhalation to set fire to his cigarette. He squatted and sucked happily before offering the red tip to Daniel. They hid the glowing ends in their hands to keep off the rain and in order not to attract the attention of some diligent sniper still on duty.

"Christmas soon," said Billy Reader.

"I suppose so."

They heard a shell that seemed much closer than the others. One thing the veterans had told Daniel from the day he joined up was that you never heard the one that had your name on it; but as Billy suddenly grabbed his wrist, and Daniel could make out his ferrety expression from the light of his cigarette end, it was clear that the same thought had occurred to him: this one was theirs and they were hearing it every inch of the way. As Daniel was lifted from the duck-boards by the blast, he knew that Billy Reader was dead; he had seen or sensed the red pieces of him in the marshy, yellow night air.

———

THERE WAS a letter for Sonia and Jacques from a Major Bartelot at the Infantry Record Office at 4, London Wall Buildings, London EC2, telling them that Private Rebière, D 2210824727, was reported missing in action at Passchendaele, but that they had had reports unconfirmed, based on an eyewitness report of a Sergeant Kimber, that he had been taken down the line by stretcher bearers to a casualty clearing station. An examination of the wounded lists at all the likely hospitals had so far proved fruitless, but further information would be passed on to them as soon as it was forthcoming. The major offered his sympathy at a time of what he knew must be "great suspense."

A LETTER came many weeks later to the address of Dr. T. Midwinter in Bayswater, London. It was not the first communication, but it was one that was much pored over by the family.

It began, "Dear Uncle Thomas and Aunt Kitty," and continued,

> Don't ask me how or why, but I appear to be in Italy. After my little adventure in the mud at Passchendaele, I was unconscious for quite a long time, and when I came to, I asked the MO where I was. He, being a typical MO, if you will forgive my saying so, was impatient about my wish to know where I was (not a <u>terribly</u> unreasonable question, I felt) but eventually said, 'Well if you must know, young man, you are in Abbeville.' I do not know how I got to Abbeville, which is in France, or why I came here, except that the hospital has very good facilities for treating those with shell shock, memory loss and head wounds.
>
> It transpired that my wounds were slight. Poor old Billy Reader had been blown into a thousand pieces, but I was simply lifted clear by the blast and dumped in another hole. I broke an arm and had some slight burns. I have gone rather deaf in one ear, but that might be useful in later life (if I marry a Madame Valade, for instance). The problem is my memory, but I suppose it does not matter too much. Perhaps there are some things it is better to forget. Eventually I was sent to rejoin my unit, who had

been moved from Belgium down to Amiens. I was surprised and
very pleased to see Jack Turney alive and I managed to be polite
to Capt. Denniston who had held his little pillbox more or less
single-handed until the battle was declared over. How could they
tell it was 'over'? Nothing was gained, nothing was lost but a few
hundred thousand lives. They told me Field Marshal Haig paid
his first visit to the chosen site of his offensive in January, after it
was finished. He surveyed the swamp and said, 'God, did our
men really have to fight in this?' And he wept.

(I do not know whether to believe that or not. Some say it
was Kiggell, his second in command.)

Anyway, the boy who bakes the bread heard from a man who
drives a train that we were off to Italy. The cook told Tommy who
told the corporal, who told the sergeant, who told the sergeants'
mess, where it was thoroughly discussed. On a majority vote, the
sergeant was detailed to tell the adjutant, who, five days later,
received his top-secret written orders to that effect from Staff
headquarters. We packed up our kit and marched to the station
where we climbed into cattle trucks, marked "Chevaux 8,
Hommes 40." Tommy mystified by this inscription. What it is to
be bilingual!

As well as the cattle trucks, there were two passenger
coaches for the elect. The CO had half of one coach to himself,
but let other officers into the other half; the second coach was
occupied by other Great Men, such as the Sergeant Cook and the
Armorer Sergeant.

I never thought I could be so glad to see the back of France,
but as the train crawled south and east, I felt my spirits lift. We
broke open a section of the truck to make a window and soon we
were passing along the valley of the River Aisne, in view of a
ridge called the Chemin des Dames, where a French king—I
forget which one—encouraged the ladies of his court to exercise.
It is better known now as the place where the French infantry
mutinied after General Nivelle sent too many off to die. (As you
will see, this letter is in a so-called green envelope and not

subject to censorship, except the remote chance of a random check at base, as at the time of writing I am in an area of low risk. So I can <u>say what I like</u>.) But back to the story—

We eventually left French soil through one of the great mountain tunnels, at Mt. Cenis, and in the morning pulled into our first Italian village. Young women poured onto the platform, throwing flowers through the open doors of the trucks (which greatly improved the atmosphere inside). They gave us oranges to eat and were happy to kiss the most repulsive-looking men. The mayor of the local town came onto the platform, a small brass band played and bottles of vino rosso were opened. I looked at the faces of my comrades from the Ypres Salient, such as are still with us, and they were filled with wonder. This Italy, they were thinking, is a kind of heaven.

Eventually they put electric engines front and back onto our train to get us down from the mountains, then steam took over again in the plain of Lombardy. There seems to be no coal here, so the stoker throws logs onto the fire. This works well enough, and I was sent to ask him if we could have hot water from his boiler for a brew of tea, as there was no other provided. "You go, Frenchie, you speak the foreign lingo." Vain to point out that it is a different "lingo"—though I do speak a little Italian, because of having lived so near the border. But I am doing my best to keep that <u>very</u> quiet.

When the train had gone as far as it would go, it was everybody out and back on foot. We were all in good spirits and no one minded a march, though I do not see why the train could not have taken us a bit further. Our line here is about 80 miles long from the Adriatic to the Alps; it starts on the River Piave, then curves up northwest. The Italians were much further east, but were driven back by the Austrians at the Battle of Caporetto, as they call it. Caporetto is in fact Karfreit, where all those workmen on the Wilhelmskogel came from. The Italians fought very well, they say, but the retreat from Caporetto was a disgrace, apparently, with discipline breaking down in a *sauve-qui-peut* rush to safety, women and children abandoned, trampled underfoot or left on the mountain roads, along with vast numbers of guns and equipment, to the mercy of the advancing Austrian enemy. How strange and sad it seems, after all these years, to write those last two words. I think of Freddy and the other boys from school and wonder where they are.

Anyway, there has now been a considerable regrouping and stiffening of the line with French and British divisions in it. The War is going about as badly as it could be for the Allies on the Western Front. We are out of men. Even what my CO would call the "runts"—the 1917 conscripts with their bandy legs and gig-lamps—are dead. We wait for more tanks and more Americans.

But here in Italy, there is a better atmosphere. Our Italian allies have regained their composure, apparently. The French troops are hard and competent and the five British divisions contain men from some of the great regiments—Royal West Kents, Durham Light Infantry, Bedfords, Cheshires, Norfolks, Warwicks, Sherwood Foresters and King Edward's Horse among others. It is a large presence, and most of these are men who have survived the Western Front and know what they are doing. That must include me, Uncle Thomas. Or at least it <u>half</u> includes me: I have survived the WF; I have never had the smallest idea what I am doing. . . . Sorry about these digressions; perhaps it is my "concussion"; anyway, now definitely back to the story:—

The plain of Lombardy is a dull place: pale, flat fields with green poplars and variegated-red-brick campaniles the only vertical marks in its horizontal sweep. The Roman roads are straight with the villages attached at a short distance; after a while we are told to march "at ease," which means you can push back your cap, loosen your buttons, smoke and chat to the men around you. Usually there is a song, but the men have not had time to think up filthy words with Italian connections yet. The first night we slept in a cattle shed in a farm and were surprised when all the women of the village came to join us at night with their sewing. Jack Turney was rubbing his hands in delight, but it seems they like to sit among the cows for warmth, there being no coal here and they want to save the wood as much as they can for their cooking stoves. Jack brokenhearted when this was explained; but there is a good feeling because the women bring vino rosso. In return, we have given them some spare army blankets, which return the following day in the shape of quite fetching khaki skirts.

The Italians are greatly taken by the sight of our shire horses (which are used for pulling wagons), as they have never seen such beasts. We also use oxen at the tail of the column and when a man's feet are so bad from marching that it is thought dangerous for him to carry on, he is allowed to deposit his pack on an "oxo wagon" and continue thus lightened. I have fortunately never reached that stage, because I dread to think what the teasing would be like.

Now I have to tell you something rather odd. We arrived on the third day of marching at a town with a huge red sandstone clock tower and battlements at its entry joined to medieval walls. (This is Cittadella. I now remember I can tell you such things in a "green envelope.") I went to the church after lunch and saw the most beautiful paintings by Veronese and Giorgione. I cannot believe that this is "allowed" in time of war. I feel so fortunate to be alive. When I think of all the men in my section, only Jack and me still living (Mac, I heard, was killed in the Salient); and not just living but able to go into this enchanted country and stare at the walls of its churches, while Billy lies in tiny pieces in the mud of Belgium. It made me want to cry, though whether with happiness or grief I could not say. I was sitting in a café, thinking about these things, when Capt. Denniston comes up and says he wants to talk to me.

Capt. D.: "Rebière, I have something to tell you."

DR: "Yes, sir."

CD: "We are going to have to make you an officer. There is simply no one else left. You are good at languages, you can read a map and although you are apparently still only about sixteen you count as a veteran now, God help us."

DR: "Thank you, sir. Do I have to go on a course?"

CD: "Good God, man. We are fighting a war. Do you think I am going to send you back to bloody Camberley? The reason I am promoting you is that you are the best I have left, God help us, not so I can send you home!"

DR: "I thought everyone had to go back to Sandhurst for training. Or I think maybe at Verona, there's—"

CD: "Don't think. You will take charge of a platoon as soon as we get to Montebelluna. The way things are going you may have command of the whole company before long."

DR: "Yes, sir, certainly, sir, etc., etc."

When the news reached the others, Jack Turney said I must be the first officer in the British Army who doesn't have to shave. This is not true, as you know, because I shave every day with the other men; but I have decided to grow a mustache to show him anyway, and to frighten the enemy.

We took up our positions on the west bank of the Piave, where we lived in caves like the forty thieves. March is the wettest month in Italy, and the Piave was very full and rapid. It is about a hundred yards across and forms a compelling no-man's-land, not much wetter than that at Ypres, but a lot less muddy! The object of our existence is a) to cross the river; b) in Denniston's words "to make a bloody nuisance of ourselves." The latter is surprisingly easy to achieve, the former rather difficult.

At ten o'clock sharp each morning, the Austrians send over about twenty shells, then stop. In the evening, they come down to the river to get water. I imagine those detailed to do so must be on some sort of charge or are voluntary members of the suicide squad, because they offer excellent sniper targets—just agile and distant enough to be sporting.

Making a nuisance of ourselves means building boats and paddling over at night on raids, like a trench raid, except there are no trenches. As the company—indeed battalion—linguist, I am considered indispensable to all such operations and I am always chosen for any boat party. Do I imagine a gleeful look in

Denniston's eye when he tells me, "First name on the team sheet, as ever, Lieutenant?" We paddle over using spades or trenching tools as paddles on rickety rafts knocked up by the RE. Sometimes the Austrians (the "Aussies," as my men call them) put up a flare, and then we dive into the water and swim like hell (very cold: to be avoided if possible). But if they do not hear us, we can get in amongst them and take a prisoner back for questioning. One of the men we brought back came from Villach and knew Herr Geissler, the railway engineer! He was delighted to have a chat about the old days and to be taken prisoner at last. "What does he say, Mr. Rebière?" Denniston kept asking, when we had been talking about how much we missed good Carinthian cooking. Anyway, he gave me the details of all the units in this part of the line. They included Poles, Ruthenes, Rumanians, Magyars and Serbians. He told us there was no major offensive planned here. So that put an end to "trench raids" for a time, rather to Denniston's disappointment.

All went very well for a bit until he hit on a better idea. If they were not going to attack us, we should build a bridge and attack them. I broke the news to Jack Turney. "What a ******g stupid idea!" "My views exactly, Private. Ours not to reason why, however." I have become very swanky in the way I talk to the men and I must say I thoroughly enjoy it. I just wish they wouldn't still call me "Daniel."

The Engineers excelled themselves by building several concrete pillars which they somehow contrived to float out into the river at dead of night without being seen by the enemy. Do not ask me how, but I swear to you they did it. The idea was that on top of these pillars, they would erect a wooden pontoon—which is the sort of thing the RE can do in about twenty minutes, putting up wooden pontoons being exactly what the RE does. Two companies were then to cross the bridge and attack. Our battalion occupies approx. 3,000 yards of the riverbank; it has three companies with one in reserve. The chances of my company (D) being chosen were what Billy Reader would have called "two-to-one on." But God—He alone knows why—was merciful, and B and C got chosen for the "stunt." Denniston utterly crestfallen since he claims the whole thing was his idea, but a bigger bloody fool than he, Col. Tucker, is the battalion commander and he made the decision. Over they went one night. Huge firefight and unpleasant bayonet work at close quarters. Inadequate support and forward planning, however, meant that the considerable advance made by our troops could not be maintained, and they were obliged to withdraw to their previous line after severe loss of life. Does that pattern of events sound at all familiar to you?

The next week, the Piave flooded and the concrete pillars were swept away; I do not think that we will try to cross the river again in the foreseeable future. I mean, we had already established—at considerable personal risk—that no enemy attack was imminent, so what on earth were we doing?

Next day it was reported to me that several of my platoon were drunk on vino rosso, and I went to investigate. This local wine must be stronger than I had thought, as some of the men were quite ill. One of the sergeants was out of control, and mutinous. I got the worst of them locked up in the guard detention room and had a guard placed outside my billet. The sgt. will be reduced to the ranks, which is a pity, as he was a good man and someone less worthy will have to be promoted corporal. I have a mind to make it Jack Turney.

Soon after that, we were told to prepare to move up into the mountains. It was said that German reinforcements had been spotted by one of our planes and that we expected an attack in the next few weeks. It was by now the end of April, and I was not sorry to see the back of the Piave.

I am writing this letter, therefore, in the pleasant town of Cittadella, my favorite of the cities of the plain. I am sitting in the restaurant where Denniston came to promote me, and I have just had a good lunch of spaghetti and chicken, with two dark black coffees to follow. I will be out of the "green envelope area" soon when we go up into the mountains and all I shall be able to send is some silly card on which I tick a box saying I am a) all

right, b) suffering from venereal disease/wind/fallen arches, or
c) dead.

I do miss you all very much. Please give my love to Aunt Kitty
and to C and M, whom I miss most of all. I will see you all again
soon, I know. Please also tell Ma not to worry, and that my next
long letter will be to her and Pa.

I am sorry this letter is so long, but I only hope that it gives
you half as much pleasure to read as it has given me to write.

The sun is out, my belly is full and the mountains are calling.
I see a Fiat motor lorry in the square and I think it has my name
on it. I embrace you all. Daniel.

Lieutenant Rebière was told to march his men to their position in the
line on the Asiago Plateau at a thousand meters above sea level. There
was an adequate metaled road up the mountain over a long series of
hairpin bends, but it was reserved to the gunners and their fifteen-
hundred-weight lorries pulling six-inch howitzers, ammunition and
other stores; the infantry were to scramble up the mule tracks in as
straight a line as they could manage.

To someone who had spent much of his childhood at exactly that
altitude, the five-hour climb was not daunting, even with a full pack,
though there were moments when he longed for Herr Geissler's cable
car. The men grumbled continually and he allowed them to stop for ten
minutes each hour, if possible at a place where a mountain stream
enabled them to fill their water bottles. As they moved up through the
pine forests, Daniel felt his spirits rise; it was hard not to feel exhilarated
by the thinning of the air, the chill that came with it and the sense of
being removed from the flat lands below. They watched the convoy of
lorries on the switchback road, pausing occasionally as it passed
through huge draped camouflage curtains that had been suspended
between the pines to fool the enemy spotter planes; some of the vehicles
carried anti-skid barbed wire on their solid rubber tires and the Italian
and British drivers pushed them hard through the bends, close to
the edge.

It was bizarre how uplifting it was after the brown and saturated
plains of Belgium, thought Daniel. On a few steep sections there was a

"teleferica," an aerial ropeway of endless steel cable attached to electrically driven steel drums; these, however, carried only small cars, about six feet by two, clamped to the cable and held on by their own weight. They transported light stores, though had been used to ferry down the seriously wounded, a hazardous journey since they were unstable in the wind and the up-car passed close to the down-car, dislodging any load that stuck out.

The men begged to stop at Granezza, where an ugly modern *osteria* promised food and warmth, but it had been requisitioned as the battalion headquarters by some other brigade, and Daniel's company followed A and C on through the woods. When they had pushed up through the mist and low cloud, he made his men pause and look behind them: there, just visible on the southeast horizon, floating in its misty lagoon, was the city of Venice.

"I am Captain Gregorio, but if you take my position you may call me Luca," said the officer who handed over his trench on the plateau. He was a man of about thirty, dark and quick of movement. He spoke in English, and was amazed when Daniel introduced himself in Italian.

"My Italian is not good," he said, "but I try. Do you speak German?"

"I try not to," said Gregorio. "We are fighting for the ownership of these mountains and the right to speak our own language, but I was brought up near Arabba, and many people in my village spoke German. So . . . a little."

"Then we will get on very well," said Daniel, in Carinthian-accented German.

Gregorio smiled widely. "I think so. We are going into reserve near Castelfranco, but some of my company will stay halfway up the mountain at Granezza. You must come and visit me. Come and have dinner."

"I will. I must settle in first. Then I will see what I can do with some lorry-hopping."

"Good. You collect water from the reservoir. It is pumped up from the plain. There is more than enough for your men—unless the pipeline is hit. Then you will have to drink wine."

"Do they bomb it?"

"Yes, they do. But we have hidden it well. We are quite good engineers, you know. Good luck, Daniele."

"Thank you, Luca. I will see you as soon as I can get down."

"We shall have pasta with wild boar. I shall shoot it myself. With a mortar if necessary."

He disappeared, laughing loudly, and Daniel could see how relieved he was to be out of the line.

The Italian trenches they took over had been blasted out of the rock because the earth covering was not deep enough to be dug into a defense. For the first four days the men set to work to extend and improve the system; they had to punch a cold drill into the rock with a sledge-hammer to make a hole for the charge. The noise of the explosions was the only sound of warfare.

From on top of a promontory, Daniel surveyed the entire plateau of Asiago. The allied line ran in and out of pine woods on the west and southern edges; the Austrians and their allies were mostly in open country in front of the small town of Asiago itself and were thus easily observed by airplane. The entire plateau was about eight miles from east to west and two or three miles in breadth, ringed with higher mountains. There was the occasional flash of an artillery piece from the enemy line, followed long afterward by a rumbling report; but after the Western Front, it hardly looked like war at all.

The company cook baked polenta from the local maize flour, which made a change from the pork and beans and tins of stew, though somehow did not taste as good as when the men had had it made by the farmers' wives in the villages of the plain. Accommodation for the officers was not in dugouts but in various wooden huts concealed in the pine forests, and on the first evening Daniel was invited, with the other platoon commanders, to dinner with Captain Denniston.

"I don't want your men thinking this is a cushy billet," said Denniston, pouring himself a glass of whisky. "We expect an attack, and meanwhile the time we have must be spent profitably. Do you understand?"

His servant, a silent, unsmiling man called Rampton, brought in the food, which included Italian sausages he had bought in Cittadella.

"Wine, Lieutenant?"

"Thank you, sir. Just a little."

Daniel had hardly ever drunk wine before and had seen its effects on his men, but he wanted to get used to it before he had dinner with Luca.

It is quite odd, he mused, as the alcohol loosened his thoughts: last month alone I bayoneted three men to death on the Piave and a few days ago I marched a platoon for five hours up a mountain to the exact spot marked on a map; but I have never made love to a woman and I do not know if I can manage to drink wine.

In the course of the next week, the men continued to improve their living conditions, though their first duty, Daniel was happy to notice, was toward their officers, and he was invited to sleep in a sort of cave, dug into the side of the hill with a smart opening made of white stone fragments left from trench detonations and a lintel of sawn pine. A wooden bed was provided inside and, since there was room for three, Daniel insisted that the newly promoted Corporal Turney join him there along with Sergeant Shields, when they were not on duty elsewhere. When he himself was resting, Daniel admired the view across the plateau.

He took out a notebook to write down the names of all the flora that he knew his father would be interested to know about on his return. On the lower slopes were wild rhododendron or *Alpenrosen*, though the red bushes, lovely as they were, did not look like roses to him. Near his own "cottage," as he secretly called it, was a pink plant; he thought perhaps it was thrift, but he had never paid much attention to botany. The blue flowers, he was sure, were harebells, and they grew profusely. When a parcel arrived from home containing not only some of his mother's cake but, from his uncle Thomas, the works of Shelley with the note "See 'Lines Written Among the Euganean Hills,'" a happy solution came to him: he would take specimens of all these wildflowers and press them between the pages of Shelley as a gift for Charlotte and Martha. He thought of their blond heads leaning over the book together, and was a little anxious that they would laugh at him.

There were no animals in the mountains—though lower down there must be wild boar, or he sincerely hoped there were for his dinner's sake; nor were there any birds, which was disappointing, as he had somehow expected buzzards or eagles; but at least there were no rats.

Odder and odder, he thought, as he laid a small pink flower carefully between the pages of "Ode to the West Wind," breathed deeply on the Alpine air and rested his eyes on the long view over the plateau: seldom have I felt so tranquil as now I do, at war; seldom have I felt more at ease with the world, or more content.

HE SAW Luca Gregorio whenever he could get down the mountain. The wild boar proved elusive, but there was always something good to eat at Granezza and Daniel invited him back to his "cottage," where he served him Maconochie's stew and polenta, with oranges, which were now a staple of the ration. Luca asked to see the company cook, and explained to him that he needed to put olive oil and herbs with the polenta next time; luckily he had brought plenty of wine, so they could wash down the glutinous mixture. They sat up till late, while Luca told him about his family in Arabba and his work in Verona, and his wife and two daughters. He seemed fascinated by the fact that Daniel could speak even a little of his language and wanted to know more about his family. Luca was the first person Daniel had told since joining up that his father was a psychiatrist.

In late May, by dint of some fortunate "lorry-hopping," Daniel was able to profit from the day off that Denniston had given him. He met Luca at nine, and they set off down the mountain in a Fiat lorry that was bound for Vicenza. Daniel wanted to buy some boots better suited to the mountains and an electric torch to replace the one blown off him at Passchendaele, so that he could more easily read Shelley; Luca told him that the modern town of Schio, the other side of Thiene, would be able to help. In return, Daniel planned to spend the first installment of his extra officer's pay on buying them the best lunch that Schio could provide.

"Don't be too hopeful," said Luca.

In Thiene, they were deposited at Mario's bar, where any passing traffic stopped for an exchange of news on road conditions and the progress of the war. Luca persuaded a post office van to take them on up the narrow roads of the mountain again, through the green meadows, to Schio, which they reached at noon. Luca made some inquiries at the post office, and by lunchtime Daniel had his new boots and a bicycle lamp, which was the nearest thing to a torch that Schio could manage; the shopkeeper allowed him a spare bulb, but had no extra batteries, so Daniel conceded that Shelley's longer poems would have to be read by day. The restaurant that had been recommended to Luca entailed a walk through the center of the modern town.

As well as a large textile works, Schio was famous for its hospital, which they stopped briefly to admire. It was a large three-story white building, with tall cypresses in its gardens. It was only as they were about to move off that Daniel noticed that the place proclaimed itself, in large letters beneath the pediment, to be a Hospital for Neurasthenics. He smiled to himself. Where English asylums invariably had an Italianate design, the Schio madhouse had a bell tower with a spire that might have come from rural Sussex.

There was no wild boar at the restaurant, but there were ribbon strips of pasta with hare, which Luca told him were the next best thing; there were also numerous dried and cured meats to start with and, after the pasta, veal from the mountain pastures cooked in sage and butter. Luca tried to pay, but Daniel insisted. "I wouldn't have ordered all that wine if I had known," said Luca.

"Too bad," said Daniel. "You are the best friend I have had since . . . well, since Billy Reader, a man who was with me in France. And before that, Freddy, who is now, alas, the Enemy."

When they had drunk coffee, Luca said he had some private business to attend to, and that he would meet Daniel at the post office at four, when the van would take them back to Thiene.

With red wine and coffee competing in his system, Daniel felt a little disorientated, especially without his companion. He sat down on a bench opposite the hospital for neurasthenics and tried to gather his thoughts. He had believed himself settled in his "cottage" in the mountains; he had found a role for himself in the army and the respect not only of his men but perhaps even of his commanding officer. It was very beautiful at that altitude, it was serene, and the Austrian guns held no fear for him. Yet as he watched the patients shuffle out from a side door of the hospital, he had an uneasy feeling.

In another life, or in a part of this one that he no longer remembered, he had been one of them. Perhaps after Passchendaele, his "shell shock" had turned to madness and his hospital had been for the insane. Or maybe it was merely that having spent his life with lunatics, he knew too well that bitter world that lay across reality at its awkward, unforgiving angle, where voices were true and memory was false. It was not that he had himself been mad, it was just that he could too easily imagine the lives of the patients. That must be it. . . . In any event, he was pleased to see Luca again and to be on the way home.

That evening, at the *osteria* in Granezza, where Luca was billeted for the time being, Daniel met a young woman called Laura, who lived in Padua but was helping the Italian war effort because she spoke French and enjoyed being in the mountains. She worked in the battalion commander's office as a secretary, but sometimes joined the other officers for dinner, where she was treated with exaggerated courtesy.

Daniel sat next to her and stared into her dark brown eyes, fascinated. She wore a tailored army jacket and a blue scarf with her black hair loose to her shoulders; she spoke French to him and occasionally placed her hand on his for emphasis. She laughed a good deal and seemed pleased to talk to someone new, as though the good manners of the Italian officers had become wearisome to her and she wanted to confide in someone the powerful secret feelings that living so close to death had stirred in her heart.

Daniel returned in a dream to his cottage by lorry at midnight, to find Jack Turney in his bed complaining that he had caught flu.

ONE MORNING in mid-June Daniel was awoken by the loud crash of an Austrian gun. He sat up in the darkness and knocked his head against the roof of his cave. The Austrian artillery never started up this early and they never shelled his part of the line. A moment later, there was another crash and bits of earth tumbled from the ceiling of his cottage. He put on his helmet and went outside. Shells were crashing into the mountainside all round and the reverberations were magnified by the rocks, so that they echoed from one peak to another, making a continuous roar. He picked up a rifle and ran to the trench where his platoon were hastily assembling, cramming on helmets and peering forward into the mist of the plateau that prolonged the darkness of the night. A number of his men were off sick with influenza and had been sent into a reserve position; many of those remaining were weakened and feverish. The noise of the bombardment made it impossible for him to gain any sense of what was going on, but in the comparative quiet between shell explosions he began to hear the rattle of machine-gun fire and rifles coming from the French part of the line.

"Christ, Christ, Christ," he said, suddenly seeing through the yellow mist a line of Austrian infantry coming toward the line. "Fire! Fire!"

His depleted platoon, sweating and surprised, had hardly had time to re-load before they were fighting with bayonets against the Austrians, who piled through the thin defense of wire, then set up machine guns with which to enfilade the British position. With no chance of communicating with Denniston and no idea of what was happening in other parts of the line, Daniel signaled to his men to withdraw at once to a prepared position about ninety yards further back in the woods.

The Austrians had broken through so quickly that their own artillery barrage had not stopped but was still piling shells into the forest, so that Daniel's progress was impeded by crashing pines and the shrapnel of exploding rocks. They joined a company of Fusiliers in the reserve trench and managed to hold the line for half an hour with two Lewis guns and as many rifle rounds as they could get off through the woods.

Soon, however, they found themselves under fire from behind and higher up the slope.

A messenger came weaving through the trees and shouted in Daniel's ear: "They've broken through on the right for half a mile. The flank of the company is being held by cooks and orderlies. You have to retire again. General's orders. A and C are behind that ridge."

"Is Denniston alive?"

"Yes, he sent me."

"All right. Let's go."

In the second withdrawal they met mustard gas curling through the tree trunks and the men became disorientated as they fought for their respirators. There were now Austrian snipers in the woods and it was difficult to know which way they were meant to be going, as machine-gun fire pursued them and rifle bullets ricocheted off the pines. The Austrians must have got word back that they had broken through because their artillery barrage ceased, but not before a final shell buried a British gun emplacement beneath a rockfall. Daniel heard the screaming of the men inside, but could not stop. He thought he saw where his company had regrouped and was shouting to his men to run for it.

When he dived down into his third position of the morning, he recognized only one man there, a private called Addison.

"Where are the rest of the men, Addison?"

"Don't know, sir. We was well and truly fucked. Couldn't see the bastards coming in the mist. I saw the corporal with his head blown off."

"Corporal who?"

"Turney, sir. Apparently they're through our line for half a mile, but the Frogs have held off the Magyars in their sector."

"All right. This is where we hold the line. Get firing."

By noon, the ferocity of the assault had died down, though there were still pockets of the Austrian Landwehr behind them as well as in full occupation of the two forward British trenches. At two o'clock a company was despatched to clear the rear, and at four the first counterattack was begun on Daniel's right. By five it had been fully rebuffed.

An hour later, word was sent from Denniston that D company was to be part of the next counterattack, due in fifteen minutes. Daniel went along the line and urged his men to prepare to go over the top, back through the woods; but the flu-stricken troops were exhausted and pleading for water.

"You can have all you want to drink when we're back in our own trench," he said. "Now get up and get ready for the whistle."

As they moved forward, the fire came from so many angles that it seemed the trees themselves were shooting at them. None of them had fought in the mountains before, and while it was harder for the guns to find them, the sense of being fired on from all sides was somehow more nerve-testing than the slow plod into death on the plains of Picardy.

Daniel saw his men hiding behind trees only to find themselves shot at from the side they had thought safe; some just kept running forward, though few of them made it back to their own support trench. Within an hour the counterattack was called off and they crept back to their reserve position in the rocks, where they flopped down exhausted on the pine needles.

At eight o'clock another section of the British line was stirred into action and charged forward to regain the ground it had lost twelve hours ago. Once more the woods and mountains echoed to the sound of the enemy machine guns, now well emplaced in their new positions. Daniel wondered vaguely who had his cottage and if his bed and books were now being used by a man from Vienna or Linz.

When night fell, the shooting stopped and they tried to get the wounded down the mountain to the regimental aid post. Daniel despatched stretcher parties and went with them into the woods to bring back as many men as they could. In the course of the night it became clear that the Austrian success had been limited to a section of the Allied line no more than a mile long, where they had pushed through to a depth of about half a mile and entrenched. It was curious, Daniel thought, that although they were more or less encircled by the enemy, there was something about the summer night at altitude that made it possible to rest; perhaps the men were simply too drained by loss, by fear and illness, and by the physical strain of battle to stay awake. At any rate, soon after midnight, Daniel, lying huddled with the remaining men of his platoon, also fell asleep. He dreamed of Laura, the girl at the Italian base.

Someone was shaking his shoulder. It was Denniston.

"Wake up, Lieutenant. We are to launch another counterattack at 04:30 hours. Having missed out on the last one, D company will be at the front of this show. It is now three. Have your men stand to at four and be ready to go."

"Sir."

Daniel dragged himself up into a sitting position, then stood and went to find the NCOs, shining his new torch, which had survived the day, among the sleeping bodies, looking for a stripe. In the course of the next hour, the men were readied: grumbling, feverish and reluctant. But as the time drew near, they fell silent, knowing what they had to do, knowing there was no way out for them now. As Daniel walked among the men, he saw them take out photographs of home and kiss their children's faces; the unmarried ones fingered lucky tokens or moved their lips in silent prayer.

For himself, Daniel felt quite calm. Soon after he had arrived in France, he saw that the way he had lived until that point was no longer possible. As a child, he had clung emotionally to his own life, acting as though it were highly valuable, sacred—or at least unique. He organized each day with passionate care, first to find comfort and to do something well, then, if there was time over, to make himself agreeable to others. In the Salient at Ypres, planning was pointless. It was worse than pointless, in fact; it was foolish and disrespectful to those who had died.

Instead, he tried to cultivate a kind of serenity, to trust to providence and to place a much lower value on his life, because to have too high a care for it was to suggest that he believed his own existence, his own little breathing hopes, to be more important than those of the millions of the dead; and insufficiently to respect the dead, and the lives and loves they had forsaken, was, so far as he could see, the worst of war crimes.

The minute hand on his watch went through the horizontal and began to drop toward the half hour. He thought of Charlotte and Martha, asleep in London. One of them was at art college, the other had a job teaching infants; to his shame he could not remember which was which. He thought of his father, who had always been so kind to him—severe, sometimes, but encouraging—and saw his dark, anxious face with its fringe of untidy white hair. And he thought of his mother, picturing her as she leaned over him, pretending to be strict, but always laughing; seeing him, apparently, as the source of some never-failing, never-ending comedy of mysterious and cosmic proportion. He smiled at the thought of her. Then Freddy, Billy, Luca and that girl Laura—

The whistle blew. He jumped and leapt up from the rocky trench. "Let's go!" he screamed. "Let's go!"

EDGAR MIDWINTER invited his sister to join him at Torrington for a few weeks in the summer and Sonia arrived in the last week of June. It was planned that Jacques would come over later when business in Paris began to fall off in the summer. Sonia stopped off in London on the way and discovered a notable change in attitude since her last visit. Where previously the people had seemed anxiously patriotic about their soldiers—if unsure of how to treat them when they actually met them face-to-face on leave—now they seemed openly proud of them and impatient for the victory they felt confident was coming. Thomas and Kitty were living in rented rooms, but hoped to buy a house soon; Thomas was finding it difficult to establish himself in private practice and his money was still tied up in the Wilhelmskogel.

There was not much to do at Torrington, but Sonia was able to work in the garden and to help Lucy with the domestic arrangements. In the afternoon, she went riding in the fields, along the ridge and down to the river. Then, in the evening, after supper, she usually wrote to Daniel, though she feared to bore him when she had so little to relate. One afternoon, she had returned from her ride and was arranging some flowers on the circular table in the hall, when the front doorbell was pulled. Outside was a telegram boy, whose bicycle was leaning against the front steps of the house.

"Mrs. Rebière?"

He held out a small envelope, then jumped back onto his bicycle and pedaled off down the drive as fast as he could. The telegram was from Paris. Sonia went up to her room and sat down. She placed the envelope unopened on the table beneath the window that looked over toward the duck pond and the church. If she did not open it, then all was still well. Then, not a religious person, she knelt at the end of the bed and prayed. She stood up, wiped her hands down the front of her dress and with shaking fingers unstuck the paper. It was from Jacques. Daniel was reported missing presumed dead following action near Asiago, Italy, June 15/16, 1918. Jacques was on his way to England as soon as he could get a boat. He had cabled to the War Office and Infantry Record Office asking them to communicate at once with Sonia at Torrington.

The following day came a letter from a Mr. R. C. Fowler at the War Office, Finsbury Court, Finsbury Pavement London EC2, on cheap yellowish paper with her name and address correctly spelled in the bottom left-hand corner. It offered condolences, but no hope. The missing accounted for a large proportion of the dead in this war; while no burial could take place, these men were honored in the same way as those whose bodies were recovered. There would in due course be a divisional memorial, he assured her, on which her son's name would appear, and it would be possible to visit it when hostilities were concluded.

It seemed that Daniel had slipped through the hands of death once at Passchendaele, but had not managed it a second time. Jacques arrived a week later to find Sonia in a state of shock; although she had shown the telegram to Edgar and Lucy, she had not spoken since the day it arrived. She had nothing worth saying. He put his arms round her, but after a mumbled greeting she remained silent.

In August, they received a letter from Daniel's former commanding officer.

Dear Mr. and Mrs. Rebière,

I am writing to offer you my sincere condolences on the loss of your son, Lt. D. Rebière. As you will know, he served in my company from the autumn of 1916 and was a dutiful and valued member of the regiment. Like many men who have served the King in this war, he was not by nature a soldier. However, he did not complain or make trouble; nor did he shirk his duties when he served with me in the autumn of 1917 in the Ypres Salient in the most trying circumstances.

When he had recovered from his wounds, and the battalion was moved to Italy, your son seemed to develop as a soldier, and I was pleased to be able to recommend him for promotion. As a platoon commander, he was dependable, prompt and resourceful. His linguistic ability made him an "ever-present" in night raids across the River Piave and a lesser soldier might have resented this continuous exposure to danger.

However, it was in the mountains, in our final Italian posting, that the true measure of the man was seen. He seemed to have a keen affinity for the terrain and to know by instinct what was required. At first, he was diffident about commanding men, but he won their trust in the best way that an officer can: by showing an example.

By the time of the Austrian offensive in June, in which your son gave his life, I had come to rely on him as my unofficial second-in-command.

His men loved him, and his inspiring example in our
successful counterattack was an important factor in our victory.

Yours sincerely,
John Denniston, Lt. Col.

With no body to bury, it was difficult to know what do about a funeral.
Jacques returned to Paris in September, but Sonia did not wish to leave Torrington. In October, it became clear that the Allies were close to a final victory and Jacques suggested that any service for Daniel should wait until
after an armistice. In his heart he was hoping that the light of peace might
reveal his son still living. The Asiago Plateau was cleaned up and the debris
of war was taken down the mountain on the snaking roads; every dead soldier from the dozen different countries who had fought there was found
and buried. In December, sheep were put to graze; and soon after Christmas, when the snow fell, the Italians ventured out with toboggans and skis.

Through the regimental headquarters, Sonia was able to be in touch
with Denniston, and asked if Daniel had any friends who would like to
come to a service at Torrington. He replied that there was an Italian captain called Gregorio and he would try to make contact with him; the
others of his original platoon, alas, were all dead.

It was not until February 14 that the village church tolled its bell and
a small group of mourners gathered at the lych-gate. In addition to the
family, there was Lieutenant Colonel Denniston for the regiment, Captain Luca Gregorio and, from Carinthia, Freddy, Daniel's childhood
friend, who had survived the war.

Sonia had prepared a small box of Daniel's belongings, including the
copy of Shelley's poems that his uncle had sent to Italy, from which various bits of dried flowers fell out; a couple of the toy animals that he had
carried in his wicker basket as a child; and his first tooth, which she had
kept in an enameled box on her dressing table and which was the only
part of his body that survived.

It was a cold, blustery day and the snowdrops on the grassy graves in
the churchyard bowed and swayed on the undulating waves of grass. A
small grave had been dug next to those of Sonia's parents.

The mourners stood about the opened earth. Kitty gripped Thomas's hand as hard as she could. Charlotte and Martha wept as they clung to one another. Denniston and Gregorio stared straight ahead, the muscles of their jaws occasionally seen to clamp or to release.

Jacques closed his eyes and tried to imagine himself elsewhere, but could see only Daniel's face.

When he had been working late, he sometimes used to go into Daniel's bedroom to say good night. As he bent over the sleeping child, he would lay his closed eyes, sore from reading, against his son's forehead, so that the soft swell of the boy's brow would fit into the sockets of his aching eyes and cool them.

As Jacques stood in the wind, he remembered, too, the way that Daniel, normally so careless with possessions, would sometimes try to clean things; how he had knelt over his skis and carefully wiped each flake of snow from them with his handkerchief, lost in concentration, even though he was shortly to set off again through the powder.

He had his arm tight round Sonia's shoulder and felt he must somehow reach her. He leaned down and whispered in her ear, "I wonder what his mustache looked like"; but her face showed no answering smile.

Little Herr Frage, thought Jacques: not a nail, not an eyelash left of him. It is as though he might never have been; it is as though he was not a human being, but just an idea of one after all.

Sonia knelt on the grass and lowered the small wooden box into the hole in the ground while the vicar read a prayer.

She stood up and held tight to Jacques, squeezing the rough serge of his coat in her hand. Her face was driven into a thin line of anguish; her eyes were dry and staring. The blood had drained from her skin, but she could feel it in her head, pounding at her temples, as though time itself were rising up inside and drowning her. She felt her lips part. "Hmm," she said in a dry, rough voice, and it was almost the first time she had spoken since he died. "Be my Valentine."

XXIII

IT WAS A COLD, DARK MORNING IN ZÜRICH. JACQUES TOOK A CAB from the railway station, past the restored guild houses, then watched the first sudden flakes of snow swirling in a light breeze across the stone façades of the palaces on the Bahnhofstrasse. It was more than two years since the Armistice, and while Paris still resembled an outsize field dressing station, its transports thronged with the maimed and limbless, the trams of Zürich were filled with whole people in plump coats; the cathedral tolled its twelve o'clock bell as it had each day since the Middle Ages, and the councillors of the Rathaus planned no monument to the dead.

In the private clinic at which Jacques alighted from the cab, Herr Fischer gathered a small team together in the patient's room. He sat down on the edge of the bed and gently took the hand of the woman who sat propped up on white pillows.

"This," he said, "is Maria. I am taking the trouble to introduce you because the operation we are about to perform is not like an appendectomy or even a straightforward cranial procedure in which the inhalation of ether renders the patient unconscious. On the contrary, in the course of the next few hours, Maria will be wide awake."

Although Fischer had been pleased to accommodate the request of a distinguished psychiatrist to be present at an operation, Jacques felt out of place in the small room. He had grown a beard and had been surprised to see it come out white; he felt old and shell-shocked in comparison to these Swiss people with their banal streets under silent snow.

Fischer squeezed the woman's hand; there was a charming benevolence in his manner, though Jacques could also see that the geniality served a purpose: Fischer needed the patient's help.

"Throughout the operation," he said, "Maria will be guiding us. That is why it is important for her to feel at ease with those of us who will be in the operating theater."

Standing up, Fischer introduced the anesthetist, the assistant, two students from the university and two nurses. "We also have a distinguished visitor from Paris, Dr. Rebière."

Jacques shook hands with Maria, a plump woman of about forty whose head had been completely shaved. She looked anxious as she took his hand, but managed a faint smile. Jacques did his best to look reassuring and confident, though he had seldom been in an operating theater.

"To recapitulate for the benefit of Dr. Rebière," said Fischer. "Since late adolescence, Maria has suffered focal epileptic seizures causing paralysis of the right arm and speech interruptions. We have therefore deduced that the site of the epileptic discharge is somewhere near the motor strip and the speech area in the left side of the brain." He pointed toward the area of Maria's bald head with a long forefinger. "We shall be performing a craniotomy here. It is hoped that by administering a small electric current to the exposed area of the brain, the seizure can be reproduced and the site of the lesion can thus be located. It is envisaged that a small amount of damaged tissue can then be removed and that the patient will subsequently experience relief from her seizures. Is that not right, Maria?"

"Yes, indeed." Her voice was small and uncertain, with a strong rural accent.

"Do we have any questions?" said Fischer.

"Yes, sir," said one of the students. "Is this a new procedure?"

"Yes and no," said Fischer genially. "The famous English neurosurgeon Sir Victor Horsley was prevailed on by John Hughlings Jackson to do something similar about twenty years ago. Sadly, Sir Victor died in Mesopotamia in the course of the war and was not able to build on his pioneering work. However, the celebrated American Dr. Harvey Cushing has picked up the torch. Before the war, he had stimulated the motor cortex in more than fifty patients. Now, perhaps Dr. Artzmann will tell us about the anesthesia."

The anesthetist, a ruddy, sportive-looking man, stepped forward and coughed. "Well, the joy of it is," he said, "as I am sure you all know, that the brain has no sensory nerves. We could remove half the good lady's brain with a spoon and she would not feel a thing. Though I imagine her behavior might be somewhat affected!" He gave a throaty laugh and the students smiled uncertainly. Jacques glanced at the patient.

Artzmann coughed. "Anyway, I shall be injecting a local anesthetic here and here and here," he said, pointing to spots round the base of the skull. "The scalp of course is innervated, so there we shall be most watchful, but once we are through the dura mater, which is a tough customer, it should be plain sailing. At any rate, I shall be doing all I can to minimize the discomfort."

"Thank you," said Fischer, evidently relieved that Artzmann had finished more tactfully than he had begun. "Now, if there are no further questions, I suggest that we reconvene at two o'clock."

When Jacques returned in the overalls and mask provided by the hospital, he found the patient had been moved to a trolley, where she lay beneath a green surgical sheet. She looked like a convict about to be transported. On the left side of her shaved head there had been drawn the outline of a rectangle using iodine-soaked cotton wool wrapped round a wooden stick; it was the size of a picture postcard, though its shape, Jacques could not help noticing, was rather like a map of France.

Two orderlies came into the small room, followed by Herr Fischer.

"Are you ready, Maria? Your friends are all waiting for you."

"I am scared," said Maria.

Fischer perched on the edge of the trolley. "I know. But listen. Your life has become very difficult, has it not? 'Unbearable.' Was not that the word you used? When we have finished, I do believe you will have something like a normal life again. In return, all I ask is that you should be brave. A little courage for a couple of hours. I shall be with you all the time. If anything hurts or does not feel right, then you must tell me. I promise we shall take the best possible care of you. Is that not right, Dr. Rebière?"

"Of course it is right. We shall all look after you."

"Are you agreed, Maria? Maria?"

"Yes."

"Thank you. Take her through, please."

Artzmann was waiting in a small anteroom off the main theater. Jacques could see his eyes crease into a grin of welcome, though his mouth was mercifully hidden beneath his white mask. He injected Maria at four points in the base of the skull and in the dotted lines of the planned incision; Jacques went through into the main room while they waited for the anesthetic to take effect. He nodded to the assistant and the students, then took his place where Fischer instructed him.

The trolley was pushed through the door feet first, then the orderlies swung it round so that the patient's head was beneath a strong circular light.

"I am going to keep talking to you all the time, Maria, and I want you to talk back," said Fischer, while the nurses secured the patient and draped sterilized towels about her head and body. A raised table, also draped with a towel, was placed above her abdomen. "I want you to tell me everything," said Fischer. "Is that clear? Sometimes I shall say something to the students, so if you hear some Latin word you don't understand, please do not concern yourself. Are you with me? Good."

Fischer leaned forward and took a scalpel from the nurse. He held it with his right forefinger on top and steadied his wrist with his left hand. As he began to cut along the marked line, his assistant followed, applying steady pressure with his fingers until Fischer had clamped the incision at short intervals with arterial forceps, bundles of which, as they grew intrusive, were then taped and tied away from the opening. When the three sides of the incision were finally complete, Fischer painstakingly pulled down the flap of scalp with tweezers, so that it hung over Maria's left ear. He stood back while the assistant then clamped the edges of the flap and wrapped it in soaked, sterilized gauze.

"We are using all these clamps here," said Fischer to the students, "to compress the blood vessels at the edge of the galea. Are you all right, Maria? Can you feel anything?"

"No."

"Good. You are being brave. You are now going to feel an unpleasant vibration. Please do not feel alarmed. It is quite normal. We are going to make some holes, Maria, then I am going to cut between them and then we are going to turn back the section of bone. Do you remember I drew a picture of it for you yesterday? Here we go."

Jacques noticed that Fischer came in from out of Maria's eyeline and wondered if it was to spare her the sight of the primitive brace and perforator attachment with which he set to work. In the skull he drilled seven holes about three centimeters apart whose positions on the notional map of France were roughly, going clockwise from the southwest, at Biarritz, La Rochelle, Brest, Caen, Calais, Mulhouse and Marseille. He enlarged the holes by attaching a burr to the brace and redrilling each one; he then plugged the cavities with wax. Between the skull and the dura mater beneath it, he gingerly inserted a metal guide which, having gone under at Biarritz, emerged at La Rochelle. Through the groove of the guide he ran a thin flexible saw; when that too had reemerged, he attached T-bars to its ends, so that it was like a serrated cheese wire. Standing squarely and locking his shoulders, he then sawed carefully upward with gentle rocking movements on a slight outward angle, till Biarritz was joined to La Rochelle by a clean cut through the bone. All the holes at the edges of the map were thus joined except the southern line from Biarritz to Marseille, where although the bone was cut, the muscle was left attached, so that the flap of skull, like that of scalp, could be turned down while remaining attached to its blood supply.

"Note," said Fischer proudly, "the slightly beveled edge of the reflected section which will make replacement more snug. This is a true osteoplastic flap. Maria, are you still all right? That grating is now over. Are you feeling pain? Maria?"

"It's all right."

"I am going to ask my colleague to give you a little more anesthetic. The next part of the procedure can sting a little."

Fischer stood back with his hands held aloft like a priest making a blessing, while Artzmann injected the patient once more. The section of skull was protected by layers of soaked and sterilized gauze, like the attached flap of scalp at Maria's ear.

As they waited for the drug to take effect, Fischer encouraged Maria, telling her how well she was doing. "But you must speak to me, Maria. Tell me what you feel."

"I feel all right. It feels odd lying here with all of you staring at me, and I didn't like the noise in my head. But I feel nothing strange. No pain."

"Good. We are now at the dura mater. This is the first and toughest of the meninges, the membranes that cover the brain. You have a splendid dura, Maria. Nice and thick and well supplied with healthy blood vessels. I am going to 'reflect' it, by which I mean that I am going to cut it, then fold it gently back."

Fischer kept up his commentary, half-facetious, half-reassuring, as he explained his progress in "reflection"; while the dura was held back with silver clips inserted by his assistant, Fischer exclaimed at the health and beauty of the lower meninges—the arachnoid and the pia mater.

He stepped back at last. "And now, my dear Maria, we can see your wonderful brain."

The students leaned forward and Fischer turned to the nurse, who wiped his forehead. The other nurse fitted a pair of magnifying glasses to his head, while the assistant tidied once more round the edges of the opening.

The brain was exposed to the light. Jacques looked at the rippled organ, the color of uncooked sweetbread, roped with black veins and delicate crimson capillaries, and then at the face of its owner, the skin of her cheeks quite pale, her brown eyes wide open.

"I am looking for signs of gliosis," said Fischer, lowering his head to the brain. "Some shriveling or yellowing of the gray matter, but I do not see anything yet. We have exposed part of the frontal lobe, here, the parietal here and the temporal down here. The appearance is normal. We shall now move on to the important part of our procedure."

Fischer's assistant passed him two electrodes and went to a black faradic box on a trolley to which they were attached.

"Are you comfortable, Maria? Are you ready? You must tell me everything you feel. Do you understand?"

"Yes."

"One of the things we are doing with the electrical stimulus is to establish an exact map of the motor and sensory areas so that they can be protected during any excision of epileptogenic matter."

Fischer nodded to his assistant, who rotated a knob on the machine; then he touched the electrodes lightly to the surface of the naked brain. It had a shimmering luster given to it by the cerebrospinal fluid, which gathered in small pools in the troughs of the sulci, like fresh dew.

"Talk to me, Maria."

"My hand is shaking. Twitching."

"Yes. We can see."

"Now numb. Feel numb. My arm. It has gone to sleep."

"What about this?"

"I . . ." Maria's voice stopped. Her jaw shuddered a little, but did not make the shape of words or syllables.

"Keep talking, Maria."

No words came.

"Broca's area, we presume," said Fischer. He removed the electrodes. "Why did you stop talking, Maria?"

"I . . . tried. I . . . had no words . . . no words."

"Are you all right? Does it hurt?"

"No. It is all right."

"What do you feel now?"

"My tongue is tingling. Blue, very bright. Now I can. Field, you see gone. Match and something. Frank, frank. Tutupic. Tamia. Tamia. Avalli."

Fischer lifted the electrodes again. At each place that he touched the brain he afterward stuck a small numbered ticket, designed to be photographed later, making sure one of the students had the number correlated in a notebook with the effect it produced. "Possibly Wernicke's area," he said. "I am not finding what I want to find. I am going to move to the other side of the Sylvian fissure. Keep talking to me, Maria."

"My leg now. It is kicking."

"Good. Anything else? I am going to move a little. Now?"

Suddenly, for the first time, the grim and wary look vanished from Maria's thick features; the skin flushed and the eyes filled. Her face became suffused with joy.

"What is it?"

"I am in the bedroom. . . . It is home. My father is lifting me on his shoulders and showing me a star through the small window. I can smell . . . yes, gas from the lamp on the landing. Outside someone is singing. My mother is sitting at the end of the bed. . . . Wait . . . I can hear the knock of the brass handle on my bedside locker. On the mantelpiece is a china giraffe. And my brother is asleep. . . . And my father has me still, is leaning down so I can kiss my brother good night. . . . And the song in the street, I can sing it, I can hear it. . . . Wait, wait . . . 'The king sits in his castle, the maid is gone away. The raven . . . something . . . the farmer cuts the hay.' And I can see the star, my father pointing. And, and . . ."

As Fischer lifted the electrodes, her voice tailed away. A look of puzzlement came across her face.

"What happened?"

"You are still here, Maria," said Fischer. "Everything is all right. I am going to move on now so I can find the source of your seizures, so—"

"No, no. You have taken me away. I want to go back. Take me back to my room. Take me back. Take me back."

Jacques saw a look of concern in Fischer's eyes above the rim of his mask. "I cannot do that. Even if I replaced the electrodes in the same place, some different images would occur. Something random."

"No," said Maria loudly, the vigor of her denial making the exposed brain tremble slightly. "That is exactly as it happened. I had not thought of it for all these years, but it was true and I was there again. It was real, Doctor. I was there."

KITTY WAS sitting alone, reading, in the drawing room of her house in Bayswater. It was a short walk from Hyde Park, conveniently placed for access to Wimpole Street, where Thomas had a room, and to the more fashionable areas south of the park where he occasionally went on house visits. It was situated in a cobbled backstreet that was reassuringly quiet at night; it was small, but with both girls living away from home they needed only one spare bedroom. Kitty herself was out at work most of the day, teaching German and French in a school near Primrose Hill, so while the house lacked the drama of the Wilhelmskogel or the atmosphere of the old schloss it served them well enough; and she liked to fall asleep to the sound of traffic from the rainy streets of Gloucester Terrace and Craven Hill.

Without telling Thomas, she had been to see a heart specialist, who had told her that he believed the valves of her heart were damaged by rheumatic fever and that she should not expect to live a full life. As to the extent by which her days might be abbreviated, he would not be drawn; nor could he say for sure whether the fevers to which she was more than normally prone in the winter were connected with the original condition or were merely the results of a weakened immune system's inability to fight off seasonal colds and infections.

At times, sitting in her London drawing room, Kitty felt frustrated by her poor health. It was not, after all, as though one had several chances at living and might reasonably expect to shoulder a fair proportion of the world's sickness in one of them; she had one life only and it had been blighted. Yet her disposition usually saved her from despair. She had only to think of Charlotte and Martha, grown tall and elegant yet still essentially the little girls, the inexplicably doubled blessing that had dropped on her when she had reason to think she might not have children at all. In the year after she had sat at her dying father's bedside, watching this lovely man dragged out slowly through the gate of death, she had once or twice thought of killing herself because she could no longer bear to have the random pointlessness of existence held quite so close to her face. Yet her subsequent cure and release from illness had filled her with a kind of levity she felt would last forever, or at least for the rest of her somewhat shortened life. She knew that there was something frivolous in her refusal to engage with the subjects that her husband had worn himself away in contemplating, but she felt that her illness had bought her the right to live as she pleased. The chance of making a living for the family was one she seized with pleasure; she planned the lessons she would teach her pupils in advance and enjoyed the release of a profession beyond medicine, of having colleagues who never thought of death, and charges who were not ill, but filled with childish optimism.

The telephone rang on the table in the hall and Kitty, unused to the noisy eruption of the instrument into her private thoughts, went to answer it with thudding heart.

"Is that Mrs. Midwinter?"

"Yes."

"This is Sergeant Moore, Paddington Green. We have a gentleman here, madam, who I think may be your husband."

"What are you talking about?"

"Is your husband missing, madam?"

"He is a little late coming home, but I would not say he was 'missing,' no."

"Well, he has been found."

"What do you mean, 'found'? He is not a stray cat."

"A gentleman was found in the Sussex Gardens area. He was in a confused state. Constable Delaney at first believed him to have been drinking but I believe this was not the case. A doctor was called but he advised the gentleman was fit to be taken home. I would be obliged if you would come to the station, madam."

"How do you know it is my husband?"

"We took the liberty of examining the contents of his pockets, where we found a letter addressed to him at number twenty-nine—"

"Very well. I am coming."

THREE DAYS after the operation in Zürich, back in their rented rooms overlooking the Thames in Pimlico, Jacques told Sonia about the procedure.

"What was so striking," he said, "was that it seemed to suggest that past experience has a continuing physical existence in the brain."

"Not just a memory?" said Sonia.

"Yes, it is a memory, but if a memory is stored in cells and can be reactivated so that the experience is relived, then memory is very much less abstract than we had supposed. It is more like a cardboard box in a brick warehouse."

"And was the patient all right?"

"Yes, I believe she did well. Fischer was able to find a small amount of dead tissue. He removed it and she is making a good recovery. But that is not really the point. The point is that our past experience is stored and can be relived."

"What was the name of that man in Paris, at the Salpêtrière, who—"

"Pierre Janet! Yes. Exactly. 'In the human brain nothing ever gets lost.' It seems as though he was right."

"But how does this change anything?"

"In two ways. We had thought that the hippocampus, another part of the brain, stored memories, but it now seems they may be spread about the brain. But more importantly, my darling, don't you see?"

"See what?" said Sonia, looking up, baffled, at Jacques's flushed, imploring face. With his unkempt white hair and his beard he looked like an illustration she remembered from her Bible of the prophet Elisha.

"Don't you see that if nothing gets lost, all is remembered and all is physically accessible, then it is really only a question of how we get access to it. The past does not die or vanish. It can be relived."

"Oh, my love, that is a forlorn hope."

"We had believed that access to memory came from a conscious effort of recollection—or an unconscious effort in a dream. Now it seems it could be quite mechanical."

"That does not sound right."

"No, no. It is quite rational. On the train back from Zürich I had a brilliant idea. In the name of science, I am going to offer myself as a guinea pig. I am going to see if someone will do the procedure on me. I doubt whether Fischer will. He is too . . . cautious. Too involved with his clinic and the university. But I shall find someone. And it's not a particularly complicated procedure."

"But no one will operate on a man who is not sick. It is far too dangerous—opening up your skull, for heaven's sake."

"But they must. Don't you see? I want to remember. I want to relive. And when he puts the electrodes on I shall tell him to leave them there until I have finished."

"You do not know what memory you might release."

"No. But I would like to try. In case . . . in case . . ."

Sonia stood up and crossed the room. She laid her hand on Jacques's sleeve. "This is quite mad, Jacques. You are meant to be a scientist. You must accept what has happened. Daniel is dead."

"It is not mad. It is neurological fact, proved in one of the best clinics in Europe and I intend to profit from it. And it is not just Daniel. I want to go back. Back to . . ." He tailed off.

"To what? To the day of your birth?" Sonia held Jacques by the wrists. "You are tormenting yourself and you are tormenting me, Jacques. Please, please stop it. Daniel is dead. Your mother is dead. Olivier too. Your father. They have all gone. Let them rest in peace."

"I cannot," said Jacques. "Not while there is hope."

THE NEXT day Sonia sat at the desk in the window overlooking the river and wrote:

> Dear Thomas,
>
> May I come to tea tomorrow? I am worried about Jacques and wd like to discuss it with you. Shall you be in at 4?
>
> Your loving sister, Sonia

Meanwhile, in the course of a conversation with the landlady of his lodgings, Jacques was given the name of someone who might help him. It was a Mrs. Hockley in Camden Town. It was not really what he had had in mind; she was no neurosurgeon; but he was inspired and desperate enough to try anything.

The motor omnibus from Victoria stopped at Euston Station, where he took a cab onward. He had never heard of Camden Town and did not like the look of what he saw: vast railway cuttings had been driven through the narrow streets, and the sooty terraces that clung onto the edge were like rescue huts at the site of an earthquake. There were one or two villainous-looking taverns with improbable names, the Swan of Avon or the Horse and Hounds, through whose steamed windows he could see capped laborers with outsize beer mugs. The cab continued north, past a large roundhouse for turning locomotives, then swung into a small and comparatively respectable street, with curtains and potted plants at the windows.

Jacques rapped the knocker at number thirty-five and heard a dog yap briefly before it was silenced. He watched the cab depart and felt glad he had engaged it to return.

A maid in a uniform answered; she looked him up and down nervously.

"I have come to see Mrs. Hockley."

"You're to wait in the parlor, then. In here."

"Thank you."

Jacques found himself in a cold front room overlooking the street. There was a gas fire, but it was not lit; on a gateleg table were some old copies of *Strand* magazine and *John o' London's Weekly*. There were half a dozen hard chairs ranged round the walls, on one of which was sitting a man in a bowler hat who nodded but said nothing. Jacques kept his coat on and rubbed his bare hands together. In the course of the next ten minutes they were joined by a couple of about sixty years old, and a young woman on her own. None of them introduced themselves or shook hands, so Jacques, assuming this was the English way, merely nodded to each newcomer.

"Mrs. Hockley is ready for you now," said the maid. "I just need to collect your money first. Ten shillings each, please. You can leave it in the plate on the side there. Thank you. Now follow me." She led them down a narrow passage, past the foot of the stairs; Jacques could see what looked like a scullery ahead of them, but before they reached it, the maid opened the door into a large dark room to one side.

"Thank you, Sarah. Now I want you all to come in and make your-selves feel at home. I am Mrs. Hockley. You may call me Venetia."

A large woman was seated at a circular table. It was so dark in the room that at first Jacques found it hard to locate a seat. As they all settled themselves, he was able to see that Mrs. Hockley wore some sort of tur-ban or headdress, perhaps of the kind worn by a concierge or cleaner but perhaps something more exotic—it was too dark to say. Behind her, thick velvet curtains obscured the window which would have given onto the backyard or garden. A few coals were glowing in a tiny fire in the grate, but the only other source of light was a candle on the mantel-piece. There was a faint smell of soap or perfumed oil. He could hear the dog yapping upstairs, then footsteps, presumably the maid's, on their way to silence it.

"Now then," said Mrs. Hockley. "If you are all nice and settled we are going to see what we can do. Is everyone comfy? I haven't asked for your names and I'd rather not know. It makes it simpler. Shall we begin with you, dear?" She looked toward the young woman.

"Very well."

"Is there someone you want to be in touch with? Is it a loved one? Do you want to tell me his name?"

"Timothy. He was my fiancé."

"Do you have something of his with you?"

"I have his signet ring."

"That's lovely, dear. Would you like to pass it over? There we are. Now I want you all to join hands with the person sitting next to you."

Jacques extended one hand to the young woman on his left and the other to the older woman on his right.

"Now we are all going to close our eyes and concentrate."

With his eyes shut, Jacques thought of Mesmer and his animal magnetism; he thought of Bernheim, Charcot and the Nancy School of hypnotism, of doctors at the Salpêtrière moving symptoms from one side of the body to the other with magnets; he thought of the whole fraught, rococo edifice of psychosomatic medicine at which so many brilliant men had labored for so long, and he had a strong desire to laugh at this plump lady in her back sitting room.

Then he felt the grip of the young woman on his left, the desperation with which she squeezed his hand. He tried to picture her Timothy, probably some hapless subaltern on the Western Front who had walked out one morning with a pistol and colored officer flashes on his uniform to make himself unmistakable to the German machine gunners in their first lazy sweep along the line . . . and he saw Daniel's face instead, only Daniel's face, and found his hand had returned the desperate squeeze of his neighbor.

"I am hearing someone," said Mrs. Hockley. "Someone ever so nice. A young man, I think. He has lovely manners."

The table, which was covered by a tasseled cloth, began to shake. Jacques lifted his hand a little in case the ferocity of his grip was somehow responsible, but it made no difference.

"Jennifer," she said. "He wants to speak to Jennifer."

Jacques felt his left hand being crushed.

"That's my name!"

Mrs. Hockley's head was thrown back and a row of beads wobbled beneath her jowls.

"He says . . . he says . . . he misses you. And he remembers Margaret. Is it Margaret, Marget—"

"Margate! That's where we got engaged."

"The voice is getting fainter again. What do you want me to ask him?"

"Ask him . . . does he love me still?"

"Timothy? Timothy? Can you hear me? Jennifer wants to know, do you love her still?"

The table shook thunderously and there was the sudden sound of glass breaking, somewhere unseen in a corner of the room. Mrs. Hockley screamed, and the noise made both other women scream in reaction. A powerful smell of old rose leaves and lavender came into the air. Mrs. Hockley lowered her head onto the table, panting.

The others sat in uneasy silence. Jacques tactfully withdrew his hand from Jennifer, who took a handkerchief from her bag and sobbed into it.

Eventually Mrs. Hockley stood up, said, "Pardon me for a minute," and went over to a small side table where she poured herself a glass of water from a carafe. She lit a second candle on the mantelpiece and sat down again.

"The spirit world has its own laws," she said. "The people who live there, they are not the same as us. You don't know what they are going to do next. They are unpredictable. We must be understanding of them. We must be careful in the way we talk to them. Is there anyone here who doubts that they live on after death?"

Gloomy looks were exchanged. If they doubted it, they kept quiet; this was the last moment they would choose to voice their skepticism, thought Jacques, with their money in Mrs. Hockley's collecting plate.

"Very well. We are going to try again. This time I am not going to ask for a name, I am just going to see if there is someone there. Please all join hands again."

Jacques replaced his hands in those of his neighbors. He noticed that Jennifer's was moist and trembling.

He closed his eyes. He saw Daniel's face again, though it was only a memory of the face; he could not quite bring its distinctive human wholeness, the character, into focus. Then he saw him as a child, walking past the fountains at the schloss in his corduroy hose, stopping to speak with one of the patients; he saw the rash of eczema at the back of his knees, the curl of hair on the nape of his neck. He pictured him in uniform, the man's features so recently acquired, provisional—the strong jaw and nose, the cleanly shaved skin, through which Jacques could see all the stages of his childhood, like half-effaced stories in a palimpsest.

"I am starting to see a strange light or aura," said Mrs. Hockley. "The color of sapphire. It is floating in the room. Keep your eyes closed, all of you. It is trying to settle, to pick someone out."

The table suddenly heaved off the floor and thumped down again. Jennifer gave out a little scream.

"Yes, I believe there is someone who is trying to make contact with one of us here. I am going to speak to the spirit. Who are you? What is your name? Who are you trying to reach? Oh de-ea-r. Oh de-e-a-r."

Mrs. Hockley threw her head back as far as her stout neck would permit. A tremor seemed to run through her upper body.

"Can you hear me? Make yourself known! I see your aura very bright. You are a lost soul. Please speak to me. Yes . . . yes, I am hearing something now. What? Yes, yes . . . continue."

An aroma of burnt pudding wafted into the room, quite distinct and different from the previous perfumed smells.

Mrs. Hockley spoke in a tremulous voice. "It is a man. . . . His name begins with the letter . . . D. . . . He speaks of mountains. . . . He is going to speak through me . . ."

Her voice adopted a lower timbre and a vibrato effect. "'I am in the mountains. . . . It is cold and snowing. . . . A man has fallen from the mountain. . . . Guns firing . . . forgive me . . . forgive me, forgive me.'"

Then in her normal voice, Mrs. Hockley said, "He said something to me about twins. I did not catch it. No! he is here again. Speak, spirit, speak to me."

From the corner of the room came a crash as of a tin tray with glasses being overturned; Mrs. Hockley let out a cry and held her hands to her throat.

"Let me be! Let me be!"

Jacques stood up, wrenching his hands away. "You stupid bitch," he shouted.

There was a gasp from the older woman.

"How can you play with people like this?" he said.

"Please, please—"

Jacques began to curse her in French, using the foulest words of the Breton ports, then turned and left the room. As he went out into the passage, he saw a male figure hurriedly going into the scullery and heard another crash of glass.

He marched to the front door and wrenched it open, then ran down the steps into the dark street. He threw back his head and lifted up his eyes to the black sky over London, hoping for relief; but all he could see was the face of his son, lit by the white moon, pressing its outline through the dark clouds and bearing down on him.

"AND THAT is why I came to see you," said Sonia, putting down her teacup.

"No one will operate. They would be struck off," said Thomas. "But I sympathize with the poor fellow. Abandoned by science, you might say. Like me. Would you like me to talk to him?"

"Not yet. I will let you know. Let's talk about happier things. Your house is looking nice."

"Yes. Kitty has done a wonderful job. Bayswater is not where we would have chosen. I suppose we might have preferred . . . what was the name of that place you lived with Mr. Whatsit? Your first husband?"

"Mayfair."

"Yes. Exactly. Anyway, I still can't get the funds out of Carinthia. I shall manage one day, I am sure. Bernthaler is working at it for me. Did I tell you, Kitty has taken a job? She has become a schoolmistress!"

"Where?"

"In a girls' academy near Regent's Park. She studied for a diploma at night school and now she teaches them German and French. She had to do it, poor girl. I make a little in private practice, but it has been difficult to pick up a clientele at my age, starting from nothing. And I am still paying for the girls' lodging in Chelsea until they can afford it themselves. So Kitty rolled her sleeves up."

"I bet she is good at it."

"Are you suggesting my wife is bossy, Sonia?"

"On the contrary, it was always she, I felt, who thought I was rather a dragon."

"No, she doesn't. She loves you. How long are you staying in London?"

"We go back to Paris on Friday."

"I would love to come and see your new apartment one day. I suppose it is very grand."

Sonia smiled. "It is like any other Parisian apartment in those big streets that Haussmann built. Large rooms, a little gloomy, long shutters, pleasant wooden floors. It is still a wonderful city."

"I don't suppose I shall go again."

"Why on earth not?"

"I don't know," said Thomas. "I get tired very easily. I lose my way."

"Don't be absurd! You talk as though you are an old man. You are only just sixty. That is no age at all."

Thomas looked down into his lap and said nothing.

Sonia looked at him curiously. She said, "One of the conditions on which I agreed to move back to Paris with Jacques was that I should spend holidays in England. Now do you think that at Easter you and I could invite ourselves and our families up to Torrington?"

"Oh, Queenie, I should love that. A big family party. I shall write at once to Edgar and . . . and . . . dear God, I can't remember what his little wife is called."

"Lucy."

"Lucy. Of course. I shall write tomorrow."

"I must be off now, Thomas. I am meeting Jacques at six."

"Will you write from Paris?"

"Of course. I always do."

"Let me show you out. Here we are. I can't see the blasted key."

"It's here. In the lock."

"Goodbye."

Sonia held her brother's hands between her own, then kissed him on the cheek and squeezed him hard.

———

IN MARCH, Thomas received a letter from Pierre Valade, asking if he might come and visit him in London. He replied that he would shortly be taking his family to Lincolnshire for the Easter holiday, but that he would be happy to entertain Valade at Torrington if Edgar had no objection. He foresaw none, since Edgar had in fact been receptive to Sonia's request that there should be a large family reunion at Easter.

Guests began to arrive on the preceding Tuesday. The first was Edgar and Lucy's daughter Emily with her sardonic husband, Charles, who worked for a newspaper in London and affected to be at a loss in what he referred to as "the provinces." He helped himself to whisky from the butler's pantry (still unused by any butler), smoked cigarettes, yawned a good deal in company and disappeared for long periods to his bedroom. At the age of forty, Emily was herself the mother of three children whose ages ran from five to fifteen, the eldest being a moody boy called Stephen, and the younger two a pair of shy, round-faced girls. Emily's twin sister, Lydia, arrived on Wednesday with her four children and her husband, John, a farmer from Northumberland, where they had lived since their marriage fifteen years earlier. He complained of the flatness of Lincolnshire, but made himself pleasant to his hosts and brought offerings of northern delicacies—Harrogate toffees, fine woolen shawls, cured fish from Whitby—for Lucy, who thanked him kindly and set them aside for the church fête.

Lucy instructed May to make sure the bedrooms were all well aired and the fires laid; there were often late frosts at this time of year and she did not want her guests to be cold in their rooms.

"Quite right," said Edgar. "Otherwise they'll be under our feet in the library the whole day."

"Edgar, you promised me that—"

"I know. I shall be the soul of hospitality. Have we had all the replies for Saturday?"

"Yes. Not a single refusal, I am happy to say."

On Wednesday came Sonia with her French mad-doctor, who, as Edgar remarked to Lucy that night in bed, looked more and more like a lunatic himself these days with his white beard and shaggy locks.

"Are he and Thomas speaking to one another? I can never remember," said Edgar.

"Yes," said Lucy. "Sonia told me it is all quite forgiven. They are like Tweedledum and Tweedledee. They have fought to a standstill and now they cannot quite remember what the argument was about."

"Is that what Sonia told you?"

"No. It is my interpretation. Sonia said that Thomas wrote a letter when Daniel died and Jacques's heart was melted by it."

"Well, he was always good with words, my little brother. If nothing else."

On Thursday, a day ahead of schedule, Pierre Valade arrived. Sonia detained him with a short tour of the garden while Lucy sent the new maid running up and down the landing with clean sheets and blankets to make up the old blue room at the back.

Valade was enthusiastic about England, which he had never visited before. He had asked for a case of St. Julien to be sent up by Berry Brothers of St. James's, anxious that his hosts would be unfamiliar with the fruit of the vine, and was astonished to find himself served with a passable burgundy at dinner. Jacques related to him the story of his first visit and of how he must not rise from dinner when his hostess stood up; he explained that there would be meat at breakfast, horses to ride and, if the weather held, a game of lawn-tennis.

"Mercifully, I have brought a sketchbook and intend to do some drawings of the house," said Valade. "Now tell me, where is this butler's pantry where one finds the Scottish whisky?"

Jacques gave him directions.

"I see. And who is the supercilious fellow with the cigarette in his mouth at all times? Am I obliged to be polite to him?"

"I fear so. He is Edgar's son-in-law. He is married to Emily."

"Ah yes. The dark one I sat next to at dinner. She was most interested in my work. Clearly a woman of resounding intelligence."

On Friday morning Herr and Frau Hans Eckert arrived from Nottingham, where they lived, bringing their son Paul and their friend Mary with them. Lucy was nervous about having a blind person in the house in case she should injure herself or fall into one of the many open fires.

Sonia was on hand to welcome them and to reassure Lucy that Mary was capable of looking after herself.

"I shall just show her round a little bit myself until she has the feel of it," said Sonia. "Daisy, you come too. Hans does not speak very good English yet, Lucy, so you may have to ask Jacques to translate."

Daisy looked about her in astonishment, both at the house and the number of people coming and going in it. Her mouth fell open, as it had done when the long corridor of the lunatic asylum first opened up to take her in.

"It's ever so nice, Maisie," she whispered in Mary's ear. "It's a little bit like the old schloss, but more English like." Mary held on tight.

Then in the evening, about seven, the double doors burst open and Charlotte and Martha came rushing in—tall, fair-haired women of twenty-three, still young enough to be euphoric at the release from their long journey. They had already found their aunts Sonia and Lucy, their many cousins at various removes, and were well into an account of their life in a Chelsea bedsitting room by the time their parents finally stepped through the front door.

Edgar embraced Kitty with the tactile enthusiasm he had always shown toward her, clasping her to him a moment longer than necessary; Lucy offered Thomas her cheek.

Friday night was an informal occasion. Lucy was concerned that her guests should not think her irreligious and had made sure that only fish was served at supper, a late meal at which all were invited to help themselves from the long table in the dining room.

At midday on Saturday, a large number of local people came to lunch. Among them was young Meadowes, the doctor, a man in his sixties still known as "young" even though his father, cantankerous old Meadowes, was long dead. Afterward, the family guests dispersed about the house and garden, the children playing tennis noisily, most of the older ones retreating to their bedrooms. Tea was on offer at five, but Lucy had made it clear that she did not expect to reappear before seven in the library. At six o'clock her son and heir, Henry, arrived from Lincoln with his wife and two sons—more males, Edgar had been pleased to note, to secure the family's name and fortune.

SONIA AND Jacques had been put in her old bedroom at the front of the house. As she went up to change in the evening, Sonia stood for a moment looking through the leaded lights of the window toward the church and the village pond.

She was pleased to be back at Torrington, to be "home," as she could not stop calling it; yet the visit felt like a ritual with little meaning. It was possible, she thought, to have too much access to the past. Although she had very much responded to that part of Thomas's lecture at the schloss which talked of our yearning to be reunited with a lost world, glimpsed imperfectly through time and the limits of our perception, there were perhaps places, people or experiences which really ought to remain behind us, she thought. If their intangibility was frustrating or raised a yearning that could not be satisfied, then so be it. The angle of a brick arch or corridor, the sensation of smell or taste that released a state of being; or here, the very floorboard on which her bare feet had stood on the morning that Mr. Prendergast was due—surely these things should no longer be habitable. It did not feel quite healthy that she could stand here now, an old woman who did not feel old—stand here as though nothing had happened, as though there were no such thing as time.

She put on her dressing gown and prepared for the cold walk to the bathroom. Since the birth of Daniel, her life had passed so quickly that she had not had time to catch the different years. When she was a child, each year had been distinct, the long days of seven quite different from the slow weeks of eight; but recently, she had barely had time to pack away the Christmas decorations before the summer was on them, then past, and the leaves were yellow in the trees again.

In the bathroom, she pushed back the window on its hinge and the very motion as the wooden frame caught on the creeper seemed to open up the rush of overpowering love she had felt for that beautiful and somehow unhappy man, her brother's friend, who walked that summer evening in the garden. She had relived this moment so often, on the heights of the Wilhelmskogel, on the floor of the bathroom of the schloss when she clasped the vanished life of her son in the bloody towels between her legs—and still it had the power of association, still the opening window opened up her heart. Yet was it possible, she now thought, that at each physical revisitation something of the numinous was lost?

She smiled at her fancies; it was enough to be alive and in good health with one's family and their friends. Soon they would all be gathered downstairs among the candles at the table she herself had decorated. What more could anyone of her age ask? Why were the rims of her eyes starting to turn fiery with the coming tears?

THOMAS WENT to see that his daughters were settled. They had been put in his old room on the top floor and were arguing about which one of them should have the bed and which the blankets on the couch.

"Why don't you both get in the bed?" said Thomas. "It's big enough for two."

"Charlotte snores."

"Martha makes funny licking noises."

"Oh dear, what a dilemma for you both. What a test of your altruism and negotiating skills. A veritable League of Nations with—"

"Daddy, don't be sarcastic."

"It is something about being in my old room," said Thomas, going over to the window. "It brings back the callow youth I was. Good heavens," he said, bending down to the long fitted shelf, "they still have all my old books here. *History of the Conquest of Peru* by William Prescott. My goodness, how I loved that. And the *History of the Conquest of Mexico.*"

"I can hardly wait to read it," said Charlotte, stifling a laugh.

"No, no, I've already reserved Peru," said Martha.

"Oh, look," said Martha. "Hind's *Algebra and Trigonometry.*"

"I have heard it's a very exciting story," said Charlotte.

"And it looks as though we'd be the first people to read it."

"Daddy, you never even opened it."

"I never cared much for trigonometry."

"Look, Charlotte, here's another penny dreadful. *Personal Narrative of Travels in South America* by Alexander von Humboldt."

"Oh, Martha, you naughty girl. It looks far too racy for you. It's positively blue!"

"Tell you what, Charlotte," said Martha, "you can have the bed, because then I can sit up all night under this light and read *Essays on the Principle of Population* by Thomas Malthus."

"As a matter of fact," said Thomas, "that is one of the most important books of the last century. Without it, Darwin—"

"After you, darling. But I shan't be letting go of *Vestiges of the Natural History of Creation* without a struggle."

"Who is it by? Ethel M. Dell?"

"It appears to be anonymous."

"Perhaps it was too racy."

"As a matter of fact," said Thomas again, "that, too, was a very important book in the history of the theory of natural selection. It turned out to have been written by Robert—"

"Daddy, was this also a very important work of the last century?" She handed him a blue notebook with his old Cambridge college crest on it.

"For social historians it may be like the Dead Sea Scrolls. It is my accounts book. 'To Buttery, one and sixpence (claret and dried fruit).'"

"Let me have a look."

"You seem to have given up in January."

"It wasn't a very thrilling volume. Not like this one. Shakespeare. Do your pupils study Shakespeare, Martha?"

"Daddy, they are only seven years old."

"Ah yes, I had forgotten."

Martha and Charlotte retreated to the bed so that they could study his accounts book more closely. As their laughter came to his ears, Thomas looked across his old bedroom at them, their fair heads bent over the pages. They were so like their mother that he sometimes wondered if any of his "genes" had passed to them at all.

When you came to think of it, had not life given him everything he could have hoped for? Not one, but three such women. He shook his head and wondered how much longer he could hold on to them.

IN THE kitchen, May was putting the finishing touches to an enormous roast turkey. She loved to see Sonia and Thomas again, the friends of her youth—her childhood, really, because, though a stout mother of two grown daughters and soon to be a grandmother, she had been a girl of thirteen when she first went into service.

"Jane, you take the gravy boats out now and warm them up," she said to the new maid. "They're in the dresser there."

"I don't know how we're going to manage with all these people. Them Frenchies and all," said Jane. "He's a funny one, that Mr. Whatsit."

"Don't be silly, Jane. We've sat down more than this. And if we can't manage, Miss Sonia will always come and help. When she was little she used to come out here to escape. She'd come and talk to me and old Miss Brigstocke so she could get away from the grown-ups. And she'd talk to Dido and Amelia."

"And Mr. Thomas. He seems nice, but he's a bit funny too."

"The trouble with Mr. Thomas," said May, "is that's he's wore himself out with thinking."

At a quarter to eight, as instructed by Lucy, they took the soup through to the dining room and the dinner began. The table had had two extra leaves inserted, but still some of the children were jammed close together at one end. There were small decorations of spring flowers at intervals among the thronged and polished glasses.

Through the shifting candlelight, Thomas could make out the face of Hans, smiling nervously, though he had been placed compassionately close to Daisy. Kitty was far away, but looked up at that moment and her silver-rimmed glasses caught the light as she smiled up the table at him. There was Jacques, sitting next to Martha, who had always secretly adored him; and there was Valade pontificating to blind Mary about oil painting. Almost everyone who had meant something to him in his life was gathered there, it occurred to him—all except Faverill, whose short obituary notice he had read in the newspaper a few days earlier. "A distinguished asylum superintendent," the paper called him, "who had a strong sense of the direction he wanted psychological medicine to take as the new century approached." "Sense of direction": he would have laughed at that, thought Thomas, the chartless helmsman steering by the stars . . .

Who else was there in the shifting light? Charlotte doing her best with that man who smoked cigarettes. Dear Daisy, and Mary. And his niece Lydia. And her many children whose names he could not remember. And then through the shadow there, the flicker and glow caught the chin of someone else he did not know. A man a little older than he was, though not unlike himself, now he came to think of it, in features: he seemed very familiar with Lucy and he had a rather proprietorial air; he kept passing the decanter round, urging people to drink, then ordering the maids to clear as though he owned the place . . .

"You haven't drunk your soup, Mr. Thomas."

"What?" Thomas looked down in surprise. He did not remember being given soup. People expected so much of him these days.

"Shall I take it away, then?"

"Yes. May? It is May, isn't it?"

"Yes, love."

"Thank you."

At the end of the main course, Edgar stood up and made a brief speech of welcome. Thomas looked at him curiously, then scanned the faces of those he knew; no one seemed to think it odd that this fellow was making a speech, so Thomas said nothing about it. He had a speech of his own in his pocket which Kitty had helped him to prepare that afternoon.

When Edgar sat down, Valade sprang to his feet. "Thank you, sir, for your very kind words of welcome and for the hospitality that you and your wife have shown us." Valade's English was much better than Thomas had expected. "To welcome a foreigner, a stranger—in my language it is the same word. Is that not shameful? To welcome me, at least, is a gesture of great kindness. I have been much impressed by the beauty and intelligence of the women in your family, monsieur. The fame of the women of England had not yet reached me, but I shall waste no time in spreading word of it when I return home. As for the men in your family, I can offer you no higher compliment, monsieur, than to say that in my view you stand as the equal of your brother, a man I have known for more than thirty years. Once we sat on a mountainside in Carinthia at a strange little guesthouse where I painted the view because it was one thing and everything. We called it Art. In all the years that followed we never found that place again. But in all that time I have never seen in your brother an ungracious deed. I have loved him as though he were my own brother. Meeting you here, monsieur, here in your Englishman's castle, has made me understand what honor I had done myself by claiming that title of 'brother.' I salute you, sir, and your beautiful wife, and I offer you the warmest thanks that my poor grasp of your language permits."

Thomas looked down the table and saw Kitty's face earnestly looking at him. "Go on," she mouthed silently. He stood up and coughed.

"I also . . . also wanted to say something. First I should like to add my thanks to Monsieur Valade's. We all appreciate the hospitality and kindness shown us by . . . our hosts."

Kitty's smiling face was still on him. It was all right. "Of course, what Valade said about me was absolute piffle. Unkind acts . . . Ungracious, was it? Once in Africa I lost my temper with a man and . . . and many other times . . ."

He looked up and forced himself to regroup. "Yes. Yes. I just have to say, while I am still able, a sort of goodbye, or at least an au revoir. Some weeks ago I . . . er, I suffered a peculiar experience. I do not wish to go into it except to say that I appeared to lose my memory. I was in a police station with no recollection of how I had got there. I was not unhappy, I just did not know what was going on. I was like King Lear. 'Methinks I should know you, and know this man;/ Yet I am doubtful; for I am mainly ignorant/What place this is; and all the skill I have/Remembers not these garments; nor I know not/Where I did lodge last night.' Anyway, to . . . to cut a long story short, I have been to see various distinguished gentlemen at the hospital in Queen Square and it appears that I am in the early stages of some kind of senile or presenile dementia.

"Rather interestingly, it has been named after Alois Alzheimer, with whom my colleague Franz Bernthaler once studied along with Franz Nissl, another formidable talent at the microscope. Oddly enough, Bernthaler assured me in his last letter that it was not in fact Alzheimer who first described the disease, but his mentor Emil Kraepelin. This may be the first time in medical history that a discovery has been voluntarily assigned by one scientist to another."

Thomas looked down the table at all the strange faces in the orange light. "Or," he said, "perhaps Kraepelin just forgot."

He consulted the notes that Kitty had made on a postcard. "So. Yes. I just wanted to say to all of you . . . Yes, a most interesting ailment, as a matter of fact, in which the plaques among the neurons are visible under a Zeiss lens without staining, though Franz tells me you get the best results with magenta red and indigo carmine. And . . . and . . ."

He looked back to his postcard. It said: "Age."

"Yes. Age. I am rather young to have this sort of thing, though perhaps sixty does not seem so young to the children at the far end of the table. The truth is that we know very little about this illness. We know very little about anything, as a matter of fact. Never mind. It is really not important. It is just that one day I may no longer know your name, and I ask you to forgive me if I pass you in the street or on the stairs and my face does not light up with love or recognition. Please forgive me. I shall no longer be myself. I am going into a dark country and I very much wanted to say goodbye to those that I have loved before I go. My dear Jacques, whose dreams of greatness I so passionately shared from the moment he embraced me on a beach somewhere in France. Sonia . . . dear God, what a sister you have been. I remember a boat in Deauville. And my own family. What can I say?"

He gazed once more down through the mist of faces until he saw the features of the woman he had loved—no longer young, but red and twisted with grief, shining with tears.

"I have been blessed beyond what any man could hope or wish for," said Thomas. "All I ask now is somewhere safe to live. I must pull in sail and lower my sights from the horizon. I am quite content to do so because I have been so fortunate in my life. I always felt that if I had to make a speech like this I should find some Shakespearean eloquence. But it is too late and the plain words will have to do. As a doctor, I have achieved absolutely nothing. Nothing at all, though God knows I tried. But in love I have been rich. Once long ago I finished a lecture in another place by saying we should try to make our lives a hymn of thanks—or some such phrase. I do not think it was a very memorable phrase, even to someone without my difficulties. I shall do my best to follow my own advice. All I ask is for your forgiveness."

He looked one last time down the table of anxious faces. "My mind may not know you," he said, "but in my heart you are remembered."

THE NEXT day, after they had come back from church, Thomas went to sit in the library with Humboldt's *Personal Narrative of Travels in South America*. One of the advantages of his disease, he thought, would presumably turn out to be that you could read your favorite books again and again, and each time would be the first. Certainly, nothing of Humboldt's story seemed familiar.

There was a knock on the door, and Daisy put her head round it. "Can I come in?"

"Of course."

She perched on the edge of a low table in front of the fire, close to Thomas's armchair. "I just wanted to say . . ."

"Say what, Daisy?"

"You know who I am?"

"Of course I do. I shall never forget you of all people, Daisy."

Daisy twisted her fingers in her lap. "About what you said last night. You know. You said you hadn't done anything as a doctor."

"Well, I haven't."

"Of course you have. Think of all the people you helped."

"I doubt whether I cured a single person. The diseases of the mind have so far proved—"

"Listen. Please listen to me. What you did for me and Mary was something wonderful. You took us from out that place. Do you remember it?"

"Yes I do, it was—"

"Good. I'm glad you remember. It was a prison. We was locked in the wards with them women moaning and messing theirselves and banging their heads against the walls. And the smell of it, the pity, the disgusting mess of it all. And we was trapped in it and locked away. And little Mary, there was nothing even wrong with her except she was blind and she had spent her whole life in this kind of place. And do you know what you did?"

"I merely—"

"You gave us a life. Me and Mary. It was like being born again into a better world. Look at us now. We both do our work at the hospital, I'm a married lady with a nice husband and a house and a fine boy. If you had done nothing else in your life, then—"

"Daisy, are you trying to make me cry? You will not succeed."

Daisy grabbed his hands in hers. "Oh, Tommy, Tommy. Don't you know how we worshipped you? You were our god. You saved us. And we watched you walking in the courtyards, down that colonnade, smiling at them patients, and me and Mary we just wanted to go down on our knees and kiss the place you'd walked on. Don't you see, you foolish, stupid man? Don't you see how much we loved you? Don't you see the . . . the . . . size of what you did for us?"

"Listen, it is kind of you to—"

"No, you listen, because it breaks my heart to hear you say you never done anything good in doctoring. If you are going to lose your memory, like you say you are, then the last thing you should know before you go is all the good you did. Maybe you didn't cure all the lunatics, but maybe no one ever will. Maybe there are some things that men will never know. And I will not let you tell yourself that you have failed because you didn't do what no man has ever done before or since. Do you understand me?" She squeezed his hands harder. "Thomas, do you understand me?"

"Dear Daisy. I do understand. And I thank you for what you have said. You can let go of my hand now."

"I'm sorry." She released him and sat back on the table. "And I think I did make you cry a little bit."

"It was just that you squeezed my hand so hard that—"

"Ssh. I wanted you to remember what I said. Will you remember? When you go into your dark place. Will you remember?"

"I will try, Daisy. I promise I will try."

IN THE evening, the guests began to depart. Jacques had an appointment with a psychiatrist in London and could not linger; when Sonia had been assured by Lucy that she did not need her help, she packed her own bag to accompany him. A cab was waiting for them outside, where it had started to rain.

It was difficult to make sincere farewells in the throng of people and luggage in the hall, but they managed to distract Lucy and Edgar's attention long enough to thank them. Jacques had a particular word for Henry, who he always thought had been responsible, as a child, for bringing him and Sonia together, though Henry said he remembered nothing of it. Kitty and her daughters, who were staying another night, were on hand to say goodbye, though there was no sign of Thomas until they got outside. He was standing alone on the far side of the crescent of grass in front of the house, where the drive set off toward the village street. He was wearing a coat and a wide-brimmed black hat. Sonia asked the driver to stop.

Jacques climbed down from the cab and held his arms out to Thomas, who embraced him. When Sonia had done likewise, she asked the driver to wait so that they could make sure Thomas returned safely to the house and did not wander into the village.

"Kitty's waiting for you," she called through the window of the cab.

"Oh yes," he said, and began to walk off.

Sonia and Jacques watched him until he reached the steps up to the front door, where he turned, raised his hat and waved it in their direction. Then he stood for a little, looking uncertain in the rainy outdoor world, till Martha came out, took him by the elbow and led him back into his father's house.

IN THE FOLLOWING MONTHS, THOMAS'S CONDITION DETERIORATED slowly. The Bayswater house was filled with notes reminding him of what to do and when to do it—different lists in different rooms. He had to give up work when a depressed patient complained that after five consultations Thomas began the sixth by asking his date of birth and family history before offering to examine his chest. In the drawing room, the note said: "Kitty returns at five. Mrs. Coyle comes at nine and will make lunch. Book is in the chair by the fire. Dr. P's number next to telephone." In the bathroom, the note said: "Teeth, shave, wash. Ointment on foot. Important." The notes sometimes helped remind him what to do when he had come into a room, but seldom said why; and they never told him who he was.

His last letter to Sonia in Paris had long passages of lucidity, however, and he seemed able to arrange his thoughts better on paper than in speech. He told Sonia that on the doctor's advice, Kitty now locked him in the house when she went to work in the morning and that he preferred it that way. In June, Jacques and Thomas finally received their share of the money in the Wilhelmskogel partnership. It was enough that Kitty could stop work if she wanted and enough to buy a flat for each of the twins; for Jacques and Sonia, it was more than they needed.

Jacques continued in private practice and helped at an outpatients' clinic at the Salpêtrière. His quest to find a neurosurgeon who would operate on him was unsuccessful; when the fourth man he approached not only rebuffed him vigorously but threatened to report his request to the medical authorities, Jacques began to see how forlorn his hope had been.

"I went a little mad," he said to Sonia. "I see that now. It was my grief, my way of feeling it."

Their apartment was on the first floor, and in the warm evening, the long windows were open to the street below. Despite the clank of trams and the roar of motor cars, they could still hear the birds in the plane trees by the side of the road and the cry of the waiters at the café opposite as they shouted their orders from the outside tables.

"I have another thing to confess," said Jacques.

"Oh yes?"

They had finished dinner by the window and Jacques poured the remains of the wine into their glasses.

"When we were in London I went to see a medium, a clairvoyant. To see if I could . . . you know, speak to him."

"But that is against everything you have ever believed."

"I know. I was desperate."

"You poor thing. Why did you not tell me?"

"I was ashamed. And then . . . and then he was there. She found him."

"What do you mean?"

"It was awful. Can you bear it?"

"Yes. Tell me."

"She said there was a young man whose name began with D. He was in the mountains. There was snow. A man had thrown himself off. There was gunfire. And he said, 'Forgive me, forgive me.'"

Sonia said nothing. Jacques was trembling.

"I cannot tell you how awful it was," he said. "I am sure she was a charlatan. I expect there is a simple explanation of how it was done. But I could not be sure at the time. I couldn't know for certain. And I believe I felt him reach out to me. Little Herr Frage. I felt him calling for me. He needed me. He was alone. My heart was torn out of my body."

For the first time since Daniel had died, Jacques began to cry. It began with a few half-stifled sobs, then acquired a mounting rhythm. Sonia put her arms round him, but the force of his grief soon became too great for her to hold. He lay on the floor in front of the fireplace and the exhalation of the sob turned into a shout, a kind of howl. Sonia closed the windows onto the street and sat with him. He could not bring himself under control. As the noise grew louder and the shaking of his body more convulsive, Sonia wondered if she should call a doctor or administer some sort of shock. She brought him water, but he could not hold it. She splashed some in his face, then held his hand tightly. For almost half an hour the storm continued, and every time it seemed to have passed, it built again. The neighbor from the next flat rang the bell to see if everything was all right; when Sonia had reassured him and sent him on his way, Jacques staggered to the spare bedroom at the end of the corridor to muffle his noises in the pillows.

Toward midnight he regained control of himself and came exhausted to the marital bedroom. Sonia, pale and anxious, helped him to undress and fetched him pills from the bathroom for his headache.

When he was calm at last and sitting up in bed, she said, "You never understood, did you?"

"Understood what? What do you mean?"

"You did not need a brain surgeon or a medium. You did not need to chase the dead members of your family. All you needed was here."

Jacques thought for a moment before answering. "In you?"

"Yes. In me."

He looked at her closely. "But you could not be everything to me. That was too much to ask. There were other people that I needed, others to share the load . . . the load of being human."

"I think I could be everything. I think I was."

"Sonia . . ."

"So far as I know, that is what it means to love someone. To bend all your powers to their happiness. All of them. To be everything."

"Everything . . ."

"Who do you think left the copy of *The Lancet* and that French novel to make you feel at home when you first came to Torrington?"

Jacques's mouth opened a little, but no sound came.

Sonia, pale but serene, stood by his side. "Everything," she said again.

But she did not tell him quite everything she had done. She did not say how, seeing his deep unhappiness in the weeks after Roya's final departure for St. Petersburg, she had eventually decided to act; how she had gone to the post office and paid the clerk at the counter to write the message and address, then taken the unsent telegram home.

She was tempted to tell Jacques there and then how she had paid Josef to deliver it to the hospital one night; but seeing the condition he was in, she merely sighed. She remembered how restored he had been in the days that followed the arrival of the telegram, how a certain lightness and eventually an equanimity had returned to him. Her subterfuge had worked as well as she could have hoped, and if she had desisted at the time from telling him, there seemed no reason to break her silence now.

IN THE autumn, Jacques had a letter from a lawyer in Lorient concerning properties that had belonged to his father's former employer. This man's son had recently died. He had fallen out with his own children and had left instructions to dispose of various smallholdings. Old Rebière's long service meant that Jacques had inherited not only his own father's house, no longer wanted by Tante Mathilde's family, but two other cottages and a parcel of land between.

"It is too late," said Jacques. "It is a kind thought but I have no wish to own these places. What would we do with them? And we have no one to leave them to. They would be an encumbrance. It is better to let a family have them."

"Perhaps one of the cottages will be by the sea and would be a good place for holidays. We could leave it to Martha and Charlotte. Or Daisy."

"Perhaps."

"Are you not intrigued even to look at them?" said Sonia.

"I swore that I would never return to Saint Agnès. I broke my vow once, for my father's funeral, and that was enough."

"In that case," said Sonia, "I shall go alone. I like Brittany. It is a lovely autumn and I shall walk along the beach and eat oysters in Vannes."

Jacques smiled. He thought it was an absurd idea, but these days he did everything he could to humor Sonia. "I shall go and book you a first-class train ticket this afternoon," he said. "You should buy a new coat. It can be very windy in October."

Four days later, after a long and uncomfortable train ride, the cab from the nearest station dropped Sonia at the foot of the main street in Saint Agnès. The lawyer had arranged for the keys to the three properties to be deposited at the pharmacy, though the shop was closed when Sonia tried the door. It was lunchtime, she supposed. In the café opposite she ordered a sandwich and a glass of wine, braving the inspection of the old men playing cards inside. "Curious" would have been a polite word for their gaze, she thought; "hostile" was really closer to the mark; but after a life of dealing with lunatics, she was not daunted by a few half-drunk old men in a bar.

"Does Abbé Henri still live here?" she said.

The barman grunted. "Top of the hill and down the track. But you won't get much sense out of him."

Sonia rapidly calculated how old he must be by now. Perhaps eighty, she thought.

"Do you know what time the pharmacy opens again?"

"When old Roland wakes up," said the barman.

"And when is that?"

"Generally about three."

She might as well go and pay her respects to Abbé Henri; it would at least pass the time.

"Thank you," she said, and set off up the street.

From the blacksmith's on the right she heard the sound of a hammer on the anvil.

The next door gave on to a small area, not really a shop, more the front room of a house, that sold wood and tools for carpentry.

At the top of the hill, Sonia paused and looked down. She was a little out of breath. The bright sky was darkening and clouds were gathering in the direction of the sea.

She went down the track to Abbé Henri's house and knocked on the door. It was opened by a housekeeper, who asked Sonia to wait while she went to see if the Curé was at home. She returned with good news: he would be pleased to see her. Sonia followed the woman down a dark corridor and into a pleasantly furnished sitting room with filled bookcases and double doors onto the garden.

An old man sat by the fire and waved his hand in welcome. "Sonia. What a pleasure. Please forgive me if I—"

"Please don't stand up. I quite understand." She took his hand.

"Make yourself at home. Why are you in Saint Agnès? Are you moving back?"

"No, no." Sonia laughed. "I have come to look at some properties that have been left to Jacques."

"How is he? He has not written for a little while."

"He is well. We live in Paris now."

"Yes, I know. He wrote to me a few months ago and sent me a very generous amount of money. My church has a mission in Africa, you see. He has always kept in touch." Abbé Henri laughed. "He was such a funny boy. So passionate. So argumentative. I worried what he would be like if he ever got to medical school."

"He was always grateful for what you did for him. He could not have done it without your help."

Abbé Henri waved a tired hand, dismissively. "I enjoyed it. It gave me pleasure."

"Though I suppose he has not achieved all that he wanted."

"Well, that is a different matter. No one ever does. No one who truly dares and hopes."

The housekeeper brought tea, but as she leaned over Sonia to put down the cup whispered to her not to stay too long. When they had drunk the tea and Sonia had told Abbé Henri a little of what had happened at the schloss, then at the Wilhelmskogel, which he had never visited, she noticed that he seemed to be finding it hard to concentrate.

"I must leave you now," she said. "Jacques asks to be remembered to you."

"And I to him. Thank you for visiting me. I remember you both in my prayers. And the one you lost."

Sonia kissed his hand, then made her own way to the front door and back onto the track. By the time she reached the pharmacy, it had reopened and a red-faced man in a slightly soiled apron, presumably Roland, gave her the keys, accompanied by a letter telling her how to reach the cottages.

It seemed that the first was indeed by the sea, and it took her twenty minutes' hard walking from the village to find it. It was a fisherman's dwelling, not much more than a hut, set back a little from the beach. The lock yielded and she found herself inside a room with stone walls and an earth floor. There were nets and pots scattered about inside, with an old bicycle propped against a stone sink. She had been in a room like this once before, but she struggled to remember when or where.

She walked along the beach a little and heard what she thought must be a curlew's harsh cry on the gathering wind. She looked at the letter of instruction and the small map attached; they flapped noisily in her hands as she breathed in the sea air. The second cottage appeared to be between the first one and Jacques's old house, so that if she followed the map carefully, it was on her way.

An early mist was gathering on the low hills, on the reed-spattered dunes that ran up from the rocks then back into the gorse. Sonia quickened her pace until she saw another small, dilapidated building, whitewashed and derelict at the edge of some woods. She took only a cursory look inside. It contained just two rooms and seemed to have belonged to a woodsman; the value of it lay presumably in the land that came with it, though that land itself was poor, so poor, she had once heard Jacques say, that the stones called out for God's mercy.

She was now skirting the edge of the village where strong gusts of wind made the shivering pine trees shed their needles on the dark, sanded earth. A badger rolled across the track and disappeared into the bank with a slow, self-important walk. She heard the first drops of rain explode against a windowpane of a gray stone cottage by the road.

Now she could see Jacques's house, which she remembered from the day of the funeral; she had to go down through a field to come round to the front of it. She crossed the cobbles of the yard, already glistening from rain, and went past the stable on the right with upper half-door open, turning in the wind. Inside, she could see rafters where a hen was roosting and some lengths of rusted chain lying against a wall.

At the door, anxious to be out of the rain, she fumbled with the keys, forgetting which ones she had already used. Eventually, the lock turned and she pushed her way into the hall. It was light enough still to see the almost vertical stairs, unbanistered, that rose in front of her. Nothing seemed to have changed.

The air was pressingly cold; it was restless with absence.

In the parlor, with its smoke-stained wooden paneling, was the old white stone chimneypiece with the ineptly carved head of a wild boar. There was no furniture in the room, but on the end wall was a gilded mirror whose glass was cracked in silver-green shards, and on a side wall was an oil painting of a nobleman who gazed with timeless indifference at the uninhabited room.

Something was not right, and Sonia stood quite still, sniffing the air, her ears straining to catch a sound. It was empty. They were dead. Old Rebière and Tante Mathilde and Grand-mère: all gone under the ground.

She heard a squealing from the unoiled half-door of the stable in the yard as the wind blew outside. It was just an old door that no one had looked after. The house needed people in it, that was all.

Yet still she stood tensed, aware and waiting, till at last she heard it, and she knew what she would hear.

It was a voice, quite soft, and it was not calling her; it was engaged in conversation; it was talking to another. It was a woman's voice, low and melodic, but somehow unsettled.

Sonia began to move slowly toward the sound, which seemed to be coming from the next room—what had once been the scullery. She went silently to the doorway and looked in.

The shutters were closed and it was hard to see at first, but then she was gradually able to make the outline of a figure: a young woman, slight, dark-haired, elegant in a white summer dress and with eyes full of laughter. She was speaking to someone who was not there. Then, aware, it seemed, of Sonia's presence, she turned toward her. For a moment, in the half-light, the two women looked into one another's eyes. Sonia thought the other woman smiled, a little. Still talking softly, she moved and walked away, through the door into what had been Grand-mère's room. Sonia waited for a moment, not sure what to do, then followed quietly; though she knew, really, what she would find when she looked into the room. There were no doors from it but the one that she herself stood in; the windows were closed, the shutters barred, and there was no one there.

She returned to the parlor and stood for a moment looking up at the stained stripes of ceiling between the gray-painted beams. When her heart had resumed a normal pulse, she found a feeling of peace beginning to spread through her limbs. There was no fear, and she was content not to understand what she had seen; she was more than content: she was reassured to know that there were things that could not be explained.

One last time she looked about the room, then left and locked the front door behind her. Her watch told her she had half an hour in which to get back to the pharmacy, where she had engaged the cab to return for her, but she did not want to go back just yet: she wanted to be outside, in the rain, on the earth that Jacques and Olivier had trodden as boys. So she set off toward the headland, thinking of the two brothers and their brief time of innocence together.

After a minute, it was the voice of her own brother that she seemed suddenly to hear. "We must turn our lives, so near as we can manage it, day by day, into an extended rapture . . ." She remembered when he was a child of five or six, and if it was cold, how he would climb into bed with her: the pattern of the candle shadows on the wall, the fiery little boy who needed her arm round him to make him sleep. And now he too was gone: gone into a different world contained within this one, and she was left almost alone to carry on.

The rain beat into her face, but she did not feel it; she was unaware of the wind that flattened her clothes against her.

One day, when he was small, about three or four years old, she had given Daniel a bath with her; he sat at the other end of the tub describing the story that he wanted her to tell him, specifying how much of the fox and the rabbit, how much of the bear and the bird, he wanted in it, like someone ordering from a menu in a magnificent restaurant. When she had finished the prescribed story to his satisfaction, got out of the bath, dried and dressed herself, she plucked the small boy from the water and wrapped him in a towel, then carried him through to her bed. She put him gently down, then laid herself on top of him, so that her eyes were against his. She felt the thrumming of the laughter in his tiny rib cage against hers, and her soul moved within her as every cell in her body shuddered with her ravening love.

And was it worth it? Was it worth the agony of loss? Was this the best that the random evolution of physical matter had thrown up?

Her jaw hardened a little as she walked onward. It was enough. It was enough, because nothing in any other world that might by chance have existed could have surpassed in majesty what she had felt; and she was transfigured by that joy, always, and even beyond death.

She turned to walk back toward the village, stiff with age. Beneath her clothes, her breasts hung flat against her ribs, the flesh of her upper arms was loose and the joint of her hip ached. She plodded on, an elderly Englishwoman in a foreign country, though still feeling in her mind a refusal to admit the years, aware of an appetite for whatever lay ahead, still hoping to go on.

And as she walked, with the faint taste of Abbé Henri's tea in her mouth, she could feel the ghosts of her dead boys, one unborn, one killed among the mountains: they lay along her nerves like dew on morning grass. She heard Daniel's voice; she saw the flesh of his boy's arm creased by the weight of his wicker basket full of toys. The bones of his beautiful hands lived in the cells of her mind, preserved, and open to remembering. The rain was pouring from her hair; and while her eyes were fixed on the path beneath her feet, she accidentally brushed her arm against the extended twig of a larch tree rooted in the earth, which, when it rebounded, sent drops of water over her hair and face.

She flinched; she was alive, and so was he. In the rain, she kissed the skin of his neck and laid the back of her hand against his cheek. "My love," she said.

With difficulty, she raised her head from the path in front, her neck and shoulders seized with damp, and through the drifting columns of rain, she lifted up her eyes to the uninhabited low hills. This is what it means to be alive, she thought again; this is what it feels like to be human. There were questions to which her husband and her brother had bent their minds—had sent themselves as good as mad in trying to answer; but it seemed to Sonia at that moment, drenched and tired as she was, that, perhaps for quite simple reasons connected to the limits of their ability to reason, human beings could live out their whole long life without ever knowing what sort of creatures they really were. Perhaps it did not matter; perhaps what was important was to find serenity in not knowing.

Her footprints now were in the mud: left and right, the regular, shortish pace of an adult female—clear marks for a moment on the earth. She watched carefully where she placed her feet, not wishing to slip and damage her brittle bones; she saw the pools of water and the white stones that punctured the dark soil ahead of her.

Then the long trail of her footprints, stretching back toward the sea, became slowly indistinct as each one filled with water and edged in upon itself; and in a matter of minutes, as darkness began to fall, the shape of the foot was lost at every pace until the last vestiges of her presence were washed away, the earth closing over as though no one had passed by.

Notes and Acknowledgments

THE MAIN CHARACTERS IN THIS BOOK ARE FICTIONAL, BUT READERS might like to know that all the doctors whose work is either quoted or referred to were real people and did hold the views ascribed to them.

The actual words of the lectures on hysteria and traumatic hysteria given by Professor Jean-Martin Charcot in chapters VII and VIII have been invented, but they are intended to reflect accurately what Charcot taught and are based on the content of his published lectures. Professor Charcot's renown, his style of lecturing and his audience were as described here. My depiction of the Salpêtrière at that time is as close to the reality as I can make it, and the various disciples of Charcot, including Georges Gilles de la Tourette, Pierre Marie and Joseph Babinski, existed as described, as did Mlle. Cottard and Blanche Wittmann. Of the many books on Charcot, the one on which I drew most was *Charcot: Constructing Neurology* by Christopher G. Goetz, Michel Bonduelle and Toby Gelfand (New York and Oxford: Oxford University Press, 1995), and I acknowledge this debt with thanks.

Throughout the novel I have aimed for factual accuracy in matters of real people, dates and so on. To this end, I enlisted the help of several specialists in their field, all of whom, I hope, are thanked below.

Dr. Wilhelm Fliess held the views ascribed to him on page 407 and published the book whose title is there mentioned; he was a minor but significant figure in the early days of psychoanalysis. The letter quoted on page 527 was indeed received by him on the date mentioned.

Jacques Rebière's theory of psychophysical resolution, outlined in chapter X, is intended to bear a close resemblance to that of its famous contemporary, psychoanalysis. I am indebted to *The Discovery of the Unconscious: The History and Evolution of Dynamic Psychiatry* by Henri F. Ellenberger (Paris and New York: Basic Books, 1970) for its description of the published nineteenth-century French and German writing that could have enabled a pupil of Charcot's with an appetite to read further to develop his own theory without reference to work in Vienna. I should like to thank Richard Webster for his many stimulating thoughts, particularly on traumatic hysteria. I am also grateful to Dr. Michael Neve at the Wellcome Trust Center for the History of Medicine at University College, London, for directing me to the work of Pierre Janet as providing further historical precedent for this kind of procedure outside strictly psychoanalytic circles.

Readers unfamiliar with early case studies in psychoanalysis may be surprised at the flexibility of some of the logical connections made in the course of the fictional history of Fräulein Katharina von A. Those who have read these gripping documents, on the other hand, will recognize that the use of paradox is central to their method—as is a willingness to move between conscious and unconscious, concealed or transparent motivation, or to invoke a mixture of the two, according to what the circumstances of the narrative appear to require. My rule of thumb in this chapter was that every leap of connection made by Jacques should have in the published literature of psychoanalysis a precedent (preferably several) that was more energetic or more fanciful.

I do not think that novels should contain bibliographies, because making lists of books at the end of a work of fiction is usually an attempt to shore up a flimsy text—as though all art aspired to the condition of a student essay. However, I feel that, in this instance, because I have had to draw on expert opinion to an unusual extent, I must make an exception and acknowledge a few selected people on whose work I depended. *The Origins of Consciousness in the Breakdown of the Bicameral Mind* by Julian Jaynes (Boston: Houghton, Mifflin, 1977) is a controversial book, sometimes referred to, with due warning lights, as a "cult classic." One does not have to accept all Professor Jaynes's speculations in neuroscience, archaeology or anthropology to be stimulated by his main thesis: that the hearing of voices was once commonplace and that the loss of the ability to hear them coincided with the generation of modern human consciousness. What Thomas Midwinter tells Hannes Regensburger in Africa is inspired by Jaynes's remarkable book as well as by Thomas's education and personal experience.

For the theoretical backbone of Thomas's lecture in chapter 20, I also drew to some extent on *The Madness of Adam and Eve: How Schizophrenia Shaped Humanity* (London: Bantam, 2001) by David Horrobin; and on *Medicine, Mind and the Double Brain: A Study in Nineteenth Century Thought* by Anne Harrington (New York: Princeton University Press, 1987). The latter was recommended to me by T. J. Crow, professor of psychiatry at Oxford University and director of the SANE Prince of Wales Center for Research into Schizophrenia and Depression. Professor Crow considers that the concept of the genetic predisposition to schizophrenia as a component of the variation generated in the speciation event was first introduced in his papers "Constraints on concepts of pathogenesis; language and the speciation process as the key to the etiology of schizophrenia" (*Archives of General Psychiatry* 1995, 52: 1011–14) and "A continuum of psychosis, one human gene, and not much else—the case for homogeneity" (*Schizophrenia Research* 1995, 17:135–45). He kindly invited me to one of his graduate seminars in Oxford and drew my attention to the quotations that I have used from the work of J. Crichton-Browne and E. E. Southard. Professor Crow's work in this field is extensive; I am indebted to it, as was David Horrobin.

Oscar Baumann led expeditions to German East Africa at the times stated for the German Anti-Slavery Committee. He left a diary of his travels and an elegant, though sketchy, map. Hannes Regensburger is a fictional character, so Baumann's mention to him of a specific site is invented, though the existence of a rift valley had excited the interest of paleontologists by this time. The actual footprints described in the novel are based on those discovered by Mary Leakey at Laetoli in 1978. Although they differ in some respects and are not in exactly the same place, I was so taken by Mary Leakey's book, written with J. M. Harris, *Laetoli: A Pliocene Site in Northern Tanzania* (Oxford: Clarendon Press, 1987), that I wished to include some of her detail, and I acknowledge this debt with admiration and gratitude. The site itself is hard to find and has been covered to protect it from the elements and the Masai cattle, but there is an accessible replica, cast in plaster, in the nearby Oldupai Gorge museum. (This name is more usually written "Olduvai," though local scholars assured me this was a faulty transliteration by early German visitors.) I would like also to thank Professor Michael Benton of the Department of Earth Sciences at Bristol University, Professor Jeffrey Schwartz at the University of Pittsburgh and Professor Ian Tattersall at the American Museum of Natural History.

The operation described in chapter XXIII was made famous by Wilder Penfield at the Montreal Neurological Institute in the mid-1930s. A detailed description was given in *Epilepsy and the Functional Anatomy of the Human Brain* by Wilder Penfield and Herbert Jasper (Boston: Little, Brown, 1954). However, Sir Victor Horsley had undertaken similar procedures in London before the First World War, and the operation was carried out in Vienna and Zürich in the 1920s. I would like to thank Michael Powell of the National Neurological Hospital in Queen Square, London, who talked me through some aspects of brain surgery.

My thanks are due to a number of other doctors and medical practitioners, notably: Lawrence Youlten, Martin Scurr, David Sturgeon, James Anderson, the late David Horrobin, Trevor Turner, Gwen Adshead, Professor Vichy Mahadevan, Professor Uta Frith and Professor Christopher Frith.

The Imperial War Museum, not for the first time, was exceptionally helpful, and I must thank Dr. Roderick Suddaby, Dr. Simon Robbins, Dr. Christopher Dowling and the staff of the documents department. I am grateful to Alice Ford-Smith and other staff of the peerless Wellcome Trust Library in London, and to the National Maritime Museum, whose beautiful photograph of the *City of New York* took six weeks to reach me by post from Greenwich—exactly the time, oddly enough, that the vessel herself took to cross the Atlantic in 1896.

Other institutions which helped me were the Library of the Institute of Psychiatry at the Maudsley Hospital in Denmark Hill, London; Bethlem Royal Hospital in Kent and its archivists Patricia Allderidge and Colin Gale; Springfield Hospital in London, particularly Hazel McElligot and John Cheetham; and the public relations office of the Salpêtrière Hospital in Paris.

Books I would further like to acknowledge are: the works of Andrew Scull, particularly *Masters of Bedlam* (New York: Princeton University Press, 1996), written with Charlotte MacKenzie and Nicholas Hervey; *Psychiatry for the Poor* by Richard Hunter and Ida Macalpine (London: Psychiatric Monograph Series, reprinted by Wm. Dawson and Sons, 1974); *A History of Psychiatry* by Edward Shorter (New York: John Wiley & Sons, 1997); *Presumed Curable* by Colin Gale and Robert Howard (London: Wrightson Biomedical Publishing, 2003); and *Hearing Voices: A Common Human Experience* by John Watkins (Melbourne: Hill of Content Press, 1998). *Mapping the Mind* and *Consciousness* by Rita Carter (London: Weidenfeld and Nicolson, 1998 and 2002) are sometimes called "laymen's" guides, but perhaps only because they are so clearly written.

My thanks for help in locating source material to Kate Roach, David Loveday, Liz Sturgeon and Charlie Miller; also to Rethink, a British charity that helps those with severe mental illness, including schizophrenia, and can be found at www.rethink.org.

For assistance in other areas, I am grateful to Andrew Ferguson and Electra May; William Sieghart; Gillon Aitken, Sue Freestone and Rachel Cugnoni. Claire Tomalin and Margot Norman made many helpful comments on an early draft of this novel.

In Carinthia I was helped by Julian Turton, Olivia Seligman and Linda Hardy; in California, by Jane and Stephen Moore and by Diana Faust; in Tanzania, by Anael and Olle Moita; in Brittany, by Caroline d'Achon. I would like to thank my wife, Veronica, for many things, but particularly for accompanying me 3,207 feet up Echo Mountain in a rainstorm and going with me one afternoon into the remotest, trackless parts of Masai country, where the Land Rover broke down in the dark.

My mother, Pamela Faulks, did not live to read this book, but convinced me many years ago that it was legitimate to have an interest in the way the mind works.

The individual to whom this novel owes most is Janey Antoniou, for whose assistance this acknowledgment can be only a token of what I owe her.

The Mount Lowe railway existed as described in chapter XV, and the remains of Echo Mountain House and the machinery at the top of the incline can still be seen today if you walk up from Pasadena. The railway carried millions of visitors into the hills, but after a succession of characteristically Californian disasters, including fire, flood and bankruptcy, the entire system closed for good in 1937.

They never did reach the top of Mount Lowe.

S.F., London, April 20, 2005

CHARLOTTE GRAY

In blacked-out, wartime London, Charlotte Gray develops a dangerous passion for a battle-weary RAF pilot, and when he fails to return from a daring flight into France she is determined to find him. In the service of the Resistance, she travels to the village of Lavaurette, dyeing her hair and changing her name to conceal her identity. Here she will come face-to-face with the harrowing truth of what took place during Europe's darkest years, and will confront a terrifying secret that threatens to cast its shadow over the remainder of her days. Vividly rendered and tremendously moving, *Charlotte Gray* confirms Sebastian Faulks is one of the finest novelists working today.

Fiction/Literature/978-0-375-70455-0

THE GIRL AT THE LION D'OR

On a rainy night in the 1930s, a young girl appears at the run-down Hotel du Lion d'Or in the seaside village of Janvilliers. She calls herself Anne Louvet; she is looking for work. And although her openheartedness charms everyone but the inn's forbidding proprietress, it is clear that she has a secret. Soon Anne falls in love with Charles Hartmann, a married veteran of the Great War who harbors his own burden of tragedy. As it follows their torrential affair, *The Girl at the Lion d'Or* weaves an unbreakable spell of narrative, mood, and character that evokes French masters from Flaubert to Renoir.

Fiction/Literature/978-0-375-70453-6

ON GREEN DOLPHIN STREET

Faulks's heroine is Mary van der Linden, a pretty, reserved Englishwoman whose husband, Charlie, is posted to the British embassy in Washington. One night at a cocktail party Mary meets Frank Renzo, a reporter who has covered stories from the fall of Dien Bien Phu to the Emmett Till murder trial in Mississippi. Slowly, reluctantly, they fall in love. Their ensuing affair, in all its desperate elation, plays out against a backdrop that ranges from the jazz clubs of Greenwich Village to the smoke-filled rooms of the Kennedy campaign.

Fiction/Literature/978-0-375-70456-7

BIRDSONG

This intensely romantic and yet stunningly realistic novel spans three generations and the unimaginable gulf between the First World War and the present. As the young Englishman Stephen Wraysford passes through a tempestuous love affair with Isabelle Azaire in France and enters the dark, surreal world beneath the trenches of No Man's Land, Sebastian Faulks creates a world of fiction that is as tragic as *A Farewell to Arms* and as sensuous as *The English Patient*. Crafted from the ruins of war and the indestructibility of love, *Birdsong* is a novel that will be read and marveled at for years to come.

Fiction/Literature/978-0-679-77681-9

THE FATAL ENGLISHMAN
Three Short Lives

In his first work of nonfiction, Sebastian Faulks explores the lives of three remarkable men. Christopher Wood, only twenty-nine when he killed himself, was a painter who lived most of his life in the beau monde of 1920s Paris, where his dissolute life sometimes frustrated his ambition and achievement as an artist. Richard Hillary was a gallant WWII fighter pilot who wrote a classic account of his experiences, but died in a mysterious training accident at twenty-three. Jeremy Wolfenden, hailed as the brightest Englishman of his generation, rejected academia to become a hack journalist in Cold War Moscow. A spy, alcoholic, and open homosexual, he died at the age of thirty-one, a victim of his own recklessness. Through their stories, Faulks paints an oblique portrait of English society as it changed from the Victorian era to the modern world.

Fiction/Literature/978-0-375-72744-3

VINTAGE INTERNATIONAL
Available at your local bookstore, or visit
www.randomhouse.com